Organizational Communication
in an Age of Globalization

Organizational Communication in an Age of Globalization

Issues, Reflections, Practices

George Cheney
University of Utah

Lars Thøger Christensen
University of Southern Denmark

Theodore E. Zorn, Jr.
University of Waikato

Shiv Ganesh
University of Montana

Long Grove, Illinois

For information about this book, contact:
Waveland Press, Inc.
4180 IL Route 83, Suite 101
Long Grove, IL 60047-9580
(847) 634-0081
info@waveland.com
www.waveland.com

Cover illustration: Juan Gris, Bottle and Glass on a Table, 1913–1914

ISBN 1-57766-271-7

Printed in the United States of America

8 7 6 5 4 3 2

This book is dedicated to our parents:

Mary and George Cheney

Elsa Palsov† and Svend Thøger Christensen

Patricia DeAntonio Zorn and Theodore E. Zorn, Sr.

Indu and Ravi Ganesh

CONTENTS

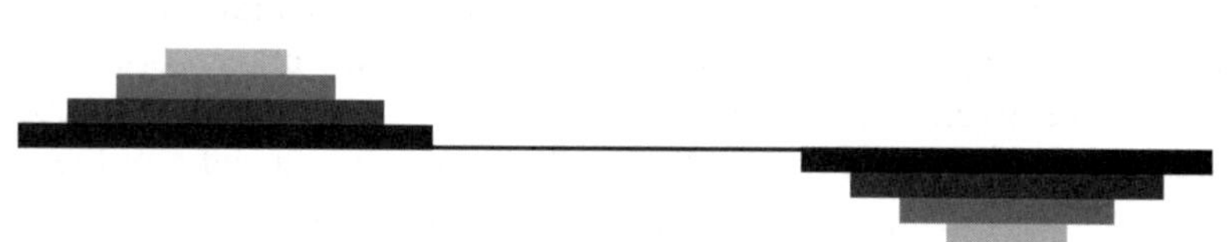

PREFACE

Why and how did we write this book?

The terms "communication" and "organization" mean lots of different things to different people. That's true even for the four of us writing this textbook. We accept that ambiguity as a part of life; in fact, we will mine some of that ambiguity for interesting insights and understandings into communicating in organizations. Still, our book does have a focus and several themes, as we'll explain in a moment.

Two of us, George and Ted, have been teaching organizational communication for two decades. We've done this in the classroom, in public colloquia, and in training seminars. Ted and George have also been heavily engaged in organizational communication research. For most of those years, "organizational communication" has meant to us what it has meant to the sub-field of communication studies that takes that name: the study of symbols, messages, media, interactions, relationships, networks, persuasive campaigns, and broader discourses *within* an organization—be it a corporation, governmental agency, religious institution, social movement, or whatever. However, Ted's move to a comprehensive department of management communication in New Zealand and George's long-term interest in organizational rhetoric—of various types—pointed both of us toward a broader consideration of the roles of organizations in society.

Lars came to organizational communication in the late 1980s, by way of sociology and then marketing. As he explored the world of advertisements and organizational strategies for positioning them in markets, he became increasingly interested in what was going on inside the "black box." Most scholars and practitioners of marketing, public relations, and advertising ignored communication within the organization. His research crosses the boundaries between what was traditionally seen as "internal" organizational communication (like leadership behavior, employee relations, group meetings, etc.) and what was deemed "external" (that is, advertising, public relations, marketing, lobbying, and so forth).

Shiv, a relatively new scholar, recently joined this project in large part because he shared the same vision of an undergraduate textbook in organizational communication—topically organized, strongly connecting theory and practice, and engaging important social and political issues while considering the "inner workings" of communication in the organization. Shiv's research in non-governmental organizations in India and nonprofit organizations in the United States convinced him that it makes little sense to consider organizations apart from the larger cultural, economic, and technological contexts in which they operate.

Organizational communication as an area of study has enjoyed rapid expansion in recent years: in communication departments, in management schools, journalism programs, departments of sociology, and other formats. While the area explicitly designated "org. comm." has had a U.S. base as well as a U.S. *bias* for most of its 50-year history, at the turn of the twenty-first century many other countries are pursuing the study. Part of our enthusiasm about writing this textbook together came from the fact that we live in three different parts of the world. This gives us the opportunity to make the book truly international in scope.

There are five overarching themes woven through the chapters in this book:

- the interdependence of internal and external forms of organizational communication,
- global and multicultural perspectives on organizational communication,
- the "disciplinarity" and multi-disciplinarity of organizational communication,
- the unity of theory and practice in organizational communication, and
- critical thinking in the analysis of organizational messages and discourses.

In addition to explaining our five themes, we want to mention the structure of the book. We have deliberately departed from the typical chronological structure of textbooks in organizational communication, as well as the containment of theory in certain chapters. Instead, we have adopted a topical structure, where important issues in organizational communication (and the study of organizations generally) are addressed, with history and theory interwoven throughout the topical discussions. For example, our chapter on rationality (chapter 3) deals with the rise of efficiency as an overarching goal in industrial societies, while it also considers various theories of rationality from Weber to contemporary critiques. That chapter, like the others, is organized around what we see as key issues or concerns in the study and practice of organizational communication. Likewise, we have tried not to compartmentalize issues of "difference"—for example, race, class, and gender. Rather, we bring those concerns to the forefront of discussion as valuable examples of real-world experiences of the issues raised. Of course, in some cases, the adoption of a gendered, or culturally-conscious, or class-based point of view may completely reconfigure an "old" issue or bring an entirely new issue into view—as we explain in chapter 14 on ethics.

We view organizational communication as both a sub-discipline of communication studies and as an exciting arena for multi-disciplinary investigation, recognizing influences from and on disciplines as diverse as anthropology, marketing, and literary criticism. We draw from a variety of different resources while focusing on some central problems and questions, such as how to develop sound and ethical leadership strategies that are inspirational and effective for both employees and external constituencies of a firm.

When we talk about the unity of theory and practice, we really mean it. Students often treat "theory" as if it were a four-letter word, and they're not entirely to blame for this. In general, scholars have often failed to demonstrate just how practical theories can be and how practice itself contributes to theoretical development. All of us carry around theories in our heads—like assumptions we have about "human nature"—but we seldom recognize those assumptions as theories. Some of our greatest experiences in the classroom have been when students really engage a theory—testing it against their own experiences and other data—or when they try to develop new theories from their lived experiences or the experiences of others. If we really want to understand the potential for new organizational forms, for example, let's put real cases in dialogue with existing theories of organizational structure and process and then see what the conversation produces.

The term "practical" merits a bit of attention here. We hear the word all the time, but it's hardly ever the case that anyone examines the different ways in which we mean it. Here, we'd like to suggest three levels of practice, all of which are relevant to the study of organizational communication. Being practical includes: (1) the development of specific, concrete skills, such as interviewing, public speaking, and small-group discussion; (2) the refinement of analytical and critical abilities—to solve problems successfully or to construct an effective persuasive campaign; and (3) the fostering of positive social change—for example, at the level of personal vocation, at the level of organizational restructuring or reorientation, or at the broader level of social betterment. This textbook is most concerned with the second and third meanings of "practical" mentioned above. However, in our discussions you will also find lots of tips and tools relevant to the day-to-day work of organizations. Our primary aim is to stimulate critical thinking about contemporary work and organizational life.

"Critical thinking" appears frequently as an element in general education requirements at many universities, but few people take the time to explain what they mean by that term. As with communication and organization, there are multiple meanings and differences of opinion about the definition. For us, *critical thinking means getting beyond the taken-for-granted assumptions about communicating with others at work and about the way we do things in organizations*. We invite students to render unfamiliar what is familiar—like the way their university or college is structured—and to consider different, perhaps more imaginative, even more noble, ways of getting work done together. Despite all the emphasis on innovation, change, and "cutting edge" organizations today, we find a great deal of conformity out there. We urge you to ask probing questions about so-called "common sense," to consider your own cultural assumptions as strange, and to investigate issues about work and life of interest to you. In terms of communication, critical reflection means looking at multiple levels of messages. For instance, we can look at a meeting in several ways: in terms of the agenda, what is said, what is not said, how people relate to one another interpersonally, how nonverbal aspects of interaction fit or don't fit with verbal ones, group-level system dynamics, meeting process, and even the fact of the meeting itself as a "message" for those involved. Through critical reflection, a course in organizational communication can be practical in the highest sense of the word—helping all of us to be better citizens of this complex, crazy, delightful, and troubling world.

You'll notice that we have written much of this textbook in a conversational, accessible style, making use of contractions, colloquial expressions, and even some incomplete sentences (on that last point, please do as we say and not as we do!). This is a deliberate strategy so that the book prompts oral presentation and discussion. When we introduce theoretical concepts and terms, we include definitions and illustrations so that the conversation incorporates the theory as another tool in the analysis.

The book is organized in a topic-by-topic format. Rather than proceeding historically, or geographically, or treating different perspectives, we have tried to distill what we think are the most important topics in the study, understanding, and practical engagement of organizations today. Chapter 1 lays out some of our assumptions in greater detail than we have here. You will find the following issues addressed, chapter by chapter:

- Introduction: Why Organization *and* Communication?
- Organizational Structure and Process
- Rationality, Decision Making, and (Ab)Uses of Information
- Culture, Subcultures, and Organizational Socialization
- Communicating Identity Individually and Collectively
- Connecting through Social Relationships and Networks
- Leadership Old and New
- Participation, Teams, and Democracy at Work
- Power and Control in Organizational Life
- Encountering, Interpreting, and Managing Conflict
- Organizational Change and Change-Related Communication
- The Meanings and Uses of Organizational Communication Technologies
- Communicating in Global and Multicultural Contexts
- Speaking of Ethics and Values in Organizations
- Analyzing Organizational Communication*

In keeping with some our most cherished values—such as putting theory into practice and an invitational, participatory approach to communication—we have decided to create and offer a Web site as a forum for exchanging ideas about teaching and learning about organizational communication. You can visit our Web site at http://www.organizationalcommunication.com. Our goal is for this Web site to facilitate a community of practice among organizational communication students and teachers—both a discussion forum and a clearinghouse of tools that can be used in the classroom. It will also serve many of the functions of a traditional instructor's guide with the added advantage of being updated continually and enriched by contributors.

*Instructors and students should note that while the chapter on analysis (15) makes reference to a number of topics previously explored in the textbook, its primary purposes are (1) to offer a wide perspective on methods for research and practical intervention and (2) to present a "tool kit" of strategies and techniques for the reader/user of this text.

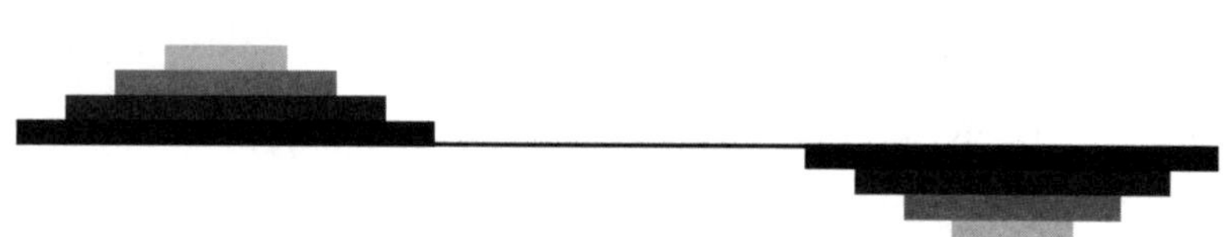

ACKNOWLEDGMENTS

George can hardly believe that this seven-year project is over—how's that for strategic ambiguity! I am deeply grateful for the opportunity to collaborate on this with Lars, Ted, and Shiv; although much of our interaction was virtual, it was nevertheless engaging and stimulating. Also, I am grateful for many enriching conversations with teachers, peers, and students over the past two decades and more. You folks are too numerous to enumerate here. In various ways, those interactions have helped to shape my thinking about organizational communication, and my contributions to this text are surely the better for them. Finally, let me offer deep thanks to Sally Planalp for her supreme patience as well as her love and support.

Lars is happy to have been part of a truly interdisciplinary project that has helped him supply flesh and blood to the idea that internal and external forms of organizational communication really *are* interdependent. Working within the field of marketing, I am grateful for the freedom that my departments have provided me over the years to explore the other sides of the marketing institution, including its interplay with dimensions of organizational life such as identity, leadership, (ir)rationality, and change management. In addition to George, whom I've enjoyed working with on many projects over the years, I would like to thank my other great co-authors, Ted and Shiv. Finally, I'd like to thank Jette Brockstedt for her sweetness, understanding, and loving support.

Ted thanks his co-authors for the intellectual stimulation and good humor; in particular, he would like to thank George for coordinating and gently pushing the project along. I would also like to thank my many students at the Universities of Waikato, Louisville, and North Carolina for their insights and challenges and my colleagues in the Department of Management Communication at the University of Waikato for their patience while I took on this project among many others during my tenure as department chairperson. Thanks most of all to Brenda (CEO) and Andrea (Vice President of Mess-making) for their support and for lessons about communication in our family organization.

Shiv would like to thank George, Lars, and Ted for inviting him to work with them on this project and giving him the opportunity to truly merge scholarship and pedagogy. My special thanks go out to the students of COMM 320 at the University of Montana, who willingly (and even excitedly!) incorporated draft chapters of this textbook as part of their learning, thereby providing us with their thoughts, opinions, and support. I'd also like to thank the various teacher-scholars in our field (especially those at Purdue University) from whom I've learned everything that I know about organizational communication; and finally, I'd like to thank my colleagues at the University of Montana for their support.

We would also like to celebrate the contributions that a range of scholars actively engaged in studying and teaching organizational communication all over the world have made to this project. Most of those colleagues are acknowledged explicitly within the text. If we forgot anyone, please accept our apologies (and do let us know before the second edition!).

We thank Mary Simpson for test-driving the book manuscript in her classes at Waikato; the feedback we received from her and her students was very helpful to us in refining certain chapters. Also, we want to thank Dan Lair who assisted all of us in the final stages of the preparation of this book, cheerfully treating our pressures as his own and giving us a fresh perspective on what we were trying to accomplish.

Finally, we wish to say that working with Carol and Neil Rowe has been a joy, even when we severely challenged their concept of a deadline. Their good humor and encouragement as well as meticulous work provide a model of professionalism with grace.

Salt Lake City, Utah, USA
Odense, Denmark
Hamilton, New Zealand
Missoula, Montana, USA

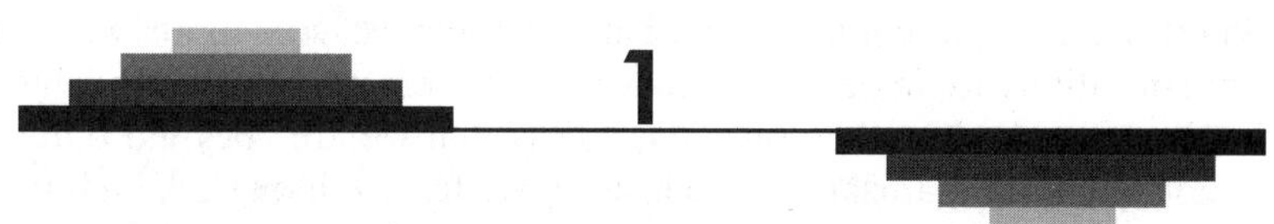

INTRODUCTION

- In the late 1990s, the London-based company The Body Shop determined that it had lost part of its "marketing edge." Ironically, its emphasis on social responsibility was no longer a distinguishing feature because so many other organizations were presenting themselves exactly the same way.
- In 2000, a number of high-tech companies in India began retraining their customer service representatives in the "appropriate kind of techie talk" so that they would sound appealing and credible to potential clients in other countries.
- In late 2001, a group of brokers employed by Merrill Lynch in the United States disrupted a golf tournament sponsored by the company by flying a plane over the golf course with the banner "Merrill Lynch Discriminates against Women."

What do these three examples have in common? In each case, we can see boundaries of work and organizations shifting, members of organizations choosing new ways to communicate with outside audiences and with each other. At the same time, each example shows the roles of history and culture in understanding what's going on. Organizations *are* changing. Some are becoming flatter and less hierarchical; some are becoming more responsive to their markets. Some are linking up with other organizations to form strategic alliances or flexible manufacturing networks. And some are just plain new—or so they seem—as when we look at so-called "virtual organizations."

To understand work and organizations today, we must look at what's going on *inside* the organization *and* at the larger culture in which an organization operates: the economy, the current business culture, changing lifestyles and expectations, the family, consumption, and technology. In general, we have to get beyond the idea of an organization as something that simply "contains" people, technologies, and work.[1] Organizations have fluid boundaries, and people's lives flow through those boundaries. So, we can't talk about organizations as if they were islands and their members and activities as set apart from what's going on in the larger society.

How We Think and Talk about Organizations

We know that things are not always what they seem, yet sometimes we forget how complex organizations are in our desire to try to put them into understandable models or molds. For example, it's common today to say that we are "beyond bureaucracy" and that *those* kinds of organizations are history. We tend to look back on bureaucracy as some quaint relic of the past—a past when we were less enlightened than we are now. *Bureaucracy* has become such a "devil" term that no one can imagine a successful candidate for public office, anywhere in the industrialized world, who would argue "What we need is more and better bureaucracy!" Condemning bureaucracy has become so accepted that we've completely forgotten its good sides or why it developed in the first place. Elements of bureaucracy first appeared in ancient China about 5,000 years ago, with the first use of written records (forerunners to our "files"); bureaucracy gradually became the dominant form of organization by the middle of the twentieth century. Something with so lengthy a history must have satisfied *some* needs. At a minimum we should *consider* its advantages while we decry its disadvantages.[2]

Bureaucracy was celebrated in the late nineteenth and early twentieth centuries for initiating standards to replace arbitrary decisions about work processes and personnel. But those very standards have their downsides: rigidity, depersonalization, and the diffusion of responsibility. When we look closely at what's happening today even in supposedly post-bureaucratic organizations, we find that bureaucracy continues—though perhaps in new forms or under new guises. For instance, newly formed teams in organizations will often reproduce some of the very aspects of bureaucracy that they're trying to eliminate.[3]

Popular Prescriptions

Popular books on organizations sell best when they simplify an idea or promote catchphrases like teamwork, flexibility, or high-speed management.[4] We all want to find the "New and Better Organization" or the "Secrets to Effective Leadership." We feel a strong need to cut through all the complexity and sum up what's going on in a few simple principles. We seek to be the "one-minute manager"[5] or leader of a "total quality organization." And why not? After all, we're awfully busy these days, and we certainly support the idea of excellence. Moreover, we have to have some guiding vision, some models, some ways of organizing the zillions of priorities that face us. In the process, we end up aligning ourselves with one trend or another—to simplify our decision making and to announce to the rest of the world that we're up to date. So, yesterday's corporation that pursued management by objectives and quality circles may well be today's corporation that is customer-oriented and *continuously* improving. Popular books, videos, and training seminars keep us current with the techniques of the times. But, in an effort to be brief and clear, such resources often oversimplify things, and then the ideas get further simplified as they are put into practice.

This isn't to deny the value of many practical, prescriptive guides. Rather, we're saying that when we take a good, long look at ourselves and these organizations we've made, we find that we're not as rational as we'd like to think we are. The customer-oriented organization may be serving customers, but it may also be fooling itself when it simply projects its own plans on consumers through surveys.[6] There's a lot to learn from reflecting on the ironies and contradictions associated with some dominant trend. Just because everyone's jumping on a bandwagon, like reengineering in the 1990s, doesn't mean *your* organization ought to go there. And, even if it does, you would do well to consider the particular circumstances of your work, your product or service, your goals, and the kind of organization you want it to be. In trying to make a university more efficient by creating lots of large lecture classes and reducing the size of faculty and staff, we may make it dramatically less effective in terms of offering highly personalized educational opportunities to students. Under the slogan of "more competition," a company may actually work to *limit* competition and to gain monopolistic control of an industry. The worker cooperative that began as fully democratic may find itself confronting authoritarian behavior from its leaders as they attempt to direct employees' values.[7] Similarly, the new computer-mediated technologies in organizations can be simultaneously liberating and constraining.[8]

Refining Perspectives

What all this suggests is that we should look at each organization and organizational problem on multiple levels and from multiple perspectives. We can take a government agency's commitment to innovation and change seriously, but at the same time we can see how some of the organization's activities seem to contradict that commitment. Alternatively, we may find that parts of the organization are changing a lot while others are staying pretty constant.[9] In addition, we may reflect on how that organization's plans and slogans are part of a larger movement that celebrates change over stability.[10] This multi-dimensional view helps us understand better how change really operates and how our very messages about change make a difference.

Going even further, we can consider how our ideas about change have themselves, well, changed. That is, how do we think about change in organizations, as compared to the ways previous generations thought about the same issue? If we then make comparisons across cultures, we can learn more about what we're doing by studying the perspectives of others who might be quite different from us. Could it be that we are so dazed by change today that we've forgotten the values of continuity, loyalty, and stability? At the very least, asking this question helps us to locate our own point of view on the spectrum of viewpoints. After confirming, denying, or perhaps refining our own perspective, we can better define a problem and possible approaches to it. This is the practical "payoff" of critical thinking, regardless of whether we are "movers and shakers" or feel that the decisions that shape our lives are basically out of our hands.

Making the Invisible Visible

Much of this book is about getting beyond the taken-for-granted—and that includes not taking our own critiques for granted. If there's anything the four of us have learned from our various experiences, it's that we should not approach organizations as fixed or monolithic, as being unchangeable or as operating the same way all the time—even organizations as large as Toyota or the Roman Catholic Church or the United Nations or Greenpeace. Taken-for-granted ideas can be so powerful that they seduce us into overlooking the origins of the idea, its different forms, its many uses, or the fact that some people may not share the idea or may see it completely differently.

When George visited Denmark in 1993 to teach a graduate seminar on organizational communication, he assumed that the concept of "efficiency" had a perfect corresponding translation in Danish and in other Nordic languages. But that was not the case. Throughout Scandinavia and in Finland, writers and speakers on management have simply adopted the English term. That led George to look a little deeper into the history of efficiency in the United States and elsewhere to explore both the specific meanings and the ambiguity of the term. Something that seemed so basic in one culture had no equivalent in another.

When something is very familiar to us, it can become transparent. We may look right through it, just as when we can take a partner for granted. When a new technology is introduced into a society it is *not* transparent. The first users of the telephone, in the 1880s, *looked* at it and found it hard to figure out what to say. Gradually, conventions for talking on the phone developed around the world, and people forgot about the medium they were holding and talking though. Similarly, people would gather around the first televisions, just after 1950, sometimes intrigued even by the test pattern. Today, computer-mediated technologies are a bit like the telephone and the TV in their early days. At the turn of the twenty-first century, we are still "looking" at online conferencing, as customs are emerging for its use. We're still trying to figure out appropriate contexts and means for this new way of interacting; we don't yet take it for granted.[11] At the same time, certain norms and customs have emerged for the early adopters, that is, for those who have been using the Internet to communicate via e-mail since its introduction in 1985.

Assessing Metaphors

Commonly used metaphors are like that, too. As we become accustomed to their usage, we begin to overlook that they are representations of some part of experience. "Skyscraper" in English is a *dead* metaphor, simply because a building scraping the sky is no longer a novelty. In this case, the practical implications for people and their relationships are not terribly important. In other instances, though, choosing a particular metaphor and then running with it makes a huge difference in social relationships. If a mutual friend uses the simile that John is "as sly as a fox," we may not be thinking of an actual fox, but we get the point and are probably fairly conscious of the metaphor in use. We may also begin to act more cautiously when we're around John. But a lot of our metaphors—and their associated assumptions about life and people—go unnoticed.

Take, for example, how ingrained are the ideas of "up" and "down" in organizations, in phrases such as the "career ladder" or "her power rose yesterday." We're so accustomed to thinking in terms of up and down that we have a difficult time modeling an organization any other way—say, for example, with concentric circles. Stop to think about the implications of other metaphors that frequently pop up in board meetings, appraisal interviews, or hallway conversations at work: "deadwood," "price war," "re-engineering," and "whistle-blower." What all metaphors have in common is that they help us to understand one thing in terms of something else.[12] But every metaphor is like a flashlight that illuminates some parts of a darkened room and leaves others obscured.

Because organizations are so complex, we need metaphors to describe them. By far the most commonly used metaphor to characterize an organization is the machine. However, the organization-as-person, -as-team, -as-organism, -as-system, and -as-culture have also made their way into popular usage (see box 1.1). If your boss at work describes your department as "running like a well-oiled machine," does that expression influence how he or she relates to employees and how they treat each other?[13] A machine usually has replaceable parts, lacks feeling, isn't very adaptable or changeable, and doesn't have the capacity to think for itself (although recent developments in computer technologies challenge these assumptions somewhat). Yet, it's easy to see why we find the machine metaphor appealing for organizations, and the metaphor fits well with the model of bureaucracy described by Max Weber at the beginning of the twentieth century.[14] Several years ago, one of our students pointed out a real *advantage* of the machine metaphor at work for the employee who doesn't want to get too involved with the organization: unlike the family metaphor, the machine metaphor suggests that the person-as-part can be left alone, as long as she is doing her job. A machine part, in contrast with a family member, isn't someone who is bound to the organization in a deep or lasting way. This implication of the machine metaphor is often overlooked.

Box 1.1 Metaphors

A metaphor can be:

- One whole in terms of another whole: ***standard metaphor*** ("the human machine"; "the corporate jungle"; "time is money"; "my boss is a snake")
- The part for the whole: ***synecdoche*** ("there are a lot of good heads in the university"; "the White House announced today"; "it's owned by the Crown")
- One thing reduced to another, related thing: ***metonymy*** ("the *Times* hasn't arrived at the press conference yet"; "the ham sandwich is waiting for his check"; "she likes to read Stephen King")
- Human qualities given to something not human: ***personification*** ("life has cheated me"; "the company is kind"; "corporate character")

Metaphors commonly applied to organizations are:

- The organization as an ***organism*** (which is actually the root of the term *organization*)
- The corporation as a ***person*** (that is, its legal status in many industrialized nations, since the 1880s)
- The organization as a ***machine*** (the most common metaphor in theories and writings about organizations)
- Business as ***war*** (common practice)
- A profession as a ***game*** (a cynical way of talking)
- The world of work as a ***network*** (emphasizing strategy and connections)
- The office as a ***family*** (highlighting intimacy and interdependence but perhaps also control)
- Corporate ***culture*** (popular since the early 1980s)
- ***Team*** (all the rage in the 1990s)

Some alternative metaphors for organizational life include the following. What are the advantages and disadvantages of seeing an organization this way?

Drama	Zoo
Tribe	Fiefdom
Recipe	Onion
Circus	Spider Plant
Brain	Mirror
Political Arena	Community
Story, Narrative, or Saga	Garbage Can
Mirror	Watermelon

Think of your own metaphor for organizations. What kinds of organizations or situations does your metaphor help to explain best? What does your metaphor overlook? How might your metaphor be useful in a practical way—say, for example, in a meeting?

"I was on the cutting edge. I pushed the envelope. I did the heavy lifting. I was the rainmaker. Then I ran out of metaphors."

What Is Communication?

We use metaphors to describe the communication process—often to simplify our understanding of it. But the useful simplification can also get us into trouble. Think of how often we conceive of communication in terms of the simple *transmission* of information, as if we were packaging up ideas and then giving them to others like a present.[15] We use this metaphor for communication when we talk about "giving her a message" or "sending them some information." The transmission-oriented view of communication makes good sense, and it does explain an important aspect of our dealings with others. But it does not begin to account for the subtleties and complexities of the larger process by which we make sense of our world, relate to one another, exert influence, maintain cultures, and sometimes affect the course of human events.

Think about the process of sending a memo. We often forget that the memo can only be understood in terms of a larger context of messages and that the persons sending and receiving the memoranda may well bring their own histories to bear on the situation. So, what the sender thinks is a simple matter of, say, introducing an idea for a new project may be perceived by the receiver as an attempt to take control of the situation and thus increase the sender's power. If the message is transmitted by e-mail and copied to the *whole* department—as George found to be common practice with reprimands in a city government organization a few years ago—the process becomes more complicated. Some of the receivers may ignore the sender's request for further discussion. This leads the sender to talk up her idea even more, and the spiral continues. This is just one example of how our everyday understanding of communication needs to be broadened beyond simple transmission in order for us to get a grip on all that's going on when people relate to one another at work and in other organizational settings.

Box 1.2 Metaphors for Communication Itself[16]

There are a number of ways to conceive of that thing we call "communication." In part, we need metaphors to describe it because it's so complex. Also, we are surrounded by communication and are to some extent products of communication. So, to talk about communication is like asking a fish to comment on the water! Still, it's interesting to see how we try to capture communication and what various metaphors we use to tell us about ourselves and our relationships to others.

Some of the metaphors we use to describe organizational communication, along with their associated terms, are:

- ***Conduit:*** for example, container, transmission, line, tool, object
- ***Lens:*** for example, eye, scanning, filtering, distortion
- ***Linkage:*** for example, relationships, connections, networks, patterns, cliques, isolates
- ***Performance:*** for example, episode, display, ritual, role, audience, actor
- ***Symbol:*** for example, representations, artifacts, narratives, shared meaning
- ***Voice:*** for example, chorus, expression and suppression, participation
- ***Discourse:*** for example, language, conversation, text, "reading"

Some of these metaphors (like "voice") appear explicitly in everyday talk, but others (like "discourse") may not. Still, every one of them is reflected to some extent in the way people treat communication in organizations. Consider, for example, how a union's request for representation on a particular management committee embodies the "voice" metaphor for communication. Or, think of how a company picnic can be an important symbol of camaraderie at work.

Can you identify other examples of the various metaphors from your own organizational experience?

Organizations as Communication

When we really come to terms with what an organization *is*, we find that much of it is communication. In a sense the organization exists as a pattern or network of energies and interactions—not only the identifiable memos or meetings, but also an entire fabric of relationships. In fact, when we speak of organizational communication, we mean to include a whole array of things, such as symbols, messages, interactions, relationships, networks, and larger discourses. The communication of an organization is something we "step into" like the flow of a river but also contribute to as we affect that flow or throw something into the stream. (Notice how we cannot escape metaphor!)

This understanding of communication is exactly why management theorist Chester Barnard chose to define the organization as "a system of consciously coordinated activities or forces of two or more persons."[17] Organizations are not simply things (like a corporation's headquarters) or abstractions (like the idea of a multinational governmental agency, such as the World Trade Organization), although organizations have both of these elements. So, a university is neither the actual, physical campus where many classes are held nor is it the sum of the people who work in it. Instead, it is a complex system of symbols, messages, efforts, and activities—a network of contributions from its members and from people and groups outside of its boundaries.

An organization's efforts are directed at specific goals—such as making cars, educating students, providing sound health care, serving the needs of disadvantaged segments of society, governing a nation, matching up singles, selling magazine subscriptions, creating new software, coordinating a sports league, and so on. But in all these cases, a network of relationships and messages enables those specific goals to be achieved.

Organizations are all around us, and we are often working with them and through them. We are used to big corporations and government agencies, to political parties and religious denominations, to health clubs and labor unions, to charities and social movements. It's natural to see organizations as solid—that is, as discrete, definable things, having boundaries we can see and touch—because that's the way they appear to us much of the time and that's the way any self-interested organization wants to be seen. When the Wizard of Oz is revealed near the end of the film by the same name, he says, "Pay no attention to that man behind the curtain! *I* am the great and powerful Oz!" He's asking Dorothy and her friends to focus on the image of something bigger—and, in a way there is something bigger because people have been acting on that assumption. So it is with organizations. Why should we expect any organization *not* to be interested in its own survival, growth, and power?[18] Organizations are all about increasing the capacity to get something done, doing more than separate individuals could do otherwise.

But, here's the rub: once we get together to form a club, or a corporation, or a religion, we create something new. We have both an easy and a hard time comprehending organizations because, on the one hand, they are products of our efforts and, on the other hand, they "take on lives of their own" (see box 1.3). When we form a new campus club, we want it to have influence, and we hope to see it last. But, if the organization starts to drift away from our original purposes or take on trappings of formality and status that we founders don't like, we say that "the club is no longer ours"; that "things aren't what they used to be"; that "it's time to move on to something else." This problem points to one of the most basic issues in the social sciences and humanities: how to reconcile large-scale social forces with individual capacities to act in a certain way.[19]

Expanding the Boundaries

No organization is an island; as a matter of fact, none ever were. For a long time, it made sense and was certainly more convenient to think about or talk about distinct organizations as having definite boundaries and "containing" people, technologies, and messages. This view is challenged daily as organizations assume new forms to adapt to rapidly changing environments and markets.

We've briefly looked at what is meant by "organizational communication." As an area of study, organizational communication grew up with management, organizational behavior, and the human relations movement (roughly from 1930 to 1970). Thus, questions that were asked early in the field's development were aimed at describing in general terms how communication operates within an organization. There was, and continues to be, a strong concern for practical outcomes. Some important questions have been:

- What effects do downward-directed organizational messages have on employees? (1940s)
- What is the relationship between the attitudes and performance of workers and the feedback they receive from their supervisors? (1950s)
- What is the relationship between subordinates' job-related attitudes and productivity and the extent to which they perceive that they participate in decision making? (1960s)

Box 1.3 The Power Metaphor in Practice: Corporations: Just Like You and Me?[20]

When U.S. courts granted corporations legal *personhood*,[21] there were profound implications for the power dynamics between people, governance, and corporations. Corporations were released from the traditional legal view that held them to be creations of state legislation, simple legal fictions granted privileges (such as limited liability) yet existing under strict public control. Over time, U.S. corporations won additional Constitutional rights including equal protection, due process,[22] search and seizure protections,[23] free speech,[24] and even negative free speech.[25]

The logic asserted by corporations was that the Constitutional rights of individual persons do not vanish when they act in groups of persons. Therefore, denying them to corporations is tantamount to denying them to their constituent parts, specifically the natural persons who are their owners. Few question rights for persons,[26] but what are the implications of providing and then expanding rights to corporations?

The government, in its role of protecting rights, became the protector of corporations. With the Constitution now on their side, corporations succeeded in challenging hundreds of state laws that had controlled corporate activities. Silence corporations on political issues?—that violates corporations' *free speech rights*.[27] More stringent labeling laws for food?—that violates corporations' *negative free speech rights*. Surprise safety inspections?—that violates a corporation's right to *privacy*.[28] The exercise of legislative authority over corporations, which had been the practice in the United States for over 100 years, was rapidly replaced with court battles.

Rights not only protect, they also empower. Corporations often use their rights, especially that of free speech, to promote new laws. Is it a surprise that prison corporations lobby for mandatory sentencing laws and resource extraction corporations push for weaker environmental protections? It is good for their business. But when, if ever, should corporate interests be superior to those of the general public? And, in the realm of largely private speech, how can we discern "the public interest" and who is representing it?

Conflicting claims of authority impact the workplace, too. Employees do not usually enjoy free speech or freedom of association in the workplace. Corporations, on the other hand, can have employees urinate into cups for drug testing. How are these power differentials justified, on legal, ethical, or practical levels? The status of corporations as persons evolved over decades of great flux about the nature of institutions and democracy, specifically the responsibilities and liabilities between people, the corporate entity, corporate directors, and shareholders.[29] Today, many social justice organizations have redirected their campaigns away from challenging corporate harms one-at-a-time and toward challenging the corporate claims of rights and authority.[30]

Think of how far-reaching the metaphor of the corporate person has become. What aspects of this metaphor do you think are beneficial—for example, in the diffusion of financial liability? What aspects are harmful to individuals or to society as a whole?

- What are the communicative components of healthy organizational climates?
- What are the characteristics of key communication roles within organizational networks? (1970s)[31]

These kinds of questions are still being explored, and their answers are not easy. But the study of organizational communication today means more than just channels and messages and relationships *within* an organization—important as those things are.[32] Communication is now understood to be much more than discrete messages that we can isolate and examine. And organizational communication research is being conducted far beyond the boundaries of the United States. A small sampling of current organizational communication research questions illustrates our points vividly:

- How do organizations with no center or headquarters or office maintain the mutual understanding, group cohesion, and individual commitment necessary for success?
- In what ways do certain practices in the leadership of many avowedly democratic organizations undermine the very values embodied in the visions and values of such organizations?
- How do certain discourses (or patterned ways of seeing and talking) about the customer infuse organizational activities with both advantages and disadvantages?
- How do organizations imitate one another, both within and across industries, all in an effort to be "different," "cutting edge," and "flexible"?
- How do certain symbols, stories, myths, take hold in an organization, a community, or a market, and how are such narratives used to establish identities and control over members by organizations?
- In what ways is the rationality of organizations something that is constructed and projected by them—for example, when businesses all engage in surveys, forecasting, and future studies only to ignore those reports and do what they wanted to do in the first place?
- How are leadership and control enacted at the workgroup level, particularly in organizations where leadership is understood to be shared and the supervisor has become a facilitator?
- How is emotional expression understood, proscribed, and "managed" in a variety of work settings, and with respect to different cultures?
- How do aspects of organizations emerge out of informal conversations, relationships, and language itself—as when we decide to speak for a group or some collective body and not just for ourselves as unaffiliated individuals?

Why Theory?

What is theory, and why is it important to us? Kurt Lewin, a German-American social psychologist (who conducted research on groups and organizations in the middle of the twentieth century), believed that "there's nothing so practical as a good theory."[33] What did he mean, really, by this slogan? Theory can be thought of as generalizing across different situations or cases or, for our purposes, organizations. Formal theories are what researchers develop over time to make sense of various aspects of the world.

While sometimes very abstract, every theory is supposed to be tied to real cases or examples. Researchers don't have a formal or scientific theory of Microsoft, or of the Church of Jesus Christ of Latter-Day Saints, or of The European Parliament, but researchers might develop a theory of some dimension of organizations—say, about an organization's mission—that would apply to all three of these organizations. (In some cases, of course, it might actually make sense to speak of a "theory" of one organization, if that organization is large enough and spans time and space. Thus, we have lots of theories about how the U.S. or French or British governments work.)

So, theory takes us beyond particulars toward universals—or at least toward speaking more generally about various cases. In this sense, theory is a useful tool. It can be used more than once. It keeps us from having to start all over again in our understanding of the world, each time we face something new. Also, a theory can be a tool for predicting trends (take, for example, a theory of organizational strategy), or for making sense of lots of things going on simultaneously (for instance, a theory of multiple goals), or for deciding the best course of action (e.g., a theory of decision making). That's why good theory is so practical. Max Weber's theory of bureaucracy, for example, continues to help us explain the promise and pitfalls of many different types of organizations—from governmental agencies to religious denominations to labor unions (as we will discuss more fully in the next chapter).

So, what other things do theories about organizational communication "say"? What issues do they deal with? Listed below are several questions theories about organizational communication try to answer:

- What happens when people come together to create a new organization?
- How can the members of an organization work effectively together?
- How should an organization be governed, led, and managed?
- What values should an organization embody and promote?
- How do organizations relate to one another in society?
- What is "good organizational communication"?
- What groups are excluded by any particular theory or model of organization?

These are not new questions but enduring ones. They resurface in most of the societies of the world. Today, more than ever, we're asking ourselves these kinds of questions as we reconsider how best to work together, to solve problems, and to maintain some semblance of community in a fast-changing world.

We all carry around theories with us, even though we don't always call them that. Each of us has a theory of love, of friendship, of money, of power, etc. We use these frameworks of understanding, or *lay theories*, to approach situations so that we don't have to start from scratch with new ideas all the time. Thus, you may have a lay theory of work or education. And that theory may or may not correspond with some formal theory that researchers have written about.

Think about what you see as a good or effective organization. When have your basic understandings of how organizations work been challenged by specific experiences? That is, when have you learned something new about organizations because one of your experiences didn't fit your preconceptions—your own theory of organizations? For example, if you work with the assumption that the best kind of leadership is charismatic, you may find that idea challenged when you observe that your club has become too dependent on its charismatic founder. You notice that all the members of the club wait to see what the leader's "word" will be on any issue, and they all try very hard to please her. Seeing the limitations of charismatic leadership may lead to modifications of your theory to allow for other forms of leadership.

How do you define theory? What should a good theory do—what criteria should it meet? Can you think of an existing theory that you find especially appealing or valuable? Here are some qualities of a good theory:

- internally consistent and coherent;
- explanatory in lots of different situations;

Box 1.4 Reengineering and Its Variations

Let's look at one popular book on organizations and what it says about theories of organizations: *Reengineering the Corporation—A Manifesto for Business Revolution* by Michael Hammer and James Champy.[34] First, what do you notice about the title? What assumptions might underlie the terms being used? What expectations does the title lead you to have for the book?

Reengineering tries to get away from "functional" specialization, where the organization is structured into departments, each with one specific function. Reengineering also rejects the usual "line vs. staff" distinction between groups of employees. Under this traditional distinction, "production" areas in a manufacturing firm were "line functions," and personnel and accounting were "staff functions." Hammer and Champy contend that the traditional emphasis on job specialization is outdated and should be replaced with emphasis on the most central work processes in the organization.

Traditionally, most organizations consisted of departments that corresponded to recognized professions: accounting, engineering, marketing, personnel or human resources. Suppose we change departments like "accounts payable" and "billing" to groups connected with "procurement" and "customer service." Also, treat these new groupings as flexible and subject to change, based on the organization's most pressing needs. What if the organization were reorganized around the basic tasks it wishes to complete and the key problems it needs to deal with? What would have to be different about communication patterns? What new groupings (for example, teams) and new means of coordination would be required?

Hammer and Champy have created a theory of organizational effectiveness that revises or replaces some older theories. But the burden of proof is on their shoulders. Job and departmental specialization have been taking a particular course over the past two centuries. To test their theory, Hammer and Champy have to demonstrate that their theory has the potential for strong, practical results. Now, think further about what Hammer and Champy are proposing. What are some of the possible advantages and disadvantages to their approach to reorganization? Can you think of organizations or departments where reengineering would work better or worse? Finally, assuming you were supporting their idea, how might you try to "sell" it? (Imagine that you are a decision maker in a manufacturing firm that makes bicycles. As another example, consider yourself to be an advisor or consultant on the restructuring of a university.)

In a later book called *Beyond Reengineering* Hammer complained that many practitioners had misunderstood the first book on the subject and that many people had equated reengineering with downsizing while forgetting about the basic principles of restructuring.[35] Indeed, some people used reengineering as a synonym for downsizing: reducing the size of the workforce without altering the basic structure of the organization. This is a good example of how a theory can be transformed by the users and also how an idea, when popularized, becomes interpreted through cultural and political lenses. How and why does this happen?

"*Sir, the following paradigm shifts occurred while you were out.*"

- understandable or accessible to many people;
- simple and straightforward, not cumbersome;
- provocative, inspiring further research and debate;
- relevant to different cultures and historical periods;
- useful as a tool of application in daily life;
- suggestive of answers to basic human questions; and
- capable of being challenged and/or modified to accommodate new information.

Throughout this book, as we consider different theories and perspectives on organizational communication, we will revisit these criteria. We urge you to use them to determine whether perspectives presented are accurate and reasonable.

Thinking Critically

Theories and practice should be in conversation with one another. Just as certain theories may develop out of practice, certain practices can be informed by our theories. We may learn a lot about leadership from participating in work teams, but we can also try to apply different models of leadership when offered opportunities to lead. Interestingly, our practice sometimes prevents us from seeing the larger picture (the forest for the trees). That's another reason why theories are useful—they allow us the freedom not to get too immersed in day-to-day practicalities and to understand similarities and differences across situations.

We can translate theories from one domain to another, in an effort to be more creative in our approaches to organizations. In a way, this happens in everyday life, quite apart from what researchers are doing. Recently, for example, we can see how some religious institutions are behaving more like businesses, with the use of sophisticated marketing and public relations strategies. Conversely, lots of businesses are behaving more like religions, as they emphasize missions, values, and ethics. In this case, practical developments in the real world challenge our traditional theories and encourage us to explore old organizational models in new ways. This is exactly the kind of creative exploration that we encourage you to do as you move through the rest of our textbook.

Box 1.5 Current Trends in Work, Business, Organizations, and Societies

- Globalization of trade and economic interrelationships, along with changes in domestic economies
- Increasing influence of transnational corporations on domestic economies and domestic policies
- Increasing professionalization and commercialization of historically nonprofit sectors
- Shrinking government roles in welfare and development across the world
- Stronger linkages between various activist groups around the world
- Rapid advance of communications and computer technologies, with a strong emphasis on creating, accessing, and controlling information
- Growing concern for customer/consumer service in all sectors, especially in terms of the marketing function and the marketing organization
- Streamlining of organizational structures, with attendant downsizing, hierarchical flattening, attempts at de-bureaucratization, etc.
- Team-based restructuring and reengineering of work processes through a variety of popular programs (e.g., TQM, *Kaizen*, SDWTs, etc.)
- Tighter linkage between internal organizational affairs and external ones; consolidation of communications functions: e.g., linkage of public relations to employee relations
- Emergence of complex interorganizational relationships: joint ventures, strategic alliances, network structures, "adhocracies," and flexible manufacturing networks
- Lengthening work weeks in many nations and shortening weeks in others
- Heightened stress with both new work responsibilities and multiple tasks; "entrepreneurship" on the job along with greater monitoring of work (especially electronically)
- Increasing reliance by organizations on outsourcing (contract-based, project-based, temporary and part-time employment), stressing organizational and individual flexibility and adaptability (with many people becoming "free agents")
- Confronting issues of diversity, including recognition of changes in composition of workforce, emergence of international and domestic organizations with diverse workforces, and the pursuit of various approaches to "diversity management"
- Differential access to the Internet, educational institutions, informational and entertainment sources, opportunities to telecommute, access to databases, and network/community participation
- The rise of business for social responsibility, environmental awareness, and "green marketing"—in both sincere and cynical forms

Endnotes

[1] See, for example, George Cheney and Lars Thøger Christensen, "Organizational Identity: Linkages between Internal and External Communication," *The New Handbook of Organizational Communication: Advances in Theory, Research and Methods*, ed. Linda L. Putnam and Fredric M. Jablin (Thousand Oaks, CA: Sage, 2001) pp. 231–269; Ruth Smith, "Images of Organizational Communication: Root Metaphors of the Organization-Communication Relation," paper presented at the annual meeting of the International Communication Association, May 1983, Washington, D.C.; and James R. Taylor, *Rethinking the Theory of Organizational Communication: How to Read an Organization* (Norwood, NJ: Ablex, 1993).

[2] Max Weber, *Economy and Society*, ed. and trans. Guenther Roth and Claus Wittich (Berkeley: University of California Press, 1978).

[3] James R. Barker, "Tightening the Iron Cage: Concertive Control in the Self-managing Organization," *Administrative Science Quarterly* 38 (1993): 408–437; and Graham Sewell, "The Discipline of Teams: The Control of Team-based Industrial Work through Electronic and Peer Surveillance," *Administrative Science Quarterly* 43 (1998): 397–428.

[4] Donald Cushman and Sarah King, "High Speed Management: A Revolution in Organizational Communication in the 1990s," *Communication Yearbook* 16 (1993): 209–236.

[5] Kenneth H. Blanchard and Spencer Johnson, *The One Minute Manager* (New York: William Morrow, 1982).

[6] For an explanation of this point in reference to the field of marketing, see Lars Thøger Christensen, "Buffering Organizational Identity in the Marketing Culture," *Organization Studies* 16.4 (1995): 651–672.

[7] See Theodore E. Zorn, "The Uncooperative Cooperative," *Case Studies in Organizational Communication 2: Perspectives on Contemporary Work Life*, ed. Beverly D. Sypher (New York: Guilford, 1997) pp. 312–336.

[8] For an interesting discussion of assumptions about and effects of new technologies in organizations, see Joseph Walther, "Computer-mediated Communication: Impersonal, Interpersonal, and Hyperpersonal Interaction," *Communication Research* 23 (1996): 3–43.

[9] Theodore E. Zorn, Lars Thøger Christensen, and George Cheney, *Do We Really Want Constant Change?* (San Francisco: Berrett-Koehler, 1999).

[10] Richard Sennett, *The Corrosion of Character: The Personal Consequences of Work in the New Capitalism* (New York: Norton, 1998).

[11] See, e.g., John Seely Brown, *The Social Life of Information* (Boston: Harvard Business School Press, 2000).

[12] George Lakoff and Mark Johnson, *Metaphors We Live By* (Chicago: University of Chicago Press, 1980).

[13] Gareth Morgan, *Images of Organizations,* 2nd ed. (Thousand Oaks, CA: Sage, 1997).

[14] Weber.

[15] Stephen R. Axley, "Managerial and Organizational Communication in Terms of the Conduit Metaphor," *Academy of Management Review* 9 (1984): 428–437.

[16] Linda L. Putnam, Nelson Phillips, and Pamela Chapman, "Metaphors of Communication and Organization," *Handbook of Organization Studies*, ed. Stewart R. Clegg, Cynthia Hardy, and Walter R. Nord (London: Sage, 1996) pp. 375–408.

[17] Chester I. Barnard, *The Functions of the Executive, 30th anniv. ed.* (Cambridge, MA: Harvard University Press, 1968) p. 72.

[18] For a provocative treatment of the rise of the modern organization, see James S. Coleman, *Power and the Structure of Society* (New York: Norton, 1974).

[19] For a thorough discussion of the structure-versus-agency problem in social theory, see Anthony Giddens, *The Constitution of Society* (Berkeley: University of California Press, 1984).

[20] Adapted from Dean Ritz, ed., *Defying Corporations, Defining Democracy* (New York: Apex, 2001).

[21] *Santa Clara County v. Southern Pacific Railroad*, 118 U.S. 396, 1886. This "right" was granted in a simple statement made by the Chief Justice prior to the hearing. In 1949 Justice Douglas commented on this grant of corporate personhood: "There was no history, logic or reason given to support that view nor was the result so obvious that exposition was unnecessary."

[22] See *Minneapolis & St. Louis Railroad Co. v. Beckwith*, 129 U.S. 26, 1889, for 14th Amendment due process protections; see *Noble v. Union River Logging*, 1893 for 5th Amendment due process protections.

[23] See *Hale v. Henkel*, 201 U.S. 43, 1906.

[24] *Virginia Board of Pharmacy v. Virginia Consumer Council*, 425 U.S. 748, 1976.

[25] *International Dairy Foods Association v. Amestoy*, 92 F.3d 67, 2nd Cir., 1996. The Supreme Court overturned a Vermont law requiring the labeling of all products containing bovine growth hormone. The right *not* to speak inheres in political and commercial speech alike and extends to statements of fact as well as statements of opinion.

[26] It is interesting to note that corporations received substantive constitutional rights before women, blacks, and native Americans (rights are still denied to immigrants, children, criminals, and the insane). It took longer for these *natural* persons to acquire them because they had to be secured through constitutional amendments. Corporations on the other hand, acquired rights through comparatively quick adjudication in federal courts.

[27] *Virginia Board of Pharmacy v. Virginia Consumer Council*, 425 U.S. 748, 1976.

[28] *See v. City of Seattle*, 387 U.S. 541, 1967.

[29] See Morton J. Horwitz, *The Transformation of American Law, 1870–1960: The Crisis of Legal Orthodoxy* (New York: Oxford University Press, 1992). See also Martin J. Sklar, *The Corporate Reconstruction of American Capitalism, 1890–1916* (Cambridge: Cambridge University Press, 1988).

[30] As examples see organization Web sites for the Program on Corporations, Law & Democracy (www.poclad.org), Rainforest Action Network (www.ran.org), and the National Lawyers Guild (www.nlg.org). Some local governments have asserted their authority over corporations by outlawing corporate-owned farms. As examples see the work of Community Environmental Legal Defense Fund (www.celdf.org), and the Northern Plains Resource Council (www.nprcmt.org). In 2000 the city of Point Arena, California, passed a non-binding resolution declaring its opposition to corporate personhood.

[31] This list is adapted from Fredric M. Jablin, "Superior-subordinate Communication: The State of the Art," *Psychological Bulletin* 86 (1978): 1201–1222.

[32] For one review of past and then-emergent trends in organizational communication research, see Linda L. Putnam and George Cheney, "Organizational Communication: Historical Development and Future Directions," *Speech Communication in the Twentieth Century*, ed. Thomas W. Benson (Carbondale: Southern Illinois University Press, 1985) pp. 130–156.

[33] Kurt Lewin, *Field Theory in Social Science* (New York: Harper, 1951).

[34] Michael Hammer and James Champy, *Reengineering the Corporation: A Manifesto for Business Revolution* (New York: HarperCollins, 1993).

[35] Michael Hammer, *Beyond Reengineering: How the Process-Centered Organization is Changing Our Work and Our Lives* (New York: HarperCollins, 1996).

2

ORGANIZATIONAL STRUCTURE AND PROCESS

Draw a *picture* of an organization you're very familiar with—perhaps where you've worked or where you've been a member. If you can't think of another example, use your college or university. What does the organization look like to you? What are its main features? What "holds the organization together"? What is "solid" or sure about the organization? What parts of the organization are "fuzzier"—more fluid or more changeable? Where do you locate yourself and how do you represent your role in the organization? Is your picture a "snapshot" of the organization at one specific time, or does it capture some of the continual process of participants working together? These questions are fun to ask, but they also get at deeper and more important questions about the life of any organization. In our consulting in recent years, we use this exercise with organizational members at all levels of an organization. It's a good way to prompt discussion in an interview because, as you draw the organization, you are forced to put some things in the foreground and other things in the background. Also, the resulting picture may reveal a lot about how the organization is functioning—or not, as the case may be.

For example, a few years ago one of George's interviewees in a consulting project drew his organization as a set of camps, with quite a bit of distance between and fences separating them. Members lived in tents, and the camps were transient. Very occasionally a member of one camp would drift into another; these drifters were not well received and were regarded as strangers. This picture said a lot about how the interviewee understood work and life in the organization. Departments and project groups were not well integrated; there were walls or obstacles between them; the groups were insular; the relative locations of the groups with respect to one another changed continuously; there was little stability in group members' work

"Wentworth, could I take another look at that reorganization plan?"

experiences; and the overall shape of the organization was subject to constant revision. Now, this was just one member's picture of the organization. By putting it together with the drawings of many other organizational members, one could see and understand much better where individuals' perceptions differed and what they had in common. With this simple exercise, we can begin to learn more about two of the most basic dimensions of any organization: *structure* and *process*.

Defining Organizational Structures

What do we mean by structure in specific terms? Think of a building or the human body, for just two examples. Consider the structure of a skyscraper. We might conceive of the structure as the architecture of the building—the main parts that make the building what it *is* and serve to hold it together. But that says nothing about what's going on inside the building or its relations to the surroundings. The same is true of the human body. We can discuss the basic structures of the human body, the contours of it. We can see skin, for example, as something of a container for the body. We can talk about the skeletal system, the muscular system, and various other systems of the human body. But if we just describe the body in structural terms, we haven't said much about the processes going on inside these different systems—let alone what's occurring beyond the body's boundaries. In the remainder of this chapter, we are going to be talking about the relationship between organizational structure and process: what the terms mean, how they are interdependent, and what their influences are on the practical problems we face in contemporary organizational life.

In one sense, structure refers to the solid parts of an organization—the *framework* that gives the organization a shape, not just at this moment but also over time.

An organizational chart gives us a snapshot of the organization's structure, at least in terms of different members' positions, various departments, and the lines of authority or chain of command. We know that the organizational chart is not the whole story, but we also sense that it's important. It gives us an idea of what to expect in terms of how the organization and its members fit together.

More specifically, the structure of an organization includes *those aspects of an organization that are pre-specified for a given situation*. So, the agenda of a meeting gives structure to a group's discussion by laying out expectations of topics and goals and relevant pieces of information. As organizational communication researcher Bob McPhee (see box 2.1) explains, structure often becomes a *substitute* for spontaneous or unplanned communication.[1] In this way, we can think of structure as a kind of communication shortcut.

What we perceive as structure in any group or organization was at some time *decided upon and put in place.* In other words, organizational structures emerge from communication processes and may, in turn, replace future communication processes. Today's rules and regulations, or even the technology that shapes how we do work, were not *given* to founding members. All of these things emerged as decisions made by individuals and groups. After decisions have been reached, components of the organization seem more solid. Accepted patterns shape or govern behavior. Once the types of issues to be discussed at regular staff meetings are determined, they become part of the structure for future interaction and communication at work. The structure works like an icon on the computer desktop or a link on the Internet—a shortcut. The icon takes you to the program; the structure eliminates the necessity to repeat discussions at every meeting. This is both good and bad, as we will see.

Structure gives shape to our actions over time. If we *know* that every week at our staff meeting we'll discuss recent expenditures, then we don't need to decide each time to add budget discussions to the agenda. The meeting's format becomes predictable, reliable, and perhaps even ritualistic. Established structures like regular agen-

Box 2.1 Functions of Organizational Communication Structures[2]

Organizational structures serve a number of functions and have a variety of effects, some welcome and some unwelcome.

- *A general point of reference*: e.g., Max Weber's model of bureaucracy, which is the most commonly applied model of organizational structure.
- *An information-processing mechanism*: e.g., a standard operating procedure that helps an employee deal with a new piece of information.
- *A system form*: e.g., an open systems model of organizations that sees the many parts of an organization as interconnected in certain ways.
- *A resource* for power: e.g., an agenda that precludes discussions that might challenge the powers that be.
- *A carrier of beliefs and attitudes* that the individual carries around: e.g., a lay theory about "how organizations work" that structures one's management approach.
- *A set of rules with unintended, negative consequences*: e.g., rewarding A, while hoping for B.
- *Something enacted or continually accomplished*: e.g., confirming an agenda or justifying a decision.
- *Something constraining,* something to be resisted, or something to overcome, e.g., the chain of command, which may prevent an employee from talking directly to the boss's boss.

das often bypass the need for elaborate conversations or discussions. Structures save us time and trouble, while they help us build on past experience. In this sense, structures substitute for communication. We don't need to revisit discussions of policies that have already been decided. But the repeated use of an agenda for a meeting may also be a power strategy, as suggested in box 2.1, because it can be used systematically to prevent new voices or ideas from being heard. Alternatively, those who use the agenda may simply lack the creativity to come up with alternative structures—and thus are less powerful than they appear.

All organizations have structures, and any organization needs a certain amount of structure in order to maintain itself over time. Otherwise, the burden of spontaneity and "reinvention" becomes too great. This is why organizations develop standard operating procedures: for purchasing agreements, for evaluating new research proposals, for considering internal promotions, for dealing with customer complaints, etc. Ironically, some organizations even have *structures* for handling innovation and change (see chapter 11).

To understand structures, we need to consider what sociologist Anthony Giddens referred to as the *duality of structure*. This idea includes two critical facts. First, it is important to remember that structure is both an *outcome* of and a *resource* for interaction. While structure emerges out of the communication process, it also helps to influence future patterns of communication. A structure such as a set of by-laws for a student intramural sports team is both an outcome of founding members' discussions as well as a guide (or resource) for the team's future interaction. If the by-laws include an attendance policy (say, you can't miss more than two of ten games per season), this will become a point of reference for the members, and it will likely be the focal point of some future arguments. Some members will develop reasons why the rule should or shouldn't apply in a specific case. Deadlines or length requirements for class papers provide another example: the established expectations become a point of reference for both defenders and critics of the policy.

The second important fact is that structure is both *enabling* and *constraining*. Giddens suggested that structure helps us to accomplish things, yet it sometimes gets in our way.[3] Certain structures, like rules or habits, tend to take on a life of their own. In creating a new campus club, for instance, be careful not to burden the organization with too many structures, such as rules, procedures, and formal positions. A well-conceived rule makes it easier to initiate new members without continually reassessing how to do things, but over-reliance on such rules may contribute to the new members feeling "just like numbers." Giddens used the term *structuration* to mean the process by which structures emerge from interaction and then become resources for and constraints on future interaction. His concept helps us see how structure and process are interdependent. Structures enable us to do things more easily—like running a meeting—and hinder us by keeping our future talk and ideas within certain boundaries. This is why a number of sociologists use metaphors of cages and webs in their theories; indeed, the fact that we create structures that then constrain us is one of the main ironies of society itself.[4]

Key Elements of Organizational Structure

With respect to organizations, we commonly look at the following structural elements: *hierarchy, differentiation and specialization,* and *formalization*. Each of these aspects of structure shows up in the organizational chart, but each also has important implications for communication and the flow of information.

Hierarchy

Hierarchy usually refers to the vertical levels of an organization. It represents the distribution of authority among organizational roles or positions.[5] One of the most common images of an organization is the pyramid, placing some persons and groups in positions of power with respect to others in the organization. Generally speaking, we expect larger organizations to have more levels than smaller ones. However, there have been efforts in many industrialized countries recently to reduce the number of hierarchical levels of large organizations—through strategies such as "flattening," "restructuring," and "team-based" management. This change in structure is intended to make organizations more nimble and adaptable to changes in their markets and environments.

Hierarchy has huge implications for communication patterns and the flow of information. A very "tall" organization, with many hierarchical levels, can block the flow of messages upward (see box 2.2).

Differentiation and Specialization

Differentiation and specialization are terms that describe the division of labor in an organization. Specifically, they refer to the degree to which labor is divided into

Box 2.2 Why Bad News Has Trouble Going Up the Ladder[6]

There are a number of reasons why bad news (in particular) has trouble making its way upward in an organizational hierarchy. One explanation is the sheer number of levels that a message has to pass through. At each level, there's an opportunity for distortion of the original message or the possibility that the message will just "sit there" and go no further. In an interesting study, Athanassiades found the following reasons for the "upward distortion" of negative messages in organizations.

- A record of poor performance *in the part of the organization where the bad news originates, since the poor performance colors others' interpretations of the messages*
- *Lack of security and trust* on the part of the employee or department sending the negative message
- *Outright fear* of retribution by one's "boss" or higher-ups who might react negatively to the bad news
- *Ambition, impression management,* or a particular desire to present oneself and one's unit in the best light
- *Bad experiences* from the past with the sending of bad news
- *Lack of an open-door policy* in higher levels of the organization

Leaders and managers have to be especially careful about how they react to reports of problems in the organization. It is very easy to discourage the upward transmission of bad news. In fact, we would say that an effective leader has to be proactive in soliciting information and opinion about organizational problems, while at the same time having the wisdom to distinguish between "normal complaining" and what some consultants have called "golden gripes"—the problems that really matter for the organization and its members.

Now take the opposite vantage point. Can you see how some of these reasons also affect the upward transmission of good news?

various units, departments, and divisions to perform specific tasks. In an entrepreneurial, start-up organization, one or two people may do everything, thus reflecting a low level of specialization or differentiation. However, in large corporations, we typically find a high level of specialization, reflected in departments like production, planning, engineering, accounting, finance, personnel or human resources, marketing, public relations, and so forth. Specialization has a significant impact on communication, primarily because each specialty has its own language or jargon. While this shared language binds together people in that division, it often mystifies and excludes those in other departments. Computer experts sound very different from accountants, and both have trouble talking to personnel or human resource managers.

These different ways of talking and seeing the world reinforce the sense that different forms of specialization, or expertise, are domains unto themselves, making collaborative projects very difficult. A focus on *the expert* in any field can be a barrier to the participation of other employees in the organization, who may have good ideas about policy but lack the credentials or the accepted vocabulary to feel confident about participating in collaborative solutions.[7] Specialization, of course, also affects communication by establishing physical boundaries between different departments. The marketing people, for example, are typically located in different quarters than those in finance.

Sociologist Émile Durkheim observed over a century ago that one of the principal features of modern societies is job specialization. Generally speaking, modern societies are more heterogeneous than pre-industrial or tribal societies, and one of the most important factors that holds the society together is the interdependence fostered by job specialization. We call on the expertise of others when we need specific help—a plumber, an electrician, an automotive mechanic, and so forth. Durkheim saw such specialization as both a blessing and a curse. The interdependence of people who rely on others for functions outside their expertise (what he called and we still call "the division of labor") is an advantage when it holds society together and a disadvantage if it leads to alienation.[8] Specialization can lead to alienation when it separates people from one another, pulls them away from the products of their labor, and creates a division between the "professional" classes of society and those who are comparatively uneducated, unskilled, or untrained. Scholars and politicians imply these sorts of divisions when they use terms like "digital divide."[9]

Formalization

Finally, *formalization* refers to the degree to which interactions in the organization are characterized by rules, regulations, and norms. Formal communication is highly specified and prescribed. In the extreme form, members of the organization know what's going to happen before it does—the pattern becomes a ritual. This isn't necessarily a problem; both formal communication and ritual serve important functions in organizations (see chapter 4).

We easily recognize a very formal meeting or social situation. We take cues from the way people look and act and may even notice elements of the room itself. We can tell right away if the atmosphere in a meeting room is stiff or relaxed. A meeting with rows of seats facing a raised platform, a speaker on the raised platform with a podium and/or gavel, attentive audience members dressed in business suits, the use of rigid meeting procedures such as *Roberts Rules of Order*—these are all elements that would indicate a highly formal setting.

All other factors being equal, hierarchy, differentiation, specialization, and formalization tend to become more prominent in an organization over time. We seek to preserve our organization, and we do so by creating positions, establishing levels, and setting up formal procedures. When we consider a large organization with many formal structures, like Nike, Lufthansa Airlines, or the United Nations, it's difficult to remember that the organization today is *the product of many processes and interactions over time.* Almost all organizations are born out of informal interaction, no matter how established they look to us now.[10] In fact, people like to romanticize the beginnings of companies—for example, repeating tales of how Apple started in Steve Jobs's garage or how Microsoft began with a spark of an idea between Bill Gates and Paul Allen.

Ironically, even though hierarchy, differentiation, specialization, and formalization are put in place to preserve an organization, they also can threaten the long-term vitality of an organization. Max Weber, the German sociologist and father of organizational theory, understood this principle well. He examined the tendency of religious organizations to go overboard with structure, thus dampening some of their members' enthusiasm and spirit.[11] Any religious organization confronts the dilemma of preserving itself and what it stands for while also maintaining the kind of informal devotion and energy that characterized its beginnings. With too little structure, an organization is doomed to be only a footnote in history. Yet too much structure, doctrine, and rules can be stifling or can become an end in itself. Pope John XXIII initiated the Second Vatican Council, 1962–65, for these very reasons. He wanted to inspire a "rebirth" of the Roman Catholic Church, which he felt had become overly structured and lacking in vitality.

Parallel to the advantages and drawbacks of formalization in the structure of an organization, the formalization of communication can be beneficial or ruinous. Organizations attempt to structure communication to gain the maximum benefit, but the task is neither simple nor straightforward. Formal and informal communication depend on one another. For example, organizations need formal communication such as written rules or policies, but they also need informal means of interpreting and administering them, such as relatively informal discussion. Similarly, new ideas about policies may well come out of informal chats around the coffeemaker. The very life of some organizations may depend on an informal communication structure, especially organizations that focus on the generation of new ideas, such as research labs, advertising agencies, and software firms.

In the interest of keeping the tone of interaction serious, offering a professional "face" to customers, and generally being more efficient, some organizations try to eliminate or reduce the impact of informal communication at work. Some large department stores and various retail chains in the United States have employment contracts that specify no conversation except with customers, no obvious romantic relationships with any colleagues or coworkers, no arriving at or leaving work with fellow employees. Rocky Mountain Records and Tapes, a Denver-based music chain, had such a policy in the 1980s and early 1990s. Rather than increasing overall efficiency, however, the misguided policy exacerbated job dissatisfaction, increased employee turnover, and probably resulted in less enthusiastic interaction between employees and customers.

One of the most important findings of organizational communication research in the 1950s was that there is a positive relationship between the quality of the informal communication network and that of the formal one. In studies of how rumors spread through an organization (as they inevitably will!), management researcher Keith Davis found that the organizations most effective in terms of their formal communication also had healthy patterns for handling informal communication. These organizations could readily see the interdependence of the two types of communication. The informal network helped the organization accomplish its formally specified plans and tasks, while the formal network kept the organization on track. The issues surrounding informal interaction and the grapevine in any organization remind us again of the ways in which formal structure and communication process are two sides of the same coin.

Putting Structure and Process Together

Structure really only makes sense in relation to *process*, what we might describe as the ongoing flow of interaction. Structure is like the "figure" to the "ground" of process. For example, the organization's chart is often used as an example of structure, yet we know that the chart does not represent all that is going on. At its very best, the organizational chart is a snapshot of certain aspects of formally defined relationships in the organization. In a sense, the chart represents a structure that specifies certain processes, such as who reports to whom.

To understand structure in terms of process, think of the different forms that water takes: oceans, lakes, rivers, streams, trickles. The water flows continuously, and we know that stepping into a stream a second time is never quite the same experience as the time before. Yet, the river has a shape, even if the form changes gradually over time. The shape is reliable and recognizable. We can distinguish one river from another. The Danube, the Nile, and the Amazon look different—have different shapes, patterns, and structures. But, the process—the flow—of a river is harder to explain, draw, or capture.

Life is like that. We live in the flow of experience, but when we tell our "life's story" we can only highlight certain things, creating a narrative of what happened. We thus give structure to our lives by discussing "main events," "turning points," "principal characters," etc. We punctuate or structure our lives by highlighting these features in our story. When we are asked in a job interview to explain how we chose our major area of study, decided on a field, and picked a career path, our response is far more orderly in most cases than what really happened. Karl Weick, an organizational psychologist, describes this as *retrospective sensemaking.*[12] Once we've told the story a few times, *the narrative becomes part of us*, part of who we are, and we draw on that story line again and again as a resource for conversation with others.

The same is true when we try to describe an organization. This is precisely why it's hard to realize that a seemingly solid organizational structure has substantial change going on within it. But no process can exist without some degree of structure. Once a structure—like a dress code in a company—is created, it becomes part of the process of activity in the organization; it helps to shape the life of the organization from then on. But the process can also *alter* the structure, as when some employees decide one day to violate the dress code in favor of more casual, less specified attire. As the rhetorical and literary critic Kenneth Burke once put it, structure and process are like "the container and the thing contained."[13] They are the solid and the spontaneous elements of organizational life—those things that give the organization both shape and substance. Too little structure leaves us floating around, looking for moorings in our work world.[14] Too much structure constrains, limits creativity, and leads to alienation and boredom.

Further, one person's essential procedural rule to guarantee smooth progression is another person's useless "hoop" to jump through and waste valuable time. Your university or college may seem to have a lot of structure—especially in terms of chain of command—but when you visit another institution, yours may seem "loose" by comparison.

As mentioned earlier, many organizations are experimenting with new structures. A large New Zealand timber and wood products company, Fletcher Challenge, went through major restructuring *once a year* in the 1990s. It is impossible, however, for employees and organizations to adapt to or to *learn* new structures in a limited amount of time. Constant change results in lower job satisfaction, high turnover, and more inefficiencies than those the policy was designed to correct. As we'll discuss in chapter 11, some organizations get so carried away with the idea of change that they forget about the value and necessity of some stability. On the other hand, a lot of organizations talk a great deal about change without ever altering their structure! So, each case must be looked at carefully.

Some social-activist groups try to eliminate *all* hierarchy and structure in their organizations. The ideology of democratic principles, equality, informality, and intimacy guides their efforts. However, most soon learn that some structures are necessary for the organization to survive. For instance, some worker-owned cooperatives start up with radically direct democratic models, where every member votes or has input on every decision. Most quickly realize that they need to employ some sort of committee or task force structure, even if there is no single elected leader. The very successful manufacturing co-op, Burley Design Cooperative of Eugene, Oregon (United States), makes the brightly colored bicycle trailers now seen in many parts of the world. Today the company has nearly 200 employees and several hierarchical levels, although all employees make basically the same salary. When the company began in the late 1970s, there were a lot of growing pains. The group had a strong commitment to direct democracy. However, when every employee became involved in an extended discussion of what size dumpster was needed for the co-op, the members recognized the necessity for a committee structure for some issues.

Systems, Structures, and Processes

The system metaphor helps us analyze the complex interactions of the parts of an organization. We observed in chapter 1 that the idea of a system is a mixed metaphor, in that it can refer to both a living organism and a machine. This characteristic makes the system metaphor both flexible and a bit ambiguous. We all talk about systems of this or that: from prison systems to audio and video systems to computer systems. The system metaphor is now used so pervasively in both the academic research and in everyday talk that, like "skyscraper," it has become very nearly a dead metaphor. However, some researchers are using the concept in some very interesting ways.

Ludwig von Bertalanffy, who hoped to articulate a unifying scheme for all areas of human inquiry, popularized systems *theory* in the 1950s.[15] But, the *idea* of a system appeared much earlier. Recall from chapter 1 the use of the term in Chester Barnard's famous definition of organization: "a system of consciously coordinated activities or forces of two or more persons."[16] Barnard's definition was important because he explicitly recognized the fact that the organization consists of *interconnected interactions and energies*. The systems idea encourages us to look at the parts of a whole and the whole in terms of the parts, emphasizing that neither can be fully understood without reference to the other.

Systems theory has been important in calling the attention of scholars and practitioners to such things as: the *interdependence* of the various parts of an organization; the fact that an organization has relations with its larger environment and may be viewed on a continuum from "closed" to "open"; the idea of *equifinality*—the principle that there are multiple paths to the same outcome; and *entropy*—the principle that stresses the need for an organization to "import" new energies in order to avoid deterioration and disintegration (see box 2.3). While early organizational theories approached the organization as a closed system, throughout *most* of the history of organizational studies, researchers have emphasized system openness, advising organizations to be attuned to their environments. The idea of a complete "marketing organization" exemplifies the ideal of openness, in that the organization is expected to adapt constantly to what its customers want and even to *anticipate* what they will want in the future.

Lately researchers have noted the value of some degree of system "closedness." From German sociologist and system theorist Niklas Luhmann,[17] we learn that organizations must not become *too* open toward their environments, or they will lose coherence, boundaries, and identity. It's like using a sieve or a filter with holes that are too big: you can't retain the things you need. This is what happens to some religious organizations that attempt to bend too much to the attitudes and values of those around them. They may succeed by expanding, but their message becomes watered down, and their membership less committed. Organizations may be open toward their surroundings in the way they collect information but closed in the way they interpret and use it, or vice versa. To be open in all these processes is impossible.[18] Openness and closure, thus, are closely related.

Although the term *equifinality* doesn't roll off the tongue with ease, it is a very practical idea that emphasizes the possibility of achieving the same goal in many ways. Thus, if cost cutting is the goal in your office, you may well find that there is more than one way to achieve it. Likewise, if encouraging innovation is the objective for your organization, you may consider not only the traditional solution—investing more in the research and development (R&D) department, but also stimulating other parts of the organization to contribute to the innovativeness of the company. Thinking along these lines is helpful to break out of accustomed patterns of dealing with issues. Remembering the principle of equifinality can be very useful in handling issues as diverse as conflict, rewards, and leadership.

The systems metaphor can bias us toward assumptions of harmony and unity, simply because it suggests that all the parts should necessarily be working together.[19] That is, simply by calling a collection of different institutions a system may obscure the fact that they don't really work *together* all that well, in the sense of coordinating their efforts. For instance, the U.S. justice system consists of varied organizations and institutions, including the police, attorneys, courts, prisons, and other correctional institutions. In practice, however, these are often working at cross-purposes with one another. The courts frequently want to limit the number of cases they hear. But police may be rewarded (at least informally) for bringing more alleged violators into the system. Attorneys, similarly, may seek more rather than fewer cases. Within the range of correctional institutions, we will also find differences in goals and perspectives. Some facilities for youth, for instance, may be genuinely interested in reform, while most of the adult institutions are primarily punitive. Since the prisons do little to rehabilitate offenders, many become repeat offenders, further burdening "the system."

Organizational communication scholar Marshall Scott Poole summarizes two of the major advantages of thinking from a systems view: "first [systems theory] attempts to explain how unintended consequences are generated by our lack of knowledge of the implications of our actions. Second, it attempts to account for properties that

Box 2.3 Open Systems Theory

Background:

General systems theory began as an attempt to unify all fields of inquiry. In sociology, structural functionalism attempts to understand the structure and function of each constituent part of society. Systems theory incorporates lessons from both organisms and machines and applies them to society.

Key Concepts and Principles:

- Input, Throughput, and Output: Every open system takes in elements from the environment (inputs), uses and changes them in some way (throughputs), and puts elements into the environment
- Interdependence of Parts: The parts—or subsystems—interact, such that each part affects and is affected by the other parts.
- Holism/Totality: The whole may be greater, lesser, or the same as the sum of the parts.
- Equifinality: There are multiple paths to the same outcome.
- Equilibrium: Open systems seek a balance in interaction between the system and its environment.
- Homeostasis: The tendency of open systems to strive to maintain equilibrium, or constant conditions, even in the face of environmental changes.
- Entropy: There is a natural tendency toward disorder, randomness, and the dissipation of energy.
- Feedback: Open systems have mechanisms for monitoring and self-adjustment.
- Variable Coupling: There may be "loose" or "tight" relationships between parts of a system.
- Continuum from closed to open: Systems such as organizations are rarely completely open or closed; rather, they may be seen as being on a continuum, that is, *relatively* open or closed.
- Process/Change/Phases or Stages of Development: Open systems are dynamic, not static; they change, sometimes in discrete phases or stages.

Sample Applications:

- Social-Technological Interfaces: For example, seeing people and the technologies they use as a system, as in computer-assisted group decision support systems.
- Conflict Management: For example, exploring causes of conflict in the relevant system, rather than focusing on individual actions or personalities as the source of conflict.
- Leadership: For example, viewing leadership as distributed across the organization rather than residing in an individual.

emerge at the collective level from the interaction of many individuals."[20] In other words, looking at an entire system helps us to appreciate that there are "side effects," or secondary results, of many actions. One word of caution—even with fairly complete knowledge of a situation, we will always be subject to unintended consequences.

So far we have emphasized the "big picture" with respect to systems ideas, especially the interrelatedness of parts. However, such connections are seldom equal in strength within an organization. Parts of an organization—such as departments—may be tightly or loosely "coupled" in terms of the overall structure. Tightly coupled parts of a system influence each other always and very directly—that is, "mechanically," like pulling a lever or pressing a button on a candy dispensing machine and having a treat pop out. Only man-made machines are completely tightly coupled. All living systems are loosely coupled—at least to some degree.[21]Loosely coupled parts of a system are somewhat or even largely independent of one another. Think of the metaphor of train cars and how they are linked or coupled. If they're too tightly coupled, the train loses its ability to negotiate curves. But if the cars are too loosely coupled, the train won't stay linked while going up a hill. The trick is to find balance, or a happy medium.

If one department is experiencing a crisis, to what extent should others in the same organization share the disturbance? For some issues, problem sharing is definitely a good idea, particularly if the organization's long-term survival is at stake. For many day-to-day business difficulties, however, there is no utility in having every department reacting to another's troubles like a cue ball hitting other billiard balls. Think of a chameleon. A chameleon changes its colors on the outside to adapt to its surroundings, but its insides stay the same. To survive in a changing environment, the chameleon is loosely coupled. And the changes it undergoes on its surface can be thought of as changes in order not to change (see also page 323).[22] Consider various types of organizations: a university, a hospital, a governmental agency, a manufacturing company, etc. What are the advantages and disadvantages for organizational subunits being tightly versus loosely coupled?

Bureaucracy: The Structure We Know Best and Like the Least

Now, let's turn to the most common structure for an organization and explain how it arose, its advantages and its disadvantages, and what might be reasonable alternatives to it. Max Weber, the German theorist most often credited with explaining the dynamics of bureaucracy, worked for a variety of private and public organizations, often as a consultant. He also traveled extensively. His experiences and his studies gave him a very broad view of the different possibilities for organizational structures and processes at different times and in different societies. Weber was interested in what he considered one of the most basic questions in society: How, and under what circumstances, do people obey others, especially institutions, even when no force is applied? Weber wrote extensively on the topic of power and specifically on what he called legitimate power or authority. He distinguished three basic authority types: charismatic, traditional, and legal-rational. Let's talk about the first two briefly, and then spend more time on the third to understand the roots and dynamics of bureaucracy.

Types of Authority

Weber's notion of *charismatic authority* was based on the personal characteristics and power of an individual or a small group—in the same sense that we now use the term *charisma*. The messages that matter in an organization relying on charismatic authority are highly personal; they emanate from one person and feature inspiring values and goals.[23] Authority is exercised in a highly personal way. For Weber, the prototype of charismatic power was the religious sect. Each of the world's major religions (as well as smaller ones) was originally centered on the characteristics or personal power of an individual. That person was often perceived as a manifestation of goodness, a prophet, perhaps even divine, and the organization developed through the charismatic power of that individual.

The greatest challenge for charismatic authority occurs when the leader disappears from the scene. Because the authority of the organization is so centered on that person, his or her absence presents a crisis. In corporations, as well as in many other kinds of organizations today, this problem is known as the problem of *succession*. The difficulty in making the transition from the charismatic founder or group of founders of an organization to a new source threatens the stability of the organization.

Another challenge for charismatic authority, which Weber called the *routinization of charisma,* is how to capture some of the spirit, energy, and dynamism of the founders of the organization and preserve those things in the institutional structure of the organization. Any organization based on a mission, or a set of core values, has to deal with this concept. One solution is to attempt to institutionalize the activities of the organization—to fill the absence of the original charismatic authority by creating lots of positions, rules, and regulations. Ironically, what we preserve may not be what we intended. The organization will change as a result of the addition of hierarchy, specialization, and formalization.

The second type of authority that Weber identified is *traditional authority*. The classic example is the *monarchy.* While monarchical systems of government are gradually disappearing from the world, this type of authority dominated for centuries. Think of the film *The Last Emperor* (1987), for example, where a four-year-old child comes to the throne as the last member of the Ch'ing dynasty in China at the turn of the twentieth century. In the film, many people, including governmental officials, try to do the bidding of the child because authority is believed to reside in the familial lineage. The child himself is the repository for authority.

It's easy for us to dismiss traditional authority as irrelevant in the modern world until we examine our experiences in organizations. Think of when you enter an organization for the first time and begin to learn the ropes. One of the most important activities you engage in is to ask questions of the people in the organization about what to do and what not to do. After you've been there six months or so, you may begin to feel like you can probe a bit further, perhaps even questioning some of the practices of the organization. Common responses to your questions may be: "Don't worry about that" or "That's the way we do things around here and that's the way we've always done it." This is the logic of traditional authority in the organization. It is authority for authority's sake: authority based in tradition and a desire not to rock the boat, with the intention to keep things going as they've always gone. Messages that appeal to or reinforce the idea of the organization's continuity are part of the logic of traditional authority. The idea is that the organization has power in itself and that power is worth preserving.

The third type of authority, *legal-rational*, is best exemplified by bureaucracy. Weber observed several worldwide trends just after the turn of the twentieth century: further industrialization, increased use of new technology in the automation of industry (like Henry Ford's assembly line, which first appeared in 1912); greater reliance on record keeping; and especially a push toward the standardization of work processes. Rules and procedures were taking precedence over arbitrary decision making and intuition. Weber predicted that this "march of rationality" (the general logic by which an organization or a society operates) would mean that bureaucracy would become the dominant form of organization regardless of the economic basis of any particular society.

Key Elements of Bureaucracy

Given the multiple examples of red tape and problems we've encountered or read about, we often equate bureaucracy with inefficiency. But it's important to probe more deeply, to ask questions about why we have bureaucracy, what its basic elements are, and what its advantages and disadvantages are.

Some of the key elements of bureaucracy from Weber's perspective follow.

- A fixed division of labor (that is, specializations are specified as jobs, positions, or roles)
- A clearly defined hierarchy of positions, each with its own sphere of competence
- Job applicants selected on the basis of technical qualifications
- Employees remunerated (paid) by fixed salaries
- The position as a primary occupation of the office holder, who will make a career in that position
- Promotion granted according to seniority and/or achievement and dependent on the judgment of superiors
- Separation of day-to-day workers from higher authorities through the creation of management or administration
- Separation of work from home and family life
- Written rules governing the performance of duties and behavior at work[24]

Together, these elements form what Weber called "an ideal type" of bureaucracy—not ideal in the sense of something perfect or an ultimate good but in terms of something in a pure form. Weber understood well that no complete or pure bureaucracy could ever exist. He also knew that some of its features would change, even though he couldn't imagine the specifics (for example, how "telecommuting" would affect employees' relationships with their organizations). Instead, he saw the bureaucratic model as a "template" one could place over an organization when analyzing it to see which parts were bureaucratic and which were not. Weber expected that any largely bureaucratic organization would also have other characteristics, including other forms of authority. Consider the many large corporations that are managed by charismatic CEOs (like IBM in its first few decades) or a bureaucratic religious organization such as the Roman Catholic Church steeped in traditional authority.

Sociologist Alvin Gouldner's work on bureaucracy in the 1950s helps us understand the relationship between process and structure in the context of bureaucracies.[25] Gouldner, whose work followed from the writings of Max Weber, conducted his study of bureaucracy in a gypsum plant outside the village of "Oscar Center" in the state of Illinois. In his study, Gouldner identified several types of bureaucracy present in that one factory and identified several processes that led to the formation of a bureaucratic structure. Specifically, he found that bureaucratization was a result of managerial succession and the desire to solve problems. The new manager of the plant, "Vincent Peele," implemented a range of rules in order to cut costs, increase productivity, and prove himself to the head office in Lakeport. Gouldner also attributed bureaucracy to the influence and power of particular individuals and as a response to status-generated tensions. In his study, this was particularly visible in Peele's efforts to try to rid the factory of the "old guard," consisting mainly of foremen who had been around a long time and controlled how things were done in the factory. Finally, Gouldner found that bureaucratization occurs when all the people concerned give equal importance and value to a rule and thus form a "representative" bureaucracy. As a case in point, he discusses the formation of safety rules in the plant that were implemented by both workers and managers.

In terms of communication, the model of bureaucracy is very important. The overall *ethos* or character of Weber's model is rationality. Weber's theory sees organizations as a means to overcome individual cognitive limitations and biases by appealing to a higher system of rules and procedures. In this way, bureaucracy is designed to protect us and our group from too much weight being given to the whims of one person, who may simply be acting on intuition or pursuing self-interest. In principle,

"It's always cozy in here. We're insulated by layers of bureaucracy."

bureaucracy is intended to promote fairness; it is designed to treat everyone the same—at least within the bounds of considerations of merit. In this sense, bureaucratic principles, such as hiring and promoting on the basis of *bona fide occupational qualifications* (or BFOQs) have often benefited women and minority groups trying to break into certain institutions or professions that were traditionally run by "old boys' clubs." On the other hand, even with a well-run bureaucracy, the rules of fairness may be limited in scope and exclusionary in other ways. Fairness is one of the most important features of bureaucracy, a feature often lost in contemporary discussions.[26]

Bureaucracy—like other forms of structure—is a type of communication shortcut. Bureaucracy gives us a system of rules, regulations, and procedures for dealing with a variety of situations. It helps us set standards that will apply across the board, or at least in most instances that we can imagine. The rule we use is an outcome of many deliberations, and we don't have to repeat all the discussion that went into creating it each time we try to apply it. (On the other hand, the reasons for the rule can get lost over time as more and more people apply it; a standardized system invariably translates to a loss of individuality. See the discussion of disadvantages below.)

Advantages of Bureaucratic Structure

So, there are good reasons why we have bureaucracy, reasons that get lost today in our rush to demonize it. As sociologist Charles Perrow summarizes, bureaucracy exists in large part to implement universalistic or common standards, and it tries to purge particularistic ones that are tied to specific individuals or situations.[27] This logic is very modern, and it echoes the concerns of science for uncovering general laws and principles to explain the world. In the case of bureaucracy, as Weber himself recognized, we're seeking generalizable, rational principles for structuring our work activities. Listed below are some of the principles that made bureaucracy so appealing:

- Bureaucracy is based on merit, is non-arbitrary, and is systematic. This differs dramatically from an organization governed by the desires of one person who happens to be in charge.
- Bureaucracy can be used to organize large systems. For example, governmental agencies, multinational corporations, and global religious denominations are usually run according to bureaucratic principles. The principles of bureaucracy are generalizable and can be used in many different contexts.
- Bureaucracy offers a set of rules and practices that can be learned, applied consistently, and passed down over time.

Disadvantages of Bureaucratic Structure

Now let's turn to three major disadvantages of bureaucracy: (1) In a bureaucratic structure that exists over time, there's a great risk of overcentralization of power at the top of the pyramid. (2) There's a threat to individuality, the danger of everyone becoming, in Weber's own words, "merely a cog in the machine." (3) Bureaucracy elevates what Weber called formal rationality over substantive rationality; people become more concerned about calculating little tasks and less aware of the big picture.

The first disadvantage, the overcentralization of power, may be seen in nearly any large organization that has existed for a number of years. Many large U.S. corporations in the 1960s and 1970s are particularly good examples. Some of these organizations, like Ford and General Motors, had developed more than 10 levels in their organizational hierarchies, creating a huge gulf between those at the top and those at the bottom of the hierarchy, and an enormous amount of power for those at the top. It's not coincidental that "planned obsolescence"—the idea that products are designed to have a limited life so they have to be replaced—was coined within industries interested in maximizing sales.

To understand the second disadvantage, the threat to individuality, imagine yourself as a student in the following situation. You intend to apply for financial aid for the next semester, and you've just learned that the deadline was yesterday. Without assistance, you're not sure you're going to be able to continue in school. When you go to the financial aid office, what sort of appeal do you make? Think carefully because your initial impulse might be to talk about *fairness*. But the deadline was published. If you invoke the principle of fairness, the response may be very simple: "I *am* being fair. The deadline was published, and I'm applying the rule to you as I've applied it to everybody else." You probably have a better chance if you use individualistic appeals: "My dog died yesterday"; "I was sick"; or, "My partner just left me." These particularistic appeals focus on you as a person, as an individual—dimensions normally ignored the bureaucratic perspective. And there we find the threat to individuality: the conflict surfaces because the organizational rules become more important than the individuals they were designed to serve. When we sense as employees or members of an organization that we're replaceable, we are disturbed that our unique qualities seem to have no relevance.

The third disadvantage involves conflict between formal and substantive rationality. To put it another way, people become preoccupied with the measurable *means* to achieve certain goals—a system for filing, a technology, or a specific work practice—and less concerned with the content of those larger goals. The midlife crisis is often the result of this type of conflict: A person who is busy going about the day-to-day routine of his or her life suddenly has a crisis of meaning. We sometimes structure our world and organize our time to make deadlines, show up at meetings, and so on, without thinking about the ultimate goals. We can become obsessed with squeezing in a number of activities without asking ourselves if they are really important to us. If we eventually recognize that we have structured our lives around activities that aren't fulfilling, we can experience a crisis. Many organizations suffer the same sort of malady and need to reflect on what's really important. Consider, for example, the hospital that is so concerned about processing forms correctly that it forces patients to wait before being treated. While there may be legal and institutional pressures on hospital employees to "get the forms done right," that concern has to be balanced against the larger goal of offering necessary treatment to patients.

From Weber's perspective, organizations *should* experience crises of meaning. On a daily basis, the members of an organization are wrapped up in doing what they do, worried about the little details of getting their job done; the same can be true for the organization as a whole. When a person or a department is concerned primarily about how to move a stack of paper from one side of the desk to another, it is easy for them to lose sight of what might be the larger purpose involved in their work. This is exactly what Weber warned against: the structure of work activities can overwhelm the purpose and the basic processes of work. Weber used the metaphor of the iron cage to depict bureaucracy, showing how it both protects and traps us inside a structure we have created.

Box 2.4 Bureaucracy: "Can't live with it; can't live without it!"

When George was a new assistant professor at the University of Illinois in the mid-1980s, he was asked to be an informal consultant for Students for Mutual Arms Reduction Talks (SMART). At a time when concern about the threat of nuclear warfare between the United States and the Soviet Union was alarmingly high, this group of student activists was interested in working on the problem at the level of citizen participation. When George attended their three-hour meeting one evening, he was astonished at the organization's purpose, its structure, and how it went about getting its work done. The organization's leader outlined on the blackboard three hierarchical levels, six departments, and even included a position of "Xeroxer" for one of the club association members whose job would be to make photocopies for all of the other members of the organization. This was an organization with only twelve core members and about 25 others associated with it, yet they were intent on implementing a highly structured bureaucracy. At first, George was shocked by this, but upon reflection reasoned: "Why not? Isn't this the most common organizational structure available?" Soon this small group of activists was going to resemble AT&T or IBM. No doubt the designated Xeroxer was one of the first to be dissatisfied and did not remain committed to the organization very long! In fact, the organization itself probably didn't last long because it was too weighed down by its own structures.

It's easy for us to look at a case like this and laugh, thinking that the organization wasn't so smart after all. But the larger lesson here applies to many organizations and to many of our experiences. Given that the student activist group needed some kind of structure, how do you think they should have structured their work? Specifically, what would you recommend for an organization dealing with each of the following dimensions of the organizational structure? Especially consider how an organization like this one can best inspire its members while also preserving itself.

- Authority and Hierarchy
- Decision-making Methods
- Rules for Active Members
- Job Specialization and Specifications
- Degree of Formality in By-laws and Meetings
- Reward Structure: Benefits and Penalties

Searching for Alternative Organizational Structures

Today many observers speak of "non-bureaucratic" or "post-bureaucratic" organizations.[28] In California's Silicon Valley, for example, there are many high-tech firms that organize themselves around a set of principles that include:

- a relatively flat organizational structure;
- a high level of education and training for most organizational members;
- no fixed positions for individuals (except, perhaps, the founder!);
- project-centered organization (in contrast to a traditional functional structure);
- a high degree of interdependence;
- little regard for seniority;
- innovation as priority;

- rewards tied to performance; and
- strong emphasis on ad hoc rules, procedural flexibility, and adaptation to the market environment.

This is the very kind of organization popularized in the early 1980s by Tracy Kidder's book *The Soul of a New Machine*, which described the joys and the pressures of work life inside a highly dynamic and demanding computer hardware firm.[29] Organizations that follow these principles tend to be more nimble than traditional, bureaucratic organizations. Industries like high tech, advertising, and research and development, where work is fundamentally about new ideas, often use this form of organization, as do team-based sectors in government and education. In some ways, non-bureaucratic organizations are nothing new. Organizations ranging from social movements to student groups to small labor unions to worker co-ops have experimented with flat structures and flexible processes for a long time. As we'll discuss in chapter 8, non-bureaucratic models are often seen as being compatible with egalitarian and democratic philosophies of organizing. With respect to communication, non-bureaucratic models of organizations are less predictable and more fluid than Weber's model. Now, let's look at so-called alternative models of organization more carefully. They're called "alternative" precisely because they want to be different from bureaucracy. As we'll see, that is not an easy goal to achieve.

As we depart from the bureaucratic form, the organizational structure gets more fluid, more flexible. The hierarchy becomes flatter, and people are released from the moorings of the traditional division-and-department structure. At the same time, however, the boundaries of the organization as a whole, and the boundaries of individual units within the organization, become much less apparent. Thus, there is less predictability in people's work behaviors. Also, there are much higher demands placed on the individual in terms of being able to work with a variety of different people and not necessarily the same people today as yesterday, or as tomorrow.

Organizational theorist Gareth Morgan (see box 2.5) uses diagrams to help us visualize some of the key differences in structure and what they mean in terms of work and communication patterns within the organization. Note that the hierarchical structure of the organization becomes less structured from the first to the last model. Work is *re*organized—activities become centered not so much on traditional departments but on important projects and tasks that need to get done. In chapter 1 we talked about reengineering as a theory of organizing work and organizing people's relationships within the organization. As Hammer and Champy point out, the essence of the idea of reengineering is to consider the basic work processes of the organization, and then organize work and employees' relationships around those basic functions.

Procurement, developing new products, serving the customer, representing the organization to outsiders, and so forth are all basic activities. We can think about these as work processes that might bring together representatives of many traditional departments in a bureaucracy. Thus, under "representing the organization to outsiders," we might bring together personnel from areas traditionally thought of as external communication functions—sales, advertising, public relations, and marketing. But we could also include employees from a variety of internally focused departments (like human resources, production, quality, accounting, etc.). Indeed, it may be argued that today these latter departments are as important as the former when

Box 2.5 Bureaucracy and Other Organizational Forms[30]

Rigid Bureaucracy

Matrix Organization

Project Organization

Loosely Coupled Organic Network

organizations represent themselves to outsiders. The point in moving toward a project-based structure is to allow the organization to orient itself toward its most fundamental concerns at a given time and to bring together all the necessary expertise and resources.

In moving from model to model, we see the need for different relationships and different communication. Each model can be viewed as a pattern for communication. The *rigid bureaucracy* highlights standard operating procedures, emphasizes rules and established procedures, and relies on stable positions and departmental boundaries. Much of the work that goes on in such an organization is likely to be carried out through formal relationships and messages. The *matrix organization* calls for a break from established patterns of interdepartmental communication and requires a great deal of ad hoc, on-the-spot organizing. In this form, we would expect a complex weave of formal and informal relations and messages. In the *project organization*, boundaries between departments are largely eliminated; members of project teams often come from widely differing parts of the organization. In some instances, the entire organization may function as a team. The high premium placed on coordination means that there would be relatively little predictability in relationships, work activities, and messages—although distinct patterns of employee relations may develop within and across projects. The project organization may not last over time. This type of team-based structure parallels what management scholar Henry Mintzberg calls "adhocracy."[31] The *loosely coupled organic network* has no clear blueprint. This kind of organizational structure emerges when a set of groups or organizations with common interests try to form an alliance or a larger working group transcends the specific organizations that make it up.

Emergent Structures and Self-organizing Systems

We have emphasized how the structure and process of an organization are interdependent. It's easy to forget this interdependence when what we *see* of an organization is some architecture, the formal organizational chart, logos, or handbooks of rules and procedures. These things can keep us from seeing how organizations develop over time and especially how structure emerges through communication processes. With today's stress on adaptability in a turbulent environment, researchers as well as practitioners are beginning to pay close attention to the ways various organizational structures emerge and especially to how organizations can learn to modify their structures over time to meet changing needs and a host of situations.

Ideas about *emergent* structure run counter to the definition of structure we offered near the beginning of this chapter, which emphasized what's *pre-specified for a situation*. Structure in that sense is something we carry around with us to help shape new situations using familiar tools. Still, as we have seen, structure doesn't simply come down from above; it is created and has a history—like a set of rules that we apply faithfully to the way we design public speeches. In talking about emergent structure, we are being deliberately ambiguous. We're trying to capture some recent trends both in organizations and in researchers' understandings of them that are a bit complicated, but we see them as important not only theoretically but also practically.

We mean "emergent structure" in at least three senses. The first meaning is the idea that a fairly unstructured, informal, and spontaneous set of work relationships can become an effective structure that works for the people involved and allows them to adapt that structure as needed. This is the idea of *order arising out of relative disorder*, sometimes even out of chaos. In a sense, all organizations begin this way. With this point, we call attention to the fact that order and disorder are interdependent. One implication of chaos theory for organizational communication,[32] for instance, is that certain levels or areas of the organization may be less structured than others, thereby allowing greater creativity. Those parts of the organization then act as incubators for new and potentially useful structures. Moving away from the belief that every level and every department of an organization needs to have the same *degree* of structure allows initiatives to be tried and tested. New patterns of work may emerge that will help the entire organization achieve its common purpose.

The second sense of emergent structure involves the idea that systems, such as organizations, manifest tendencies to "know" their relevant environment and help to determine how the system will act and react to a range of situations. Any system, from a biological cell to a society, has a "generative mechanism" that helps to shape even its seemingly unexpected behaviors. Cells have built-in mechanisms for sensing themselves and repeatedly clarifying their relationship with the environment. Established systems have certain "logics" that may not be evident at first.[33] For example, think of how some operating procedures in an organization are never really stated but are apparent to an outside observer who watches how the organization reacts to news from headquarters. When asked, organizational members usually explain these mechanisms by saying "that's just how things happen around here." Any system may reveal a tendency to become more organized in particular ways. The movement from informal to formal procedures in organizations is the most obvious aspect of this. But there may be built in (but non-obvious) ways in which a group or organization responds to the environment, deals with change, and resolves crises.

The third meaning of emergent structure is that communication practices themselves produce certain structures and that organizational frameworks, accordingly, arise from extended interaction for specific purposes. Thus, rather than seeing communication as happening *in* organizations, we should also look to the organizational properties of communication itself. For example, the placement of nouns and pronouns in talk at work often tends to *reify* (treat as "real") authority—as when "a committee announces" some conclusions. Repeated use of the same verbs (often converted from nouns), like "dialoguing" or "brainstorming" or "conferencing," has the effect of making certain processes, activities, and procedures seem important and well established. Communication scholar James R. Taylor and his colleagues urge us to consider not just how communication occurs within organizations but also how organization arises out of communication—as when groups of people begin to recognize that they are an organization only after they start calling themselves a "coalition" or a "band" or a "workforce" or a "network."[34]

Snapshot Synthesis

We hope the examples in this chapter have provided a new perspective on structure and its interaction with process. Structure often serves as a symbol. We use it to convince others (and ourselves) that we are doing things the right way—being systematic. Structuring some activities allows us the freedom to contemplate others.

Effective structures enable choice and are self-adaptive. If there are built-in mechanisms for reflection in the organization, members can influence the current structure to adapt to needed changes. Structure can be reframed but it requires careful analysis and the ability to see beyond accustomed responses. Now that you are more familiar with structure and process, we hope you will think a bit differently about organizational structure than you did in the past—recognizing that what may appear quite solid is actually more fluid and what seems malleable may in fact be rigid.

Key Concepts

- **Structure**: those aspects of an organization that are pre-specified for a given situation; these become a *substitute* for spontaneous or unplanned communication
- **Process**: the ongoing flow of interaction; exists in an interdependent relationship with structure
- **Duality of Structure:** the notion that structure is both an *outcome* of and a *resource* for interaction; as a resource, structure both enables and constrains interaction
- **Hierarchy:** usually refers to the vertical levels of an organization; represents the distribution of authority among organizational roles or positions
- **Differentiation or Specialization:** describes the division of labor in an organization, the extent to which labor is divided into specialized units, departments, and divisions
- **Formalization:** the degree to which interactions in the organization are characterized by rules, regulations, and norms; formal communication is highly specified and prescribed
- **Open versus Closed (Systems):** amount of influence of the environment on a system; applied to organizations, open systems are often considered the ideal in that they adapt constantly to the environment, yet some degree of "closedness" may be desirable to avoid losing coherence, boundaries, and identity
- **Authority:** the basis for securing people's compliance in organizations; Weber distinguished three basic authority types: charismatic, traditional, and legal-rational
- **Bureaucracy:** the most common type of organizational structure in contemporary organizations; based on legal-rational authority; includes (among other features) fixed division of labor and a clearly defined hierarchy of positions
- **Post-bureaucratic Structure:** contemporary organizational forms based on principles such as a relatively flat organizational structure, no fixed positions for individuals, project-centered organization, and little regard for seniority
- **Emergent Structure:** the idea that structures, or order, may emerge somewhat spontaneously from interaction; also, unstructured, informal, and spontaneous set of work relationships can become an effective structure that works for the people involved

Endnotes

[1] See Robert D. McPhee, "Formal Structure and Organizational Communication," *Organizational Communication: Traditional Themes and New Directions*, ed. Robert D. McPhee and Phillip K. Tompkins (Thousand Oaks, CA: Sage, 1985) pp. 149–178.
[2] Adapted from McPhee.
[3] Anthony Giddens, *The Constitution of Society* (Berkeley: University of California Press, 1984).
[4] Clifford Geertz, *The Interpretation of Cultures* (New York: Basic Books, 1973).
[5] Mary Jo Hatch, *Organizational Theory: Modern Symbolic and Postmodern Perspectives* (Oxford, UK: Oxford University Press, 1997) p. 164.
[6] John C. Athanassiades, "The Distortion of Upward Communication in Hierarchical Organizations," *Academy of Management Journal* 16 (1973): 207–226.
[7] See Frank Heller, Eugen Pusic, George Strauss, and Bernhard Wilpert, *Organizational Participation: Myth and Reality* (Oxford, UK: Oxford University Press, 1998).
[8] See Émile Durkheim, *The Division of Labor in Society* (New York: The Free Press, 1964).
[9] See, for example, William E. Loges and Yoo-Young Jung, "Exploring the Digital Divide: Internet Connectedness and Age," *Communication Research* 28 (2001): 536–556.
[10] Chester I. Barnard, *The Functions of the Executive, 30th anniv. ed.* (Cambridge, MA: Harvard University Press, 1968).
[11] Max Weber, *Economy and Society*, trans. Guenther Roth and Claus Wittich (Berkeley: University of California Press, 1978).
[12] Karl E. Weick, *The Social Psychology of Organizing*, 2nd ed. (Reading, MA: Addison-Wesley, 1979).
[13] Kenneth Burke, *A Rhetoric of Motives* (Berkeley: University of California Press, 1969).
[14] Jo Freeman's essay "The Tyranny of Structurelessness" was first printed by the women's liberation movement in the United States in 1970.
[15] Ludwig von Bertalanffy, *General System Theory: Foundations, Development, Applications*, rev. ed. (New York: Braziller, 1976).
[16] Barnard, p. 73.
[17] Niklas Luhmann, *Essays on Self-reference* (New York: Columbia University Press, 1990).
[18] E.g., Weick.
[19] David Silverman, *Interpreting Qualitative Data* (London: Sage Publications, 1993).
[20] Marshall Scott Poole, "A Turn of the Wheel: The Case for the Renewal of Systems Inquiry in Organizational Communication Research," *Organization–Communication: Emerging Perspectives, Volume 5: The Renaissance in Systems Thinking*, ed. George A. Barnett and Lee Thayer (Greenwich, CT: Ablex, 1997) pp. 47–64.
[21] Robert B. Glassman, "Persistence and Loose Coupling in Living Systems," *Behavioral Science* 18 (1973): 83–98.
[22] Gregory Bateson, *Steps to an Ecology of Mind* (New York: Ballentine Books, 1972).
[23] Phillip K. Tompkins, "Communication Implications," *Handbook of Organizational Communication*, ed. Fredric M. Jablin, Linda Putnam, Karlene Roberts, and Lyman Porter (Thousand Oaks, CA: Sage, 1987).
[24] Weber.
[25] Alvin Gouldner, *Patterns of Industrial Bureaucracy* (Glencoe, IL: The Free Press, 1954).
[26] Paul du Gay, "Organizing Identity: Entrepreneurial Governance and Public Management," *Questions of Cultural Identity*, ed. Stuart Hall and Paul Du Gay (London: Sage, 1996). Compare Karen Lee Ashcraft, "Organized Dissonance: Feminist Bureaucracy as Hybrid Form," *Academy of Management Journal* 44 (2001): 1301–1322.
[27] Charles Perrow, *Complex Organizations: A Critical Essay*, 3rd ed. (New York: Random House, 1986).
[28] See Peter F. Drucker, "Toward the New Organization," *The Organization of the Future*, ed. Frances Hesselbein, Marshall Goldsmith, and Richard Beckhard (San Francisco: Jossey-Bass, 1997); Charles Heckscher and Anne Donnellon, eds., *The Post-bureaucratic Organization: New Perspectives on Organizational Change* (Thousand Oaks, CA: Sage, 1994).
[29] See Tracy Kidder, *The Soul of the New Machine* (New York: Avon Books, 1981).
[30] See Gareth Morgan, *Creative Organization Theory: A Resourcebook* (Thousand Oaks, CA: Sage, 1989) pp. 64–67.
[31] See Henry Mintzberg, *The Structuring of Organizations: A Synthesis of the Research* (Englewood Cliffs, NJ: Prentice-Hall, 1979).
[32] Matthew W. Seeger, "Chaos and Crisis: Propositions for a General Theory of Crisis Communication," *Public Relations Review* 28 (2002): 329–337.
[33] See especially the forum on self-organizing systems in the August 1999 issue of *Management Communication Quarterly.*
[34] James R. Taylor and Elizabeth van Every, *The Emergent Organization* (Mahwah, NJ: Erlbaum, 2000).

3

Rationality, Decision Making, and (Ab)Uses of Information

Rationality has been a prominent concept in Western philosophy and in human history since Aristotle defined the human being as the rational animal over 2,400 years ago in ancient Athens. Since the Enlightenment in the late eighteenth century, the idea of being modern has been tied to a progressive march toward a more and more rational society. "Progress" has implied the application of rational methods to our ways of doing work, business, raising a family, and even planning for leisure time. Rationality implies ordering our world based on reason—using observable facts and logical reasoning to reach objective conclusions. Only recently, as the limits of rationalism in Western thought have been realized and as Eastern philosophy has come into direct contact with Western traditions, has the privileged place of rationality been seriously questioned.

The Idea of Rationality

Aristotle emphasized that human beings have the capacity to think about and to articulate connections between means and ends, between premises of an argument and a logical or reasonable conclusion.[1] The idea of rationality suggests that we can reflect on what we're doing and thinking—and reflect on those reflections. Expressions such as "I know that you know that I know" illustrate this kind of rationality. While Aristotle focused on the rational side of human experience, he also gave an important place in his theorizing to emotions. This fact has been generally overlooked in Western philosophy, and certainly in the study of organizations, resulting in the neglect of important aspects of the human experience at work. The centerpiece of Aristotle's rhetorical theory, the *enthymeme*, incorporated both "rational" and "intuitive" (emotional) thinking. The rise of bureaucracy, the legacy of scientific management, and the overemphasis on "the bottom line" have pushed out of view a number of the "softer" aspects of organizations, business, and work life.

Rational usually connotes the ideas of being reasonable, sensible, sane, and systematic. We make rational plans: schemes that show relatively direct paths to the accomplishment of our goals. Because we want to be accepted and successful in society, we usually want others to see us as rational. In heated arguments, one of the surest put-downs is to declare the other "irrational." This is also the way we commonly label unusual business practices, unpredictable policies, and enemy nations. In a detailed study of U.S. war discourse from 1812 through the 1970s, rhetorical critic Robert Ivie found consistent examples of U.S. politicians and media portraying the enemy as irrational (as well as barbaric and evil).[2] That is, we tend to see our opponents as *both* mad and bad! We would no doubt find parallel results for the wartime language of other nations. Our very idea of rationality is not something objective; rather, it is colored by attitudes, preferences, historical trends, and politics.

In modern organizational life, rationality is epitomized by the bureaucratic order. As we discussed in chapter 2, Max Weber viewed the legal-rational system as the superior form of workplace organization because it replaced the arbitrary decisions of individual monarchs, prophets, or CEOs with clearly stated rules, regulations, and practices that help the organization function effectively and efficiently.

Box 3.1 The Enthymeme

The enthymeme is an element and a structure of communication that operates chiefly as a form of deduction, although it also relies on induction. It is similar to the syllogism in logic, but it does not insist on the same precise form as the often repeated *All men are mortal; Socrates is a man; therefore, Socrates is mortal.* This and other syllogistic forms must adhere to certain "formal" rules; they are not correct if they are not structured properly. In that sense, syllogisms are ideal models; they do not depend on context, social situation, or everyday interaction. Syllogisms are structures by which we try to organize our thinking, and they can serve as ideals for how we think we ought to reason.

The *enthymeme*, by contrast, is by its very nature embedded in interaction; it is not an abstract or formal model. In this way, it is called the rhetorical syllogism, and it derives its persuasive force from more than its adherence to rules for formal structure. Above all, the enthymeme draws upon given beliefs or attitudes of the audience. For example, commercials for cosmetics for a Western audience do not need to state explicitly the *major premise:* We admire youth and beauty. The *minor premise* would be something like, "Our product will make you (look) young and beautiful." And the *conclusion* would take the form of an imperative, even if only implied: "Buy this product!" Enthymemes are interactive; they are also imperfect, in terms of the rules of formal logic. Finally, enthymemes often make use of all three of Aristotle's artistic proofs: *ethos*, the credibility of the persuader; *pathos*, the emotional responses of the audience; and *logos*, the logical and substantive aspects of the message itself. This is evident in many political ads, which don't explicitly state their purpose but urge the viewer, listener, or reader to "make the necessary connections." Brief TV spots, for example, seldom explain an issue, but they attempt to create associations with credible and respected people (even if they're from outside politics), with emotional responses, and with a *shorthand* definition of an issue—be that employment, or crime, or the environment.

After all, it is *reasonable* that individual members should be hired, promoted, and fired on the basis of merit; it is *reasonable* that there should be a clearly defined chain of command and responsibility, so that the organizational decision-making process doesn't collapse in chaos; and it's *reasonable* that organizations should listen to their consumers when planning change.

Part of the logic of bureaucracy—especially its de-emphasis on personal relationships and intuition—goes directly against many cultural understandings of the ways to do business. In many Latin American countries, for example, the relational basis for making decisions, appointing personnel, and accomplishing tasks is captured in the term *palanca*. Palanca is a broad concept that highlights the interdependence of people and the fact that they need each other to do work.[3] From the perspective of palanca, why would you want to hire someone who is a total stranger, however qualified they might be, when you have a friend or relative at hand? Rationality is, to a great extent, a relative matter; we can learn much about its advantages and disadvantages by putting various cultures and perspectives in conversation with one another. Culture influences every aspect of life; bureaucracies will look different in Sweden or Colombia or Indonesia than they do in the United States or the United Kingdom. (We will discuss cultural differences in much greater detail in chapters 4 and 13.)

Making Management Systematic and Scientific

By the 1880s when the economies of the United States and western European nations were on roller coasters of recession and boom and labor strife was rampant, some owners and analysts began to look for more systematic approaches to conducting business. In particular, they were concerned about the lack of specialized training and knowledge in supervisory positions. Until the closing years of the nineteenth century, very few people considered that a manager or owner ought to receive training. That's hard to imagine now, with the number of MBAs in all kinds of organizations. The new emphasis on applying science to management went hand in hand with the trend toward greater bureaucratization and rationality. Businesses attempted to be less arbitrary and more systematic—in other words, more organized. Popular magazines of the late nineteenth century (some of which are still in circulation today, such as *Harper's* and *The Atlantic*) in the United States announced an almost unbounded faith in the possibilities for human reason, science, and technology to serve us and to solve our problems. Although we have similar aspirations today, they have been tempered by wars, fascism, concentration camps, and industrial disasters like Three Mile Island, Pennsylvania (1979), Bhopal, India (1984), Chernobyl, Ukraine (1986), the *Exxon Valdez* oil spill, Alaska (1989), and the space shuttles *Challenger* (1986) and *Columbia* (2003).

Scientific Management

Just after 1900, a U.S. engineer named Frederick Taylor (1856–1917) launched a widespread effort called *scientific management*. While a young engineer at Bethlehem Steel in the late 1880s, he had tried to convince owners, managers, and to some extent workers of the importance of having everyone adhere to some kind of standardized system for doing work. Taylor was tirelessly dedicated to making businesses more organized and more efficient. This was the first major development in management thought (see box 3.2), breaking with the tradition of the owner simply

Box 3.2 Timeline of Major Trends in and Approaches to Management in the Twentieth Century and Beyond

- Systematic Management (circa 1880–1910*)
- Scientific Management (circa 1900–1950)
- Human Relations Movement, including emphasis on participative management (circa 1930–1970)
- Open Systems Theory (circa 1960–1985)
- Management by Objectives (circa 1965–1980)
- Organizational Culture/"Theory Z" (circa 1975–1990)
- Quality Circles (circa 1975–1990)
- "Toyotism," including Lean Production (circa 1975–1995)
- Total Quality Management and its variants (circa 1980–present)
- Marketing Orientation/Customer Service Focus (circa 1985–present)
- Business Processes Reengineering (circa 1990–present)
- Learning Organization/Knowledge Management (circa 1990–present)
- Self-Organizing Systems/Network Organizations (circa 1990–present)

*Indicates period of most significant influence.

being "the boss" (a term passed down from slavery, incidentally). Taylor's program included "time and motion" studies—attempts to measure exactly how persons and technologies interfaced. For example, his famous description of the shoveling of pig iron into a blast furnace at a steel mill in Pennsylvania included detailed calculations and calibrations of every physical motion involved in that process. Taylor worked on developing his program for many years before it started to become accepted in the U.S. economy and also in the economies of many other industrialized nations.

Scientific management confronted strident opposition in the beginning. Taylor faced protests from *both* workers and owners in many firms; he was fired from several of his positions. Owners were often angered when Taylor criticized them for relying too heavily on intuition and their own personal experience; like many chefs, they were unable to explain to others exactly what their practices were. Nevertheless, by 1910 his theory was implemented in dozens of major industrial firms in the United States. Through the efforts of members of the International Taylor Society, the techniques of scientific management were later incorporated in many firms in Western Europe and even in the Soviet Union.

In 1911 Taylor published *Principles of Scientific Management*.[4] That same year, workers at the Watertown Arsenal in Pennsylvania struck over the introduction of the techniques of scientific management, seeing the system as oppressive. Taylor was called to testify in the House of Representatives about the turmoil. In its basic form, scientific management was a philosophical movement resting on four principles.

- Codifying workers' skills into scientific laws (versus relying on intuition to accomplish tasks)
- The scientific selection and training of labor

- The unity of work processes through the systematic application of standards to all employees—managers as well as workers
- The resulting development of a "harmonious and just relationship" between management and labor

The first two principles received the most attention in the majority of factories where scientific management was implemented.

Efficiency

Above all, scientific management (or Taylorism as it was commonly called) was directed at expanding the output of industry, especially heightening its efficiency. The value of efficiency is so highly elevated in most industrial societies today that it's hard to imagine that it did not play the same central role in our culture *before* Taylor as it has *since* Taylor. It's important to consider what Taylor meant by efficiency and then talk about some of the many different meanings for the term that have since evolved.

Taylor and his followers had succeeded in installing efficiency as a supreme value in U.S. business and organizations by 1930. In the 1950 film *Cheaper by the Dozen*, the principles of scientific management are applied to domestic life. The movie portrays many different situations where the twelve children are subjected to the principles of scientific management with hilarious results. In one scene, the household begins to look like a machine in terms of how everyone is performing tasks, showing the absurdity of an overemphasis on efficiency in work or home life (see box 3.3).

An important aspect of the development of scientific management was that the application of the means became divorced from its ends. Issues about human cooperation, for example, seldom got much attention when the principles of scientific management were applied on the shop floor in dozens of factories around the United States and Europe. Taylorism cast human motivation in almost completely negative terms. According to its principles, people constantly needed external rewards and penalties to make them work effectively. Intrinsic love of work or commitment to lofty goals wasn't considered motivation.

Theory X and Theory Y

Douglas McGregor described two competing views of work and management.[5] Theory X, like the aspect of scientific management described above, assumes that work cannot really be intrinsically or inherently satisfying and that organizations therefore must rely on external rewards to motivate employees. Theory Y, by contrast, envisions possibilities for making work truly enjoyable and assumes that employees can derive intrinsic satisfactions from doing their jobs. A Theory X manager would be more likely to insist on monitoring employees closely than a Theory Y manager.

Today Theory X is often presented as a "foil" for more complex understandings of human motivation for work. However, this is a bit misleading, since many organizations still operate as though employees respond mainly to external rewards and threats. In fact, the prevalence of electronic monitoring on the job today (see chapter 12) is not much different from the scene in Charlie Chaplin's film *Modern Times* (1936) where our hapless hero discovers that he's being watched by his boss through a video screen in the bathroom! And management sociologist Graham Sewell has found a surprising and disturbing coincidence of team-based organizational restructuring *with* electronic and over-the-shoulder monitoring in many organizations.[6]

Employees today often receive a mixed message: emphasis on freedom, initiative, and entrepreneurship from the notion of teamwork, yet constraint, top-down control, and lack of confidence from heightened surveillance. One major lesson from the history of modern organizations is that ingrained patterns and actual practices do not change as easily or as often as the trends and theories about work do.

Efficiency Reconsidered

Let's pause to consider different meanings and different values attached to the term *efficiency*. Unquestionably, efficiency is one of the most important values in contemporary industrialized societies. Efficiency makes good sense in that we have only limited time, resources, and energy for accomplishing the things that are important to us. Individuals today are just as caught up with the idea of being efficient as organizations are. Witness the popularity of "multi-tasking," where a person talks on a cell phone while working on a notebook PC and perhaps trying to cook something on the stove. We are so accustomed to trying to make things more efficient that we seldom consider exactly what the term means. Efficiency, thus, functions much like what Kenneth Burke calls a "god term" in popular discourse.[7] Arguing for "efficiency"—without explaining any specific meaning—often gains the assent of others. In a corporate board meeting, for example, when different options for expansion of the firm or cutting costs are being considered, a person simply describes his or her plan as "more efficient" than another and may win the argument. A recent article in

"The dip in sales seems to coincide with the decision to eliminate the sales staff."

The International Herald Tribune argued that all European nations are about to be put in competition over tax and interest rates, wages and employment levels, welfare systems, and industrial output. The editorial went on to say that the most efficient countries will "win."[8]

But efficiency can mean many different things. Think what efficiency means to you. The term can refer to getting the greatest amount of output for a given amount of input. During World War II, the phrase "getting the biggest bang for the buck" was coined to describe the efficiency of different bombs and bombing strategies. Efficiency can refer to cutting waste, or it can mean doing something speedier or faster. It can mean doing something without consuming very many resources. We can set up certain ratings that individuals or organizations must meet in order to be considered efficient.

Think for a moment about restructuring the university with efficiency as the *supreme value or goal*. What would the university look like? What is efficient in terms of higher education? Would reorganization result in a select number of departments or disciplines with very few faculty and staff and extremely large classes? This would be efficient, in a certain sense, but would it be effective—in terms of offering the best educational experience possible? Would the loss of interaction among students and professors affect the educational experience? A television program in the late 1980s depicted changes in surgical procedures in the then Soviet Union. Patients waiting to have cataract operations were lined up prone on a conveyor belt. The conveyor belt moved them into the room; a team of doctors and nurses performed the cataract surgery; and then the conveyor belt moved them out of the surgery room. We wish that

Box 3.3 The Senses (and Non-Sense) of Efficiency

Consider how efficiency is used in both vague and specific ways in organizational decision making. For example, efficiency applied to counseling or psychotherapy could result in little sustained attention to each client. So, what might be efficient from the standpoint of serving many clients could actually diminish the nature of client contact. Think of ways each meaning below can be applied either sensibly or foolishly (sometimes to the effect of great harm).

- The maximum output for a given input ("getting the biggest bang for the buck")
- High quantity of production (i.e., mass production, mass availability)
- Smooth operations and reduction of errors, with predictability and control
- Limited waste in production processes/low environmental impact/consumption of few resources
- Increased speed of production
- Total focus on objective(s), with no distractions
- Incremental profit increase for a given organizational change
- Uniform production standards or consistency of practices
- *Kaizen*, or "continuous improvement"
- Lean Production: responsive to demand, with no slack and no backlog
- Precise and standardized measurement of individual and group performance, to be used as a benchmark for future work

Now, consider the impact on all the other functions of an organization while the basic objective of efficiency is being pursued. When does efficiency make the most sense? When is it counterproductive?

we had this episode on videotape because it is a stark reminder about the excesses of concern for efficiency. When you describe this surgical procedure to most people, they recoil in horror and say, "I wouldn't participate in something like that." Yet it meets many of the criteria for an efficient procedure. When Lars was a kid in Denmark, medical doctors used to pay visits to patients in their private homes at night and on weekends. Today, the patients need to visit the doctors at a central clinic in town. Because it's considered more efficient—that is, for the doctors, whose time is valued very highly, as opposed to the patients whose time in this case is not considered an important resource.

Effectiveness and Efficiency

In his book *The Functions of the Executive,* Chester Barnard offered an unusual but very helpful perspective on efficiency. He defined it as attention to and satisfaction of individuals' goals within the context of an organization's pursuit of its goals. For Barnard *effectiveness* is the extent to which an organization meets its *primary* objectives: making cars, offering seminars, selling groceries, creating computer software, etc. Efficiency was secondary, but nevertheless crucial, and included negative as well as positive effects. Embracing the values, goals, and hopes of the organization's members would lead to greater job satisfaction and therefore achievement of both individual and organizational goals. From this standpoint, organizations must be *both* effective and efficient in order to insure long-term survival.[9] Organizations that focus on the pursuit of system-level goals to the exclusion of individual satisfactions are inefficient and doomed to fail in the long term, according to Barnard. Conversely, if we focus too much on job satisfaction and fail to accomplish the key organizational goals, then our organization won't last very long (see table 3.1).

What do you think of Barnard's conception of efficiency? Consider how it differs from typical notions of efficiency (box 3.3). Think of group projects you've been involved in; you can probably think of examples of the two extremes portrayed in quadrants 1 and 4. In the first quadrant, the group doesn't accomplish its main goal—for example, putting together a class presentation on an organizational case study—and the members of the group aren't very happy. In quadrant 4, we find a group that both attains its collective goal(s) and keeps members fairly satisfied and committed. This group does a great job on both dimensions. But, in the other two quadrants, we see the more complicated cases of where the group does well on one major dimension but not the other. Quadrant 2 depicts the group that gets a lot done but leaves its members dissatisfied—perhaps because *all* the group did was focus on task achievement. This group may get the project completed, even at a high level of achievement, but the peo-

Table 3.1
Effectiveness and Efficiency in "Conversation" with One Another

	Low Effectiveness	*High Effectiveness*
Low Efficiency	**1** Failure at Group Goals; Unhappy Members	**2** Success at Group Goals; Unhappy Members
High Efficiency	**3** *Failure at Group Goals;* Happy Members	**4** Success at Group Goals; Happy Members

ple in it are not eager to continue to work together and are likely to feel disappointed despite a high grade on the assignment. In a way, this characterization applies to many organizations today that are preoccupied with narrow conceptions of the "bottom line" and fail to remember that they're employing human beings. In terms of leadership in groups and organizations, we can think of people who are terrific task masters but fail to inspire or be sensitive to others (see chapter 7). Quadrant 3 is a happy group; perhaps they enjoy beer and pizza together, but they don't accomplish anything.

The model illustrates that the two dimensions of effectiveness and efficiency are interdependent. They can and often do influence each other. A group's continued success with reaching its targets may end up producing very satisfied members. Likewise, a group that is happy for a while just getting together may find their energy gradually disappearing if they don't get something done. In fact this relationship between what small-group scholars call *task* and *socio-emotional* dimensions to group process helps explain some of the inconclusive results from three decades of research under the human relations movement. The movement arose following the famous Hawthorne Studies of 1927–32. Elton Mayo, a sociologist from Harvard, conducted a series of experiments with workers at the Western Electric Plant in Cicero, Illinois. Six female employees were placed in a separate room with the same production equipment as their colleagues. Only the levels of illumination were manipulated to determine the effects on production. The researchers discovered that production went up whether the lighting was lower or higher. The conclusion was that the condition responsible for increased production was the special attention. After these studies, the movement focused on such things as group norms, job satisfaction, and other employee attitudes in part as a reaction against the technical excesses and heartlessness of scientific management.

During the years of the movement's popularity, there were more than 3,000 studies conducted that tried to establish a positive correlation between job satisfaction and work productivity. Researchers looked for clear evidence of what was intuitively appealing to many people: that the happy worker is the productive worker. Curiously, that huge volume of research resulted in an average positive correlation of only about .17. What that means, statistically speaking, is that knowing that someone is happy at work tells you a little bit but not a whole lot about whether or not they are productive. Linking job satisfaction to work productivity is far more complicated than previously thought. Sometimes, it *is* the happy worker who is productive; other times, being productive makes one happy. Plus, there are a variety of other factors, or variables, that figure into this relationship: the reward system, physical working conditions, the social climate of work, and time.

Barnard's novel way of reframing efficiency reminds us to look at the big picture of what's going on in any organization. When we focus on one goal, we should also look at what's happening "around" that goal. We may be making lots of widgets but have miserable working conditions. We may be teaching lots of students but the quality of their experience may be unsatisfactory. We may be processing more health-care patients with the aid of advanced technologies, but they may prefer another hospital's treatment. In particular, we should examine institutional goals, the means to achieving those goals, and the degree to which the sum total of organizational activities are directed toward addressing important human goals and needs.

In his book *The Market Experience*, political scientist Robert Lane[10] says we should broaden and deepen our understanding of the market, given that so many discussions of business and economics move quickly toward abstractions about system-wide performance ("market indicators") and away from more basic human concerns ("Is this system producing betterment for all or most people?"). There is a tendency to forget about people in our attempts to calculate inflation rates, cost-cutting measures, and the marginal utility of a particular policy. This can even lead to conclusions like "high unemployment is good for the economy" or "a rise in the rate of cancer causes the Gross Domestic Product (or GDP) to go up because of the increased use of health care services." What evidence does Lane offer for his view? In his latest book, *The Loss of Happiness in Market Democracies*, he explains how people in Western industrialized countries are on the average less happy today than 50 years ago, despite the spectacular performance of the market in generating wealth for many segments of society. This leads Lane to ask: "In what specific senses is the market rational? Or not rational?"[11]

Decisions, Decisions

The idea of rationality (and its ramifications) is the key element in the study of decision making. Much of organizational research—across the fields of business, sociology, psychology, and communication—has been devoted to describing, critiquing, and struggling to improve decision-making processes for individual members and for organizations considered as entities.

In 1948 Herbert A. Simon, the Nobel prize-winning economist and author of *Administrative Behavior,* pointed out that the idea of efficiency is a *master premise* in business culture.[12] He meant that efficiency is often treated as a goal above many other goals such that it usually goes unquestioned in policymaking discussions (as we mentioned earlier). According to Simon, the *decisional premise*, a value that guides decisions—such as safety first, efficiency is good, or customers before anything else—is the basic building block of organizations. Simon's model of organizational decision making depends heavily on communication, both in terms of how decisional premises are expressed and received (for example, some corporate slogans are taken very seriously by employees) and in terms of how they are communicated at each level of the organization.

This means that we would look at an organization vertically as a chain of decisional premises, running from very broad ones at the top of the organization to fairly specific ones at the bottom. In fact, an organization as a whole may then be seen as a hierarchy of decisional premises, with the broadest value and factual premises residing at the top where presumably those in charge have the widest view of the organization's activities and goals (e.g., prioritizing profit, service, long-term viability, or image). Simon's idea of a well-functioning organization of any kind is when these broad ideas at the top are translated into, or aligned with, specific goals down the ladder. That is, we would expect a company policy like "Safety first!" to lead to some specific practices and procedures on the shop floor. If the top administrator of a hospital talks repeatedly about cost reduction, then we would expect that the overriding concern of doctors, nurses, and technical personnel is keeping costs down. The overarching premise thus shapes the decision-making environment for organizational members: it channels their thinking and helps them choose from among an array of options.

When analyzing decision making in an organization we can evaluate whether a decision maker's premises are in line with the interests of the organization as a whole. We can also look at clashes between different sets of value premises, say between managers and scientists. In assessing decision making, we talk about where best to locate a decision in an organization. Consider the university, with its many disciplines and departments. Where would we want to locate the decisions to determine exactly what the budgets would be for individual departments for the upcoming fiscal year? Would we allow each department *complete autonomy* in making those decisions? Probably not, because each is likely to try to maximize its own resources without considering the needs of other departments within the organization. Thus, while we would want departments to participate to some extent in this decision-making process with respect to the budget, we would ultimately locate the decision at a higher level in the organization where there was a broader vision of the organization as a whole and its many different interests.

Information Processing

From the standpoint of decision making, organizations may be viewed as information-processing entities. This means that the organization can be broken down into little bits of information but also conceived of holistically in terms of how it manages uncertainty and attains the level of confidence in information that it needs to move forward, similar to the functions of the human brain.

As an example of how to think about the organization in information-processing terms, take the traditional idea of *span of control*, which usually refers to the number of persons that one manager supervises. From an information-processing (or a cognitive) perspective, conclusions regarding the ideal span of control are often linked to the limitations on the human capacity to "chunk" and process information. First, we can only keep so many ideas or idea clusters in mind at the same time—analogous to the number of balls that a juggler can keep in the air. Second, from a communication perspective, there's an added constraint, related to the number of people with whom we can effectively communicate at once. That is, we are limited by such things as talk time when we try to relate to too many other people at a meeting. Third, not everyone can participate effectively when the group grows too large. These are three things we appreciate intuitively, and this is one place where three different aspects of social science converge. Organizationally speaking, the upper limit on effective span of control is 7–9 persons.[13] The same is true of our capacity to chunk or cluster bits of information, like credentials of candidates for a job.[14] Finally, the same number is suggested by small-group communication studies as the upper limit for a work or project team, or a policy-making committee.[15]

The only formula we'll offer in this entire textbook is a handy one that helps to support our intuitions about the growth of any group. The total possible number of two-person or dyadic relationships in any group or organization can be expressed as $N(N-1)/2$, where N is the number of persons in the group. So, with just 5 members, there are 10 possible two-person links. But, when our little club grows to 10 members, the corresponding number of two-person links possible is 45! We experience that difference, practically speaking, when a committee expands, or when we are asked to supervise more people than usual, or we try to keep too many projects under control at the same time.

These practical limitations to managing information and relationships tell us a lot about how to design organizational structures and also what reasonably to expect of individuals and groups in positions of decision-making responsibility. For example, too large a committee can hinder effective deliberations and decision making. Also, a manager cannot realistically be expected to stay familiar with the important objectives and problems of too many units or departments.

Box 3.4 Organizations as Brains, Computers, or Information-Processing Entities

One of the most important perspectives on organizations and communication draws analogies between the organization, the "thinking machines" of the human brain, and the computer. The decision is the locus for studies of organizations conducted from this perspective, which emphasizes the cognitive, rational, and information-related aspects of organizational life. We'll refer to this family of perspectives simply as "information processing." This perspective focuses on the creation, identification, flow, management, and use of information.

- The central concept within this perspective is the control of uncertainty, or at least ways to deal with it.
- From this view, organizations are seen in direct analogy to the human brain and to the computer. As Gareth Morgan writes: "From this vantage point, we come to see that the various job, departmental, and other divisions within an organization do not just define a structure of work activity. They also create a structure of attention, interpretation, and decision making that exerts a crucial influence on an organization's daily operation. Departmental and job divisions [we would add functional and project specializations] segment the organization's environment, compartmentalize responsibilities, and thus simplify the domains of interest and decision making of managers and operatives."[16]
- With the brain as a model, we can begin to think of organizations as self-aware and self-organizing. That is, organizations are capable of reflecting on their own activities and habits—at least on good days!
- The brain metaphor relates closely to today's popular idea of the "learning organization": the notion that an organization can have mechanisms built into it that allow it to adjust to changes in the environment and to actually benefit from the organization's mistakes.[17]
- With the computer as a model, we can begin to simulate organizations and various scenarios for their future developments. By inputting numerical values for key variables—say, about the economy, politics, and culture—we might be able to predict within certain bounds the overall well-being of a city in the future.
- Artificial Intelligence (AI) is now being used to simulate organizational functioning and to consider complex decision-making paths over time.

Prior to the pioneering work of Simon, decision-making models tended to presume an almost perfect, rational "man." It was commonly assumed that human beings were almost infinite in their capacities to calculate decisions in such a way as to maximize specified outcomes. Corresponding to this view, sometimes encapsulated in the term *homo economicus*, was the stress on the rules of formal logic in philosophy. Often these rules, such as those that define the elements and features of a syllogism (major premise, minor premise and conclusion) were seen to represent both the reality and the height of human decision-making achievement. Human beings were seen as capable of calculating the advantages and disadvantages for any decision in a fairly systematic way, just as we might look carefully at a transaction in buying a television or some other expensive item. Relationships between people were seen in terms of "exchanges" of benefits and contributions, just as governments do in assessing potential allies.

But, we may ask: If rationality is an inherent part of "who we are," why do we work so hard to present ourselves to others as highly rational? And if rationality is so natural, why must it be encouraged, cultivated, and promoted? The answer is that we are *partially* rational, in the usual sense of that word. However, our goal is often to

"Are we thinking here, or is this just so much pointing and clicking?"

present ourselves as being *highly* rational. Organizations are especially prone to this kind of impression management, as we will see later in this chapter.

While by no means an anti-rationalist, Simon sought to redefine the human being as "boundedly rational," while drawing an analogy between human cognitive processing and the structure and workings of an organization. To Simon, maximization is a Utopian goal, but *satisficing* (as he called it; think of "suffice" plus "satisfy") is what we mere mortals can hope to achieve. Whether we are talking about the forces of supply and demand in the marketplace or the interrelationships of organizational members, maximization can be considered as a point of reference but not as a realistic goal. Instead, satisficing represents the making of a reasonably good decision within the limits of time, information, and foresight. For Simon, this is the best that can be hoped for in most situations, whether the decision maker is an individual, a group, or an organization. A rational organization, in Simon's view, is one that controls the premises for decisions and locates decision-making power in such a way as to satisfice in the pursuit of the organization's key interests. That's the best we can expect to do.

Quality and Quantity of Information

Simon's colleague James March has explored organizational decision making in a variety of situations in order to specify the conditions under which information becomes the basis for decision making.[18] A major part of this process, according to March, is simply determining what counts as information. Put another way, when does something get labeled as "information" and then as "good information"?

In a very interesting essay, Martha Feldman and James March show that it's not just the pieces of information that are important; it's how we use information. Information is often used loosely, rather than being analyzed carefully to inform a decision. There's peer pressure to appear to have and use information, because information itself is an important symbol of rationality in our society. Feldman and March give many examples of organizations that gather mountains of information never to be used—all in an attempt to appear rational like other supposedly modern, successful organizations.[19] According to Feldman and March's analysis: "Organizational participants seem to find value in information that has no great decision relevance. They gather information and do not use it. They ask for reports and do not read them. They act first and receive requested information later."[20] An acquaintance of ours, who was until recently the lead scientist for a large corporation, commissioned a large-scale environmental study costing tens of thousands of dollars, which was then completely ignored—perhaps never even read, according to him—by the company's top management in making a strategic decision. As Feldman and March point out, information gathering itself becomes a sign to the rest of the world that the organization is behaving appropriately.

This issue is the reason some practitioners and theorists try to distinguish between data—a collection of messages—and true information—something to be used and valued. This reasoning counters the popular view—perpetuated by cable television and the Internet—that greater access to messages (or data) necessarily means having more information. Of course, if we add the terms "knowledge" and "wisdom" to our list, the issue gets even more complicated. These types of questions are not just academic, as organizations are faced with more and more messages that announce themselves as important. All organizations feel compelled to announce to the world: "Hey, look, we're being rational, we're taking market surveys, holding focus groups, doing the kinds of things that our leaders, competitors, and stakeholders expect of us." The point here is to assess the situations where we find ourselves gathering information, creating information, or disseminating information. Are we acting simply because that's what's expected rather than with a clear purpose in mind?

Flow of Information

Decision making in organizations relates to the "flow" and nature of messages. Thus, many researchers use terms such as *information overload*, *information underload*, and *information quality* to describe the decision-making environments of individuals and groups in organizations. While it is difficult for anyone to make a decision in a state of complete uncertainty, researchers have also found that too much information can be paralyzing for the individual or group confronted with a choice. In a way, this idea goes against the current desire for more and more information through surveys, forecasting, etc. But organizations, like individuals, can make effective use of only so much information. While the organization doesn't and can't use all of the information it assembles, it may be believed widely within the organization that it *has* to have all available data.

As a growing number of organizations are beginning to realize, this belief can cause problems for organization members, who become burdened with completing reports, processing data, and passing the information along to colleagues and other departments. Much of the communication and work activity of the organization becomes wrapped up with accumulating and "processing" information, even though many of the reports do not contribute to decisions and actually increase the stress on workers. If the time spent completing and submitting reports *on* work consumes the time available to *do* work, effectiveness is greatly diminished. What first appears systematic and sensible from an organizational perspective can actually be counter productive. In this regard, it is important in both theory and practice to make a distinction between information *acquisition* and information *use*, recognizing that many decision makers are much more diligent about the former than they are about the latter.[21] Not surprisingly, most people in organizations report a desire for a moderate amount of information—but determining the right amount—and what type will be useful—for a particular unit or department can be a difficult matter. The recognition of such issues has led to the development of *knowledge management* as a major trend in contemporary organizations, as explained in box 3.5.

Another way of thinking about the flow of information in an organization puts a spotlight on the communication process. Recent research on highly coordinated decision-making structures shows how the bases for making decisions may reside not with any individuals in the group but with the group as a whole. The idea of *socially distributed cognition* illustrates the change of focus from information residing with individual persons to its location in a network. This perspective draws us away from the idea of thought and talk as produced totally by individuals or collections of them and into a world of understanding how coordination is possible. For example, Edwin Hutchins and Tove Klausen studied communication between airline pilots and air traffic controllers to show how information processing occurs in a complex network of mutual understanding.[26] In many cases, there is no one person or "node" in the network where all of the information is held. The knowledge that is shared and the mental representations that are made as a result of each interaction work together as a system in ways that cannot easily be explained by an examination of each utterance. The idea of socially distributed cognition for analyzing organizational communication is useful in that it reconceives cognition beyond the boundaries of the individual human brain and instead views it as occurring between and among people.[27] Cognition itself is interwoven with interaction and language.

Systems theorist Niklas Luhmann[28] even suggests that the idea of an individual decision maker is misleading. While he defines organizations as systems that communicate through and about decisions, he's reluctant to ascribe the ability to make decisions to individual persons. First, it is impossible to decide when a decision begins and when it ends—and thus to determine who's actually making the decision. For example, you might consider yourself the decision maker when you go out to buy a new stereo system, but every part of that process—your budget, the salesperson you encounter, the sorts of stereos on sale, and even your desire to buy a stereo—are the result of other processes. Secondly, Luhmann claims, no decision makers have a general view of themselves or the organization. Thus it's unclear whether it's the individual or the organization that decides. What we do know, however, is that by ascribing decisions to persons, the complexity and mystery of decisions are obscured. While doing so helps us sum up a complex set of actions and events, the danger is that we may oversimplify what actually occurs.

Box 3.5 The Benefits and Ironies of Knowledge Management

Knowledge management (KM) is one of the current buzzwords among managers. KM has been defined as "developing and exploiting an organization's tangible and intangible knowledge resources."[22] A major factor in the emergence of KM is the increasing capacity and use of information and communication technologies (ICTs). First, the increased use of ICTs has led to an explosion of available information that often overwhelms users. The challenge is how to sift through the barrage of available information to find what is most useful to a given goal. Second, the increasing capacity of ICTs has enabled more and more information to be stored, and to be retrieved in more user-friendly ways.

There are some benefits with KM initiatives. KM tries to make the acquired knowledge of the organization available to its staff when needed to make decisions. More broadly, managers hope that KM will give their organizations a competitive advantage. This hope is based in the popular assumption that we are now experiencing a "knowledge-driven" economy, one in which competitive advantage for organizations is obtained by developing and managing *intellectual capital.* However, managers should enter into KM initiatives with open eyes. Many management change programs promise benefits that are not necessarily delivered.

KM is in part a reaction to the massive downsizing and reengineering of the 1990s. Many organizations recognized that a dangerous consequence of those trends was the loss of organizational knowledge. Thus, KM is often framed as *re-valuing employees* who were de-valued by downsizing and business process reengineering (BPR). However, one could also argue that KM is a continuation of those trends, in that it is in part an attempt to "extract" or "capture" and *commodify* that part of the employee that is valued (his or her knowledge), thus making the organization less vulnerable to the employee's loss and making the employee more expendable.

KM, like many other frameworks for management, may be considered a management fad.[23] While there is something real, tangible, and useful about the concept of KM, there is also a strong sense that the concept is appealing because it is new and symbolic of being cutting edge. When Ted asked a group of managers at one organization why they were pursuing KM, one laughingly responded, "A bandwagon drove by, so we hopped on."[24]

KM seems to take for granted that organizations 1) know what their knowledge is, and 2) know where it's located. Organizations, in other words, are expected to be transparent to themselves. This, however, is hardly the case—organizational knowledge is often tacit, and self-transparency requires a perfect self-consciousness that's practically unattainable.[25] An interesting question debated tirelessly in the KM literature and by managers attempting to implement the concept is: Where does knowledge reside? For example, is it in individuals, groups, organizations, or texts? Knowledge is not equivalent to information, we are told by KM practitioners, yet the two are often combined in the theoretical literature and in practice. For example, a KM task force at one organization had as their objective: "To identify critical knowledge and facilitate access to and use of existing information." As written, the objective could be read as explicitly distinguishing information as something that can be stored while critical knowledge must be identified. However, the group (as do other groups implementing KM) talked frequently about knowledge (not just information) being stored.

Models of Group Decision Making and Communication

So far we have been discussing rationality and decision making in a general way, emphasizing both limits and possibilities. But, there are a number of different models of decision making that we can perhaps best see in the context of a group and then apply to a larger organization. The logics of different decision-making models are often quite similar, although the actual decision-making processes may look a bit different depending on the size of the group or organization we're examining. Notice that some of these models are descriptive, while others are prescriptive or normative. Also, consider how some models emphasize the phases that groups can or should experience.

Group communication researchers have devoted a great deal of energy to rational models of decision making. In particular, they have investigated what sort of communication distinguishes effective from ineffective group decision-making processes in so-called task groups (groups whose primary reason for being together is accomplishing tasks). Naturally, people are interested in which kinds of group processes or decision-making procedures are going to be the most effective. But this is not as simple as it may first seem, because we quickly find many factors that influence effectiveness. In fact, the complexity begins with the question: What do we mean by "effectiveness"?

Effectiveness is usually defined in this research in terms of accuracy (or correctness), quality, or the evaluation of a group's decision by external experts. So, with either an experimental group or a group in a field (naturalistic) setting, a model will be tried and then evaluated by an unbiased third party with some knowledge about the problem.

Functional Theory

One theory that has been researched perhaps more than any other is called functional theory. This theory can be seen as a "normative" theory—it suggests a standard, or norm, for effective groups to follow. In a general way, the model follows from John Dewey's "reflective thinking sequence," which recommends that a group move from more general considerations of goals to specific considerations of means of implementation, and then evaluate the options according to some agreed-upon criteria.[29]

Functional theory typically assumes that all task groups face similar tasks and relational obstacles to effective decision making and that certain functions, or vital activities, are necessary to overcome these obstacles. Functional theory advocates the value of "vigilance"; that is, it suggests that groups should be vigilant in carefully scrutinizing the problem situation, the criteria, and the alternatives. Communication is seen as a social tool used to serve these functions. Communication can have an inhibiting or facilitating influence on effective group decision making—either by exacerbating problems or overcoming obstacles.

A group's decision, according to functional theory, is the result of a series of smaller decisions, each of which serves one of the following necessary functions of effective decision making.

- Assessing the problem: groups must explore thoroughly the situation they face
- Specifying goals: groups should identify their objectives and the criteria for a good decision
- Identifying possible solutions: groups should consider a range of alternative ways to solve the problem
- Evaluating the positive and negative features of the alternatives: groups should consider the pros and cons, the advantages and disadvantages of the alternatives under consideration[30]

Functional decision-making theorists claim that communication is most important in ambiguous tasks. When decisions are relatively straightforward, the functions or stages shouldn't matter as much. When decisions are ambiguous or amorphous, it is more important to communicate about all four functions. For example, a few years back, Weaver Street Market (WSM), a small, cooperatively owned grocery store in Carrboro, North Carolina in the United States learned that a large health and gourmet foods grocery store was opening a branch near them. This created concern, since WSM was already struggling financially. What, if anything, should they do? For the next several months, the meetings of the board of directors focused on this new development and how WSM should respond. Some directors argued that nothing needed to be done, since the stores were likely to attract different customers. Others strongly believed a large portion of their customer base would be taken away. This was an ambiguous problem situation; it was not clear whether there was a problem and whether or how the store needed to respond. So, the directors spent hours assessing the problem situation and performing the other functions specified in functional theory. Eventually, they decided there was a real threat and agreed on several strategic responses that included expansion of the store.

Research has found some support for the claims of functional theory, although results have been inconsistent. The most consistent finding is that decision-making effectiveness is related to communication that evaluates available alternatives. Fulfilling the problem analysis and criteria-setting functions has also been positively related to effectiveness.[31] Functional theorists have suggested that the theory can be more complete and consistent by specifying the relationships of functions to situational contingencies, a process they have only begun. They argue that the functional requirements for decision-making effectiveness probably differ depending on the nature of the decision-making task and the nature of the group itself.[32]

Some tasks have a "positive bias," meaning it's more important to carefully evaluate the positive qualities of alternative choices. For example, in deciding who deserves the employee-of-the-month award, it's probably more important to consider who has exhibited the most significant accomplishments. Their negative qualities or failures would matter, but you probably wouldn't want a group to decide such an award based on who is least objectionable. Other tasks have a negative bias. For these activities, it's more important to carefully evaluate the negative features of the alternatives. A tourist board deciding whether or not to approve public access to a volcano after increased seismic activity is an example of decision making with a negative bias. The best decision in this situation is likely to be based on careful scrutiny of the negative features—the dangers—of the alternatives.

Some critics argue that functional theory is simply too narrow in its current form for application to real-life groups. They make a number of suggestions to broaden and enhance the theory's application.[33] In particular, they suggest that important functions are neglected by the theory. For example, a *historical function* (creating a shared understanding of the historical context of the decision) directs groups to consider more than the immediate decision. What decisions have been made in the past that might constrain a group's choices? An *institutional function* would help a group situate its decision within the larger institutional context. For example, in a study of a university's top management team, previous decisions made by the team—particularly regarding the organizational vision—influenced subsequent decisions by suggesting what sorts of decisions the group should favor.[34] Another study showed top management repeatedly ignoring the organizational vision in decision making and suffering dire consequences as a result.[35]

Additional Perspectives on Group Decision Making

Communication researchers have recently attempted to develop an integrated model of group decision making. Randy Hirokawa and Abram Salazar posit that when groups adopt structures (norms and rules) such as a high-achievement focus, vigilance, and a collaborative climate, they are more likely to perform the functions necessary to reach effective decisions.[36] Marshall Scott Poole and colleagues found that groups adopting decision paths most similar to logical, normative models (as specified by functional theory) perceived their decisions to be of higher quality and were more satisfied and unified with their decisions than groups that used more complex paths.[37]

Box 3.6 Group Decision Making: Structure and Process

In a series of studies, Poole and his colleagues researched the developmental processes of decision-making groups in an attempt to go beyond traditional phase models of decision development. This work has developed two separate but related theories.

Developmental theory is a contingency theory that describes decision development in groups. Poole and Holmes summarized the intent and results of this research program as follows: "Most theories of decision development have posited a simple, normative sequence of phases to follow, such as Bales's orientation/evaluation/control sequence. However, empirical research indicates that groups follow multiple paths. . . . The normative sequences are best thought of as ideal models that group members try to follow in organizing their activities. Generally about 30% of groups are observed to follow simple, normative sequences, whereas the remainder follow more complex decision paths, often recycling to previous phases or taking phases 'out of order.' Both the nature of the group task and social factors such as group size and cohesiveness are related to the complexity of group decision paths, with social factors accounting for a greater share of the variance."[38]

The second theory that these scholars have developed is an adaptation of Anthony Giddens's structuration theory to explain how groups create structures—for example, norms and rules—that serve as resources and constraints in their subsequent interactions.[39] While this is a complex theory, the essence of it is that "groups select, adapt, and develop their own working structures"[40] and then reproduce (and stabilize), alter, or eliminate them. These working structures are made up of generative rules and resources that group members use in their interactions. For example, Zorn and Ruccio demonstrated how sales teams developed shared norms (i.e., structures) for communication competence and then consequently interpreted their managers' leadership practices in light of those norms.[41] Structuration theory is especially interesting because it reminds us of how structure and process are interdependent (as we discussed in chapter 2). This keeps us from seeing any particular rules, norms, or procedures as fixed or eternal—we remember that all of them have sources, potential uses, and possible pitfalls.

Constructing Rationality

Since Simon first published *Administrative Behavior* more than 50 years ago, other theorists have tried to show that we're not even as boundedly rational as Simon claimed. Social psychologist Karl Weick,[42] for example, reminds us that often we do not proceed neatly from consideration of the problem to development of criteria for identifying the best solution to careful assessment of alternative solutions. Rather, we often take action and then "rationalize" after the fact. This tendency does not make our actions irrational, but it reminds us that decision making is not just a linear or one-way process.

The inconsistency between "practice and preaching" isn't always due to dishonesty, hypocrisy or bad planning, however. Much of it has to do with the retrospective sense making, discussed in chapter 2.[43] We make sense of decisions after the fact, as we reconstruct them and especially as we recount them to others. Karl Weick shows how we are often not the rational creatures that we seek to be or that we present ourselves to others as being. Frequently, he says, the thought sequence is a direct reversal of the usual image we have of ourselves. For example, while we might like to believe that we carefully analyze problems and generate tailor-made solutions, Weick suggests that we carry solutions in our heads and look for problems to fit them. What we remember worked for us in previous decisions becomes the *frame* for viewing the next decision. Our plans, like our memories, are selective.

Organizations do this often. They use maps from earlier situations in new situations because that's the best they can do. For example, labor unions can develop patterns by which they approach all problems in the same manner. Thus, they have preferred solutions or approaches that they apply regardless of the specific company. Such a pattern of behavior, however, often overlooks differences in companies and how strategies ought to be adjusted to address those variations. But when you're lost, as Weick says, any map will do. And mostly, we're lost when facing a new environment or a new organization. To counter this tendency, however, some labor organizers have begun to tailor "corporate programs" to the specific situations found in factories and offices, rather than pursuing a blanket strategy.

Garbage Can Model of Decision Making

Michael Cohen, James March, and Johan Olsen go a step further in their now-famous *garbage can model* of decision making.[44] In the 1960s and 1970s, they examined universities as cases of "organized anarchy," arguing that educational institutions (among others) can be seen in many cases as collections of: solutions looking for problems; issues and feelings seeking to be aired; and decision makers looking for decisions to make.

Thus, when a problem or issue emerges in an organization, various stakeholders dump their solutions, feelings, related issues, etc. into the garbage can in a rather haphazard fashion. A decision is made when an acceptable match is seen between problems, solutions, resources, and participants. Through retrospective sense making, the process may be framed as a rational analysis followed by logically developed solution. According to the garbage can model, what actually happens in many cases is a far cry from that. For example, recent studies of Total Quality Management show that many managers use it as a way of legitimizing what they already intended to do all along. In this way, what might be seen as simple arbitrariness is cloaked in the ethos of careful thought and "being systematic."[45] After two decades of research, many organizations have claimed to practice TQM but have done little more than increase monitoring of production while demanding that employees work harder.

Equivocality, Enactment, Selection, and Retention

Central to the study of decision making in organizations today is the idea of uncertainty and its cohorts, ambiguity and equivocality. Weick discusses the decision-making environment in terms of *equivocality*—that is, when two or more possible interpretations exist for a situation. Consider, for example, how economic indicators are treated by governmental and business planners and by the mass media. A single statistic, say about the prime interest rate, can often be interpreted in at least two different ways, either as reflecting an economic downturn already in progress or as revealing the beginnings of new economic vitality. During an early draft of this chapter, the U.S. Federal Reserve Board was debating whether to interpret rising unemployment as a sign of a continued economic boom or as an indication that a recession is just around the corner. (It looks like the latter was the correct interpretation!) We're not saying that economics has no material or objective basis, but we are saying that the same piece of information can often be interpreted in multiple ways. Thus, what becomes policy has a lot to do with attitudes, preferences, and frameworks of reference held by decision makers and analysts. One person's acceptably high (even "necessary") unemployment rate is another's sign of an unjust society.

Decision makers in organizations must constantly interpret data. Think of how you might conduct a market analysis if you wanted to launch a new small business in your community. What pieces of information would you search for and which would you pay the most attention to? Weick uses the following terms to describe three key stages of decision making.

- *Enactment,* the process of actively producing (or enacting) the information environment we inhabit, such as deciding what information is relevant for attention (e.g., market price or a new crisis abroad)
- *Selection,* the choices we make about how to interpret that information (e.g., "Is this a serious problem or not?")
- *Retention,* what we remember from the process of having made a decision, or what we retain for future decisions (at the level of the organization, what goes into the institutional memory)

The choice of the term *enactment* is very important. Weick emphasizes that we don't just react to an environment that's "out there." Rather, we construct it, by paying attention to certain things and not to others. Weick reminds us that we play a much greater role in constructing the environment for a decision than we think we do. Facts don't just show up in our offices or work areas. We often "plant" them ourselves. The captain of the ill-fated *Titanic* in 1912, for instance, chose not to heed iceberg warnings and instead increased the ship's speed. The iceberg that sunk the ship a few hours later was an important part of the physical environment, but safety concerns were not an important part of the ship's decision-making environment. It had been described as "unsinkable," and the goal was to cross the Atlantic in record time. By enactment, Weick means that we set the scene, or literally "carve out" a relevant world, for our decision.

When we decide what statistics are important or choose certain forms of evidence for our decisions, we create a specific environment for decision making. When we, for example, make an outline for a thesis or convene a meeting to solve a problem, we define the territory for our subsequent actions. If we already have a sense of where we want to go, it is very easy to enact this projection. Weick argues for flexibility and complexity at each stage of the process so that an organization can adapt well to a changing world. He also urges us to "complicate ourselves" in the sense of surrounding ourselves with many different pieces of information and many potential options. That is, we should be open to a variety of possibilities, so that we don't unwittingly become trapped by our own habits or patterned responses. This prescription is in direct recognition of the idea of *equifinality* (discussed in chapter 2), where there are usually multiple paths to the same goal.

Organizational Goals and Ways to Achieve Them

Organizational goals are an important consideration in looking at the rationality of organizations. The most common notion of rationality is that the ends and means we choose to accomplish goals are reasonable. But the problem of goal *displacement* has been observed for many types of organizations over the decades. In the early twentieth century, German political theorist Robert Michels believed that over time all organizations move toward oligarchy, or rule by a few. He focused his analysis on a variety of German political parties, but he intended his conclusions to apply broadly to many types of organizations. Michels believed that regardless of the value orientations of large organizations, they would eventually move toward concentration of power at the top of the pyramid. This tendency is so overwhelming in large organizations that a concern for power can override even the most socially conscious organization that preaches equality and democracy.

If Michels is right, organizations will inevitably lose sight of basic goals (making good refrigerators, providing effective job training, curing disease, helping the poor, etc.) and will become preoccupied with their own continuance, their own power, or their own prestige. Michels's principle, *the iron rule of oligarchy*, suggests that organizations such as religious organizations, charitable trusts and worker-owned cooperatives should dissolve themselves rather than experience the inevitable drift away from their basic goals over time.

Related to this is the charge that organizations in fact do not have *any* real goals beyond system maintenance—beyond their own growth and power. Organizational theorist Petro Georgiou makes this argument, in part to shake up our perspective on organizations as being rationally directed toward the objectives they say they are pursuing.[46] The claim is radical: not only do organizations, like individuals, work to maintain themselves but also they come to see survival as *the* overarching goal. When we consider how rarely organizations commit "suicide," or decide to dissolve themselves or cease operations without outside pressure (from the market or a court or someone else), we can see the kernel of wisdom in this view.

In addition to having reasonable goals, rational organizations are expected to have goals that are mutually supportive and *consistent*. According to March, however, this is rarely the case.[48] Most often, March claims, organizations don't even have consistent preferences. Preferences change over time not only because future circum-

Box 3.7 When We Hope for A but Reward B

Psychologist Alfie Kohn, in his provocative book *Punished by Rewards*, offers many examples of when we reward one thing while desiring something else.[47] This is true, for example, of grading systems used in our colleges and universities—they often encourage students to focus on getting good marks rather than on the process of learning. People in individualistic, industrialized societies often focus on salary and benefits, thinking that every new increment will bring greater happiness. One of the best examples of where organizations reward one thing while desiring something else is in the relationship between extrinsic and intrinsic forms of motivation. We want people to be intrinsically motivated to do their work, to find great satisfaction in doing their jobs, to find their jobs enriching, and to be dedicated to the organization and their larger profession. Yet we often focus on extrinsic rewards, particularly money and status. This is exactly why many employees who are contemplating a move to another employer ask for a raise when what they may really want is praise and recognition, or camaraderie, or a better work climate.

Still another common example is organizing into teams and/or expressing the value of teamwork, but basing rewards on individual achievements. People often interpret the organization's message in such cases as being, "Talk up the value of teams, but if you really want to get ahead, you have to stand out and promote yourself as superior to your teammates."

What other examples can you cite where an organization rewards something other than what it really seeks? Think of creativity, for example. How many organizations promote creativity, foster innovation, and encourage a healthy attitude toward change? Do their policies and practices match their communication?

stances are difficult to predict but also because unclear preferences allow decision makers the flexibility to adapt to or define new situations. When preferences are unclear, organizational goals often conflict. For example, organizations aim for long-term customer satisfaction while rewarding short-term sales. Such inconsistencies are well known in our personal lives as well. Think of examples from your own life.

Arguments such as these bring us back to one of Weber's basic fears about bureaucratic life (discussed in chapter 2): that substantive rationality, with its concern for collective reflection on ultimate ends, would be overtaken by formal rationality, with its calculating and often myopic perspective. While the critiques may have dissenters, they clearly indicate that the task of evaluating the "effectiveness" of an organizational decision is a daunting one.

From Rationality to Rationalities

A different, more communication-oriented perspective on rationality and organizations suggests that there are multiple rationalities in any given organization. Consider, for example, how a concern for economic efficiency and an ethic of care clash with one another in a contemporary hospital. Or look at the different ways men and women sometimes go about working on tasks in groups: men stressing the accomplishment of the task over more people-oriented concerns and women emphasizing the maintenance and cultivation of sound relationships. Indeed, Deborah Tannen's socio-linguistic research points out these different rationalities by which men and women are typically socialized in U.S. society and also in many other societies of the industrialized world.[49]

To understand the issues surrounding rationality, decision making, and information even better, think of the ways we view *different kinds of messages* in the organization. For example, how do *lists* and *stories* function in persuading others with whom we work to a particular course of action? Larry Browning, an organizational communication researcher, has written that lists are rooted in science and are thus technical communication used to convey certainty, standards, and accountability. We expect lists of information to be presented in a particular way in order to be credible, to be perceived as rational, and to be perceived as systematic or scientific.[50] Stories, however, are more personal, romantic, and dramatic. Given these characteristics, it's quite tempting in contemporary organizations to equate lists with "rational" and stories with "non-rational." However, sometimes a compelling story can be extremely persuasive in bringing an audience to a particular point of view.[51]

These two types of messages relate not only to different individual preferences but also to cultural patterns. In more oral traditions, stories or narratives seem the natural (or rational) way to express important ideas. On the other hand, the memo with its stylistic partner, the list, is a modern, Western creation developed for managers to disperse directives to a large number of people without the need for face-to-face communication. Based on our personal and cultural preferences, we may make unconscious judgments about who is the more rational, logical, and competent communicator. For instance, we may automatically assume that speakers who use PowerPoint slides know a lot about their subject.

Similarly, Leslie Baxter, a communication theorist and interpersonal scholar, has described the ways we "talk things through" versus "put them in writing."[52] These two everyday expressions suggest different ways of viewing the communication process and ultimately suggest different forms of rationality. In many North American organizations, for example, things are not considered real until they are written and become, as the saying goes, "etched in stone." But this is in stark contrast to many other societies, where talking things through, especially face to face, is what gives the relationship, as well as the content of the messages, a certain hard reality.

While the Basque region of Spain has been industrialized since the mid-to-late nineteenth century and is in many ways very modern, there remains a legacy of an oral tradition in the culture such that talking things through is much more highly valued than putting them in writing. What this means for large businesses and other organizations in this region is that the most "real" or sure form of communication is still the face-to-face agreement: the giving of one's word to another person in a meeting or over a cup of coffee. Certainly, Basques have adopted various forms of written and electronic communication, and memos are quite common in their large organizations. Still, they retain a very strong emphasis on face-to-face interaction as the most real, the most valid, and the most trustworthy form of communication. (This is also true of many other societies of the world, including indigenous cultures in Asia, Australasia, the Pacific, Africa, and the Americas.) For George's research on worker cooperatives in the Basque Country, Spain from 1992–1999, this meant that interviews with employees of worker cooperatives were much easier to arrange than questionnaire surveys were to conduct. In part, this is because paper-and-pencil questionnaires are seen as isolating, alienating forms of data gathering. "After all, why would you want someone to fill out a questionnaire for you when you could just ask him or her, in person, the questions you want to ask?" This is in marked contrast to large U.S. organizations, where researchers and consultants alike find it more convenient and more accepted to pass out copies of a survey than to set up time-intensive, one-on-one interviews.

Thus, when we consider the whole issue of rationality, decision making, and the uses of information, we need to keep in mind the worldviews within which we operate, and how those worldviews influence what counts as real, what counts as valid, and what counts as trustworthy in terms of relating to one another in organizations. In recent years, *multiculturalism* (which we discuss further in chapter 13 on globalization) has had important effects on how we conceive of multiple organizational rationalities. Multicultural critiques of Western instrumental rationality advance the idea that many concepts taken for granted about doing business in nations such as the United States, the United Kingdom, and Germany, especially notions of effectiveness and efficiency, are actually culturally situated and embedded.

For instance, organizational communication scholar Kathleen Krone and her colleagues have studied Chinese bureaucracies, arguing that effective and efficient communication practices are rooted in cultural contexts and political ideologies as well as the "instrumental" structure of the bureaucracy.[54] The cultural formulation of rational practices in such organizations was evident in a range of communication practices, notably conflict resolution. When managers attempted to handle issues of absenteeism or honesty among workers, they usually initiated "education" efforts, involving a combination of cajoling, threats, and promises. Such education could even involve approaching the worker's family and asking them to participate in the effort. Most Western college students would be horrified at the idea that a manager

Box 3.8 Studies of Time in Organizations

Organizational communication researchers Dawna Ballard and David Seibold have questioned the idea of time as something that is pre-given in organizations.[53] Instead, they focus on time—in terms of the way we measure it, divide it up into discrete units, and orient ourselves collectively toward it—as a cultural construction. They elaborate on Edward Hall's work on the temporal (time-related) nature of culture, focusing especially on distinctions between monochronic cultures and polychronic cultures. *Monochronic cultures*, as the term implies, focus on the accomplishment of one task at a time and value tasks over relationships. These cultures are characterized by a low level of flexibility, a desire to control time, and a rigid adherence to schedules. *Polychronic cultures* value relationships over tasks and are more flexible when it comes to scheduling.

Ballard and Seibold used this framework to explore the social dimensions of time and conducted a study of ways in which work groups oriented themselves differently toward time. Based on the responses of 337 employees in various work groups and multiple locations of a national cable installation company, they identified three significant dimensions of time on which work groups varied: flexibility, separation, and concurrency. *Flexibility* refers to the rigidity involved in time structuring in areas such as scheduling, daily routines, etc. *Separation* refers to the desire of the members to filter out "extraneous" factors in the completion of a task and is reflected in the need to "screen out distractions." *Concurrency* is related to the number of tasks engaged in at any given time. Ballard and Seibold's research demonstrates that even such a seemingly objective and rational notion as time is dealt with differently by different groups of people.

(or professor) would consider it appropriate or efficient to contact their families each time they didn't show up for work or for class!

The cultural nature of rationality is not only visible in communication practices, it is also evident in our assumptions about what counts as knowledge. In classes that you take—including your organizational communication classes—you are probably used to learning models of effective practice or management. Elizabeth Gowdy argues that such models usually conceive of professional practice as instrumental problem solving through the application of scientifically tested, universal methods. Indeed, we think of knowledge itself in these terms.[55] This is problematic because it obscures our awareness of the cultural origins of bodies of knowledge. As Morgan and Krone show, the "techno-scientific" language that saturates medical situations encourages medical students to think of knowledge and expertise in terms of detached concern, objectiveness, and universality.[56]

Another example is social work intervention. Models of practice tend to be geared toward increasing client "self-sufficiency." While this might seem normal and universally applicable, the self-sufficiency is grounded in the rhetoric of individual rights to self-determination, which in turn is based in individualism! Many social workers have begun to emphasize the importance of "practice wisdom," or culturally grounded notions of effective social work. Social worker Donna Hurdle writes about social work practice in Hawaii where social workers, rather than follow technical models of conflict resolution that emphasize the roles of individuals in mediation processes, have appropriated *Ho'oponopono*, a family-based process that emphasizes harmony and the restoration of goodwill, or *aloha*.[57]

The concept of technical and unitary rationality has been prominently reassessed from the point of view of culture, and it has been criticized from a number of other perspectives as well. Box 3.9 summarizes some recent programs of research that have further articulated the idea of multiple rationalities.

Emotionality in Organizational Life

We have already suggested that part of the *ethos* or character of bureaucracy is to minimize the role of emotion and the less controlled parts of ourselves when we're at work. This is part of what people on the street mean when they say to one another, "Now, behave professionally!"[64] In fact, there are a lot of assumptions and expectations relating to dress, manner, emotional tone, etc. built into that simple phrase. We've probably all been in meetings when someone violates the emotional ethic of the group or organization—say, with an "outburst" of tears, anger, or laughter. In many cases, a committee or work group doesn't know how to deal with such expressions of humanity, and the person is simply ignored with a transition like "Moving to the next item on our agenda . . ."

One of the major criticisms of bureaucracy and related forms of organization is that they downplay the more emotional and social aspects of human work—sometimes by denying that they exist and other times by seeking to control them. Two public administration writers, Ralph Hummel and Robert Denhardt, both of the United States, have sharply criticized the prevailing emphasis on rationality to the exclusion of emotionality in organizations.[65] Denhardt, for example, says that the information-processing model of organizational life is limiting and even oppressive because it neglects important parts of being human. In the industrialized world, the most valued communication is technical in orientation: it asks "How" in preference to "Why?"

Hummel views bureaucratic language as dysfunctional when it "abstracts" issues away from people and what he sees as fundamental human concerns. For example, cases in social agencies are often discussed in terms very distant from the personal concerns of clients. To some extent, of course, this kind of "abstraction" is necessary in order to move from individual instances to general categories, but Hummel reminds us that the basic motivations for the work and the lives of real people can get lost in

Box 3.9 Rationality Reevaluated

Creative survey research demonstrates that the language used to describe possible options shapes the choices made by respondents. For example, psychologists Daniel Kahneman and Amos Tversky have found in their research using scenarios that the subject's evaluation of financial risk varies a lot depending on how the situation is described. Economist Richard Thaler finds tremendous inconsistencies in everyday reasoning about money. For example, a person will often mow her own lawn to save $20, but she would seldom agree to mow a neighbor's lawn to make an additional $20.[58] A recent U.S. poll on income taxes found that a simple rephrasing of the primary question changed the responses greatly, even though essentially the same question was being asked in both cases.[59]

Studies of **classification and categorization**—in fields from physics to public administration to psychiatry—reveal that choices of labels to characterize types of behavior create "filters" that affect how we see things and make decisions subsequently. For instance, Mary Douglas's fascinating book *How Institutions Think* offers case studies from subjects as varied as the penal system and winemaking. The systems of terms take on a life of their own, often removed from their original purposes. In communication studies, Majia Holmer-Nadesan shows how the personality testing in human resources management embodies certain political choices and ideologies. Steve May shows how the same thing is true for supposedly benevolent employee-assistance programs (or EAPs).[60]

Research on **aphorisms or cultural slogans** like "Act professionally" or "Get a real job!" or "This is just business" tell us a lot about what things are valued within the society or the speech community where the slogans pass as common sense. For example, Robin Clair has explained the assumptions about what goals and activities are legitimated (or deemed valid) by the phrase "Get a real job."[61]

Feminist critiques of phenomena as diverse as childhood socialization and bureaucratic decision making show how *male tendencies to privilege abstract categories over personal examples* colors the decisions that are made in areas such as law, welfare, and leadership. Carol Gilligan's *In a Different Voice* relates the biases of a great deal of developmental research toward competition and achievement and against collaboration and relating to others. Kathy Ferguson's *The Feminist Case against Bureaucracy* explains how thinking bureaucratically can often work against the very values that an organization is supposed to embody.[62]

Postmodern interpretations provide a number of important lessons about the limits of rationality. For example, if the modern world is defined in part by a radical questioning of assumptions, then the very idea of rationality (and for that matter, modernity) itself should be questioned. Recently, some theorists have reframed taken-for-granted Western ideas of progress, suggesting that modern notions of advancement and "rational" decision making are subject to enormous contradictions and blind spots.[63]

What do you see as some of the most important implications of these theories for our self-awareness as organizational members and decision makers?

the process. While Hummel's critique is probably overstated a bit, he does call our attention to the peculiar patterns of communication that sometimes are encouraged in large organizations. Often, these ways of talking and being do not "feel right" to the participants, yet the patterns persist because of reasons of power, habit, or the inability of a group to see other alternatives (see our discussion of power in chapter 9).

Emotional Labor

Many kinds of jobs demand that we control our emotions; sociologist Arlie Russell Hochschild refers to this effort as "emotional labor."[66] Interestingly, employees can be asked to shape their behavior in one of three ways: to heighten their expression of joy (e.g., the infamous smiling customer service representative or Disneyland employee), to appear mean or indifferent (as is emphasized in the training of tax collectors and some debt counselors), or to present a vaguely pleasant professional demeanor (what historian Peter Stearns calls "American cool").[67] However, displays of trained and memorized behavior are as likely to frustrate customers as to please them if the salesperson seems merely to be acting out a script. Perhaps you've worked in jobs where the amount of emotional labor expected was great. Studies of airline attendants reveal not only corporate expectations for their behavior but also some creative strategies of resistance—like "accidentally" spilling coffee on the lap of an obnoxious customer.

The very idea of emotional labor reminds us of how organizational expectations can shape our feelings, at least on the surface level, as we try to perform the roles expected of us in supposedly rational workplaces. As organizational communication theorists Dennis Mumby and Linda Putnam explain (playing on Simon's concept of "bounded rationality"), we sometimes experience "bounded emotionality."[68] This concept has both theoretical and practical significance, as we consider life in the modern organization. For example, there are certain defined limits that shape how we are allowed to act in an organization, and these limits may be reflected as well in how we conceive of "acceptable" organizational behavior. In day-to-day practice, the emotional side of our role is suppressed or controlled, presumably in the interests of the organization. In the United States waitpersons are expected to project a particular kind of friendliness accompanied by broad smiles, self-introductions, and explicit references to being willing to serve. In contrast, servers in France are expected to show their respect for the customers by remaining at a distance until asked for service.

Partial Inclusion

There are some good reasons why roles should be performed in ways that are aligned with the goals and culture of the organization. In the interests of coordination and unity of impression, there's a need for some degree of consistency across individuals, situations, and departments. It's in the interests of a department store to have customers get the same kind of friendly service from the cosmetics department as they do in home appliances. Also, as we learned in our discussion of bureaucracy in chapter 2, *roles* are very important in most large organizations. Except for total institutions (like prisons and some monasteries where the individual truly is "inside" the organization) most organizations do not completely "contain" the people that work for them. Instead, we talk about people being "partially included" in organizations, recognizing that they are filling roles and that they "have a life" outside the organization.

The principle of partial inclusion cuts both ways, positively and negatively, for the organization and the individual. For the organization, the idea of replaceability is preserved. Partial inclusion allows the organization to protect itself against the loss of employees, while also expecting that the employees will leave big parts of themselves behind when they come through the door. A dynamic restaurant owner in Missoula, Montana used to practice just such a philosophy of management by insisting that employees come to work devoted to their roles completely and serving the customers "perfectly." It's not that she is unsympathetic to bad days or to personal loss; it's that she would tell the employee who is grieving over a friend's bad auto accident simply "to stay home."

On the other hand, even in the case of a fairly benevolent version of this philosophy, a manager may find her employees less committed than they might otherwise be. So, some of them would stay home—but for good! For the individual, there's the obvious disadvantage that he must leave behind "personal" matters as he conforms to a professional role. This may be hard when someone wants to appeal to personal circumstances to explain why they were late or why their work on the last project was less effective than usual. However, the partial inclusion also protects the individual by giving him or her boundaries between work and "life" and keeps him or her from being completely absorbed in the organization. When our students tell us that they really like companies and agencies that offer such things as day care, wellness programs, intramural sports, and other programs, we remind them that there may be a personal cost as well.

As more and more of an employee's activities and "mental space" become tied up with the work organization, the complete identification leaves little flexibility if circumstances change and the company moves to another country or goes out of business, for example. The extreme example of total rather than partial inclusion is the corporate burial plot that some Japanese corporations offer—the employee never really retires! Non-western organizations might also embody different relationships between rationality and emotionality. Krone and her colleagues found that managers in Chinese factories dealt similarly with both pleasant and unpleasant emotions, reflecting their beliefs that emotion is part of reason rather than something distinct from rationality.[69]

In our studies of organizations and communication, we are beginning to revalue the role of emotion at work. Many organizations are doing this with policies that allow for—or even encourage—a more casual atmosphere. In the United States, for instance, Southwest Airlines has built a reputation for employees who joke, laugh, and have fun. In recent decision-making studies, it has been found that emotion helps "push" us toward some options and "pull" us away from others. Without our emotional selves, we would often be lost in seas of data, choices, and options.[70] This is exactly why one of our friends highlights the need for groups to capitalize on "epiphanies"—those special moments of collective enthusiasm when an idea spreads, and the energy can be harnessed to make it happen.[71]

But our emotions still can "get the better of us" in the sense that we lose perspective on a problem when we don't stop to examine it carefully. We can short circuit the reasoning process when we become too enamored of a cute label or a clever-sounding slogan. In political discourse, terms like "freedom," "equality," and "progress" are often used to the advantage of politicians. Neither they nor any of their constituents pause to ask what's really under discussion. The idea sounds great, and its invocation (say in a rally) excites people in a way that they all feel unified. The many possible differences in meaning for the slogan aren't even considered. "Family values" has become a buzzword in U.S. politics, for both the Republican and the Democratic parties. The specific values aren't specified, but the idea of *having* values becomes a cherished image for political and business organizations, just as for religious institutions. The push for businesses and corporations to present themselves as emotionally sensitive to their customers can result in somewhat incoherent messages. For example, the corporate slogan of India-based Sahara Airlines—"Emotionally Yours"—is printed on every ticket they issue.

Business and management fads are often like this, too. Whether the trend is management by objectives (as it was in the 1970s) or "strong" culture (as in the 1980s), or teamwork (still hot today), people want desperately to find *the* answer and are often willing to surrender their good judgment as well as their resources to consultants who profess to hold the key to success. These trends, as well as many others, have kernels of truth. But, as they spread and become implemented in all sectors, people often forget about local wisdom, born of experience and expertise. Ted and George, for example, have each been asked to help implement "teamwork" in organizations where top managers had little idea of what doing so would mean in actual practice. These clients could only articulate vague references to liking teamwork in basketball! Again, we return to one of the central themes for this book; we need to get beyond the taken-for-granted aspects of organizational life.

Snapshot Synthesis

Our purpose in challenging prevailing notions of rationality is not to dismiss the concept altogether—far from it. We all like to deal with people who are predictable, confront situations that can be explained from past experience, and find reliable ways to achieve goals. To say that organizations are not perfectly rational is to remind ourselves that they are made up of the plans, energies, and dreams of human beings. We recommend a perspective on rationality that recognizes the limits, paradoxes, and ironies of "the best laid plans." Just as unintended consequences have arisen with the introduction of each new technology in our world, so should rationality be understood as a domain of human activity that is fraught with surprise and setback as well as success. When Aristotle defined humans as "rational animals," he probably meant that on a good day we can lay out plans and move confidently toward them—and especially that we can reflect on those plans themselves!

A look at something as seemingly straightforward as how data serve as argument in a human resources management decision reminds us of the vagaries of rationality in practice. The same piece of data about the performance of an academic department—say, that it has increased its level of productivity by 25% over the past three years—can be used *either* to justify keeping personnel the same ("You're doing fine with the people you have") or expanding the unit ("You need more help"). Similarly, consider budgetary decisions in U.S. universities about sports programs, especially North American football. If the team is winning, that information can be used to justify a budget increase, as a form of reward. However, repeated losses by the team can be used as a call for further investment! The examples are endless. The cautionary tale is to evaluate carefully what data count as information, how people make arguments, and what forms of rationality win the day. This is where cognition and communication really come together.

Key Concepts

- **Rationality:** ordering our world based on reason; using observable facts and logical reasoning to reach objective conclusions; usually connotes the ideas of being reasonable, sensible, sane, and systematic; in modern organizational life, epitomized by bureaucracy
- **Scientific Management**: Frederick Taylor's system to standardize work intended to make businesses more organized and more efficient, especially through the use of "time and motion" studies; the first major development in management thought
- **Efficiency:** while it has multiple meanings, often refers to getting the greatest amount of output for a given amount of input; a supreme value or "god term" in rationalistic views of organizations
- **Decisional Premise:** a value that guides decisions, such as "safety first"; according to Herbert Simon, the basic building block of organizations, such that an organization may then be seen as a hierarchy of decisional premises, with the broadest value and factual premises residing at the top and more specific ones following logically at lower levels
- **Information-processing Theory:** a perspective on organizations that focuses on decision-making processes, especially the cognitive, quasi-rational, and information-related aspects of organizational life; tends to place emphasis on controlling uncertainty
- **Bounded Rationality:** a focus on the emotional experience of organizational life, based in the inter-subjectivity of relationships and seeing both constraint and possibility in the non-rational aspects of work
- **Socially Distributed Cognition:** the idea that information resides not with individual persons but within a network of people who interact regularly
- **Functional Theory**: a rationalist and "normative" theory of group decision making that suggests a standard, or norm, for effective groups to follow by identifying the functions that group members should perform to be effective in decision making
- **Garbage Can Model**: a non-rationalist explanation of how decisions are made in organizations that suggests that when a problem or issue emerges, various stakeholders dump their solutions, feelings, related issues, etc. into the garbage can in a rather haphazard fashion, and a decision is made when an acceptable match is seen between problems, solutions, resources, and participants
- **Equivocality:** in Weick's theory, the key element of the organizational environment to be managed in decision making; when two or more possible interpretations exist for a situation
- **Enactment:** Weick's notion that when we reach out to discover and understand the world around us we unavoidably "plant" part of the reality we discover

- **Iron Rule of Oligarchy:** Michels's principle that, regardless of the value orientations of large organizations, they would eventually move toward concentration of power at the top of the pyramid
- **Bounded Emotionality:** the notion that there are certain defined limits that shape how we are allowed to act in an organization, with the emotional side of our being typically suppressed in favor or the "rational" side

Endnotes

[1] See Aristotle, *Rhetoric*, trans. W. Rhys Roberts (New York: Modern Library Random House, 1954).

[2] See Robert L. Ivie, "Images of Savagery in American Justifications for War," *Communication Monographs* 47 (1980): 279–294.

[3] See Lecia Archer and Kristine Fitch, "Communication in Latin American Multinational Organizations," *Communicating in Multinational Organizations,* ed. Richard Wiseman and Robert Shuter (Thousand Oaks, CA: Sage, 1994).

[4] See Frederic Winslow Taylor, *Principles of Scientific Management* (New York: Harper Brothers, 1911; New York: W. W. Norton & Co., 1967; Dover Publications, 1998).

[5] See Douglas McGregor, *The Human Side of Enterprise: 25th Anniversary Printing* (New York: McGraw-Hill/Irwin, 1985).

[6] Graham Sewell, "The Discipline of Teams: The Control of Team-Based Industrial Work through Electronic and Peer Surveillance," *Administrative Science Quarterly* 43 (1998): 397–428.

[7] See Kenneth Burke, *A Rhetoric of Motives* (Berkeley: University of California Press, 1969).

[8] See John Schmid, "Tietmeyer's Parting Advice to Europe: New Watchword Will Be Competition, Retiring Bank Chief Predicts," *International Herald Tribune* 23 (Aug. 1999): 1.

[9] Chester I. Barnard, *The Functions of the Executive, 30th anniv. ed.* (Cambridge, MA: Harvard University Press, 1968).

[10] Robert E. Lane, *The Market Experience* (Cambridge, UK: Cambridge University Press, 1991).

[11] Robert E. Lane, *The Loss of Happiness in Market Democracies* (New Haven, CT: Yale University Press, 2000).

[12] See Herbert A. Simon, *Administrative Behavior, 50th anniv. ed.* (New York: Free Press, 1997).

[13] See Henri Fayol, *General and Industrial Management* (New York and London: Pitman, 1949).

[14] See Allen Newell and Herbert A. Simon, *Human Problem Solving* (Englewood Cliffs, NJ: Prentice-Hall, 1972).

[15] Sunwolf and David R. Seibold, "The Impact of Formal Procedures on Group Processes," *The Handbook of Group Communication Theory and Research*, ed. Lawrence R. Frey, Dennis S. Gouran, and Marshall Scott Poole (Thousand Oaks, CA: Sage, 1999).

[16] Gareth Morgan, *Images of Organization* (Thousand Oaks, CA: Sage, 1989) pp. 81–82.

[17] Peter Senge, *The Fifth Discipline: The Art and Practice of the Learning Organization* (New York: Doubleday, 1990).

[18] See, e.g., James G. March and Johan P. Olsen, "The Uncertainty of the Past: Organizational Learning under Ambiguity," *European Journal of Political Research* 3 (1975): 147–171.

[19] See Martha Feldman and James G. March, "Information as Signal and Symbol," *Administrative Science Quarterly* 26 (1981): 171–186.

[20] Feldman and March, p. 182.

[21] See Charles A. O'Reilly, Jennifer A. Chatman, and John C. Anderson, "Message Flow and Decision Making," *The Handbook of Organizational Communication,* ed. Fredric M. Jablin, Linda L. Putnam, Lyman W. Porter, and Karlene H. Roberts (Thousand Oaks, CA: Sage, 1987).

[22] This definition was used by a manager in a company Ted studied. The manager used the definition in his efforts to persuade top management to support a major knowledge management initiative.

[23] Eric Abrahamson, "Management Fashion," *Academy of Management Review* 21 (1996): 254–285.

[24] Theodore Zorn, "The Brief Rise and Quick Fall of Knowledge Management in a New Zealand Organization," *Cases in Organizational Communication*, ed. Pamela Shockley-Zalabak and Joann Keyton (New York: Roxbury Publications, in press).

[25] Gianni Vattimo, *The Transparent Society* (Cambridge: Polity Press, 1992).

[26] Edwin Hutchins and Tove Klausen, "Distributed Cognition in an Airline Cockpit," *Cognition and Communication at Work*, ed. Yrjö Engeström and David Middleton (Cambridge, UK: Cambridge University Press, 1998) pp. 15–34.

[27] See James R. Taylor and Elizabeth J. Van Every, *The Emergent Organization: Communication as Its Site and Surface* (Mahwah, NJ: Lawrence Erlbaum, 2000).

[28] Niklas Luhmann, *Organisation und Entscheidung.* (Opladen: Westdeutscher Verlag, 2000).

[29] See John Dewey, *The Essential John Dewey*, ed. Larry A. Hickman and Thomas M. Alexander (Bloomington: Indiana University Press, 1998).

[30] Randy Y. Hirokawa and Abram J. Salazar, "An Integrated Approach to Communication and Group Decision-Making," *Managing Group Life: Communicating in Decision-making Groups*, ed. Lawrence Frey and J. Kevin Barge (Dallas: Houghton Mifflin, 1997) pp. 156–181; Dennis S. Gouran, "Effective versus Ineffective Group Decision Making," *Managing Group Life: Communicating in Decision-making Groups*, ed. Lawrence Frey and J. Kevin Barge (Dallas: Houghton Mifflin, 1997) pp. 133–155.

[31] Randy Y. Hirokawa and Abram J. Salazar, "Task-Group Communication and Decision-making Performance," *Handbook of Group Communication*, ed. Lawrence R. Frey, Dennis S. Gouran, and Marshall S. Poole (Thousand Oaks, CA: Sage, 1999).

[32] Hirokawa and Salazar, "Task Group Communication."

[33] Cynthia Stohl and Michael Holmes, "A Functional Perspective for Bona Fide Groups," *Communication Yearbook* 16 (1993): 601–614.

[34] Dennis A. Gioia and James B. Thomas, "Identity, Image and Issue Interpretation: Sensemaking during Strategic Change in Academia," *Administrative Science Quarterly* 41 (1996): 370–403.

[35] Theodore E. Zorn, "The Uncooperative Cooperative: Attempting to Improve Employee Relations at Weaver Street Market, *Cases in Organizational Communication Vol. 2*, ed. Beverly D. Sypher (New York: Guilford Press, 1997).

[36] Randy Y. Hirokawa and Abram J. Salazar, "An Integrated Approach to Communication and Group Decision Making," *Managing Group Life: Communicating in Decision-making Groups*, ed. Lawrence R. Frey and J. Kevin Barge (Boston: Houghton-Mifflin, 1997).

[37] Marshall S. Poole and Michael E. Holmes, "Decision Development in Computer-Assisted Group Decision Making," *Human Communication Research* 22 (1995): 90–127; Marshall S. Poole and Jonelle Roth, "Decision Development in Small Groups IV: A Typology of Decision Paths," *Human Communication Research* 15 (1989): 323–356.

[38] Poole and Holmes, p. 95.

[39] Marshall S. Poole, David Seibold, and Robert McPhee, "The Structuration of Group Decisions," *Communication and Group Decision Making*, 2nd ed., ed. Randy Y. Hirokawa and Marshall S. Poole (Thousand Oaks, CA: Sage Publications, 1996) pp. 114–146.

[40] Marshall S. Poole, Gerardine DeSanctis, Laurie Kirsch, and Michelle Jackson, "Group Decision Support Systems as Facilitators of Quality Team Efforts," *Innovations in Group Facilitation*, ed. Lawrence R. Frey (Cresskill, NJ: Hampton, 1995) p. 305.

[41] Theodore E. Zorn, Jr. and Sarah E. Ruccio, "The Use of Communication to Motivate College Sales Teams," *Journal of Business Communication* 35 (October 1998): 468–499.

[42] Karl E. Weick, *The Social Psychology of Organizing*, 2nd ed. (Reading, MA: Addison-Wesley, 1979).

[43] Weick.

[44] Michael D. Cohen, James G. March, and Johan P. Olsen, "A Garbage Can Model of Organizational Choice," *Administrative Science Quarterly* 17 (1972): 1–25.

[45] Mark J. Zbaracki, "The Rhetoric and Reality of Total Quality Management," *Administrative Science Quarterly* 43 (1998): 602–636; Qi Xu, "TQM as an Arbitrary Sign for Play: Discourse and Transformation," *Organization Studies* 20 (1999): 659–681.

[46] See Petro Georgiou, "The Goal Paradigm and Notes toward a Counter-paradigm," in *Complex Organizations: Critical Perspectives,* ed. Mary Zey-Ferrell and Michael Aiken (Glenview, IL: Scott Foresman, 1981).

[47] See Alfie Kohn, *Punished by Rewards: The Trouble with Gold Stars, Incentive Plans, A's, Praise, and Other Bribes* (Boston: Houghton Mifflin Company, 1999).

[48] James G. March, "How We Talk and How We Act: Administrative Theory and Administrative Life," *Leadership and Organizational Cultures*, ed. Thomas Sergiovanni and John E. Carbally (Urbana: University of Illinois Press, 1984).

[49] See Deborah Tannen, *You Just Don't Understand: Women and Men in Conversation* (New York: William Morrow & Company, 1990).

[50] Larry D. Browning, "Lists and Stories as Organizational Communication," *Communication Theory* 2 (1992): 281–302.

[51] See e.g., Walther R. Fisher, "Narration as a Human Communication Paradigm: The Case of Public Moral Argument," *Communication Monographs* 51 (1984): 1–22.

[52] Leslie A. Baxter, "'Talking Things through' versus 'Putting It in Writing': Two Codes of Communication in an Academic Institution," *Journal of Applied Communication Research* 21 (1993): 313–326.

[53] Dawna I. Ballard and David R. Seibold, "Time Orientation and Temporal Variation Across Work Groups: Implications for Group and Organizational Communication," *Western Journal of Communication* 64 (2000): 218–242.

[54] Kathleen Krone, Mary Garrett, and Ling Chen, "Managerial Communication Practices in Chinese Factories: A Preliminary Investigation," *Journal of Business Communication* 29 (1992): 229–252.

[55] Elizabeth Gowdy, "From Technical Rationality to Participating Consciousness," *Social Work* 39 (1994): 362–370.

[56] Jayne Morgan, and Kathleen Krone, "Bending the Rules of Emotional Display: Emotional Improvisation in Caregiver Performances," *Journal of Applied Communication Research* 29 (2001): 317–340.

[57] Donna Hurdle, "Native Hawaiian Traditional Healings: Culturally Based Interventions for Social Work Practice," *Social Work* 47 (2002): 183–192.

[58] Roger Lowenstein, "Exuberance Is Rational," *The New York Times Magazine* 11 (February 2001): 68–70.

[59] See Daniel Kahneman and Amos Tversky, *Judgment under Uncertainty* (Cambridge: Cambridge University Press, 1982).

[60] See Mary Douglas, *How Institutions Think* (Syracuse, NY: Syracuse University Press, 1986); and Majia Holmer-Nadesan, "Essai: Dislocating (Instrumental) Organizational Time," *Organization Studies* 18 (1997): 481–510.

[61] See Robin Patric Clair, "The Political Nature of the Colloquialism, 'A Real Job': Implications for Organizational Socialization," *Communication Monographs* 63 (1996): 249–267.

[62] Carol Gilligan, *In a Different Voice* (Cambridge, MA: Harvard University Press, 1982); Kathy Ferguson, *The Feminist Case against Bureaucracy* (Philadelphia, PA: Temple University Press, 1984).

[63] See Bruno Latour, *We Have Never Been Modern* (Cambridge, MA: Harvard University Press, 1993).

[64] See Michael W. Kramer and Jon A. Hess, "Communication Rules for the Display of Emotions in Organizational Settings," *Management Communication Quarterly* 16 (2002): 66–80.

[65] Robert B. Denhardt, *In the Shadow of Organization* (Lawrence: University Press of Kansas, 1981); Ralph G. Hummel, *The Bureaucratic Experience*, 4th ed. (New York: Bedford/St. Martin's Press, 1994).

[66] See Arlie Russell Hochschild, *The Managed Heart: Commercialization of Human Feeling* (Berkeley: University of California Press, 1985).

[67] See Peter Stearns, *American Cool: Constructing a Twentieth-Century Emotional Style* (New York: New York University Press, 1994).

[68] See Dennis K. Mumby and Linda L. Putnam, "The Politics of Emotion: A Feminist Reading of Bounded Rationality," *Academy of Management Review* 17 (1992): 465–486.

[69] Kathleen Krone, Ling Cheng, Diane Sloane, and Linda Gallant, "Managerial Emotionality in Chinese Factories," *Management Communication Quarterly* 11 (1997): 6–50.

[70] See Antonio Damasio, *Descartes' Error, Emotion, Reason, and the Human Brain* (New York: G. P. Putnam's Sons, 1994).

[71] See Ernest G. Bormann, "Fantasy and Rhetorical Vision: The Rhetorical Criticism of Social Reality," *Quarterly Journal of Speech* 58 (1972): 396–407.

4

Culture, Subcultures, and Organizational Socialization

Consider how much you learn about an organization from attending a meeting. How do people dress? How do they sit, who defers to whom, who talks the most? Is joking common? Do people make personal comments? Are arguments taken personally? Such communication patterns make up an organization's culture. The culture of an organization is embedded in and expressed by habits of communication. Everyday habits display what we take for granted in our lives; this is also true for organizations and their communication. For example, in many organizations, "professionalism" is a taken-for-granted value. We often notice such values only when they are breached, as when someone engages in an "unprofessional" emotional outburst in a formal meeting. As mentioned in the last chapter, we've probably all experienced a situation where emotional expressions were ignored by the group; decorum was not broken.

People in organizations often are not aware of some of the most basic aspects of their relationships with one another: patterns of interruptions in conversation, the avoidance of conflict, and taboo topics, to name a few. Sometimes we find certain values and attitudes at the deepest level of an organization: for example, unspoken but nevertheless important commitments to "cut corners" or to take shortcuts in order to meet pressing deadlines. We often don't realize that we're "inside" a culture—at least not until we step out of it. Most of the time we are like the fish that can't see the water in which it is swimming. When we visit other countries for the first time, however, we notice details of the environment and behavior because they are not familiar or customary. We are strangers and suddenly aware of differences and similarities. The same awareness can surface if we change jobs after a long time period with the same employer. We suddenly see what we took for granted in a new light.

What do organizational members take for granted when they communicate with each other and/or with the organization's surroundings? Think of an organization with which you are familiar. What would an outsider notice that insiders overlook? What are the advantages and disadvantages of this "taken-for-grantedness" for the organization? Since an organization's culture shapes its communication, managers often want to influence the culture. To what extent is that possible? And how is the culture passed on to newcomers—especially if some values or norms are not stated explicitly? Let's look closely at the idea of organizational culture, trying to move beyond its taken-for-grantedness.

In this chapter, we will discuss these and related questions. We will continue our exploration of how organizations make sense of themselves and their surroundings through communication—that is, how "organizational life is accomplished communicatively."[1] First, however, we need to take a closer look at the concept of culture. What is culture and how does it influence organizations?

Defining Culture

The idea of culture originated in the study of botany and referred to the process of growing and cultivating plants. Its etymological origins are Latin: *cultura* (cultivate) and *colere* (to care for). For many years, culture was seen as the opposite of nature, which was understood as something raw, wild, or non-manufactured. This distinction echoes the "nature-versus-nurture" debate, which asks whether biological inheritance (genetics) or experience in the world (socialization) has the most influence in shaping an individual's personality. Culture was also used to refer to the arts and amusement, as it often is today. Ministries of culture in many countries oversee funds for the arts or support new styles of music. We still speak of "high-brow" and "low-brow" culture, referring to different forms of arts and entertainment.

The notion of culture within the fields of anthropology and sociology, however, is broader since it encompasses *all* characteristics that humans have *in common* and that distinguish them from other animals, including symbol systems such as language, dress, rituals, myths, metaphors, stories, values, and attitudes. Based on this wider interpretation, *culture is a system of meaning that guides the construction of reality in a social community.* For example, our meanings for time structure how we act. Thus, the habit of looking at a clock or a watch punctuates the lives of most people in the modern industrialized world. People schooled in this habit take for granted that days are time-structured; as a consequence, they have a hard time imagining societies that operate(d) on more natural and longer rhythms—the seasons, sunrise, sunset, and the weather. Even knowledge is cultural. Think about the relationship between the early European assumption that the Earth was flat and its conceptualizations of heaven above and hell below. Or consider our knowledge about what makes up a healthy meal. This knowledge has certainly changed over the years and in various ways in different societies. We deal with cultural systems of meaning from our most fundamental beliefs about why things are done the way they are to our definitions of things and events.[2]

According to sociologist Talcott Parsons, culture is one of the basic institutions of society, and studying culture helps us see how a society perpetuates itself.[3] To survive, a culture must ensure that individual members internalize its values, beliefs, and norms—in other words, speak the "proper" language. All collectives, thus, set up systems for cultural reproduction. For example, schools instruct, media distribute information, and legal institutions monitor behavior, including laws and regulations. Although such systems are never able to regulate behavior completely, they provide the culture with a certain amount of stability and predictability. This is perhaps the most crucial feature of culture: it defines a space within which certain behaviors are expected and, to a large extent, taken for granted.

A cultural system of meaning, however, is dynamic. It helps communities make sense of themselves and their surroundings, while being simultaneously informed and shaped by those sense-making activities. Culture, thus, is both the cause and the effect of human activity. As anthropologist Clifford Geertz puts it: "Believing . . . that man (sic) is an animal suspended in webs of significance he himself has spun, I take culture to be those webs . . ."[4] This may sound circular, and in a sense it is. We construct the world that constructs us. Even when our ability to change our culture seems limited, the meanings we refer to as culture only live through us. Whereas Geertz used the metaphor of the web, Kenneth Burke said life is like a conversation: we enter it after it is already going on, we gradually get the hang of it, then we leave and the conversation continues—in some ways influenced by our own participation in it.[5]

Very few cultures are monolithic entities based on just one system of meaning. In fact, the existence of differences within the culture is an important source of its dynamics. Differences may originate in family background, religion, education, occupation, wealth, status, lifestyle, interests, etc. We refer to cultures within a larger culture as "subcultures." The members of a subculture identify themselves with a distinct group within the larger culture, interact regularly with this group, and often share perceptions and understandings of central problems.[6] For example, communication scholars Shirley Willinghanz, Greg Leichty, and Joy Hart found that two distinct subcultures developed in a company called Auto Tech as it was going through a major organizational change. One of these subcultures had a strong allegiance to the organi-

Box 4.1 Degrees of Cultural Integration and Differentiation

Organizational theorist Mary Jo Hatch[7] illustrates the variations in the interplay between a general culture and its subcultures.

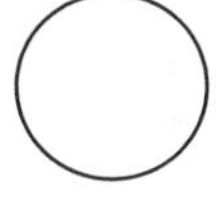

Unitary:

Diverse: Integrated

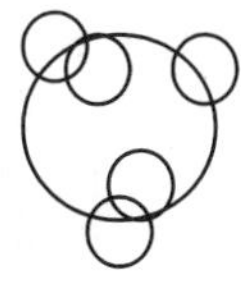

Diverse: Differentiated

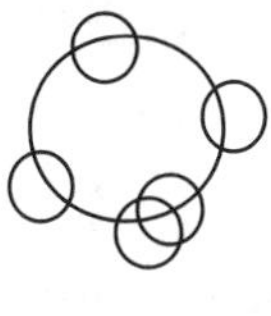

Diverse: Fragmented

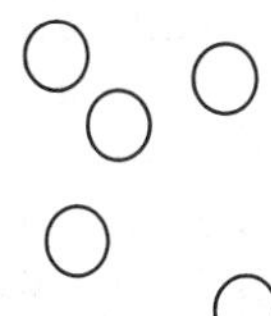

Disorganized: (Multi-cephalous)

Whereas the unitary culture may appear strong because all members subscribe to the same values and meanings, it may be too *closed* to change. At the other end of the continuum, the disorganized culture manifests multiple differences, but it may not have enough similarities to qualify as a culture.

Look at these variations and think of concrete examples of each. What are their strengths and weaknesses? Which model best represents how you see your culture(s) and society?

zation's traditional egalitarian values and structure, and one developed around a new group of executives who were committed to a hierarchical structure and accompanying values.[8] In other cases, subcultures develop in an organization around professions (like accounting, engineering, or advertising), departments, or regions. Sometimes subculture members are identifiable through dress, or manner, or preferred symbols—this can be true in a manufacturing firm just like it is in the music industry. Think about differences among academic departments in terms of level of formality, hierarchy, and student-friendliness. Or think about how differently salespersons often see the world from the ways engineers commonly do. Other professions, of course, could be described using similar terms. Think of examples of subcultures other than professions. What make these groups distinct? Is it vocabulary, style, a way of seeing the world? While the general culture needs differences to flourish and grow, subcultures need the general culture and its dominant values in order to differentiate themselves. The notion of culture, thus, refers not only to what is held in common by the human race but also to what differentiates societies or groups of people from each other. As we will see in chapter 5, the idea of multiple cultures, and subcultures, has an important parallel in the realm of organizational identity.

Organizations as Cultures

How appropriate is it to compare an organization with something as complete as a culture? Clearly, organizations are in some respects bounded entities concerned with making sense of themselves and their surroundings. These processes are to a great extent informed and shaped by organizational values, norms, and beliefs rooted in a specific organizational language(s) and expressed in organizational symbols and rituals. Thus, following the anthropological and sociological traditions, scholars of organizational culture urge us to study such phenomena in order to discover what "holds an organization together." To what extent, however, are languages, symbols, and rituals unique to individual organizations? In what respects can organizations claim to "own" specific cultural features?

According to management scholar Edgar Schein, any culture exists at three levels.[9] At the most fundamental level are the *core beliefs and assumptions* that members of the culture see as truth. At this level, the culture is usually blind to itself. Although core beliefs and assumptions may change over long periods of time, they are rarely discussed explicitly. Among organizational core beliefs and assumptions we find, for example, the idea that organizations are controlled by external, anonymous forces of the market ("the invisible hand"), that organizations need to grow to exist, or that employees need to be controlled in order to work hard enough. The second level of culture consists of *values and behavioral norms*. Here we find a greater level of self-awareness; the culture's members discuss, confirm, or challenge existing values. Such challenges, however, most often come from marginal members of the culture, like newcomers, visitors, or outsiders. Examples of organizational values and associated norms are efficiency, flexibility, service mindedness, and ethics. These values and norms are often influenced by trends in the general business culture. The third level of culture, *artifacts*, is the most visible and tangible level. Artifacts include buildings, dress, décor, and logos; they also include rituals, ceremonies, traditions, stories, and jargon. Schein regards organizational artifacts as manifestations of the

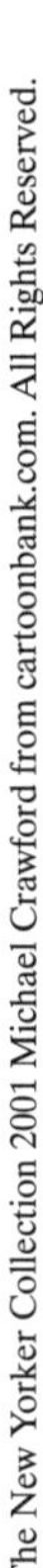

"And the dim fluorescent lighting is meant to emphasize the general absence of hope."

deeper levels of culture. Thus, architecture, office layouts, slogans, and bumper stickers reflect both behavioral values and basic assumptions in an organization. An open office landscape may be seen as a representation of an open culture where ideas and problems are discussed freely. The same office landscape, of course, may be seen as a manifestation of managerial control. While artifacts are more visible than values, we may not be able to interpret easily their full meaning.

Together, assumptions, values, and artifacts constitute the complex phenomenon of culture. Whereas assumptions shape values that in turn are reflected in artifacts, the influence goes both ways. The introduction of new artifacts, such as new information technologies or a new office layout, can reshape organizational values and, over time, be incorporated into new assumptions. Think about an organization with physical spaces for informal communication, such as a coffee area or a courtyard. Now imagine the effect on the culture of the organization if those meeting spots are eliminated. In addition to Schein's three levels, an organizational culture can be described as a system of *demarcation, identification*, and *control.* Culture "does" all of these things, as we will discuss further. *Demarcation* refers to setting and maintaining boundaries—either literally, as with a building or a campus, or figuratively in terms of the bounds of acceptable behavior. For instance, the culture may structure meetings to begin with chitchat about personal matters, in which everyone is expected to participate. If newcomers step outside these bounds of group norms—say by not laughing loud enough at the boss's jokes—other members send signals such as frowns or whispers to clarify the boundaries of expected behavior.

Identification refers to the appropriation of and commitment to a particular identity. A culture needs its members to identify with its basic values. As we discuss in chapter 5 there are many ways in which organizations get their members to identify with the culture—by praising and emphasizing certain values that employees already hold, by getting members to see other values as "threats," or simply by just encouraging the belief that "we're all in this together."

Control refers to the order of a system that not only "keeps people in line" but also helps them maintain predictability. Although culture isn't often thought of in connection with control or power (see chapter 9), even the more ancillary aspects of an organization—such as storytelling by the coffee machine—may be quite revealing about power relations at work. Culture controls in part by identifying what is seen as normal—and therefore what's allowed or prohibited, encouraged or discouraged.

Box 4.2 Voices from the Field

Organizational Culture and Commitment in Guatemalan Organizations
Federico Varona, San José State University

A study conducted in several Guatemalan workplaces in the 1990s found that one of the most important components of one's association with her or his employing organization for Guatemalan employees is *the cultural work ethic*, that is, dedication to the idea of being a productive member of society. This ethic is traditionally undergirded by Christian teachings (as recognized a century ago by Max Weber and others), and this is still true in Guatemalan organizations run by Catholics, such as the school and the hospital investigated in this study.[10] This finding reveals an important cultural characteristic of Guatemalan workers and has theoretical implications for research in other countries. It challenges the research trend that has treated work ethic independently from *organizational commitment* or *loyalty* or *identification with the organization* (Morrow, 1983).[11] The results support Reichers's (1985) perspective on *multiple* forms of commitment (and identification)—in that we must specify the precise "object" of commitment or identification, be that the work itself, a job or position, a supervisor, colleagues or coworkers, the organization, or a profession.[12] In this case, the sense of loyalty is directed even more broadly—to the idea of work in general, to doing a good job, and being responsible to the community. The two most important dimensions in the conceptualization of overall organizational commitment by the Guatemalan employees and supervisors were: *identification with the organization's mission (or values and principles)* and *putting forth one's best to do a good job* (again, we see the importance of a work ethic). These aspects of the individual's relationship with the organization must be understood within the larger context of Guatemalan society and the culture of its organizations. Here we find just one example of how national-level or ethnic culture can influence and interplay with the experience of work.

The work ethic, in any form, is hard to appreciate until you really probe it. It involves deep-seated assumptions about what it means to be a good worker and a good citizen. It also defines our collective notions of ambition, industriousness, and laziness, and affects how we evaluate the work of others. The work ethic also shapes our very idea of what it means to be busy.

After reading this chapter, return to this box and ask yourself the following questions: Do you think that the findings listed above translate into other cultural contexts? How do you think Varona's work is related to box 4.3 on Hofstede's research on national culture? How would you describe Varona's perspective on organizational culture? What does "the work ethic" mean in your own country today?

One of George's students investigated gender and leadership within a regional agency of the U.S. Forest Service, a traditional male environment. More than one of the female managers related the same story: the experience of a male manager from another region walking into a room before a meeting, seeing only women, and then asking "So, where are all the foresters?" (a number of the women present *were* in fact forest rangers).[13] In this case, control operates through the assumption that what's "normal" is that foresters should be male. It's easy to imagine that such an assumption would guide staffing decisions—for example, leading to a preference for hiring men—and how it would control the everyday choices of women employees, given that the norm is male behavior.

Studying Culture

In our daily lives, we all "study" culture in the sense that we frequently observe differences and similarities between systems of meaning—at the workplace, among ethnic groups, or in religious communities. Ethnographers, however, specialize in the study of human cultures. Defined as a branch of anthropology, ethnography deals with the scientific description of specific human cultures, for example a tribal society in the Amazon, a street gang in Chicago, or a group of professionals at a Russian hospital. Through direct or participant observation (see chapter 15) of the culture and interviews with its members, ethnographers try to discover how cultures organize, experience, and interpret their specific worlds. Ethnographers, in other words, study how social realities are constructed *locally*. In carrying out their studies, some ethnographers "go native," that is, become a full member of the culture they're studying. For example, some organizational researchers have joined the social movement organizations they were investigating. While such an approach gives the ethnographer access to valuable information about the culture, it simultaneously makes it difficult for him or her to keep the analytical distance necessary to detect differences and similarities to other cultures. The true ethnographer is a "professional stranger"[14]—close enough to the culture to witness detailed information and distant enough to be aware of key elements taken for granted in the culture. Obviously, this is often a difficult balance.

Thick Description

In studying culture, ethnographers develop "thick descriptions" of local communities (tribes, villages, or organizations). According to Geertz, a thick description is highly detailed and attempts to identify the systems of meaning through which individual and collective actions are produced and interpreted. This is at the heart of an interpretive perspective on research: to aim at what academics call true "intersubjective understanding"—to represent the world as seen by the participants in the research. Geertz says thick description describes the difference between an involuntary twitch of the eye and a meaningful wink, even though the two actions themselves are quite identical.[15] Ethnographers focus on the artifacts, values, beliefs, norms, symbols, stories, myths, rituals, ceremonies, and other practices through which the communities describe and maintain themselves vis-à-vis their surroundings.

Understanding such dimensions of a community, it is believed, reveals the social bond—that is, the "glue"—that holds the community together. Whereas dominant U.S. culture would typically be associated with values like individuality and freedom of speech, a culture like the Balinese (of Indonesia) would be linked with such values as piety, adherence to tradition, and a sense of responsibility to the collective heritage. In many strongly collectivist cultures, emotional expression is understood to be more of a group concern than an individual one.[16] Likewise, while general suffrage and recurrent elections are significant dimensions of democratic societies, cultures founded on religious principles refer to ecclesiastical rituals and ceremonies as the key to their social bond. Although such descriptions are often too simplistic, they illustrate the point we made earlier that the notion of culture at once refers to patterns of *similarity* and patterns of *difference*—similarity within the culture and difference among cultures. When we study a specific organizational culture, we are interested in

Box 4.3 Organizational Cultures and National Differences

One of the more influential scholars of organizational culture is Geert Hofstede, whose studies of subsidiaries of IBM in 53 nations in the 1970s and 80s revealed some important links between organizational and national culture. Based on questionnaire-oriented data (much of it already collected by IBM itself), Hofstede proposed four dimensions to identify differences among national value systems and to explain different cultural orientations to work.[17]

The first dimension, *power distance*, refers to the cultural emphasis upon the amount of power that superiors can acceptably have over subordinates. China, for example, has relatively high power distance as compared to some other countries (e.g., Israel or Austria where it is less acceptable for superiors to dominate the behavior of subordinates). *Uncertainty avoidance* denotes the extent to which a culture can deal with uncertainties about the future without experiencing stress. Japanese culture, according to Hofstede, ranks high on uncertainty avoidance, meaning that Japanese culture places a high premium on avoiding uncertainty. A third dimension, *individualism-collectivism,* differentiates between those national cultures that emphasize individual identity, welfare and goals, and those that emphasize group welfare. In Hofstede's survey, the United States ranked highest on individualism, with Australia and the United Kingdom closely following. Finally, *masculinity-femininity* differentiates between those cultures that emphasize assertive and competitive orientations toward work (masculinity) and those that emphasize cooperative, interdependent orientations toward work (femininity). In this regard, Denmark and the Netherlands are considered "feminine" cultures. In the late 1980s, Hofstede and his coauthors proposed a fifth dimension, which they referred to as "*Confucian dynamism*."[18] This distinguished between those cultures that emphasize a short-term orientation to work and those that emphasize a long-term orientation.

Many organizational studies use Hofstede's dimensions. In the early 1990s, the success of East Asian economies, for example, was attributed to their long-term work orientation. And the so-called Protestant work ethic (with an emphasis on hard work, business success, the accumulation of goods, and the maximization of material prosperity) has been related to cultures that feature low power distance and high individualism.[19] Still, it is difficult to explain all differences between individuals and organizations with reference to national culture; actual cultural expectations and prescriptions might vary from organization to organization in more complicated ways. And, of course, there are methodological concerns with trying to reduce cultural complexities to linear dimensions as assessed through a questionnaire.

Think of organizations where you have worked. Can you find examples of behavior based on characteristics of the national culture? What other factors could explain the culture of your organization? What do you see as the merits and the limits of a typology like Hofstede's?

discovering relevant differences and similarities in order for us to see what sets the culture apart from its surroundings and what constitutes important links.

In studying the corporate or business culture of Japan, for example, we might examine the dominant or majority national culture of the country. Then, we could consider what parallels or connections exist between the national culture and the corporate culture. Anthropologist Dorrine Kondo considered a subculture within the Japanese business world: small, family-owned workshops in Tokyo.[20] Contrasting her work with a bias in the research toward the study of Japan's large corporations, Kondo looks at micro-businesses. Kondo observed a variety of aspects of the culture within those organizations, including factors related to gender, neighborhood, and industry. Through a vivid account of training seminars, she explained how culture sets limits not only on the visible activities of members but also on the options that they consider. Through participation in what are called "ethics seminars," organizational members, for example, learn discipline of the body and the mind, with physical exercises and programs that promote company loyalty. At the same time, the seminars reinforced traditional gender roles (emphasizing the subservience of women through their many expected chores) and maintained a clear hierarchy within the organizations that, not surprisingly, privileged family members over others. Kondo demonstrated how family-owned businesses have characteristics that are both parallel to and different from those of large corporations in Japan—the kinds of organizations that are usually discussed for that country. In many different kinds of organizations in Japan, loyalty to the organization (as "family"), for example, remains an important though gradually diminishing value.

In fact, "family" and "community" interact in important ways in many different national and cultural contexts. Community at work and in the public sphere begins with family connections, with solidarity in each domain reinforcing that in the others. For example, in a study of three private firms and one public agency in Mexico, Hector Díaz-Sáenz and Patricia Witherspoon explain:

> An unexpected finding in this study was the role of the family in influencing a sense of community. The desire to belong in a community emerges from the family. Thus, many Mexicans may expect to find a sense of community in their work organizations. Participants said that the worst thing that could happen to anyone is being socially isolated in their workplace. "We spend more time in our work than in our house, but the sense of family or community we have is deep-rooted . . . and I believe that it is those values, that way of life we bring to the firm." Another participant said: "When the family is strong, very united, then communities develop similar to them." In other words, organizational members take their talents and experience in creating strong familial relations into the workplace with them, and attempt to develop similar webs of supporting relationships there.[21]

The larger culture is both reflected in and supported by relationships at work.[22] Although some cultures live a more isolated existence than others, most organizational cultures are affected or shaped by socio-historical forces or processes. Thus, to study a specific organizational culture it is necessary to look beyond the organization's formal boundaries and consider some of the most important structures, beliefs, and values that hold cultures together. Communication researcher Patricia Covarrubias demonstrates this point well in her study of issues of cooperation and coordination at Grupo Industrial Gutiérrez de Velasco (GDV) in Veracruz, Mexico.[23] She found that when employees at this organization addressed each other when they communicated, they called upon complex cultural "codes" or prescriptions that cued them toward culturally appropriate modes of communication. For example, the act of uttering the word "*tú*" (an informal way of saying "you") instead of "*usted*" (a more formal mode of address) demonstrated parity and invoked family and friendship ties, helping achieve generative joint action and cooperation. Of course, employees also used the terms *tú* and *usted* in subversive and provisional ways, constructing messages that communicated playfulness, distance, sarcasm, or hierarchy. In all situations, the meanings and interactions were deeply embedded in a cultural and linguistic context that had to be understood in order to figure out issues of cooperation and coordination in organizational contexts.

Language and Narratives

Cultures create and maintain patterns of similarities and difference largely through language. As a system that informs and guides the way we orient ourselves in the world, language is not a passive medium by which we simply record our experiences. It is a dynamic system of meaning through which we construct our world.[24] Once again, Kenneth Burke offers us a useful scheme for understanding how our language groups certain things together and pulls other things apart (he calls these basic processes "congregation" and "segregation"). As Burke explains, there are four categories of words: terms for things (such as objects), terms for relationships (like friendship), terms for belief systems and ideologies (such as capitalism, or democracy, or socialism), and terms for the "ineffable" or things beyond our experience (such as spirits or deities).[25]

This straightforward scheme is helpful in reminding us of all "the things that words do," as British linguistic philosopher John Austin famously put it in his book, *How to Do Things with Words*. Words don't just name; they also create. As we discuss elsewhere in this book, talking about terrorism in terms of a "war" is quite different from calling it a "crime," since the words allow for or imply different systems of action. Indeed, the sheer act of naming or labeling can help to bring the very thing it references into being. For example, the term *sexual harassment* only emerged in the 1980s. The common use of the term changes what we see; thus, naming an action or pattern of actions "sexual harassment" brings it into being, in the sense that its use leads us to *see* something quite different from what we would have seen before the term was used.

We need to be especially sensitive to how language is used in the organizational setting. Language includes categories, classes, hierarchies, and distinctions that both order and create our world. In organizations, think of the many ways we categorize members: professional versus non-professional, management versus employees, supervisory versus non-supervisory, paid versus volunteer, permanent versus temporary, "fast track" versus "mommy track,"[26] and so on. These categories are human creations. As we noted in the preface, some terms and metaphors—such as "up" and "down"—are so ingrained in our thinking that we often believe they are *natural* rather than expressions of human preference in organizations.

Anthropologist Mary Douglas makes connections between the organization of everyday life and overall social patterns.[27] Douglas focuses on how we, as individuals and collectivities, divide and thereby order the world. According to Douglas, the functions of labeling and classification direct us in answering questions of "what is" and "what ought to be." The simple acts of labeling and classification, she says, are infused with moral significance and moral direction. For example, consider the difference in labeling an action "harmless flirting" versus "sexual harassment." One of the most important things to notice about categories is that they are human creations that may or may not *fit* the phenomena they are supposed to capture. Douglas, for example, compares wine classification systems between France and California, noting that the French system of classification that emphasizes geographic areas was producer-oriented and based on connoisseurship. The California system, based on the type of grape, is driven by a classification system that emphasizes large-scale marketing. These differences, in turn, imply other differences in style, image, and taste. Thus, the world of wine and winemaking is as socially constructed as it is rooted in climate and the earth.

By categorizing and labeling the world in which we live, we indirectly make decisions about *inclusion* and *exclusion* and thus set boundaries for our own—and others'—existence. We decide what things go together and what things ought to be apart, what's consecrated and what's profane, what's "hot" and what's not. In addition to ascribing significance to the world, language helps us define and confirm our place and belonging within the boundaries of the culture. Think, for example, of the language of high school cliques, of gendered styles of speech in the boardroom, or of disciplinary or professional jargon.

A well-known example is the "us" versus "them" feelings that surround competition between sports teams at local, regional, national, or international levels. "We won" applies not only to the players of the winning team but also to their supporters. Here is one of many instances where identity and culture come together. Teams have characteristic uniforms, mascots, and other paraphernalia, along with rituals. For example, in the 1990s, a concerted effort was made to market the New Zealand All Blacks rugby team as a national symbol. This occurred both through official advertising on television and in magazines to brand the team as authentically Kiwi and through the players' adoption and adaptation of the traditional Maori war dance, the *Haka*. Through these and other developments, the All Blacks have become more visible within NZ and abroad. Part of this visibility includes, not surprisingly, the mass marketing of products with the All Blacks logo, a white on black representation of a fern.[28]

Box 4.4 An Organizational Vocabulary

In a 1975 case study of a neighborhood bar in Minneapolis, authors James Spradley and Brenda J. Mann asked waitresses about the different kinds of customers they encountered.[29] The waitresses had devised a number of categories for their customers. The labels chosen reveal the world of the waitresses, their experiences with customers, and the lens they developed to make sense of and cope with their work. Some of their many vivid descriptions include: girl, jock, animal, bartender, greaser, businessman, redneck, bitch, creep, bastard, obnoxo, regular, real regular, person off street, policeman, party, zoo, bore, pig, slob, hustler, Annie, cougar, sweetie, waitress, loner, female, drunk, Johnny, hands, couple, king and his court.

What do you think the terms say about the formal social structure of the bar or about the informal networks that waitresses developed as a part of their work? Think about why waitresses developed such vocabulary and what sort of attitude toward customers this list reflects and reinforces. What do the names say about power relations between the waitresses and customers? Have you noticed specialized vocabularies in organizations? Why do these vocabularies exist? What do they "do"?

In addition to language, organizational culture is communicated through other symbols, artifacts, ceremonials, legends, stories, and rituals. Management scholars Harrison Trice and Janice Beyer[30] discuss six types of rites found in the organizational setting.

- *Rites of passage* (used to facilitate the transition of persons from one role to another)
- *Rites of degradation* (used to fire or replace organizational members)
- *Rites of enhancement* (used to provide public recognition of an accomplishment)
- *Rites of renewal* (used to reinvigorate the culture with new ideas or practices)
- *Rites of conflict reduction* (used to reduce conflict or deflect attention away from it)
- *Rites of integration* (used to encourage a feeling of community and commitment)

Studying rites is not easy. Where, for example, do they start and where do they end? Rites are pervasive; they are everywhere among us. Through rites and ceremonies we express who we are, where we belong, where we come from, and where we are headed. Rites and ceremonies communicate more than what we see on the surface, more than their literal content. Thus, they also have meta-communicative dimensions. For example, the monthly board meeting may ostensibly be about furthering the organization's agenda but it may also communicate something to members about their relationships with one another and to the leader of the organization. Similarly, informal gatherings that employees openly call "bitch sessions" may be important opportunities to share information and for cooling down.

The same is true for organizational stories and narratives. They simultaneously convey information about heroes and villains, projects and goals, and success and failure. Stories are thus both informational and persuasive. Scholars of organizational stories focus on scenic elements, drama, action, and characters with reference to what each aspect has to say about collective perceptions.[31] Stories play multiple roles in organizational cultures. For example, stories about crisis situations in organizations serve to reinforce ideas about good and bad responses to crises.[32] In intra- and inter-organizational conflict situations, stories help simplify complexities and point to courses of action; stories can rally people toward courses of action. In this sense, it's hardly surprising that the war metaphor is so commonly used in business and in the market: it allows for a sense of urgency and a clear demarcation between "us" and "them" as it mobilizes support for group action. In both urgent and non-urgent situations, organizational members use stories—for example about the greatness of the founder or about recent difficulties all have weathered—thereby strengthening the sense of in-group and out-group. Recognizing that stories have the potential to reinforce a feeling of community and belongingness in organizations and sometimes even inspire change, many contemporary management consultants now include corporate stories in their portfolio of strategic communication tools. Management consultant Dave Snowdon, for example, is lecturing extensively for organizations across the globe about the power of stories to generate a strong "we" feeling and to inspire change.[33]

In this section, we've looked briefly at key dimensions of social life—language, rites, stories, and narratives—important indicators of differences and similarities within and among cultures. Next we discuss how dimensions of culture apply to organizations and, more specifically, to the complex phenomenon we call organizational communication. How do organizational cultures communicate and how do they communicate culture?

Culture and Communication in Organizations

For more than a quarter of a century, culture has played a prominent role in the organizational literature—reminding both managers and scholars of the human side of organizational life. In the early 1980s, the term *culture* was popularized, especially in the book *Corporate Cultures* by Terrance Deal and Allan Kennedy,[34] and by a growing body of research comparing business practices in Japan with those of the United States. As Japanese industries successfully penetrated world markets, Western industries became increasingly concerned about how to maintain productive economies. They confronted crises about efficiency and sought answers in how productivity and other aspects of organizational life are related to culture. Consultants began selling the idea of "strong cultures" versus "weak cultures" and how they could transform the latter into the former.

The "Functionalist" Perspective on Organizational Culture

Many different authors explored the topic of organizational cultures. Most prominent, perhaps, were Thomas Peters and Robert Waterman with their now famous book *In Search of Excellence*.[35] In their study of Fortune 500 corporations, Peters and Waterman concluded that excellent—effective, winning, and achieving—organizations are characterized by a careful cultivation of shared meanings and attention to the collective spirit of the organization. In a similar vein, other writers concluded that a well-managed corporate culture focused on social integration, motivation, and commitment would help organizations achieve an innovative spirit and, as a consequence, productivity and competitive advantage.[36] The common thread in these writings characterized the *strong* organizational culture as a system of *unique* ideas, values, and symbols organized and *controlled* by management in its effort to integrate the organization's members around a *shared* set of meanings. In other words, organizations would be able to control their employees by managing the culture in which they worked.[37] *Weak* cultures, by contrast, were less integrated and unique, and thus poorly controlled.[38]

The focus on the cultural dimension of organizations reflected a growing awareness of the fact that "more things are going on in organizations than getting the job done." The growing managerial interest in culture since the late 1970s, however, was not *separated* from concerns about getting the job done. Edgar Schein, for example, whose theory of organizational culture we mentioned earlier, is convinced that leadership is so intertwined with the formation of organizational culture that the most essential function of leadership is what he calls "manipulation of culture."[39] Organizational culture, he claims, is embedded in leaders and potentially strengthened by them. Good leaders create and shape their organizations' cultures by embedding their assumptions in missions, goals, structures, and work procedures.

This perspective on culture is sometimes described as "functionalist"[40] because it conceives of culture as something an organization *has,* as a tool that functions to accomplish organizational objectives. A functionalist perspective, in this sense, emphasizes instrumentality and isolates features of a culture for their practical utility.[41] Thus, we can think of Nokia, Vivendi, McDonald's, and your university as rational systems that adopt, design, and use cultural values in order to achieve specific goals. While the pool of values and beliefs in the organization may have additional purposes, they primarily serve, according to this perspective, to help the organization integrate its members, adapt to its surroundings, and survive in a changing environment. To what extent is such a view on culture valid? Are certain aspects of an organization's culture functional to its survival? And to what extent can they be shaped and managed by the organization or used as a tool?

In an interesting study of Disneyland, communication scholars Ruth Smith and Eric Eisenberg describe how shared values and images can be instrumental to an organization's performance—at least for a period.[42] Their focus on "root" (or basic) metaphors of organizational life led them to identify two central images of the Disney experience: drama and family. Whereas the former reflects Walt Disney's wish to stage his amusement park as "the happiest place on earth," the latter refers to the friendly, informal, and caring atmosphere of the Disneyland culture. These images, partly manufactured by management, were widely shared by organizational members and contributed for many years to the success and prosperity of Disneyland. However, when a strike hit the park in 1984, dissatisfied employees used the same images *against* management to argue that the organization had abandoned the spirit of Walt Disney. From the perspective of management, cultural traits that used to be functional to the organization suddenly became dysfunctional.[43]

Of course, this problem is not confined to conflict situations. In times of change, many organizations see values and perspectives that were formerly advantageous mutate into liabilities that prevent the organization from undertaking its necessary adjustments. For example, how can an emphasis on a solid tradition be a hindrance to innovation, creativity, and flexibility? What is potentially lost in the process? How can organizations undergoing change combine the strengths of the past with their aspirations for the future? What happens when an organization announces a "new set of values"? How can that effort in image-making backfire?

Although the notion of culture has made management more aware of the informal dimensions of organizational life, the largely mechanistic assumptions about culture that we find in most management writings seem to preclude a deeper insight into the phenomenon. In academic writings, the functionalist approach to culture has been critiqued extensively. The critique[44] has focused on the following assumptions.

- A culture is a *consistent* pattern of values and practices
- Cultural values, symbols, and perspectives are *shared* by *all* organizational members
- Management can use culture to *control* employees
- The manifestations of a culture are *unique* for a particular organization

The "Symbolist" Perspective on Organizational Culture

To counter the functionalist or instrumental perspective and its idea of culture as something an organization *has,* management scholar Linda Smircich[45] and other students of organizational culture advance the view that organizations *are* cultures. According to Smircich, the idea of culture directs our attention to the non-rational, subjective, and interpretive aspects of organizational life. From this perspective—sometimes referred to as the symbolist perspective[46]—culture becomes a metaphor for describing the whole organization, its structures and processes, and its imaginary as well as its material dimensions. Organizational culture is seen as a complex and ever-evolving totality of people, goals, actions, experiences, and interpretations. In this sense, it may rarely manifest the consistency, sharedness, and control assumed in the functional perspective.

In contrast to managerial ideals, *complete consistency is not a prominent feature of organizational life*. For example, while many organizations claim they value innovativeness, they most often reward safe, well-known, and easily measurable solutions. Some say they want decentralization and participation but impose more control. Many large companies and government agencies foster identities of themselves as being both large enough to offer a wide array of services and small enough to "have a friendly face." Some declare that they are market-driven but ignore customer complaints. These are just a few examples of inconsistencies that symbolists point to in objecting to the usual emphasis on consistency.

Why do we usually think of inconsistency as a problem? The nineteenth-century U.S. essayist Ralph Waldo Emerson did not. He said: "Foolish consistency is the hobgoblin of little minds." Can we apply that provocative statement to organizations and imagine situations where insistence on consistency would be detrimental to organizational survival? How can an emphasis on consistency, predictability, integration, and order actually limit an organization's creativity and adaptability—not to mention diminishing the joy of its members? Also, consider how consistency traps an organization by not allowing it the flexibility to adapt to changing circumstances. Think of universities, or sports teams, or religious organizations as diverse case examples.

The Roman Catholic Church experienced this very trap. The church embraced *risorgimento* (in Italian, roughly translated as "resurgence") through the Second Vatican Council of 1962–65. Under the leadership of Pope John XXIII, the Church maintained its basic doctrine and structure while at the same time updating itself in other ways to better fit the modern world, though not without great controversy. Like all organizations that try to stand firmly on longstanding tradition, the Church had to manage its cultural change very carefully to avoid the perception that it was abandoning core commitments in doctrine, rituals, and other practices. An organization as large as this one will inevitably include many groups who are walking a tightrope between adherence to organizational norms and exploration of alternative ways of doing things.[47]

Although inconsistencies often appear hypocritical, they allow organizations the flexibility to adapt to multiple audiences and to changing and conflicting norms and demands. As management professor James G. March has pointed out, hypocrisy is a transition period during which we learn to balance and integrate different goals and evolving preferences.[48] Based on these observations—and the recognition that people become members of organizations for many different reasons, bring different skills and capabilities to their workplace, have different preferences, and pursue different interests and goals[49]—it becomes increasingly difficult to maintain that organizational cultures are completely consistent.

If organizations have inconsistent values and practices, how can their members be expected to share ideas about what their cultures represent? Well, they probably can't—at least not fully. Proponents of a symbolist perspective argue that organizations consist of many different and sometimes competing value systems that constitute what organizational theorist Gareth Morgan calls "a mosaic of organizational realities rather than a uniform corporate culture."[50] Some of these realities are created by subcultures (for example, professional work groups) within the organization that develop their own specialized languages, task-related priorities, and extra-organizational allegiances. Consider, for example, the different universes of engineers, accountants, marketing people, computer analysts, administrative assistants, and public relations officers. What differences in language, priorities, and allegiances would you expect to find among these various professions? What values can they be expected to have in common? Stereotypical jokes about their jargon or different manners of dress highlight how language and other symbols express identity and create a sense of belonging to a distinct group. The differences among the worldviews of engineers, accountants, and marketing people can be regularly witnessed in many organizations.

Many manufacturing firms experience tension between the subcultures of production and sales, given that the former department sees itself at the "center" of the firm and the latter perceives its role as being "close to the customer"—both perspec-

Box 4.5 Baseball and Culture

A good example of an analysis that reflects the symbolist perspective is that of communication scholar Nick Trujillo's work on U.S. baseball/ballpark culture.[51] Trujillo attended 67 home games in two seasons, observed games, off-season luncheons, banquets, autograph appearances by players, press boxes, ticket offices, security posts, and interviewed a range of employees and spectators. He distilled three dominant interpretations of baseball culture reflected in various workers' and other participants' communication: baseball as business, as community, and as drama. Ballpark culture can be interpreted as a *business* in that it exhibits features of industrial production, including standardization of procedures, highly specialized roles, a hierarchy, and reliance on technology. Baseball as a business is also evident in the *commodification* of ballpark culture itself, evident in workers' interpretation of the game as a commodity for generating revenue and their experiences of themselves as commodities—upper management knew that a lot of workers would do anything to get involved in baseball, and could therefore take advantage of them. Ballpark culture can also be interpreted in terms of *community*, as a place where groups of people could come together to play, celebrate, work, interact, develop interpersonal relationships, and in a sense, engage in symbolic worship. Finally, the culture can also be interpreted in terms of *drama* or *theatre*: the staging of a show. This is evident in a number of interpretations of baseball as being not merely a game, but an entire "entertainment experience." In this sense, the game becomes a play, the spectators an audience, and employees stagehands.

The number of possible interpretations highlights the competing, somewhat inconsistent views of those integrally involved in the organization. It also points to the need for people who examine organizational culture to adopt multiple perspectives. Trujillo identifies at least three such academic perspectives. A *romantic* perspective interprets baseball in an idyllic, celebratory way, focusing on the enjoyment of baseball as an experience in and of itself—as portrayed in films such as *Field of Dreams*. A *functionalist* perspective focuses on what the culture of baseball does in terms of perpetuating society, by way of teaching participants important social values about teamwork, achievement, success, and family. A *critical* perspective emphasizes the constraining aspects of such culture, including its emphasis on masculinity and militarism, and its promotion of dominant ideologies about capitalism and consumerism—especially as it and other sports become more commercialized.

Think about your favorite hobby or sport. How does it function as a culture? What would it look like from romantic, functionalist, and critical perspectives?

tives lead members to believe they know what's best. Other organizational subdivisions are based on social or ethnic background, tenure, geographic location, age, or gender. Each of these divisions may produce differences in norms and behaviors, which can be used to identify or to distinguish different organizational subcultures.

Organizational communication scholar Patricia Riley, in a study that explored how organizational culture structures political activity in two subsidiaries of a large organization, found that members of different subcultures conceived of political practices differently. One group conceived of acceptable politics as involving covert practices and informal networks, whereas another group had a "politics is nonsense" approach. Riley used such differences to argue that organizational culture is better thought of as a system of integrated subcultures rather than a unitary set of values.[52]

Other studies from a symbolist perspective have found support for such differences. For example, in his study of Proteus Rainwater Limited in Great Britain, Ed Young[53] found that an emphasis on shared values and sentiments in an organization sometimes hides divisions. He identified the organizational culture through interviews with and observations of female shop-floor workers at the organization's production facility. The culture was evident in various patterns of behavior, ranging from the wearing of roses on St. George's Day, the collection of pictures of the Royal Family on a centrally placed bulletin board, to the frequent informal gatherings among the female workers. His analysis of these cultural manifestations, however, uncovered an interesting division within this claimed unity.

Although the shop-floor workers could be regarded as a distinct group in the sense that they shared a common work location, in practice the group was divided along the lines of product specialization, age, and tenure. While the older women worked as highly specialized machinists on products with a steady customer demand, the younger women worked in groups on products with a more fluctuating demand. As a consequence, the stability in the group of older women was much higher than among the younger women. The differences in stability were reflected in attitudes

"I don't know how it started, either. All I know is that it's part of our corporate culture."

toward work. The younger women typically saw their engagement with the organization as a passing chance to earn some money; lengthy tenure resulted in stronger relationships for the older women. These structural differences were exacerbated by each group's image of the other group as less competent or professional and by the fact that the collective rituals of wearing roses, displaying pictures of the Royal Family, and arranging social outings were largely organized by the group of older women. The official sharedness, thus, was tempered by strong tendencies to fragmentation. According to Young, it is exactly this tension between fragmentation and unity that constitutes an organizational culture. What does this observation tell us about the values, rituals, and symbols that organizations present as manifestations of their culture?

In a similar vein, organizational culture scholars Joanne Martin and Debra Meyerson[54] point out that the notion of a shared culture presupposes an integration perspective on organizational life that rarely fits reality. Organizational unity is often challenged and fractured by subcultures. They propose two alternative perspectives on organizational culture: a differentiation perspective and a fragmentation perspective. The *differentiation* perspective presents organizational culture as a collection of coexisting subcultures each with stable, shared, and consistent values. The *fragmentation* perspective challenges both the integration and the differentiation perspective by suggesting that subcultures are dynamic and unstable and that the dominant organizational culture as a consequence is multi-faceted and in constant flux.

If people don't share values and beliefs, there's little chance that culture can be used as a management tool to control and monitor employees. In light of this fact, the need for organizations to declare "our values" may sometimes take on greater importance, even urgency. Another reason to question the idea of using culture as a management tool is that culture develops through numerous kinds of social interac-

Box 4.6 Different Cultures
Durkheim's "Organic" and "Mechanical" Solidarity

Émile Durkheim observed in the 1880s that the basic "logic" of modern, Western, industrialized societies was fundamentally different from that of pre-industrialized, tribal, and "traditional" societies. Durkheim described the social order of pre-industrial societies in terms of "mechanical solidarity" versus the "organic solidarity" of modern societies.[55] These terms are somewhat confusing initially because "mechanical" sounds more modern than "organic." But in this context, mechanical refers to the nature of social relationships. Relationships work in a mechanical, almost automatic fashion in a tribal society where nearly everyone adheres to the same set of beliefs and practices (religious, cultural, political, and social). By contrast, relationships are not so predictable, coherent, or unified in a social order based on organic solidarity. People have a variety of worldviews, and their behaviors are not deducible from one common set of beliefs and practices. With the rise of organic solidarity, we find a strong faith in reason, science, and human control. There is a technical approach to solving problems and a corresponding desire to master nature and the world. In terms of the division of labor or how human activities are organized, organic solidarity features the interdependence of various functions performed at work, in professions, and for organizations. In this way, an organic society is far more differentiated and fragmented than is a society characterized by mechanical solidarity. In fact, Durkheim was concerned that the hierarchies and strata of modern society would lead to alienation and segregation: separating educated experts from those who were not highly trained.

tion. Organizational cultures typically have been developing over many years; they are embodied in different employees; they are reproduced daily through rituals and ceremonies; and they're often influenced by developments in the general culture of a society or by conditions within a specific industry.[56] As a consequence, symbolists contend that culture cannot be easily planned or manipulated.

This is not to say that managers and other change agents cannot, or should not seek to, influence culture. Certainly some norms, practices, and values are at least partly shared. As a consequence, we can effect certain changes from either the top or the bottom of an organization—for example, by supporting certain initiatives or traditions or by encouraging employees to participate in the development and nurturing of certain values or norms.[57] Cultural change efforts, however, are rarely easily accomplished or completely predictable.

In addition to questioning the degree to which culture can be reliably managed, symbolists also question the uniqueness of individual organizational cultures. Many organizations today talk about their cultures as vehicles for setting them apart from their surroundings, and they often make claims to be "different" in their orientation toward business practices, the environment, employee relations, and a host of other business practices. The current emphasis on branding (developing a unique and memorable image or brand) reflects this trend. The Body Shop, for example, makes claims to uniqueness based on its environmentally friendly practices. Think about the nature of such claims for a moment. Why are some manifestations of uniqueness more readily accepted than others?

Interestingly, the strong emphasis today on organizational uniqueness in the corporate landscape implies that organizational members and decision makers tend to recognize only those dimensions of their local culture that they feel set their organization *apart* from other organizations, while ignoring the shared cultural dimensions across organizations.[58] Thus, organizations find uniqueness in their language, logos, uniforms, corporate architecture, design, job announcements, myths, sagas, stories, etc.[59] It is possible, however, to view these expressions of uniqueness as manifestations of a *common* managerial culture—a culture that demands that all organizations today cultivate and communicate the same kind of symbolic dimensions.

Since the ability to "stand out" has become an imperative in a cluttered communication environment, the propensity to focus on differences rather than similarities is understandable. If we want to figure out whether an organization's emphasis upon a particular value is truly an expression of uniqueness, however, we need to realize that an organization is not a "box" within which a unique culture grows. Rather, we should pay attention to societal-level issues such as language, history, ideology, myths, and even science and art in order to understand how individual organizations understand and create their realities.[60] In this sense, many so-called "unique" organizational symbols, stories, myths, rituals, and ceremonies represent the larger culture as much as they represent the organization.[61]

On Doing Culture: Reproducing and Altering Culture

Some scholars refer to the common and shared aspects of culture as its "deeper," contextual dimensions.[62] Assuming for a moment that such a description is accurate, what will count as the more *superficial* dimensions of a culture? Buildings? Uniforms? Advertising campaigns? If we accept the idea that culture is *multi-layered*, we see how the notion of culture as something that can be managed (the functionalist approach) cannot be separated from the notion of culture as something deeper and more fundamental (the symbolic approach). The two approaches are related in other ways as well. While each of these perspectives captures a different dimension of organizational reality, they both treat organizational culture as a bounded phenomenon, confined within the organizational setting. And this is true whether we conceive of culture as something an organization *has* or something an organization *is*. Both these perspectives concentrate their focus on the *internal* aspects of an organization.

Another alternative is to look at culture as something an organization *does*. Organizations *do* culture—or communicate culture—simultaneously at several levels. On the one hand, and as we've discussed above, organizations are constantly in the process of constituting their cultures through rituals and ceremonies. Some of these rituals and ceremonies (such as advertising campaigns and marketing analyses) are part of official strategies through which organizations relate to their surroundings. Other rituals and ceremonies take place more or less unnoticed as part of daily routines and standard operating procedures. Here we find *unwritten* procedures for managing meetings, recurrent discussion themes at lunch hour, or ways of joking during breaks. Thus, rituals and ceremonies help organizations create and confirm their culture. On the other hand, organizations are "doing" culture in the sense that their actions and ideas are not only confirming but also shaping the wider culture in which they are embedded. By subscribing to a new management ideal (e.g., total quality management), organizations do not simply reproduce a trend in the managerial culture but help construct that culture in new ways. To do culture thus means to create and recreate at once the reality of the organization and the cultural environment in which it is located.

If organizations both reflect and shape the general culture, we should question the idea of organizational culture as a *strictly bounded* system of meaning. The cultures of organizations are at once organizational and social phenomena. We could also question the claim that the cultural meanings of organizations are subjective, as scholars within the symbolist tradition often suggest.[63] Usually, we think of subjectivity as individual meanings (perceptions, opinions, ideas, etc.) relatively unaffected by the facts of the external world. While the people who hold the meanings treat them as real, those meanings cannot be verified scientifically, that is, objectively. There's more to subjectivity and objectivity, however, than this conventional perspective suggests.

Most of the "subjective" meanings that we subscribe to in our daily lives—who we are, what we believe in, what we hope for—are validated by the communication and behaviors of others. While we all have our idiosyncrasies (and this is true for organizations as well), our so-called subjectivity is socially grounded and confirmed. We are, in other words, granted subjectivity by society. By analogy, the cultures of organizations are so rich with current *social* values (e.g., diversity, participation, efficiency, etc.) that their "subjectivity" becomes a social phenomenon. While organizations do culture, cultures simultaneously do organizations. This, of course, doesn't make the cultural meanings of the organizations objective in any universal sense. But the meanings aren't subjective either. They are shared and thus objective (or intersubjective) in a sociological sense.

The systems of meaning that we create and recreate in our daily lives—in and outside of organizations—are *objective* in the sense that we as a collectivity take them

Box 4.7 The Social Construction of Reality

In a now famous treatise written almost four decades ago, sociologists Peter Berger and Thomas Luckmann[64] described how subjectivity and objectivity are related in a human society. Subjectivity and objectivity, they said, are linked through three central processes: externalization, objectification, and internalization. Our subjectivity is *externalized* when we unfold our physical and spiritual beliefs into action. The products of this activity are *objectified* when we treat them as external reality: for example, when they become institutionalized as habits, rules, or regulations (that is, when preferences move to the level of general knowledge or practice). Finally, this reality is *internalized* through processes of socialization, through our appropriation of language and even through our attempts to change the world around us.

While externalization makes our reality a human product, it is through the processes of objectification and internalization that our constructions obtain a reality of their own and through which our subjectivity becomes a product of society. *We create the world that in turn creates us.* As a consequence, and in certain senses, our reality is socially constructed. This is true even for so-called scientifically proven facts. Consider, for example, how we reexamine history (designated heroes), or economics (assignments of value), or psychology (the evolution of what we call forms of mental illness). Such facts are validated (tested, challenged, or confirmed) by a community of scientists who communicate among themselves through the use of consensually authorized "grammars" (research methods).

Berger and Luckmann did *not* make a case for a total relativism, as social constructivism is sometimes taken to mean. All constructions are not equally valid—as we find in everyday life when our interpretations "bump up against" situations where they don't fit very well.

Can you think of personal or organizational experiences that are treated as objective facts but which are in fact collective constructions? Are there limits to the idea of "the social construction of reality"? When do our constructions "bump up against" a reality where our individual or collective interpretations don't fit very well? What sorts of experiences cause us to change our interpretations of conflict, success, or work?

for granted, relate to them as immutable objects capable of shaping our destiny, and regard them as capable of achieving a momentum of their own. These are what Durkheim called "social facts." Organizational members, thus, often perceive the values, beliefs, categories, symbols, rituals, ceremonies, etc. that we typically refer to as "the organizational culture" as objective features of organizational life, similar to how they view the buildings and offices in which they work. For example, many business organizations treat marketing categories such as "lifestyle groups" as an objective reality rather than recognizing the category as a label that they have constructed to view the public.

This perspective is easily validated by the behavior of other organizations. The question becomes: what does the term *lifestyle group* do for marketers? How does it aid them in their work? Where does the concept lead them, practically speaking? Other organizations view systems of accounting in an almost sacred sense, instead of looking at them as something that they themselves have created. The multiple auditing scandals experienced in the United States in 2001–2002—and the (brief) public outrage that accompanied them—reveal just how internalized mythical images of accounting had become. The idea that something so seemingly solid and factual as accounting could in practice create illusions of profit or solvency contributed to the shock. Think of additional examples of cultural significations in organizations that are read (or interpreted) as objectively as our physical environment.

From a communication perspective, organizations do culture by determining the general conditions for communication within the organizational setting, by setting standards for how new members are integrated, and by projecting images of the organization both within and outside its boundaries. Although organizations do culture in numerous ways, we can capture some important cultural processes through the notions of *communication climate, socialization,* and *marketing.* We will explore the first two processes for the remainder of this chapter, and we will turn to a discussion of marketing and image management in chapter 5.

Organizational Climate

Organizational communication climate became a widely used way of characterizing the experiences of members of an organization in the 1960s and 1970s. In fact, it predates the concept of organizational culture itself.[65] However, until the emergence of cultural approaches to organizations, research on organizational climate did not have any single concept or set of concepts that linked various studies together. The term *culture* stepped into this gap.[66] The original applications of the notion of climate were inspired by the cognitive field theory of psychologist Kurt Lewin and the concern of human relations proponents investigating the nature of informal communication in organizations. W. Charles Redding of Purdue University directed numerous projects that explored and applied this concept to organizations. These studies represented some of the first systematic attempts to examine the communicative life of an organization and its members rather than studies limited to messages, events, or media.

We use the term *climate* to try to capture the totality of life within an organization, just as the metaphor implies. Specifically, we can define climate as the psychological environment in which organizational behavior occurs.[67] It is often assessed as the aggregate or "average" perception of organizational members on dimensions such as openness or supportiveness. Whereas organizational communication studies traditionally had focused on the formal communication structures of organizations, the climate concept introduced an emphasis on relationships and interaction. To illustrate this difference, we can point to organizations that have loose and informal structures on paper yet seem to foster rigid and formal relationships among their members.

Linking the idea of organizational communication climate to leadership functions, Redding developed a prescriptive model for managers known as the "Ideal Managerial Climate" (IMC).[68] The five components of the IMC are *supportiveness, trust, openness, emphasis on high-performance goals,* and *participative decision making.* Based on his extensive research and experience as a consultant, Redding offered this model as a comprehensive way for an organization to be productive while having a healthy atmosphere. This model is very useful not just in evaluating management but in assessing an organization as a whole. Think of how communication will unfold in an organization if some of these components are missing. How, for example, will lack of trust affect the way organizational members interact with each other—or with their superiors?

Research on sexual harassment has shown that organizational climate is critical in determining whether or not sexual harassment will occur.[69] In a study of narratives of victims of sexual harassment in U.S. universities, scholars Charles Conrad and

Box 4.8 The Informal Side of Organizational Life

In the 1950s, Keith Davis investigated the informal communication patterns of organizations. He found that the informal "grapevine" was important to the vitality of the organization as a whole and that managerial attempts to stamp out informal communication end up failing because they are unrealistic and sap valuable energy from the organization's culture.[70] Chester Barnard had observed in the 1930s that formal organizational structures are born out of informal communication and that the two must exist in a dialectical interdependence—that is, a "push and pull" in which each influences the other—for any organization to flourish.[71] Informal communication networks offer valuable feedback about how things are going at all levels of the organization; they help keep people "at the top" in touch with those "below" them. Informal dimensions of organizational life, thus, do not exist as separate and delimited spheres in organizations. Informality flows through all processes and infuses them with meaning and significance.

As organizational communication researchers Michael Pacanowsky and Nick Trujillo note: "People do get the job done, true (though probably not with the single-minded task-orientation that organizational communication texts would have us believe); but people in organizations also gossip, joke, knife one another, initiate romantic involvements, cue new employees to ways of doing the least amount of work that still avoid hassles from the supervisor, talk sports, arrange picnics."[72]

What other activities in an organization's life would you describe as informal? What is the organizational significance of informality and how can we claim that informality serves important functions for an organization?

Bryan Taylor argue that the outcome of harassment complaints is influenced by an aspect of climate that they call "the organizational conspiracy of silence."[73] The formal and informal silencing of sexual harassment occurs in organizations that refuse to admit the existence or seriousness of sexual harassment or insist on the secrecy of sexual harassment complaint procedures. Such silencing results in maintaining sexist ideologies that allow for the occurrence of harassment in the first place.

The assessment of organizational climate is typically accomplished through the use of individual questionnaires asking about conditions of the organization such as interpersonal trust, accessibility to information, and amount of time spent communicating with people at different levels of the organization. One of the dilemmas is how to pull together the many individual characterizations into a holistic assessment of the organization. In other words, how do we "add up" many different descriptions of life in an organization to develop a complete picture? More specifically, what do we do with widely variant opinions? Can we simply "average" them? Should some opinions be weighed more heavily than others? Is there a single, dominant climate or atmosphere in any organization? If not, how should we think about climate? These questions have both theoretical and practical implications.

Of course, the problem of how to link the individual level of analysis to that of the group is not unique to research on organizational climate. It is a fundamental problem for the studies of organizations (and societies) generally, and it surfaces in other metaphors of organizations: systems, network, and culture. Organizational communication researcher Cynthia Stohl reminds us that we need to establish clearly the bridge between organizational phenomena such as structures and interpersonal phenomena such as conversations between superiors and subordinates.[74] Micro-phenomena ("externalization" in box 4.7) contribute to the development of organizational patterns and structures, as when informal interactions lead to formalized procedures ("objectification"); conversely, organizational patterns, such as rules for rational behavior, shape to some extent individual attitudes and interactions between, say, superiors and subordinates ("internalization").

In spite of methodological problems, the notion of climate is important because it looks at the conditions for communication in the daily workings of an organization. Also, like the metaphor of culture, "climate" is applied to the study of the entire organization. Although the conditions may seem external to individual members' control—if we trace out the implications of the climate metaphor and think of the weather—they can be affected in different directions both by management and by other members of the organization. Some recent research indicates that a positive communication climate has a moderating influence in the relationship between human resources practices such as training, job performance reviews, detailed job descriptions, and systematic hiring practices, and the overall extent of customer satisfaction.[75] Essentially, positive internal communication practices, such as training and performance appraisals, contribute to a positive communication climate in the organization, which in turn improves the communication between the organization and its customers.

Socialization

One of the most important processes by which organizations communicate their culture is through the *socialization* of new members. From a functionalist perspective, socialization refers to the ways a member of an organization learns the norms, values, and skills necessary for adopting a particular role and performing a particular function within the organization.[76] For smooth organizational functioning, it's important that recruits and new members *fit* the organization. This view on socialization, of course, ignores the concurrent reality that organizational members are actors who also create, interpret, and make sense of their world. Thus, the culture of any organization is created and recreated by its members over time.

While each member entering the organization learns the values, beliefs, and practices of the organization, he or she simultaneously shapes the organization through his or her "reading" of those values, beliefs, and practices (a symbolist perspective on organizational socialization). If the organization has a strong emphasis on tradition (with, for example, a rigid hierarchical structure), new members can often do very little to alter the culture. However, if the organization leans toward innovation and change, we should expect members to be able to do more to shape the culture of the organization with their own personal values, beliefs, and practices. Most studies of organizational socialization have analyzed the organization's point of view, but this can lead to a kind of blindness about what members are thinking and doing, and how they affect the organization. In box 4.9, Sarah Tracy looks closely at employee socialization and discusses some contradictory expectations. Consider what Tracy's work says about the relationships between rationality and emotionality discussed in the chapter 3.

Writings on organizational socialization emphasize different dimensions of the socialization process, but most focus on the changes and transformations that new organizational members go through as they experience and adapt to a new work situation.[77] Socialization to work life, of course, begins much earlier. In childhood we learn about careers and workplaces through interaction with family members, teachers, and friends. The media later become important sources of information about organizations and organizational life. Plus, we learn about specific jobs through interviews, job descriptions, and various work experiences.

Box 4.9 Voices from the Field

"Locking Up Emotion"

Sarah J. Tracy, Arizona State University

Most jobs require some "emotion labor," which includes knowing about and managing one's emotional demeanor in line with organizational expectations.[78] An ethnographic study of organizational culture on a cruise ship found that service workers on the ship continuously labored to smile whenever they set foot in passenger areas.[79] However, emotion labor extends beyond putting on a happy face. As part of their job, some employees must *hide* their emotions or even show a variety of negative as well as positive emotions in attempting to meet various, and sometimes contradictory, organizational norms.[80]

Another yearlong ethnographic study of a prison and jail identified eight core organizational expectations linked to emotional expression and construction among correctional officers.[81] Employees faced the following diverse and often mutually contradictory expectations: respect inmates, nurture inmates, suspect inmates, be tough and maintain detachment, follow the rules, be flexible, rely on others, and don't be needy. Administrators passed on the norms as straightforward and obvious edicts and discouraged officers from asking questions or discussing the norms. The emergent tensions are summarized below.

Contradictory Tensions that Mark the Correctional Officer Job

Contradictory Tension	*Organizational Norms Encompassed by the Tension*	
Respect-Suspect	Respect inmates	Suspect inmates
Nurture-Discipline	Nurture inmates	Be tough Maintain detachment
Consistency-Flexibility	Follow rules and procedure	Be flexible
Solidarity-Autonomy	Rely on others Handle problems among officers	Don't be needy Inform on fellow officers

In an attempt to manage these organizational norms and tensions, correctional officers were subject to a number of unintended emotional consequences. Among other constructions, correctional officers evidenced states such as withdrawal and paranoia—emotional responses common among people faced with double binds caused by contradictory organizational expectations.[82]

In order to avoid the debilitating emotional constructions associated with such double binds, correctional settings should perhaps do more to encourage discussion and questioning about organizational norms and tensions. While communication does not dissolve contradiction, talk allows employees to acknowledge, consider, and conceptually escape the "frames" of double binds and to see other possible responses to work expectations.

Think about some different ways in which the socialization process could be adapted to help correctional officers deal with contradictions in their organizational settings. How might communication about organizational dilemmas and paradoxes be related to less debilitating emotional constructions? For example, can communication about puzzling aspects about organizations help people to feel "I'm not alone" or "I'm not crazy"?

Work-specific socialization is generally conceptualized as developing through three sequential stages:

1) the anticipatory stage;
2) the encounter stage; and
3) the metamorphosis stage.[83]

The *anticipatory* stage refers to everything we learn about a specific job and a specific organization prior to the first day at work. By reading brochures, manuals and annual reports, watching organizational videos and advertisements, and interacting with employees (for example in the job interview) new members develop expectations about the work situation. Such expectations, however, are often biased and unrealistic because initial contacts with the organization are staged in a more positive light. In the *encounter* stage, the newcomer confronts the organizational reality through day-to-day experiences with tasks, colleagues, and superiors. In this phase, the newcomer is subjected to the official policies of the organization and its members and also experiences a number of surprises or discrepancies between expectations and reality. In this early stage of employment, messages from colleagues and superiors about rules, procedures, and practices are usually very important and taken very seriously. In the *metamorphosis* stage, the newcomer seeks to become an accepted and participating member of the organization by learning and adapting to the organization's expectations. Also in this period, the newcomer creatively seeks to individualize his or her

Box 4.10 Memorable Messages, Turning Points, and Critical Junctures

Professor Cynthia Stohl has studied the structure, form, and nature of *memorable messages* in the process of organizational socialization.[84] Asking employees in a Midwestern corporation to talk about "any messages [they] recall which seemed to have a significant impact on [their] life," Stohl found that memorable messages are brief oral injunctions, delivered by "older and wiser" colleagues, regarding important issues in the respondents' lives, prescribing rules of conduct or offering strategies for dealing with varied situations, and often reflecting conservative social values important for the maintenance of the organization. More specifically, the memorable messages analyzed by Stohl provided information about norms, values, expectations, rules, and rationality of the organizational culture. In addition, the analysis showed that people tend to recall primarily messages given in equivocal situations and messages provided by the "establishment" of the organization. Memorable messages, thus, have important socializing functions. By transmitting the cultural heritage of the organization, memorable messages provide new members with the social skills and knowledge necessary to behave and perform as competent members of the organization.

The idea of memorable messages is akin to the notions of "turning points"[85] and "critical junctures"[86] in relationships. These are definite moments at which something happens—the message "hits home" or "strikes a chord"—that then transforms the relationship. Such memorable messages can produce "paradigm shifts" for individuals, pairs, groups, or organizations, as when a great speech (a "pep talk') helps a group see the task ahead of them in a wholly new light than they had previously.

Can you recall messages that have been significant for your experience of work life? Who were the sources of these messages? For example, did you ever get a great piece of career advice from a mentor that changed your life? What about messages that have had a significant impact on your life in general?

role in the organization, for example by developing methods to distinguish the relative importance of various messages from management or by negotiating definitions and methods related to specific tasks. Learning how to socialize new members effectively may help organizations establish stronger and more satisfying relationships with their employees—which could, in turn, result in a change in the culture.

While stage models of organizational socialization are useful, they depict a more standardized process than may actually occur. Also, the idea of "anticipatory socialization" potentially devalues a number of forms of labor to marginal positions. Robin Clair, in an analysis of the powerful colloquialism "a real job," found this to be true.[87] Most often, participants in Clair's study associated a "real job" with one that provided them with lucrative salaries or utilized their education fully.[88] In many cases, this resulted in people framing their current jobs as not quite "real" enough, despite the fact that they were firmly entrenched in an organization or well established in a line of work. Thus, to tell someone to "get a real job" says a lot—not only about the

Box 4.11 Building a Strong Individual-Organizational Relationship

Organizational communication analyst Charmaine Wilson[89] has developed the following list of stages that newcomers experience during the early months in a position and has proposed a number of issues for organizations to consider to build a strong relationship with their employees:

1. *Pre-entry:* It is important to offer the new employee as realistic a preview of the job as possible. The more that uncertainty can be reduced, the more effective and comfortable the new employee can be.
2. *Entry:* This is typically a stressful time both for the individual and the organization. Here it is especially important that the employee is helped to see the "big picture" of the organization and his or her role in it.
3. *Learning:* This phase, which refers to the first 6 months on a job, is characterized by the newcomer's sensitivity to messages and information from others in the organization. Many different kinds of events and interactions can become "critical incidents" for the newcomer during this time. As a consequence, it is important that the organization follow through with promises and ideas aired when the person was hired.
4. *Negotiation:* When a new employee has demonstrated his or her competence on the job—for example, through a "probationary period"—it is important to allow for mutual feedback between the employee and the organization and to set up opportunities for negotiation of procedures and tasks.
5. *Mutuality:* This refers essentially to the plateau reached by the new employee when he or she finds life in the organization to be "business as usual." The individual has "learned the ropes" and now talks like an insider in the work group, team, department, or unit. At this point, it is important to offer the individual ongoing opportunities for input into decisions and to provide new training options to enrich the job experience and enhance the organization's effectiveness.
6. *Commitment:* At this point, the individual and the organization have demonstrated loyalty to one another. And the employee's special achievements and sacrifices have been recognized. To reinforce the positive sides of this situation, openness about expectations, plans, and hopes is crucial.

Think about where and how a successful socialization process can go wrong. Have you personally experienced jobs where one or several of these stages were missing? What are the consequences? Can you think of cultures where Wilson's prescriptions would be less applicable?

people involved but about the larger society. What other expressions, sayings, or aphorisms can you identify that have deep-seated and persuasive meanings like this phrase? Once again, this points to the complexities of culture and the importance of examining how larger cultural emphases can affect individuals in organizations.

Snapshot Synthesis

As a metaphor for the taken-for-granted dimensions of an organization, organizational culture invites us to pay attention to the blind spots in our daily worklives. Since our perception is shaped by our language—an essential dimension of culture—this is not an easy task. The reality of our workplace is at once a construction in which we all participate and an objective fact that confines us and ensnares us within its systems of values, assumptions, and beliefs. To think beyond those systems requires for us to act, at least occasionally, as "professional strangers," able to pose the "silly" questions to each other and to our leaders. Why do we do this or that? Why is such-and-such practice considered rational or objective? Why do we pursue *these* goals? And so on. This methodological strategy has been called "garfinkeling," after U.S. sociologist Harold Garfinkel, and it is useful in uncovering buried assumptions guiding the way we live. Thus, we can walk up to someone at work on the job and ask, "So, *what* are you doing?"[90]

The acknowledgement of multiple cultures within a single organization, however, leads us to be cautious about assuming the existence of shared values in an organization. Members of organizations may act in concert without sharing some basic values and ideas. Behind an integrative facade we may find differentiation or fragmentation. Realizing this impels us to look for the dominant culture of the organization. If we think of culture, along with organizational theorist Gareth Morgan, as "an active, living phenomenon through which people create and recreate the worlds in which they live,"[91] we cannot ignore the fact that some people have more power and influence to shape this creative process than others. Obviously, formal leaders have a special advantage in defining and developing the reality of the workplace. By articulating shared values and prescribing codes of behavior, formal leaders are in a privileged position to say what the organization and its culture is or should be. And while culture—in the broad sense of reality construction—cannot be imposed unilaterally on a social setting, some constructions clearly receive more attention than others.

Key Concepts

- **Culture**: a system of meaning that guides the construction of reality in a social community. Its manifestations include languages, habits, rituals, ceremonies, myths, stories, beliefs, values, attitudes, and artifacts
- **Subculture**: a culture within a larger culture whose members share perceptions and understandings of central problems and interact regularly within this distinct group
- **Schein's 3 Levels of Culture**: core beliefs and assumptions; values and behavioral norms; artifacts

- **Hofstede's Cultural Dimensions**: power distance, uncertainty avoidance, individualism-collectivism, masculinity-femininity, Confucian dynamism
- **Language**: a system of meaning that not only labels our world but also helps us co-create it continuously through the use of categories, classes, hierarchies, and distinctions; language helps us orient ourselves in the world and maintain patterns of similarities and differences
- **Rites**: ceremonial acts that are prescribed or customary for a culture; in organizational settings, we find rites of passage, rites of degradation, rites of enhancement, rites of renewal, rites of conflict reduction, and rites of integration
- **Corporate Culture**: a term used to describe the managerial interest in managing an organization's culture
- **Functionalist Perspective on Organizational Culture**: the notion that organizations *have* cultures that leaders should seek to nourish, shape, and ultimately control in the interest of accomplishing instrumental goals
- **Symbolist Perspective on Organizational Culture**: the notion that organizations *are* cultures, a complex and ever-evolving totality of people, goals, actions, experiences, and interpretations; an organizational culture, according to this perspective, is rarely monolithic and can therefore not be controlled by management or embraced by a strategy
- **Martin's 3 Perspectives on Culture**: integration, differentiation, fragmentation
- **Organizational Climate**: the cultural conditions for communication in the organizational setting, including levels of supportiveness, trust, openness, emphasis on high-performance goals, and participation
- **Socialization**: the process through which an organization communicates its culture(s)—especially to new members
- **Memorable Messages**: messages—typically prescribing rules of conduct—that organizational members recall to have had a significant impact on their lives

Endnotes

[1] Michael E. Pacanowsky and Nick O'Donnell-Trujillo, "Organizational Communication as Cultural Performance," *Western Journal of Speech Communication* 46 (1982): 121.

[2] Sonja A. Sackman, *Cultural Knowledge in Organizations: Exploring the Collective Mind* (Newbury Park, CA: Sage, 1991).

[3] Talcott Parsons, *Sociological Theory and Modern Society* (New York, Free Press, 1967).

[4] Clifford Geertz, *Interpretation of Cultures: Selected Essays* (New York: Basic Books, 1973) p. 5.

[5] Kenneth Burke, *A Rhetoric of Motives* (Berkeley: University of California Press, 1969).

[6] John Van Maanen and Stephen R. Barley, "Cultural Organization: Fragments of a Theory," *Organizational Culture*, ed. Peter J. Frost, Larry F. Moore, Meryl R. Louis, Craig C. Lundberg, and Joanne Martin (Beverly Hills, CA: Sage, 1995) pp. 31–54.

[7] Mary Jo Hatch, *Organization Theory: Modern, Symbolic and Postmodern Perspectives* (Oxford: Oxford University Press, 1997).

[8] Shirley Willinghanz, Joy L. Hart, and Greg Leichty, "Telling the Story of Organizational Change," *Responding to Crisis*, ed. Dan Millar and Robert Heath (New York: Lawrence Erlbaum, 2003).

[9] Edgar H. Schein, *Organizational Culture and Leadership* (San Francisco: Jossey-Bass, 1991).

[10] Federico Varona, "Conceptualization and Management of Communication Satisfaction and Organizational Commitment in Three Guatemalan Organizations," *American Communication Journal* 5.3 (Spring 2002) < http://acjournal.org>; Federico Varona, "Relationship between Communication Satisfaction and Organizational Commitment in Three Guatemalan Organizations," *The Journal of Business Communication* 33.2 (1997): 111–140.

[11] Paula C. Morrow, "Concept Redundancy in Organizational Research: The Case of Work Commitment," *Academy of Management Review* 8.3 (1983): 486–500.

[12] Arnon E. Reichers, "A Review and Reconceptualization of Organizational Commitment," *Academy of Management Review* 10.3 (1985): 465–476.

[13] Suzan Czajkowski, "'Where Are All the Foresters?' A Study of Gender, Leadership and Power," M.A. thesis, U of Montana, 2000.

[14] Michael H. Agar, *The Professional Stranger* (New York: Academic Press, 1996).

[15] Geertz, pp. 6–7.

[16] Sally Planalp, *Communicating Emotion* (New York: Cambridge University Press, 1999).

[17] Geert Hofstede, *Culture's Consequences* (Beverly Hills, CA: Sage, 1980).

[18] See Geert Hofstede and Michael Harris Bond, "The Confucius Connection: From Cultural Roots to Economic Growth," *Organizational Dynamics* 16.4 (1988): 4–21. This perspective has also been developed by Guo-Ming Chen and Jsensen Chung, "The Impact of Confucianism on Organizational Communication," *Communication Quarterly* 42.2 (1994): 93–105.

[19] Adrian Furnham, Michael Bond, Patrick Heaven, Denis Hilton, Thalma Lobel, John Masters, Monica Payne, R. Rajamanikam, Barrie Stacey, and H. Van Daalen, "A Comparison of Protestant Work Ethic Beliefs in Thirteen Nations," *Journal of Social Psychology* 13 (1993): 185–198.

[20] Dorrine K. Kondo, *Crafting Selves: Power, Gender, and Discourses of Identity in a Japanese Workplace* (Chicago: University of Chicago Press, 1990).

[21] Héctor R. Díaz-Sáenz and Patricia D. Witherspoon, "Possessing a 'Sense of Community': A Study of Employee Perceptions in Selected Work Organizations in Mexico," in *Organization ↔ Communication: Emerging Perspectives, Volume 7: International and Multicultural Approaches*, ed. George Cheney and George A. Barnett (Cresskill, NJ: Hampton Press, in press).

[22] This point is crystallized in the title of the book by James R. Lincoln and Arne L. Kalleberg, *Culture, Control, and Commitment: A Study of Work Organization and Work Attitudes in the United States and Japan* (Cambridge, UK: Cambridge University Press, 1990).

[23] Patricia Covarrubias, *Culture, Communication and Cooperation: Interpersonal Relations and Pronomial Address in a Mexican Organization* (New York: Rowan and Littlefield, 2002).

[24] Ernst Cassirer, *Language and Myth*, trans. Susanne K. Langer (New York: Dover Publications, 1953).

[25] Kenneth Burke, *The Rhetoric of Religion* (Berkeley: University of California Press, 1961).

[26] "Mommy track" is sometimes used to describe a career path—often associated with slower career advancement—for women who simultaneously work and raise children.

[27] Mary Douglas, *Natural Symbols: Explorations in Cosmology* (New York: Vintage Books, 1973).

[28] Judy Motion and Shirley Leitch, "Equity in Corporate Co-Branding: The Case of Adidas and the All-Blacks," *European Journal of Marketing*, (in press).

[29] James P. Spradley and Brenda J. Mann, *The Cocktail Waitress* (New York: McGraw Hill, 1975) p. 61.

[30] Harrison M. Trice and Janice M. Beyer, "Studying Organizational Cultures through Rites and Ceremonials," *Academy of Management Review* 9.4 (1984): 653–669.

[31] Mary Helen Brown and Jill J. McMillan, "Culture as Text: The Development of an Organizational Narrative," *Southern Communication Journal* 57.3 (1991): 49–61.

[32] Mary Helen Brown, "Defining Stories in Organizations: Characteristics and Functions," *Communication Yearbook* 13 (1990): 162–190.

[33] *Børsen,* (June 21, 2002): 6.

[34] Terrence E. Deal and Allan A. Kennedy, *Corporate Cultures: The Rites and Rituals of Corporate Life* (Reading, MA: Addison-Wesley, 1982). See also Anthony G. Athos and Richard T. Pascale, *The Art of Japanese Management: Applications for American Executives* (New York: Simon and Schuster, 1981); William Ouchi, *Theory Z: How Americans Business Can Meet the Japanese Challenge* (Reading, MA: Addison-Wesley, 1981).

[35] Thomas J. Peters and Robert H. Waterman, Jr., *In Search of Excellence, Lessons from America's Best-Run Companies* (New York: Harper & Row, 1982).

[36] John P. Kotter and James L. Heskett, *Corporate Culture and Performance* (New York: Free Press, 1992).

[37] E.g., Deal and Kennedy; Ralph H. Kilmann, Mary J. Saxton, and Roy Serpa, *Gaining Control of the Corporate Culture* (San Francisco: Jossey-Bass, 1986).

[38] Deal and Kennedy.

[39] Schein, pp. 316–17.

[40] Majken Schultz, *On Studying Organizational Cultures, Diagnosis and Understanding* (Berlin: Walter de Gruyter, 1994).

[41] The term "functionalist" has been employed in the research literature in many different ways. In fact, in recent discussions in organizational communication, functionalism has been inappropriately used as a catch-all term for empirical, post-positivist, quantitative, and managerially-oriented forms of research, as if all those terms referenced the same thing or as if they were all to be dismissed out of hand. We use "functionalist" to stress an instrumental perspective on culture, where particular features are isolated and assessed for their practical utility. The term "functionalism" owes its origin to the sociological tradition of structural functionalism in the early twentieth century, in which society was understood as having many interlocking dimensions serving particular roles. That perspective is perhaps most closely associated with U.S. sociologists Talcott Parsons and Robert Merton, although the perspective was broadly influential in anthropology as well.

[42] Ruth C. Smith and Eric Eisenberg, "Conflict at Disneyland: A Root Metaphor Analysis," *Communication Monographs* 54 (1987): 367–379.

[43] For a similar study of SAS (Scandinavian Airlines System) see Peter Dahler-Larsen, "Organizational Identity as a 'Crowded Category': A Case of Multiple and Quickly-Shifting We-Typifications," *Cultural Complexity in Organizations: Inherent Contrasts and Contradictions*, ed. Sonja Sackman (Thousand Oaks, CA: Sage, 1997) pp. 367–390.

[44] E.g., Joanne Martin and Debra Meyerson, "Organizational Cultures and the Denial, Channeling, and Acknowledgment of Ambiguity," *Managing Ambiguity and Change*, ed. Louis R. Pondy, Richard J. Boland, and Howard Thomas (New York: Wiley, 1988) pp. 93–125; Ed Young, "On the Naming of the Rose: Multiple Meanings as Elements of Organizational Culture," *Organization Studies* 10.2 (1989): 187–206; Debra Meyerson, "Uncovering Socially Undesirable Emotions: Experiences of Ambiguity in Organizations," *American Behavioral Scientist* 33.3 (1990): 296–308; Schultz, 1994; Dahler-Larsen, pp. 367–390.

[45] Linda Smircich, "Concepts of Culture and Organizational Analysis," *Administrative Science Quarterly* 28 (1983): 339–358.

[46] Schultz.

[47] George Cheney, *Rhetoric in an Organizational Society: Managing Multiple Identities* (Columbia: University of South Carolina Press, 1991).

[48] James G. March, "How We Talk and How We Act: Administrative Theory and Administrative Life," *Leadership and Organizational Cultures*, ed. Thomas Sergiovanni and John E. Carbally (Urbana: University of Illinois Press, 1994). See also Nils Brunsson, *The Organization of Hypocrisy* (Chichester, UK: John Wiley & Sons, 1989).

[49] Karl E. Weick, *The Social Psychology of Organizing* (London: Addison-Wesley, 1979).

[50] Gareth Morgan, *Images of Organization* (Beverly Hills, CA: Sage 1986) p. 127.

[51] Nick Trujillo, "Interpreting (the Work and Talk of) Baseball: Perspectives on Ballpark Culture," *Western Journal of Communication* 56 (1992): 350–371.

[52] Patricia Riley, "A Structurationist Account of Political Culture," *Administrative Science Quarterly* 28 (1983): 414–437.

[53] Young.

[54] Debra Meyerson and Joanne Martin, "Cultural Change: An Integration of Three Different Views," *Journal of Management Studies* 24 (1987): 623–647; Joanne Martin, *Cultures in Organizations: Three Perspectives* (New York: Oxford University Press, 1992).

[55] Émile Durkheim, *The Division of Labor in Society* (New York: The Free Press, 1984).

[56] Mats Alvesson and Per Olof Berg, *Corporate Culture and Organizational Symbolism* (Berlin: Walter de Gruyter, 1992).

[57] Stanley A. Deetz, Sarah J. Tracy, and Jennifer Lyn Simpson, *Leading Organizations through Transition: Communication and Cultural Change* (Thousand Oaks, CA: Sage, 2000).

[58] Mats Alvesson, "A Flat Pyramid: Symbolic Processing of Organizational Culture," *International Studies of Management and Organization* 19.4 (1989): 5–24.

[59] This topic will be elaborated in chapter 5 on organizational identity.

[60] Ernst Cassirer, *An Essay on Man: An Introduction to a Philosophy of Human Culture* (New Haven, CT: Yale University Press, 1944); Cornelius Castoriadis, *The Imaginary Institution of Society,* trans. Kathleen Blamey (Cambridge: Polity, 1987).

[61] Joanne Martin, Martha S. Feldman, Mary Jo Hatch, and Sim B. Sitkin, "The Uniqueness Paradox in Organizational Stories," *Administrative Science Quarterly* 28.3 (1983): 438–543.

[62] Mats Alvesson, "Cultural-Ideological Modes of Control: A Theory and Case Study of a Professional Service Company," *Communication Yearbook* 16 (1993): 3–42.

[63] E.g., Smircich, pp. 339–358; Barbara Gray, Michael G. Bougon and Anne Donnellon, "Organizations as Constructions and Destructions of Meaning," *Journal of Management* 11.2 (1985): 83–98.

[64] Peter L. Berger and Thomas Luckmann, *The Social Construction of Reality. A Treatise in the Sociology of Knowledge* (New York: Doubleday, 1966)

[65] According to Geert Hofstede et al., the first systematic treatment of "organizational cultures" appeared in *Administrative Science Quarterly* in 1979. Geert Hofstede, Bram Neuijen, Denise Daval Ohayv and Geert Sanders, "Measuring Organizational Cultures: A Quantitative and Qualitative Study across Twenty Cases," *Administrative Science Quarterly* 35 (1990): 286–317; Andrew M. Pettigrew, "On Studying Organizational Culture," *Administrative Science Quarterly* 24 (1979): 570–581.

[66] Eric Eisenberg and Patricia Riley, "Organizational Culture," *New Handbook of Organizational Communication*, ed. Fredric M. Jablin and Linda L. Putnam (Newbury Park, CA: Sage, 2001) pp. 291–322.

[67] Harrison M. Trice and Janice M. Beyer, *The Cultures of Work Organizations* (Englewood Cliffs, NJ: Prentice-Hall, 1993).

[68] W. Charles Redding, *Communication within the Organization* (New York: Industrial Communications Council, 1972).

[69] Joann Keyton, Pat Ferguson, and Steven C. Rhodes, "Cultural Indicators of Sexual Harassment, *Southern Communication Journal* 67 (2001): 33–50.

[70] Keith Davis, "The Care and Cultivation of the Corporate Grapevine," *Dun's Review* 102 (1973): 44–47.

[71] Chester I. Barnard, *The Functions of the Executive, 30th anniv. ed.* (Cambridge, MA: Harvard University Press, 1968).

[72] Pacanowsky and O'Donnell-Trujillo.

[73] Charles Conrad and Bryan Taylor, "The Context(s) of Sexual Harassment: Power, Silences and Academe," *Conceptualizing Sexual Harassment as Discursive Practice*, ed. Shereen Bingham (Westport, CT: Praeger Publishers, 1994), pp. 45–58.

[74] Cynthia Stohl, *Organizational Communication: Connectedness in Action* (Thousand Oaks, CA: Sage, 1995).

[75] Kirk L. Rogga, David B. Schmidt, Carla Schull, and Neal Schmitt, "Human Resource Practices, Organizational Climate, and Customer Satisfaction," *Journal of Management* 27.4 (2001): 431–449.

[76] See, for example, Martha S. Feldman and James March, "Information in Organizations as Signal and Symbol," *Administrative Science Quarterly* 26.2 (1981): 171–186; John Van Maanen and Edgar H. Schein, "Toward a Theory of Organizational Socialization," *Research in Organizational Behavior* 1 (1979): 209–264.

[77] E.g., Theodore Caplow, *The Sociology of Work* (New York: McGraw-Hill, 1964); Edgar H. Schein, "Organizational Socialization and the Profession of Management," *Sloan Management Review* 30 (1998): 53–66; John P. Wanous, *Organizational Entry, Recruitment, Selection, and Socialization of Newcomers* (Reading, MA: Addison-Wesley, 1980).

[78] Arlie Russell Hochschild, *Emotion in Organizations*, ed. Stephen Fineman (Thousand Oaks, CA: Sage, 1993) pp. ix–xiii.

[79] Sarah J. Tracy, "Becoming a Character for Commerce: Emotion Labor, Self Subordination, and Discursive Construction of Identity in a Total Institution," *Management Communication Quarterly* 14 (2000): 790–827.

[80] Sarah J. Tracy and K. Tracy, "Emotion Labor at 911: A Case Study and Theoretical Critique," *Journal of Applied Communication Research* 26 (1998): 390–411.

[81] Sarah J. Tracy, "Emotion Labor and Correctional Officers: A Study of Emotion Norms, Performances and Unintended Consequences in a Total Institution," *Dissertation Abstracts International* 6107A (2001): 2519 (University Microfilms No. AAI99–79409).

[82] Paul Watzlawick, Janet Beavin Bavelas, and Don D. Jackson, *Pragmatics of Human Communication: A Study of Interactional Patterns, Pathologies and Paradoxes* (New York: W. W. Norton & Company, 1967).

[83] E.g., Fredric M. Jablin, *Handbook of Organizational Communication: An Interdisciplinary Perspective* (Newbury Park, CA: Sage, 1987).

[84] Cynthia Stohl, "The Role of Memorable Messages in the Process of Organizational Socialization," *Communication Quarterly* 34.3 (1986): 231–249.

[85] Connie Bullis and Betsy Wackernagel Bach, "Socialization Turning Points: An Examination of Change in Organizational Identification," *Western Journal of Speech Communication* 53.2 (1989): 272–293.

[86] Sally Planalp, "Critical Junctures in Interpersonal Relationships," unpublished paper, U of Utah, 2003.

[87] Robin Patric Clair, "The Political Nature of the Colloquialism, 'A Real Job': Implications for Organizational Socialization," *Communication Monographs* 63 (1996): 249–267.

[88] Clair.

[89] Charmaine E. Wilson, "A Communication Perspective on Socialization in Organizations." Paper presented to the annual meeting of the International Communication Association, May 1984, San Francisco.

[90] Michael Lynch and Wes Sharrock, eds., *Harold Garfinkel* (London: Sage Publications, Ltd., 2003).

[91] Morgan, p. 131.

5

Communicating Identity
Individually and Collectively

Today, employees increasingly care about the way their employing organization communicates with them and with the larger world. At the same time, a growing number of organizations are concerned about the behavior of their employees and the way they represent the organization, even after hours. In addition, organizations in most sectors are preoccupied with their standing on a number of social, environmental, and ethical issues. Consider, for example, advertisements by General Motors in the weeks after September 11, which focused on the company's commitment to U.S. patriotism. The common denominator in all these situations is *identity*. While many employees think of their workplace as an integral dimension of their personal identity, organizations are increasingly involved in the question of who they "are" and how their different audiences—including employees, customers, and other external stakeholders—perceive them. Organizations, just like individuals in the modern world, are often immersed in issues of identity to the point of obsession. While this concern is not entirely new, the renewed focus on identity creates an intensified engagement of organizations with planned communication across their formal boundaries.

Defining Organizational Identity

At the broadest level it is useful to think of identity as something every living system is *doing*—and in fact must do—in order to maintain itself. As systems theorists have made clear, identity is closely related to the ways living systems make sense of themselves and their environments.[1] Any living system needs to delineate boundaries between itself and its surroundings and to monitor and maintain those boundaries constantly. Just as we need to have some awareness of the boundaries of our bodies (one characteristic of some forms of schizophrenia is that people are unable to tell where their bodies end and the rest of the world begins), so do organizations require a sense of "self" to maintain coherence. There's nothing mystical about this—it's a matter of keeping track of *who* and *what* you are. To do less means schizophrenia for the individual and loss of the capacity to "hold things together" for the organization. (Obviously, the whole issue of boundaries for organizations is greatly complicated by economic globalization, networks, and technological advancement; we will discuss those implications here and in later chapters).

What do we mean when we talk about identity and, in particular, organizational identity? Identity has become such a widely used term that we rarely consider its specific meaning. In the context of everyday language, we typically talk about identity when we want to refer to something special or unique that characterizes a social entity and sets it apart from its surroundings. In this common-sense understanding, identity is what makes it possible for us to recognize an individual or an organization as distinct. Think carefully about what makes you distinct as an individual. Or your partner. Or a close friend. Consider the same question with respect to your university or an organization. What's distinct about these organizations and how stable and persistent are the identities that we perceive?

Social psychologists talk about identity as structures or patterns—of, for example, behaviors, looks, or opinions—that can be recognized and validated as unique, autonomous, and relatively stable in time and space.[2] But what does this mean when we talk about organizations? Management scholars Stuart Albert and David Whetten view identity as the consistent thread that runs through an organization over time: the organization's "core," if you will. More specifically, they refer to organizational identity as the *central, distinct,* and *enduring* dimensions of an organization.[3] What, however, makes an organization special or perhaps unique? And how stable does it need to be in order for us to perceive and accept its identity? Is it even realistic to say that any organization *has* an identity—in the sense of something essential or enduring? There are no simple answers to these questions.

First, organizations are not really unique in and of themselves. When we think about organizational uniqueness, we realize that this notion refers to differences *between* or *among* organizations—a fact that reminds us just how dependent an identity is on its surroundings. For example, how would we describe the identity of the UK-based Body Shop without referring to other, less environmentally friendly, cosmetics and personal products manufacturers? And how can we understand the unique position of Italy's Benetton without acknowledging the differences between its advertisements and those of other clothing companies? Clearly, "difference" presupposes "sameness," and there is no way we can understand one without the other. Interestingly, in their pursuit of identity and difference, many organizations end up demonstrating conformity and imitation. For example, in efforts to render themselves distinct, organizations often describe themselves as "interactive" or "participatory" and under such labels initiate a range of programs including diversity seminars, suggestion boxes, "lunch with the boss," and employee shareholding packages. Yet the actual structure and content of such programs do not differ significantly from one organization to another. As we have stressed elsewhere in this text, there's nothing so common as an "innovative organization" these days!

Second, stability with respect to organizational identity begs the question of what it means to be "stable." Change, variation, and even conflict are inevitably part of organizational identity because, like human identity, it is shaped by multiple resources (social, political, psychological, material). From a communication standpoint, perhaps the most provocative formulation of identity comes from the late nineteenth-century German philosopher Friedrich Nietzsche. He conceived of messages about who we are in terms of narrative.[4] From this point of view, the stories that organizations tell about themselves, their work, and their world construct their identity—that is, the stories themselves fold into the identity and in a very real sense become the identity. Nietzsche's conception of identity is much more fluid than our usual, everyday sense of identity as something solid, reliable, and immutable. In line with this general perspective, management scholars Blake Ashforth and Fred Mael define organizational identity as "unfolding and stylized narratives about the 'soul' or essence of the organization."[5] Other organizational theorists argue that organizational identity is fluid and unstable because it is related to the organization's image, which is constantly shaped by external pressures and interpretations.[6] The dependence on external images makes organizational identity dynamic and mutable and, thus, adaptable to environmental changes. However, what shapes the images that organizations import from their surroundings? Is the influence clearly external or the result of efforts to project a particular image?

Interestingly, the managerial literature typically describes organizational identity *both* in terms of continuity and essence *and* as something that can be managed and adapted to changing circumstances.[7] Indeed, these views are often mixed so that organizations are expected to emphasize their history and continuity while simultaneously updating and continuously fine-tuning their expressions of identity. This latter view may seem paradoxical and even illogical but reflects the complex situation facing most organizations today: in order to endure in a turbulent marketplace, organizational identities need to be flexible.

As organizations become more concerned about who they are and what they stand for, we see an increasing focus on notions like corporate *personality*, corporate *profile*, corporate *reputation*, and corporate *image*. Think about the personality and profile of a well-known organization, say, McDonald's. Does the profile of McDonald's differ from its identity? Then consider the image and the reputation of McDonald's. Are these the same? What are the differences? How do the French, or the Indonesians, or the Egyptians see McDonald's, as opposed to its image, its identity, and its reputation in the United States? If you compare your answers with those of your friends you'll see how difficult these questions are and how much your answers depend on the implied definitions.

Identity in Historical Context

It's interesting to look at the history of the term *identity*. The ancient Greek concept of *tautotes,* rendered into classical Latin as *identitas,* referred not so much to differences between individuals but rather to sameness. Identity in the pre-Western past pointed mainly to what was shared and in common—the bonds that tied people together. The idea of a unique special self emerged from the ideas of the Enlightenment writers in England and France in the late eighteenth century.

In the late nineteenth century, Émile Durkheim observed a marked contrast between tribal or preindustrial societies and modern or industrialized societies. He used the term *social solidarity* to capture this difference. In tribal or preindustrial societies, identity was largely *ascribed* to the individual by the social group or the collectivity. Rather than having choices available, every individual in that society subscribed to the same beliefs, religion, economic system, culture, etc. Individual identity was virtually inseparable from collective identity. Thus, many languages of the preindustrial world, some of which still exist, did not have the first person pronoun "I." An individual expressed his beliefs or her opinions indirectly through reference to the group.

The French philosopher Olivier Mongin uses the body (or corpus) as a metaphor for traditional society. He describes modernity as a process of "decorporation," that is, a process that dissolves the ancient relations of community and authority through which people traditionally defined their status, their roles, and their positions in society. Modern society, according to Mongin, has no "corporeality" and thus no capacity to ascribe enduring positions to its members. Having lost its obvious relation to others, the modern "decorporated" individual lacks a stable source of identity. While in traditional societies identity was ascribed, in modern or industrialized societies identity is essentially undefined. (We'll discuss some implications of this change in the next chapter, particularly in box 6.1). This issue is not confined to the individual (in, say, her "identity crisis" or his need to "find himself") but reflects a collective identity crisis of modernity.[8] Interestingly, contemporary organizations often see themselves as providers of corporeality, that is, community, identity, and power.

While Durkheim described the fundamental difference between preindustrial societies and industrialized societies as residing in how individuals express themselves vis-à-vis the collectivity, he could probably not have imagined the extent to which identity would become a preoccupation in modern society. And he certainly could not have predicted the extraordinary availability of identities provided by organizations today either through membership in them or through identification with the images projected in their external communications.

Box 5.1 The Rise of the "Corporate Person"

The Latin word "corpus" (body) is the root for "corporation," which means a body authorized as a separate legal entity with rights, privileges, and liabilities distinct from those of its members (see box 1.3) Thus, a corporation is an entity that goes beyond individuals in time, resources, and power. In the late Middle Ages in Europe, tradesmen formed guilds to enhance their power vis-à-vis the Church and the State (which were themselves intertwined). These budding organizations, which set standards and prices, were the forerunners of *both* the modern corporation and contemporary labor unions. The important point is that a "corporate" person emerged as a new kind of social actor that allows individuals to accomplish things they couldn't do otherwise—through the pooling of resources initially, the prestige accumulated through cooperative efforts, and the leverage such efforts create. Incorporation also limits individual liability (as expressed in the abbreviation Ltd.) *and* personal responsibility (as suggested by the French or Spanish *S.A.*—"anonymous society").

What do you see as advantages and disadvantages to legal incorporation? And, what features or characteristics does the metaphor of "corporate personhood" highlight about organizations in general?

Organizational Identification

Many organizations—corporations, governmental agencies, nonprofit groups, religious denominations, universities, etc.—are preoccupied with their identities and images. They use those images to gain attention in the marketplace of symbols. Through organizational efforts to craft identities, individuals are presented with many possible sources of personal identity. Advertising is a prime example. With advertising, organizations attempt to shape their own identity, and in doing so, offer individuals a resource for personal identity. One of the central messages of modern advertising is that the individual can express who he or she is through the purchase of a branded product or through identification with a group of people who express themselves with the same style.

Creating Identities with the Organization

In addition to mass-communicated symbols of identity, modern organizations make explicit attempts to create specific identities for their members. And clearly, organizations have become important sources of identity for the citizens of twentieth-century industrialized societies. In the 1960s, "I'm an IBMer" defined and distin-

"I can't decide. I'm having a brand identity crisis."

guished a sizeable portion of the workforce. Can you think of other slogans that express allegiance to an organization? Careerism developed as a modern phenomenon, and many large corporations began to dominate the identity landscape of the United States, Japan, and Europe after World War II. Attachment to employing organizations, as well as to brand names, became more and more common. *The Organization Man*, written in the 1950s by William H. Whyte, pointed to the paradox of rampant conformity within a supposedly individualistic society (the United States). To put it in other terms, it is ironic that many of us express our uniqueness primarily through affiliation and identification with particular *groups*, organizations, classes, brand names, nations, etc.

Because we generally define who we are through attachments to organizations, we are keen to protect and affirm positive perceptions of the organizations to which we belong. Knowing that we can acquire a more positive identity in the eyes of our significant others through associations with popular or respected organizations, we tend to experience threats to those organizations as threats to our own identities. In addition, we tend to associate more strongly with organizations that have a strong and positive image.[9] Thus, there is a tendency for our organizational attachments to become self-reinforcing.

Knowing that they have become important sources of identity for the individual,[10] organizations increasingly seek to extend the corporate community beyond the workplace. In addition to using the pronoun "we" in advertising and other forms of official communication, a growing number of organizations organize daycare centers, social clubs, or fitness centers for their employees. By organizing such activities, organizations hope to build stronger bonds with their members, to stimulate motivation, and to heighten loyalty—in other words, to increase identification. An extreme example of this extension of the "organizational self" to the individual is the creation of corporate burial plots in contemporary Japan.

Identification with an employer is apparent in behavior that communicates loyalty to the organization, its values, and policies. It is also visible in artifacts like uniforms, logos, plaques on the wall, etc. All these emblems of identification express the bond of the individual to the organization. Social theorist Nelson N. Foote defined identification this way in the middle of the twentieth century: "We mean by *identification* appropriation of and commitment to a particular identity or series of identities. As a process, it proceeds by *naming*; its products are ever-evolving self-conceptions . . . that is, upon ratification by significant others . . . it is only through identification as the sharing of identity that individual motives become social values and social values, individual motives."[11] Identification, in other words, is a process through which our personal identities achieve social currency.

The concept of *identification* first surfaced in the psychoanalytic writings of Sigmund Freud. He viewed the process as a defense mechanism, as when a person identifies with his boss as if the boss were his father. To Freud, this tendency was a natural though problematic extension of one kind of social bond to another; it is an inappropriate, although understandable, "transference" of affection and authority that helps to protect the ego. Psychologists and sociologists have emphasized the important role of identification in personal development, stressing how the individual internalizes or reflects the identities of certain groups or the larger society while also trying to shape something distinctive and unique.

Harold Lasswell, a U.S. political scientist, saw identification as an important link between individual feelings, attitudes (including the need to belong and feel proud by virtue of connection to something larger), and global politics.[12] For example, Lasswell revealed how people's sources of *personal shame* sometimes made it more likely

Box 5.2 Voices from the Field

"Virtually Identified"
Craig R. Scott, The University of Texas at Austin

There are a growing number of possible targets of identification for workers—including one's employer, work team, local office, and/or occupation. Sometimes these loyalties all align nicely, but in other cases people may be more identified with one aspect of work than another. In a study of geographically-dispersed workers in Colorado's Cooperative Extension Service (which serves counties of the state), more immediate targets, such as one's local office, are usually identified with most strongly (so, county office employees identified more strongly with the county office, and people in headquarters identified most strongly with the headquarters).[13] Although organizational members exhibited fairly strong identification with several relevant targets, conflicts between various identification targets were most likely for members at the most dispersed (county) level of the organization.

Another feature of organizations today is that significant numbers of people are working somewhat virtually—as teleworkers, virtual team members, or contract employees who are connected to others in the organization through various new communication technologies. For these "virtual workers," issues of dispersion and the use of communication technologies affect identification with various workplace targets. In a survey of teleworkers, Erik Timmerman and I discovered that those who teleworked part-time (more than one day per week, but no more than 50% of the week) were more identified with their work team, employer, and occupation than those who teleworked less than one day per week or those who teleworked more than 50% of the week.[14] Additionally, although virtual workers even today tend to rely quite heavily on basic landline phone and voicemail technologies, we found that the use of more advanced phone technologies (e.g., audioconferencing, mobile phones) was actually most predictive of organizational and occupational (but not work team) identification.

The relationship between technology and identification applies not only to virtual workers, but also to certain key communication technologies. A set of experiments conducted with student and organizational teams using group decision support systems (GDSSs)[15] revealed that groups involved in computer-based meetings exhibited lower identification with all workplace targets as compared to teams meeting face-to-face. Additionally, tools like GDSSs that provide people with the ability to interact anonymously contributed to less self-reported identification with one's work team, more online comments revealing a lack of identification, and fewer expressions of identification with multiple targets of attachment.

Thus, issues of identification are important to consider for the dispersed and increasingly virtual worker in organizations today. As employees and/or managers, we would be wise to consider how the various forces changing the world of work today impact our sense of connection to organizations, teams, occupations, and other aspects of work.

How might the use of various communication technologies by employees enhance or detract from their sense of identification with an employing organization? What communication strategies might you use to keep people identified in such situations? As organizations increasingly utilize teleworkers and virtual teams, how is this likely to affect identification with various aspects of the workplace?

want to demonize other countries and to go to war. A recent book on French-Lebanese journalist Amin Maalouf, goes even further with this ent to suggest that there's a terrible intensity of identity that can express ɜnce against an out-group; in fact, he finds this aspect of modern identity ɛ both tempting and frightening.[16]

In chapter 3 we introduced Herbert A. Simon and his work on decision making and bounded rationality. Simon established a clear linkage between organizational identification and decision making, insisting that identification necessarily narrows the individual's range of choice and in fact precedes the act of selecting from among many alternatives.[17] Extending Simon's ideas, Tompkins and Cheney defined the process this way: *A person identifies with an organization when he or she seeks to select alternatives with the interests of the organization—as best they can be determined—uppermost in mind*.[18] This definition is useful in analyzing day-to-day decision making in organizations as well as the accounts (or explanations) that decision makers give for their actions. We can ask people at work what things matter as they make their decisions—assuming, of course, that they are sufficiently self-aware to answer such a question!

Organizational identification occurs when "an individual's beliefs about his or her organization become self-referential or self-defining."[19] When organizational members identify with their workplace, they define themselves in terms of the organization; they internalize its mission, ideology, and values, and they adopt its customary ways of doing things. Eventually, the member may see him- or herself as an exemplar or microcosm of the organization. Organizational identification, in other words, suggests a feeling of *oneness* with the organization.[20] Think of the number of times you or your friends have defended criticism of your workplace (or your university, or your favorite sports team), and then think about how you felt when you were doing so.

Such feelings rarely develop by themselves. Employee identification is a central management issue in today's world. With mergers and acquisitions and new organizational arrangements like virtual offices and telecommuting, the nature of managerial control is changing radically (see chapter 12). In contrast to the traditional manager supervising subordinates through his or her physical presence, contemporary managers need more symbolic means to build loyalty and commitment.[21] As a consequence, most organizations use multiple means to foster employee identification, including speeches, uniforms, reward systems, rituals, ceremonies, advertisements, or other symbols of community.

In a study of corporate house organs (periodicals distributed by organizations to their employees), George found four strategies used frequently to integrate members into the organizational body: the common ground technique, identification by antithesis, the assumed "we," and unifying symbols.[22] The first strategy usually involves explicit connections—as when an urban politician tells farmers, "You know, I used to work the land." Organizations do this all the time by featuring individual employees in their ads expressing their love of the company. Identification by antithesis is when the in-group's identity is supported by opposition to an out-group's, for example, when a company blames its competitors or the government for its misfortune. The cohesion of one's "in group" is likely to be reinforced by the competition with or the blaming of the "out group." The assumed "we" is a bit more subtle; an example is the CEO of a company commenting in an annual report: "We at ACME believe that . . . "Unifying symbols can be seen in corporate brands, logos, rituals, and architecture—all the cultural features that attempt to capture the *essence* of an organization.

Building on Bullis's earlier research on the identifications of forest rangers, James DiSanza and Connie Bullis analyzed employee responses to identification inducements in a newsletter from the U.S. Forest Service.[23] Refining the identification categories discussed by Cheney above, DiSanza and Bullis document four types of identification responses to the newsletter ranging from very positive to very negative responses. More specifically, they found the following response types: *non-identification* responses (the responses did not indicate feelings of either identification or dis-identification), *textual identification* (responses were based explicitly on newsletter content), *contextual identification* (the responses referred to incidents or experiences beyond the newsletter text), and *dis-identification* (responses expressed feelings of separateness from the organization). While most Forest Service employees interviewed responded positively to the newsletter articles, some felt that the stories didn't match their experience with the organization. DiSanza and Bullis concluded that newsletters like the ones analyzed tend to reinforce previous feelings of identification or dis-identification.

Unintended Consequences

While we have mentioned the advantages of employee identification to the organization several times in this chapter, the unintended consequences or dark sides of identification are perhaps less obvious. High levels of identification among employees can produce a lack of organizational flexibility and creativity, over-conformity to organizational dictates, and tyrannical behavior on the part of leaders. Highly identified individuals could experience a lack of risk taking, loss of an independent self, and burnout.[24]

A manager and owner of a Danish advertising agency, Jesper Kunde, has written a book that describes strong employee identification as essential in today's business world. The book, called *Corporate Religion*,[25] promotes a management style that prescribes *100% loyalty* to corporate values and intolerance to critical voices in the organization. How do you imagine Kunde's agency *selects* its employees? And how will employees—if they choose to stay in the organization—adjust their behavior to fit his philosophy? Alternatively, can you imagine strong employee identification in an organization that allows or even appoints one or several "devil's advocates" charged with the job of questioning established values and practices?

Most organizations need some system that forces the organization to reevaluate regularly the images and values it takes for granted. This is necessary because identity is a lens through which organizations make sense of the world.[26] As a consequence, the official identity of an organization may produce inertia or, in some cases, fatal blind spots that prevent it from perceiving important threats or changes in its environment. The Lego Corporation's conception of itself as a toy brick producer, for example, prevented it from perceiving important changes in the patterns of how kids play. Thus, it wasn't until the early 1990s that Lego realized that it was competing for kids' time and attention not so much with other toy producers but with the computer and electronics industry. Today after some years of financial hardship, Lego has managed to integrate its world of toy bricks with elaborate computer programs. To arrive at this point, Lego not only needed to redefine its identity as an organization but also to help its members transfer their loyalty and commitment from the old toy producer to the new electronics corporation.

Box 5.3 Identification as Sense-breaking and Sense-giving

In his interesting study of Amway distributors, management scholar Michael G. Pratt presents a rather extreme case of organizational identification.[27] Amway is a network marketing organization that operates through approximately three million distributors worldwide. These distributors sell Amway's products and services face to face; there is no central business location. In order to help its geographically dispersed workforce retain a sense of common purpose, Amway has established an elaborate system of identification. Pratt reports that Amway fosters allegiance to the organization through the use of two types of practices: *sense-breaking* practices that break down meaning and self-images held by members before they entered the organization and *sense-giving* practices that provide meaning by helping members build new visions and identities for themselves.

The practice of sense-breaking at Amway involves a fundamental questioning of who one is, often by linking the sense of self to material possessions—or rather the lack thereof. Newcomers are assigned to mentors (successful higher-level distributors) who demonstrate—through their behaviors, lifestyles and wealth—what the newcomer can achieve. Sense-breaking also involves helping new members identify and build dreams for themselves or their loved ones. Amway stimulates what Pratt calls "motivational drives for meaning via identity deficits." The most common dreams at Amway center around financial and lifestyle issues like, for example, buying a new car or going on a vacation. Mentors help lower-level distributors articulate dreams and identify barriers to their fulfillment. As part of this dream-building process, distributors are told to replace a dream come true with an even bigger dream: "Keep climbing, never reach your peak." To the extent they buy into this philosophy, Amway distributors get caught in an ongoing dream-building process in which their social lives gradually become more and more entangled with their identity as distributors.

The practice of sense-giving takes the form of positive programming through which the distributor is taught to concentrate on "uplifting and edifying" things and avoid relationships (including those with family members) that prevent them from achieving their goals. By focusing exclusively on relationships that support their dreams and engagement with Amway, the distributors seal off their new identities from a critical environment. Dream building and positive programming, as Pratt points out, work together to produce positive identification to the extent that many distributors describe their relationship with their mentors in parental terms.

In the case of Amway, identification went beyond commitment and loyalty to include fundamental beliefs about one's self. Interestingly, Pratt also reports very high turnover rates at Amway. While some employees described themselves as Amway "zealots," others had a more ambivalent or critical attitude toward the organization. Some former distributors even organized an anti-Amway Web site where harsh critique of the organization's identification practices was aired (for example, see http://members.tripod.com/~nomorescams/links.htm). Pratt talks about *de-identification* when there is virtually no connection with the organization and *dis-identification* when one identifies oneself in opposition to the organization. In contrast to Amway zealots, ambivalent and critical distributors did not cut themselves off from non-supportive relationships. Instead, they maintained such relationships and, eventually, gave them more significance in their identity-building process than they gave to Amway's sense-breaking and sense-making efforts.

Are you familiar with organizations that use identification practices similar to those of Amway? What are the advantages and disadvantages of such practices? Can you think of organizations that are less dependent on creating identification that explicitly?

Organizational identification rarely implies that members become mindless machines or over-socialized functionaries. Even in organizations with strong values there's usually considerable latitude in the ways in which these values can be enacted.[28] Fortunately, many organizations are aware that such latitude is an important source of creativity and organizational development.

Conflicting Identities

Even when organizations consign individuals to rather narrowly defined identities, individuals find spaces of their own for alternative forms of self-understanding. For example, after studying women service workers in a U.S. university, organizational communication researcher Majia Holmer-Nadesan argued that the formal role ascribed by the university to women service workers urged them to "remember their place" and emphasized their subordination to a largely male system of authority.[29] The women themselves voiced their identities in *alternative terms* by talking about themselves and their roles using metaphors of motherhood. They called themselves "mothers away from home" and talked about "being there for the kids." They viewed their work as primary care for students and did not describe it in subordinate terms.

This brings home an important point with respect to organizational identities and identifications: the fact that they often conflict. The classic example that has been researched heavily since the 1960s is the clash between identification with the organization (an employer) and identification with a profession. Professionals like architects, lawyers, nurses, consultants, teachers, firefighters, etc., for example, often find that their professional expertise and experience (constructing buildings, teaching, putting out fires, etc.) conflict with the marketing ethos—exalting an organization-wide orientation towards the needs and wants of the customer. While these professionals may respect the democratic thrust of this ethos, they often find that it prevents them from giving the customers what they really need.

Likewise, scientists in industry often find managerial policies conflicting with scientific values. Their beliefs, values, and attitudes are often associated more closely with their profession than with the administration of their employer. An interesting case study of the implementation of the Bay Area Rapid Transit System in San Francisco in the 1970s showed very vividly how such a clash can occur. A number of scientists and engineers who worked on the project alerted their bosses, administrators, and managers just prior to the implementation of the system that certain aspects were unsafe.[30] The scientists and engineers fully expected that the administrators of the project would respond by saying "Let's close the project down, rather than risk public safety." However, the administrators and managers were identified more with values such as expediency and efficiency than with safety. This is a classic example of a conflict between two groups grounded in different visions of what is relevant and appropriate, based on their identification with a particular profession. Thus, professional identities can strongly imply certain values and practices as well as characteristic bases of knowledge.

Challenges to Organizational Identity

We are exposed to continued messages from organizations: messages about products and services, messages about images and values, messages about identities. In addition, we receive messages about changes within organizations: corporate restructuring, downsizing, and the spread of general job insecurity. Recent books such as *The Death of the Organization Man*[31] capture a world of work in flux, with a large segment of the workforce in temporary services, self-employment, and contract-based jobs.[32] With so many messages, it is difficult for corporations to establish and maintain a recognizable identity. References to "the information age" or the "communication explosion" seem to imply that more is better. As postmodernist theorists have noted, more communication may actually involve *less* communication.[33] Consider this scenario from a cartoon that we came across a number of years ago. A man is abandoned on a deserted island. He writes a message and puts it in a bottle. He then walks to the beach to throw the bottle into the ocean, and discovers that *the ocean consists of nothing but other messages in bottles!* To some extent, this describes the situation organizations confront when trying to craft messages to express themselves and to gain the attention of others.

Struggling Just to Be Heard

Think about the number of corporate messages you encounter daily and the variety of media that announce those messages. Where do the messages originate? Many of them are advertisements from business corporations trying to sell a product or service. The top 100 marketers in the world (the biggest spenders are in the automobile, food, and personal care industries) spent more than $70 billion on media advertising in 2001. Almost half of this amount was spent in the United States alone. Among the top 100 advertising spenders, Procter & Gamble headed the list with media spending of almost $4 billion, followed by General Motors and Unilever. Other major advertisers include Ford, Toyota, AOL Time Warner, Philip Morris, Daimler-Chrysler, Nestlé, Volkswagen, Honda, McDonald's, and Coca-Cola. Europe is the second biggest advertising region with a total spending of $24 billion, followed by Asia with $9 billion and Latin America with almost $2 billion.[34]

So far we've only talked about the sheer quantity of messages around us. When we take a closer look at what the corporate messages say, we encounter another challenge to organizational identity. In a marketplace crowded with organizations struggling to stand out and be heard, few messages can expect to gain attention in and of themselves. As a consequence, a growing number of messages are designed to "lean" on other messages and exploit their more prominent position. The classic example is the famous campaign by Avis rental car company: "We're #2. We try harder." Although Avis did not mention its competitor explicitly by name, there was no doubt that the campaign referred to Hertz. This trend, which is often referred to as "positioning," has moved beyond such relatively simple comparisons. Today we find computer companies leaning on IBM's slogan "Think," as when ICL computers years back suggested "Think ICL" and when Apple urges us to "Think Different." Likewise, Sisley—a producer of underwear—trades on Nike's slogan when suggesting "Just *Un*do It." When the clothing company Esprit claims that it supports the fight against AIDS, it plays on Benetton's famous depiction of misery, including a person dying of that disease. In today's marketplace, messages play creatively on each other, often crossing product categories in their "inter-textual" allusions.[35] As a consequence, identities of products and organizations are constantly challenged and redefined.

Box 5.4 Marketing, Advertising, Promotions, and Public Relations

The American Marketing Association defines *marketing* as "the process of planning and executing the conception, pricing, promotion, and distribution of ideas, goods, and services to create exchanges that satisfy individual and organizational goals."[36] However, marketing may also be seen as a business philosophy. What sets marketing most clearly apart from previous business philosophies is its explicit focus on the customer. Whereas most organizations historically have been production or product oriented or driven by salesmanship, marketing prescribes an organization-wide focus on *customer satisfaction*.

Advertising and sales promotions are classical subfields of marketing. *Advertising* usually refers to any form of *paid, non-personal* communication about products or ideas in the prime media, such as television, newspapers, magazines, posters, cinema, and radio. But we find advertising in many other media today including banner-ads on Web sites, CD-ROMs, coupons, telephone solicitation, billboards, posters, and commercial messages on clothes and on vehicles. *Sales promotions* are incentives to consumers or vendors designed to stimulate purchase. Sales promotions include coupons, point-of-sales displays, and samples.

Over the last four decades, marketing has broadened its perspective to include many of the activities and perspectives traditionally associated with the field of *public relations*. This implies a broader view of target groups (from markets, customers, and consumers to politics and stakeholders) and a redefinition of marketing's goal—traditionally seen as attracting and satisfying customers through the exchange of goods and services—to include the development and maintenance of positive and beneficial relationships between various groups in society.[37]

What are some advantages and disadvantages to organizations from this expanded version of marketing? How has marketing infused many different aspects of culture in industrialized societies? Has it affected the way individual professionals present themselves?

Blurred Boundaries

When we talk about the identity of an organization, we need to imagine that the organization has some relatively clear boundaries. To what extent is that true? Members of a work organization are simultaneously members of other organizations—including family, sports associations, etc.—and spend a considerable amount of time outside the workplace. They are sometimes customers of the products or services produced by their own workplace. At the same time, many of an organization's activities have a direct impact on its surroundings—its products and services, salaries to its employees, collaboration with other organizations, networks, etc. Thus, it is not quite clear where an organization begins and where it ends. In these respects, organizational identity is difficult to pinpoint. In fact, there are a variety of reasons why organizational boundaries are blurred today, including: the roles of technologies (especially, computer-mediated communication) in creating new linkages; the establishment of interorganizational networks (partnerships, alliances, etc); and the expansion of the marketing orientation (for example, by creating closer relationships with stakeholders).

Traditionally, most organizations have identified themselves through their name, their product(s), their location, or the people they employed. Together, these dimensions constituted what the organization "was." These dimensions, however, are not so stable any longer. With frequent mergers and acquisitions, many organizations change not only their names but also their range of products, their location and, sometimes, their staff. With mergers and acquisitions, what used to be external—a competitor, for example, or a supplier—can become part of the organization. Boundaries, it seems, are in constant flux. For this reason, organizations are especially keen to assert their identity after a merger. In many countries large bank conglomerates continually acquire smaller private banks. Even universities are not immune to the impulse to merge and consolidate. Management at Lars's institution (The University of Southern Denmark) strongly emphasized the necessity of *abandoning previous names* after a recent merger. As organizations grow and change, the certainty with respect to names, products, locations, and personnel is replaced by new identities based on more abstract concepts such as visions or mission statements.

Even for organizations that keep the same name and the same range of products, boundaries are often uncertain. Some car manufacturers, for example, allow the customer to design his or her own car from a set of available options. Recently, Volvo (of Sweden) made it possible to handle this design process on the Internet. In a similar manner, Motorola produces personal pagers by letting the customer co-design the product on a laptop together with a sales representative. In such cases, the boundary spanner is not only the front-line personnel of the organization but also the customer. As a consequence, it may be difficult to clearly demarcate where the organization begins and where it ends.

So-called "network organizations" often face the same kind of difficulties. Defined in large part by the interactions between the involved organizations (see

Box 5.5 Missions and Boundaries

Ideas about organizational identities have changed historically. As organizational theorist William Bergquist[38] points out, this is related to differences in the ways organizations have conceived of their missions and boundaries over time from premodern to modern to postmodern organizations.

Premodern organizations had unclear boundaries and unclear missions. Since work and family life were closely interrelated and mostly organized to provide food and shelter for the family, it was unnecessary to define missions and boundaries. The early shoe or clothes manufacturers of the industrial revolution in England exemplify such organizations, which we still find in many developing countries.

Modern organizations have clear boundaries and unclear (sometimes inconsistent) missions. In the industrial world of factories and manufacturing systems, clear distinctions between work life and leisure activities were established. With frequent mergers and acquisitions, however, the missions of organizations—except in broad terms of financial gain—are rather vague. Examples are organizations that produce consumer goods, such as the automobile industry.

Postmodern organizations have unclear boundaries and clear missions. With new organizational forms, networks, and virtual offices, the boundaries of contemporary organizations are increasingly unclear. To compensate, many organizations attempt to define their missions in clear and distinctive ways. Organizations that produce, for example, health care products often find themselves in this category. Rather than defining themselves in terms of the products they produce, they typically build their identities on broad social values like well-being, quality, or security.

Can you find other examples of organizations that fit these three types of organizations? Think across sectors and industries and domains of activity. Can you think of arguments against Bergquist's scheme for categorizing organizations?

chapter 6), the identities of network organizations are neither tied to physical location nor to products.[39] When the collaboration between organizations has lasted for many years and when the network of interactions across formal borders is sufficiently complex, it makes little sense to assume clear boundaries between each participating organization. New communication technologies, "telework," and virtual offices exacerbate this problem. When boundaries fade, employees sometimes feel closer to their profession or to employees in other organizations than to their own employer. The more the realities of contemporary organizational life erase the sharp lines around an organization's identity, the more it seems that the organization attempts to reestablish them. While traditional physical boundaries break down, psychological boundaries related to identity, values, authority, and tasks, are painstakingly created.[40]

Growing Stakeholder Scrutiny

Interest groups, growing media attention to scandals and hypocrisy, and new demands from so-called "political consumers" challenge the identities of organizations. Although consumer unrest and criticism have existed since the 1950s—especially toward industries like oil, chemical and tobacco—it wasn't until the 1990s that organizations on a wide scale began to see their identities as being closely tied to social and political issues. Today, organizational identity is probably best understood, as management scholars Susanne Scott and Vicki Lane suggest, as a set of beliefs, which are "contested and negotiated through iterative interactions between managers and stakeholders."[41] Without powerful stakeholders granting legitimacy, contemporary organizations will have great difficulties sustaining their distinctive characteristics.

Stakeholders are generally understood as groups of people "whose collective behavior can directly affect the organization's future, but which is not under the organization's control."[42] Such groups include consumers, investors, suppliers, grass roots organizations, employees and their families, host communities, local governments, state and national governments, general society, and sometimes even foreign governments. While consumers, for example, have stakes in fairly priced products and services, employees are affected by issues like working conditions, salaries, and security of employment. Consider also the interests of groups like local governments and local communities.

The idea that certain groups have a stake in an organization implies that other groups (organizations) have the ability to grant such stakes. According to corporate communication theorist Robert Heath,[43] the notion of "stake seekers" encourages us to articulate issues and controversies in terms of available resources in society. This view makes it clear that environmental responsibility, for example, costs industry and citizens money, or that workplace democracy may have implications beyond the organization's formal boundaries in terms of how internal decisions affect the use of natural resources. This perspective also implies that there is some kind of market for stakes where prices are cleared and stakes exchanged. In a sense, we can think of courts, commissions, and legislatures as institutional representations of such a market. These institutional bodies formulate policies and rules concerning the exchange of stakes between stakeholders and stake seekers.

One of the organizations that has been subjected to substantial public scrutiny is Royal Dutch Shell. Over the years, Shell has been criticized extensively for both its products and for its activities in a number of different countries (for example, in Nigeria and Turkey).[44] In 1995, Shell faced a rash of negative reactions from consumers and grass roots organizations following its decision to dump the oil platform Brent Spar into the North Sea. While Greenpeace occupied Brent Spar to force Shell to scrap the platform on land, consumers started a boycott of Shell in many European countries. After weeks of boycott and bad press, Shell finally gave up its plans. Although not all charges against Royal Dutch Shell have been entirely fair, the Shell name now connotes cynicism and unethical business practices to many people. Other organizations have faced similar reactions or boycotts from consumers. The decision in 1995 by the French government to resume its testing of nuclear bombs, for example, made many European consumers leave French wine on the shelves, increasing the market share of wine produced in other countries. More recent examples of stakeholder scrutiny include the growing media focus on socially responsible investing. Whereas investment decisions used to be relatively detached from ethical or political concerns, contemporary investors increasingly make demands on organizations to align their behaviors with ethical standards of the day. Their identity, they feel, is at issue.

In their study of the Port Authority of New York and New Jersey, Jane Dutton and Janet Dukerich illustrate how the issue of identity is closely related to the ways organizations define, diagnose, and respond to problems in their surroundings.[45] Dutton and Dukerich found that the organization's identity served as a significant reference point that members used for assessing the importance of external issues. When they studied the organization's response to homelessness in the 1980s, they found that the organization's internal communication activities were affected by how organizational members thought outsiders perceived their organization. Dutton and Dukerich also found that the organization's treatment of homelessness to some degree affected how employees thought outsiders were judging their individual characters. The Port Authority case, thus, reveals the extent to which an organization's response to an issue can be framed by perceptions of a collective identity.

Other organizations are equally at risk of having their identity linked to social and political issues. Industries as diverse as banking, transportation, and insurance are all vulnerable. For instance, neither Nike nor Starbucks Coffee wanted to be targets of anti-WTO protests in Seattle, Washington, in December 1999, even though images of their stores were flashed around the world during the rallies and subsequent riots. The number of stakeholders or potential stakeholders has increased exponentially. With the increased numbers, corporations must justify their existence in terms of broader social, political, and environmental needs.

Managing Organizational Identity

There is a growing industry offering services to organizations that worry about their standing and visibility. Although identity has been a salient corporate issue for more than a century,[46] the identity industry came into its own in the 1970s. In 1973, for example, a group of oil companies needed to find a new corporate name and logo. They spent over $100 million dollars using focus groups to research consumer reactions to possible names for the new company. The name eventually chosen, "Exxon," tested well with the public. It created a sense of uniqueness (a double "x" appears naturally only in the language of Maltese) and power.

Organizations are especially sensitive about their identities in periods of rapid growth or during mergers and acquisitions. When new people with different back-

Box 5.6 Major Developments in External Organizational Communication (U.S. Context)

1860s: Early developments in advertising (e.g., Macy's)

1870s–1910s: Anti-monopoly sentiments

1880s: Early developments in public relations responses to public criticisms of oil, railroad, and meatpacking industries

1900s: Public criticism of numerous industries by prominent authors ("muckrakers")

1920s: Advent of radio; expansion of advertising; systematic study of persuasion and propaganda (between the wars); birth of the term *lifestyle*

1930s: The Great Depression; widespread questioning of capitalism and its inequities

1950s: Rising expectations and standard of living; development of the suburbs; TV; first appearance of marketing as a distinct discipline

1962–1973: Era of social protest; emergence of consumer protection movement; challenges to consumerism and materialism; the broadening of the concept of marketing; the emergence of social and public marketing

1975: Emergence of corporate issues management (as a proactive form of PR)

1980s: Rise of identity and issue advertising

1990s: Dominance of marketing discourse and a reformulation of the classical, adaptive marketing concept to more proactive forms of marketing; the emergence of integrated marketing communications and corporate branding as unifying strategies

Turn of the 21st century: Consolidation of corporate communications as the integrative communication practice *par excellence*

grounds, different skills, and different expectations enter the organization, they need to be socialized to the organization's culture. The need to manage identity, however, is felt in other situations as well. For example, to ensure a steady flow of capital, an organization needs to demonstrate to existing and potential investors what it stands for and what it is. As sociologist Michael Schudson points out, investors want identity messages in addition to assessments of their prospective return on investment.[47]

Moreover, to support their sales personnel and retail outlets, organizations need to communicate professionally and consistently about their products. Sales people and retailers typically work much harder for a product that has a well-established and distinct identity. To create goodwill among stakeholders and in the media, organizations couple corporate visibility with a sense of purpose and legitimacy. Stakeholders increasingly demand more explicit communication that links corporate identity with social values. Finally, to attract and keep good employees, organizations need to create a cohesive identity and a sense of community and belongingness. As we have already discussed, there is a growing expectation that organizations will provide their members with clear points of identification. Thus, there are many different audiences for an organization's identity efforts.

Integrated Marketing Communications

Organizations can handle the need to assert their identities in many different ways. Common to most efforts is an attempt to communicate systematically and consistently across different audiences. To do that, a growing number of organizations embrace what is called "integrated marketing communications." In its most wide-ranging sense, this means organizing and controlling whatever is said about the organization internally and externally.

By coordinating and synthesizing visions, strategies, and identity themes across different departments (for example, marketing, public relations, and human resources), organizations pursuing integrated marketing communications hope to speak with *one voice* in order to create a unified impression of what the organization is and what it stands for.[48] Although marketing communications are often integrated only at the level of specific campaigns in order to create synergy between messages or between different marketing communication parameters like advertising, sales promotions, point-of-purchase communications, etc., more and more organizations have begun to think of their communications in their entirety. Moreover, there are attempts to manage communication holistically in order to maintain a clear and consistent image of all the organization's activities. How realistic is this kind of centralization, in a corporation, a government agency, a lobby group, or a university?

Assessing Organizational Identity Programs

In his book *Corporate Identity: Making Business Strategy Visible through Design*,[49] corporate identity and design consultant Wally Olins describes three different structures of corporate identity management:

1. *Monolithic identity*: The organization uses one name and one visual style. Examples: Shell, Q8, The Body Shop, SAS (Scandinavian Airlines System),

"As board members, we need to speak with one voice. I'm suggesting Donald Duck."

BMW, IBM, and Yamaha. Increasingly, the monolithic identity structure is referred to as "corporate branding."[50]

2. *Endorsed identity*: An umbrella organization consists of multiple groups or companies, each of which has its own name and identity plus that of the parent organization. Example: General Motors (Chevrolet *GM*, Pontiac *GM*, Oldsmobile *GM*, Buick *GM*, Cadillac *GM*).
3. *Branded identity*: The company operates through a series of brands that may be unrelated to each other or to the corporation. Examples: Procter & Gamble (Pampers, Tide, Fairy Liquid), Philip Morris (Kraft, General Foods).

Why would a corporation choose one identity structure over another? Many choices are, no doubt, based on tradition. In other cases, the structure chosen reflects an explicit identity strategy. (Branding even extends to individuals in the job market, as recommended by management consulting guru Tom Peters.[51]) When airlines and big oil companies base their organization on a monolithic identity strategy, it is typically because they are concerned about external visibility and internal cohesion. To allow a multiplicity of names for its different products and in different parts of the world would detract from the name recognition and its positive connotations. In periods of crisis, however, the attention can be a liability. Procter & Gamble's branding strategy is very different in that it has the potential advantage of buffering the identity of the organization from the names of its many individual products. While this has an obvious advantage if an individual product fails, the organization may have difficulties communicating one clear message.

Many models and programs have been devised to guide the management of corporate identity. Each model reflects the particular interest or profession of its creator. Thus, design consultants approach identity as a design problem; corporate communication scholars put an emphasis on consistency between messages and symbols across the organization; and organizational theorists and practitioners focus on organizational behavior. Each perspective has an interesting and important story to tell, and each should be included when considering what an organization is and what it can be. Most corporate identity programs prescribe a fundamental reflection on what the organization is.[52] This reflection serves several important purposes, including:

- Establishing the *raison d'être* ("reason for being") of the organization
- Defining its corporate mission
- Determining the desired corporate identity

After reflecting on these fundamental concepts, most corporate identity designers prescribe a *situation analysis.* The analysis looks at competitors to determine the organization's strengths and weaknesses relative to them and to detect possible gaps between its actual and desired identity. Based on the situation analysis, strategic *communication objectives* are decided and specific measures to change, adjust, or maintain the organization's identity position are chosen. After the identity program has been implemented and carried out, the process is evaluated.

Most corporate identity programs, thus, build on conventional management action plans. As a general framework or checklist, *sequential* ordering of activities makes a lot of sense. But can organizations really manage their identities this way? Is it possible, for example, to establish an organization's "actual" identity? Many scholars and consultants think yes. They urge us, for example, to look at the products and services of the organization, the behavior of its staff, the values of management, and the many symbolic and practical manifestations of the organization. If we agree that the sum of these dimensions constitute an organization's identity, we can then provide some account of what an organization is. Still, how do we weigh these dimensions against each other? Even more complicated, how do we systematically interpret and assess what an organization says and does?

Consider, for example, how Starbucks established its unique position in the coffee market. In contrast to most on-the-go coffee places, where coffee of low quality is served in an instant (at least in the United States), Starbucks decided that its raison d'être was to sell a high-quality coffee experience. Rather than speeding up the brewing and serving process, Starbucks defined its mission as providing coffee to connoisseurs. More specifically, it took the part of the coffee experience that the typical consumer was expected to hate the most—the waiting line—and turned it into a central dimension of its identity. Whereas a conventional situation analysis would have demonstrated that such a strategy is senseless in a busy world, Starbucks realized that there's more to coffee than the brown liquid. The anticipation of choice, the smell of the coffee, and the many different blends are essential parts of the experience. Moving from there, Starbucks realized that its communication objective was to convey exclusiveness and sophistication associated with coffee. This objective implied charging relatively high prices for a cup of coffee, designing beautiful interiors in its cafés, and presenting its different blends in an exotic and appealing language.[53] Although all the corporate identity dimensions (or stages) mentioned above are present in the Starbucks case, their success was not a result of following a prescription. The success of Starbucks was in large part a result of original thinking.

Interestingly, identity management is carried out not only by managers with communication responsibilities but also by rank-and-file members who identify with the organization. Since identification, as we have seen, implies that threats to the organization's identity are experienced as threats to the self, members sometimes find themselves driven by impression-management concerns. Management scholars Kimberly Elsbach and Roderick Kramer, for example, analyzed how members from eight "top-20" business schools responded to the 1992 *Business Week* survey rankings of U.S. business schools.[54] Their analysis showed that the rankings challenged established self-identities of business schools as research-driven institutions and called into question internal beliefs about the schools' standing relative to other schools. Most members made sense of these threats by affirming positive perceptions of their school and by focusing selectively on favorable identity dimensions not recognized by the ranking survey. Can you think of similar examples where *employees* become involved in identity management?

To a large extent, however, corporate identity management is a matter of precise handling and controlling of corporate messages and their interpretations. Corporate identity management has a tendency to become sequential, sender-oriented, and top-down communication activity that leaves little room for the perceptions, interpretations and interests of employees, consumers, and other stakeholders. The implications of this limitation are the topic of the remaining part of this chapter.

Box 5.7 Voices from the Field

Corporate Identity, National Identity, and Rugby

Shirley Leitch and Judy Motion, The University of Waikato

There are numerous definitions of corporate identity but the most comprehensive definition is probably that of the International Corporate Identity Group, which reads in part: "Every organization has an identity. It articulates the corporate ethos, aims and values and presents a sense of individuality that can help to differentiate the organization within its competitive environment."[55]

Sport holds a special place within many societies and provides a potent vehicle for the expression of national identity and pride. Sport is much more than just a game. It is a multi-billion dollar business funded by governments and major corporations, and it is a source of passion and excitement for millions of people. In New Zealand, rugby is the national sport and a central element of national culture. The New Zealand Rugby Football Union, the NZRFU, is rugby's governing body and its corporate identity is closely tied to that of the national team, the All Blacks. The NZRFU is a largely faceless organization, but the All Blacks have, arguably, the most famous faces in the land. Every aspect of All Black life—from the selection of players to the design of their uniforms—is the focus of intense media attention. Thus it is the All Blacks and their successes—and failures—that serve to differentiate the NZRFU from other sports organizations.

Given the strength of feeling attached to rugby and the All Blacks, the NZRFU has always been constrained by public opinion. Its corporate identity is derived from its rich historical past and from the traditions of the game. Thus, the advent of professionalism and "marketization" in rugby in the 1990s presented the NZRFU with a major challenge. New Zealanders cherished the myth of rugby players as amateurs who played purely for the love of the game but the NZRFU was faced with the reality of multi-million dollar contracts luring top players to other teams.

A large sponsorship deal with Adidas (a multinational company headquartered in Germany) provided the NZRFU with the financial support necessary to survive within the world of professional rugby. Part of the sponsorship process was to apply a marketing discourse to the national icon, the All Blacks. The identity was distilled and transformed into a brand; brand values were articulated; and the team was promoted *as* a brand. However, the deal was secured at the expense of New Zealand-based Canterbury International, the company that had provided the All Blacks' jerseys since 1905. Ironically, Canterbury continued their contract with the Australian national team, the Wallabies, who went on to victory in the 1999 World Cup of rugby.

The loss of the World Cup that year resulted in a day of unofficial national mourning in NZ and much media criticism of the NZRFU. Some of the criticism focused on the coach and players, but an equal amount was directed at the NZRFU's new identity as a professional sports organization. The advent of professionalism was said to have ruined the game and resulted in the production of a team more concerned with money than with playing rugby.

How do cultural icons (celebrities) turn into commodities, like many other objects of advertising and marketing? What other organizations have similar stakeholder relationships and hence similar constraints on changes to their identities? Are there ways to avoid the kind of market-based transformation of organizational and national identity chronicled here?

Ironies and Paradoxes in Corporate Identity Management

Most contemporary managers know the significance of communication in the management of organizational identity. They realize that their organization's identity is not self-evident or pre-existent but must be constantly constructed through unfolding narratives about what the organization is or aspires to be. Organizational identity in this sense becomes a selective and motivated claim that a group of people makes about an organization.[56] It is thus important to ask who is making that claim—who is articulating what the organization is and further, who is expected to be guided and shaped by that articulation?

Integration without Voice

One central purpose of corporate identity management is to make sure that organizational members identify with the organization. Today, many organizations are aware that such identification requires that the organizational member be in some respect *heard* and *involved* in the articulation of the organizational identity. In his classic study of the U.S. Forest Service, Herbert Kaufman showed how newly

Box 5.8 The Voice of the Employee

American Airlines publishes short stories told by their employees in *A Spirit of Greatness,* described as "a blueprint for any executive in any company who wishes to explore and understand the enormous difference that committed employees make to providing exceptional customer service." Read the following excerpts[57] carefully and comment on their significance for organizational identification.

Thanks for Looking After My Wife
I'm a mechanic, and while working in Houston, I received a routine call from a 727 flight engineer to fix a loose bolt on a panel in the wheel well. I tightened the bolt, checked for any other problems, and returned to the office. Later, I was walking through the terminal, and an older gentleman approached me. He had a big smile on his face and extended his hand. "I want to thank you," he said. "What for?" I asked, shaking his hand. "I was looking out the terminal window and saw you tightening that bolt on the 727 the other day," he answered. "My wife was on that flight. Thanks for taking care of her." As he walked away, a powerful feeling of satisfaction came over me. I really did take care of his wife, and that man made me feel very proud.—Doug Cardwell, *Mechanic/Tay Shop, Alliance Maintenance Base*

Look What I Started
"I try to treat every customer as though they owned the company."—Mark Hawkins, *Reservations Agent, Dallas*

All Our Passengers Are First Class
At the airport, when assigned to the "First Class check-in" position, it is customary for agents to assist the Economy check-in line when there are no First Class passengers. On many occasions, passengers who are next in line hesitate to approach when called, explaining, "Ma'am, I'm not traveling First Class." My reply, "All American Airlines passengers are First Class; we just don't have that many seats in front," always brings a smile. —Lurain Murray, *Passenger Service Agent, Montego Bay, Jamaica*

Whose voices are articulated here? Does it make a difference that American Airlines has published these stories? How do readers/listeners typically process organizational stories like these?

employed forest rangers were socialized into the organization by having them give public talks in the local community. Hearing themselves articulate the values and missions of the organization, these forest rangers were able to relate to and internalize those values in a more active way than if the values had simply been conveyed to them via traditional internal media. Having a voice in external communications helped to solidify organizational identification for those employees.[58] The Danish state-owned train corporation DSB pursues a similar strategy. Its external magazine, available on all passenger trains, presents stories and several pictures of employees in both their professional and private lives. By giving voice to rank-and-file members, DSB hopes to personalize its organization and to strengthen identification across several organizational functions.

Clearly, the social and emotional involvement that we call identification presupposes participatory involvement. However, only a few organizations allow for such participation in establishing corporate identity. Although "participation" and "diversity" have become management buzzwords (see chapter 8), few managers today seem willing to tolerate unfettered communication about the organization's identity by employees and external stakeholders. Despite the lack of general participation in the articulation of corporate identity, it's interesting to note that commonality and sharing across the organization are taken for granted when organizations talk about who they are. Managers tend to assume that whatever is expressed officially will more or less automatically be shared by everyone.

Corporate identity management is typically the domain of a relatively small clique of decision makers speaking on behalf of the rest of the organization. In stark contrast to the passive role left for other organizational members, these select few enjoy a great deal of creativity in the expression of corporate identity—especially in times of change. As mentioned earlier, the LEGO Corporation has for many years been in the process of redefining its identity from toy bricks to a broader range of products. In this process, top management has displayed remarkable freedom of interpretive creativity. What used to be fixed and almost sacred corporate symbols—the brick, the colors, and the corporate history—are now viewed as replaceable signifiers. This, of course, is only the case until a new official definition of identity has been decided.

With its emphasis on integration and cohesion, conventional identity management mutes multiple voices and rarely leaves room for more than one identity. Although this approach makes sense in a cluttered communication environment, it overlooks the fact that environmental complexity often calls for dual or multiple identities.[59] When organizations are facing many different audiences each with different expectations of the organization—for example, employees, investors, customers, and environmental groups—a more pluralistic definition of the corporate identity would allow the organization the flexibility to adapt to changing circumstances and preferences. Indeed, it may be argued that abstract or ambiguous definitions of the organization may help minimize conflict between messages to different audiences.[60]

Some organizations use "strategic ambiguity"[61] when formulating visions and mission statements—for example, highlighting vague value terms such as "excellence" or "creativity" or "friendliness." Such ambiguity, it is believed, allows different stakeholders inside and outside the organization the latitude to read their own values and preferences into the document. Still, most organizations rarely allow for more than one official interpretation of their identity. While the organizational identity is

Box 5.9 Articulating the Identity of Corporate Buildings

Identity is a serious matter, and management typically tries to monopolize and control interpretations of what the organization "is." Although this may not always be possible,[62] we see corporate managers and consultants of corporate identity eager to expound the *exact* meaning of corporate symbols to the world around them. This is evident in design manuals, mission statements, and corporate videos where organizations carefully craft their exact identity to both internal and external audiences. Members are expected to embrace the chosen interpretation. It is ironic that so many organizations still issue controlled, top-down messages that are expected to be "owned" by all segments of the organization's membership.

Like other corporate identity parameters, corporate buildings are rarely left to speak for themselves by top management.[63] Typically, CEOs, communication managers, and other architects of organizational identity try to explain to internal and external audiences (including journalists and the business press) how new buildings and design should be interpreted. Describing the significance of Volvo's pentagon-shaped plant in Kalmar (Sweden), the vice president of corporate planning suggested, rather curiously, that "it was a signal to the whole company that we were fully backing up what we were saying about work democracy, technological innovations, etc."[64] A marketing manager of a leading Swedish office furniture manufacturer explained the round shapes used in the organization's headquarters: "The domed roof, in its form and design, consequently symbolizes the rounded details in our assortment. In the interior we have rounded doors and some corners are similarly rounded instead of being right-angled in order to accentuate the identity of the product. . . . In the exterior, logo, architecture, and product program we are everywhere confronted with the same round basic form. From the moment we enter the reception we are also confronted with the positive sense of well-being associated with success. No communication problems here."[65]

Why do you think that top managers put so much emphasis into "correct" interpretations? Is it a problem if designers and other groups perceive corporate buildings and design differently?

often couched in rather abstract and general terms—for example, many organizations, describe themselves as service providers dedicated to quality, development, and responsibility—organizational decision makers are anxious to make sure that their identities are communicated, received, and interpreted in ways that match the officially approved version. Do you think tolerance for multiple voices would strengthen or weaken organizational identity?

External Involvement

External audiences are expected to be interested and involved in what organizations say about themselves. To what extent is that true? We know that Coca Cola used to be "The Real Thing" and perhaps we are aware that its slogan of the 1990s was "Always Coca Cola." But what difference does it make to us? We know that McDonald's has a clown called Ronald McDonald, but do we really care if they change to a rabbit called Oscar? And even when we (or our kids) care, how long does it last?

Clearly, with the advent of critical stakeholders and so-called political consumers, organizations confront rising expectations that they live up to accepted standards for production, leadership, and social responsibility. The inquisitive nature of these concerns, however, is not necessarily an indication that consumers, interest groups, and other stakeholders are interested in the more detailed identity considerations of contemporary organizations. One interesting exception, perhaps, is the emotional way we often relate to our favorite sports teams (see box 5.7).

In most other situations, however, our involvement is low. Although we recognize the colors and symbols of many large corporations (e.g., BMW, BP, Virgin), how interested are we if they decide to change these symbols—especially given that they *have* already been changed several times? Or if Procter & Gamble decides to assemble all its products under one corporate identity umbrella, what would this mean to us as outsiders? Probably not a great deal.[66] We may feel a certain loyalty to some products, (although signs indicate that customer loyalty is dwindling), we may feel attached to certain global brands, and perhaps we even feel attracted to some corporate slogans or popular catchwords. How do such feelings and attractions translate into corporate identity programs? They probably don't—at least not in any simple or direct ways.

Most consumers are happy to know that responsible and respected companies produce the products they buy, that these companies are generally sensitive to social and environmental issues, and perhaps even that these companies are able to produce some interesting and entertaining commercials. Other than that, consumers rarely care about what organizations say about themselves. As consumers and citizens we are mostly engaged in our own lives, in our families, our careers and, perhaps, our local community.[67] Although products and brands often figure prominently in these interests and concerns, it would be a mistake to assume that this reflects an interest in corporate identity.

Auto-communication and Corporate Self-absorption

When formulating their identity programs, organizations assume the existence of external interest. Indeed, in order for corporate identity programs to have an internal impact—in terms of cohesion, motivation, loyalty, and identification—they need to be communicated consistently and regularly in the organization's surroundings. External presence and visibility grants the identity program status and authority and commits the organization to take its own words seriously. We can illustrate this with an example from personal communication. Uttering resolutions to oneself in front of a mirror does not have the same impact as declaring them in front of an audience that one respects. Although the message is primarily internal, the external audience makes all the difference. And the more engaged and interested the audience is imagined to be, the stronger the impact on the sender. We call this kind of communication—self-referential acts of communication through which senders relate to *their own messages*—"auto-communication." Auto-communication can be seen as analogous to what some system theorists call "self-reference." According to Chilean biologists Humberto Maturana and Francisco Varela, all living systems communicate with their surroundings primarily in order to confirm and maintain themselves as autonomous entities.[68] Self-reference, in other words, is a systemic "drive" through which the living system preserves its identity.

Organizations auto-communicate whenever the messages they project in their surroundings are received as messages to the organization itself. Some organizations use this strategy consciously. Chemical Bank, for example, addresses its own members in ads showing a smiling employee, her signature, and the slogan "Expect more from us." In a similar manner, airline companies like Lufthansa Airlines and Thai

[...]-communication

[...]ist Yuri M. Lotman[69] tells [...] young poet whose work [...]blished. When he receives [...]s each poem carefully sen[...]e, word-by-word, noticing details [...]er audiences would typically ignore. The poet is probably the most involved receiver of this piece of work. Reading his own words in a high-status medium accessible to all other readers adds another dimension to his experience. He suddenly sees himself as a member of a community of writers. Lotman points out that this type of communication—auto-communication—is not about messages *per se* but about meta-messages, that is, messages about situation and context rather than content.

What role does the published book play in this process? What are the advantages of auto-communication? And what are the disadvantages? Think about the medium used in the Merrill Lynch protest discussed at the beginning of chapter 1. Consider advertisements, annual reports, job announcements, etc. Which media would help organizations communicate effectively with themselves? And why?

Airways use ads to remind their employees about desirable qualities and duties. This is done by articulating a common "we" on the behalf of all organizational members. Clearly, managers and other architects of corporate identity are often more involved in articulating the "we" than anyone else. And sometimes ordinary members join in—if not always with the same exuberance—to extol the virtues of the organization. To the external spectator, however, this articulation often seems unduly loud, irritating, and self-absorbed. Self-absorption is one of the most interesting paradoxes of corporate identity management.[70] In a complex and cluttered communication environment, organizations need to manage their identity in order to stand out, yet the more successful they are in achieving that goal, the greater the possibility that the audience will resent the repetition.

The Danish shoe producer Eccolet, for example, is carefully designing its retail outlets all over the world using an identical type of maple wood. Managers at Eccolet have told students of Lars that it is imperative for the organization to use this wood in order to convey the same image to consumers in all countries and to increase global awareness and recognition of the Ecco brand. Although the strategy of standardizing communication and design across different cultures may have a number of advantages in terms of coordinating the dissemination of corporate symbols and controlling communication costs, these measures are usually not dictated by *consumer* interests or concerns. Eccolet managers presume that their target consumers are highly enough involved in their company to compare store design across different countries. This, however, is quite unlikely and demonstrates how easily corporate vanity turns into self-absorption.

The idea of self-absorption explains how an organization's preoccupation with itself has dysfunctional consequences for the organization's ability to respond to its environment. It represents, in other words, an explicitly "pathological" form of auto-communication. Self-absorption can be observed not only when an organization is explicitly communicating with, or collecting information from, its environment but also as it builds internal programs and policies.

We can talk about organizational narcissism when the organization is so caught up in polishing its image, programs, and practices that the original purpose for communicating its values and goals becomes secondary. Shiv studied a not-for-profit institution in India that worked on issues of rural poverty. The NGO (non-government organization) demonstrated organizational narcissism as it developed a system of information and communication technology (ICT) and began to see itself as absolutely central to solving problems of rural poverty. Ironically, this resulted in the organization focusing on self-improvement at the expense of addressing the needs of local communities. As the ICT system developed, the organization saw it primarily as a means of enhancing its own legitimacy vis-à-vis funding agencies rather than as a means of improving its accountability to local communities.[71]

Snapshot Synthesis

Contemporary organizations struggle to assert distinct identities in their surroundings for many different reasons: to "break through the clutter" of corporate messages, to unite their members around shared symbols, and to establish themselves as recognized and legitimate players in the marketplace. Although organizational identity typically refers to something that sets an organization apart from its surroundings, such differences usually hinge on similarities amongst organizations. As a consequence, organizations are often more alike on central dimensions than they themselves believe—even when their identities are managed carefully and changed over time.

The social need to identify with something bigger than oneself allows organizations to develop a high degree of loyalty and devotion among members. Such identification, however, rarely surfaces by itself. Most organizations need to manufacture commitment carefully through the use of symbols, speeches, uniforms, reward systems, rituals, ceremonies, advertisements, etc. And even when such means are employed, there's little guarantee that employees will stay involved in the organization's identity in the long run. The major reason for this is that most organizations expect involvement without involvement, that is, commitment to symbols and strategies without giving voice to its lay members. Even external audiences—customers, interest groups, and other stakeholders—are expected to participate in the identity game of contemporary organizations. And while some clearly do through their loyalty to certain brands or their devotion to certain organizations (for example, sports teams), most external audiences care little about what organizations say about themselves. Most marketing and advertising efforts, however, tend to assume the opposite with the consequence that many organizations today become absorbed by their own expressions of identity.

Key Concepts

- **Identity**: in everyday usage, what makes it possible for us to recognize an individual or an organization as distinct; from a systemic perspective something every living system does in order to maintain its boundaries and thus itself
- **Organizational Identity**: according to Albert and Whetten, the *central*, *distinct*, and *enduring* dimensions of an organization; according to Ashforth and Mael, "unfolding and stylized narratives about the 'soul' or essence of the organi-

zation; alternatively, that which *represents* an organization—from either the "inside" or the "outside"

- **Organizational Identification**: a feeling of oneness with an organization, such as when members define themselves in terms of the organization, internalize its mission, ideology, and values, and adopt its customary ways of doing things
- **Identity Conflicts**: when allegiances to different organizations or subgroups are experienced as incompatible, such as when the customer orientation of one's workplace is at odds with the orientation of an outside professional group to which the employee belongs
- **Identity Challenges**: problems facing the previously stable identities of contemporary organizations due to over-communication, blurred organizational boundaries, mergers and acquisitions, critical stakeholders, etc.
- **Identity Management**: the systematic creation and handling of "corporate" signifiers
- **Positioning**: an image strategy than leans on and, to some extent, exploits the positions of other players in the marketplace of products, services, and symbols
- **Stakeholders**: groups of people who have a stake in the organization's activities and performance; their collective behavior can directly affect the organization's future
- **Integrated Marketing Communications**: the notion of aligning and coordinating all communication activities across formal organizational boundaries in order for the organization to speak with one voice
- **Monolithic Identity**: an identity strategy where the organization uses one name and one visual style in all its communications; sometimes referred to as corporate branding
- **Corporate Identity Programs**: strategies to build and organize—often in a sequential manner—an organization's identity on the basis of its *raison d'être,* its mission statement, and its desired image
- **Auto-communication**: self-referential acts of communication through which the sender relates to its own messages; although auto-communication is essential in building an identity, it often implies self-absorption
- **Organizational Narcissism**: when an organization is so caught up in polishing its identity that the original purpose for communicating its values and goals are forgotten

Endnotes

[1] E.g., Humberto R. Maturana and Francisco J. Varela, *Autopoiesis and Cognition: The Realization of the Living* (Dordrecht, Holland: D. Reidel, 1980); Niklas Luhmann, *Essays of Self-Reference* (New York: Columbia University Press, 1990).

[2] Erik Erikson, *Identity: Youth and Crises* (New York: Norton, 1968); George Herbert Mead, *Mind, Self and Society* (Chicago, IL: The University of Chicago Press, 1934).

[3] E.g., Stuart Albert and David A. Whetten, "Organisational Identity," *Research in Organisational Behaviour* 7 (1985): 263–295.

[4] Friedrich Nietzsche, *Daybreak: Thoughts on the Prejudices of Morality*, ed. Maudemarie Clark and Brian Leiter (Cambridge, UK: Cambridge University Press, 1997).

[5] Blake E. Ashforth and Fred A. Mael, "Organizational Identity and Strategy as a Context for the Individual," *Advances in Strategic Management* 13 (1996): 21.

[6] Dennis A. Gioia, Majken Schultz, and Kevin G. Corley, "Organizational Identity, Image, and Adaptive Instability," *Academy of Management Review* 25.1 (2000): 63–81.

[7] E.g., Klaus Birkigt and Marinus M. Stadler, *Corporate Identity: Grundlagen, Funktionen und Beispielen* (Landsberg an Lech: Verlag, Moderne Industrie, 1986); Wally Olins, *Corporate Identity: Making Business Strategy Visible through Design* (London: Thames and Hudson, 1989). For a critique of this view see Lars Thøger Christensen and Søren Askegaard, "Corporate Identity and Corporate Image Revisited: A Semiotic Perspective," *European Journal of Marketing* 35.4 (2001): 292–315.

[8] Olivier Mongin, "La Democratie à Corps Perdu," *Esprit* (Feb. 1982): 206–214; see also, Anthony Giddens, *Modernity and Self-Identity: Self and Society in the Late Modern Age* (Cambridge: Polity Press, 1991); Christopher Lasch, *The Culture of Narcissism: American Life in an Age of Diminishing Expectations* (New York: Norton, 1978).

[9] Kimberly D. Elsbach and Roderick M. Kramer, "Members' Responses to Organizational Identity Threats: Encountering and Countering the *Business Week* Rankings," *Administrative Science Quarterly* 41 (1996): 442–476; Jane E. Dutton et al., "Organizational Images and Member Identification," *Administrative Science Quarterly* 39 (1994): 239–263.

[10] Kenneth Burke, "The Rhetorical Situation," *Communication: Ethical and Moral Issues*, ed. Lee Thayer (London: Gordon & Breach, 1973) pp. 263–275; George Cheney and Phillip K. Tompkins, "Coming to Terms with Organizational Identification and Commitment," *Central States Speech Journal* 38 (1987): 1–15; Lars Thøger Christensen, "Buffering Organizational Identity in the Marketing Culture," *Organization Studies* 16.4 (1995): 651–672.

[11] Nelson N. Foote, "Identification as the Basis for a Theory of Motivation," *American Sociological Review* 16 (1951): 14–21.

[12] Harold D. Lasswell, *World Politics and Personal Insecurity* (New York: Free Press, 1965).

[13] Craig R. Scott, "Identification with Multiple Targets in a Geographically Dispersed Organization," *Management Communication Quarterly* 10 (1997): 491–522.

[14] Craig R. Scott and C. Erik Timmerman, "Communication Technology Use and Multiple Workplace Identifications among Organizational Teleworkers with Varied Degrees of Virtuality," *IEEE Transactions on Professional Communication* 42 (1999): 240–260.

[15] Craig R. Scott, "The Impact of Physical and Discursive Anonymity on Group Members' Multiple Identifications during Computer-Supported Decision Making," *Western Journal of Communication* 63 (1999): 456–487.

[16] Amin Maalouf, *In the Name of Identity* (New York: Arcade Publishing, 1996).

[17] Herbert A. Simon, *Administrative Behavior: A Study of Decision-Making Processes in Administrative Organizations* (New York: Free Press, 1997).

[18] George Cheney and Phillip K. Tompkins, "Communication and Unobtrusive Control in Contemporary Organizations," *Organizational Communication: Traditional Themes and New Directions*, ed. Robert D. McPhee and Phillip K. Tompkins (Thousand Oaks, CA: Sage, 1995) pp. 179–210.

[19] Michael G. Pratt, "To Be or Not to Be: Central Questions in Organizational Identification," *Identity in Organizations: Developing Theory through Conversations*, ed. David Whetten and Paul C. Godfrey (Thousand Oaks: Sage, 1998) p. 172.

[20] Blake E. Ashforth and Fred A. Mael, "Social Identity Theory and the Organization," *Academy of Management Review* 14 (1989): 20–39. See also Cheney and Tompkins; Ashforth and Mael.

[21] Linda Larkey and Calvin Morrill, "Organizational Commitment as Symbolic Process," *Western Journal of Communication* 59 (1995): 193–213.

[22] George Cheney, "The Rhetoric of Identification and the Study of Organizational Communication," *Quarterly Journal of Speech* 69 (1983): 143–158.

[23] James R. DiSanza and Connie Bullis, "'Everybody Identifies with Smokey the Bear': Employee Responses to Newsletter Identification Inducements at the U.S. Forest Service," *Management Communication Quarterly* 12 (1999): 347–399; see also Connie A. Bullis and Phillip K. Tompkins, "The Forest Ranger Revisited: A Study of Control Practices and Identification," *Communication Monographs* 56 (1989): 287–306.

[24] Ashforth and Mael (1996); Janet M. Dukerich et al., "The Dark Side of Organization Identification," *Identity in Organizations: Developing Theory Through Conversations*, ed. David Whetten and Paul C. Godfrey (Thousand Oaks: Sage, 1998) pp. 245–256.

[25] Jesper Kunde, *Corporate Religion: Building a Strong Company through Personality and Corporate Soul* (London: Financial Times Prentice Hall, 2000).

[26] Karl E. Weick, *Sensemaking in Organizations* (Thousand Oaks: Sage, 1995); Ashforth and Mael; George Cheney and Lars Thøger Christensen, "Organizational Identity: Linkages between 'Internal' and

'External' Organizational Communication," *The New Handbook of Organizational Communication*, ed. Fredric M. Jablin and Linda L. Putnam (Thousand Oaks: Sage, 2001) pp. 231–269.

[27] Michael G. Pratt, "The Good, the Bad, and the Ambivalent: Managing Identification among Amway Distributors," *Administrative Science Quarterly* 45.3 (2000): 456–493.

[28] Ashforth and Mael.

[29] Majia Holmer-Nadesan, "Organizational Identity and Space of Action," *Organization Studies* 17.1 (1996): 49–81.

[30] Robert M. Anderson, Robert Perucci, Dan Schendel, and Leon Trachtman, *Divided Loyalties: Whistle-blowing at BART*, (West Lafayette, IN: Purdue University Press, 1980).

[31] Amanda Bennett, *The Death of the Organization Man* (New York: Morrow, 1990).

[32] See review by Vicki Smith, "New Forms of Work Organization," *Annual Review of Sociology* 23 (1997): 315–339.

[33] See e.g. Jean Baudrillard, *The Ecstasy of Communication* (New York: Semiotext(e), 1988).

[34] "World's Biggest Ad Spenders: P&G and GM," *AdAge.com*, (November 11, 2002) (http://www.adage.com/news.cms?newsID-36485).

[35] Lars Thøger Christensen, "Intertextuality and Self-Reference in Contemporary Advertising," *Advertising Research in the Nordic Countries*, ed. Flemming Hansen and Lotte Yssing Hansen (København: Samfundslitteratur 2001) pp. 351–356; Lars Thøger Christensen, *Reklame i Selvsving* (Frederiksberg: Samfundslitteratur, 2001).

[36] Peter D. Bennett, ed., *Dictionary of Marketing Terms* (Chicago: American Marketing Association, 1998).

[37] George Cheney and Lars Thøger Christensen.

[38] William Bergquist, *The Postmodern Organization: Mastering the Art of Irreversible Change* (San Francisco: Jossey-Bass, 1993).

[39] Note that we can label a single organization as a "network organization" in that its structure resembles a network. Or, we can identify a "networked organization" as one that is embedded in a larger group of interconnected organizations.

[40] Larry Hirschhorn and Thomas Gilmore, "The New Boundaries of the 'Boundaryless Company,'" *Harvard Business Review* (May–June 1992) pp. 104–115.

[41] Susanne G. Scott and Vicky R. Lane, "A Stakeholder Approach to Organizational Identity," *Academy of Management Review* 25.1 (2000): 43–62.

[42] James E. Grunig and Todd Hunt, *Managing Public Relations* (Forth Worth, TX: Harcourt Brace Jovanovich, 1984) p. 297.

[43] Robert L. Heath, e-mail conversation with author Lars Thøger Christensen, Spring 2000.

[44] Sharon M. Livesey, "The Discourse of the Middle Ground: Citizen Shell Commits to Sustainable Development," *Management Communication Quarterly* 15 (2002): 313–349.

[45] Jane Dutton and Janet Dukerich, "Keeping an Eye on the Mirror: Image and Identity in Organizational Adaptation," *Academy of Management Journal* 34.3 (1991): 517–54.

[46] Roland Marchand, *Creating the Corporate Soul: The Rise of Public Relations and Corporate Imagery in American Big Business* (Berkeley: The University of California Press, 1998).

[47] Michael Schudson, *Advertising, the Uneasy Persuasion: Its Dubious Impact on American Society* (New York: Basic Books, 1993).

[48] Don E. Schultz, Stanley I. Tannebaum, and Robert F. Lauterborn, *The New Marketing Paradigm: Integrated Marketing Communications* (Chicago: NTC Business Books, 1994); see also Lars Thøger Christensen and Lars Thording, "The Corporate Anatomy of Integrated Communications: Challenging an Expanding Organizing Perspective," work-in-progress.

[49] Wally Olins, *Corporate Identity: Making Business Strategy Visible through Design*. (Boston: Harvard Business School Press, 1990) pp. 1–224.

[50] Nicholas Ind, *The Corporate Brand* (London: Macmillan Press Ltd., 1997).

[51] Thomas J. Peters, *The Brand You 50: Or 50 Ways to Transform Yourself from an Employee into a Brand that Shouts Distinction, Commitment, and Passion!* (New York: Alfred Knopf, 2000).

[52] See e.g. Russell Abratt, "A New Approach to the Corporate Image Management Process," *Journal of Marketing Management* 5.1 (1989): 63–76; Cees B. M. van Riel, *Principles of Corporate Communication* (London: Prentice Hall, 1995); Cees B. M. van Riel and John M. T. Balmer, "Corporate Identity: The Concept, Its Measurement and Management," *European Journal of Marketing* 31.5–6 (1997): 340–355.

[53] Adam Morgan, *Eating the Big Fish: How Challenger Brands Can Compete against Brand Leaders* (New York: John Wiley & Sons, 1999).

[54] Elsbach and Kramer.

[55] van Riel and Balmer.

[56] Ashforth and Mael.

[57] John M. Capozzi, "Excerpts from *A Spirit of Greatness. Stories from the Employees of American Airlines*" (Fairfield, CT: JMC Publishing Services, 1998).

[58] Herbert Kaufman, *The Forest Ranger* (Baltimore: Johns Hopkins University Press, 1961).

[59] Albert and Whetten; Cheney.

[60] Michael G. Pratt and Peter O. Foreman, "Classifying Managerial Responses to Multiple Organizational Identities," *Academy of Management Review* 25.1 (2000): 18–42.

[61] Eric Eisenberg, "Ambiguity as Strategy in Organizational Communication," *Communication Monographs* 51 (1984): 227–242.

[62] Peter Dahler-Larsen, "Organizational Identity as a 'Crowded Category': A Case of Multiple and Quickly-Shifting We-Typifications," *Cultural Complexity in Organizations: Inherent Contrasts and Contradictions*, ed. Sonja Sackman (Thousand Oaks: Sage, 1997) pp. 367–90.

[63] Per-Olof Berg and Kristian Kreiner, "Corporate Architecture: Turning Physical Settings into Symbolic Resources," *Symbols and Artifacts: Views of the Corporate Landscape*, ed. Pasquale Gagliardi (Berlin: Walter de Gruyter, 1990) pp. 41–67.

[64] Berg and Kreiner, p. 57.

[65] Berg and Kreiner, p. 49.

[66] D. Kirk Davidson, "Consumers Really Don't Care about Brand Products' Owners," *Marketing News* 32.24 (1998): 5–6.

[67] Morgan.

[68] Maturana and Varela. See also Klaus Krippendorf, "An Epistemological Foundation for Communication," *Journal of Communication* 34 (1984): 21–36; Luhmann.

[69] Yuri M. Lotman, *Universe of the Mind: A Semiotic Theory of Culture* (London: I. B. Tauris, 1990).

[70] Lars Thøger Christensen and George Cheney, "Self-Absorption and Self-Seduction in the Corporate Identity Game," *The Expressive Organization*, ed. Majken Schultz, Mary Jo Hatch, and Mogens Holten Larsen (Oxford, UK: Oxford University Press, 2000) pp. 246–270.

[71] Shiv Ganesh, "Organizational Narcissism: Technology, Legitimacy and Identity in an Indian NGO," *Management Communication Quarterly*, 16 (in press).

6

Connecting through Social Relationships and Networks

In this chapter, we'll consider the nature of workplace relationships and networks. We start with relationships, since they are the building blocks of networks. Consider the frequent advice to "network"—to build a set of relationships that can be advantageous to your career success. Similarly, organizations build networks of suppliers, distributors, and other partners. This often boils down to a set of relationships among individuals—even though such partnerships may also involve binding legal contracts. Work relationships and personal or social relationships are not always easily separated. In addition, communication at work is about much more than just the work itself! There are all sorts of things we talk about other than how to get the work done. Social talk is an integral part of our experience of organizations and organizational communication. We will also discuss some of the most important organizational functions of relationships and networks and some of the implications for relationships outside of work and the workplace.

Workplace Relationships

How can we describe relationships at work? Let's consider the following scenario.

> Cassandra, the on-duty manager of Habersham Kids' Clothing, is leaning over the checkout counter doing paperwork. She is white, in her late 20s, smartly dressed. There are no customers in the store. A 19-year-old Polynesian salesperson, Kara, is rearranging some clothing on a rack. A group of three women come in, one holding a baby. Cassandra immediately straightens up, tugs at the sides of her blouse to straighten it, changes her facial expression to a cheery smile, and tries to

> make eye contact with the customers. Her face is bright and cheerful. She then looks to Kara, who takes her cue from the manager.
>
> Kara leaves the rack and approaches the customers. "Hello, how're you?" The customers smile and nod politely but don't say more than "Hi." "Can I help you find something?" Kara asks. The woman with the baby says, "No, we're just looking." Kara turns her attention to the baby, reaches gently to take his hand, and says with exaggerated cheerfulness, "Well, you're a cutie, aren't you?" She looks back to the women: "Let me know if I can help you."
>
> The women stay together at first, looking at, touching, and commenting on the clothes, the sizes, and the prices. Kara returns to rearranging clothes but to a different rack closer to the shoppers. After a minute or so, Kara says to the women, "We've gotten in quite a few new items for winter this week. Those on display against the wall are quite nice." The three women all look to her and smile. The one with the baby says "thanks" and moves toward the display that Kara mentioned. Apparently taking this response as encouraging, Kara walks with her and points out one style of color-coordinated shirts and pants sets. "Mmm," the woman responds. The other two women have continued to look in other parts of the store. Cassandra has come out from behind the counter and moved closer to them. The woman with the baby seems very interested in the outfits to which Kara has led her. Kara holds a blue version up. They discuss the appropriate size. All the while, Kara is being very attentive, smiling, and occasionally playing with the baby. "That will look darling," Kara says at one point. Shortly after, the woman buys the outfit.

This may seem like a strange case to introduce a chapter on workplace relationships, but we want to challenge how you think about relationships, particularly in the context of the workplace. The scenario in this case is recognizable by all of us as the sort of ritualistic customer-salesperson interaction we expect when we enter a retail store. However mundane it may be, there's a lot that's interesting about this interaction that took place in a downtown shop in Hamilton, New Zealand. What do you notice about the roles, the relationships, and the communication?

One way to look at the brief relationship is by considering its importance to the organization. Jan Carlzon, former CEO of Scandinavian Airline Systems (SAS), called the interaction between salespeople and customers "moments of truth."[1] What he meant is that in these interactions the customer—or potential customer—forms a vivid and lasting impression of the organization. Customers decide, for example, if the organization is one they'd like to return to. So, from the organization's perspective, relationships like the one between Kara and the woman with the baby are critical to attaining organizational goals. But that's not the only reason to consider such a relationship.

From another, quite different, point of view, such interactions are important to consider given that we are often described as living in a "consumer culture" in which sales interactions may be seen as defining moments. There's a ritualistic aspect to such interactions; the way they unfold is familiar and comfortable, almost scripted. In a consumer culture, sales encounters can be thought of as *rituals of reification*, semi-scripted activities that maintain or reinforce existing social norms. We use the theoretical concept of reification here because it highlights the human tendency to see norms or rules as solid or unchangeable—creating the impression that "things are like that" or "things have always been this way." These are also sometimes *rituals of reproduction*, in which individuals in an otherwise impersonal world interact in order to establish and maintain a sense of community or bonding.[2] Basically we're suggesting that sometimes the ritualistic aspects of the sales encounter reinforce our understandings and acceptance of social reality, and sometimes they provide a sense of belonging or identity. We feel momentarily connected to the other person, even if it is brief and fleeting and perhaps somewhat "synthetic."

Many kinds of relationships exist in organizations. We all have been or will be a part of many different types of relationships: superior-subordinate, coworkers or teammates, buyer-seller, or friends, just to name a few. The ones that have received the most attention from researchers are those that are seen as instrumental to the success of the organization. Superior-subordinate relationships are frequently studied because many people believe that such relationships play a key role in the organization's productivity.

Much of the research on relationships at work has focused on their instrumental role in career success—the networks that people form and the role of those networks in advancing careers. From this perspective, relationships are resources we compete for with others in order to help us "get ahead." While there is no question that many of the relationships we form do have a substantial impact on our careers, we form relationships for other reasons as well. For example, one study that explored the relationships people considered significant in their professional lives found that many people cited relationships themselves as important, not as a means to some end. Among the most common reasons they gave were collegiality, admiration for the other person, personal friendship, and pleasure and satisfaction in the relationship.[3]

Social-Historical Trends in Relationships and Networks

Are relationships and relational communication at work pretty much the same today as they always were? There's evidence to suggest that these phenomena have changed in some fundamental ways in recent times. A key facet of organizational life today is *negotiating* relationships and identities. Relationships and identities are actively constructed. They are dynamic and fluid, not stable or unitary. Relational communication in the contemporary workplace is expected to take on an egalitarian, interactive (versus one-way) nature. People don't always fulfill those expectations, of course, but these expectations shape our views about what sorts of communication we consider competent. Thus, we expect meetings to have a friendly, informal feel versus being highly formal and structured (such as using *Roberts Rules of Order* for parliamentary procedure). Similarly, managers are advised to use informal and personalized practices such as "Management by Wandering Around" (MBWA), and to listen, connect with, and develop rapport with staff.

The "container model" of organizations (see chapter 1) points us toward considering our lives and our relationships inside and outside the organization as separate—with professional, hierarchical relationships inside and family and friendships outside. Just a brief reflection, however, suggests that such a model doesn't describe our experiences very well. The demarcation between work and non-work life has evolved over the years. Prior to the Industrial Revolution in the late 1800s, the two domains were closely intertwined. In societies based primarily on agriculture and crafts, families often worked together; work and home life were not clearly distinct. The Industrial Revolution changed all that. Factories had strict rules and procedures to be followed, many of which discouraged non-work related interaction. Now, there are some signs that the lines between work relationships and the social/personal are being blurred again, albeit in somewhat different ways.

For example, the number of hours worked has increased significantly in many countries in recent decades. This is true, for example, for university educated full-time workers and especially for women.[4] This has important implications for relationships and relational communication. First, if we have less leisure time and we spend more hours at work, the chances are increased that our social and personal relation-

Box 6.1 Communication in Post-Traditional Societies

Building on the work of other social theorists, British critical discourse analyst Norman Fairclough has identified several characteristics of communication in "post-traditional" societies. Note the parallels in Fairclough's claims to Olivier Mongin's description of the "decorporation" of society, which we discussed in chapter 5.

1. *Assumed (or traditional) roles, identities, and relationships have been lost or discarded.* In traditional societies, people "knew" their roles and identities and thus their relationships with others. For example, you were either noble or common, aristocracy or working class. The type of relationship one had with other members of society was accepted as a given. Now, however, rather than a fixed feature of societies (and organizations), roles, and positions, identities and relationships must be negotiated.[5]
2. *There is an increased demand for emotional labor and "communicative labor."*[6] Because negotiating identities and relationships can be a delicate matter, communication has become more important to everyday life and especially to organizational life. For example, superiors have to work to treat staff with respect, courtesy, and sometimes warmth, even when they might feel like doing otherwise. As Fairclough stated, "A consequence of the increasingly negotiated nature of relationships is that contemporary social life demands highly developed dialogical capacities."[7]
3. *Social interaction has become more conversational, informal, and democratic.* That is, we expect less formality and fewer power markers, or displays of power in our speech (e.g., calling someone "Mister" or "Sir"). That doesn't mean there aren't power differences, of course. But, the power differences typical of, say, manager-subordinate relationships are not so easily recognized in conversation.[8] So, for example, each of the authors—in three different countries (and continents) at four different universities—addresses the dean by his first name, even though in each case the dean is older and of a higher organizational rank.
4. *There is an increase in promotional discourse;* practices of advertising seep into other realms of social life. Since identities and relationships are not fixed and must be negotiated, we have come to expect some self-promotion as normal. Consider how people today have personal Web pages that are often quite similar to advertisements.
5. *Discourse has become more "technologized."* "Technology" doesn't just refer to machines, of course, but also to technique (see chapter 12). With the recognition of the importance of communication in contemporary society, researchers and consultants who study organizational communication, write "how to" books, and train members of organizations to communicate. More than likely, your university offers workshops on how to conduct yourself in employment interviews. Perhaps you've learned in your communication courses some guidelines for conducting meetings, making presentations, or developing persuasive proposals. All of these are examples of "technologizing" discourse.
6. One result of the trends above is *an increase in "synthetic personalization,"* sometimes called "manufactured friendliness," which is a kind of emotional labor. You may have noticed some of this in Kara's treatment of the customers in our earlier example. The effect of synthetic personalization is the potential for increased questioning of authenticity and perhaps even increased cynicism.[9]

ships will be with coworkers. We simply have less time to spend with those with whom we do not work. Despite developing deeper relationships with coworkers, the increase in stress that accompanies increased working hours[10] may strain work relationships (as well as non-work relationships). Also, as Arlie Russell Hochschild reports, some people *use* work to escape stresses at home—thus inverting our usual assumption about people trying to be home and away from work as much as possible.[11]

Changes in the use of communication technology have important implications for work-related relationships and networks. First, such technology has enabled an increase in working virtually, either from home or other remote locations. This can further blur the distinction between personal and work domains, as someone may, for example, simultaneously work on a report and care for children. Second, more of our work-related interaction is mediated by technology as we use e-mail, videoconferencing, faxes, and mobile phones to cooperatively accomplish tasks. We are thus simultaneously more connected and available to our network of work associates and more distanced from coworkers.

The trend toward flattening organizational hierarchies and more team-based work also has implications for workplace relationships (as we will discuss in chapter 8). Many organizations today use self-managing teams or self-directed work teams (SMTs or SDWTs), meaning that groups of coworkers may work together without a clearly designated supervisor. This changes the nature of organizational control, as we will discuss later in the chapter. Many supervisors have been troubled by the change to SMTs, since

"O.K., step away from the laptop and hold up your end of the conversation."

such a change often requires them to learn new ways of relating to coworkers. Even if the organization doesn't use SMTs, workers today find they are working in teams more often, with more emphasis on teamwork skills and less reliance on clearly defined hierarchies.

Finally, the trend toward increasing workplace diversity and globalization has interesting implications for relationships and networks. People often find they are interacting with a diverse array of people from different cultural, ethnic, and religious backgrounds. Because of technology, coworkers are often geographically distant. For example, India has developed a strong international business in software design, such that many firms from around the world outsource information processing work to Indian partners. Thus, someone in Europe or Australia may be communicating daily via e-mail with a colleague in India.

Key Elements of Relational Interaction

Communication between people in organizations is never as simple as the labels we typically use to describe it: for example, "making a sales pitch," "placing an order," or "gathering some information." These descriptions each suggest a simple, one-way transfer of information. But there's always much more going on. A few important communication concepts can be helpful to thinking about such processes in more sophisticated ways.

Definition of the situation and communication goals. As we've discussed before, our view of organizational communication highlights that reality is *socially constructed*. We develop our understandings of things through interacting with other people. But that doesn't mean we always reach the exact same meanings. Whenever we have a conversation with another person or group, each of us has a *definition of the situation*, which includes an understanding of the kind of conversation we're having, the goals of the conversation, and the kind of relationship we have with the other(s) in the conversation.[12] Sometimes our definition of the situation is quite similar to that of others involved in the conversation, and sometimes it's quite different. For example, let's say you and a coworker are discussing an issue at work. In your mind, you may think what's happening is a lively discussion or perhaps a friendly debate. However, if your coworker becomes agitated, it could signal that from her perspective the discussion is turning into a fight. Different definitions of the situations determine the realities experienced.

Part of what makes these situations complex is that people almost always have *multiple goals* when they communicate. Three types of goals are clearly identifiable in most conversations: instrumental (or task), identity, and relationship goals.[13] The *instrumental* goal is easiest to determine; it's usually the primary reason given for a conversation. Examples include persuading, gathering information, instructing, informing, selling, and teaching, just to name a few. But even when we're focused primarily on these instrumental goals, we simultaneously try to achieve identity and relational goals. *Identity goals* include presenting yourself in a desired way and treating others *as if* they are certain kinds of people. How would you describe Kara's identity goals in the scenario at the beginning of the chapter? Perhaps she wants to present herself as a friendly, competent, child-loving professional; she talks to the woman with the baby *as if* she is an important, valued customer, and mother. None of this is to say that Kara is insincere. She may or may not be. But we are constantly pursuing identity goals in communication—both in conversations like Kara's as well as in public relations messages that try to shape a corporate identity. Sometimes this happens with very little thought or "strategy." At other times, it may be well rehearsed and planned. Closely related to identity goals are *relationship* goals. Our messages in communication constantly reflect what we think of the relationship and, sometimes, how we want to shape or modify that relationship. As with identity goals, this process can be quite spontaneous or strategic; it may be subtle or blatantly obvious. Often identity and relational aspects of messages are sent nonverbally. For example, notice that Kara's facial expressions and touching the baby all suggest she is trying to create a bond with the customer.

One of the ways that identity and relational goals are closely intertwined is that we seek *legitimation* for valued identities in our relationships.[14] For example, if you desire an identity as a competent professional, you would like supervisors and coworkers to treat you *as if* you are such a person. One of the factors that stimulate relationship development is the *exchange* of legitimation. Continuing the example, you would probably show respect for a supervisor who treats you as if you are competent and efficient. Relationships, like other meanings, however, are situated, fluid, and dynamic. As these examples show, identities and relationships are integrally connected. The identity one wants to convey—for example, expert, leader, or adviser—is closely connected to the kind of relationships established with others. The reverse is also true. Relationships are based on perceived identities. Managers and subordinates, salespeople and shoppers, coworkers, and friends all construct, perform, and negotiate identities and relationships.

In order to converse and work cooperatively, communicators must *negotiate* shared definitions of the situation, including shared definitions of identities and relationships. That is, while each of us has a subjective point of view, we try to achieve "*intersubjectivity*," or a mutually understood view of the situation. That doesn't mean people always reach shared definitions, of course. But communicators typically try to understand each other and make themselves understood. Socio-linguist H. P. Grice suggested that the *cooperative principle* underlies our attempts to communicate.[15] By this he meant that we typically assume that people are trying to be cooperative—by making themselves understood—even when it's quite difficult to figure out what they mean. He suggests that when someone isn't clear, we still search for a meaning that would make sense. This is why communication can work even when, on the surface, it may seem irrelevant or incomplete. So, for example, if someone asks you if you support a proposal and you reply, "Is the Pope Catholic?" most of us will know that you mean "Yes, I do support it." Even though your reply is seemingly irrelevant, we search for a meaning that makes sense given our assumption that you're trying to be cooperative.

Dialectics. The concept of *relationship dialectics* is a particularly useful way to examine prominent, recurrent tensions experienced in relationships. Let us start with a few examples.[16]

- *Scenario # 1*: You've socialized with the same group of workmates the past two weekends in a row. One of them talks about plans for the coming weekend assuming you'll be joining them again. While you've greatly enjoyed your time with the group, you're uncomfortable with that assumption, and you are considering doing something else.
- *Scenario # 2*: Your supervisor reveals a bit of confidential information to you about another member of your department. You're definitely interested but wonder about the appropriateness of his sharing that information.
- *Scenario # 3:* You are chairing a weekly status-update meeting of your project team. Your team has a comfortable, routine agenda for these meetings, but you're thinking about trying something different.

In each of these scenarios, there is a tension between attractive choices (see box 6.2). In scenario one, you could strengthen your *connection* with your workmates or establish your *autonomy* from them. In scenario two, your supervisor is being very *open* with you, but you wonder if being a bit more "*closed*" in this case would be appropriate. In scenario three, the *predictability* of the routine is comfortable, but some *novelty* might spice up the meeting a bit. Relational dialectics are tensions (opposing forces) that are both interdependent and mutually negating.[17] They are interdependent in that they are necessarily linked. For example, we can only know what being *open* looks and feels like in relation to being *closed,* and vice versa. But pursuing one end of the dialectic necessarily negates the other. That is, by being more open, you're necessarily being less closed; by injecting novelty, you necessarily lessen predictability.

Box 6.2 Relational Dialectics

Dialectic	Essential tension	Organizational examples
Connection–Autonomy	The desire to establish connection with others vs. the desire to establish freedom of action	• Wanting to be part of a team yet wanting to stand out as an individual • In a networked organization, wanting to establish closer links to a partner organization, yet not wanting to limit your business choices by the partnership arrangement • Establishing rapport with a salesperson, but not wanting to feel obligated to purchase
Openness–Closedness	The desire to allow information to be disclosed or free flowing versus the desire to maintain privacy	• Talking about your work with a colleague who works for a competitor, but being careful not to disclose organizational "secrets" • Telling a member of your team about organizational plans, but trying not to disclose information you were asked to treat as confidential • Chatting with your boss about your weekend, but wanting to keep some things private
Novelty–Predictability	The desire for the relationship to be predictable versus the desire for it to be new and fresh	• Enjoying your friend's ritualistic gossip about work, yet feeling a bit annoyed at his complaining about "the same old things" • Being comforted by a vendor's standardized service procedure, yet wondering if it's time for it to be updated • Feeling excited about a restructuring of the organization, but anxious that it will disrupt familiar routines and relationships

Dialectics help explain why relationships constantly change and why, to make relationships successful and satisfying, they constantly need our attention. While we all experience the tensions, we don't necessarily experience them in the same way. So, while the usual routine in the third scenario may be reassuring to some members of the team, others may get bored with it or question whether there's a better way to do things. People differ in terms of what they consider the right balance at a given time, and an individual could change his or her interpretation of the right balance as well. Too much of one desired feature (e.g., openness) pushes us toward the other end of the dialectic (e.g., "closedness"). So, I may appreciate the routine of the status meetings for a while, and even work to maintain the routine by suggesting a standard agenda, and then later feel the agenda is too constraining. Or, a public relations practitioner who chooses to leave a company to work as a freelance consultant may cherish the increased autonomy at first, only to find later that she misses the connection to the larger group. Often, successfully pursuing one end of a dialectic makes the other more appealing. So, because individuals differ from each other *and* differ in terms of their own preferences over time, relationships are constantly in flux, ebbing and flowing between the opposing forces. A move by one person to create more autonomy means less connection within the relationship, which may spark a move to enhance connection, and so on.

Notice how relationship dialectics help explain why conflict occurs even in the best of relationships. We are different from each other in what we consider the right

Dialectic	Essential tension	Organizational examples
Equality–Inequality	The desire to have people considered equals versus the desire to have some considered superior	• Feeling excited by a promotion, yet anxious that it will strain relationships with coworkers in your former work group • A CEO downplaying status differences (e.g., "Call me Karen") but cultivating a larger than life image • Arguing for equitable benefits for organizational members, but making exceptions for contract workers
Instrumentality–Affection	The desire for liking/affection to be an end in itself versus the desire to use liking/ affection as a means to an end	• Inviting a coworker to lunch with the intention of asking for support on a controversial work issue • Wondering why a supervisor has suddenly started being so attentive and considerate
Impartiality–Favoritism	The desire to have people treated fairly and impartially versus the desire to be "special"	• Wanting to get the "inside scoop" from the boss (who is also a close friend), while wanting to portray the workplace as fair and impartial • Establishing a policy to address lateness, yet making exceptions for certain people

amount of connection versus autonomy in a particular relationship, so we may act in ways that are not preferred by the other person. Furthermore, since typically our communication is focused on instrumental goals, the relational messages that manage dialectical tensions are often implied, not explicit. So, for example, I probably would *not* say to the coworkers in the first scenario above "I'm feeling the need for more autonomy, so I think I'll stay away from you this weekend." Rather, I might just say "I have other plans." The focus is on the instrumental goal, giving enough information to deal with the situation but not acknowledging the underlying relational goals: the coworker's request for enhanced connection and your desire for more autonomy. However, the coworker may very well "read into" your response a relational message that is asking for some autonomy.

The connection–autonomy dialectic is perhaps most basic to relationships. To speak of any kind of relationship implies connection. Indeed, we only become humans through our relationships. Yet, to be an individual requires a certain degree of autonomy. While connection–autonomy, novelty–predictability, and openness–closedness are the most common relationships, three other pairs (included in box 6.2) have emerged: equality–inequality, instrumentality–affection, and impartiality–favoritism.[18]

Communication is the means by which dialectics are manifested in the relationship, and it is also the means to manage them. We notice the tension in a relationship and we experience the choices that move a relationship toward one or the other end of a dialectic through communication. Similarly, we can work to improve relationships by raising awareness of (a) the natural tensions faced in relationships, (b) what is being experienced in the particular relationship, (c) the individuals' goals vis-à-vis the dialectics, and (d) the array of choices available to the participants.

Communication competencies. People aren't equally competent at managing the complexities of relationships. Some people handle difficult situations effortlessly, accomplishing their instrumental goals and at the same time leaving people feeling good about themselves and their relationships. Others struggle with this. As discussed above, many analysts suggest that communication skills and abilities are more important than ever. For example, based on a large-scale analysis of changes in the workplace, one group of authors concluded: "New work systems demand substantially more from employees than did traditional arrangements. Employees need more skills, particularly team-related behavioral skills, to succeed in these new systems."[19]

What sorts of communication skills are necessary? Researchers disagree on what constitutes competent communication, or indeed how to conceptualize competence.[20] One of the reasons for this is that what constitutes competent communication depends on, among other things, the context and the evaluator. That is, someone may seem very competent in a one-on-one counseling situation, yet hopeless as a public speaker. Or, one can seem incompetent to other participants in a meeting because he seems to ramble on and on without making his point, while he evaluates himself as brilliant in the same context since his goal was to stall for time so a decision was delayed to a future meeting. The organization's values will also make a difference. For example, if the organization values being competitive and standing out from the crowd, someone who is assertive and flamboyant may be seen as a competent communicator, whereas the same person might be considered embarrassingly incompetent if the culture valued a more low-key, self-effacing, group-oriented approach. While we cannot isolate one set of competencies as mandatory, research does suggest some communication skills and abilities that are important to most organizational contexts. We will focus on three sets of competencies: social perception skills, message design skills, and interaction management.

Social perception skills involve assessing people and situations: being able to think about people and social situations in complex ways; being able to pick up on the subtleties of social situations and adapt to them. Someone skilled in social perception would be likely to try to imagine the situation from others' points of view, consider their goals, values, feelings, and beliefs, and use this knowledge to consider how to interact with them. Research shows that social perception skills are a key factor for success in the workplace. For example, people with such skills tend to rise up the organization hierarchy more quickly than those with lesser skills.[21]

Message design skills are closely related to social perception skills, in that one's perception of the situation will influence the messages one crafts. For example, in public speaking, one of the basic principles is to analyze and adapt to the audience. We do the same sort of thing at the interpersonal level, sizing up the context and the other person(s) participating, then adapting (at least somewhat) to them. In fact, research has shown that people with advanced social perception skills adapt to their audiences more than do those with less developed perception skills.[22]

A basic dimension of difference in message design skills is listener adaptation: the degree to which a speaker adapts messages to the goals, values, and beliefs of the listener. The importance of listener adaptation is obvious in the example of a salesperson-customer relationship. A salesperson who successfully adapts to the interests and values of a customer has a much greater chance of being successful in making a sale (the likely instrumental goal of a salesperson-customer interaction) and also in achieving relational and identity goals.

There are many other important dimensions of message design skills: how well we use evidence, the degree to which our messages are vivid and novel, the degree to which our messages are confirming or disconfirming to others, and so on. Messages that are disconfirming—such as having one's suggestion ignored or rejected, or being interrupted—can be very damaging to relationships. The degree to which messages are clear versus ambiguous—and the degree to which ambiguity is intentional, or strategic, is another dimension. Interpersonal communication scholar Barbara O'Keefe describes differences in messages in terms of the primary *message design logics* they embody.[23] Summarized in box 6.3 are the three message design logics she has identified.

Finally, a third set of skills focuses on *interaction management*, which includes managing the flow of conversation. Appropriate turn taking and topic switching are two key elements of this set of skills. While they may seem rather mundane, they can be crucial in relating comfortably with others. If you've had a recent conversation with someone who interrupts you mid-sentence or tries to switch topics when the rest of the group is clearly enjoying the exchange of information on a topic that obviously interests them, you'll understand the importance of competence in interaction management.

These communication competencies are crucial to being able to achieve instrumental, relational, and identity goals in conversations with others. We will identify other competencies and strategies that are specific to particular goals in other chapters. For example, in chapter 7, we will discuss strategies for enacting leadership, and in chapter 10, strategies for managing conflict.

Box 6.3 Message Design Logics

Message Design Logic	Definition	Interpersonal Influence Examples
Expressive	Simply expressing one's thoughts and feelings, with no attempt to adapt to situational or relational constraints	"I want that report done by tomorrow or else!" "I *really*, **really**, REALLY want that report tomorrow!"
Conventional	Adapting one's message to shared conventions or norms for communication	"Would you please have the report ready by tomorrow?" "As your supervisor, I'm going to have to ask you to have the report in tomorrow."
Rhetorical	Reframing or redefining the situation to avoid threats to identities and relationships	"I know getting the report in by tomorrow is as important to you as it is to me." "How about we plan to celebrate getting that report completed tomorrow afternoon?"

Varieties of Organizational Relationships

Most research on relationships in organizations focuses not on relationships per se, but on particular kinds of relationships: superior-subordinate relationships, customer-salesperson relationships, and coworker relationships, to name a few. In this section, we look at some of the major categories of relationships found in organizations and consider particularly useful and provocative research findings on each.

Superior-subordinate relationships. We use the traditional terms "superior" and "subordinate" to refer to dyads in which one person supervises another. However, we do so with a bit of discomfort. Given the sensitivity to language and meanings we are trying to bring to this book, calling one person superior to another because of his or her job is a questionable practice. Many organizations today have become sensitive to this issue as well, commonly replacing terms like "subordinate" or "employee" with "associate," "team member," or "colleague" (see box 6.4). For clarity, though, we'll stick with the traditional terms.

Structurally speaking, communication between superiors and subordinates consists of *upward and downward communication flows*. Downward communication, according to systems theorists Daniel Katz and Robert Kahn, includes five categories of messages: (1) job instructions, (2) job rationales (the reasons justifying particular jobs), (3) information on procedures and practices, (4) feedback on performance of subordinates, and (5) indoctrination messages, which are intended to convey the organization's cultural assumptions and build employee identification.[24] Of course, Katz and Kahn were focused on messages that served clear organizational functions. Certainly downward communication includes other kinds of messages, too, such as humor and messages that serve primarily identity and relational functions—boasting and bonding, for example.

Similarly, a number of functions have been identified for upward communication. These include messages conveying (1) job status and problems in performing work, (2) information about coworkers, (3) perceptions of organizational policies and practices, and (4) ideas and suggestions. Again, beyond these work-related messages, subordinates also communicate upward about personal and social matters. Of course, there are obstacles to the flow of accurate and timely upward communication, including such things as impression management ("I want our department to look good"), careerism ("I've got everything under control here"), and fear of relaying bad news to superiors ("She told me never to complain like that again").[25]

Organizational communication scholar Phillip Tompkins refers to the process through which stories change as they are communicated to different levels in the organization as *uncertainty absorption*. As in the example above, if problems are reported to a supervisor who doesn't want to paint a bleak picture to executives, he can portray problems as minor concerns. In his long-term investigation of NASA's Marshall Space Flight Center, Tompkins found that the use of a regular feedback mechanism, called "Monday Notes," proved to be one of the most useful channels of communication between levels of the massive space agency in the 1960s and 1970s.[26] The director of the program, Wernher von Braun, asked each lab director to submit a one-page summary of the week's progress and problems every Monday morning. Von Braun read all the summaries, made comments, and circulated copies to all lab directors. All the units thus had knowledge—and responsibility—that extended beyond their specific areas of expertise (penetration/sensing). Listening to people from various levels in the organization plus people outside the organization, such as suppliers, contributed to effective communication—and to a successful organization. After von Braun's departure, the flight center stopped using the Monday notes. The change in leadership contributed to what Tompkins calls *organizational forgetting*—abandoning founding values.

The superior-subordinate dyad is by far the most studied relationship by organizational communication researchers. Much of the early research on organizational leadership focused primarily on supervisory communication toward subordinates (rarely considering communication from subordinates to superiors). In some respects, this attention seems justified. Research shows, for example, that superiors spend from one-third to two-thirds of their time communicating with subordinates.[27] Research also shows that people in organizations prefer to hear messages about organizational change from their immediate superiors and that they generally trust superiors to give them the most accurate information about organizations.[28] We will consider some of these concepts in chapter 7 on leadership; for now, we will focus particularly on concepts that are helpful in explaining the *relationship* between superiors and subordinates.

One consistent finding is that superiors and subordinates have different perceptions of their relationships and that these perceptions are influenced by the nature of their roles. For example, research shows that superiors tend to believe they spend more time communicating with subordinates than subordinates believe. Also, superiors tend to believe they initiate interaction with subordinates more than do subordinates, whereas subordinates believe the opposite.[29] Most people in organizations perceive that their superiors provide them with inadequate information. This is often true even though many of the same people complain of information overload.[30] It is easy to see how these differences in perception both contribute to and are influenced by the dialectical tensions we described above.

Because of such tensions, relationships are dynamic and change over time. For example, George Graen and Mary Uhl-Bien's model of superior-subordinate relationship development suggests three phases of superior-subordinate relationships,

"Keep up the good work, whatever it is, whoever you are."

each characterized by different patterns of communication.[31] First, there is a *stranger* phase, characterized by communication that fulfills the contractual obligations of their roles. That is, superiors provide the direction and resources (including information) subordinates need to perform their roles, and subordinates do as required to perform theirs, and not much more. Second, there is an *acquaintance* phase, often prompted by one party's offer to improve the working relationship by exchanging favors, thus increasing interaction and allowing each to "test the waters" with the other. The third phase is called *maturity*, which is characterized by a partnership in which the partners exchange loyalty and support.

Of course, not all superiors and subordinates follow the same trajectory in the development of their relationships. Extensive research prompted by George Graen's[32] leader-member exchange (LMX) theory suggests that superiors develop *in-group* relationships with some subordinates and *out-group* relationships with others. In-group relationships are much like what's described in the maturity phase of the three-phase relationship development model. In-group subordinates and their superiors establish mutual trust, respect, and support. In-group members can communicate informally about work and non-work matters with their superiors; they can disagree with and challenge each other without damaging the relationship. (Notice here how our success in attaining relational goals is constrained by the type of relationship we have with the other person). Out-group subordinates, on the other hand, have relationships with their superiors characterized by low trust and low support, often avoiding communication or limiting it to task-related matters. Communication is often antagonistic, characterized by high face threats and competitive conflict. We'll have more to say about LMX theory in the chapter on leadership.

Sometimes in-group relationships between superiors and subordinates develop beyond work relationships to become friendships. Such *blended relationships*[33] can be beneficial to both parties. For example, Nancy Boyd and Robert Taylor argue that the "highest quality work experiences for both leader and follower potentially occur when both a close leader-follower friendship and a high LMX are present."[34] However, blended relationships present special challenges, too, both for superiors and subordinates. For example, the *impartiality–favoritism dialectic* is especially prominent, since superiors usually do not want to give the impression of giving preferential treatment to friends. Subordinates may feel uncomfortable being labeled the boss's "pet" if it's widely known that the blended relationship exists.[35]

Trust is a key element of strong superior-subordinate relationships, just as it is in most other types of relationships.[36] While it is difficult to state a universal set of principles that determine effective superior-subordinate relationships, one of the founders of organizational communication, Charles Redding, attempted to do so. Trust is central to Redding's framework. Based on a series of studies on the communicative characteristics of effective supervisors, Redding concluded that more competent supervisors are:

1. *"Communication-minded."* For example, they enjoy talking and speaking in meetings, they are able to explain instructions and policies, and they enjoy conversing with subordinates.
2. *Empathic listeners*. They respond understandingly to so-called "silly" questions from employees. They are approachable and will listen to suggestions and complaints with an attitude of fair consideration and willingness to take appropriate action.
3. *Persuasive*. They tend (with some notable exceptions) to "ask" or "persuade," in preference to "telling" or "demanding."
4. *Sensitive* to the feelings of others. For example, they are careful to reprimand in private rather than in public.
5. *Open*. They share information and give advance notice of impending changes, explaining the "reasons why" behind policies and regulations.[37]

Substantial research suggests that effectiveness in superior-subordinate relations also depends on situational factors. Like effective communicators generally, effective superiors have to adapt their communication to target listeners as well as to the context.

Peer relationships. The relationships we form with peers—both within and external to the organizations in which we work—are critical to our career success and to the quality of our work lives. Coworkers are often a source of information and guidance, as well as emotional support. In addition, relationships with professional peers outside one's employing organization may be as important to one's satisfaction and success as relationships internal to the organization. On the other hand, while we usually think of peer relationships as a positive thing, close connections to others can provide the organization with a form of unobtrusive control by providing a reason for people to stay with the organization and not risk upsetting the status quo for fear of losing valuable relationships.[38]

While there has been much more research on superior-subordinate relationships, most of us interact more with coworkers than with supervisors. This may be increasingly the case as organizations move toward flatter structures and team-based work arrangements. Relationships with peers can be quite influential in shaping attitudes, beliefs, and assumptions. As we have emphasized in the previous two chapters, identities and cultures are socially constructed entities. As people interact with coworkers on the job, they jointly construct beliefs about the organization, the work they do, and each other. For example, some research suggests that peers' expressed attitudes toward work are more influential than that of supervisors.[39] One study demonstrated that peers within teams of university students working together on summer jobs co-constructed norms for what constituted competent supervisory communication.[40] Thus, in what may seem like a strange twist, subordinates can sometimes set standards for supervisors.

Relationships with peers can take multiple forms, ranging from enemies, to casual work relationships, to friendships, to romantic partners.[41] And of course, relationships are dynamic, moving to different states as we interact, subtly negotiating the dialectical tensions in the relationships. Relationships typically begin as casual work relationships, but may develop into other forms. Organizational communication researchers Patricia Sias and Daniel Cahill[42] interviewed pairs of coworker-friends to explore the factors that led them to become friends (from their initial, casual work relationships) and the ways their communication changed as their relationships deepened. Their analysis showed that the most prominent factors contributing to their relationship development, as well as their patterns of communication, changed as the pairs became closer friends:

> Friendships tended to develop early due to the co-workers simply being around one another, working together on shared projects and tasks, and perceiving common ground. At this point the variety of communication topics discussed increased; however the co-workers were somewhat cautious about sharing information and opinions with one another. Relationships developed into close friendships usually because of important personal or work-related problems, although perceived similarity and extra-organizational socializing continued to impact relational development. At this point, the co-worker became a trusted source of support with communication becoming increasingly more intimate and less cautious. Over time, this trend continued into the third transition where the co-workers became an important part of each other's personal and work life.[43]

As we discussed earlier in this chapter, sometimes we value relationships in and of themselves and sometimes we value them because we see them as means to an end (the *instrumentality–affection dialectic*). Often in organizations, relationships are strategically developed to help individuals accomplish personal or professional goals, ranging from garnering social support to attaining promotions. For example, one study found that fast-track women managers strategically sought two kinds of relationships: close, instrumental relationships with others inside the organization and relationships with women outside the organization. The internal relationships were intended to increase men's comfort with them and to lessen gender bias; the external relationships were intended to share strategies for overcoming obstacles unique to women.[44] As organizational communication scholar Fredric Jablin says, communication among peers may serve either *formal-organizational functions* (such as communication focused on task accomplishment) or *psychological-individual functions* (such as communication that meets one's need for affiliation).[45] Our individual relationships with peers are the building blocks of our social and professional networks and an important element in the quality of our work lives.

Internal-external relationships. When we think of workplace relationships, we often think first of relationships between coworkers or between superiors and subordinates. But there are many important relationships that bridge the "internal-external divide." People in organizations sometimes consider relationships with suppliers, consultants, and customers as important as their "internal" relationships. Several recent trends reinforce the importance of such relationships.

First, there is an increased emphasis on being "customer-driven" in the last decade or so. Businesses, as well as government organizations, often organize with the key principle of being "close to the customer" or "customer responsive." Such organizational strategies place immense value on creating close relationships with customers and potential customers. One manager in a city government organization we studied occasionally invited "customers" (local citizens) to meetings to be interviewed by his staff to find out what his department was doing well and where it could improve.[46] A clear example of a trend toward being customer responsive is what marketing professionals call "customer relationship marketing" and "relationship selling." These terms refer to a strategy that assumes that successful sales and marketing result from developing close relationships with key customers and clients, solidifying sales and identifying opportunities for repeat business. For example, many organizations spend substantial sums for their staff to entertain clients and potential clients, assuming that such money is well spent if close relationships develop that then result in sales.

Because of the importance of customer relationships, organizations spend substantial sums to train staff to initiate and manage these relationships. The Disney organization is renowned for its orientation and training of new employees—"the cast" as Disney refers to members of its organization.[47] Many companies, particularly service organizations, use training programs to teach employees to develop positive and upbeat (although brief and superficial) relational interactions with customers. Sales and service staff are employed and trained to perform "emotional labor" (discussed in chapter 3), a key task of which is to convey positive emotions such as happiness, excitement, or a sense of fun. The training is an example of the "technologizing" discourse discussed in box 6.1 Workers are taught specific strategies and tactics for performing emotion work (see box 4.9). The training typically encourages the use of a personal, informal, conversational style—the style we might use with close friends—and is intended to make customers feel special and connected to the organization's employees (and thus, to the organization). This is what we referred to as the synthetic personalization of communication. While such emotional labor is often effective in creating a positive experience for customers, it can be stressful to employees.[48] And, some critics argue that emotional labor can have more serious negative consequences than stress. Workers may become more callous or manipulative in their other relationships. As a result, society can be negatively affected by the technologizing of relational encounters, perhaps becoming more cynical, or perhaps expecting superficial relationships and synthetic personalization to be the norm.[49]

With postmodern irony, marketing professor Stephen Brown from the University of Ulster, Northern Ireland, suggests that today's customers are sick and tired of customer relationship marketing (CRM)[50] and its implications for their shopping experience. People, he claims "miss the days when a transaction was just a transaction, when purchasing a bar of soap didn't mean entering into a lifetime value relationship." Customers, he continues, want old-fashioned products and services and old-fashioned marketing. "Wary of CRM-inspired tactics, which are tantamount to stalking, they appreciate the true transparency of a blatant huckster." Rather than listening to customers in order to give them what they want (customers, he claims, neither know what they want or what they don't want), Brown proposes a retro approach to marketing that implies new relationships between producers and their customers based on exclusivity, secrecy, amplification, entertainment, and tricks. While some may question his unconventional and rather cynical view of the market, his perspective brings fresh air into a field that keeps importing—and thus diluting—notions and perspectives from real relationships, like dialogue and interactivity.[51]

A second set of trends likely to promote more internal-external relationships has to do with changing organizational forms. Organizations have attempted to become "leaner," often outsourcing some functions that would formerly have been performed internally or hiring contract workers from temporary agencies such as Manpower (now the single largest employer in the United States). A closely related trend is that organizations today often "partner" with suppliers and vendors, developing long-term relationships with other companies. (We return to these trends later in this chapter in the discussion of network organizations.) These two trends make it more likely that staff in one company will have ongoing working relationships with staff from another company. In fact, people employed by an outside company often work for a year or more on the premises of another company, working more closely with staff from the host company than they do with staff from their own company. While internal-external relationships may be analyzed and influenced by many of the same constructs—dialectics, communication competencies, and so on—they take on their own special dynamics. Our main point here is to encourage you to think of work relationships more broadly and more critically.

Changing and Reframing Relationships

Often, relationships change from one form to another without a great deal of conscious thought or intention as people interact over time. As people respond to the ebbs and flows of the dialectical tensions in their relationships, relationships evolve to a point where reframing is necessary, for example, re-labeling workmates as friends. However, sometimes relationships are reframed strategically. The many different kinds of relationships we experience in organizations can retain their initial characterization or they can morph into new types of relationships. If the frame we construct to categorize the nature of the relationship no longer adequately describes the roles, expectations, and obligations, we choose a new frame. Relationships are not "given" by the roles or positions we are assigned or develop. Rather, relationships evolve in response to individual, relational, and contextual factors. The variety of relationships and their dynamic nature is one of the joys—and one of the challenges—of organizational life.

Communication Networks

You have probably been advised to use your *network* of relationships to help your chances of landing a job. You may also already understand the value of developing and extending that network as a means for advancing your career. Such advice is predicated on the belief that networks of relationships can (a) make you aware of

Box 6.4 What's in a Name?

Citizens of a town or students of a university are often called "customers" and the executive group of an organization might be called the top management "team." Someone hired to work for an organization might be referred to as an associate, a colleague, a teammate, or even an internal customer, as well as an employee. *What strategies are behind such labels?*

Terms like "associate" and "colleague" have come into vogue through the trend of employee empowerment. Advocates of employee empowerment argue that employees should be treated as thinking, autonomous professionals and that "associate" and "colleague" symbolize the power and autonomy they are granted, as well as their relative equality to, and shared goals with, management. *Employee* highlights the fact that one is employed, but it also connotes being used for instrumental ends (as in to "employ" a tool or procedure).

Teammate obviously comes from the trend to structure organizations into work teams, and highlights the team-based relationship of employees to each other and their shared goals (since team is usually defined as a group of interdependent people working toward a common goal). This term also is intended to create a positive image of one's role, since we associate it with sports, leisure, and fun.

Internal customer comes from the push to be customer-oriented. The logic of this reframing is to highlight that each person in the organization provides services to others and is provided services by others.[52] If they are considered "customers," they should be treated with the same importance accorded external customers.

Each of these terms frames employees' identities and relationships to highlight certain aspects of their roles and to redefine their relationships to the organization, to management, or to each other. Of course, just giving someone a different name by itself doesn't change the person's job, relationships, or identity.

What would need to happen to make these changes meaningful? What are the potential drawbacks to such re-labeling? Which labels seem the most "real" or authentic to you?

opportunities, (b) pass on valuable knowledge of trends or events that may affect your career, and (c) act as a base of influence to help you take advantage of opportunities as they arise. Organizations that emphasize relationship marketing may actively encourage network building by their members. Thus, professionals who depend on relationship marketing often strategically join social and professional clubs and have an active social schedule in order to develop their professional networks.

Most of the discussion in the first part of this chapter focused on relationships between two individuals, *dyads*. Dyads are the building blocks for communication networks, by which we mean patterns of contact between individuals that are created by exchanging messages.[53] The last part of this chapter is devoted to exploring the role of communication networks in and between organizations. First, we'll take a look at networks of individuals, then we'll take a look at networks of organizations or, more simply put, network organizations.

Network linkages are created through people communicating with each other and establishing relationships. A single individual can be part of many communication networks. Some of these networks may be comprised totally of members of the organization such as a group of young professionals who socialize together or a group of people in various parts of the organization who have a strong interest in a particular technology. The same individual may belong to networks comprised of people totally unconnected to the organization, such as a community improvement association or a church group. The individuals may belong to groups that include people from "inside" *and* "outside" the organization such as professional associations that may include colleagues and others.

Network analysis has a long history in organizational communication studies, just as it has been used in a variety of other fields ranging from studies of political socialization (e.g., "How do we predict your voting patterns by knowing the people with whom you associate") to mental health (e.g., "How do we understand your difficulties with respect to your roles in certain networks of family and friends and coworkers?"). Network studies began in the 1940s and '50s when social researchers asked school children to name "your best friends in this class." Today, network analysis is amazingly sophisticated and combines examinations of the content of messages with the nature of linkages between people (or "nodes") in a system. Network analysis is useful for assessing the flow of communication in a group or organization, the strengths of relationships, and the topics discussed. For example, if you were trying to influence a group of people to accept a major organizational change, a network analysis could give you a sense of how information flows in the organization, who the key opinion leaders or gatekeepers of information are, and who is outside the network and thus not privy to regular information updates. Interestingly, the very idea of "networks" is now a part of everyday vocabulary, borrowed originally from television networks and then applied to an array of social and technologically mediated interconnections.

Network concepts such as those listed in box 6.5 can be useful to analyze the communication patterns within a group or even an entire organization (see appendix for a template for analysis). Researchers have used these concepts to understand the structural and process features of groups and organizations. For example, sociologist Mark Granovetter developed an insightful analysis based on the "strength of weak ties"[54]—which has to do with network density and strength. Granovetter argues that while we typically value strong ties, for some purposes we should value and cultivate weak ties. For organizations to be innovative, for example, weak ties are essential. Apply this reasoning to your own experiences. Think about those with whom you have the strongest ties—your closest friends; they are likely to share your views, have access to many of the same information sources, and so on. Where do you encounter challenges to your taken-for-granted routines and assumptions? We are more likely to be exposed to very different points of view and different information sources from those with whom we have weak ties—people such as occasional acquaintances or friends of friends. Additionally, the concept of network density has applications in job-seeking (where weak ties are often the ones that give you the most leads), grieving (where individuals tend to need some "new blood" in their social networks after an initial period of loss), and innovation (where new ideas often come from comparatively removed or distant sources).

Communication scholar Richard Farace and colleagues differentiated three important types of networks in organizations. First, there are *production* networks, which exist primarily to accomplish work tasks. Second are *innovation* networks, which emerge around the creation, development, and diffusion of new ideas. Finally, *maintenance* networks exist to develop and maintain social relationships. Of course, these types may overlap, such as when a group of coworkers in a production network begin to bond and socialize together, forming a maintenance network. Often, however—and this is where network analysis can be particularly helpful—there will be

Box 6.5 Key Concepts in Network Analysis[55]

Network roles (the positions that individuals occupy within networks).

- *Group or clique members*: those connected to others through interaction
- *Isolate*: an individual who doesn't regularly interact with others
- *Bridge*: an individual who is a member of two or more groups
- *Liaison*: an individual who interacts with two or more groups but is not a member of them
- *Communication Star*: an individual who is highly central to a network; stars are key points of contact for their group
- *Gatekeeper*: an individual who controls the flow of communication between parts of a network

Dimensions of analysis for individuals

- *Centrality*: the degree to which an individual is "at the crossroads of information flow" in a group[56]
- *Connectedness*: the number of contacts an individual has
- *Range or diversity*: number of links with individuals different from oneself
- *Accessibility*: the degree to which an individual can easily communicate with others in his/her network

Dimensions of analysis for dyads

- *Strength*: the amount of interaction between two individuals
- *Symmetry*: degree to which the exchange of support or resources is relatively equal or unequal
- *Direction*: degree to which communication is from actor A to B, or vice versa.
- *Stability*: degree to which the tie has lasted over a period of time
- *Multiplexity*: degree to which the actors interact on more than one issue, or for more than one reason
- *Openness*: degree to which the individuals in a dyad have interaction with others outside the dyad

Dimensions of analysis for whole networks (Note that some of these can be applied to dyads, just as some of the dyadic dimensions can be applied to networks.)

- *Size*: number of individuals in the network
- *Heterogeneity*: extent to which members in the network are similar or different from each other
- *Mode of communication*: the primary means by which members communicate
- *Density*: the ratio of actual to possible within-group links
- *Clustering*: degree to which the network is composed of subgroups or cliques

differences, sometimes subtle and sometimes blatantly obvious, between such networks. Finding the isolates, the bridges, and other network indicators can help us understand why a network is functioning well or not.

Communities of Practice

One interesting form of network in the workplace today is what has been labeled "communities of practice." These are networks of relationships that bind people together with a focus on particular projects or professional interests. Etienne Wenger and William Snyder define community of practice as "a group of people informally bound together by shared expertise and passion for a joint enterprise."[57] Consulting firms, who sometimes work within client organizations for months or even years, propagate such communities. Consultants and their clients may come to see themselves as coworkers after working together for relatively long, intense periods on projects. Similarly, contract employees may become part of a community of practice as they work on long-term projects. Wenger and Snyder argue that people in organizations form communities of practice for a variety of reasons—to maintain connections with peers when the company reorganizes; to respond to external changes such as e-commerce; or to meet new challenges when the company changes strategy. Whatever the basis for forming the community, members share knowledge creatively. The free-flowing exchange fosters new approaches to problems.[58] Wenger and Snyder emphasize that communities of practice are emergent, not created. However, organizations that value innovation and knowledge sharing should create the conditions for them to flourish and nurture their growth.[59]

Box 6.6 A Case Study of "Virtual Community"

There are three major arguments about the state of community in the modern world. The *community lost* argument holds that traditional forms of community are rapidly eroding (that is, membership in civic organizations is declining). The *community saved* argument finds that traditional forms of community have merely shifted (for example, in the United States, involvement in little league baseball teams has shifted to youth soccer)[60] Finally, the *community-liberated* argument contends that traditional forms of community are being replaced by entirely new forms.

Central to the community liberated idea is the emergence of a relatively new form of social organization, the online community. Coined "virtual communities," this form of organization has been the center of a heated debate, revolving mainly around the question of whether members of such collectives are capable of forming relationships meaningful and sustainable enough to be properly termed communities.

Communication scholar Dan Lair studied one such online community, dedicated to the trading of live concert recordings: Phishhook.com.[61] Phishhook provides its roughly 25,000 members with Web space to store their collection of concert recordings and a series of discussion boards, where members can talk about everything from their hobby to hockey games. Several of Lair's findings illustrate the nature of this kind of community.

Members do connect in meaningful ways, often using the discussion boards to arrange meetings at concerts. From these meetings, stories of parties, lasting friendships, and even the occasional romantic relationship subsequently circulate on the discussion boards.

A strong set of norms operates, affording members a high degree of trust when investing their time, money, and energy in trades with partners whom they have usually never met in person.

Members share a value system, connected to the music they trade, which encourages them not only to "spread the music" but also to "spread the good vibes" associated with music.

"Community" is used in members' discourse to highlight the connection between members, encouraging positive behaviors and discouraging negative ones. Interestingly, members who act aggressively on the discussion boards (often referred to derisively as "trolls"), frequently argue that Phishhook is not a "real community," but rather "just a discussion board."

Think about the characteristics of communities in the "real world." Where are these communities? How do community members interact with one another? To what extent does the "community experience" translate into the online world? Why do members of online groups refer to themselves as "communities"?

Interorganizational Relationships

Some of the most important organizational relationships involve people, resources and procedures from several organizations. In order to conduct their businesses, a growing number of organizations are entering into more or less formal relationships with other organizations. Sometimes such relationships are short term and loosely formed; at other times, they become long-lasting partnerships.

Interorganizational relationships are established for a host of reasons, including strategic, institutional, symbolic, personal, etc. Although such relationships vary in intensity, closeness, and scope of collaboration, they are typically designed to increase the competitiveness of the involved partners by creating synergy between their individual resources, strategies, and skills. Most writers, however, seem to agree that interorganizational relationships are established primarily because organizations hope (1) to reduce risk and uncertainty by linking up with other players in the market and (2) to improve their resource base, including both material resources and the information they use to guide their decisions and actions.

Many organizations today find that their plans and strategies increasingly depend on the decisions of other organizations, that the problems they face are bigger than they alone can solve, and that their attempts to manage environmental contingencies often create unanticipated problems.[62] With increased environmental complexity and turbulence, organizations expand their boundary-spanning activities to include collaboration with other organizations. Barbara Gray defined collaboration in interorganizational domains as "the pooling of appreciations and/or tangible resources, e.g. information, money, labor, etc., by two or more stakeholders to solve a set of problems which neither of them can solve individually."[63] Collaboration, Gray points out, is based on the recognition that organizational activities are truly interdependent and that organizations in order to reduce risk and uncertainty need to come together to identify salient problems, develop shared interpretations of the situation and generate joint frameworks to structure and, eventually, control the situation.

Box 6.7 Some Types of Interorganizational Relationships

Strategic Alliance: a close association of organizations, formed to advance common interests or causes

Coalition: alliance, typically temporary, between business organizations

Cartel: combination of independent business organizations formed to regulate production, pricing, and marketing of goods by the members

Conglomerate: a corporation made up of a number of different companies that each operate in a specific market

Joint Venture: partnerships or conglomerates, often formed to share risk or expertise

Licensing: official or legal permissions to manufacture a product developed and owned by another organization

Franchise: authorization granted to someone to sell or distribute a company's goods or services in a certain area

Research Consortium: an association or a combination, as of businesses, financial institutions, or investors, for the purpose of engaging in research of common interest

Network Organization: two or more organizational units involved in a (semi-)formalized long-term relationship

In addition to risk reduction, interorganizational relationships offer participating organizations access to resources (material, information, know how), technologies, markets, skills, or scale economies that would otherwise be beyond the reach of a single organization.[64] Indeed, the relationships between organizations may well be termed "access relationships"[65] because they extend the reach of individual organizations. For example, since most cars today have fairly sophisticated information technologies, a producer of automobiles may establish a partnership with a producer of computer chips in order to stay competitive.

Interorganizational relationships may also help organizations share important knowledge, so-called "intellectual capital." A buzzword for this type of knowledge sharing is "c-commerce" (collaborative commerce). Collaborative commerce refers to the development of interorganizational teamwork, where organizations open their internal information systems to their business partners. A Danish producer of work clothes (uniforms), for example, has access to databases of several of its major customers including the police and the postal service. C-commerce also exists where several organizations collaborate on the development of a new product.

Interorganizational relationships are also used to build public confidence in the value of an organization's products or services. By linking up with well-known and respected partners, organizations entering relationships hope to attract customers and other corporate partners, develop their reputations and, perhaps, improve their performance.[66] In order to improve the quality of its customer orientation, JCPenney, for example, sends point-of-sale information not only to its suppliers but also to its suppliers' suppliers.[67]

One useful way to understand interorganizational relationships is in terms of vertical or horizontal integration. Organizations are *vertically integrated* when one organization provides parts or services needed by the other organization in order for it to produce or deliver its products or services. Intel, for example, provides the processors for many computers today. Conversely, organizations are *horizontally integrated* when their customers are passed from one organization to the other in the service cycle. Some physical therapy clinics, for example, are horizontally integrated with hospitals in the sense that patients are referred to those clinics when discharged from the hospital.

We can also distinguish interorganizational relationships by identifying two general types: *symbiotic* and *pooling* relationships.[68] In symbiotic relationships the partners combine different yet complementary products, resources or capabilities to form an entity that is qualitatively different from each of the participating organizations. This is the case when, for example, Procter & Gamble (a consumer-goods company) and Wal-Mart (a retailer) invest in a joint information system in order to coordinate their different activities and competencies (production and sales, respectively).[69] Sometimes, symbiotic relationships also involve public organizations. For example, universities form strategic partnerships with industries and governments in order to facilitate innovation. In pooling relationships, by contrast, the cooperation partners bring in *similar* resources and capabilities in order to realize economies of scale or to augment their quantitative presence and power in the marketplace. For example, Scandinavian Airlines System (SAS) has established alliances with several other airlines, including Thai Airways, Singapore Airlines, and United Airlines. The resulting pooled relationship is dramatically called "The Star Alliance."

Since these types of interorganizational relations are established for different reasons, they imply different kinds of challenges to the organizations involved. While symbiotic relationships are established to exploit complementary differences and facilitate mutual learning, these very same processes potentially undermine such relationships. If, for example, one of the partners learns faster or more effectively than the other(s), the differences and mutual interdependencies that gave rise to the relationship in the first place may disappear and thus propel that partner to leave the relationship or, alternatively, to take over the other organization(s). As a consequence, organizations in symbiotic relationships may choose to be very strategic and selective in the way they disclose information to their partners. Indeed, such selectivity may be a prerequisite for the organizations to retain their specific identity and, thus, survival within the alliance. Interorganizational relationships, thus, are highly dynamic and often need to be revaluated and adjusted. As organizational sociologist Mark Ebers[70] points out:

> Because in an inter-organizational relationship the partner organizations regularly exchange resources and information, the parties' resource and information bases indeed are affected by the inter-organizational relationship. The outcomes of an inter-organizational relationship thus change the conditions under which the cooperating organizations act.

Box 6.8 Voices from The Field

Assembling Cross-Skill Teams with "IKNOW"

Noshir Contractor, University of Illinois at Urbana-Champaign

Information technologies provide alternative (potentially less hierarchical) tools for intra- and inter-organizational coordination. Yet, the pervasiveness of Internet technologies makes it increasingly difficult for individuals to discern the scope and shape of their "virtual" knowledge networks.[71] In other words, while information technologies can greatly expand networks for information gathering and problem solving, the range and patterns of these networks become less visible to the participants. Specifically, it is increasingly difficult for individuals to accurately determine: "Who knows who?" "Who knows who knows who?" "Who knows what?" and "Who knows who knows what?"

Together with colleagues at the University of Illinois at Urbana-Champaign,[72] I have developed "community-ware" or "collaborative filtering" tools that are especially beneficial for assembling cross-skill teams to address specific tasks or projects. By visualizing knowledge networks, the IKNOW (Inquiring Knowledge Networks On the Web) community-ware tool helps people identify potential collaboration partners. The knowledge network links could be based on shared interest, expertise, membership in professional associations, co-occurrence of words between individuals' Web sites, links from one individual's Web site to another's, or links from two individuals' Web sites to the same third party Web sites.

IKNOW helps enhance individuals' ability to access an organization's knowledge network. (For articles, presentations, and samples of IKNOW sites, see http://iknow.spcomm.uiuc.edu.) IKNOW can assist in creating, sustaining, and growing knowledge networks by providing (1) a set of visual tools to inspect, identify, and critically analyze the existing and potential collaborations; (2) the ability to track the growth characteristics of the knowledge network including its size, density of interconnections, and content areas; and (3) the ability to efficiently and effectively identify potential partners who share common or complementary interests. Versions of IKNOW have been designed for use in a number of settings, including the PrairieNet Community Networking project, Illinois Tourism, and a U.S. Army installation.

Still, interorganizational relationships may be stable for other reasons. For example, partner-specific investments (such as specific computer hardware or software) may lock the partners into existing relationships. Or, an organization may rely on multiple links if it does not have sufficient information to make new decisions on its own. Finally, personal relations between individuals in the partnering organizations may prevent the organizations from investigating possibilities for partnerships with other organizations. Ebers argues that symbiotic interorganizational relationships are more stable if the relationship involves complex processes that organizations cannot replicate on their own. Management scholars David Whetten and Howard Aldrich suggest that interorganizational relationships characterized by "multiplex linkages" (that is, connections between the partnering organizations on multiple dimensions) are more likely to be stable than those connected only by "uniplex" (one-dimensional) strands.[73] Interorganizational relationships, in other words, are more stable the more the partnering organizations have to talk about. Interorganizational relationships based on friendship or professional affiliation between individuals in the participating organizations are more likely to continue; in fact, they often become the basis for more formalized partnerships.

The Network Organization

The network organization can be regarded as the pinnacle of interorganizational relations. Network organizations are comprised of two or more organizational units from different organizations involved in a long-term, and more or less formalized, relationship. The relationships of network organizations are often global in scope and reach.[74] The typical objective of a (global) network organization is to bring together the resources controlled by different organizations to create a new and stronger organization, one that is better equipped for a new market, a new technology or a new service.

Network organizations typically emerge from relationships among individuals or groups of individuals rather than from formal organizational structures. In contrast to the emergent networks discussed in relation to individuals, however, several dimensions of a network organization's life—e.g., its legitimate authority, its strategies, and its visions—are prescribed and imposed by management and reflected in organizational charts and formal contracts.[75] In other words, as the network is formalized, its emergent nature is usually contained within a narrower frame of control. Still, compared to the traditional organizational hierarchy, the network organization is highly flexible.

Before the 1980s, markets in the Western world were typically dominated by large, hierarchically organized firms that were able to obtain and sustain advantages of scale through growth, central planning, and control. Often, those companies were able to use their size and experience to expand into—and to dominate—overseas markets as well. Many such firms still exist. Their advantages, however, are gradually waning. Although the efficiency traditionally associated with scale economies is still central in today's market, contemporary firms also need to be flexible and adaptable in order to stay in business. This change can be attributed to a number of related developments, such as globalization, technological change, deregulation, and demographic changes in the workforce.[76]

New information technologies eliminate, to a large extent, the constraints of time and space (see chapter 12). New technologies shorten product life cycles and lower barriers to market entry. The latter trend is augmented by recent legal, policy, and deregulation changes. Globalization (see chapter 13) has intensified competition and lowered profit margins. Add to these market conditions the demographic fact that the workforce of the Western world is generally becoming older, and the need for organizations to become flexible without losing the advantages of scale economies is evident.

Core Competencies

Many organizations today focus on the functions for which they have expert skill—their *core competencies*—and *outsource* those activities that can be performed more quickly or cheaply by others. When organizations learn to do "fewer things better with less"[77] they simultaneously need to search globally for opportunities, resources, and partners. Often this search leads to vertical integration, the formation of strategic networks and alliances with companies *upstream* or *downstream* on the value chain. Upstream integration means developing ties of coordination with suppliers, while downstream integration means developing ties of coordination with distributors and customers. For example, the first firm in a network may research, plan, and design a product; the second may engineer and manufacture it; while the third, fourth, and fifth may handle marketing, sales, distribution, and service.

Box 6.9 The Case of Cisco and the Value Chain

Organizations today place a great deal of emphasis on value chain analysis and the creation of a network of alliances. These two features are closely related. Value chain analysis starts with the recognition that a series of events happens in the creation and delivery of a product or service, and each of these events can be seen as a link in the value chain. That is, each event contributes value to the process. So, to oversimplify a bit, a manufactured products business (for example, tires or computers) involves research and development, purchasing and procurement, design and engineering, manufacturing and production, sales and marketing, and finally, delivery and distribution. When organizations engage in value chain analysis, they ask, "On which parts in the value chain do we want to focus our business?" That is, where do we as an organization want to add value and extract value? What are we good at and what is sustainable? Then, they may decide to be involved in some links in the chain and to create a network of partners to handle the other parts.

A clear example of this is Cisco, which is often praised as the prototypical "New Economy" Corporation. For example, there are 38 factories making Cisco products. Cisco owns two of them. Many Cisco products sold are never touched or seen by a Cisco employee. Rather, Cisco contracts with partner organizations to do much of the manufacturing and distribution of its products (mostly, computer networking equipment). Cisco focuses on those parts of the value chain that they consider their specialties—their core competencies, which include the design and marketing of products. Then, they *outsource* the other functions in the value chain, including manufacturing and distribution, to partner organizations.[78] This trend for organizations to outsource all but core competencies to create a network organization is referred to as "*dis*-aggregation," which some pundits describe as a central characteristic of the new economy.[79]

Some authors believe there is as much evidence for aggregation as for dis-aggregation—in other words organizations joining together in mergers and acquisitions.[80] Can you find examples of both trends? Which seems to be dominant? What are the possible social and economic consequences of dis-aggregation?

By choosing the right partners, organizations operating in networks hope to be both efficient and flexible and to remain competitive throughout the value chain. Efficiency is attained by housing specialized expertise in specific locations, and adaptiveness is secured by networking with many different specialized organizations. In addition, many network organizations now establish clear performance measures for internal divisions so that their performance can be continuously compared to that of external suppliers. Often this implies converting each division into a business unit that is encouraged or forced to sell their products on the open market. Charles Snow, Raymond Miles, and Henry Coleman describe the philosophy behind this system:

> For the network to operate properly each of its nodes must interact regularly with outsiders—trading, buying, or selling products or raw material to other firms in order to bring real prices to bear on internal transactions. Thus, inside the company, clusters of business units, grouped by region and product category, can be seen buying and selling from one another as well as from outside firms.[81]

As competition intensifies in the twenty-first century, organizations will regularly be subjecting their activities to so-called "market tests"—that is, letting virtually all departments compete with external providers—in order to justify their ownership. How do you imagine that the introduction of such regular market tests will affect life in contemporary organizations and the way their members communicate? (Think both in terms of interpersonal and interdepartmental communication and in terms of how organizations collect and use information from the environment.) What do you see as the advantages of this trend? What are the possible pitfalls?

Although network organizations are usually established in order to meet a number of critical needs—like getting access to technologies, products, skills, and knowledge—the implications for the organizations involved are considerably more far-reaching than these functional goals. In particular, ideas of "organization" and "environment" need to be redefined considerably. As we have seen, organizations are traditionally regarded as bounded entities defined by their physical structures, their resources, their markets, and their legal statuses. Following this line of thought, an organization's environment is understood as *non*-organization, that is, everything that is not comprised by these definitions. In the network perspective, however, it becomes meaningless to disconnect the organization from its environment. Although all groups and organizations create their identity through interaction with their surroundings, this is especially the case for the network organization that explicitly defines itself through a complex set of *interdependencies*.

In contrast to the traditional, hierarchical firm, the network organization is embedded in a web of relationships that is not simply external to the organization but integral to its definition and existence. While resources, for example, traditionally considered "internal" to the organization are now available to partners in the network and thus not entirely controllable by the organization itself, a number of resources from *other* organizations in the network, typically seen as "external," now become subject to the organization's influence and control. In fact, one could claim that the network *itself* is one of the organization's most valuable resources.[82] By making resources and activities available to the organization, the network becomes an integral part of the organization's definition. As a consequence, the notion of organizational boundaries changes its meaning quite radically.

Box: 6.10 The Domesticated Market

A quarter of a century ago, marketing theorist Johan Arndt declared that the buying and selling process in the Western world had become domesticated.[83] The traditional image of competition in the marketplace determining success or failure is gradually being eroded from within. Arndt claims the vagaries of unrestrained competition are being replaced by voluntary, long-term, and binding commitments among a growing number of organizations. Within such arrangements—which we have called network organizations—transactions are "tamed." By internalizing a large number of market transactions within its boundaries, network organizations transform the anonymous market clearing process into an administrative procedure where routines and agreed-upon rules replace market negotiation. As Arndt puts it: "More and more transactions are conducted not in ad hoc promiscuousness, but in the context of often surprisingly stable long-term corporate matrimonies, allowing for some discreet asides."[84]

Think of examples of network organizations that support Johan Arndt's notion of domesticated markets. Think of limitations to Arndt's perspective based on what you know about contemporary organizations.

Communication in Interorganizational Relationships

No matter how interorganizational relationships are organized, they challenge our conventional notions about organizational communication. Traditional organizational structures were developed to simplify and minimize communication needs; indeed, they sometimes were a substitute for communication (as discussed in chapter 2). In contrast, we expect interorganizational relationships to be highly communication intensive.[85] This is especially true for global network organizations that depend on sophisticated communication linkages between its partnering organizations.[86]

Organizational communication scholar Eric Eisenberg and his colleagues distinguished between "types" and "levels" of interorganizational linkages.[87] They identified two *types* of interorganizational linkages: material and information. *Material* refers to the flow of tangibles (money, goods, and personnel); *information* refers to symbolic exchanges (data, ideas, goodwill). One organization, for example, may lend equipment (or some of its members) to another organization. Or it may make its databases available to its business partners—as in the case of c-commerce mentioned above.

Eisenberg and his colleagues found three *levels* of linkage: institutional, representative, and personal. An *institutional* linkage refers to exchanges of information or materials between organizations without the involvement of specific organizational roles or personalities, for example routine data transfers between banks. Although few studies treat institutional exchanges explicitly, such exchanges—where transactions occur automatically—are very important in contemporary organizations. In some countries, tax authorities, for example, automatically receive information about people's income. A *representative* linkage is when an official representative of one organization has contact with an official representative of another organization, for example in a negotiation situation. Representative linkages have been studied in terms of boundary role occupants or overlapping memberships. Boundary roles are occupied by people who represent the organization to its environment, including other organizations. Such people filter input and output, search for and collect information, represent the organization to external constituencies, and protect the organization by buffering it from external threats and pressures. For example, public relations professionals often represent organizations to the media, and employee relations professionals often represent organizations to unions. A *personal* linkage takes place when an individual from one organization exchanges information or material with an individual from another organization in a non-representative capacity. One example would be two marketing people who know each other through a professional association socializing or exchanging ideas. Personal linkages may sound less important than more formalized linkages; most decision makers, however, are aware of the fact that interorganizational relationships often depend on informal contacts and goodwill in the business community. A prime example is the weekly golf match between business leaders. In some countries, interorganizational relationships are often intermingled with kinship relations. Can you think of other examples of informal communication between people from different organizations?

Communication in interorganizational settings, and networks in particular, often cross traditional functional boundaries and hierarchical layers. Thus, information flows are potentially more efficient—fast and economical. The information exchanged, however, is simultaneously more complex. In addition to receiving information faster, current communication technologies allow their users to modify, enhance, or manipulate the received information in numerous ways.[88] As a consequence, the quality of communication exchanges becomes the most central concern in interorganizational relationships. Interorganizational communication centers around three important issues: trust, identity, and coordination.

Trust. When organizations establish far-reaching interdependencies with other organizations—implying mutual access to each other's information, skills, and resources—trust is an essential element in the relationship. Trust among organizational partners involves *goodwill*, *commitment*, and *equity*. Organizations need to trust that their partners enter the relationship with good intentions, that they are sincerely interested in contributing to the relationship, and that they are motivated to deal fairly. This is not always the case. Some organizations enter partnerships with the intention of absorbing the skills and activities of the other organizations, unfairly taking more than they contribute to the collaboration.

Trust is established through frequent communication between the partnering organizations. As Peter Ring and Andrew Van de Ven point out, "Trust in the goodwill of other parties is a cumulative product of repeated past interactions among parties through which they come to know themselves and evolve a common understanding of mutual commitments."[89] Trust often builds on interpersonal relationships already established between individuals in those organizations. The individuals may, for example, have established strong ties through a shared professional affiliation or through other shared interests. Or perhaps they are simply friends. The transition of trust from one type of relationship to another, however, is not easy. The fact that a person is willing to attribute sincerity and trustworthiness to another individual *as a person* does not necessarily imply that the same characteristics will be attributed to the individual in his or her role in the organization.[90] In fact, the very institutionalization of the relationship through a formal agreement may weaken the trust on which it was established in the first place.

Conversely, interorganizational relationships established through formal channels may over time develop into more informal relations. Research has shown that as interorganizational relationships become institutionalized, personal relationships gradually supplement formal role relationships, that psychological affiliations increasingly substitute for formal, legal contracts, and that over time formal agreements increasingly mirror informal understandings and agreements.[91] Formal and informal communication, thus, are interwoven in complex ways in interorganizational relationships. In fact, it may be argued that an imbalance between formal and informal processes may lead to dissolution of the interorganizational relationship.

While partners in an interorganizational relationship rely on trust, they may fear that the information they exchange will become accessible to competitors *outside* the network. As a consequence, the openness that organizations encourage within the network may be counterbalanced by carefully closing the network to outsiders.[92]

Identity. While transparency in transactions and decisions and an open communication climate between members of the partnership generally facilitate trust, it is equally important that each participating organization has a clear sense of itself and its stakes in the relationship. As we discussed in chapter 5, organizational identity has

Box. 6.11 Trust in Interorganizational Virtual Organizations

The importance of trust in interorganizational relationships is even more pronounced when the relationship only exists in a virtual environment. Eva Kasper-Fuehrer and Neal Ashkanasy define an interorganizational virtual organization as a "temporary network organization, consisting of independent enterprises (organizations, companies, institutions, or specialized individuals) that come together swiftly to exploit an apparent market opportunity. The enterprises utilize their core competencies in an attempt to create a best-of-everything organization in a value-adding partnership (VAP), facilitated by information and communication technology (ICT). Virtual organizations act in all appearances as a single organizational unit."[93] A good example is *Virtuelle Fabrik Euregio Bodensee* (www.virtuelle-fabrik.org), a virtual network of companies that helps other companies create temporary interorganizational relationships.

In contrast to other types of organizational relationships, the virtual organization lacks the dimension of nonverbal communication usually regarded as essential in trust building. As a consequence, this type of interorganizational relationship needs to find alternative ways to establish trust. Also, the absence of hierarchical control and a legal framework to regulate the formation, operation (and dissolution) of the organization makes producing and organizing trust in different ways even more important. Finally, the temporality of these types of virtual organizations makes trust building essential.

According to Kasper-Fuehrer and Ashkanasy, interorganizational virtual organizations must use what they call "appropriate ICT" to communicate trustworthiness among its members. Appropriate ICT, in this context, refers both to a technical and a human dimension. First, ICT equipment needs to be standardized, in terms of products and interfaces, to enable stability and reliability in the relationship. Second, it needs to allow its users to transmit as many nonverbal cues as possible, including facial expressions. The use of "emoticons"—such as :-) or :-(is one possibility. In addition to the use of appropriate ICT, interorganizational virtual organizations need to establish a *common business understanding* in order to compensate for the lack of legal sanctions and formal control. Such an understanding involves clear communication about what the partners stand for, about the nature of their business transactions (in terms of production, cooperation, and agreements), and about the expected outcomes of their relationship. Finally, Kasper-Fuehrer and Ashkanasy emphasize that high standards of *business ethics* are essential to build trust in these relationships. Such ethics can be established, of course, by agreeing on shared codes of ethics but also through concrete behavior such as payment habits.

become a growing issue for organizations of all kinds. Interorganizational relationships intensify this issue considerably. If given the option, many organizations would probably prefer not to engage in interorganizational relationships. Such relationships constrain their autonomy by limiting their actions and challenging their identity.[94] There is always the risk that one party absorbs the skills and activities of another party and abandons the network. In fact, this is often the case. For example, Zenith, a producer of television sets, lost the manufacturing and design of color television and VCR technology to its Korean partner Goldstar. General Electric lost several of its domestic home appliance products to its partner Samsung. Because of this risk, organizations are often advised to enter a network with clearly defined identities and strategic cores so that the competencies and skills in the network are truly complementary and so that each partner is considered indispensable by the others.[95]

On the other hand, it is through interaction with others that organizations develop their own identity. Through the process of projecting themselves onto their surroundings, organizations get to know themselves and appreciate their identity. Relationships with other organizations, thus, can be instrumental for organizations to develop their identities and core competencies. Think of examples of organizations with strong and unique identities that would be difficult for partners to emulate or take over. Then think of organizational identities that would be too vague or fragile to retain their autonomy within an interorganizational network.

Coordination. In contrast to the classical organization arrangement, interorganizational relationships typically have unclear lines of authority and control. As a consequence, processes of coordination within such relationships are potentially marked by confusion and ambiguity. Interorganizational relationships therefore require a strong commitment to cooperation. Although professionals are hard to supervise because they often are more loyal to their profession than to their organization,[96] coordination is crucial. While the motivation for organizations to enter relationships with other organizations is frequently to become more flexible, the reality of the new network is that activities—both within each organizational unit and across the network—must be monitored closely and coordinated precisely. As W. Graham Astley and Richard A. Brahm[97] put it:

> On the one hand, the need for greater flexibility is requiring organizations to disaggregate their activities and externalize certain functions to be performed by collaborating partners, domestically or internationally. On the other hand, the need for greater integration and coordination of activities across interdependent markets, industries and countries is requiring organizations to manage their exchange relationships through negotiated arrangements designed to stabilize operations.

To accomplish these tasks, many network firms have assigned key managers to operate across rather than within hierarchies, creating and assembling information, skills, and resources from all parties.[98] While one may question the implicit assumption that organizations in the network will be willing to fully disclose information to each other, the task of organizing information across the network and communicating it in relevant ways to all participants becomes a highly important activity in all phases of the network's life cycle. We conclude with an example (box 6.12) to help you think "outside the box" in terms of our traditional understandings of work relationships, organizational boundaries, and network linkages.

Box 6.12 Voices from the Field

The Case of Anti-Globalization Activism
Juliet Roper, The University of Waikato

The World Trade Organization (WTO) was set up in 1995, as a product of the Uruguay Round of GATT (General Agreement on Tariffs and Trade) talks. Its policies of deregulation and liberalization of markets and services beyond developed Western nations were supported and enforced by the World Bank and the International Monetary Fund (IMF). The introduction of the WTO coincided with growing criticism of the concept of a global free market, as the negative effects of free trade policies became evident: infringements of human and labor rights; public health and environmental issues in relation to food production and environmental damage. While the promise was of universal prosperity, there is now increasing evidence of growing poverty for many while small numbers of people accumulate vast wealth. As a result, the legitimacy of the policies and their supporters has been called into question.

The IMF, the World Bank, and the WTO have been slow to modify their policies, in spite of growing opposition that culminated in the protests in Seattle, 1999, at a WTO meeting of trade negotiators. These protests (and subsequent demonstrations in Quebec City and Genoa) were the result of individuals and organizations networking via the Internet. The Internet was the tool for disseminating information and organizing protesting factions. Most of the activist Internet sites are based on the premise that people can be empowered only if they have the information required first for awareness and then for debate on issues of public concern and if they have the means of joining together in sufficient numbers to influence public policy. The activist sites fulfilled both these requirements. Beyond the provision of information on what was happening in other parts of the world, the sites put people in touch with others of similar concerns and enabled them to coordinate protest action.

The global and national alliances that have developed through the agency of the Internet continue to grow in their capability of generating mass responses to events and policies that might otherwise have passed unnoticed. This was first apparent in the global protest against the proposed Multilateral Agreement on Investment (MAI) in 1998. As their power grows these networks of activists can increasingly exert pressure on organizations and corporations to bring their policies more in line with what is publicly acceptable and hence legitimate.

What is the nature of the power employed by Internet activists? Could the activists have exercised such power in other ways? What do you see as the future for Internet-based social movement organizing across international lines?

Snapshot Synthesis

The relationships we form are important for the success of our work—that is, accomplishing tasks—as well as for the quality of our work lives. These relationships are created, developed, sustained, and sometimes terminated through communication. The relationships form the building blocks of networks—from personal networks to organizational networks. In this chapter, we have tried to explore relationships and networks in their cultural and historical contexts. Understanding the dynamics of relationships and networks and developing skills for managing them are essential to our personal and professional effectiveness, as well as the effectiveness of organizations.

Key Concepts

- **Discourse "Conversationalization":** the tendency in contemporary times for discourse to be more informal and democratic, with less formality and fewer power markers
- **"Technologization" of Discourse:** the tendency in contemporary times for discourse to reflect more strategizing, based on research and/or training that focuses on communication techniques that are effective in achieving communicators' goals
- **Synthetic Personalization:** sometimes called "manufactured friendliness" this is a kind of emotional labor in which organizations train and encourage their employees to use a friendly, informal, conversational communication style with customers
- **Definition of the Situation:** a communicator's interpretation of the situation, which includes an understanding of the nature of the interaction, the goals of the interaction, and the nature of the relationships between or among the communicators
- **Multiple Communication Goals:** when people communicate, they *simultaneously* attempt to achieve instrumental or task goals (such as persuading or informing), identity goals (including self-presentation and treatment of the other party), and relationship goals (such as increasing or decreasing intimacy)
- **Intersubjectivity:** a mutually understood view of a situation or other phenomenon
- **Relational Dialectics:** tensions, or opposing forces, in any relationship that are both interdependent and mutually negating
- **Communication Competencies:** individuals' abilities that include social perception skills, message design skills, and interaction management
- **Leader-Member Exchange (LMX) Theory:** a theory that suggests (among other things) that superiors develop in-group relationships with some subordinates and out-group relationships with others
- **Blended Relationships:** relationships that combine both a work and personal relationship, such as a superior–subordinate dyad who are also friends
- **Formal-Organizational Function of Communication:** communication that serves formally sanctioned organizational purposes, such as communication focused on task accomplishment
- **Psychological-Individual Function of Communication:** communication that serves the needs of individual members, such as communication with peers that meets one's need for affiliation
- **Network Analysis:** analysis of the structural or process features of a network or networks, such as assessing the flow of communication in a group or organization, the strengths and types of relationships
- **Network Roles:** the positions that individuals occupy within networks
- **Strength of Weak Ties:** the idea that for some purposes, such as encouraging the flow of innovative ideas, we should value and cultivate weak ties in a network

- **Community of Practice:** a type of network of relationships that binds people together with a focus on particular projects or professional interests
- **Virtual Community:** a network of people with common interests who interact primarily online
- **Interorganizational Relationship:** a (typically formal) relationship formed by two or more organizations to share resources in order to achieve their individual and shared goals
- **Network Organization:** an organization that brings together the resources controlled by different organizations to create a new and stronger organization, one that is better equipped for a new market or a new service

Endnotes

[1] Jan Carlzon, *Moments of Truth* (Cambridge, MA: Ballinger, 1987).

[2] Brenda Gainer, "Ritual and Relationships: Interpersonal Influences on Shared Consumption," *Journal of Business Research* 32 (1995): 253–260.

[3] Connie J. G. Gersick, Jean M. Bartunek, and Jane E. Dutton, "Learning from Academia: The Importance of Relationships in Professional Life," *Academy of Management Journal* 43.6 (2000): 1026–1045.

[4] Peter Cappelli, Laurie Bassi, Harry Katz, David Knoke, Paul Osterman, and Michael Useem, *Change at Work: How American Industry and Workers Are Coping with Corporate Restructuring and What Workers Must Do to Take Charge of Their Own Careers* (New York: Oxford University Press, 1997) pp. 193–194.

[5] Norman Fairclough, *Critical Discourse Analysis: The Critical Study of Language* (London: Longman Publishers, 1995) p. 137.

[6] Fairclough, *Critical*, p. 137.

[7] Fairclough, *Critical*, p. 137.

[8] Norman Fairclough, *Discourse and Social Change* (Cambridge, UK: Polity Press, 1992).

[9] Fairclough, *Critical*, p. 136.

[10] Cappelli et al., p. 195–198.

[11] Arlie Russell Hochschild, *The Time Bind: When Work Becomes Home and Home Becomes Work* (New York: Henry Holt & Company, 1998).

[12] Donald W. Ball, "'The Definition of the Situation': Some Theoretical and Methodological Consequences of Taking W. I. Thomas Seriously," *Journal for the Theory of Social Behavior* 2 (1972): 61–82.

[13] Ruth Anne Clark and Jesse G. Delia, "Topoi and Rhetorical Competence," *Quarterly Journal of Speech* 65 (1979): 187–206.

[14] George J. McCall and J. L. Simmons, *Identities and Interaction: An Examination of Human Associations in Everyday Life* (New York: Free Press, 1978).

[15] H. Paul Grice, "Logic and Conversation," *Syntax and Semantics, Vol. 3: Speech Acts*, ed. Peter Cole and Jerry Morgan (New York: Academic Press, 1975) pp. 41–58.

[16] Leslie A. Baxter and Barbara M. Montgomery, "Rethinking Communication in Personal Relationships from a Dialectical Perspective," *Communication and Personal Relationships*, ed. Kathryn Dindia and Steven Duck (New York: John Wiley, 2000) pp. 31–53; see also Kenan Bridge and Leslie A. Baxter, "Blended Relationships: Friends as Work Associates," *Western Journal of Communication* 56 (1992): 200–225; and Theodore E. Zorn, "Bosses and Buddies: A Constructive/Dramaturgical Analysis of Simultaneously Close and Hierarchical Relationships in Organizations," *Under-Studied Relationships: Off the Beaten Track*, ed. Julia T. Wood and Steven Duck (Newbury Park, CA: Sage, 1995) pp. 122–147.

[17] Baxter and Montgomery, pp. 31–53.

[18] Bridge and Baxter, pp. 200–225; Zorn, pp. 122–147.

[19] Cappelli et al., pp. 8–9.

[20] Fredric M. Jablin and Patricia M. Sias, "Communication Competence," *The New Handbook of Organizational Communication: Advances in Theory, Research, and Methods*, ed. Fredric M. Jablin and Linda L. Putnam (Thousand Oaks, CA: Sage, 2001) pp. 819–864.

[21] Beverly Davenport Sypher and Theodore E. Zorn, "Communication Related Abilities and Upward Mobility: A Longitudinal Investigation," *Human Communication Research* 12 (1986): 420–431; Theodore E. Zorn and Michelle Violanti, "Communication Abilities and Individual Achievement in Organizations," *Management Communication Quarterly* 10 (1996): 139–167.

[22] Sypher and Zorn, pp. 420–431.
[23] Barbara J. O'Keefe, "The Logic of Message Design: Individual Differences in Reasoning about Communication," *Communication Monographs* 55 (1988): 80–103.
[24] Daniel Katz and Robert L. Kahn, *The Social Psychology of Organizations* (New York: John Wiley, 1978).
[25] John C. Athanassiades, "The Distortion of Upward Communication in Hierarchical Organizations," *Academy of Management Journal* 16 (1973): 207–226.
[26] Phillip K. Tompkins, *Organizational Communication Imperatives: Lessons of the Space Program* (Los Angeles: Roxbury Press, 1992).
[27] Fredric M. Jablin and Kathleen Krone, "Task/Work Relationships: A Life-Span Perspective," *Handbook of Interpersonal Communication*, ed. Mark L. Knapp and Gerald R. Miller, 2nd ed. (Thousand Oaks, CA: Sage, 1994).
[28] T. J. Larkin and Sandar Larkin, "Reaching and Changing Frontline Employees," *Harvard Business Review* (May–June 1996): 95–104; Helena Economo and Theodore E. Zorn "Survivor Perceptions of Communication during Downsizing," *Asia Pacific Public Relations Journal* 1 (1999): 19–41.
[29] Jablin and Krone, p. 632.
[30] Stephanie Zimmermann, Beverly Davenport Sypher, and John W. Haas, "A Communication Metamyth in the Workplace: The Assumption that More Is Better," *Journal of Business Communication* 33 (1996): 185–204.
[31] George Graen and Mary Uhl-Bien, "Relationship-Based Approach to Leadership: Development of Leader-Member Exchange (LMX) Theory of Leadership over 25 Years—Applying a Multi-Level, Multi-Domain Perspective," *Leadership Quarterly* 6 (1995): 219–247. (They actually refer to their model as focusing on leader-follower, not supervisor-subordinate relationships, but that seems to be what they're talking about.)
[32] Graen and Uhl-Bien, pp. 219–247.
[33] Bridge and Baxter, pp. 200–225.
[34] Nancy G. Boyd and Robert R. Taylor, "A Developmental Approach to the Examination of Friendship in Leader-Follower Relationships," *Leadership Quarterly* 9 (1998): 4.
[35] Zorn, pp. 122–147.
[36] For example, Eva C. Kasper-Fuehrer and Neal M. Ashkanasy, "Communicating Trustworthiness and Building Trust in Interorganizational Virtual Organizations," *Journal of Management* 27 (2001): 235–254.
[37] W. Charles Redding, *Communication within the Organization* (New York: Industrial Communication Council, 1972) p. 433.
[38] Gary A. Fine, "Friendships in the Workplace," *Friendship and Social Interaction*, ed. Valerian J. Derlega and Barbara A. Winstead (New York: Springer-Verlag, 1986) pp. 185–206; also Patricia M. Sias and Daniel J. Cahill, "From Coworkers to Friends: The Development of Peer Friendships in the Workplace," *Western Journal of Communication* 62 (1998): 273–299.
[39] Jablin and Krone, p. 641.
[40] Theodore E. Zorn and Sarah Ruccio, "Motivational Communication in College Sales Teams," *Journal of Business Communication* 35 (1998): 468–499.
[41] Zorn, pp. 122–147.
[42] Sias and Cahill, pp. 273–299.
[43] Sias and Cahill, pp. 288–289.
[44] Herminia Ibarra, "Paving an Alternative Route: Gender Differences in Managerial Networks for Career Development," *Social Psychology Quarterly* 60 (1997): 91–102.
[45] Fredric M. Jablin, "Organizational Entry, Assimilation, and Disengagement/Exit," *The New Handbook of Organizational Communication: Advances in Theory, Research, and Methods*, ed. Fredric M. Jablin and Linda L. Putnam (Thousand Oaks, CA: Sage, 2001).
[46] Theodore E. Zorn, Deborah Page, and George Cheney, "Nuts about Change: Change-Oriented Communication in a Public Sector Organisation," *Management Communication Quarterly* 14 (2000): 515–566.
[47] John Van Maanen, "The Smile Factory: Work at Disneyland," *Reframing Organizational Culture*, ed. Peter J. Frost, Larry F. Moore, Meryl Reis Louis, Craig C. Lundberg, and Joanne Martin (Newbury Park, CA: Sage, 1991) pp. 58–76.
[48] Arlie R. Hochschild, *The Managed Heart: Commercialization of Human Feeling* (Berkeley: University of California Press, 1985); Sally Planalp, *Communicating Emotion: Social, Moral, and Cultural Processes* (New York: Cambridge University Press, 1999).
[49] Fairclough, *Critical*, pp. 137–138.
[50] Note that CRM is often also used for Customer Relationship Management and in that case typically refers to electronic systems such as those that monitor customers' buying habits and use the data gleaned from that monitoring to target marketing efforts.

[51] Stephen Brown, "Torment Your Customers (They'll Love It)," *Harvard Business Review* (October 2001): 82.
[52] Paul du Gay and Graeme Salaman, "The Cult[ure] of the Customer," *Journal of Management Studies,* 29/5 (1992): 615–633.
[53] Adapted from Peter R. Monge and Noshir S. Contractor, "Emergence of Communication Networks," *The New Handbook of Organizational Communication*, ed. Fredric M. Jablin and Linda L. Putnam (Thousand Oaks, CA: Sage, 2001) pp. 440–502.
[54] Mark S. Granovetter, "The Strength of Weak Ties," *American Journal of Sociology* 81 (1973): 1287–1303.
[55] Adapted from the following sources: Monge and Contractor, "Emergence of Communication Networks"; Terrance L. Albrecht and Betsy W. Bach, *Communication in Complex Organizations: A Relational Approach* (Fort Worth, TX: Harcourt Brace, 1997).
[56] Albrecht and Bach, pp. 147.
[57] Etienne C. Wenger and William M. Snyder, "Communities of Practice: The Organizational Frontier," *Harvard Business Review* (January–February 2000): 139–145.
[58] Wenger and Snyder, pp. 139–145.
[59] Theodore E. Zorn and James R. Taylor, "Knowledge Management and/as Organizational Communication," *Key Issues in Organisational Communication*, ed. Dennis Tourish and Owen Hargie (London: Routledge, 2003).
[60] Robert Putnam, *Bowling Alone: The Collapse and Revival of American Community* (New York: Simon & Schuster, 2000); see also Robert Putnam, "Bowling Alone: America's Declining Social Capital," *Journal of Democracy* 6 (1995): 66.
[61] Daniel J. Lair, "'Just Trying to Spread the Groove': Creating and Sustaining Community Online at Phishhook.com," M.A. thesis, U of Montana, 2002.
[62] Barbara Gray, "Conditions Facilitating Interorganizational Collaboration," *Human Relations* 38.10 (1985): 911–936.
[63] Gray, p. 912.
[64] William W. Powell, "Hybrid Organizational Arrangements," *California Management Review* 30.1 (1987): 67–87.
[65] Toby E. Stuart, "Interorganizational Alliances and the Performance of Firms: A Study of Growth and Innovation Rates in a High Technology Industry," *Strategic Management Journal* 21 (2000): 791–811.
[66] Stuart, pp. 791–811.
[67] John F. Rockart, "Toward Survivability of Communication: Intensive New Organization Forms," *Journal of Management Studies* 35.4 (1998): 417–420.
[68] Mark Ebers, "The Dynamics of Inter-Organizational Relationships," *Research in the Sociology of Organizations* 16 (1999): 31–56.
[69] Stanley Baldwin, "Tying the Knot," *The Economist Newspaper, Ltd.* (May 14, 1994): 73.
[70] Ebers, pp. 39.
[71] Peter R. Monge and Noshir S. Contractor, *Theories of Communication Networks* (New York: Oxford University Press, 2003).
[72] Noshir S. Contractor, Barbara J. O'Keefe, and Patricia M. Jones, *IKNOW: Inquiring Knowledge Networks On the Web*. Computer Software. Urbana-Champaign: University of Illinois at Urbana-Champaign, 1997, <http://iknow.spcomm.uiuc.edu>; Noshir S. Contractor, Dan Zink, and Mike Chan, "IKNOW: A Tool to Assist and Study the Creation, Maintenance, and Dissolution of Knowledge Networks," *Community Computing and Support Systems*, ed. Toru Ishida (Berlin: Springer-Verlag, 1998) pp. 201–217; Noshir S. Contractor and Ann Bishop, "Reconfiguring Community Networks: The Case of PrairieKNOW," *Digital Cities: Technologies, Experiences, and Future Perspectives*, ed. Toru Ishida (Berlin: Springer-Verlag, 2000) pp. 151–164; Julie Fesenmaier and Noshir S. Contractor, "Inquiring Knowledge Networks on the Web (IKNOW): The Evolution of Knowledge Networks for Rural Development," *The Journal of the Community Development Society* 32 (2001): 160–175.
[73] David A. Whetten and Howard Aldrich, "Organization Set Size and Diversity: Links between People Processing Organizations and Their Environments," *Administration and Society* 11 (1979): 251–282.
[74] Peter R. Monge and Janet Fulk, "Communication Technology for Global Network Organizations," *Shaping Organizational Form: Communication, Connection and Community*, ed. Gerardine DeSanctis and Janet Fulk (Newbury Park, CA: Sage, 1999) pp. 71–100.
[75] Monge and Contractor, "Emergence of Communication Networks."
[76] Charles C. Snow, Raymond E. Miles, and Henry J. Coleman, Jr., "Managing 21st Century Network Organizations," *Organizational Dynamics* (Winter 1992): 5–20; Monge and Fulk.
[77] Snow, Miles, and Coleman, Jr., pp. 5–20.

[78] Don Tapscott, David Ticoll, and Alex Lowy, *Digital Capital: Harnessing the Power of Business Webs* (Boston: Harvard Business School Press, 2000).

[79] Tapscott, Ticoll, and Lowy; see also Kevin Kelly, "New Rules for the New Economy," *Wired* (Sept.1997): 1–12. <http://www.wired.com/wired/archive/5.09/newrules>. [9 August 2002].

[80] John Seely Brown and Paul Duguid, *The Social Life of Information* (Boston: Harvard Business School Press, 2000).

[81] Snow, Miles, and Coleman, Jr., p. 13.

[82] Håkan Håkansson and Ivan Snehota, "No Business Is an Island: The Network Concept of Business Strategy," *Scandinavian Journal of Management* 5.3 (1989): 187–200.

[83] Johan Arndt, "The Market Is Dying: Long Live Marketing!" *MSU Business Topics* 27 (Winter 1979): 5–13.

[84] Arndt, p. 6.

[85] Rockart, pp. 417–420.

[86] Monge and Fulk.

[87] Eric M. Eisenberg, Richard V. Farace, Peter R. Monge, Erwin P. Bettinghaus, Ronnie Kurchner-Hawkins, Katherine I. Miller, and Lynda Rothman, "Communication Linkages in Organizational Systems: Review and Synthesis," *Progress in Communication Sciences*, ed. Brenda Dervin and Melvin Voigt (Norwood, NJ: Ablex, 1985) pp. 231–258.

[88] Monge and Fulk.

[89] Peter S. Ring and Andrew H. Van de Ven, "Developmental Processes of Cooperative Interorganizational Relationships," *Academy of Management Review* 19.1 (1994): 110.

[90] Ring and Van de Ven (1994), pp. 90–118.

[91] For a review of this research, see Ring and Van de Ven, pp. 90–118.

[92] Søren Skafte Overgaard, "Uvilje til videndeling," *Børsen Informatik* (Apr. 24 2001): 7.

[93] Kasper-Fuehrer and Ashkanasy, pp. 235–254.

[94] Joseph Galaskiewicz, "Interorganizational Relations," *Annual Review of Sociology* 11 (1985): 281–304.

[95] Håkansson and Snehota, pp. 187–200.

[96] Eisenberg et al., pp. 231–258.

[97] W. Graham Astley and Richard A. Brahm, "Organizational Designs for Post-Industrial Strategies: The Role of Interorganizational Collaboration," *Strategy, Organization Design, and Human Resource Management*, ed. Charles C. Snow (Greenwich, CT: JAI Press, Inc., 1989) p. 253.

[98] Snow, Miles, and Coleman, Jr., pp. 5–20.

7

Leadership Old and New

Direction, Coordination, Facilitation, and Inspiration

Leadership is one of the most studied phenomena in the multi-disciplinary arena of organizational studies. The 1990 *Handbook of Leadership* had over 10,000 citations.[1] That's 10,000 books, articles, and other publications written on the topic of leadership—and the total would be much higher if it were updated today. Even with all those ideas, drawing firm conclusions about what makes leadership effective—or great—is still difficult. In this chapter, we'll talk about leadership as an important dimension of organizational communication. We'll discuss its significance, how it's defined, along with major theories of leadership and their value in helping us to understand and practice leadership communication.

The Importance of Leadership

In the late 1970s, SAS (Scandinavian Airline Systems) was in trouble. In 1981, Jan Carlzon was appointed company president. By the mid-1980s, the company experienced a dramatic turnaround in its fortunes.[2] How did that happen? Should *Carlzon* get credit for the success? These are questions we ask about all kinds of organizations, not just businesses. Sports teams that have a couple of bad years usually prompt discussions about sacking the coach. Religious congregations and social clubs that experience significant increases in membership or enthusiasm often engender praise for the pastor or president. We like to be able to credit (or blame) individuals "at the helm" of organizations. While this simplifies our world, do these individuals in fact *deserve* the credit or the blame? See the case study in box 7.1 for an example.

Box 7.1 The Blame and the Credit Go to Leadership!

Dean Smith, the legendary University of North Carolina basketball coach, is recognized as one of the greatest coaches in U.S. college basketball history. By the time he retired in 1997, he had more wins than anyone in the history of college basketball (879, to be exact). His teams had won two NCAA championships, 13 conference championships, and an Olympic championship (at a time when only college players played for the United States). His UNC teams won more than 20 games per season—a common standard for a successful season—27 years in a row. But there were many indicators of success beyond winning. A number of his innovations changed the way the game was played and became common practices with other teams. His players had a 97% graduation rate (one of the highest of any university sports programs) and many of them sought his advice and stayed in regular contact with him long after their playing days. By almost any measure, he was a great leader of his organization. However, public opinion wasn't always on his side. In his first season—his only losing season in 36 years—his team lost several games, and he was hung in effigy by angry fans on the UNC campus. They attributed the team's loss to poor leadership. Of course, that was before he had established a record of success. People wouldn't make that mistake again, right? Well . . . wrong. After establishing some pretty lofty expectations, less successful seasons often led to grumbling. When his teams fared "poorly," the letters to the editor would often include comments such as "Dean's over the hill," "He's lost touch with his players," or "The game has changed and passed him by." With the next fabulously successful season, Smith was given as much credit for the team's success as he was blame for the team's "failures" in previous years.

Think critically about this case. What other explanations could be given for the success or failure of sports teams or other organizations? How would you describe the discourse—the logic embedded in conversations and media reports—used in discussing sports organizations? What lessons from sports organizations are relevant to other kinds of enterprises?[3]

Ironically, there's disagreement about whether or not leadership is even important in organizations. That may seem strange given the emphasis we place on leaders and the volume of literature on the subject.[4] The development of academic majors devoted to leadership studies (at several U.S. universities) and advice from management gurus for "more leadership and less management"[5] are further testimony to the value placed on leadership. On the other hand, some scholars argue that contemporary industrialized societies *over*emphasize the importance of leadership. They say we attribute too much importance to leadership as an influence on groups and organizations. As organizational communication scholar Charles Conrad observes, this has important implications for the study of ethics and for the practical aspects of leadership; we become blind to dynamics between individuals and their institutions.[6] In this argument, leadership is a myth that we perpetuate and "reify" (treat as real and tangible that which is actually abstract and intangible). We try to encapsulate all the abilities and processes associated with leadership in the body of a person. There is some evidence that, even when there are other logical explanations, people prefer to explain organizational performance in terms of leadership—*who's in charge*.[7]

If this is true—and it probably is at least some of the time—why do we do this? A deceptively simple answer is that contemporary discourse encourages it. The underlying assumptions in everyday conversation and in media representations are that leaders *cause* organizations to succeed or fail. Leadership takes on a "mythological significance."[8] The human tendency to seek something grander than oneself results in seeing leaders as being larger than life. Ironically the search for something grander often results in oversimplification. Organizational performance is an overwhelmingly complex and ambiguous phenomenon. Why does a business have great success for a while and then experience a downturn? There could be many factors—changes in the market, a recession in the economy, new competition, loss or retirement of key staff members, just to name a few—but it's often the person considered the "leader" who takes the heat. This is as true in politics as it is for a ship's captain. It's just too difficult to take all the possibilities into consideration, even if we did have complete information (which we rarely do).[9] Besides, a good leader would take all those things into account and find a way to succeed, right?

Another reason we tend to overemphasize leadership is because many Western countries—particularly English-speaking ones—are very individualistic in their values and orientations.[10] This means, in part, that they believe individuals are autonomous, independent, and self-determining. This worldview sees individuals as powerful, capable of exerting great influence on groups and even society. Thus, if the economy is booming, the current president or prime minister tends to get credit, even though current economic conditions are no doubt a result of a complex array of variables and may be more a result of policies from years past than current ones.

Although collectivist cultures also place importance on leadership, they are more likely to attribute organizational performance to the successful collaboration of groups. This makes sense in a society where identity is understood as part of a web of social bonds. However, even in collectivist societies, a "cult of personality" can emerge, and certain leaders take on larger-than-life qualities. In China from 1949 to 1976, giant posters and billboards contributed to the aura surrounding the nation's first communist party chief, Mao Tse Tung.

More radical dissenters from the idea that leadership is important believe that society needs to be *rescued* from powerful leaders.[11] From this perspective, people in contemporary societies experience alienation and deep social anxiety—believing that they have little control over or responsibility for their lives. Leadership, these dissenters claim, is a construction that perpetuates this state. Even in democratic societies, people look for the qualities of a "messiah" in a new leader, all the while failing to see how they themselves could make a difference. This outlook puts unrealistic expectations on the new leader and inevitably leads to disappointment. Social-movement organizations, ironically, often succumb to this kind of thinking, as they watch their leaders change course, retire, or die. It's therefore no surprise that the first "theory" of leadership to develop in the West was about "Great Men," as we'll discuss shortly.

Probably a more balanced view of the contributions of leadership is reasonable. Leadership can influence the success and satisfaction of groups and teams. At times, however, we overuse leadership as an explanation—especially in our history books, which often ignore the contributions of groups and entire generations of people, preferring to focus on a few individuals considered to be great (until recently, most of these were dead white male politicians). While too much emphasis on the role of the person neglects broader social dynamics and forces at work, too little (as we discuss in chapter 9) fails to grant *agency* to individual persons. The key is to consider—and question—various alternative perspectives and alternative explanations.

What Is Leadership, Anyway?

Before we get too far, let's talk about what leadership is. Leadership is difficult to define—perhaps because most people feel they "know it when they see it," creating multiple impressions of what leadership means. Leadership scholar Joseph Rost found more than 220 different definitions of leadership and devoted two chapters in his book to a review of them.[12] Another prolific writer on leadership, John Kotter, devoted an entire book to differentiating management from leadership.[13] These scholars spent considerable energy trying to pin down just what leadership is. However, trying to determine a single definition can obscure the larger issues and processes involved. For instance, if we used Venn diagrams (with overlapping and non-overlapping circles) to depict leadership as a sphere, we could find interesting ways in which it intersects with power, persuasion, influence, achievement, and management.

Most people agree that leadership is an influence process, that it involves influencing people's attitudes and actions. But there is quite a bit of disagreement about *what* leadership influences people to do. Typically, writers describe leadership as influencing people to achieve *goals* or to *produce change*. For example, is it leadership when a manager influences an employee to meet a goal that has been set? Some would say yes, especially if the goal is difficult and interaction with the manager created increased employee motivation to do the job. Others—and this is the dominant view in contemporary writing on leadership—would not view influencing people to accomplish goals as leadership. From their perspective leadership is fundamentally about creating *major* changes—like taking a company or a nation in a wholly new direction. Only if what's attempted constitutes a substantial change—what leadership theorist Bernard Bass called a quantum leap forward in process, attitude, or results—is it leadership.

Box 7.2 What *Is* Leadership?

Think of all the ways we use the words leadership, leading, and leader. We've selected a few that present different perspectives. Which of these comes closest to how you would define leadership in an organizational context—for example, in a university or in a private firm?

a. Being in first place ("He led the entire race"; "Brand X is the market leader")

b. Being expert or the best at something ("She's a leader in her field")

c. The performance of acts *required* by the group[14]

d. An interactional process that helps people in organizations manage their environment.[15]

e. The process of influencing others toward goal achievement[16]

f. Symbolic communication that modifies attitudes and behaviors of others to meet shared group goals and needs[17]

g. An influence relationship among leaders and followers who intend real changes that reflect their mutual purposes[18]

h. A process of producing change through establishing direction and aligning, motivating, and inspiring people[19]

Can you think of others? Many of our students say that the definitions above are roughly in reverse order of preference for defining organizational leadership. The first two reflect everyday conversation about leadership. All the others are definitions offered by scholars over the years. The last definition probably comes closest to how most writers and managers today think of leadership.

Many writers focus on leadership as distinct from management.[20] Thus, there's broad agreement in the current literature that leadership and management are fundamentally different. One substantial difference is that leadership produces change and management produces stability. Managers are said to "do things right," while leaders focus on "doing the right thing."[21] We expect moral vision to come with good leadership; we want leaders who will help us make decisions about priorities. We expect some kind of reference to values from our leaders and are surprised whenever there is no mention of them. This was one of Chester Barnard's fundamental points about leadership in his classic work *The Functions of the Executive.*[22]

Notice that most definitions of leadership characterize it as an influence process, which is inherently communicative. You can't lead without communicating, whether directly, subtly, or perhaps sometimes unintentionally. So, it makes sense for us to focus our attention on this key organizational communication process. The importance of communication in leadership may be even greater in contemporary organizations that have radically different structures than traditional organizations.

Most perspectives on leadership operate under the assumption that the domain of the leader is largely internal—that leadership primarily is enacted within formal organizational boundaries. Marguerite Schneider of the New Jersey Institute of Technology, however, points out that new organizational forms with blurred boundaries, networking, flattened hierarchies, and contract labor call for new leadership perspectives and practices.

> In the radix organization, authority tends to mean power to guide cooperation for task accomplishment, rather than power to direct the actions of a predefined group or persons within the organization. This is a change from "power-over" or authority of command, to "power-to," the ability to implement.[23]

With fuzzy boundaries between internal and external operations, the concept of authority is blurred in ways that challenge conventional notions of managerial practice. As Schneider notes, leaders in radix organizations have multiple relationships outside their hierarchical domain, and they need to encourage the development of inter-organizational networks that are independent of themselves as leaders. To develop leadership skills and practices that emphasize relationship building with a variety of stakeholders is an important challenge.

Leadership is difficult to define for several reasons beyond the fact that language and meanings are inherently ambiguous, slippery, and evolving. Some of the reasons for this are interesting and can help us form a more complex, sophisticated view of leadership. Rather than try to settle the definitional debates, we'll discuss organizational leadership broadly in this chapter as a process of influencing others to achieve goals. While we'll give more attention to popular contemporary views—those that view *leadership as influencing others to create change*—sticking solely to this view would force us to ignore much of the research and theory that have shaped our understanding of leadership processes.

The Confusion about Leadership

One reason for the difficulty in drawing firm conclusions about leadership practice and leadership effectiveness is that we sometimes confuse leadership and leader. *Leadership is usually understood as a process; a leader is a person*. How do we tell if someone is a leader? The deceptively simple answer is "if they lead (or provide leadership)." But sometimes leadership is talked about as whatever leaders do, so we have a circular definition. To complicate matters more, we often designate as "leader" anyone who's in a *position* of authority. For example, because someone who occupies an official role—be it supervisor or CEO, priest or cardinal, department chair or university president—is responsible for supervising others, we assign a leadership role. But are supervising and managing the same as leadership?

A second difficulty is closely related: the confusion between leader and manager or leadership and management. We often use these terms interchangeably in everyday conversation: "Maria's our team leader" or "Maria's our group manager." As we discuss in the chapter on participation, this becomes an important concern for organizations making the transition from traditional methods of supervision (direction) to team-based facilitation. As we've discussed above, contemporary writers go to some lengths to distinguish leadership from management—usually describing leadership in positive, elevated terms and treating management as a mundane activity.

A third cause of difficulty stems from this question: *Is it leadership only if you're successful?* Because leadership has such positive connotations, and because we typically use it to explain successes and failures, the temptation is only to describe apparently successful actions as leadership. If they're unsuccessful, this logic goes, there must have been no leadership. But this again creates a circular logic; you can't tell if it was leadership until you know the outcome! And of course, the success of an outcome is often ambiguous. For example, many people said Ronald Reagan worked an economic and political miracle in his two terms as U.S. president in the 1980s. Others—looking at the same outcomes quite differently—considered Reagan's presidency a disaster, not a miracle.

Yet another factor is that we describe widely varying phenomena *as* leadership. We call things leadership that occur in many different contexts and at many different levels of analysis. For example, we may talk about a small child leading as she organizes a game with a friend on the playground, a supervisor providing leadership to a small work group, and a CEO leading a multi-national company's turnaround. While there is a similarity—influencing other people through communication—there are also great differences. The contexts—playground, factory floor, and boardroom—are very different. So are the levels of analysis: influencing one person, a small group, and a huge corporation. The fact that we label such different phenomena leadership seems to be one of the reasons leadership research has had so many inconclusive findings.

Some of the most influential early research on leadership was by Kurt Lewin and his associates in the United States in the 1940s. They looked at the effects of different styles of leadership: *autocratic* (authoritarian), *democratic*, and *laissez faire* ("hands off"). Managers and organizational theorists tried to use their findings to improve organizational practice. However, many of Lewin's studies of leadership focused on an adolescent boys club in the United States! It seems a great leap of faith to try to apply findings from such studies to the corporate boardroom, not to mention to extend them to women and to other societies.

Finally, complicating any discussion of leadership is the tension between (and sometimes the uncomfortable combination of) scholarly research and the commercialization of leadership. Leadership *sells*. For example, a search in 2002 on Amazon.com on the subject of leadership produced over 3000 books that had been published since 1998. There is a competitive mass market for books and public seminars providing the "secret" to leadership success. While books on leadership for managers have been around for many years, the business publishing industry was transformed in the 1980s with the success of one book, *In Search of Excellence*. With sales of over 5 million, this publishing phenomenon demonstrated the potential market for such books.[24] An outgrowth of the success of the book was the Tom Peters Corporation, named for the lead author, which has an annual income by now probably larger than that of many small nations!

Certainty also sells. Most people don't want to buy these books to find out that, well, after all, it's not so easy and the answers aren't entirely clear. And they certainly don't want to read a long list of definitions or reports of conflicting research studies! The desire for mass market success means that most discussions of leadership are not intended to clarify a complex phenomenon; rather, they assert simple, pithy phrases that will sell copies. So, we get the "one-minute" method, the seven habits, the 21 irrefutable laws, and a host of titles beginning with "How to." Each new book, of course, implies that former views on leadership are no longer valid, creating new uncertainties to be settled by the latest book's simple prescription.

Box 7.3 Historical Development of Popular Approaches to Understanding Leadership

- 1800s–early 1900s: "Great Man Theories"
- Same period through 1930s: Trait Theories
- 1940s–1960s: Functional Theories: Initiating Structure and Showing Consideration (or Task-oriented and Relationship-oriented Behaviors)
- 1940s–1970s: Style Theories: Notably, Democratic, Authoritarian, and *Laissez Faire*
- 1970s–1980s: Contingency Theories
- 1980s–present: Transformational and Charismatic Theories
- 1990s–present: Teamwork and Facilitation

Our point isn't that popular management books don't have value; they do. We enjoy reading many of them and often find them provocative. For example, Edward Lawler's *From the Ground Up* reduces the process of building a new corporation to six principles by identifying recent trends and how managers cope successfully with them.[25] However, the oversimplification in popular books contributes to the confusion surrounding leadership. The effort to create an impression of certainty and novelty may be appealing, but avoiding possible complications and contradictions does not lead to a complex understanding of a multifaceted topic. It is difficult to make generalizable statements about what makes leadership effective. In fact, according to some scholars, it's foolhardy to even *try* to develop a single definition or single set of principles for leadership.

Organizational sociologist Mats Alvesson of Lund University, Sweden, argues strongly against the ideal of developing a grand theory of leadership.[26] According to Alvesson, a common definition of leadership is neither possible nor desirable as it often misses the target and obstructs new and interesting ways of thinking about leadership. Moreover, it tends to "freeze" a social reality in which leaders are obliged to display certain qualities, and followers (organizational members) are expected to value them. For example, asking an employee to respond in a questionnaire to the statement: "My manager makes me proud to be associated with him/her" communicates to respondents that it's normal for subordinates to feel in certain ways about their managers, "fairly often," "sometimes," or "once in a while." As Alvesson points out, such an approach to leadership creates the impression that one *should* be proud of or *should* admire one's boss. Alvesson's critique extends beyond questionnaires to include other quantitative and qualitative methods. His conclusion is that most known methods tend to produce the object (in this case, leadership) it sets out to analyze. Are we thus better off without trying to agree on a single leadership definition or a single *best* theory? While being careful not to oversimplify, we will attempt to identify some findings from the leadership research that are useful for current and aspiring leaders.

"Visions" of Leadership in Recent History

Vision is a conceptualization or image of what something is, can be, or should be. For example, the telecommunications giant AT&T asks consumers and employees to visualize "an interconnected world." The corporation tries to present itself as the global leader in making that vision a reality—down to its logo suggestive of the planet with lines across it. Vision is an important part of our contemporary understanding of leadership—so much so that many of today's leaders are criticized for lacking a broad vision. For example, as we write, Israeli Prime Minister Ariel Sharon and Palestinian head Yassir Arafat are both being criticized for escalating the violence in the Middle East without having any clear idea of what to do next or how to move toward peace. In fact, many commentators have accused them of being so trapped in their 30-year personal feud that they have both lost sight of greater goals and possibilities. Later in this chapter, we'll discuss how leaders use visions and how visions are interpreted by audiences. First we want to talk about the visions, or metaphors, presented by theorists over the years in their writing about leadership.

Not surprisingly, given the volume of writing on leadership, many theories and models have been developed. Each of the approaches listed in box 7.3, for example, reflects a vision (or underlying metaphor, or conceptualization) of what leadership is or should be. For example, theorists from the "traits" and "Great Man" approaches viewed leadership as whatever was done by the great men and women of history. Theorists from the situational school viewed leadership as *supervision*—influencing followers to accomplish their job responsibilities. Scholars from the styles approach also saw leadership as influencing others and characterized by a pattern or *style of influence*. Many contemporary scholars see leaders as *change agents* and leadership as creating substantial changes in groups and organizations. Finally, some critically oriented scholars see leaders as *oppressors* and leadership as a means of oppressing or dominating workers. Box 7.4 suggests still other "visions" of leadership.

Many writers have tried to organize the various approaches that have emerged into a coherent set of categories. While any set of categories is bound to be somewhat arbitrary, we like a model that was developed by leadership theorist Keith Grint, as shown in box 7.5. One of the things that makes this model attractive is that it highlights the importance of leadership as a *socially constructed phenomenon*. The dimensions he outlines point to the assumptions underlying the way we think about, and talk about, leadership. Communication plays a particularly central role in his description of the most recent approach, constitutive leadership.

As the model shows, we can make *essentialist or non-essentialist* assumptions about the leader (the individual) and the context. Essentialism means that the characteristics we find are essential features (part of the nature) of the phenomena we study. An essentialist assumption, then, implies that a definitive or objective account of the phenomenon is both possible and important. At the level of a people or a society, essentialism shows up when we assume all Arabs or Muslims or all members of any group can be explained by a single account—for example, based on religion or shared cultural values. In leadership studies, both the traits and styles approaches make essentialist assumptions about the individual. They assume that we can describe the essential characteristics of the individual (her traits or his style) and that these characteristics are the key to understanding leadership. From this perspective, figuring out a list of qualities or characteristics of individuals (that is, effective leaders) is all we need to know to understand leadership. For the most part, these approaches ignored the role of context: how leaders actually interact and the roles that others around them play. Thus, they take *non*-essentialist views about *context*, assuming context is not crucial in explaining effective leadership; therefore they seem to assume that if leadership works in one setting, it would work in other settings too.

Box 7.4 Metaphors for Leaders or Leadership

What does each of these metaphors suggest for leadership practice? What are the advantages and limitations of each? Can you think of others?

- Servant
- Orchestra conductor
- Leader of a jazz band
- Dictator
- Coach
- Facilitator
- Actor
- Father/Mother
- Coordinator
- Great communicator

Box 7.5 Grint's Classification of Leadership Theories

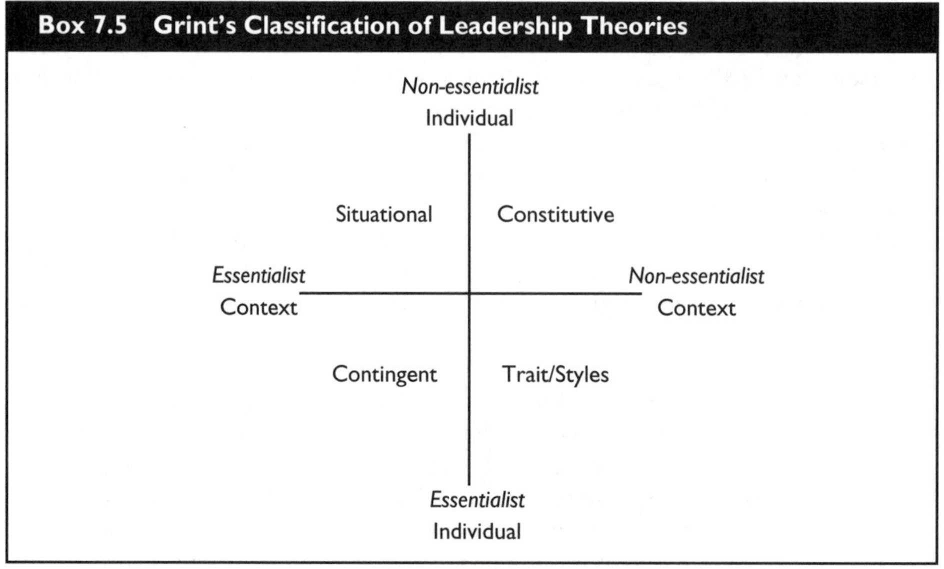

Contingency approaches (epitomized by Fred Fiedler's contingency theory, explained later in the chapter) assume that leadership is best understood by describing the essential features of *both* the leader and the context and how they match up. Situational approaches, such as path-goal theory, do not make essentialist assumptions about leaders; rather, they focus on leadership behaviors that can (in theory) be performed by anyone. However, situational approaches do make essentialist assumptions about contexts, assuming that once the essential features of the situation or context are identified, the most effective leadership behaviors can be determined. Constitutive approaches assume neither the context nor the individual leader's essential features are important or possible to describe. These approaches tend to see both individuals and contexts as socially constructed without stable, defining features. Instead, leaders, followers, and observers negotiate the meanings ascribed to leaders, leadership acts, and contexts.

In what follows, we'll talk about each of these major approaches, their assumptions, and what we can learn from each. Each of these approaches—in fact, like all theories—are products of cultural-historical moments. To some degree the metaphors used to think about and talk about leadership reflect the social and intellectual *milieu* (context) *or Zeitgeist* (spirit of the times) from which they emerge. We'll discuss the relationship of each approach to the major trends and events of the era in which it emerged.

The Traits Approach

The traits and "Great Man" approaches emerged in the late nineteenth century and were particularly popular in the first half of the twentieth century. They reflect the Western biases from which the approaches were developed and nurtured: a highly individualistic culture, one with great faith in the possibilities for individuals to "put their stamp" on organizations and societies. For example, in the United States between 1865 and World War I, there were literally thousands of studies about the leadership of Abraham Lincoln. Some of these studies were so preoccupied with "essentializing" his leadership that they spoke of head size and brain measurement! The pre-twentieth-century art of phrenology (the "reading" of the head) shows how far a trait-based or "Great Person" approach can go in trying to find leadership *inside* someone.

The prominence of the "Great Man" and trait approaches also reflects developments in the field of psychology, in which psychological tests were increasingly popular tools for assessing individual differences.[27] Just before and during World War I, IQ (intelligence quotient) and personality tests became popular for categorizing people and for determining their abilities and inclinations. In laboratories in Western Europe and the United States, this testing was an important impetus to the development of the field of industrial and organizational psychology. Today, we are so accustomed to such tests that it's hard to imagine when we didn't "type" people in that way, although in recent years the historical and cultural biases in the tests have been well documented.

Researchers in the Great Man and trait traditions hoped to identify the qualities necessary for effective leadership. Not surprisingly given what we've discussed already, this proved frustrating. While hundreds of studies failed to demonstrate that there were any qualities that were either necessary or sufficient for leadership, they did identify some qualities that made it more likely that leaders could be effective. Weber's "charisma" usually appeared near the top of such lists, though as a social construct it can be thought to be multi-faceted and subject to further breakdown into component parts. Ralph Stogdill, one of the preeminent leadership researchers associated with traits research, reviewed 163 trait studies in 1974 and concluded:

> The leader is characterized by a strong desire for responsibility and task completion, vigor and persistence in the pursuit of goals, venturesomeness and originality in problem solving, drive to exercise initiative in social situations, self-confidence and sense of personal identity, willingness to accept consequences of decision and action, readiness to absorb interpersonal stress, willingness to tolerate frustration and delay, ability to influence other persons' behavior, and capacity to structure social interaction systems to the purpose at hand.[28]

Traits research was more consistent in identifying the characteristics associated with leadership *emergence* rather than leadership *effectiveness*. Certain traits seem to predict fairly well who will be chosen or viewed as a leader, but not necessarily whether that person will get good results. This is an important distinction. We have culturally shared perceptions about what traits are needed for effective leadership, but these don't necessarily translate into effective leadership performance. People in the United States (and many other countries with a similar cultural profile), tend to pick leaders they perceive as intelligent, assertive or dominant, and masculine.[29] Even physical characteristics tend to make a difference. For example, a number of studies have found that people in leadership positions tend to be taller than average.[30] The preference for taller people shows up markedly in job interviews in many countries today.

Traits views of leadership have not disappeared. Most of us believe that there are some abilities, skills, or talents that make a difference in leadership. Communication skills may be among the most important skills necessary for effective leadership.[31] Recall our discussion of Norman Fairclough's ideas in chapter 6 that communication is more important than ever in our "post-traditional" world. Leaders must be able to influence others' views of problems, goals, and situations by producing messages (like PR, advertising, or marketing), managing communication networks (as with employee communications), and fashioning symbols to represent the organization as a whole (as we find in corporate communications and identity management). Substantial empirical research points to the importance of communication abilities—especially the ability to see others' perspectives and to adapt messages to the followers' perspectives.[32] Surveys of CEOs and administrators show a strong preference for job candidates with communication skills, recruiters' checklists of characteristics consistently reflect this.

To summarize, it is probably safe to say that there are no traits that are necessary or sufficient to be effective leaders, but some personal characteristics, like intelligence and communication abilities, certainly increase the likelihood of effectiveness in most situations. However, even if traits are much less important to leadership effectiveness than previously thought, they do seem to be quite important to leadership emergence and selection. Societies develop common beliefs about personal characteristics desirable in leaders, and these socially constructed assumptions influence who stands out as having leadership potential.

Styles Approach

The styles approach was particularly prominent in the middle part of the 20th century, although its influence continues today. (Box 7.6 is a contemporary approach that shows that a view of leadership as styles is still useful and relevant.) It is one of the most useful approaches to help students and managers understand the variety of leadership choices available in everyday situations. Think about what was happening in the era in which the styles approach first became prominent. With the emergence

Box 7.6 Voices from the Field

"(Re)conceptualizing Instrumentality and Collaboration"
Patricia S. Parker, University of North Carolina at Chapel Hill

Whom should we study to learn about leadership in the twenty-first century? With the increasingly diverse workforce, organizations would benefit from understanding and practicing leadership from multicultural perspectives.[33] In the mainstream literature, two competing models of leadership are discussed that were developed based almost exclusively on studies of white, middle-class women and men, but which are presented as culturally and race-neutral.[34] One model is based on the notion of masculine instrumentality—unilateral, directive, and distant communication aimed at controlling others. In contrast, the other is based on the notion of feminine collaboration—communication emphasizing interpersonal consideration through relationship building, empowerment, empathy, and interdependence.[35]

In an interview and observation study of 15 African-American women senior executives,[36] I challenged the universal depiction of men and women's leadership as either instrumental (control-oriented) *or* collaborative (empowering). The study revealed an interactive approach to leadership communication that (re)conceptualizes leadership in terms of *both* control *and* empowerment, where control is (re)defined as interactive and personal, rather than as competitive and distant. The five themes and their descriptions are summarized on the following page. They form the basis of leadership from the perspectives of African-American women executives in the study.

Leadership Communication Theme	Description
Interactive Leadership	• Knowing the business, its mission, and its goals, and being able to communicate that knowledge clearly, directly, and consistently • Being accessible to staff and customers • Modeling effective behavior
Empowerment of Employees through the Challenge to Produce Results	• Expecting high performance, based on the executive's confidence in the person's ability to deliver • Setting specific goals for producing high quality results
Openness in Communication	• Bringing important issues into the open • Making sure that voices (including their own), which need to be heard on a certain issue, get that opportunity • Having no hidden agendas
Participative Decision Making	• Collaborative Debate: Dialectic inquiry that involves one-to-one argument and explicit agreement and refutation for the purpose of collaboratively reaching decisions • Autonomy: Trusting employees and pushing control of the organization to the lowest levels • Information Gathering: Staying aware of multiple points of views
Leadership through Boundary Spanning Communication	• Connecting the organization to the Black community in positive ways • Articulating the organization's mission and purpose.

The African-American women executives' interactive approach to leadership provides a way for leaders in an increasingly diverse workplace to serve as conduits through which a diversity of viewpoints could be brought together, negotiated, and enacted. I theorized that the "both/and" quality of African-American women's leadership communication emerges from their cultural standpoints at the intersection of race, gender, and class oppression within the dominant culture of U.S. society. I recommend that research continue to seek diverse sources of knowledge about leadership from other cultural groups, such as African-American men, Asian Americans, Native Americans, and Latina/o Americans.

Think about the possibilities this approach suggests for cross-cultural leadership training and learning. For example how would you design a leadership training class based on the interactive model of leadership? Who should teach the class? Who should participate?

of Hitler, Mussolini, and Stalin in the 1930s and the threats their regimes created, there was a great deal of concern with totalitarian systems. People wanted to understand the appeal to followers and tried to find patterns of influence in the communication of the leaders. The most popular terms for describing leadership styles were based on the predominant types of political organization in the era: democratic, autocratic, and *laissez faire*. The last term literally means "let do," and is often translated as "hands off," suggesting that a laissez faire leader does very little to influence or lead, leaving followers to make their own choices.

The analysis of these styles is sometimes simplistic, with democratic usually the "winner" in a discussion of the behavior associated with each approach. Often overlooked is the fact that even within a largely democratic group or organization, there may be times when either autocratic or laissez faire styles are useful and even urgently needed. For instance, in some emergency situations, direct instructions are required, and many groups need a "cooling off" period after an emotionally charged episode, which calls for a less engaged style.

Small group research often makes the distinction between *task-oriented* and *socio-emotional* leaders, recognizing that those two needs may not be met by one person. The famous Ohio State Studies of the 1950s and 60s focused on these two dimensions. The studies were based on extensive surveys across the United States, which produced some 2,000 factors thought to be relevant to leadership! When the researchers used statistical factor analysis to boil down the list, they found just two principal dimensions. One was called *initiating structure*—the degree to which the leader organized and structured the task and directed followers in how to do it. The other they called *showing consideration*—the degree to which the leader showed concern for followers' feelings, sense of belonging, and so forth. Obviously both styles depend on the communication skills of the leaders.

Initiating structure is enacted by giving orders, instructing, and giving specific feedback. Consideration is enacted verbally by praising and asking questions, as well as nonverbally through smiles, physical closeness, and eye contact (among other possibilities). New Zealand business leader Stephen Tindall (owner of The Warehouse retail chain and a leader in the businesses for social responsibility and sustainability movements in New Zealand) articulates a strong preference for a consideration approach in saying, "My job is to try now and nurture the leadership in the company and the well-being through our 'people come first' philosophy and make sure it goes right through the organization . . . I see it as more important to be with our people rather than just waving the company's flag with the big people we trade with."[37]

Contingency and Situational Approaches

The mixed results of the traits and styles approach convinced many researchers in the 1960s and 1970s that they were basically on the right track, with one exception: perhaps the best style or the most appropriate set of traits *depends on the situation*. Think about that era. It was characterized by substantial social change, in which grand theoretical traditions were being challenged and belief in universal truths were breaking down. This led to what is often referred to as the contingency and situational approaches. These two are sometimes treated together because they share the assumption that leadership effectiveness must take into account contextual factors. Also, both approaches tend to focus on the same two dimensions of leader behavior that emerged in the styles approach: one dealing more with task or instrumental goals and one dealing more with feelings, people, and relationships. However, there's a significant difference between the two approaches.

Fred Fiedler's Contingency Model assumes that leaders have relatively stable motives (or traits).[38] This approach takes an essentialist view of individuals. On the other hand, the situational view assumes that individuals are not so easily and objectively described. It denies that they have an essence and assumes instead that people can choose which leadership style or behaviors to use. For example, Ted and Lars, both of whom have been heads of departments recently, have in general used a much more directive style of leadership with new members of staff and a much more *laissez faire* style with more experienced members.

Fiedler's model, however, assumes that some leaders are more people-oriented and some more task-oriented—and that these orientations make them best suited for different kinds of situations. Task-oriented leaders, according to Fiedler, are best suited to highly favorable and highly unfavorable situations. People-oriented leaders are better suited to moderately favorable situations. Fiedler used the term *favorable* to mean: (a) good leader-member relations, (b) a highly structured task, and (c) high position power for the leader. While research results are mixed, they have generally supported the Contingency Model, although it has been criticized for conceptual and measurement problems. It is useful for pointing out that we have two choices to improve leadership effectiveness: (1) select leaders who seem a good fit with a situation, or (2) change the situation to be a better fit with the leader. Of course, those two tasks are not easy to accomplish, since the leader's qualities and the characteristics of the situation are open to multiple interpretations (which is a key argument of the constitutive approach).

There are many theories that fall under the situational approach. Path-goal theory and leadership substitutes theory are two that have received a lot of attention from researchers. Box 7.7 illustrates another one of these, Paul Hersey and Kenneth Blanchard's life-cycle model.

Box 7.7 Hersey & Blanchard's Life-Cycle Model of Leadership[39]

Think of a time when you helped someone learn something new. Perhaps you've taught a child to ride a bike or a friend how to use a mathematical formula. What's your general strategy? It's probably not all that different from what's recommended by the life-cycle model. In this model, leadership is seen as influencing someone to accomplish goals. The underlying metaphor is leader as supervisor or performance manager. Leadership style is the pattern of influence behaviors used, especially *directive* (task behavior) and *supportive* (relationship behavior). The basic idea is to adapt these types of behavior to wherever the follower is in the "life cycle" of learning a task.

While Hersey and Blanchard admit that the best style depends on many situational variables, they claim the best usable guide is the match between the leader's style and the follower's task "maturity" level—the person's ability and motivation to complete a task independently. So, for example, the leader should use a highly directive style for someone new at a task, someone at a low maturity level. The logic is that someone at this stage primarily needs direction. Directive behavior is gradually reduced as the person gains skill and confidence, and supportive behavior is increased to encourage the person. Supportive behavior is reduced as the person gains confidence to work on his or her own. For someone at a high maturity level, a *delegating* style is recommended. The leader largely leaves the follower alone and allows her to make decisions and solve problems. This approach makes sense for someone who is experienced and motivated to work independently on a task.

There are several ways one might use this situational leadership model. First, the model suggests leaders should *match* their style to followers' maturity level. Second, leaders can use the model to *develop* followers' maturity level by gradually changing their style as the follower increases in maturity on a given task. Finally, the model can be used to "contract" for leadership style (that is, explicitly negotiate which style will be used under which conditions) based on various job responsibilities and levels of experience and motivation. The life-cycle model is intuitively appealing: adjusting direction and support to match the needs of followers seems like good advice. As with any prescription, it is important to be mindful of underlying assumptions and to analyze each application and outcome.

The Constitutive Approach: Social Perception and Managing Meanings

The pure version of the constitutive approach assumes we can't have an objective account of either situations or individuals and that we don't need to in order to understand leadership. Grint favors this approach (as do we) and argues that early approaches are flawed in assuming we can objectively categorize persons and situations. In this approach, neither the essential qualities of the leader nor those of the situation are important. Rather, we need to focus on how they are socially constructed—that is, how we talk about and think about them. In line with our view of organizational communication as being open to multiple meanings, readings, or interpretations, we see leaders—and leadership situations—similarly.

While there are no essential traits or skills for leadership in a constitutive approach, it does highlight the importance of the ability to manage meaning. That is, since leaders and situations are open to various interpretations, leaders should be skilled at persuading and at framing situations. The constitutive approach suggests that aspiring leaders be aware of the socially constructed nature of things, events, and ideas and that they consciously attempt to influence others' constructions or interpretations. To do that, they must have highly developed social perception skills (sometimes called social insight in the traits approach). This refers to the skill of being aware of how others see situations and being able to consider multiple views of a situation. Social perception skill enables leaders to have a sense of what's important to others; this ability is invaluable in selecting possible strategies for influence.

"Constitutive" isn't a label most people would recognize, even if they'd read quite a bit about leadership in the management literature. One theory that makes constitutive assumptions (it assume leaders and followers actively negotiate their relationships) is LMX (Leader-Member Exchange) theory, introduced in chapter 6 and discussed in box 7.8. In addition to LMX theory, some specific theories within the "transformational" approach share constitutive assumptions, particularly the emphasis on socially constructing meanings for people and situations.[40]

Transformational Leadership. Especially since the early 1980s, we have seen the emergence of a new school of leadership. Since this school is the dominant one in practice and research today, we'll devote a bit more attention to it than the others. The group of theories and models included in the transformational school is usually traced to the publication of historian James McGregor Burns's book outlining what he called transforming (as opposed to "transactional") leadership.[41] While a variety of other labels are used in addition to transformational—for example visionary and charismatic—and while there are notable differences, this group of theories shares a number of important features and can be seen as a fundamental shift in leadership theorizing compared to leadership theories from previous decades.

Prominent among the features of this group are the following assumptions. First, leadership is a *process of creating significant changes*; the underlying metaphor, thus, is leader as change agent. The term *transformational* points to the centrality of this assumption. Second is an emphasis on leadership as managing meaning through symbolism, particularly by creating and articulating an inspiring vision. In the transformational approach, leaders attempt to shape followers' meanings, especially their meanings for their work. Some transformational approaches (particularly charismatic leadership theories) also emphasize that followers' meanings for leaders—for example, a group's construction of a particular leader as charismatic or transformational—are dynamic and subject to change.[42]

Why did this theory emerge in the final two decades of the twentieth century? In the early 1980s, it became apparent that the global economy was emerging, the pace of change was increasing, and the U.S. feared being surpassed as an economic power. Japan was touted as an economic miracle, prompting the broadcast of an often cited television special in the United States: *If Japan Can, Why Can't We?* Similarly, the best seller *In Search of Excellence: Lessons from America's Best-Run Companies*[43] was published in 1982 and reflected the idea that for U.S. companies to compete, they

Box 7.8 Voices from the Field

"Not all leader-follower relationships are the same"
Jaesub Lee, University of Houston

LMX theory is used extensively by organizational communication researchers today.[44] The theory proposes that leaders (supervisors) have limited amounts of personal and organizational resources (e.g., time, energy, role, discretion, and positional power) and distribute such resources among their followers (members, subordinates) selectively. Thus, some followers receive more resources from the same leader than others in the same workgroup or unit. This unequal distribution or reception of resources over time results in the formation of Leader-Member Exchanges that vary in quality, spanning from high to low. High LMXs (i.e., "in-group," "cadre," or "partnership") are characterized by a high degree of mutual positive affect, loyalty, contributions/obligation to the exchange, professional respect, and trust, whereas the opposite is observed in low LMXs (i.e., "out-group," "hired hands" or "managership").

Communication scholars have investigated and refined LMX theory predictions of leader-member relationships. For example, some key findings include:

- Compared to those in low LMXs, leaders and followers in high LMXs expend a lot more time and energy on communication, talking to one another more openly, informally, and frequently; engaging in mutually polite persuasion, challenge, and disagreement; and listening actively and providing accurate feedback.
- Compared to out-group members, in-group followers have greater opportunities to be influential in decision making. For example, in-group followers are invited and consulted when leaders make decisions. Leaders do not force decisions on the in-group followers. They also provide the in-group followers with privileged information and/or inside scoop.
- Compared to out-group peers, in-group followers enjoy a lot more job and performance-related attention and help from their leaders, for example, by receiving challenging projects and assignments with greater job autonomy and latitude and by discussing work problems, performance details, mutual expectations, and ways to enhance performance. Therefore, they tend to be more productive, satisfied with their jobs and communication experiences, and willing to stay longer with the current organization.
- Finally, followers whose leaders have in-group LMXs with their bosses are a lot happier in their jobs and experience greater cooperative communication in their workgroups than their peers whose leaders have out-group LMXs with their bosses.

These findings suggest that the kinds of relationships we have with our superiors (and the kinds of relationships that our superiors have with their bosses) strongly affect our daily experiences of organizational life. They suggest that it is in our interest to try to develop "in-group" relationships with superiors.

Identify communication behaviors and activities that are indicative of low- vs. high- quality LMXs. What might be done to improve or change LMX quality with a boss or subordinate? Is it possible and desirable for a leader to develop in-group relationships with all subordinates?

had to change radically. Thus, transformational leadership fit the prevailing notion that leadership must change organizations radically to prepare them for the global economy and its new forms of competition.

Another factor leading to the development of the transformational approach was the dissatisfaction with the situational approach. Transformational scholars described the situational approach as "transactional" leadership.[45] They pointed to the underlying assumption in such models that the way to lead or motivate followers was through an economic transaction: exchanging reward for effort. Think of Hersey and Blanchard's model, for instance, based on the idea that gradually increasing supportive behavior in the early stages of the life cycle is rewarding and motivates the follower to continue to improve. However, using less directive behavior—allowing more freedom and autonomy—is rewarding as well. This led Bernard Bass, one of the pioneering organizational scholars in the transformational leadership school, to argue that for the last 50 years the trend had been toward more reward and less punishment (more carrot, less stick).[46] He was pointing to the underlying assumption that motivation of followers is based on contingent reward.

Bass argued that transactional theories were not necessarily wrong, just incomplete. He said they would be likely to produce "first order" (incremental) changes but not the "quantum leaps" (radical shifts) in performance or thinking produced by transformational leadership.[47] Furthermore, transformational scholars pointed to the gap between the literature on organizational and "world class" leadership. For example, they noted the sterility of transactional approaches, suggesting that terms like "task behavior" and "supportive behavior" failed to capture the energy and emotion that come to mind when we think of leaders like Gandhi or Churchill. This paralleled a recognition of the importance of emotion and the "non-rational" (notice we didn't say *ir*rational) aspects of organizations, as we discussed in chapter 3. The emergence of the organizational culture approach—with its emphasis on the symbolic, expressive aspects of organizational life—also influenced the view of leadership as transformational. After all, one of the main things transformed by a leader is people; Burns pointed to the ability of transformational leaders to help others become leaders while changing the organization's culture. As discussed in chapter 4, management scholar Edgar Schein articulated a theory that views transformational leadership as a process of creating, institutionalizing, and changing organizational culture.[48]

One of the difficulties with the transformational approach is determining the criteria for labeling leadership transformational. That is, what would make us call a process transformational leadership as opposed to transactional (or some other kind of) leadership? Change is central to the concept; if someone attempts (or succeeds at) radical organizational or social change, the leadership is transformational. CEOs are referred to as transformational leaders when they have tried to transform.

But there are dangers in using this criterion, at least by itself. For example, must the change be at the level of the organization—for example, a corporate turnaround—or might it also be dramatic individual change, such as what happens when one is inspired by a great teacher? Also, would we consider leadership transformational if change was created regardless of the means—for example, if the large-scale organizational change was accomplished through the slash and burn tactics of "corporate raiders" (see box 7.10).

A second possibility is that the use of certain behaviors is what makes leadership transformational. Popular authors James Kouzes and Barry Posner[49] interviewed numerous managers at all organizational levels in the private and public sectors and asked the managers to describe what they did when they were at their best as leaders. They concluded that five common practices are at the heart of transformational leadership.

1. *Challenge* the process, which includes questioning the status quo, experimenting, and taking risks
2. *Inspire* a shared vision, which includes facilitating a common vision by appealing to people's values, interests, and dreams
3. *Enable* others to act, which includes promoting cooperation, building trust, and sharing power
4. *Model* the way, which includes setting an example and planning "small wins" for the group to ensure momentum and progress toward the vision
5. *Encourage* the heart, which includes rewarding and celebrating group and individual achievements

Others identify similar behaviors in defining transformational leadership.[50] Box 7.9 provides an example of a leader who used many practices inherent in transformational leadership, as well as a compatible philosophy of leadership.

Finally, transformational leadership may be identified by the nature of the leader's appeals or promised rewards. James McGregor Burns suggested that

Box 7.9 The Human Touch[51]

Centennial Medical Center in Nashville, part of the HCA Hospital System, provides a great example of positive organizational culture change. When Bill Arnold, the new CEO, took over at HCA, the organization had "lost its creative juices. People had begun to believe that they didn't matter and that doing quality work did not matter." HCA needed to transform their organization into a more competitive business, and quickly. The transformation was accomplished in such a way that employees began to realize that they did matter, that their work was important, and that their ideas for helping make HCA a more profitable, better place to work were necessary and vital to HCA's success.

How did HCA accomplish the turnaround? Bill Arnold took the first step toward organizational change by literally taking the door off his office and moving coffee pots and snacks into his office. This was a symbolic act by Bill to communicate to everyone in the organization "Come by. Have a cup of coffee. Tell me your ideas and frustrations. Come in whenever you want, even if someone else is in the office. Use your judgment to determine the timing of your visit." Bill's symbolic move represented some of the principles of what he and co-author Jeanne Plas call *person-centered leadership*, which maintains that respect for individuals and their needs, concerns, and ideas are key for organizational success. Under Bill Arnold's leadership, HCA emphasized five person-centered organizational principles:

1. Pay attention to "golden gripes." The things people complain about the most are the most important to them, and they often have great ideas about how to fix those problems.
2. Encourage open communication between associates at all levels of the organization.
3. Provide all associates with access to leadership.
4. Promote an honest, open, humane culture.
5. Support employees' personal and family lives and needs.

Which aspects of transformational leadership are most apparent in this example? Is "person-centered leadership" just another name for transformational leadership, or do you see some important differences?

transformational[52] leaders appealed to a sense of moral purpose or higher level needs, versus their immediate self-interests or lower level needs. He said that transformational leadership lifted leaders and followers to a higher level of morality. Similarly, Bernard Bass suggested that transformational leaders appeal to needs other than currently prominent ones, but not necessarily higher needs (although those are more typically discussed). Usually, examples cited of transformational leadership include appealing to followers to transcend their self-interests for a higher good—making the world, or at least the organization and its relevant environment, a better place. This is why the idea of a rhetorical vision is invoked so often in discussing transformational leadership. By articulating a vision of a better world or organization, leaders appeal to followers to join in making the vision a reality. In addition to its religious undertones, this gets at the idea discussed earlier that transformational leadership implies major change—in this case, personal change. The leader encourages such change by appealing to followers to change their focus, usually away from selfish interests to a higher purpose: be that making a better car, making customers happy, setting aside an area for conservation, or working toward peace.

Leadership theorists aren't unified in their views of the criteria for what's considered transformational leadership. These differences highlight one of the attractive aspects of the theory: transformational leadership is not something objectively identified. There are multiple meanings or multiple perspectives on this phenomenon. One person's transformational leader is likely to be another's demagogue, as box 7.10 illustrates.

Box 7.10 The Corporate Leader: *Hero* or the Villain? Gandhi vs. Chainsaw Al

Popular prescriptive approaches to leadership romanticize business leaders and continually compare them to great historical leaders, such as Churchill, Gandhi, and Martin Luther King. These models emphasize humane practices, such as participation and empowerment, intended to engender commitment and motivation. The way Gandhi empowered the Indian people, in a non-violent revolution against the British Empire in the 1930s–1940s, is often used as an analogy. Martin Luther King's "I Have a Dream" speech, delivered on the Lincoln Memorial in 1963, is often used to illustrate how business leaders should use language to inspire or articulate vision. Such comparisons suggest a romantic image of the business leader's role in society, as well as illustrating the possibilities for transforming leadership.

Yet the contemporary emphasis on continuous change has led to practices such as downsizing and outsourcing, with a view of workers as disposable and an ethic of "no long term."[53] Perhaps then it's no surprise that role models greatly removed from Gandhi and King emerged in the 1990s. One of the most notorious examples is "Chainsaw" Al Dunlap, who became something of a folk hero in the business world, earning his name from his reputation for being hired as CEO specifically to "slash and burn."[54] It became common to hire CEOs, such as Dunlap, with the specific mandate to make companies profitable by downsizing, selling off, and otherwise "trimming the fat" of unprofitable organizations. Are such leaders transformational? After all, they certainly do "transform" organizations. Certainly there is something a bit uncomfortable about classifying such leaders in the same category with Churchill, Gandhi, and King. Yet the glorification of business leaders is intended to encourage similar categorization. It also contributes to the astronomical growth in CEO salaries and the growing discrepancy between salaries at the top and those at the bottom.[55]

Limitations of Transformational Leadership. One problem with transformational leadership theories is that they typically don't explain the basis of transformational leaders' influence. They specify characteristics of transformational leaders and prescribe actions for transformational leadership, yet they fail to elucidate a coherent rationale for followers' responses to these. As James McGregor Burns argued, "One of the most serious failures in the study of leadership has been the bifurcation between the literature on leadership and the literature on followership."[56] A result of this separation has been a failure on the part of many leadership theorists, especially those in the transformational leadership school, to theorize followership. That is, why do people respond positively—sometimes passionately—to some leadership attempts and not others? In our own field of communication studies, it is surprising that the research and theory on rhetoric and persuasion has not been seriously integrated with that on organizational leadership. For example, most theories of persuasion attempt to explain why people change their attitudes or behavior in response to persuasive attempts. Some of these theories might be very useful in explaining why followers are persuaded by leaders in some cases and not others.

One explanation we would offer has to do with *identity*. Transformational leadership, in articulating a vision that asks followers to join in the pursuit of a better future, is fundamentally about identity. This strategy is based on the assumption that followers will be motivated and inspired to the degree they see an appealing identity in joining the leader to fulfill a vision. The leader is essentially saying, "Here's an opportunity to do something meaningful, to be a contributor to something important. *You* can feel good about yourself because you're one of the builders of this better future." The other practices of transformational leadership support this identity-based strategy. Notice in the model offered by Kouzes and Posner that the practices focus on constructing a positive, appealing identity for followers. The third and fifth practices (*enable* and *encourage*) are the most obvious. The idea is to construct an identity for followers that helps them believe they have the power to make a difference, to create this positive future, and that this identity is recognized and celebrated by the leader.

A second, and closely related, shortcoming of some transformational leadership models is that they tend to espouse a rather one-way view of leadership. Burns described "a relationship of mutual stimulation and elevation"[57] between followers and leaders, and other theorists have paid lip service to transformational leadership as two-way communication. However, models generally view transformational leadership as what a leader does *to* followers. Kouzes and Posner advise transformational leaders to "challenge the process," "inspire a shared vision," and "model the way." Other writers studied the actions taken by CEOs and heads of large organizations; the resulting models were behavioral prescriptions for successful leadership.[58] What receives little attention in the writing is that followers don't react predictably to the prescribed actions. They interpret actions from their own perspectives and then act, which, in turn, influences leaders.

A third concern is the rather romantic picture of leadership painted by transformational theorists. The rhetoric of transformational leadership is a continuation of that popularized by *In Search of Excellence* and has overtones of the "Great Man" school of leadership from the first half of the twentieth century. Consistent with this rhetoric, leaders are called "heroes and heroines."[59] For example, Kouzes and Posner describe two leaders in their introduction by saying that they "chose a pioneering

"My goodness, if I'd known how badly you wanted democracy I'd have given it to you ages ago."

path and led their organizations to new summits of excellence."[60] The romance of leadership is very much a phenomenon associated with individualistic cultures.[61] While there is nothing inherently wrong with a romantic view of leadership, it represents a narrow perspective on leadership processes. From another perspective, for example, that of employees who lose their jobs because of the enactment of a transformational vision, the romantic picture painted by these models is unwarranted (see box 7.10).

The transformational approach to leadership, though not without its problems, continues to be an appealing and useful way of thinking about leadership today. In particular, it reminds us of the importance of communication in shaping meanings for situations. That is, rather than assuming that situations are stable and must be adapted to (like the situational and contingency approaches do), the transformational approach suggests that leaders may negotiate new meanings for situations through communication. Because of the fluid nature of meanings, leaders and followers can create new meanings for their work and themselves—achieving great things, sometimes against seemingly impossible odds.

Characteristics of Contemporary Social Life and Their Implications for Leadership

Some of the trends of "post-traditional" society identified by Fairclough have important implications for understanding leadership communication. In particular, these trends tend to support our view of transformational leadership as a process of negotiating identities. Recall Fairclough's claim in box 6.1 that there has been a loss of fixed roles, identities, and relationships in moving from traditional to post-traditional society.[62] Members of organizations do not simply assume or accept an identity; rather, they are searching and negotiating for one (or more). Nor do people assume relational definitions based on tradition; instead, they construct relational definitions personally and socially. These trends make the negotiation of identities and relationships central to contemporary leadership communication. (Notice the fit with our theory linking transformational leadership and identity.)

Leaders today rarely assume their positions because of tradition or heritage. This might happen, in the case of a family-owned business, but people aspiring to leadership usually must negotiate meanings for who they are, who they are capable of becoming, and what their role as leader entails. Less obviously, it means that the negotiation of followers' identities and relationships presents both a challenge and an opportunity for contemporary leaders. Since these are not fixed, followers cannot be assumed to see themselves in set ways (e.g., as followers) nor to view their relationship to another person as an established pattern. Most contemporary theories of leadership implicitly suggest the importance of negotiating desirable identities and relational definitions for aspiring leaders.

Fairclough argues that the nature of social interaction has changed, with trends toward being more conversational, informal, and democratic. As a result, power asymmetries typical of leader-follower relationships are likely to be masked or less obvious than in the past.[63] For example, executives and their staff in most English-speaking countries tend to call each other by first names, even when the manager is much older and of a higher organizational rank than the subordinate. Thus, contemporary leadership communication is likely to be judged positively when it is egalitarian and interactive rather than one-way or authoritarian.[64] Sam Walton, the late founder of the Wal-Mart discount retail chain, was renowned for visiting Wal-Mart stores, donning a Wal-Mart hat, and chatting amicably with customers and workers—even pitching in to help at the checkout stand if needed. The same was true for the former owner and CEO of the LEGO Corporation, Godtfred Kirk Christiansen, who would regularly walk around the production plant and chat with workers. Following that model, leaders today are encouraged to use management by walking around (MBWA),[65] to listen to, connect with, and develop rapport with followers. Yet, these democratic practices in the context of the leaders' mystified and romanticized status may actually increase their "superhuman" status, as followers marvel that the "great man" can relate to the "common man." Contemporary leadership discourse creates the situation in which leaders must simultaneously try to create a persona of greatness and one of ordinary-ness.

Also characteristic of contemporary society according to Fairclough is the increase of *promotional* discourse. Contemporary leaders often need to engage in self-promotion to create constructions of themselves as leaders, more so than leaders did in traditional societies. It places a great deal of emphasis on impression management or performing the role. Recently scholars have emphasized that effective leaders consciously manage the impressions they convey.[66] The examples of well-known corporate CEOs appearing in television and print commercials indicate this trend.

The necessity to be perceived as friendly and personable often causes leaders to seek training on methods to improve their self-presentation and relationships. Such training is an example of what Fairclough meant by discourse being "technologized." But technologizing discourse makes the creation of a leadership identity characterized by sincerity and authenticity more of a challenge. Democratization of leadership practices should make credibility a natural outcome; followers expect leaders to be "real" and personal. However, as leaders internalize the prescriptions of discourse technologists (e.g., to listen, connect and empower), they can actually create suspicion and cynicism if followers perceive that they are following a plan to produce commitment and motivation. If followers detect only the appearance of participation and listening without any real, internal desire to create a more equal exchange—only the desire to be regarded as a democratic leader—followers will question the authenticity of the leaders.[67] Practiced informal relationships can be termed "synthetic personalization.

To summarize, a key facet of leadership today is *negotiating relationships and identities*, which are dynamic and fluid—not stable or unitary. They are actively constructed and negotiated in interaction. The nature of leadership communication takes on characteristics such as informal and self-promotional qualities; the danger is that this behavior can be "technologized" by those studying it and practicing it.

Framing: Vision, Values, and Symbolism

Fairclough's analysis suggests how important communication is to contemporary leadership practice. As we've discussed, there is also general agreement that a particular kind of communication—vision—is essential to leadership. Most leadership writers today suggest that articulating an inspiring vision is important to motivate and generate commitment from followers.[68] Gail Fairhurst and Robert Sarr discuss articulating a vision as one form of "framing"—that is, using symbols to convey preferred values and meanings, including preferred interpretations of organizational problems, solutions, and goals.[69]

The importance of framing is especially obvious in crises. Aaron Feuerstein, CEO of Malden Mills, a textile company based in the northeastern U.S., faced a particularly challenging crisis when a devastating fire destroyed his textile mill. There are many ways he could have framed his response to the crisis. He could have framed it as "the last straw" that drove him to move his company to another location with cheaper labor costs, as most of his competitors had done. Or, he could have framed it in terms of searching for someone to blame. Instead, as one newspaper reported, Feuerstein framed the response as a commitment to his workers and to the community.[70]

> With one of his buildings still burning behind him, the 69-year-old owner of Malden Mills . . . spoke the words everyone in the [community] wanted to hear . . . . "We're going to continue to operate in Lawrence. . . . We had the opportunity to run to the south many years ago. We didn't do it then, and we're not going to do it now."[71]

Some writers and researchers focus extensively on the rhetorical and communicative dimensions most likely to inspire followers, which could be called the "technology" of leadership visioning. What elements are necessary to communicate vision successfully? Some evidence (and much of our personal experience) suggests organizational visions and other framing devices (such as mission statements or statements of core values) sometimes engender more cynicism than commitment.[72] Are visions overrated as leadership tools? If a clear, elevating goal is essential—as research on successful teams has found[73]—why are people often cynical about vision statements?

One reason is that vision statements sometimes seem like someone else's visions. Interestingly, in an era with so much emphasis on democracy in the workplace, many leaders seem to expect "involvement without involving." They respect commitment and loyalty to corporate visions, but do not make an effort to insure the vision is the result of joint efforts by all members of the organization. A second reason people are sometimes cynical about vision statements is that they seem irrelevant to actual work processes. Having a vision of being the industry leader may seem pretty far removed from the job of a cashier. A third reason visions are often received with skepticism is

Box 7.11 Characteristics of Leadership Visions

Following are some characteristics for an "effective" leadership vision statement, subdivided by content and presentation.

Content: The vision...

- is future oriented, but respects the past.
- embodies standards of excellence and high ideals.
- clarifies purpose and direction.
- is challenging, ambitious.
- makes sense for organization, market, and culture.
- reflects the uniqueness of the organization (or the uniqueness to which it aspires).
- creates positive identities for staff.

Delivery, Style, and Use: The vision...

- is visual; it captures the imagination with word pictures.
- uses figurative language, such as metaphors, contrast, spin, stories, and catchy phrases.
- uses puzzle-solution (or headline-punchline) format.
- takes a strong position.
- uses repetition, alliteration.
- is communicated with passion, energy.
- is communicated with confidence.
- minimizes powerless speech forms (e.g., hesitations, tag questions).
- conveys sincerity.
- is visibly displayed, or explicitly referenced in decision making.
- is consistent with leaders' actions.

Consider the properties of visions we've just presented. Try to write a brief vision statement for an organization with which you're familiar. How would it be different if you were writing it for a written or an oral presentation? Have a bit of fun with it. Then, think critically about what you've written and the guidelines above. Under what conditions would such a vision be likely to be persuasive? What ethical dilemmas does the process of constructing such visions present?

that leaders often don't "walk the talk"—that is, they say one thing in a vision ("We value people"), but their practices suggest the opposite ("We restructure regularly and fire people!").

Karl Weick makes some interesting observations by reversing the catchy "walk the talk" admonishment. Although walking the talk could encourage integration between words and action—and sounds politically correct in an era of increased stakeholder scrutiny—Weick has an alternative view. While he sympathizes with its motive—to improve the accountability of leaders—he points out that such behavior (if at all realistic) increases caution and inertia and reduces risk taking and innovation. "When told to walk their talk, the vehicle for discovery, the walking, is redirected. It has been pressed into service as a testimonial that a handful of earlier words are the right words."[74] People act in order to think, he claims, and need the flexibility to adapt their words to their actions. This is especially the case for leaders whose words are often scrutinized carefully. Those best able to walk the talk, Weick says, "are the ones who actually talk the walking they find themselves doing most often, with most intensity, and with most satisfaction."

Finally, visions may seem like a management fad—what managers do these days—and therefore contrived or insincere. Think about this concern for a moment, because it is a good demonstration of how important the social-historical context is to interpreting communication. Because of the ways visions have been used and hyped over the past two decades, meanings for them have changed. Visioning was an innovative thing for corporate executives to do in 1985; it is no longer so novel today. Vision and value statements are as common these days as Web sites.

Discourse practices like visioning emerge and take on different meanings. As they continue in use (and sometimes *ab*use), meanings for them change. So, we need to pay attention to what *receivers* of these messages, employees, think of the vision and mission statements. For example, Gail Fairhurst and her colleagues have found that some employees will turn corporate slogans upside down or inside out as an act of resistance.[75]

Just because visions sometimes engender cynicism is not a reason to shun them. They can serve important purposes. The language we use to talk about our future, our work, and our organizations is important. Vision and other skillful uses of language in leadership can be more than verbal tricks. The language we use grounds our experience, helps us make sense of situations, and thus strongly influences our actions.[76] For example, words focus our energy and aid our decision making. Visions facilitate concertive forms of control (see chapter 9) in that they suggest the premises we can use for important organizational decisions. Sometimes, visions may even inspire motivation and commitment by large segments of a workforce.

In fact, we think the problem with vision statements isn't that leaders take them too seriously; the problem is they don't take them seriously enough. Too often leaders put energy into constructing a well crafted vision and values statement, put it on a Web site and a plaque in the reception area, and then forget about it. Customers and organizational members see it, though, and if it doesn't reflect management's actions, cynicism is a likely result. We're not suggesting that every organization ought to have a vision and values statement, but we are suggesting that *if* you create one, take it seriously, use it, relate important decisions to it, and act consistently with it.

Too often we think of a vision or goal as a thing rather than a process. But the process of using the vision (and we would also include here other framing devices) is at least as important as its content. Fairhurst and Sarr argue that an appropriate use of visions and similar framing devices should follow several guidelines. First, *leaders should find opportunities to personalize visions and to adapt them to local contexts*. This means that leaders should talk about the vision not in the abstract and not just in terms of what it means for the entire company, but in terms of its relevance to specific individuals and work groups. For example, it's fine to say "Our vision is to improve people's lives through our products," but how does this relate to the people packaging or delivering those products? Gary Yukl provides a good example of how visions can matter to workers, even at the lowest organizational level. When two bricklayers were asked what they were doing, one said he was building a wall, while the other said, "I'm building a cathedral."[77] Second, *leaders should reference visions in discussing organizational problems and solutions and in introducing new programs*. That is, if a vision is to function as a guide for organizational action, it shouldn't simply be framed and displayed in the organization's reception area, it should be used to help make sense of and to generate responses to the dilemmas faced by the organization. Third, *leaders should express their enthusiasm for the vision, expressing their emotions sincerely*. Finally, *leaders should develop their own and others' mental models relevant to the vision*. A mental model is a personal theory—an assumption about how the world (or one specific part of it) is or how it works. We all carry around in our heads many mental models that help us interpret and explain all sorts of things. What Fairhurst and Sarr are saying is that leaders should develop and refine their mental models of how the vision can solve problems and lead to solutions, and they should continually share their ideas in order to develop followers' mental models.

When we think about framing and leadership, it is important to consider not only how leaders frame values and visions but also leadership. Feminist scholars have helped us understand that the way in which we frame leadership is gendered. For example, Kathy Ferguson argues that we often associate feminine values such as collaboration, sharing, and connection with subordinate organizational positions, while we associate masculine values such as competition and control with management or leadership.[78] Communication researchers Diane Kay Sloan and Kathleen Krone studied 30 U.S. women managers in sectors such as health, media, government, and manufacturing.[79] They found that these managers tended to frame the concept of leadership in terms of gendered values: viewing openness and support in terms of a feminine leadership style, and closedness and intimidation in terms of masculine style. They also found that the women had experienced masculine styles much more often than feminine styles and responded to masculine leadership styles in a number of ways: rejecting masculine power altogether; engaging in self-doubt and blame; focusing on enhancing their own competence as a coping mechanism; confronting masculine power; and, finally, resignation.

Leadership Alternatives

Are our discussions of leadership applicable to all people and groups, such as those outside of European-heritage cultures? This is a reasonable question to ask, given that nearly all the theorists and research we've cited in this chapter come from English-speaking countries—chiefly, the United States. Furthermore, most of the models have been developed with a focus on white, male leaders in business contexts. Given that groups and cultures vary on many important dimensions, these dimensions will influence how leadership is constructed and enacted.[80]

Whether or not the leadership theories and principles we have reviewed apply to a wide range of groups is an open question. We have each shared many of the ideas discussed in this chapter with students and managers from many ethnic groups and countries, and they have found value in the discussions. This is not to say they agreed 100%, but they found that the theories and principles could be useful in reflecting on and guiding their leadership choices. However, it is important to consider alternative views on leadership. Patricia Parker's work on African-American women executives, which we reviewed in box 7.6, provides such a view, as does work on leadership in organizations that define themselves as being in opposition to mainstream or traditional business organizations. Box 7.12 summarizes work by organizational communication scholar Patrice Buzzanell and her colleagues. It presents three primary rationales for establishing alternative forms of organizing and some key leadership processes that support these rationales.

Another interesting explanation of leadership that was intentionally developed with the idea of applying it across cultures is Jyuji Misumi's PM leadership theory.[81]

Box 7.12 Alternative Organizational Forms and Accompanying Leadership Processes[82]

Organizing Rationale	*Organizational Goal*	*Site of Power*	*Leadership Processes*
Anti-bureaucracy	Resist organizational practices that promote "employer" viewpoint	Member-employee-owner	• Create participatory structures/practices • Encourage, work with dissent/conflict using democratic processes
Primacy of relationships	Value caring, interdependence, and community, and resist devaluing non-instrumental relationships and non-task activities	Networks, "webs" of relationships	• Build and sustain network of relationships among stakeholders • Develop and maintain relationships that lead to power sharing, inclusion, and flexible time • Focus on goal processes (not just outcomes) and collective needs
Values/ideology-driven	Resist societal values privileging individualist, corporate, and competitive ethics	The process of articulating or representing values, especially in meetings	• Use values as basis for creating organizing structures • Facilitate discussion in ways that respect ideas and people

This theory was developed in Japan and has been applied and tested in many other countries. This theory is essentially a style theory on Grint's grid (see box 7.5) in that there are certain functions always required of leadership: P, or *performance behaviors*, which help followers to organize and accomplish tasks, and M, or *maintenance behaviors*, which help followers maintain harmonious relations. However, the situational expressions of these behaviors are culturally variable. For example, Misumi found that talking about a staff member's personal difficulties was considered a positive expression of M in Hong Kong and a negative expression of M in the United States and Britain. Misumi suggests that researchers and practitioners should first analyze the local interpretation of what constitutes P and M, and then use this information to guide practice and research.

While we might question Misumi's conclusion that a styles approach is necessarily best, we think his emphasis on identifying local interpretations of leadership behaviors is on target. It makes sense to assess the meanings people in a particular national, ethnic, or even organizational culture hold for various leadership behaviors and to use this knowledge to improve practice.

Snapshot Synthesis

Leadership is a much investigated—but not-so-well understood—phenomenon. Communication is at the heart of leadership and the complexity of communication contributes to the confusion surrounding leadership. That is, leadership is largely a process of leaders and followers interacting with and through symbols. We "do leadership" by communicating through our words and actions. Simultaneously, it is the very ambiguity of the symbols through which we communicate that leads to different conclusions about what constitutes leadership (not to mention what constitutes *effective* leadership). Thus, two people can be having a conversation about the same concept—leadership—while referring to very different phenomena.

While we have not concluded that any one approach is the best approach to leadership, we favor a constitutive approach: one that sees both individuals (such as leaders and followers) and contexts as socially constructed. However, to say that these phenomena are socially constructed is not to say that it doesn't matter what we do (since nearly *anything* can be constructed as leadership). Rather, it places emphasis on communication processes such as framing and managing meaning. We may not be able to list the actions that will result in leadership effectiveness conclusively, but we can say with confidence that one's skill in communicating is a key factor in leadership effectiveness in most situations. Effective leaders must be skilled in both the receptive processes of listening to others and interpreting their meanings and the productive processes of conveying meaning to others in ways that creates common understandings and coordinated actions.

Key Concepts

- **Vision:** a conceptualization or image of what something is, can be, or should be; in contemporary leadership theories and practice, a crucial element in enacting leadership is articulating a vision of desirable changes

- **Traits Approach**: a research tradition that focuses on the physical, cognitive, or psychological characteristics (e.g., traits, abilities, dispositions, etc.) that result in leadership effectiveness and/or emergence
- **Styles Approach:** a research tradition that attempts to classify leadership into general patterns of behaviors or orientation, such as democratic, autocratic, and laissez faire
- **Contingency Model:** assumes that leaders have relatively stable motives (or traits) and that these must be matched to certain situational characteristics for effective leadership
- **Situational Approach:** a research tradition that suggests that leaders adapt their styles of leadership to match situational characteristics for maximum effectiveness
- **Constitutive Approach:** a research tradition that suggests that both leaders' qualities and situational qualities are socially constructed; in this view, managing meaning is essential to leadership effectiveness
- **Leader-Member Exchange (LMX) Theory:** assumes that organizational leaders have limited amounts of personal and organizational resources and distribute such resources among their followers selectively; thus, they develop high LMX (in-group) relationships with some followers and low LMX (or out-group) relationships with others
- **Transformational Leadership:** a recent research tradition that suggests that leadership is a process of creating significant changes including articulating an inspiring vision for change, especially through managing meaning
- **Transactional Leadership:** a term used by transformational leadership scholars to characterize previous (especially situational) approaches based on the underlying assumption that the way to lead or motivate followers was through an economic transaction, exchanging reward for effort
- **Framing:** using symbols to convey values and meanings, including preferred interpretations of organizational problems, solutions, and goals

Endnotes

[1] Bernard M. Bass and Ralph M. Stogdill, *Bass and Stogdill's Handbook of Leadership* (New York: Free Press, 1990).

[2] Jan Carlzon, *Moments of Truth: New Strategies for Today's Customer-Driven Economy* (Cambridge, MA: Ballinger, 1987).

[3] For one example of research that gleans lessons from sports organizations and attempts to apply them to business, see Mike Pratt, Kevin Roberts, and Ed Weynes, *Peak Performance: Business Lessons from the World's Top Sports Organizations*, ed. C. H. J. Gilson (New York: HarperCollins Business, 2000).

[4] For a comprehensive analysis of writing on leadership in the twentieth century, see Joseph C. Rost, *Leadership for the Twenty-First Century* (New York: Praeger, 1991). Also, note the publication of journals devoted to the study of leadership, such as *Leadership Quarterly.*

[5] Warren Bennis, *Why Leaders Can't Lead: The Unconscious Conspiracy Continues* (San Francisco: Jossey-Bass, 1989); Lester Levy, *Leadership and the Whirlpool Effect: Why New Zealand Managers Are Failing to Deliver to Their Potential—And What Can Be Done About It* (Auckland: Penguin, 1999).

[6] Charles Conrad, "Notes on the Enron Case," unpublished paper, Texas A&M University, 2002.

[7] James R. Meindl, Sanford B. Ehrlich, and Janet M. Dukerich, "The Romance of Leadership." *Administrative Sciences Quarterly* 30 (1985): 78–102.

[8] Gary Gemmill and Judith Oakley, "Leadership: An Alienating Social Myth?" *Human Relations* 45.2 (1992): 113–129.

[9] Meindl et al., pp. 78–102.

10 Geert Hofstede, *Cultures and Organizations: Software of the Mind* (New York: McGraw-Hill, 1991).
11 Gemmill and Oakley, pp. 113–129.
12 Rost.
13 John P. Kotter, *A Force for Change: How Leadership Differs from Management* (New York: Free Press, 1990).
14 Gordon L. Lippitt, *Organizational Renewal* (New York: Appleton-Century-Crofts, 1969).
15 J. Kevin Barge, *Leadership: Communication Skills for Organizations and Groups* (New York: Bedford/St. Martin's, 1994).
16 Paul Hersey and Kenneth Blanchard, *Managing Organizational Behavior: Utilizing Human Resources* (Englewood Cliffs, NJ: Prentice-Hall, 1996).
17 Michael Z. Hackman and Craig Johnson, *Leadership: A Communication Perspective*, 3rd ed. (Prospect Heights, IL: Waveland Press, 2000).
18 Rost.
19 Kotter.
20 Kotter; Bernard M. Bass, *Leadership and Performance beyond Expectations* (New York: Free Press, 1985).
21 Kotter; Edward E. Lawler, *From the Ground Up: Six Principles for Building the New Logic Corporation* (San Francisco: Jossey-Bass, 1996).
22 Chester I. Barnard, *The Functions of the Executive, 30th anniv. ed.* (Boston: Harvard University Press, 1968).
23 Marguerite Schneider, "A Stakeholder Model of Organizational Leadership," *Organization Science* 13.2 (2002): 209–220.
24 Art Kleiner, *The Age of Heretics: Heroes, Outlaws, and the Forerunners of Corporate Change* (New York: Doubleday, 1996): p. 333.
25 Lawler.
26 Mats Alvesson, "Leadership Studies: From Procedure and Abstraction to Reflexivity and Situation," *Leadership Quarterly* 7.4 (1996): 455–485.
27 Gary A. Yukl, *Leadership in Organizations* (Englewood Cliffs, NJ: Prentice Hall, 1994) p. 254.
28 Ralph M. Stogdill, *Handbook of Leadership: A Survey of the Literature* (New York: Free Press, 1974) p. 81.
29 Robert G. Lord, C. L. DeVader, et al., "A Meta-Analysis of the Relation between Personality Traits and Leadership: An Application of Validity Generalization Procedures," *Journal of Applied Psychology* 71 (1986): 402–410.
30 See Bass and Stogdill. Bass's summary found nine studies supporting this claim, four studies finding no relationship between leadership and height, and two studies finding a negative relationship.
31 For example, see Theodore E. Zorn and Michelle T. Violanti, "Communication Abilities and Individual Achievement in Organizations," *Management Communication Quarterly* 10 (1996): 139–167.
32 For example, see Zorn and Violanti, pp. 139–167; also see Theodore E. Zorn, "Construct System Development, Transformational Leadership, and Leadership Messages," *Southern Communication Journal* 56 (1991): 178–193.
33 Patricia S. Parker, "African-American Women Executives' Leadership Communication within Dominant-Culture Organizations: (Re)Conceptualizing Notions of Collaboration and Instrumentality," *Management Communication Quarterly* (2001): 42–82.
34 Patricia S. Parker and dt ogilvie, "Gender, Culture, and Leadership: Toward a Culturally Distinct Model of African-American Women Executives' Leadership Strategies," *Leadership Quarterly* 7.2 (1996) pp. 189–214.
35 Alice H. Eagly, *Sex Differences in Social Behavior: A Social-Role Interpretation* (Hillsdale, NJ: Lawrence Erlbaum, 1987).
36 Patricia S. Parker, "African-American Women Executives within Dominant Culture Organizations: An Examination of Leadership Socialization, Communication Strategies, and Leadership Behavior," diss., U Texas Austin (1997) (University Microfilms Number 9802988).
37 Sherrill Tapsell and Stephen Tindall, "A Leader by Example," *Management* 45.3 (April 1998): 24–28, 20 Dec. 2000 <http://proquest.uni.com/pqdweb>.
38 Fred E. Fiedler, *A Theory of Leadership Effectiveness* (New York: McGraw-Hill, 1967).
39 The model has gone through revisions over the years. Blanchard offered a substantially different model, although he provided little rationale for his changes. The model presented here reflects the original version, which is quite consistent with Hersey's recent versions as well. For a recent presentation of the theory, see Paul Hersey and Kenneth Blanchard, *Managing Organizational Behavior: Utilizing Human Resources* (Englewood Cliffs, NJ: Prentice-Hall, 1996).
40 Some versions of the transformational approach seem to embody assumptions from several of Grint's categories. For example, most also emphasize the importance of particular patterns of behaviors, much like the styles approach.

[41] James M. Burns, *Leadership* (New York: Harper & Row, 1978).

[42] Jay A. Conger, *The Charismatic Leader* (San Francisco: Jossey-Bass, 1991).

[43] Thomas J. Peters and Robert H. Waterman, *In Search of Excellence: Lessons from America's Best-Run Companies* (New York: Harper & Row, 1982).

[44] Some selected references include: Gail T. Fairhurst, "The Leader-Member Exchange Patterns of Women Leaders in Industry: A Discourse Analysis," *Communication Monographs* 60 (1993): 321–351; Gail T. Fairhurst and Teresa A. Chandler, "Social Structure in Leader-Member Interaction," *Communication Monographs* 56 (1989): 215–239; George B. Graen and Mary Uhl-Bien, "Relationship-Based Approach to Leadership: Development of Leader-Member Exchange (LMX) Theory of Leadership over 25 Years: Applying a Multi-Level Multi-Domain Perspective," *Leadership Quarterly* 6.2 (1995): 219–247; Kathleen J. Krone, "A Comparison of Organizational, Structural, and Relationship Effects on Subordinates' Upward Influence Choices," *Communication Quarterly* 40 (1992): 1–15; Jaesub Lee, "Leader-Member Exchange, Perceived Organizational Justice, and Cooperative Communication," *Management Communication Quarterly* 14 (2001): 574–589; Jaesub Lee and Fredric M. Jablin, "Maintenance Communication in Superior-Subordinate Work Relationships," *Human Communication Research* 22 (1995): 220–257; Robert C. Liden and John M. Maslyn, "Multidimensionality of Leader-Member Exchange: An Empirical Assessment through Scale Development," *Journal of Management* 24.1 (1998): 43–72; Bridget H. Mueller and Jaesub Lee, "Leader-Member Exchange and Organizational Communication Satisfaction in Multiple Contexts," *Journal of Business Communication* 39.2 (2002).

[45] Bass.

[46] Bass.

[47] See our discussion in chapter 12 on first-order and second-order change.

[48] Edgar H. Schein, *Leadership and Organizational Culture* (New York: Free Press, 1997).

[49] James M. Kouzes and Barry Z. Posner, *The Leadership Challenge: How To Get Extraordinary Things Done in Organizations* (San Francisco: Jossey-Bass, 1987) p. 6.

[50] For example, see Paul C. Nutt and Robert W. Backoff, "Facilitating Transformational Change," *Journal of Applied Behavioral Science* 33.4 (1997): 490–508; Neil M. Tichy and Mary Ann Devanna, *The Transformational Leader* (New York: John Wiley, 1986); Harrison M. Trice and Janice M. Beyer, "Cultural Leadership in Organizations," *Organization Science* 2 (1991): 149–169.

[51] Adapted from William W. Arnold and Jeanne M. Plas, *The Human Touch* (New York: John Wiley and Sons, 1993).

[52] Burns actually used the term transforming rather than transformational. We use transformational here for consistency.

[53] Richard Sennett, *The Corrosion of Character: The Personal Consequences of Work in the New Capitalism* (New York: W. W. Norton & Co., 1998).

[54] John A Byrne, *Chainsaw: The Notorious Career of Al Dunlap in the Era of Profit-At-Any-Price* (New York: HarperBusiness, 2003).

[55] Ian Wilson, *The New Rules of Corporate Conduct: Rewriting the Social Charter* (Westport, CT: Quorum, 2000).

[56] Burns, p. 3.

[57] Burns, p. 4.

[58] Tichy and Devanna; Warren G. Bennis and Burt Nanus, *Leaders: The Strategies for Taking Charge* (New York: Harper & Row, 1985).

[59] Thomas J. Peters, *Thriving on Chaos: Handbook for a Management Revolution* (New York: Alfred A. Knopf, 1987) p. xiii.

[60] Kouzes and Posner, p. 6.

[61] Meindl et al., pp. 78–102.

[62] Norman Fairclough, *Critical Discourse Analysis: The Critical Study of Language* (London: Longman, 1995) p. 137.

[63] Norman Fairclough, *Discourse and Social Change* (Cambridge, UK: Polity Press, 1992).

[64] Hofstede 1991. With trends toward the globalization of culture, this trend is likely to be felt worldwide, but will certainly be more prominent currently in cultures Hofstede described as "low power distance," such as most English-speaking countries.

[65] Peters and Waterman 1982.

[66] For example, William L. Gardner and Bruce J. Avolio, "The Charismatic Relationship: A Dramaturgical Perspective," *Academy of Management Review* 23 (1998): 32–58; and William L. Gardner and Dean Cleavenger, "The Impression Management Strategies Associated with Transformational Leadership at the World-Class Level," *Management Communication Quarterly* 12 (1998): 3–41.

[67] Fairclough, *Critical Discourse Analysis*.

[68] Conger; Kouzes and Posner; Kotter.

[69] Gail T. Fairhurst and Robert A. Sarr, *The Art of Framing* (San Francisco: Jossey-Bass, 1996).

[70] Robert R. Ulmer, "Effective Crisis Management through Established Stakeholder Relationships: Malden Mills as a Case Study," *Management Communication Quarterly* 14 (2000): 590–615; Theodore E. Zorn, "Talking Heads: The CEO as Spokesperson," *Raising the Corporate Umbrella: Corporate Communications in the 21st Century*, ed. Philip J. Kitchen and Don E. Schultz (New York: St. Martin's, 2001).

[71] John Milne, "Mill Owner Says He'll Pay Workers for a Month," *The Boston Globe* (15 Dec. 1995): B50.

[72] T. J. Larkin and Sandar Larkin, *Communicating Change: Winning Employees Support for New Business Goals* (New York: McGraw-Hill, 1994).

[73] Carl E. Larson and Frank M. La Fasto, *Teamwork: What Must Go Right, What Can Go Wrong* (Newbury Park, CA: Sage, 1989).

[74] Karl E. Weick, *Sensemaking in Organizations* (Thousand Oaks, CA: Sage, 1995) p. 183; p. 182f.

[75] Fairhurst and Sarr.

[76] Susan J. Bethanis, "Language as Action: Linking Metaphors with Organization Transformation," *Learning Organizations: Developing Cultures for Tomorrow's Workplace*, ed. Sarita Chawla and John Renesch (Portland, OR: Productivity Press, 1995).

[77] Yukl.

[78] Kathy Ferguson, "On Bringing More Theory, More Voice, and More Politics to the Study of Organizations," *Organization* 1 (1994): 81–101.

[79] Diane Kay Sloan and Kathleen Krone, "Women Managers and Gendered Values," *Women's Studies in Communication* 23 (2000): 111–130.

[80] For example, see Geert Hofstede, *Cultures Consequences* (Beverly Hills, CA: Sage, 1980).

[81] Jyuji Misumi, "The Development in Japan of the Performance-Maintenance (PM) Theory of Leadership," *The Journal of Social Issues* 51 (1995): 213–228.

[82] Adapted from Patrice Buzzanell, Laura Ellingson, Christina Silvio, and Vicki Pasch, "Leadership Processes in Alternative Organizations: Invitational and Dramaturgical Leadership," *Communication Studies* 48 (1997): 285–310.

8

Participation, Teams, and Democracy at Work

The tension between organizational productivity and employee satisfaction has existed since the earliest theories about organizations.[1] Reacting to the overemphasis on technical concerns in scientific management, theorists drew attention to the "social side of enterprise"—to the dignity, rights, and full engagement of a person at work.[2] This chapter explores the ideal of having members at all levels of an organization contribute to the shaping of their own work lives. Ideas about democracy, participation, and teamwork promote a noble vision of a civilized workplace.

The Individual and the Organization

Some observers of management trends throughout the twentieth century have noted that the more things changed, the more they seemed to stay the same.[3] Many of the same issues with respect to individual involvement in the organization surface and resurface with the rise and fall of successive movements, including the current trend toward team-based restructuring of organizations. For example, although the human relations movement ushered in concerns for employee satisfaction, group norms, and job enrichment at the individual and group level, its stress on productivity contained a built-in contradiction. The two goals can and sometimes do go hand in hand, but employees often question the authenticity of the organization's commitments to their well being when productivity seems to be the primary concern. Today questions persist about the degree to which participation in *policy* making is a right of employees and the extent to which participation means contributing to the organization in ways that extend beyond the job description. For example, "entrepreneurship" on the job—one currently popular version of employee involvement—can also mean exhaustion if workload and responsibility increase dramatically. In such examples, the interests of the individual and the organization can be seen to overlap, intersect, and conflict. The tension is clearly seen in the idea of "employee participation" and its various organizational manifestations.

As with other broad terms we have discussed in this text, especially ones related to values, participation has a wide variety of meanings and uses.[4] On the one hand, employee participation signals a right, a privilege, or even a responsibility on the part of an employee to contribute to the basic activities of an organization, including having some input into policy making. Participation in this sense is based on democratic ideals and individual rights that extend when a person walks in the door of a factory or office. There are long traditions associated with this democratic sense of work participation. Some are linked to labor unions (for example, in the UK and other European nations); others have their roots in national-level institutions like the co-determination models of northern Europe, where employee associations, employers, and governmental agencies shape industrial policy at the bargaining table.[5]

On the other hand, participation can also imply a requirement that the employee give his or her "all" toward the success of the organization, including being willing to take on responsibilities beyond one's usual job description in order to increase output, efficiency, and customer service. This sense of participation is prevalent in some of the management programs we have already discussed in this book: TQM, team-based restructuring, and continuous improvement. In the highly successful Basque worker-owned-and-managed cooperatives that George followed through most of the 1990s, he found that this second meaning of employee participation was crowding out the first meaning. As the cooperatives tried to compete in a global market, the meaning of participation changed.[6]

Because value-related terms like *participation* or *democracy* have multiple meanings, however, doesn't mean these terms aren't useful or even that we should attempt to reach a definitive meaning. There is a lot of interpretive "action" in key values and ideals. As Kenneth Burke advised, we should pay close attention to "the spots where ambiguities necessarily arise" because these are places in discourse and human affairs where crucial issues get worked out.[7] We base our definition of *participation* on Cynthia Stohl and George Cheney's work. They offer a conceptualization of participation that is both theoretical and practical: "worker participation comprises organizational *structures* and processes designed to empower and enable employees to *identify* with organizational goals and to collaborate as *control agents* in activities that exceed minimum coordination efforts normally expected at work."[8] As we'll see later, this definition is wide-ranging; the italicized items highlight several important dimensions.

Each phase of the history of management and administration heralds new forms of participation; employee participation is nothing new. Historian Roland Marchand, for example, describes how major U.S. corporations established employee representation plans during the World War I era. By the mid-1920s, nearly five hundred corporations (among them AT&T, Goodyear, and Bethlehem Steel) had institutionalized various forms of nonunion work councils. Although most employee representation plans, according to Marchand, were designed as vehicles of integration, they gradually shaped expectations about employee participation and involvement.[9] Later, in the 1940s and 1950s, Rensis Likert at the University of Michigan advocated and tested *participatory management* styles, finding that these types of management were both

"We can't come to an agreement about how to fix your car, Mr. Simons. Sometimes that's the way things happen in a democracy."

satisfying and effective in a variety of settings.[10] At about the same time, Britain's Tavistock Institute examined ways that coal mining in Norway and Wales could be conducted more safely and effectively through charging work groups with key decisions.[11]

Today many business and governmental leaders, along with organizational consultants, feel sure we are on the brink of more democratic, energetic, and entrepreneurial work environments. Such leaders see organizations released from old bureaucratic constraints and envision possibilities for employee collaboration in project centers rather than in traditional departments. Similarly "customer service" is treated as a unifying symbol—a practical expression of democratic society, in that a focus on customers' needs and wants gives them more "voice" in the organization's affairs. Customer service often serves also as a model for reconfiguring the *internal* affairs of an organization—with employees viewed, alternately, as internal customers and suppliers.[12] If all of us participate, working as hard, as creatively, and as fast as we can, then better customer service will be the happy outcome for everybody. Management consultant William Halal celebrates this vision as a "democratic revolution" for business and other sectors.[13] It is democratic in the sense of emphasizing creativity and entrepreneurship on the part of individuals and groups (work teams) and also because it invites the participation of each member in many phases of work.

Simultaneously, however, there are many critics inside and outside of the labor movement who see the new workplace as depersonalizing, oppressive, and ultimately a sham as a form of democracy. This skeptical view focuses on the increased responsibilities (without corresponding rewards) for many of today's employees, the fluidity of work relations (and the lack of stability or loyalty), and the falseness of many calls to "employee empowerment" (when top-down control is maintained alongside new forms of peer pressure at work).[14] With several different case studies in the United States—ranging from a wood products company to a computer software firm—sociologist Vicki Smith illustrates the complex tension between what she calls "risk and opportunity in the new economy."[15] In each of her cases, certain dimensions of autonomy are at work, but the threat of restructuring or layoffs is ever-present. In every case, employees are required to participate more fully in their jobs than was true in the past.

So how do we recognize participation, teamwork, or democratic forms of organization when we see them? Each can be seen as a special case of *communication*. It is in patterns of communication that each of them will be real or false to us, effective or ineffective, consistent or self-contradictory.[16] For example, think about how you would *define* democratic participation in a staff meeting: perhaps in terms of whether or not members all have input into setting the agenda, or the extent to which each person has the opportunity to speak, or how the discussion is managed. Some people equate participation in decision making with the *capacity to make a difference* in terms of the outcome. But such capacity is not always determined by structures—sometimes the composition of a group prevents some individuals from participating. And, of course, many of us will sometimes use the fact that we did not get our way as evidence that our voice wasn't heard at all! In this chapter, we will talk about participation, teamwork, and democracy at work in terms of specific, concrete communication practices that make them happen.

We also want to look at the broader discourses surrounding these terms: for example, the movement toward team-based restructuring in organizations, which has become popular across sectors and in many different parts of the world. The way teamwork is defined by the top managers of a firm will determine to a great extent what policies and procedures follow from it as a way to enlist greater participation from employees. One person's model of democracy may be someone else's burdensome system—this can happen in social movement organizations, worker cooperatives, collectives, and other organizations even when the desired outcome is to gain more rights for members. Thus, we will pay special attention to the rhetoric surrounding these "master" terms in different organizations, industries, sectors, and societies. "Teamwork," for example, means something very different in Japan than in the United States, in Sweden than in Israel.

There are many ironies and surprises associated with programs that attempt to democratize work. As one example, many of the supposedly *empowering* programs for employees are decided upon and implemented in a highly top-down manner. Many organizations that announce themselves as "democratic" do not match common perceptions of the term. Here's another example of conflicting definitions. In the 1980s a traditional hierarchical agricultural firm in Papua New Guinea was transformed into a worker cooperative. The owner told employees: "You are all now managers of the company." To the owner's surprise, the employees put down their tools. When asked what they were doing, one spokesman for the worker-owners said: "Well, if we are all managers, we don't have to work anymore"![17]

The issues of participation, teams, and democracy at work relate with many of the other topics in this text: organizational structure, culture, leadership, globalization, and power. And, as we'll see later (in chapter 12), participation may even be shaped by communication technologies. You'll notice, too, how much issues of democratization of the workplace parallel broader political and social issues. We will discuss implications for networks beyond the boundaries of existing organizations, for home life, and for the larger community (what many would call "the public sphere"). We will try to chart the complex terrain of contemporary work trends to describe what exists today as well as the possibilities for the future.

Defining Our Terms

Like the meaning of many of the other key terms of organizational life, the meanings for participation, teamwork, and democracy are slippery and vague. We would like to stress several points here. First, notice that all three of these terms are commonly used in popular discourse. As we turn on TV news reports, for example, we find many conflicts around the world described as forces of "democracy" opposing something else. Because of the sheer popularity of that term, especially in Western nations, we find parties and groups all over the political spectrum claiming the mantle of democracy, saying that they are more democratic than their opponents. Democracy, thus, is a "god term"—an unquestioned good—for many societies. But other nations or groups are suspicious of the term because they see it as an excuse for the West insisting on the spread of its own ideals. U.S. government officials and spokespersons, for example, often use the term *democracy* when they really mean "capitalism," blurring the distinctions between political and economic realms. In fact, this issue of how to define democracy emerges frequently on the global stage and was part of the discussions surrounding the fiftieth anniversary of the United Nations' Universal Declaration on Human Rights in 1998.

Participation is an even broader or more diffuse term, because it references so many different forms of activity. In general, the term suggests active, voluntary involvement in arenas ranging from work to sports to politics. The United States is *structurally or institutionally* a democratic nation, yet voter turnout for presidential elections hovers around 50% in recent decades. Conversely, there can be a high level of political participation in a country with few democratic institutions or structures. In the former Czechoslovakia in November 1989, millions of people took to the streets to demand the overthrow of the Communist government; in just two weeks' time, the totalitarian government fell. Thus, democracy does not necessarily imply participation, and neither does participation mean democracy—though the two ideas are closely related to one another.

Box 8.1 The Difference between Workplace Democracy and Employee Participation

Workplace democracy generally refers to those principles and practices designed to engage and represent as many relevant individuals and groups as possible in the formulation, execution, and modification of work-related activities. Hallmarks of workplace democracy include an array of activities and indicators:

- the performance of organized bodies of governance
- equity of compensation
- the uses of social as well as technical training for employees
- allowance for dissent
- the manifestation of a genuine concern for the individual (in contrast with a simple focus on efficiency)
- the provision for multiple feedback loops in the communication networks of the organization
- the promotion of cooperative ideals externally as well as internally
- openness to the renegotiation of the meaning and practices of employee participation—not just by top managers but also by other employees.

By contrast, employee participation programs are typically narrower in scope—organizationally sponsored systems that may or may not have democratization as their primary goal or outcome. Participation usually refers to employees' involvement in decision making that is related to performing specific job tasks.[18]

A number of writers have observed the same principle for organizations. Systems such as worker councils, labor unions, or quality circles may be in operation, yet there may be little active involvement or even interest on the part of employees. Over time, of course, interest may decline even further. This is exactly what happened with the widely popular quality circles programs from about 1975 to 1990. As Cynthia Stohl found, in cases across the world, the *ex*-quality circle members were often the least satisfied with their jobs and the organization—less happy than either current quality circle members or those who never volunteered to participate in the first place.[19] The reasons for the dissatisfaction include unmet expectations, bumping up against the limits of participation, and fatigue from too many meetings. Perhaps participation in quality circles programs created a language of critique that didn't exist earlier.

As we mentioned earlier, there are different rationales or motivations for employee participation programs. But the issue is more complex than just a choice between productivity and people. In fact, we should be careful not to frame the issue in such either-or terms. In a famous study, two organizational researchers H. Peter Dachler and Bernard Wilpert found four main rationales for employee participation programs:

- increased productivity,
- job enrichment and greater job satisfaction for individual employees,
- establishment of an element of democracy in the workplace, and
- development of a more equitable and just society.[20]

While productivity is the most common emphasis in for-profit organizations and in work organizations generally, justice is the rationale most often found in organizations that define themselves as social movements (such as peace or environmental groups). Perhaps we could imagine a fifth rationale: legitimacy or social accreditation. That is, by developing employee participation programs, organizations demonstrate externally as well as internally that they recognize the value of their employees and are willing to invest the resources necessary to help them realize their full potential. As articles in the business sections of major newspapers testify, employee participation programs convey such meta-messages to a large audience.

Comparing European and North American senses of employee participation, we find that North Americans are less likely to appeal to social, political, or philosophical justifications and more likely to use productivity as the *primary* (though usually not the sole) reason for such initiatives. Justifications for specific programs framed in terms of democracy or social justice have been relatively rare in U.S. experience, except within organized labor movements. In general, employee participation refers to instances where top management or the administration initiates an effort to boost both employee involvement and productivity. In other parts of the world, differences depend on the origins of the particular programs. In an interesting study of European managers from six countries, Cynthia Stohl found that meanings and attitudes toward participation varied a great deal by nationality.[21] For example, German managers were more likely than Dutch managers to consider macro-level structures of participation such as exist under the co-determination models.

The English word *teamwork* is now surfacing on at least five continents. In some countries, the term has a lot of resonance because of the connection to athletics: cohesion within sports teams and competition with other groups. However, despite assumed similarities, cultural differences in the sense of teamwork are significant. For example, models of teamwork in the Swedish auto industry feature a high degree of collaboration and autonomy at the group level. By contrast, the model of teamwork in the typical Japanese auto plant includes a strong sense of loyalty to the company. Collaboration is emphasized at the level of team production, but autonomy is not necessarily a significant dimension. Sociologist Laurie Graham worked at a Subaru-Isuzu plant in Indiana for six months and discovered there was relatively little freedom or discretion at the shop level, despite the implementation of a quality-management system and self-directed work teams. She found that for top Japanese managers, "teamwork" became a handy justification for all sorts of requirements of workers—from mandatory morning exercises to requests for overtime hours to calls for greater output.[22]

The differences in meaning become a problem when people try to implement a program based on a vague idea of "teamwork." In an attempt to be perceived as forward thinking or in tune with current trends, some organizations attempt to apply a popular model across the organization, even where the model doesn't fit very well. In a university, for example, teamwork makes sense for some functions but not for others. We'll return to the types of conditions for (and limitations of) teamwork later in this chapter.

Employee Participation

When we examine participation programs, we need to look at such things as intentions, goals, constraints, structures, processes, outcomes, and adaptability. These features can be used as descriptive or even prescriptive criteria for assessing any particular program of participation.

Labor Organizing and Employee Participation

In the last quarter-century, the power of labor unions has declined in the United States, the United Kingdom, and a number of other industrial nations. Overall union membership dipped to a low of 17% in the United States by 1995; since then, it has risen slightly. Even in Germany, where labor power is institutionalized at the national level, the late 1990s saw a significant decrease in unions' roles and influence on the national and regional councils. Part of that decline was due to some unions growing out of touch with their rank-and-file membership. They became huge, centralized, and bureaucratic; in some of the biggest unions, there were scandals and frequent reports of corruption. Another reason was that many young people in Western industrialized countries stopped identifying with unions and started to see themselves as autonomous "professionals." As Kenneth Burke noted in the 1930s, "laborers tend to enlist our sympathies but not our aspirations."[23] We've witnessed this in our classrooms; while many university students identified themselves with workers during the 1970s, few students today want to represent labor in simulated negotiations over wages and other benefits, identifying more with management.

There are two more reasons why labor moved to the background of thinking about organizations: first, many corporations pursued active policies of "union-busting," including in some cases, programs of participation intended to dilute labor power. This is exactly what happened with some quality circle programs in major United States corporations—the circles were created to offer employees avenues of participation so that they would see the presence of organized labor as unnecessary or even undesirable.[24] A final reason was that the *language* of labor unions was out of step with the times. When "excellence," "quality," "teamwork," and "customer service" became the new buzz words, many of the oldest and most visible unions—such as the AFL-CIO in the United States or GMB in the United Kingdom—continued to stress employee benefits, working conditions, and workers' rights. Part of management's strategy became the theme of "cooperation"—in contrast with the union's adversarial portrayal of the relationship between management and labor. Driven by cutbacks in workforces and the use of outsourcing, many of the largest unions accepted sacrifices in wages and other benefits in the last two decades of the twentieth century.

Since the late 1990s, however, there has been something of a turnaround. Labor demands have been increasing, and some important contracts have included protections from sudden layoffs and extensive outsourcing of basic services. Many labor unions have adopted what they call "corporate campaigns," multi-faceted efforts to boost their images and strengthen their position vis-à-vis management. As rhetorical critic Dana Cloud notes, there is a renewed interest in class issues as the grounds for labor campaigns today, as the growing gap between the "haves" and the "have nots" becomes impossible to deny amidst the rhetoric of "classlessness."[25] In terms of employee participation, it's especially noteworthy that a number of recent labor strikes and near-strikes have been in response to increased pressures at work associated with the implementation of self-directed work teams. Examples from the United States include General Motors, the United States Postal Service, and Boeing Aircraft. A few companies like Levi Strauss have reversed their implementation plans (see box 8.2).

Box 8.2 Levi's Failed Attempt at Teamwork Implementation: Lessons for Other Organizations[26]

In the mid-1990s, Levi Strauss & Co. decided to implement team-based models of production. The company had long been known for its fairly progressive human resource policies as well as enjoying a great deal of employee loyalty. With sales of their famous jeans declining (by the early 1990s Levi's were no longer seen as "hip" by teens in many countries), the company decided to try to make its production processes both more efficient and more up to date. Although this change marked an end to disliked assembly-line technologies on the shop floor, it also created new ambiguities and new stresses. Listed below are the advantages and disadvantages of the changes implemented from the viewpoint of employees.

Advantages/Successes:

- less repetitive work/more variety in jobs
- greater employee input into work
- fewer repetitive-motion injuries
- job satisfaction tied to whole product
- development of team identity and commitment
- enhanced image of organization

Disadvantages/Barriers:

- insufficient organizational planning and employee training
- quantity of production (and therefore efficiency) falling initially
- increase in work injuries overall
- increased overhead
- speed up of work processes
- severe peer pressure for employees
- unrecognized needs and difficulties under new system

From the standpoint of many unions, employee participation programs do not create real democracy at work because the programs simply co-opt employees into acting in ways that are against their interests.[27] Some labor unions see worker-management tension as *inherent* in the workplace. This highlights an important distinction between unitary versus adversarial models of democracy. *Unitary* models assume that a great deal of consensus is possible, even involving two or more differing groups. An *adversarial model*, by contrast, assumes that the best democratic results can only come with active opposition, open debate, and a clash of interests.[28] You can see both types of democracy operating in many societies, where some assemblies work toward consensus and others fashion decisions out of conflicting views. This distinction between the two models of democracy—one grounded in oppositional voice, the other presuming unified concerns—becomes very important when we talk about attempts at creating "alternative" organizations that are more democratic and egalitarian, with truly flat and participative structures.

Managerially Driven Programs of Employee Participation

There are three main categories of management-sponsored programs of employee participation. It is important to understand these approaches before discussing a brief history and specific types of employee participation.[29]

- Employee participation as *problem-solving or decision-making groups that are to some extent outside of or beyond regular work activities*. This type of employee participation began with the human relations movement, particularly the initiatives toward what was called "participative management" from the 1940s through the 1960s. Quality (control) circles are the best known example in this category; cross-sectional groups or committees meet, often after work, to contribute ideas about productivity, efficiency, and quality.
- Employee participation as *a restructuring of work processes and activities*, using self-directed or semi-autonomous work teams. Here specific tasks are reorganized to allow for greater coordination, a widening of individual responsibility, perhaps job rotation, and sometimes involvement in the development of the entire product or service. In some cases, there is substantial independence or autonomy in group decision making, such that teams can make their own determinations about the uses of new technologies, set their own schedules, and formulate their own production strategy. This type of participation first appeared in the 1940s to 1960s in the United Kingdom under the heading of socio-technical systems (discussed later in the chapter).
- Employee ownership as *economic investment in and/or overall governance* of the organization; employee participation becomes part of the basic structure. Sometimes, employee ownership is the result of the transformation of a more traditional firm. Other times, it exists from the very beginning; the organization is built from the ground up with principles of participation to guide it. For example, in a worker cooperative the entire equity of the organization is held by employees and none by outsiders. A worker-owned cooperative may also be governed by the employees themselves, perhaps even using a one-person, one-vote principle for decisions on fundamental policies. Another example is employee stock ownership programs, many of which include economic rights without decision-making power.

When the harmful and alienating aspects of the industrial revolution first became apparent in the first half of the nineteenth century (fueling Karl Marx's critique of capitalist economies with examples of horrible factory conditions in England), social activists in Europe looked to some form of worker participation as a means of reintegrating the urban working class into society. Even before World War I, workplace democracy was a major political issue in many Western European nations (e.g., in Germany, Britain, Denmark, and France).[30] By the 1960s the European community began formal initiatives on worker participation. Today workplace democracy remains a controversial and unresolved issue within the European Union, often conceptualized as a hybrid of the ideologies of socialism, human relations, and capitalism. In some countries there are legal mandates for participation (e.g., German workers councils and co-determination policies), whereas in others (e.g., Denmark) legal regulations are scarce but various cooperative agreements are commonplace. In some nations there is an adversarial union/management undercurrent in participative initiatives, whereas in other nations cooperation between management and labor is more developed.

In the United States employee participation is typically focused more narrowly on inter-firm competition and on issues of human resources management. The human relations tradition, in the middle of the twentieth century, emphasized the value and potential of participation, cooperation, and collaboration between and among employees. Extensive, open, friendly, trusting, face-to-face encounters between workers and managers were associated with increasing psychological satisfaction, development and growth of individuals, and increased productivity and efficiency of organizations.[31]

In the 1970s job enrichment and job redesigns were undertaken in order to make workers happier, more committed, and hence more productive. Many of these programs were based on the theories of human motivation by Abraham Maslow and Frederick Herzberg.[32] Both of these theorists made distinctions between lower-order needs for security and well-being and higher-order needs for job satisfaction. Job designs typically included some form of limited employee participation that allowed workers input into the production aspects of daily work routines and provided more information to workers. At the same time, some United States companies (e.g., Lockheed and Honeywell) were impressed by the performance, success, and quality of Japanese manufacturing. They were particularly interested in J. Edwards Deming's ideas and began to implement quality-circle programs, giving workers the opportunity to participate in production and quality-related problem-solving groups.[33] By the early 1980s literally thousands of companies throughout the world developed quality-circle programs, including programs in 90% of U.S.-based "Fortune 500" firms.

By the late 1980s, however, the limitations of quality circles in non-Japanese contexts became apparent, and organizations began experimenting with more encompassing quality programs such as statistical process control and total quality management. These programs were still loosely based on Deming's famous "fourteen points" (see box 8.3) but included increased autonomy and greater employee involvement in the actual work processes. The preoccupation with total quality made U.S. manufacturing and other firms more aware of the work of the British socio-technical theorists and their focus on semi-autonomous teams or work groups. Shell Oil, Staley's, Cummins Engine, TRW, General Motors, and Procter & Gamble, for example, built new plants that minimized the distance between workers and managers and maximized workers' participation in the day-to-day decisions that affected their jobs.[34] These organizational designs are expected to make organizations more flexible, more responsive to change and quality issues, and thus more competitive in the global economy. At the same time, such programs are expected to stimulate employee participation at all levels of the organization, foster more fluid employee relations, and enhance job satisfaction.

In all these cases, note that participation refers to involvement in decision making about processes directly related to doing specific tasks. Moving beyond the small and routine decisions required by a particular job, *participation in decision making* may address involvement in broader issues such as job assignments within a given production process, the right to stop an assembly line if something is jeopardizing the quality of the product, or having a say in the way performance appraisals are carried out. This breadth of participation is rare in North America; it occurs more frequently in Western Europe. The programs discussed below give workers a substantial say in organizational decisions, but each varies according to the degree to which participation actually transforms organizational structure.

Job enrichment refers to management's effort to redesign jobs. Typically, job enrichment is a top-down process involving the analysis and reconfiguring of employees' jobs, with relatively little input by employees into the actual process of redesign. Once in place, the redesign allows greater participation by employees in the work

Box 8.3 Deming's 14 Points

W. Edwards Deming's ideas about quality improvement are given credit for Japan's economic miracle following World War II. In fact, Japan's highest award for quality improvement is called the Deming Prize. Deming's 14 points became the foundation for Total Quality Management (TQM). Following is a condensed version of them.[35]

1. Create constancy of purpose toward improvement of product and service
2. Adopt the new philosophy
3. Cease dependence on inspection to achieve quality by building quality into the product in the first place
4. End the practice of awarding business on the basis of price tag; instead, move toward a single supplier for any one item, on a long-term relationship of loyalty and trust
5. Improve constantly and forever the system of production and service; thus constantly decrease costs
6. Institute training on the job
7. Institute leadership
8. Drive out fear, so that everyone may work effectively for the company
9. Break down barriers between departments
10. Eliminate slogans, exhortations, and targets for the workforce asking for zero defects and new levels of productivity; the bulk of the causes of low quality and low productivity belong to the system and thus lie beyond the power of the workforce
11. Eliminate work standards (quotas) on the factory floor; substitute leadership
12. Remove barriers to pride of workmanship
13. Institute a vigorous program of education and self-improvement
14. Put everybody in the company to work to accomplish the transformation

process to enhance internal motivation and job satisfaction. Frequently a model developed by industrial psychologists Richard Hackman and Greg Oldman is used, whereby each job is evaluated according to the following characteristics: skill variety, task identity, task significance, and job feedback.[36] If jobs are redesigned along these dimensions, results can include greater meaningfulness of work, expanded employee responsibility, and more extensive knowledge about the process that helps in pinpointing possible areas for improvement.

Quality circles are usually comprised of 10–12 members from the same or closely interrelated work areas, who meet voluntarily and on a regular basis to deal with problems of quality and productivity. Although typically limited in the domain of problems they are permitted to consider (i.e., issues of salary, benefits, authority, and organizational structure are out of bounds), quality circle members are trained in statistical procedures, which help them analyze work-related problems and evaluate potential solutions. Members have partial access to the decision process but cannot make autonomous decisions. Solutions proposed by the circle are evaluated by a management committee that makes the final decision and determines the procedure used to implement the innovation. There is a great variation in the types of rewards associated with quality-circle programs (i.e., praise, public recognition, award banquets, and/or financial rewards based on the savings/cost reductions of implemented innovations). As we explained briefly above, quality circles and related committee structures are supplemental to the work process and are not an integral part of organizational structure. The implementation of quality circles, in other words, does not involve a restructuring of work processes, departments, or individuals' jobs.

Quality of work life (QWL) programs, in the strict sense of the term, are designed to improve relations between managers and workers by increasing the involvement of workers in various aspects of organizational life. Although many programs can fall under this rubric, it is usually used to describe participation programs that focus on management-union cooperation (rather than compensation).[37] For example, management might support paid education leave to provide workers with information about industry economics, global competition, or political climate. QWL programs also grant workers access to management discussion about specific problems in the company.

Semi-autonomous, self-managing, or *self-directed work teams* (SDWTs) are the basic building block of many presumably "post-bureaucratic" organizations. Workers take on the responsibility of former supervisors, including setting their work schedule, deciding on the best way to do the job, monitoring their own work performance, hiring additional workers, conducting inventory and ordering materials, and coordinating the team's efforts with other teams across the organization. Work teams are usually comprised of 5–15 members and are responsible for a specified task (e.g., the assembly of an appliance or the coordination of student services in a university). Team members are able to perform all required functions to complete the task. When a team member is absent, no replacement workers are provided. The team is expected to continue a high level of performance by adapting procedures to compensate for the missing member. Some work teams may have a wide arena of responsibilities, which may include contributing to the marketing of their products or services. Semi-autonomous teams are an integral part of the organizational design and rely heavily on worker motivation and commitment. SDWTs also involve a sometimes difficult transition for traditional supervisors and managers into the role of team facilitator, with considerably less formal authority.

Eric Trist and his colleagues at the British Tavistock Institute were among the first researchers to highlight the interdependence between the social system and the technical system. In the 1950s, they studied the effect of mechanization of miners in British coal mines. Prior to mechanization, work was controlled by the work group responsible for mining a particular coal seam. Through informal communication and adaptation, the members of each work group would assign and coordinate the necessary tasks among themselves, following the mining of a seam from beginning to end. Mechanization shattered the cooperative dynamics of the informal group. Division of labor was formalized, and individual miners were isolated—separated by task, by location on the coal seam, and by shift. Miners no longer had the opportunity to see their efforts carried through to completion.

Trist and his colleagues discovered that no formally designated coordination mechanism could replace the informal mutual adjustments made by the miners on their own. Direct supervision was ineffective because of the dark, dangerous conditions of the mine and the distance between miners. Output measures were ineffective because problems could not be traced to a particular worker or work process. Workers had no sense of being a part of the whole. Mechanization had eliminated an informal communication system without providing a formal replacement, resulting in both lowered productivity and increased worker alienation.

Trist and Bamforth proposed a solution to bring the formal technical system into accord with the informal communication system of the miners.[38] Work duties were organized to allow small work groups to employ the new technology. Work groups could share jobs, communicate informally, and solve problems as they arose. At the same time, the performance of the group could be measured and standardized. In a later work, Fred Emery and Trist coined the term *socio-technical system* to describe this network of semi-autonomous participatory work groups.[39] The term now designates a general concern with the interrelations of the technical and social-psychological organization of industrial production systems.

Gainsharing plans are formal, supplemental compensation programs focusing on rewarding workers for improvements in labor productivity and cost reduction. Scanlon plans are the most common type of gainsharing program. Developed in the 1940s by Joseph Scanlon, these plans provide workers with financial rewards based on organizational productivity. Workers' suggestions, innovations, and ideas are evaluated and implemented by a company-wide committee also responsible for evaluating the success of the idea and the bonus that will be given. As with quality circles, participation here is consultative: the workers cannot make and enact decisions without the "okay" of management. Unlike with circles, however, workers receive no formal training in statistical or group problem-solving processes. They have a wider decision domain than quality circles and provide a greater focus on the economic condition of the firm.

Employee stock ownership programs (ESOPs) are the most common form of employee ownership. Over 100,000 companies in the United States alone are, to some degree, employee-owned, but only about 15% of these are *majority* employee-owned.[40] In an ESOP, the company sets up a special trust in which it either contributes cash to buy stock for the employee from existing owners or contributes stock directly. As long as the employee works there and the company is profitable, the employee receives an agreed-upon amount of stock. The stock stays in the trust until the employee leaves the company or retires. In the most successful programs, employees have full voting rights on their stock and regular opportunities at shareholder meetings for input into decisions affecting their jobs. Some ESOPs give employees regular substantial stock contributions, have participation opportunities on the job, treat employees as owners, explain through a series of formal and informal communicative practices how their plans work, and frequently remind employees of their ownership stake in their firm. However, ESOPs vary widely in both the degree of formal ownership afforded employees and in the extent of control over decisions.

There are a number of dimensions of participative systems that we can use to understand how programs are enacted and especially what their practical implications are for day-to-day work experiences, decision making, and interaction.

- ***Origin:*** mandated versus voluntary program (at level of the organization as a whole)
- ***Rationale:*** orientation toward democracy or emphasis on productivity
- ***Direct or Indirect:*** forms of involvement for employees
- ***Specific Requirements:*** for employee involvement
- ***Extent of Formality***: supervision/monitoring; reporting of results
- ***Decisional Domain:*** encompassing to very limited
- ***Degree of Employee Autonomy:*** self-governance
- ***Level(s):*** of the organization at which involvement occurs
- ***Isolated versus Universal*** across the organization
- ***Temporality:*** short- versus long-term
- ***Rewards:*** extrinsic versus intrinsic, individual versus group
- ***Training:*** none to comprehensive; one shot to continual[41]

Nearly all of the dimensions of participative systems have important implications for communication. For example, both the *origin* of the design of a program and the *decisional domain* entailed by it must be assessed with respect to such issues as access to discussion, opportunities for individual self-expression, and the possibilities for the articulation of diverse groups' interests. The communicative practices associated with any formal program become important in making judgments about *the degree to which it constitutes real workplace democracy*.[42] Attention to specific communicative practices (or lack thereof) will reveal whether claims by an organization to be democratic or to have meaningful employee participation are valid.

In very concrete terms, we can think about the degree of participation on an influence power continuum. With respect to a particular decision or policy related to one's job, an employee can answer in one of the following ways:

- "I am not involved at all."
- "I am informed about the matter beforehand."
- "I can give my opinion."
- "My opinion is taken into account."
- "I take part with equal weight."
- "I decide on my own."[43]

These answers correspond to employee participation and workplace democracy in terms of decision making in the organization. They apply to situations where we can isolate a particular decision—such as when to come to work, how to meet a production target, or whether the production area should operate around the clock. Various levels of participation may be appropriate, depending on characteristics of the manager, the employee, and the situation.[44]

As we discuss in the next chapter, the extent of employee participation may also be considered in broader and more subtle terms: for example, in terms of how programs of participation are first conceived. In organizations ranging from worker cooperatives to feminist organizations to some new religious sects to many social movement organizations, a commitment to workplace democracy through meaningful employee participation is often the foundation on which other practices are built. In such cases, the entire organization is designed as a site for participation—from the very beginning.

Teamwork

It is commonplace today to think about working in "teams" in organizations. The idea of teamwork has caught on to such a degree that it has become a key means of organizing and re-organizing to become more effective. But what distinguishes a team from a group? And why is the idea of teamwork so popular in the workplace today?

The word "team" in English has been used for hundreds of years to refer to teams of horses or oxen pulling a wagon. However, the contemporary use of teams in organizations is borrowed from its use in sports. Thinking metaphorically about organizational work groups as sports teams lends an air of energy, excitement, and challenge that managers and workers often crave in otherwise mundane work. Framing work groups as teams can thus be a rhetorical strategy of management designed to increase motivation and performance, or it can be a strategy by workers themselves to make their work more meaningful or more fun.

Communication in organizational groups and teams has been a concern of increasing importance to communication scholars in recent years. As the structure of work organizations has evolved to emphasize teams, scholars have explored the characteristics of and communication processes within organizational teams. For instance, research has addressed the characteristics of communication that result in team effectiveness, changes in communication practices as a result of moving to team-based organizational structures, and the control processes typical of team-based structures.[45]

Teams versus Groups

People use the term *team* rather loosely in organizations, often to refer to a department or other organizational unit. Managers may refer to "the PR team" or "the top management team" without giving a lot of thought as to whether the entity truly exhibits the characteristics of a team. A team has been defined as *a small number of people with complementary skills who are committed to a common purpose, set of performance goals, and approach, for which they hold themselves accountable.*[46] Jon Katzenbach and Douglas Smith add that teams have shared leadership roles, mutual (in addition to individual) accountability, a specific team purpose that is distinguishable from the organizational mission, and collective work products.[47] A group, on the other hand, is simply a collection of people with something in common; six people waiting at a bus stop can be considered a group, but certainly not a team.

"Great! I put together a team and now I'm turned on by a gang."

Katzenbach and Smith contrast teams with *working groups*, which typically have a strong leader, individual accountability, a group purpose that is the same as that of the organization, and individual work products. It has been common in recent years for executives to refer to their organization as having a top management team.[48] However, the degree to which a collection of top managers truly functions as a team or as a working group (or somewhere in between) depends on two factors, according to management theorist David Nadler: the internal coordination requirements and the complexity or instability of external demands placed upon the group.[49] Nadler essentially suggests that teamwork becomes more important as both internal coordination requirements increase and external demands become more complex and unstable. Since these characteristics typify the environment in which most large organizations operate, most top management decision makers have adopted teams as an organizing form.

Making Teamwork Work

Of course, calling one's group a team does not ensure that it operates with team-like qualities or that it enacts teamwork effectively. While there is a massive practitioner literature with advice about team effectiveness, research on this topic is surprisingly scarce. Two studies point to some common qualities of effective teams.

The first study was conducted by communication researchers Carl Larson and Frank LaFasto.[50] Through interviews with members of 75 teams that had achieved a high level of success, these researchers identified eight dimensions of team effectiveness (listed and defined in box 8.4). They constructed a survey questionnaire to assess the perceptions of 32 management teams, most of which were executive-level teams. While they argued that all eight dimensions are important, their most consistent findings were that three dimensions were most prominent in effective teams: the presence of a clear, elevating goal; competent team members; and standards of excellence. Conversely, the three most prominent problems for *in*effective teams were the absence of unified commitment to the team and its mission (particularly members putting individual goals ahead of team goals), a lack of external support and recognition, and poor collaboration, (particularly the absence of open and honest communication).

The second study focused on top management teams in Europe and the United Kingdom.[51] These researchers used data acquired from interviews and questionnaires with top management team members to conclude that six team competencies were essential to high-quality team communication and that each of these competencies was linked to organizational-level outcomes. *First,* interpersonal relationships among members must be good, with members understanding and respecting one another's styles and values. *Second*, the team must have the capacity and willingness to engage in open discussion of important and potentially contentious issues. The *third* essential characteristic is a high level of trust among members. *Fourth*, the team must be approachable and open to feedback and criticism by others external to the team. *Fifth*, members must have sufficient discipline and cohesion to implement and pursue decisions on which they agree. The *sixth* competency was that members must have the capacity to discuss and understand both long- and short-term issues of concern to the organization. While there are differences in the findings of these two studies, there are also important similarities. Communication, collaboration, trust, and a clear focus stand out in both studies as particularly important.

Knowing the qualities of effective teamwork is important, but equally important is identifying how to develop those qualities. While there is not extensive research on team-building processes, communication scholar Susan Glaser's longitudinal study of a team of fire management supervisors and managers is very informative.[52] She used

Box 8.4 Larson & LaFasto's Characteristics of Effective Teams

- A clear, elevating goal: a clear sense of purpose, mission, or vision that members find inspiring and challenging.
- Unified commitment (to group and purpose): a sense of dedication to the team's goal and commitment to the team and its members
- Results-driven structure: the organization, or structure, of the team is aligned with its purpose and the nature of its task
- Collaborative climate: members have a sense of working together and a commitment to supporting each other; the focus is on achieving the team's goals, not just one's own assigned tasks
- Competent team members: in total, the team has members with the technical skills and interpersonal skills to achieve its goals
- Standards of excellence: members expect outstanding levels of performance from the team and from themselves individually
- External support and recognition: the team receives support from the larger organization by getting the resources needed to perform and by being recognized for its achievements
- Principled leadership: team leaders are respected for having a strong sense of principles or ethics

an action research approach that led her, as the consultant-researcher, to interview team members multiple times over a three-year period, feeding back her analysis to the team, and helping the team to develop new communication skills and patterns. Interviews with team members revealed consistently positive appraisals of a number of specific improvements in team functioning. From this experience, Glaser suggested that improving team effectiveness requires: (a) developing members' interpersonal/group communication competencies, (b) facilitating constructive confrontation and consensus building among team members, and (c) encouraging the group to think of its team building as a long-term process (that is, follow up regularly on skill building and on issues raised in the team-building process). Clearly, communication is not only an important quality of effective teams; it is also an important means to establish team effectiveness.

Supervision versus Facilitation

Organizing via teams leads to some important differences in managing. Managers' and supervisors' roles change from one of "commanding and controlling" to one of facilitating and coaching—even mediating. Team members are typically asked to make more decisions and to solve their own problems—functions that would typically be performed by supervisors and managers in traditional, bureaucratic organizations.[53] Thus, supervisors and managers often find that the nature of their work changes rather dramatically in team-based structures. In fact, supervisors and middle managers sometimes resist the move to team-based organizing because such changes often lead to the flattening of the hierarchy and the elimination of middle-management jobs as well as the replacement of supervisor roles with that of team leader, coordinator, or facilitator. Box 8.5 suggests some key differences in the roles of supervisors compared to team leaders or facilitators. A traditional supervisor operates much more autonomously and autocratically, whereas a team facilitator works more as a "servant" to the team, helping to create the conditions for the team to be successful in achieving their goals.

A number of procedures have been designed to enhance the ways teams interact. In an extensive review of literature on facilitation methods, communication scholars David Seibold and Sunwolf demonstrate the potential value of such methods for improving the effectiveness of group interaction, particularly for enhancing problem

Box 8.5 Traditional Supervisors versus Team Facilitators

Supervisor	*Team Facilitator*
Plans, organizes, directs, and controls	Insures available resources
Meets cost, quality, and timeline objectives	Develops team; coaches and counsels members
Manages and solves daily problems	Represents the team to outside groups, such as upper management
Plans and implements improvements	Trains and facilitates team in problem solving
Administers safety, housekeeping, and communication programs	Assumes responsibility for indirect tasks—the tasks that support the team and enable them to stay focused on their primary goals.

solving and decision making, improving conflict management within and between groups, providing feedback for empowering groups, generating high-quality information for conducting communication campaigns, and building teams.[54] In general, facilitation methods emphasize creating effective structures for interaction, such as ground rules and problem solving procedures, that are oriented toward encouraging collaboration and vigilant decision making.

Differences among Teams

While these general observations about teams are useful, it is important to recognize that every team's situation is somewhat unique. That is, we can identify the qualities of effective teams *in general*, or a process that many teams will find useful in team building, but what is most important for a given team to function effectively may be quite different from these generalizations. Perhaps the best advice is to use what management scholar Edgar Schein calls a *process consultation* approach; someone serves as a process observer during team meetings. After watching team interactions, the observer provides feedback at the end of the team meeting. The team can then discuss and agree on ways to address the observations and improve the team's process.

While every team is in some way unique, we can point to some dimensions of difference that stand out for analysis across teams. Note that some of the research we discussed above focused on top management teams, while other research focused on teams operating at lower organizational levels—for example, teams responsible for making a product or providing a service to customers. Larson and LaFasto have identified three primary types of teams (see box 8.6). Recall that one of the qualities of effective teams was "results-driven structure." Essentially, Larson and LaFasto suggest that teams can be categorized into having one of three broad objectives, which they call problem resolution, creative, and tactical. The structure a team adopts should be aligned to the broad objective. If a team's broad objective is creative, they should be organized to give them relative autonomy to create, rather than being closely supervised or required to follow a restrictive set of guidelines. Alternatively, if a team's broad objective is tactical, such as a firefighting team, they need to be organized to have clear procedures to follow with clearly defined roles for each member.

Box 8.6 Results-Driven Structures[55]

Broad Objective	*Dominant Feature*	*Process Emphasis*	*Examples*
Problem resolution (solving problems)	Trust	Focus on issues (versus personalities, or who gets credit)	Consultants who specialize in analyzing and improving organizational processes
Creative (developing new ideas, products, or services)	Autonomy	Explore possibilities and alternatives	Advertising agency; research and development team
Tactical (implementing a plan or set of structured procedures)	Clarity	Directive; highly focused tasks; role clarity; well-defined operating procedures; accuracy	Fire fighting team; engine assembly team (e.g., in a Volvo factory).

We can imagine the hazards in a member of a firefighting team deciding to freelance when other members of the team are expecting him or her to play a specific role that protects the rest of the team from danger. While Larson and LaFasto's typology is instructive, we must keep in mind that a given team may change its broad objective from one situation to the next. For example, a firefighting team may have a tactical objective when fighting fires, but a problem-solving objective when back at the fire station to identify ways to improve its procedures.

Democracy and Participation in Alternative Organizations

"Alternative organizations" is a term used to refer to groups, communities, and institutions outside the mainstream. Alternative organizations are usually outside two main sectors of the economy: government and the largest established business firms or agencies. The label "alternative" emphasizes opposition to, or divergence from, traditional structures of hierarchy and centralization. These organizations feature "flatter," more democratic, more egalitarian ways of organizing work. Alternative organizations are often found in the nonprofit (or independent) sector, within social movements, in organizations based on feminist principles, in intentional living communities, and in some electronic networks. The term *alternative* implies a comparison; we must always ask "alternative to what?" and "alternative how or in what way?" As organizational communication scholar Teresa Harrison has observed, in a variety of such organizations, the level of interdependence among members poses special opportunities and special challenges for the enactment and maintenance of democracy.[56]

Many organizations that seem well established actually began as alternative organizations. This is true of the birth of most religious organizations; they generally began as sects, usually in opposition or in separation from some larger religious institution or denomination. Thus Christianity is sometimes referred to as "the Jesus sect," which separated from Judaism. The point here is that "alternative" is a relative term. It is useful to consider organizations along various continua that position them relative to one another. Is a particular organization truly democratic in its decision-making practices? Well, let's compare it to most organizations in its sector or type of activity. Is an organization decentralized? Well, what does the typical centralized pattern of authority look like? Is an organization informal in its daily practices and interactions? Well, what kinds of practices and interactions do we see at work most of the time?

So-called alternative organizations have special challenges, at both the "micro" level and the "macro" level, as found by researchers investigating a range of cases from Israeli *kibbutzim* to worker co-ops to feminist groups to anti-globalization Internet activism. At the micro level are the issues of time, emotion, and inequality, according to public administration scholar Jane Mansbridge.[57] *Time* becomes a problem in democratic or egalitarian groups simply because of the process required to achieve true consensus or even majority agreement. Quaker or Friends' meetings are based on an elaborate rule of consensus, but this process is often multi-stage and can be frustrating for the uninitiated observer. So, there is a type of short-term inefficiency that is traded for a long-term efficiency of trust-building and securing the group's commitment to a judgment or a decision. By contrast, many organizations or groups that make swift decisions, even when not under the mantle of urgency, find later that the group doesn't really back the chosen course of action. So, many democratic or egalitarian groups prefer to do the preparatory work necessary to establish clear mutual understanding and to move the group toward a collective goal.

In many traditional, bureaucratic organizations, task concerns overwhelm attention to the attitudes, feelings, and moods of members. In fact, as we saw in chapter 3, this is almost required by the principle of "partial inclusion"—whereby it is a person's role and not the whole person who is inside an organization. But many non-traditional organizations react against this division by bringing more of the person's concerns inside the bounds of the organization; inevitably then, *emotion* becomes a recurring issue for these organizations. For example, in her Ph.D. dissertation, Hollis Glaser found in an informal theatre troupe that meetings were often emotionally charged, and the group had to make decisions about when, exactly, to "move on" from someone's issue, how to "cool off," and what kind of repair work might be necessary after a negative emotional outburst.[58] All this is in dramatic contrast to highly businesslike meetings, where, for instance, one participant's tearful breakdown might be completely ignored by the person chairing the meeting. Thus, the degree to which expressiveness is permitted or even encouraged in a meeting is one dimension along which we can assess an organization's culture and tone.

Inequality is the third challenge for democratic organizations, according to Mansbridge. By definition, many worker cooperatives and social movement organizations deem members to be equal in terms of status and participatory access. Some worker co-ops, for example, harden this commitment through flat wage scales—paying everyone the same salary or hourly rate. Other organizations rotate the roles of director, coordinator, or chair to ensure that power does not become too entrenched. For a similar reason, a socialist party that existed in Denmark throughout the 1970s, for example, didn't allow its members more than two periods of parliament representation.

Some organizations will adopt a Native American convention for meetings by passing a "talking stick" to ensure that each person thinks carefully before speaking and does not dominate discussions. Such discussions, often called "talking circles," thus proceed in a very different way than the linear paths most others expect of meetings. Equal participation—or at least equal opportunity—is ensured, and listening to others becomes paramount. George has seen this process work effectively when adopted by social-movement groups in times of great decision or great stress and emotional intensity.

Still, in almost all group discussions, of whatever structure, differences will arise. People vary by personality, interest, commitment, and mood. Some members will be more articulate than others; some will have greater expertise or knowledge on a particular issue.[59] And some simply like to talk more than others do. So, the trick for alternative organizations is how to balance differences, honoring them for what they are, while at the same time maintaining a kind of "ethical equality" at the broad level that envelops everyone in an attitude of mutual respect.

In our view, organizations (and societies) that deny real differences, pretending that no power relations are ever present among the group, will be destined to have those differences surface in some unproductive ways. This is exactly what happened at protests at the Nevada Nuclear Test Site in the 1980s, where a variety of groups came together to protest continuing underground nuclear tests by the U.S. Department of Energy. Some of these groups (which were radically egalitarian in nature and specifically rejected "asymmetrical power") actually witnessed the rise of authoritarian leaders. George experienced something similar with the nuclear freeze advocacy group in the mid-1980s (see chapter 2). When he challenged the direction of the leader and argued for consensus-style decision making, the leader insisted "we have to run a tight ship in order to get the job done." Such are the ironies of participation and power, even in many so-called alternative organizations (see box 8.7).

Box 8.7 Voices from the Field

A Case Study of Feminist Organizing
Karen Ashcraft, University of Utah

"SAFE" is a nonprofit community with a twofold mission: (1) to provide battered women and their children with shelter, support, and advocacy and (2) to end domestic violence through community education and networking. SAFE is also a self-avowed "feminist organization." This label captures more than devotion to a gender-related cause; it refers to a philosophy and method of organizing. Typically, feminist organizations seek the empowerment of members through organizational systems premised on equality and participation. One such system is collectivism—organization without hierarchy, defined by decentralized, shared control and decision-by-consensus.

For various reasons, pure collectivism can be difficult to maintain, and SAFE is a case in point. Indeed, SAFE's organizational system reflects a fundamental contradiction: a hierarchical structure that members both accept and attempt to undermine in practice. As a nonprofit organization, SAFE must demonstrate (at least for external eyes) an explicit system of accountability and efficiency. In this sense, it is a bureaucracy, complete with a hierarchy of authority, division of labor, and formal rules. At the same time, members perceive that such a structure is at odds with feminist empowerment, and they adhere to an interaction system designed to undermine or circumvent bureaucracy—in their terms, "ethical communication."

Ethical communication entails a set of corresponding individual and collective responsibilities and rights. For example, it requires frank expression, upholding the group's right to know personal agendas; it obligates the group to listen to all voices, affirming the individual's right to be heard. Members praise this system for helping them to implement feminist empowerment in the midst of bureaucratic trappings. Simultaneously, they admit that SAFE's odd mix of hierarchical structure and egalitarian communication practice creates acute dilemmas of power and participation.

Dilemma #1: How to control membership through shared beliefs and honor the expression of different viewpoints. For organizations that do not want to rely on hierarchy for control, shared beliefs offer a clear sense of community, purpose, and order. Although SAFE's feminist beliefs serve such a function, ethical communication also requires members to express and value their differences. Simply put, the rigid content of SAFE feminism clashes with a communication system that flaunts flexibility. This tension produces an ongoing difficulty of knowing when and how to discipline members.

Dilemma #2: How to foster close relationships among members without creating informal "power blocs." On the one hand, ethical communication invites intimacy among members with its emphasis on self-disclosure. Conversely, it instills suspicion, if not fear, of intimacy. For example, its list of responsibilities and rights depicts any close relationship as potential fodder for subtle, divisive, coercive alliances. Thus, members struggle to discern and enact appropriate relationship boundaries.

Dilemma #3: How to participate as equals in the midst of evident inequalities and centralized authority. How could SAFE supervisors facilitate meetings without the appearance of undue influence? How could other members follow the lead of supervisors yet act as their empowered peers? SAFE's blend of bureaucracy and egalitarianism requires members to pull off quite a feat: to at once enact and suppress the exercise of and submission to power.[60]

The *micro*-level challenges of time, emotion, and inequality are matched by three *macro*-level challenges of self-maintenance, autonomy, and goal persistence in participatory organizations. These challenges can be applied to all sorts of organizations, but they are acutely relevant to organizations that try to stay outside the mainstream.

The problem of *self-maintenance* is understood well in all organizations that rely heavily on volunteers. Simply put, how do you sustain the social commitment necessary to keep the organization going—over time and through bad times and good? While the first wave or "generation" of volunteers may be tremendously enthusiastic and feel a burst of creative energy as they shape an organization, the groups that come later may find the organization stagnant or inflexible. In addition, there is the ever-present danger of burn out. As one peace activist told George, "What good are we if we exhaust ourselves in one project and are unable to move on to the next?" In charity organizations ranging from the Red Cross to the Salvation Army to community food banks, the tendency is to rely heavily on those who are already busy—this compounds the risks of burn out and turnover for the organization. (We see this in academic departments!) The argument is sometimes made that highly motivated volunteers "do it to themselves"—that burnout is a personal issue. This argument misses the mark on the complexities of the individual-organizational relationship. For a volunteer-based organization, as for any organization, the question of balance between personal and organizational goals should be continually revisited and open to discussion.

The idea of self-maintenance applies on another level as well: the mechanisms for the organization's continuance. If the organization is too informal, too unstructured, it may not last beyond a brief moment in time—what Henry Mintzberg calls an "adhocracy."[61] As organizational communication scholar Teresa Harrison observes, the lessons of structuration theory are particularly apt here; democratic and egalitarian organizations must create the very resources that they will need to keep going.[62] Among other things, this means not always privileging spontaneity over structure and appreciating the wisdom obtained from lived experience. If the organization's very existence is equated or identified with a particular project, that may satisfy both individual and collective purposes. But as we saw in chapter 2 on structure, the trick is to set up mechanisms for continuance while not weighing down the organization with the machinery of institutionalization.

Striking the right balance is not easy, as Weber recognized a century ago. This is why periodic reflection and communication feedback loops are so valuable. No organization, no matter how passionate about or engaged with its values, can afford to rest on yesterday's enthusiasm or achievements. This is not to say that the organization needs to be constantly changing in structure or activity; rather, checks must be in place to ensure that the very vitality that gave rise to the organization can be sustained. As we discussed with respect to open systems theory in chapter 2, the tendency is for energy to dissipate and for an organization to lose its "cutting edge." This is exactly why some successful social movement organizations become nostalgic for their earlier rag-tag days when the bonds of unity were reinforced by a sense of passion and overwhelming odds. Provisions for feedback loops can help avoid behaviors that lead to stagnation and dissipation. Rotation of roles or occasional restructuring can make a positive difference, as can infusions of "new blood."

Autonomy is the second of what we're calling "macro" issues for highly participatory organizations. The issue here is the degree to which the organization can pursue its goals independently of outside influence. For example, organizations such as non-profit agencies must often compete for grant monies from government and private sources. In doing so, they sacrifice some autonomy. The very act of chasing those funds can alter the nature of the organization, complicated by the fact that there are often strings attached to the funds. In their studies of five California co-ops in the 1970s and 1980s, sociologists Joyce Rothschild and Allen Whitt found that this kind of resource dependency often diverted the organizations—including a law collective, an alternative high school, a food co-op, and an alternative newspaper—from their initial goals.[63] The lack of autonomy led some of these organizations to dissolve rather than to depart from original or founding values.

The resource dependency issue also has a communication aspect. Organizations find themselves "speaking the language" necessary to secure funds from outside sources. Thus, as Shiv has found in his work on a variety of non-government organizations (NGOs) in India,[64] often these organizations find themselves swept up in a technocratic discourse that sees technology as a salvation rather than simply as a tool. In the process, the authentic social commitments of the organizations can get lost. It's not that all these ideological imports of ideas are wrong or even inappropriate; it's more about the way they are mindlessly appropriated and applied, though often this happens under pressure from transnational organizations like the World Bank or the IMF.

Finally, *goal persistence* is an issue. It's difficult for any organization to maintain adherence to the same goals over time. Some organizations—and this is often true for alternative organizations—find that they've actually achieved their goals; that the goals themselves are outdated; or that one goal has been displaced by another. One of the most interesting changes, especially in terms of communication, is what happens to cherished values as goals shift. George observed this type of change in his study of the cooperatives in the Basque Country. The sacred term *participation* was transformed in practical meaning as the goals of the cooperative adapted to changing circumstances.

A Case for Consideration

The Mondragón worker-owned-and-managed cooperatives represent one of the most successful cases of workplace democracy in the world. Founded in 1956 by a Basque priest, along with five young engineers, the co-ops now include the tenth largest private firm in Spain and one of the largest in the Basque Country. Originally centered on industrial products and financial services, the system of cooperatives now spans the fields of consumer services, education, construction, and travel services. A hallmark of the system has been a dual structure of governance, including both one-person, one-vote assemblies and selected managers. Thus each of the more than 170 co-ops (ranging in size from eight to 9,000 employees) has built-in checks and balances to ensure that social concerns (such as employees' welfare) are considered side-by-side with issues of productivity and profit. Most employees are worker-owners, receiving dividends in the form of both salary and returns on investment. Traditionally, all equity of the firms was held within; thus, there was no outside ownership or stock. By statute the co-ops must reinvest a certain amount in the organization and its membership as well as in the community.

In recent decades, however, particularly with market globalization, the character of the co-ops has changed along with their host communities. Pressures for greater productivity and faster customer service are felt here as elsewhere, making for reduced autonomy and less of a buffer between the co-ops and the larger European and global economies. A significant change came with the dropping of most barriers to the flow of capital, knowledge, and labor within the European Union in 1992. The co-ops, thus, suddenly found themselves competing with German, Swedish, Japanese, and U.S. firms.

The co-ops have responded to market changes by being more centralized, trying to "speak to the market with one voice." The Mondragón Cooperative Corporation has also added a large managerial superstructure, reorganized according to sectors or specialties rather than by the historical geographic regions (communities and mountain valleys), and widened the wage differential between lowest and highest paid (which until the early 1990s had been quite narrow). These changes caused a schism, and one group of co-ops separated from MCC in 1992, chiefly over issues of local control.

In three separate visits to the co-ops (1992, 1994, and 1997), George found tensions over social and economic values. Two key questions reflected those values: "Given growth, financial success and longevity, can the cooperatives hold on to their soul?" and "Can a firm so democratically organized survive over the long term?" The practical form of those questions surfaced in debates over the widening wage scale, the employment of some non-owning contract workers, occasional lay-offs during economic downturns, and the co-ops' historic opposition to organized labor unions (claiming there is no clash of interests between capital and labor in an employee-owned firm). At the same time, new programs of participation aimed at enhancing productivity and customer service were evident throughout the co-ops, and employees there (as elsewhere around the world) felt the pressures associated with an increased pace of work and life. On the streets, rising consumerism was in shiny evidence, and some young people spoke about their careers more as portable possessions or achievements than as ties to land and community. Also, during the last two decades, the proportion of women in the workforce had grown tremendously and participation in the Catholic Church had dropped considerably.

Thus, the changes in values at Mondragón are both internal and external; sorting out the influences is a complex task. The economic pressure of market globalization is real, especially in sectors like automotive parts where the co-ops must compete with global giants. However, globalization is also used by management as a justification for structural and procedural changes, including the adoption of some fairly standard TQM-like practices. In many of the industrial co-ops, work teams and even larger "mini-factories" have been created that emphasize group performance and autonomy, but the reality in most instances is that the range of discretion over decisions doesn't match the pressure to produce and the electronic monitoring of production.

From a communication standpoint, the shift in meaning over time for the value term *participation* is especially interesting. Traditionally, *participación* referred to the right or even the responsibility of worker-owners (*socios* or associates) to contribute to shaping the policies of the co-ops. That right was exercised most visibly at annual assembly meetings and in preparatory "chats." But as one of the founders of the co-ops, Jesús Larrañaga argued in 1994:

> Today we need a form of neo-cooperativism. Participation means something different and more than voting on policies; it must be real participation in the daily

> work, and not something legal or political in nature. . . . We have to participate for reasons of competitiveness and the expansion of the market. And, the kind of participation we most need is not something up in the clouds, dealing with abstract issues, but something continuous and concentrated in one's job.[65]

There had been a transformation in meaning and practice, reflecting both external economic and cultural changes and a shift in managerial ideology. Can you think of other examples where the same value term was used in very different ways over time and under different circumstances? What does this lesson mean for organizations, either for-profit or not-for-profit, that are strongly based in certain values? What do you think of the possibilities for any local or regional organizations to resist the pressures of market globalization?

Ironies, Paradoxes, and Limits of Work Participation and Democracy

Since WWII, the issue of popular participation has become increasingly pressing in third world development. The push for increased participation has come from critics who charge government-sponsored social and economic development programs with being hierarchical, top-down, and unconcerned with the needs of local communities and individuals. In the last two decades, alternative organizations have become important in realizing visions of participative social change in the third world. Development communication scholar Clemencia Rodriguez observes that in an effort to be seen as more participative, international development agencies such as the World Bank have increasingly turned to third world NGOs and practitioners to design and implement development projects.[66] While this seems admirable, Rodriguez argues that an examination of the discourse of such projects reveals that they are not as participatory as they seem. In an analysis of a World Bank-driven project in Colombia to develop *Zonas de Reserva Campesina* (ZRCs) [specific rural zones where intensive social, environmental, and economic programs are initiated], Rodriguez demonstrates that the discourse of ZRC development systematically excludes Colombian women. This neglect is evident in the gendered language of World Bank development projects, Colombian law, and even in the reports of local development agents—which treat the participation of women in incidental, objectified terms. Rodriguez observes that this negation of women in development discourse lies in contradiction to the central role that women in fact play in the family, at work, and in conflicts over warfare and displacement in Colombia.

By now it should be evident that the road to democratization is a winding one, with many obstacles, blind curves, and pitfalls. Even for the best-intentioned manager, administrator, or work group, or for the most committed nonprofit agency or social movement organization, there will inevitably be tensions, contradictions, and even paradoxes. For example, can restructured work systems imposed from the top actually include democratic, team-based work practices (see box 8.6)?[67] Other paradoxes and contradictions may be more endemic to organizations that try to be democratic from the ground up: for example, there can be a tendency on the part of many social movement groups to demand that each new wave of members pass "loyalty tests" and not deviate from the founding values and practices of the organization.

This leads to what might be called "the paradox of homogeneity," where the group stamps out the very diversity that could help it flourish over time.

Another irony or limitation is related to the *range* or scope of participation. Who should participate and who shouldn't? Should participation, for example, be confined within organizational boundaries? Shareholders have some influence (often a lot of influence) on what the organization is doing, but how about other external audiences? Consider, as an example, a European company that produces chemical products in South America. For environmental reasons, the company considers replacing its production facilities with more sophisticated equipment. In addition to being more environmentally sound (and more expensive), the new equipment will result in laying off 50% of the workforce. Who should participate in this decision? Should families of the affected employees, the local government, and environmental groups (local or global) be included in discussions? Most likely, these groups will have divergent views on this issue. Whose opinion should weigh most heavily? There are no easy answers to such problems—and there's no guarantee that participation (no matter how broad its scope) will produce the best solution.

These are just three examples of intricacies related to participation and workplace democracy. The issue, as Cynthia Stohl and George Cheney explain, is not how to eliminate all these tensions or avoid them, but rather how to manage them productively. In the life of any democratic group, organization, or community, some of these challenges will arise. Some paradoxes are listed and described briefly below. Notice how each of the four major categories (structure, agency, identity, and power) deal with important aspects of organizing decisions and activities.

1. ***Paradoxes of Structure*** relate to the "architecture" of participation, e.g., "Be spontaneous, creative, vocal, and assertive in the way we have planned!"
    - ***Paradox of Design:*** imposing or mandating *grassroots* participation from the top; e.g., the board of directors decides to implement Total Quality/Participative Management
    - ***Paradox of Adaptation:*** reacting to outside forces or expectations to such a degree that the organization's "soul" is lost
    - ***Paradox of Punctuation:*** short-cutting the democratic process in practice because the process costs time; over time the vitality of the system is lost
    - ***Paradox of Formalization:*** institutionalizing democracy such that spontaneity is gone: what should be inspired becomes routine
2. ***Paradoxes of Agency*** involve the individual's (sense of) efficacy within the system; e.g., "Do things our way but in a way that's still distinctively your own!"
    - ***Paradox of Responsibility:*** relinquishing the power to make decisions to the group, particularly while insisting on the *right* to participate
    - ***Paradox of Cooperation:*** pursuing formal or informal procedures designed to further collaboration in such a way that cooperation is actually undermined
    - ***Paradox of Sociality:*** intense involvement at work limits other forms of participation (e.g., in family and community)—prevalent in mission-based organizations
    - ***Paradox of Autonomy:*** surrendering individual agency for that of the collective; the gains to the individual through adhesion to the community are soon outweighed by the sacrifices

3. ***Paradoxes of Identity*** involve issues of membership, inclusion, and boundaries, e.g., "Be *self*-managing to meet organizational goals!"
   - ***Paradox of Commitment:*** making commitment to and enactment of the group's espoused values and beliefs about voice and participation a test that ironically leads to exclusion rather than inclusion
   - ***Paradox of Representation:*** becoming co-opted by dominant interests; losing one's "voice" unexpectedly—e.g., when labor thinks like management and forgets about workers yet still insists its role is distinct
   - ***Paradox of Compatibility:*** the potential problems with exporting a particular model of democracy or participation to another society or culture
4. ***Paradoxes of Power*** concern the locus, nature, and precise exercise of power in the organization, e.g., "Be independent, just as I have commanded you!"
   - ***Paradox of Control:*** encountering less and not more freedom within team-based structures—at the group level or at the system-wide (organizational) level
   - ***Paradox of Leadership:*** waiting for a charismatic leader to inspire, create, and maintain democracy
   - ***Paradox of Homogeneity:*** failing to see the value of resistance or oppositional voices; excessive valuing of agreement, cooperation, and consensus—especially in social movement organizations—while preaching diversity of opinion

Snapshot Synthesis

Participation has been an issue of concern as long as there have been organizations. It seems only natural for members to want a voice in shaping their work lives, and organizations find participation desirable for a number of reasons, ranging from genuine concern for the welfare of employees to a desire for the productivity benefits that can follow from participative forms of management. However, even though participation is generally considered desirable, enacting participation is by no means straightforward. As we have shown, the meanings of participation and related terms such as teamwork and democracy are themselves ambiguous. Plus, there are multiple forms and degrees of participation, and a number of barriers and paradoxes that make the implementation of participation an enormous challenge. Many different forms of managerial participation programs have been designed over the years, including problem-solving or decision-making groups (such as quality circles), the restructuring of work processes (such as self-managed work teams), and employee ownership (such as employee stock ownership plans). Even so-called "alternative" organizations that are explicitly committed to participatory structures face numerous challenges to making participation work. Ultimately, it is through concrete communication practices that participation is put into practice, maintained, and evaluated.

Key Concepts

- **Workplace Democracy:** refers to principles and practices designed to engage and represent as many relevant individuals and groups as possible in the formulation, execution, and modification of work-related activities
- **Employee Participation:** organizational structures and processes designed to empower and enable employees to identify with organizational goals and to collaborate as control agents in activities that exceed minimum coordination efforts normally expected at work
- **Unitary Model of Democracy:** assumes that consensus is possible, even involving two or more differing groups
- **Adversarial Model of Democracy:** assumes that the best democratic results can only come with active opposition, open debate, and a clash of interests
- **Job Enrichment:** typically, a "top-down" process involving the analysis and reconfiguring of employees' jobs, intended to allow greater participation by employees in the work process to enhance internal motivation and job satisfaction
- **Quality Circles:** usually comprised of 10–12 members from the same or closely interrelated work areas, who meet voluntarily and on a regular basis to deal with problems of quality and productivity
- **Quality of Work Life (QWL) Programs:** designed to improve relations between managers and workers by increasing the involvement of workers in various aspects of organizational life
- **Self-directed Work Teams (SDWTs):** the basic building block of many presumably "post-bureaucratic" organizations; usually comprised of 5–15 members responsible for performing all required functions to complete the task, including the responsibilities typically performed by supervisors
- **Socio-technical Systems:** originally used to describe a network of semi-autonomous participatory work groups, the term now designates a general concern with the interrelations of the technical and social-psychological organization of industrial productions systems
- **Gainsharing Plans:** formal, supplemental compensation programs focusing on rewarding workers for improvements in labor productivity and cost reduction; Scanlon plans are the most common type of gainsharing program
- **Employee Stock Ownership Programs (ESOPs):** a common form of employee ownership program in which the company contributes stock to employees along with, in some cases, ownership privileges
- **Team:** a small number of people with complementary skills who are committed to a common purpose, set of performance goals, and strategy, for which they hold themselves accountable
- **Process Consultation:** an approach to team (or organizational) development in which someone (or everyone) observes the team process, shares their observations with the team, and lets the team discuss and agree on ways to address the observations

- **Results-driven Structure:** the organization, or structure, of the team is aligned with its purpose and the nature of its task
- **Alternative Organizations:** refers to groups, communities, and institutions outside the mainstream—emphasizing opposition to, or divergence from, traditional structures of hierarchy and centralization with "flatter," more democratic, more egalitarian ways of organizing work
- **Feminist Organizing**: a philosophy and method of organizing that seeks to empower members through organizational systems premised on equality and participation, usually subscribing to a symmetrical version of power relations

Endnotes

1 Nikolas Rose, *Governing the Soul: The Shaping of the Private Self* (London: Routledge, 1990).

2 Chris Argyris, *Integrating the Individual and the Organization* (New York: Wiley, 1964).

3 Richard Gillespie, *Manufacturing Knowledge: A History of the Hawthorne Experiments* (Cambridge, UK: Cambridge University Press, 1991).

4 David R. Seibold and B. Christine Shea, "Participation and Decision Making," *The New Handbook of Organizational Communication*, ed. Fredric M. Jablin and Linda L. Putnam (Thousand Oaks, CA: Sage, 2001).

5 Christian Berggren, *Alternatives to Lean Production: Organization in the Swedish Auto Industry* (Ithaca, NY: ILR Imprint of Cornell University Press, 1992).

6 George Cheney, *Values at Work: Employee Participation Meets Market Pressure at Mondragón* (Ithaca, NY: ILR Imprint of Cornell University Press, 1999).

7 Kenneth Burke, *A Rhetoric of Motives* (1950; Berkeley: University of California Press, 1969).

8 Cynthia Stohl and George Cheney, "Participatory Processes/Paradoxical Practices: Communication and the Dilemmas of Organizational Democracy," *Management Communication Quarterly* 14 (2001): 349–407.

9 Roland Marchand, *Creating the Corporate Soul: The Rise of Public Relations and Corporate Imagery in American Big Business* (Berkeley: University of California Press, 1998).

10 Rensis Likert, *New Patterns of Management* (New York: McGraw-Hill, 1961).

11 Eric Trist and Ken W. Bamforth, "Some Social and Psychological Consequences of the Longwall Method of Coal-Getting," *Human Relations* 4 (1951): 3–38.

12 Paul Du Gay and Graeme Salaman, "The Cult[ure] of the Customer," *Journal of Management Studies,* 29.5 (1992): 615–633.

13 William E. Halal, *The New Management: Democracy and Enterprise Are Transforming Organizations* (San Francisco: Berrett-Koehler, 1996).

14 See, e.g., Mike Parker, "Industrial Relations Myth and Shop-Floor Reality," *Industrial Democracy in America: The Ambiguous Promise*, ed. Nelson Lichtenstein (Cambridge, UK: Cambridge University Press, 1993).

15 Vicki Smith, *Crossing the Great Divide: Worker Risk and Opportunity in the New Economy* (Ithaca and London: Cornell University Press, 2001).

16 Cynthia Stohl, *Organizational Communication: Connectedness in Action* (Thousand Oaks, CA: Sage, 1995).

17 Allan Bull, letter to George Cheney, August 1998, Macquarie University, Sydney, Australia.

18 George Cheney, "Does Workplace Democracy Have a Future?" *At Work* (May/June 1998): 15–17.

19 Stohl, *Organizational Communication*.

20 H. Peter Dachler and Bernard Wilpert, "Conceptual Dimensions and Boundaries of Participation in Organizations: A Critical Evaluation," *Administrative Science Quarterly* 23 (1979): 1–38.

21 Cynthia Stohl, "European Managers Interpretations of Participation," *Human Communication Research* 20 (1993): 108–131.

22 Laurie Graham, *On the Line at Subaru-Isuzu* (Ithaca and London: Cornell University Press, 1995).

23 Burke.

24 Guillermo J. Grenier, *Inhuman Relations: Quality Circles and Anti-unionism in American Industry* (Philadelphia: Temple University Press, 1988).

25 Dana Cloud, "Laboring under the Sign of the New: Cultural Studies, Organizational Communication, and the Fallacy of the New Economy," *Management Communication Quarterly* 15 (2001): 268–278.

26 Ralph T. King, "Levi's Factory Workers Are Assigned to Teams, and Morale Takes a Hit," *The Wall Street Journal* (20 May 1998): A-1, A-6.

27 Mike Parker and Jane Slaughter, *Choosing Sides* (Boston: South End Press, 1988).

[28] Jane Mansbridge, *Beyond Adversary Democracy* (Chicago: University of Chicago Press, 1983).

[29] Much of this summary is adapted from George Cheney, Joseph Straub, Laura Speirs-Glebe, Cynthia Stohl, Dan DeGooyer, Jr., Susan Whalen, Kathy Garvin-Doxas, and David Carlone, "Democracy, Participation, and Communication at Work: A Multi-Disciplinary Review," *Communication Yearbook 21*, ed. Michael E. Roloff (Thousand Oaks, CA: Sage, 1998).

[30] George Strauss, "Workers' Participation in Management: An International Perspective," *Research in Organizational Behavior* 4 (1982): 173–265.

[31] Fritz J. Roethlisberger and William J. Dickson, *Management and the Worker* (New York: Wiley, 1939).

[32] J. Richard Hackman and Greg R. Oldham, *Work Redesign* (Reading, MA: Addison-Wesley, 1980).

[33] W. Edwards Deming, *Out of the Crisis* (Cambridge, MA: MIT Center for Advanced Engineering Study, 1986).

[34] Stohl, *Organizational Communication*.

[35] Deming.

[36] Hackman and Oldham.

[37] John L. Cotton, *Employee Involvement* (Thousand Oaks, CA: Sage, 1993).

[38] Eric L. Trist and Ken W. Bamforth, "Some Social and Psychological Consequences of the Longwall Method of Coal-Getting," *Human Relations* 4 (1951): 3–38.

[39] Fred Emery and Eric Trist, "The Causal Texture of Organizational Environments," *Systems Thinking*, ed. Fred Emery (Middlesex, UK: Penguin Books, 1969) pp. 241–258.

[40] Cory Rosen, Katherine J. Klein, and Karen M. Young, *Employee Ownership in America: The Equity Solution* (Lexington, MA: Lexington Press, 1986).

[41] Cynthia Stohl, unpublished notes, 1996. We are indebted to her for many of the ideas in this chapter.

[42] Cheney, *Values at Work*.

[43] Frank Heller, Eugen Pusic, George Strauss, and Bernhard Wilpert, *Organizational Participation: Myth and Reality* (Oxford, UK: Oxford University Press, 1998).

[44] Robert Tannenbaum and Warren H. Schmidt, "How to Choose a Leadership Pattern," *Harvard Business Review* 36.2 (March–April 1958): 95–101.

[45] See Carl E. Larson and Frank M. LaFasto, *Teamwork: What Must Go Right/What Can Go Wrong* (Newbury Park, CA: Sage, 1989); James R. Barker, Craig W. Melville, and Michael E. Pacanowsky, "Self-Directed Teams at XEL: Changes in Communication Practices during a Program of Cultural Transformation," *Journal of Applied Communication Research* 21 (1993): 297–312; Patricia Geist and Monica Hardesty, *Negotiating the Crisis: Drugs and the Transformation of Hospitals* (Hillsdale, NJ: Lawrence Erlbaum, 1992).

[46] Andrew J. Dubrin, *Leadership: Research Findings, Practice, and Skills*, 2nd ed. (New York: Houghton-Mifflin, 1998) p. 218.

[47] Jon R. Katzenbach and Douglas K. Smith, *The Wisdom of Teams: Creating the High Performance Organization* (New York: HarperCollins, 1993).

[48] Theodore E. Zorn and George H. Tompson, "Communication in Top Management Teams," *New Directions in Group Communication Research*, ed. Lawrence R. Frey (Newbury Park, CA: Sage, 2001) pp. 253–272.

[49] David A. Nadler, "Executive Team Effectiveness: Teamwork at the Top," *Executive Teams*, ed. David A. Nadler and Janet L. Spencer (San Francisco: Jossey-Bass, 1998) pp. 21–39.

[50] Larson and LaFasto.

[51] Siobhan Alderson, "Reframing Management Competence: Focusing on the Top Management Team," *Personnel Review* 22 (1993): 53–62.

[52] Susan R. Glaser, "Teamwork and Communication: A Three-Year Case Study of Change," *Management Communication Quarterly* 7 (1994): 282–296.

[53] James R. Barker, Craig W. Melville, and Michael Pacanowsky, "Self-Directed Teams at XEL: Changes in Communication Practice during a Program of Cultural Transformation," *Journal of Applied Communication Research* 21.4 (Nov. 1983): 297–312.

[54] Sunwolf and David Seibold, "The Impact of Formal Procedures on Group Processes, Members, and Task Outcomes," *The Handbook of Group Communication Theory and Research,* ed. Lawrence R. Frey (Thousand Oaks, CA: Sage, 1999): 395–431. See also Lawrence R. Frey, ed. *Innovations in Group Facilitation: Applications in Natural Settings* (Cresskill, NJ: Hampton Press, 1995).

[55] Adapted from Larson and LaFasto.

[56] See Teresa Harrison, "Communication and Interdependence in Democratic Organizations," in *Communication Yearbook 17*, ed. Stanley Deetz (Thousand Oaks, CA: Sage, 1994).

[57] Jane J. Mansbridge, "Time, Emotion, and Inequality: Three Problems of Participatory Groups, *Journal of Applied Behavioral Science* 9 (1973): 351–68.

[58] Hollis Glaser, "Structure and Struggle in Egalitarian Groups: Reframing the Problems of Time, Emotion, and Inequality as Defining Characteristics," diss., U Illinois Urbana-Champaign, 1994.

[59] Laetitia B. Mulder and Henk A. M. Wilke, "Participation and Power Equalization," *Organizational Behavior and Human Performance* 5 (1970): 430–438.

[60] Karen L. Ashcraft, "Organized Dissonance: Feminist Bureaucracy as Hybrid Form," *Academy of Management Journal* 44 (2001): 1301–1322; Karen L. Ashcraft, "Empowering 'Professional' Relationships: Organizational Communication Meets Feminist Practice," *Management Communication Quarterly* 13 (2000): 347–392.

[61] Henry Mintzberg, *The Structuring of Organizations* (Englewood Cliffs, NJ: Prentice-Hall, 1979).

[62] Harrison.

[63] Joyce Rothschild and J. Allen Whitt, *The Cooperative Workplace* (Cambridge, UK: Cambridge University Press, 1986).

[64] Shiv Ganesh, "Organizational Narcissism: Technology, Legitimacy, and Identity in an Indian NGO," *Management Communication Quarterly* (In press).

[65] Cheney, *Values at Work*.

[66] Clemencia Rodriguez, "Shattering Butterflies and Amazons: Symbolic Constructions of Women in Colombian Development Discourse," *Communication Theory* 11 (2001): 472–494.

[67] Stohl and Cheney.

9

Power and Control in Organizational Life

Power is an important issue in our everyday lives, in organizations, and in society. *All of us have theories about power.* Sometimes we think of power as bad—something to reject, avoid, or deny. Other times it becomes a goal. What are some characteristics of power and how does it work? Here are some possibilities:

- Power is held by a few people.
- Real power goes with money.
- Land ownership grants power.
- Information is power.
- Education and expertise are sources of power.
- The government is the most powerful institution in society.
- Corporations are the most powerful institutions in society.
- Power is concentrated in the hands of white males.
- The northern hemisphere has more power than the southern hemisphere.
- Power means getting others to do your bidding while thinking it's their idea.
- There is power in what is not said as well as in what is said.
- The trappings and the appearance of power don't mean anything.
- The trappings of power and the appearance of power are everything.
- Power has to be given.
- Power must be taken.
- Power is negotiated.
- Being powerful today doesn't mean being powerful tomorrow.
- Power tends to beget power or reproduce itself.
- Power lies not with what you know but whom you know.
- One institution's powers must be kept in check by other institutions' powers.

- "Power tends to corrupt, and absolute power corrupts absolutely." (*Baron Lord Acton*)
- There are lots of benevolent or well-intentioned uses of power.
- We can escape or get beyond power.
- We can have power "with" others as well as power "over" others.
- Power is an inherent part of society; we can't get rid of it.

These 25 statements express various beliefs about power. You probably agree with some of the ideas and not others. For example, we hear about lots of scandals in all the major institutions of society, so you may come to the conclusion that *power corrupts*—or at least that power tends to corrupt. If so, you might say, "I don't trust anybody who has very much power or who has been in power for a long time, because of the temptation to be corrupt." Since theory flows from generalizing across different cases, you have the foundation for a theory of power. Interestingly, most lay theories of power correspond to formal theories about power in society. We will highlight some of these parallels in this chapter.

Encountering Power

Over the past century, hundreds of definitions of power have been advanced. Probably the only unifying theme running through those definitions is: *the ability or capacity to achieve a goal even against the interests, will, or resistance of others*. This general characterization of power matches Max Weber's concern about how to explain *uncoerced obedience.* Why do we do things that institutions tell us to do? How and under what circumstances do individuals surrender autonomy to larger social units? This question was a main preoccupation of Weber's, and he addressed it in part through working out his three "ideal types" of authority (charismatic, traditional, and legal-rational) and by explaining the forces of rationalization at work in modern society. Moreover, Weber saw organizations of all kinds as being fundamentally about control—in the sense that they strive to maintain some kind of order in the ways they harness the energies of their members.[1]

Weber wasn't arguing that every organization is designed *only* to control people, but he was saying that organizations, by their very nature, do control people. From Weber's standpoint, there are legitimate exercises of power or control and non-legitimate ones. By *legitimate* he means the ones that society says are okay. For example, we are allowed to teach classes and do research because of our degrees. Because we are associated with large institutions, we are provided with certain resources to do that. *Authority* is the legitimate use of power in a society. It doesn't mean everybody sees this use of power as legitimate, and it doesn't mean it's the same across all societies or across all times. It does mean, however, that at a particular moment, in a particular society, most people agree that this exercise of power is okay. The ultimate challenge to authority is a mutiny, a rebellion, a coup, or a revolution. But authority is confronted in less direct ways as well, as we'll discuss under the topic of *resistance* later.

The general definition of power offered above is not completely satisfying or encompassing, for either theoretical or practical purposes. For example, the emphasis on *ability* seems to suggest that power rests only with individual persons. This severely limits our understanding of how we are influenced by the structures and the organization of institutions. Focusing on the "Who?" of power (however important that may be in certain cases where one person truly is "in charge") underplays the importance of the interactional dynamics and patterns of power in which people operate. Power happens between and among people in specific situations; it isn't limited to the individuals we see as powerful persons. When we're new in a job or a community, we often try to scope out "where the power is"—how the big decisions are made, which policies are taken the most seriously, which lines not to cross, etc. This is all part of "learning the ropes" in an organization. We negotiate the terrain with others to learn the boundaries.

The stress on goal-attainment, however, overlooks the fact that many exercises of power are not tied to intentions. In fact, they often seem to be part of the fabric of society itself. The Jerzy Kosinski novel (1971) and the Hal Ashby film *Being There* (1979) depicted how power can be exercised without intention. The simple-minded character played by Peter Sellers in the movie was totally without any desire to influence others, yet his words were eagerly heeded by the public. When he spoke about gardening, political and business leaders thought he was talking in metaphor about the inevitable rise and fall of the economy! So much for the notion that you have to *intend* to use power to exercise it and to have an effect on others.

Primary (childhood) and secondary (e.g., work) socialization processes shape how we think about and relate to the world. We learn certain assumptions and value premises through family, friends, and education. Sometimes we don't even know or remember where certain ideas or attitudes came from; that is, we can't recall specific messages about them. Subtle forms of racism or anti-Semitism or religious intolerance do not always have clear origins for the individuals who express those prejudices. You may be able to identify key moments, turning points, or memorable messages that led to the development of certain attitudes,[2] but you might not be able to pin down the source of other beliefs. Socialization and re-socialization are complicated matters because these processes depend on an accumulation of messages from many sources, including the mass media. Similarly, a simple association of power with identifiable actions of individual persons doesn't tell the whole story.

The "Who" of Power

One of the biggest issues with respect to power in organizations is *whom to blame*. In certain organizational structures—take a monarchy, for instance—you know exactly whom to blame, the King or the Queen and their minions. These people are visible; they're public; and they may have absolute control. To be able to point to someone or some group who is in charge is comforting in a way because you know where the power is coming from and exactly how it's being exercised. We like to be able to pin down power, to figure it out. Dorothy and her friends in the 1939 movie *The Wizard of Oz* look forward to meeting the Wizard; but at the same time they are terrified because they see him as *the* ultimate source of power.

But in a bureaucratic organization, authority is not nearly so personal or visible most of the time, and that's both positive and negative. It's good in the sense that *power gets distributed* through a system in a bureaucratic organization, but it's negative (and maddening) in the sense that we can't always tell who's responsible, who made this decision, and why. If you have read some of Franz Kafka's books (for example, *The Process*), you have an idea of how frustrating this latter feeling is. Sometimes no one can answer questions directly—not because they are trying to deceive, but because power has been diffused through many people and numerous

"If we can just get beyond this 'I'm the boss' mentality and concentrate on a simple 'What I say goes' outlook, I think this will all work out."

decisions over time. People no longer know why they did "x" yesterday. They just know that if they don't do "x" tomorrow, they might get in trouble. It would disrupt the pattern, clog up the system, and rip the social fabric. When people tell us "we're just following the rules," they're often being quite sincere and not trying to frustrate our search for the origin of the decision. Organizations, like people, thrive on a certain degree of routine, exemplified in the phrase "that's the way we do things around here." In that sense, the logic of traditional authority operates even in a bureaucracy that's supposed to be beyond such non-rational ways of justifying actions.

On the societal level, the "Who?" of power becomes even more problematic. Let's return to the power of socialization. Most U.S. citizens today routinely refer to the events of 1861–1865 as *The Civil War*, rejecting the alternative and very different labels: "War between the States," "War of Southern Secession," and "War of Northern Aggression." Each of these labels has a very distinct sense, and each reflects certain assumptions about the parties to the conflict: whether one nation or distinct groups of states were involved, who was the aggressor, etc. To the victor goes the power to label the events of history. U.S. historian Shelby Foote has uncovered old documents that show that prior to that conflict it was common to say "The United States *are*," whereas following the war people were much more likely to say "The United States *is*."[3] This is a vivid example of the power of language not only to reflect major changes in society but also to help make them happen.

Similarly, we may observe the rise and fall of certain heroes in Mexican history as depicted in school textbooks. During the Salinas de Gortari administration (from

1988–92), all primary school history books were systematically rewritten to identify different heroes other than those celebrated previously. For example, Emilio Zapata, a socialist fighter during the Mexican Revolution of 1910–1921, became a footnote. There is great power in the ability to write or rewrite history, to say what's important, to give light to certain issues or personalities and not others. Arvind Rajagopal, for example, argues that the telecasting of the 70-episode *Ramayana* in 1987 in India was especially significant because it brought diverse notions of the epic Hindu story together onto one screen and provided standardized images of "Hinduness" to an audience that was otherwise remarkably diverse in terms of language, class, and ethnicity. Followed one year later by the 94-episode *Mahabharata*, both series were stupendously successful. An estimated forty to eighty million people watched every week. During this time, the Hindu right-wing Bharatiya Janata Party gained rapid national prominence; coincidence seems an unlikely explanation.[4]

Finally, the definition of power above includes the term *resistance.* But it neglects the fact that power is often not met with resistance (or countervailing power) simply because the exercise of power is not always recognized. In many types of meetings from the boardroom to the school board, certain issues and alternative viewpoints are not placed on the agenda; they are not even considered by those who *ought* to think of them. Each of us—George, Lars, Ted, and Shiv—has been in meetings where a topic or a direct question has been raised by someone and then completely ignored by others in the room. It's a very strange feeling to witness an attempt to communicate confronted by a wall of silence.

The "How" of Power

British political sociologist Steven Lukes explains that many instances of power-in-use are extremely subtle and likely to go unnoticed (see box 9.6). There can be no resistance without first having recognition.[5] If you don't know you're being persuaded or

Box 9.1 Exercise
Developing Your Own Definition of Power

Definitions of power, the "who" of power, and the "how" of power take many forms. In addition to the aspects of power discussed in the chapter, the meanings of power are affected by culture. In Spanish, for instance, the word *poder* conveys more of a sense of "enablement" than does the German *Macht.* In Chinese and in Japanese, ideas of power are tied closely to legitimate authority and to the management of "face" on the part of an individual or a group. These are just a few examples. In the classroom, we ask students to diagram how power is related to a number of other concepts, those listed at the end of the box. Venn diagrams (circles that are sometimes distinct or that overlap in varying degrees) are useful for depicting the interrelationships. You can illustrate whether you think power is a larger domain than authority, how much of power is persuasion, etc. This exercise helps examine our assumptions about power in organizations and society. Ideas about the interrelationships of these terms will vary from person to person. The diagrams provide a good starting point for debating questions like: "Where does persuasion end and manipulation begin?"

- Authority
- Coercion
- Influence
- Coordination
- Persuasion
- Cooperation
- Force
- Compliance
- Domination
- Manipulation
- Seduction
- Enticement

even manipulated, you're certainly not going to object! This highlights the relationship between power and persuasion. While there are types of power that do not involve persuasion (e.g., coercion), there are probably not forms of persuasion outside the bounds of power. A case study of the Appalachian region of Tennessee, one of the poorest regions of the United States, explores why the poor persons in that resource-rich region have never "risen up" physically or verbally in opposition to the British and U.S. coal-mining operations that have exploited their wealth, kept their wages down, and controlled entire communities (examples of what are commonly called "company towns"). Sociologist John Gaventa, who grew up in the region, explains that the people simply have come to accept their lot in life and have suppressed their interest in trying to change things.[6] In a study of a very different part of the world, political scientist Albert Memmi, in *The Colonizer and the Colonized,* shows how some Algerians, formerly under French rule, had internalized the idea of domination and applied it to other groups—often without realizing how they were extending the lines of oppression.[7] The same thing can occur with victims of domestic violence; the abused may eventually repeat the violence with their own children, even though they resolved to be different.

Sources of Power

The list at the beginning of the chapter included several sources of power. *Land* is perhaps the most traditional of these resources. The feudal system, in Europe, Asia, and other parts of the world, illustrates this source of power. Land was concentrated in the hands of a few nobles; the rest of the population worked the land for the landowners in a relationship of outright or quasi slavery. The rise of capitalism with the increase in trade in the late Middle Ages in Europe and the movement away from barter to the abstract notion of capital opened possibilities other than agriculture for producing and securing wealth. The European middle class developed from merchants and traders who benefited from the flow of goods across borders. Aside from the Church and the empires, these were the first multinational organizations. Their emergence anticipated the rise of the first truly multinational corporations like the Dutch East Indies and West Indies Companies in the seventeenth century. One of the most interesting and influential critiques of this budding capitalism came from Karl Marx, who based his critique firmly in the material dimensions of class relationships and the capitalist economy (see box 9.2).

What is especially interesting about *capital* (money) as a source of power is its abstract nature. Even when various countries used to link their currencies directly to reserves in gold or silver, capital took on an abstract quality that was partially removed from the goods or services or labor it represented. While we often think of money as material in nature, in another sense, it is one of the most abstract resources of power. Economic systems today depend on trust, confidence, agreements, and persuasion. A good example of this is the value of one currency (say, the Euro) in relation to another (say, the U.S. dollar); the conversion rate at a given time depends on perceptions of the strength of the two economies in question.

The economy, thus, is both material and symbolic, both solid and intangible. Why is a particular item *worth* a high price? Or, why is a particular kind of work valued at only a minimum wage level? When we look at markers of economic "value," we should see the element of arbitrariness involved. For example, the salaries of administrative assistants are quite low in many countries, even though their actual work can be demanding and they have access to some of the most important knowledge of the organization.

Stock indexes go up or down in response to changes in productivity or profit or unemployment or inflation, but they are also subject to levels of confidence about the health of the economy and to decisions among groups of investors, the international bond markets, and key financiers. In the United States, for example, it used to be the case that reports of massive layoffs within an industry, like steel or auto manufacturing or communications, would result in those stocks *declining* dramatically in value. Since about 1985, the reverse has been true. "Downsizing" and "rightsizing" have become acceptable corporate practice and a sign of a positive step along the way to greater economic efficiency and higher profits. Thus, the predominant interpretation for a particular management choice can have a huge impact on economics in general.

Box 9.2 Karl Marx
The Concepts of Class and Alienation

Two aspects of Marx's work, class and alienation, are significant for the study of power in organizations. The Marxist treatment of class must be understood as a reaction to the "functionalist" treatment of class, which regarded divisions between human beings as inevitable and necessary in order for society to function. The Marxist approach sees class differences as being *material*—as arising from the relations of various social groups to the forces of production—land, capital, labor, etc.[8] For Marx, class relationships mark the progress of history itself and are necessarily antagonistic. He saw the basic tension in capitalist organizations between the *bourgeoisie*, who own the forces of production, and the *proletariat*, who are subject to it. Since the objective of capitalism is profit making, it is based on a system of exchange wherein surplus value—the difference between the exchange (or market) value of the product and the wages of the worker—is gained through the buying of labor power at a grossly inadequate price. The relation between the bourgeoisie and the proletariat is therefore highly asymmetrical, but interdependent.

Marx borrowed the concept of alienation from Hegel. For Marx, alienation was the historical outcome of the increased division of labor in capitalist organizations. In such systems, the product of labor, instead of being an expression of creativity, becomes a symbol of oppression to workers because they do not own it—instead, it owns *them*. The very nature of work becomes external to the worker, since the worker does not own either the instrument of production or the object that is produced.[9] But Marx, and many observers since, have found other kinds of alienation at work and in our larger society: including the ways we become alienated from one another in our various jobs, professions, and careers. The division of labor, where the machine dictates to the worker who becomes the object of control—as epitomized by the assembly line—is one of the most pronounced forms of alienation. For Marx, because alienation is such an inextricable aspect of the capitalist cycle, its only resolution lies in the transcendence of capitalism itself. In the *Communist Manifesto*, Marx and his colleague Friedrich Engels wrote about the revolutionary consciousness that must be established among workers in order to organize a new community where collective freedom is determined by individual freedom.[10]

Which of Marx's ideas do you think are still relevant today? How is the notion of "class" both material and symbolic (or persuasive)? How can the concept of alienation at work and in society be extended and updated? In what different ways are we alienated, or separated, from control over our work? In what ways are we alienated from one another through divisions in society?

This is exactly why economist Deirdre McCloskey (1984, 1994) speaks of "the rhetoric of economics," referring to the huge role that persuasion plays in what we often think of as the "hard facts" of the economic realm. This is not to say that all of economics is a game, or that it has no material basis.[11] Persuasion operates on two broad levels here: *first*, in terms of what happens in the economy—as when fear of higher inflation rates leads analysts and policy makers to raise interest rates for borrowing money; *second*, in terms of the very economic models we use to represent "what's going on" in the world.

Thinking back to our discussion of metaphor in chapter 1, consider how economics, like other disciplines, relies on metaphor to explain things. Economic models, and curves, and images do have a certain relationship to what we call "reality," but they are also human estimations, or sometimes sheer guesses, about whole patterns of human behavior. When we become too attached to abstract models, we forget that they are intended to be representations of human behavior and that human behavior itself can change. One generation's ideas about savings and consumption may be reversed by what the next generation does. The model, the representation, needs to be modified to reflect this. The important point is that when we move from land (a tangible) to capital (a symbol) as a resource for power, the role of persuasion increases tremendously. Power moves into the realm of the symbolic, the domain of communication.

In reviewing the movement of the key locus of power over the past 500 years (especially but not only in the West), economist John Kenneth Galbraith charts the shift from land to capital to what he terms "organized expertise."[12] Galbraith allows that land is still a very important resource (as is evident when you try to buy land, a house, or a condominium in most of the world's major cities), but he points out that the principal resource of power shifted in modern society toward capital at some point during the European Renaissance. Another huge shift took place around the middle of the twentieth century—the rise of shared knowledge about how to organize large-scale projects and institutions. With the advent of computer technologies and electronic communications of various sorts, centers of power emerged around *information*. In the distant past, it was unimaginable that knowledge or expertise or information alone could be a huge source of power. Today, the enormous computer and communications industries, where there are now literally hundreds of different professional specializations, testify to the shift identified by Galbraith.[13] It is not just an empty cliché to say that information is power. On the broadest level, Galbraith emphasizes the premium placed on professional know-how, in areas of knowledge that society decides to reward.

The Social Construction of Knowledge

Communication is a source of power because what *counts as important knowledge* is decided by people. The "packaging" (i.e., the communication about) of different sets of information makes a huge difference in what will be accepted or viewed as "hot." Knowledge and wisdom don't *come to us*; they are created and constructed as we try to figure out the world and determine what goals are interesting to pursue. This is apparent when we look at whatever management trends are in vogue. In order to be part of the crowd, we have to speak the same language of what's in fashion—whether it be "quality management" or "customer service" or "teamwork." Today's hot topic of "knowledge management" puts a spotlight on the various kinds of information that an organization has at its disposal: how to retrieve it, create it, evaluate it, and ultimately use it.[14]

While history consists of material and physical events, history as a discipline is really a set of words expressed from a particular point of view. Any discipline of study is really a vocabulary that corresponds to a certain way of viewing the world. When we choose the terms of sociology over those of psychology, the world looks different and in a sense *is* different. As Kenneth Burke explained, when we realize just how much of what we call "history" is made up of nothing but symbols, the feeling is a bit like "peering into an abyss."[15]

Box 9.3 Food for Thought
What Knowledge Counts as Important?

Think about the types of knowledge that are the most highly prized today in your society, and the advantages and disadvantages of these rankings of different forms of expertise. Ask yourself these questions: Which professions or positions are the most highly paid? Why?; Which professions or positions command the greatest respect? Why?; What categories of people occupy these privileged professions? (Think in terms of education, gender, and ethnicity, for example.); Which kinds of expertise or bodies of information are the most highly prized or are in the greatest demand? Why?; How have these rankings perhaps changed in recent years?; What do you see as positive and negative about this kind of hierarchy? Which things would you value more, or less?

Consider also the types of nonfiction books (videos, CDs, DVDs, etc.) that are most popular now. What do rankings on best-seller lists tell us about society and the things it holds important? As you answer this question, consider books about: "how to" do things; self-improvement; paths to success; celebrity lives; business; money; and power.

Relationships and Power

Another way to think about resources for power is in terms of *relationships*. In a famous article written over 30 years ago, social psychologists John French and Bertram Raven outlined what they called "the bases of social power": the strength of power in the relationship between two people, O and P, in some system *a* is defined as the maximum potential or ability of O to influence P in *a*.[16] The bases of social power thus refer to the kind of relationship that O has with P—to the ways that relationship is characterized. French and Raven identify five main bases of power.

- *Reward Power*: where O is able to grant or deny positive sanctions to P
- *Coercive Power*: where O can threaten to punish P
- *Legitimate Power*: where O has recognized authority over P
- *Referent Power*: where O has power over P because P identifies with O
- *Expert Power:* where P acknowledges that O has certain information, knowledge, or skills

Notice that in all five bases of power, the relationship between the two people is fundamentally important. So, P's *perception* of O enters into the determination of whether P has power over O. This is an important dimension of power: whether a person views another as being powerful determines, to a large degree, how much power the other actually has. In the popular media, we often can see how positional or legitimate power is limited when popular opinion turns against a particular leader. In late 1999, the power of Gerhard Schroeder as German Chancellor was greatly diminished compared to what it had been at the beginning of that year. As was his predecessor Helmut Kohl, Schroeder was blamed for being slow to deal with some of the problems associated with West Germany's absorption of the former East Germany. The decline in popularity resulted in a real loss of power. Schroeder's opposition to the invasion of Iraq by U.S. forces in 2003 restored both his popularity and his power.

In the case of a department head's relationship to her employees, we may find all five of the resources for power: reward, coercive, legitimate, referent, and expert. At various times, one or another base of power may become more important than the others. For instance, in times of crisis, legitimate power may be expanded and a leader will be granted more authority to make decisions and dictate actions of others. In mentoring relationships, which develop over time, referent power may be the most prominent aspect of the relationship. The mentor is admired and to some extent emulated by the younger, less experienced colleague.[17]

As noted in chapter 7, new conceptions of leaders are placing a greater emphasis on expertise than on legitimate power. The authority of the manager or administrator is not acquired completely through position; rather, the authoritativeness of her work has to be established over time and in the course of everyday judgments and activities. For women in many organizations, this emphasis on "earned authority" can have a sharp edge. They are frequently granted less positional authority than male

Box 9.4 Power as Finite or Expanding Tannenbaum's Model of Total Power in an Organization

Arnold Tannenbaum's detailed study of power made extensive use of what is sometimes called "the reputational method." The researcher surveyed members of an organization and asked them to indicate, along a quantifiable scale, "How much power or influence does each individual (or group) have within the organization?" This method enabled Tannenbaum ultimately to characterize power relations in an entire organization. Tannenbaum considered the *total* amount of power in an organization, arguing that the sum could increase, decrease, or remain the same. In this way, Tannenbaum viewed power as something other than a finite resource and thereby challenged the common lay perception of a power relationship (or set of relationships) as a "zero-sum" game (i.e., as power increases for one party, it must decrease correspondingly for the other party by the same amount).[18]

Consider an organization in which you have been a member or with which you are familiar. Think about how the total amount of power in that organization may increase. Ask yourself the following questions: (1) In what ways would this be possible—through some new program, through a top-down policy change, by a bottom-up initiative, through the actions of outside forces such as the market or legal frameworks, or by some other means? (2) Do you think the total increase in power in the organization is related or unrelated with the organization's "effectiveness?" (3) What would an increase in the total amount of power in the organization mean for communication patterns in the organization? Would they automatically become more open? Would there be more participation? Would there be more effective coordination?

Do you see power as a finite or as an infinite resource? Why? What are the advantages and disadvantages for the observer of organizations in treating power as a resource that can be managed? When do you think power really is just like a material resource? And when do you think such a view might limit our thinking and our ability to change a situation?

managers and feel they must constantly prove themselves. Moreover, female leaders often feel they must walk a thin line between stereotypically feminine or "soft" roles and excessively "masculinized" ones. In fields or industries that are historically male-dominated, such as the natural sciences, engineering, and airline piloting, the challenge can be a heavy and unfair burden.[19]

With reference to today's team-based restructuring, it is often difficult for many traditional supervisors and managers to make the transition to work teams where positions are not so clearly identified as they are in a more hierarchical form of organization. As we will see shortly, *control over the communication process* itself can be an important resource for power. Think of the power of gatekeepers in deciding which issues are left off the agenda for a meeting.

Getting a Handle on Power

Power is a slippery matter, both in theory and in real life. As with leadership, one of the greatest problems in analyzing power is that we tend to "reify" it (treat it as if a material thing).[20] This makes sense, in a way, because concrete things like land and other possessions are sources of power. Also, we often try to reduce complex concepts to something more easily understood. As we saw in chapter 1, metaphors help us make sense of complex issues. Saying "He gave away some power" becomes a useful way of communicating that a manager delegated some authority. Still, this kind of thinking prevents us from understanding that even in the apparently simple instance of power-*in-use*, power is often a dynamic, *interactional* phenomenon. It is a dimension of social relationships in whatever domain we want to talk about. Power has both a "surface structure," in terms of what is observed and grasped immediately about social relations, and a "deep structure," rooted in concealed but important aspects of how society functions. We'll talk more about this later, in terms of apparent versus unobtrusive aspects of power-in-use.

To illustrate our point about the complexities of power in interaction, we want to give you one of our favorite examples—a series of exchanges between a parent and a child a few weeks before the child's birthday.

Episode 1: The father says, "What would you like for your birthday?" The child takes a few seconds to think and then says, "I want a horse." The father is somewhat taken aback by the enormity of the child's request and says "No," but with an explanation about how the family can't afford a horse, doesn't have a place to keep it, can't take care of it, etc. We now have completed episode one: the child makes a request for a horse; the father denies the request. If we code this interaction using a simple scheme indicating "who's up and who's down," we would say that the score is Parent, 1; Child, 0.

Episode 2. The child comes back to the father and initiates the interaction. "Daddy, you know what I would like? A big dog." The father's response once again is negative, but this time the explanation he gives his daughter is even longer: "Well, our house isn't that big, we can't really have a dog, I'm going to be stuck taking care of it, and you know how much they eat," etc. Scoring this new episode, we now have a total of Parent, 2; Child, 0.

Episode 3: The father initiates this one, saying: "Okay, your birthday is getting really close now, so what would you like?" After pausing to think for a few seconds, the child responds: "I'd like a Guinea pig." The father quickly agrees: "Sure, you can have a Guinea pig." At this point, of course, the father may be feeling a bit guilty. "I've said 'no' twice, so I've got to say 'yes' now."

Here we see how simple coding schemes that identify "Who's in charge?" cannot account for everything that's going on—even in this basic everyday interaction. This is a classic example of where posing the question, "Who has the power?" is not enough. If we ask the question that way, we conclude that the parent had legitimate power (or authority) and retained the ability to deny or grant each request. From this perspective, we might say that the child exercised a bit of power by getting her wish in the third instance, but basically we're going to conclude that most of the power was held by the father.

Of course, there's a degree of truth in that assessment, but it overlooks the possibility that the child may have *framed or structured* the entire episode, to get what she wanted all along. This strategy is what experienced salespersons know as the "door in the face" persuasive strategy: asking for something big at first (like a huge contribution to a charity) and then moving toward a smaller request (a lesser amount that the person may well contribute). The opposite is the "foot in the door" strategy, where you ask for something small (like one magazine subscription) and then work your way up to a larger request (several magazine subscriptions). Research shows that both strategies tend to increase one's chances of obtaining a favorable response.[21]

Looking at the episode from both "macro" and "micro" levels enables us to appreciate the complexities of power in interaction. If we only asked the question of *who* has power, we've got to side with the parent and conclude, of course, the parent has more power than the child. But then we haven't learned much about what potentially went on in these three interactions. It's more useful to investigate control by each party. In cases such as this one, power is not something static, but rather an aspect of social relationships that is negotiated.

Negotiating Power

A number of theorists have helped us see the ways in which power is negotiated. Aristotle made an interesting distinction between what he called *artistic proofs*—the use of persuasion—and *inartistic proofs*. The latter included uses of force but also contracts and specified systems of rewards and punishments. Why did Aristotle lump all those things together as non-persuasion? Because they limit human choice. For example, once you sign a contract, you are legally bound, and persuasion from the other signatories or from yourself is irrelevant (unless of course you have to be persuaded to honor the contract). In fact, when relationships become more contract-based, as they are in some countries today, some of the more informal, spontaneous parts of interaction are reduced in significance. Another effect of reliance on contracts can be that trust is diminished and relationships become more colored by power. In any case, it's important to keep in mind the types of situations where power is not "up for grabs," or even under discussion. These are in contrast with cases where power can be shaped or modified by interaction, and where the outcomes of its exercise are uncertain or unstable.

Implicit Messages about Power and Authority

Chester Barnard, for example, emphasized that power or authority (as in the legitimate or socially sanctioned use of power) *must usually be granted* by those who would follow the directive of a person or group in authority.[22] Similarly, Steven Lukes identifies two levels of authority in a directive or command. The first level is the actual *content* of the message ("Do this!" or "Don't do that!"); the second level is the implicit dimension of the message that asks the receiver not to follow conflicting directives from other people (see box 9.6 for an application of Lukes's model to analyze aspects of power).[23] That is, each directive carries with it an indirect suggestion that the hearer should ignore or reject other commands that would conflict with the first directive. If this second level of the message is accepted, not only will *that* directive have force but also the hearer will likely see the giver of the directive as authoritative—perhaps for other matters. Both Barnard and Lukes cast power largely in terms of the communication process. From their viewpoints, understanding power means paying attention to what happens when people relate to one another, whether they approach the situation as equals or as members of a hierarchical relationship.

A CEO, for example, may come to be labeled as "ineffective," as the stock prices for the corporation plummet. In that case, a widespread perception of her weakness cannot be overcome by her appeals to the power of her position. Interestingly, management expert Rosabeth Moss Kanter finds that explicit appeals to power—"You know, I've got the power to make or break this company"—are often signs that the speaker's perceived power is on the decline.[24] We can see the negotiated aspects of power more clearly when we consider how comparatively less powerful members of an organization utilize certain strategies to get what they want (see box 9.5). Of course, there still are cases of brute uses of power—as in threats, physical violence, imprisonment, and the total manipulation of a situation—where it is unrealistic and very misleading to say that power is a "two-way" matter.

Box 9.5 Mechanic's "The Power of Lower Participants"[25]

In 1962 David Mechanic wrote a now-famous article that argued for a more negotiated view of power. He saw three main sources of power: (1) information and knowledge; (2) persons in authority and as sources of information; and (3) "instrumentalities" such as architecture, technology, and capital. When lower participants in an organization—those persons we ordinarily view as having limited power—gain access to one or more of these sources, *they are able to enjoy much more power than would otherwise have been predicted.* One example is the position of the administrative assistant. She often has more power than her position would imply—simply because of her access to information, her gatekeeping role in the physical setting (instrumentality), and perhaps her influence with her superior. The same thing can be said about janitors at universities, who often hold literal gatekeeping roles (for example, keys to all doors) or personnel with technical expertise, like people working in the computer service department.

"Sovereign-centered" and Strategic Visions of Power

In *Frameworks of Power,* organizational theorist Stewart Clegg addresses some of the most difficult theoretical problems related to the study of power and organizations. He traces two general lines of analysis of power. The first derives from philosopher Thomas Hobbes (1588–1679) and focuses on "the sovereign" or the "personal" and identifiable uses of power. Hobbes is famous for the characterization of life as "nasty, brutish, and short" and he believed that every society needed a powerful central force—a kind of "sovereign"—to maintain order. From this perspective, the stress is on power associated with an individual, a group, or an institution—power that proceeds from a distinct and visible source. The "Who" of power is readily identifiable. We can see or feel the power of the queen, or CEO, or president, or administrator.

Clegg sees a different sort of conceptualization of power originating with Niccolo Machiavelli (1467–1527). Machiavelli was a political advisor in early Renaissance Florence, which was then a powerful city-state in what is now central Italy. He wrote a book about strategies of power called *The Prince*. In it, Machiavelli laid out in detail the conditions for obtaining and withholding power. His perspective on power emphasizes power-in-use, the *strategic* aspects of power as a basic dimension of human relations. From this standpoint, the "How?" of power is the more important question. As Clegg points out, this question is answered by observing what actually goes on in a power relationship, such as exists in a courtroom, a staff meeting, or even between a parent and child.[26]

Clegg believes that both perspectives—the "Who" and the "How"—on power are important. He argues that it may be best to consider power*s* (plural) or various "circuits" of power in society, recognizing that different social contexts evoke different types of power (that is, different strategies, different resources, different symbols, etc.). For example, think of how various kinds of technology, material resources, and social factors come together in a work setting to determine power relations and their outcomes. Every dimension of the organization, whether symbolic or non-symbolic, can contribute to the workings of power. Capital gives a department the ability to initiate new projects. Expertise and technology allow it to execute those projects. Persuasion and authority function so that certain values, preferences, directives, and suggestions are put into action. In all these arenas, though, even with something as solid as architecture, symbolism intervenes. The configuration of a workspace, such as location of certain offices, is "translated" or interpreted by those who pay attention to these things and who use them. Thus, regardless of the intent of the overall designer, people will try to make sense of things like the accessibility, size, and setting of an office.

In this way, as French sociologist Bruno Latour explains, all aspects of an organization—even the material parts of it—enter into a larger "text."[27] And that text is full of implications for power: possibilities and actualities of influence. When the Sears Corporation moved from its famous tower in downtown Chicago to a suburban campus-style structure in the 1990s, it was both symbolizing and trying to effect change in a team-oriented direction: a literal as well as a figurative "flattening" of the organization. What happens in practice—in the complex of interrelations within the firm—can only be assessed over time and with respect to multiple "circuits of power" in Clegg's terms. Some employees might *respond* to the change in physical setting; others might *use* it; still others might try to *adapt or even transform* it further. For some, the architecture of the company might be a powerful symbol of change, while for others it could be a cynical symbol of superficial attempts at inviting participation.

Using Clegg's distinction between sovereign-centered and strategic notions of power, we can return to our example of the parent and child to understand how we could come to very different conclusions about the episode. Focusing on the *holder* of power would highlight the role of the father, who has legitimate authority ("Because I'm the dad, that's why!"). But, a strategic perspective helps us to appreciate how even a small child can try to frame an entire series of interactions to get what she wants. Ultimately, we need both perspectives to figure out what's really going on in many situations.

Power in Messages, Interactions, and Patterns of Talk

When we say that power is often exercised in strategic ways, we have to be careful. We don't mean that all exercises of power are fully conscious or tied to individuals' intentions. Otherwise, it would be impossible to explain the power of a bureaucracy or the power of socialization. Rather, we mean that there are certain patterns of communicating that have major effects on shaping attitudes and behavior—*even when people aren't fully aware of them and even when the effects aren't intended*. Take, for example, how subordinates often anticipate the wishes of their superiors. The "boss" may not say explicitly that she would like a different kind of proposal from the young advertising designer who reports to her, but the designer "gets the message" that the boss isn't happy with the current design because she has made no comment about it. It is possible that the manager is using silence to communicate dissatisfaction. But, it is also possible that she is simply allowing herself more time to evaluate the design.

Recently, we heard a story from one of our very successful former graduate students. She didn't think her application for admission to a program was highly regarded because when she ran into the director of graduate studies at a convention, he seemed to ignore her. In actuality, he was preoccupied with a conversation with someone else, and the student was the *top* applicant to the program for that year! Our messages have multiple and often unforeseen effects (unintended consequences). Moreover, as we have learned from five decades of research on communication *networks*, in settings ranging from school classrooms to the U.N. General Assembly, a message that's salient or memorable to one person might well be ignored by another. Intercultural interactions are especially vulnerable to misunderstandings stemming from anticipations of what others want or request.

An example that Shiv has used in class refers to the experience of one of his friends who worked with an Indian textile company that was attempting to link up with a German firm. Shiv's friend went to Germany to negotiate the deal. After the second day of negotiations, the head of the German firm asked the Indian representative home for dinner. The Indian didn't think anything was unusual about the invitation, given that it is the norm in India to entertain foreign guests at home. The next morning, he happened to mention the dinner to the German consultants whom the textile company had hired, and they were astounded. They told him that it was extremely important that he had been invited to someone's home because it almost never happened. In fact, this meant that they would shortly be made an offer and that the German firm really wanted to make a deal. He was told he should be thinking of ways in which he could increase his bargaining power!

Power and the Elements of the Communication Situation

This case shows how the flow of communication assumes a life of its own. Once messages are "out there," they can have effects quite unintended by the speakers or sources of the messages. A strategic perspective on power includes all aspects of

Box 9.6 Steven Lukes's Three-Dimensional Model of Power

There are hidden or unobserved aspects of power in many situations. Every one of us has been at a meeting, for example, where a decision seems to have been made even before people start talking about it! Steven Lukes developed a three-dimensional model to analyze the less apparent as well as the more obvious aspects of power. We'll apply his model to a staff meeting about a particular topic or decision. Imagine yourself as an invited guest or as a researcher permitted to observe the meeting and perhaps also allowed to interview the participants afterwards or even roam around the organization for a while.

Level one includes the most observable aspects of power. For example, person A gives a directive to person B, and B then complies or doesn't comply with A's request. Observers can assess who talks the most, who gives commands, who announces decisions, and who listens and responds to directives. This level of power concerns what is most directly observable—to both insiders and outsiders at the meeting.

Level two includes less observable aspects of power. For example, when B wants to object to A's directive, but B says nothing. Here, an observer could ask people after the meeting "What would you have liked to say or do? If you were free to say anything you wanted or felt, what position would you have expressed?"

Level three includes the least observable aspects of power. For example, when B doesn't even *think* about objecting to A's request, even though A's directive is against B's interests. This level of power is the most speculative. Basically, the researcher or observer has to prove that even though the participants do not feel in any way constrained or oppressed in the meeting, if "things were run differently," their *true interests* would be expressed. Establishing this, of course, requires an outsider taking the privileged position that she can better see others' interests than they can themselves.

Researchers or observers of meetings can engage in the following activities and reflections.

1. Note what is actually said at the meeting.
2. Is anything missing from this "text"?
3. If you ask questions of the participants, what would you probe?
4. What if group members don't seem to notice the things that you are fairly certain are going on?
5. How can you as observer or critic be sure you're not "reading" into the situation things that aren't there?
6. What are the implications for intervention by the critic-observer? That is, when do you step into a situation—a domestic quarrel, a workplace meeting, a local governmental agency—confident in the view that you can "see" something others can't and then try to help them? This is one of the most important practical questions, from a critical perspective on social life, and it pushes us beyond the goal of simply elucidating a situation.

interaction. We should pay close attention to what happens in interaction: to what is said or not said, to definitions of key terms, to who is talking, to who is excluded from conversation, and to how the rules for communication are established and applied in each particular context.

Defining Terms

Anyone who has ever formally debated knows that *the ability to define terms* is an extremely important part of the debate. If a legislative body, like a parliament or a congress, is discussing whether or not the country should intervene militarily in another nation, the labels applied to the other nation and its conflict are crucial. That's why battles over what to call certain groups—"rebels," "insurgents," "renegades," "freedom fighters," "contras," etc. are not mere word play.

Terrorism, as discussed all over the world, is a case in point. While we wouldn't suggest that the issue is a completely relative one, without the possibility for international standards, we can't help noticing how much power and interests determine who gets labeled a "terrorist" and what gets deemed "terrorism." Often the contrast in perspectives is so sharp that one country's "heroes" are condemned as "terrorists" by another. We also observe what a difference such labels make in terms of setting policy. For instance, in Washington today it's fashionable to identity certain countries as "rogue states," which immediately places them in a category of unpredictable, untrustworthy, and evil. In February 2002 U.S. President George W. Bush referred to several countries that he believed supported or harbored terrorists as an "axis of evil"—and provoked passionate debate throughout the world. As some ambassadors to the U.N. have pointed out, the United States could also be considered a "rogue" state if it violates international law.

Contested labels such as these become available resources for persuasion and power. Terms for values are by their very nature abstract, ambiguous, and full of different possible meanings. In New Zealand presently, there are maneuverings among businesses to decide if they want to be called "socially responsible" or "sustainable." At issue are alignments with certain political parties, public images, and probabilities of success or failure in terms of employing the labels in marketing strategies. Similarly, at one alternative school in Montana recently, the members of the board had a consensus on the need for "socially conscious investment" of school funds but they couldn't agree on what that would mean in practice! Sometimes there is power in *avoiding* fine distinctions and subtle differences in opinion. So, defining terms is one way to exercise power. Here is a list of strategies by which power can be accumulated or retained through the shaping of the communication process itself:

- Defining the terms for discussion
- Setting the agenda for a discussion
- Limiting the availability of information for a discussion
- Determining who can participate in the discussion and who is excluded from it
- Rewarding or paying more attention to certain speakers in the discussion
- Using up talk time during the discussion
- Silencing certain viewpoints in the discussion
- Bringing closure to a discussion by prematurely declaring agreement or consensus

"Discursive Closure"

The list of strategies above is by no means exhaustive. In fact, there are even more subtle aspects to the communication process that illustrate how power can be exercised, often without recognition on the part of participants to a discussion. Building on the insights of social theorists Jürgen Habermas and Michel Foucault, organizational communication theorist Stanley Deetz coined the term *discursive closure* to refer to the ways certain discussions or discourses feature one viewpoint and close out others.[28] This is when the scope of a discussion—say, about some value or policy—is limited to certain terms and opinions and not others.

Discursive closure may be enacted in a variety of ways. For example, certain points of view may be *neutralized*, or treated as non-social and non-political simply by saying such things as, "It's not personal, it's professional." At other times, the subject or source may be *disqualified* via such statements as "you're just whining." And sometimes inequalities can be *naturalized*, or treated as inevitable, exemplified in such phrases as, "That's just the way things are done around here." In other cases, inequality might be reinforced or *legitimated* by common socially upheld values. For example, narrowly applied notions of merit in organizations can be used to justify inequality between people ("He deserves it because he's clever.") At times such strategies are readily apparent. Discursive closure refers especially to cases where the cumulative effects of such strategies go unnoticed and result in systematic biases in discussions of particular issues.

Hegemony

The process of *hegemony*, whereby a particular way of seeing and doing things becomes dominant, was coined by the Italian political philosopher Antonio Gramsci.[29] Especially interesting from his point of view, is how a broad consensus, or a "common sense," is established and influences large groups or entire societies. Thus, we might ask why certain disadvantaged classes of people in one society or another see themselves as "deserving" their poor lot in life or as being loyal servants to the status quo. It is not that such underprivileged people are "cultural dupes," nor is it that they are necessarily completely unaware of how they have been left out of the power structure. Rather, it is a question of how certain ideologies or belief systems support a social structure and hierarchy. As theorist Dennis Mumby explains, hegemony *always* involves struggle over systems of meaning and the processes by which social reality is framed.[30] Once again, it is essential to analyze who defines specific terms and how; who determines particular ways of speaking or which styles of dress are "appropriate" or how those become accepted as conventional; and how do deep-seated notions of "that's the way things are"—in an organization or in a larger society—become entrenched.

For example, consider the rush toward privatization in recent years. Since the early 1980s, the private sector has been glorified in many parts of the world, and the public sector has been dismissed as inefficient, stale, beyond repair. So encompassing is this viewpoint in nations such as the United Kingdom, the United States, Australia, and New Zealand, that few people have been asking whether large-scale privatization really is the best path for sectors such as health care, prisons, schools, and research. Only when scandals erupt, as has happened with Health Maintenance Organizations (HMOs) and private contract-based correctional facilities in the United States do people stop to consider whether it may be valuable to separate certain societal functions from the profit motive. For example, following the terrorist attacks of September 11, 2001, there was widespread questioning of putting airport security almost exclusively in the hands of private firms, without the clear governance of national, public standards. As British management theorist Noreena Hertz asserts, today it is difficult in many countries to challenge the prevailing orthodoxy of privatization, free trade, and corporate globalization; this is terribly ironic in what are supposed to be market *democracies* characterized by freedom of discussion.[31]

Thus, we participate in broad "discourses" or patterns of talk in our lives inside and outside of organizations. These discourses are organized around certain key symbols—like some of the ones we've already discussed in this book: conceptions of the individual, of justice, of truth, of progress, success, etc. Only when we carefully consider history or probe diverse cultural or ideological perspectives can we fully know our own biases and how those are "situated" at a particular place and point in time.[32] Even then, our perspective will not be completely objective in the ways we would like it to be.

Box 9.7 Patterns of Communication and Power

Let's consider several other approaches to understanding how communication patterns can embody strategies or techniques of power.

Narratives or stories and the ways they are told, while seemingly trivial or innocuous, can serve the interest of power or may have unintended consequences—as when "the boss" casually tells a story about a past employee with a "new idea" who was "too pushy."[33]

Procedures and habits can disguise the workings of power. "Being a professional," "doing business," and "standard operating procedure" (as with the allegiance of journalists to "objective" standards of reporting as an excuse for insensitive questions).[34]

Maxims and cultural knowledge include seemingly innocent or even humorous sayings that reinforce social hierarchies by clearly ruling out certain options as being unacceptable or for "losers."[35] "Get a real job" is one example.

Micro-linguistic devices support the status quo. Certain finely tuned expressions like "That's the way he is" make change difficult or virtually impossible—as in the case of sexual harassment.[36]

Ambiguity in language can conceal differences, throw responsibility on others, and deny responsibility or culpability. It can also inspire, protect, and unify groups.[37]

Broad patterns of talk or "discourses" dominate how situations are perceived. As we've discussed, whole societies embrace these patterns at certain points in time. For example, consider how often organizational or institutional problems are defined as individual problems (such as "inability to cope" or "resistance to change").[38]

Interinstitutional or cross-sector influences are apparent when one sector (such as education) is heavily infused with the ideas, language, and symbols of another (such as business). For example, Shiv has found a rather mindless adoption of popular notions of "techno-optimism"—a belief in the capacity of technology to solve all our problems—even by supposedly reflective and independent non-governmental organizations (or NGOs) in India.[39]

Systems or Patterns of Control in the Organization

We now shift our focus to the whole organization in terms of systems of power, or more precisely, control. In a way, "power is as power does." Shifting from the noun "power" to the verb "control" stresses action and process over a more static conception of power. More specifically, we're asking the question: How is work and how are members' behaviors controlled or shaped most of the time in the organization?[40]

As we look at the modern organization, particularly at how it has developed in the industrialized world, we can see several prevalent systems or patterns of control. Analyzing organizations in terms of these systems is not merely an academic exercise. By applying these models, we come to a better understanding of the dimensions of organizational control and can make better decisions about how and when those systems should be modified to make organizations run more effectively. We can also use the models to make ethical assessments.

U.S. political scientist Richard Edwards specified three primary systems of organizational control: *simple, technical, and bureaucratic*—with each describing the basic ways that work and workers are organized and controlled in the interests of the larger organization.[41] Each of these patterns has emerged historically, and each has distinctive characteristics. Like Weber's ideal types of authority, none of these systems of control exist in their pure form; they are useful as templates to place over the organization to analyze it. The simple form of control centers on relations that are direct and personal, but also arbitrary—as we find in the relationship between an owner of a small family-run shop and his employees. In such a system, the owner can give orders and expect them to be obeyed. The technical form of control relies chiefly on the technology of the organization to structure behavior of employees; the quintessential example is the assembly line. The bureaucratic form, as discussed in chapter 2, is built on a system of rules, regulations, norms, and habits. To these three primary systems, communication researchers have added *concertive control*, a term coined by Phillip Tompkins and George Cheney. Concertive control is exercised largely in a horizontal way, as we might find in a work team.[42] The principal features of each of these control systems are outlined in box 9.8.

According to Edwards, there has been a general movement away from obtrusive (apparent) means of organizational control toward unobtrusive (subtler) means. The simple model of control involves the most obtrusive—a direct relationship between a supervisor (or manager or owner) and her employees. A technical system of control is somewhat less obtrusive, using technology to oversee human beings; the supervisor on an assembly line often has 100–300 employees and relies on technology to manage most of the work. A bureaucratic system is still less obtrusive. There are still supervisors, of

"Oh, can't complain."

course, but their roles are secondary in comparison with the system of standards, rules, etc., that govern everyone's work throughout the organization. Finally, the concertive system is least obtrusive, involving group norm-setting and peer monitoring. In concertive systems, control is exercised by people working "in concert" with accepted organizational vision, values, and norms. This is exactly what management professor James Barker found in his multi-year study of the transition to work teams in a Denver, Colorado, firm. He observed how team members could impose on one another expectations that were in some ways more stringent than those in the old bureaucracy.[43]

Importantly, the movement away from more direct means of organizational control is by no means linear or entirely predictable. Today's organizations exhibit a mix of methods. Also, there are advantages and disadvantages to each. In terms of communication, what is especially important is that each system of control features different kinds of relationships. Specifically, each model specifies three types of interaction between employees and superiors: giving directives or structuring work activities; monitoring work activities and results; and rewarding work or correcting deviations. This sounds mechanical and impersonal—and often is exactly that. But, let's look at each of the four types of organizational control in terms of what we can expect to happen typically.

Box 9.8 Systems of Control in Organizations: Ideal Types

Simple. This form is typified by the small "Mom and Pop Shop." Supervision is direct, personal, and arbitrary (not systematic), and monitoring of work processes is also direct and personal. Rewards and correction are at the discretion of the owner/manager. This system works well with a competent, fair, and benevolent head.

Technical. This form is best exemplified by the assembly line (and analogous ways of structuring work using technology). Supervision is largely indirect, impersonal, and highly standardized. Monitoring of work processes is direct (by the technology on the "front line") but also largely impersonal. Rewards and correction are variably determined (e.g., by differing incentive systems, such as piece-rate or benchmarking). The system is highly efficient, in certain senses of the term, but is generally alienating for employees.

Bureaucratic. This form is seen in most large organizations, regardless of sector, although it never exists in a pure form. Supervision exists in a variety of forms, but it is chiefly done through the implementation of rules, regulations, standards, procedures, and policies. Monitoring of work processes is conducted primarily through common adherence to the rules. Rewards and correction are non-arbitrary and distributed on the basis of clearly defined merit guidelines. The system can be used to organize large enterprises in all sectors; it can be effective and efficient. However, it may produce overconcentration of power, limitations on creativity, and institutional rigidity.

Concertive. This form is found in many types of organizations, but it is exhibited most explicitly by many high-tech and other firms that stress creativity, innovation, and adaptability (at least in their early stages of development). In large organizations it is often found in conjunction with programs such as TQM and Kaizen. Self-supervision, employee empowerment, and team-based peer supervision are encouraged within a broader mission or vision and within parameters set by top management (e.g., production targets). Monitoring of work processes occurs at the level of teams and in the upward reporting of production information. Rewards and correction tend to be a mix of performance-based mechanisms for individuals and for groups (teams). This system is appealing for a number of reasons, but it can cost the individual and the group a great deal in terms of work commitment, job stress, and less apparent means of control.

In the family-run small business, we would likely find a fair amount of centralization. There is a person or a couple of people in charge. They're not necessarily trained as managers, and they rule largely by their own preferences. The employee may hope for a "benevolent dictator" rather than a "tyrant," since there may not be much opportunity to modify the system of running things. Supervision is over-the-shoulder to a great extent; so, giving orders and monitoring work have a personal, direct, and one-on-one flavor. Rewards and any corrections would be done by the "boss," and everyone who worked there would know that. There may well be a coziness to this kind of organization, and the firm may have a strong tradition. In fact, most organizations in the early twentieth century were run this way. Such was the case even in the large, dirty factories that Marx witnessed in England in the mid-1800s. Although the organization was large, as Edwards explains, there was little "science" to management. So, when supervision was conducted by someone other than the owner, it was still his orders that were being followed on down the line. Little changed without his direct command or approval. Such simple forms of control have clear disadvantages as well as advantages. In general, they are more direct and more personal. But their arbitrariness leaves employees without a system of rules or standards to appeal to if there's a problem.

Henry Ford introduced the assembly line in Detroit, Michigan in 1912. This was not the first means of automating work. Some efforts had already been made in the areas of agriculture, textiles, and mining. But Henry Ford turned the idea of a "disassembly line" that he observed in meat packing upside down. Instead of having workers in serial process take something apart, he had them put it together. The idea of the assembly line spread fast to other industries, especially home appliances. By the 1920s, this means of structuring work through technology was all the rage, and it was heralded as a fast, efficient way to organize a huge workforce and to create mass production. This development did not mean that forms of simple control disappeared—not at all. But, it did represent a change in thinking about how work could be divided, structured, and controlled. What's distinctive about technical control is that the technology built into the workplace controls the worker much of the time. One can't just say, "Oh, I think I'll skip this round." Or, "I feel like doing things differently this time." Work is regularized and standardized through the "architecture" of the workplace—that is, the technology. There are still supervisors, but they are often distant from most workers and work activities. So, in a very real sense, the technology of the workplace directs and monitors workers—even rewards them by determining break times in some cases.

There are other forms of technical control in organizations. For example, consider the large open office where dozens of employees are lined up at their personal computers. In many types of work today, the PC is not only the principal way of doing work; it is also the employee's main link to the organization. And with the electronic monitoring of work in many organizations, the dimensions for technological control of work processes and workers actually widen (see box 9.9).

We have already talked a lot about bureaucracy and its key features. Here we simply want to emphasize that control over work processes and behaviors becomes less personal, more diffuse, and less apparent in a bureaucracy. While there is often a tall hierarchy of levels, and positions are highly specialized, it is really the *system* of rules, regulations, norms, procedures, and habits that everyone follows as their guide. The system is the boss, in a very real sense, even though workers may have one or

Box 9.9 Questions about Electronic Monitoring in the Workplace[44]

Electronic monitoring of employees' work behaviors is becoming more common in many sectors, and it takes several different forms. The means of surveying employees through electronic means include: video camera monitoring of work areas; centralized monitoring of e-mail message content; personal computer monitoring of breaks and work periods; automatic and frequent reporting of work rates (such as number of key strokes), production results, and problems; and regularized robotic interactions with employees (e.g., in a production area).

Think about the different roles that new technologies can play at work. Consider the technologies both from the perspective of the individual employee and from the perspective of the organization. Think especially about each of the applications of electronic monitoring of employees listed above.

What are some reasons for electronic monitoring of employees? What are some arguments against it? How effectively can such systems be centralized and managed? What about the margin for error? What are the practical and ethical implications of regular surveillance of employees? What might be some surprising or unexpected outcomes—in terms of effects on behavior or attitudes—of the use of electronic monitoring at work? What forms of resistance on the part of employees being monitored might we predict or imagine? What do you think about electronic monitoring in the workplace or of work?

several others to whom they report. This has the advantages we spoke about in chapter 2: non-arbitrary decision making, clear standards for work outcomes, predictability, and the capacity to structure large and far-flung enterprises. But, it can also result in the over-centralization of power, rigidity, and depersonalization.

Concertive control is present most clearly in fairly flat organizations or units, where there is a high degree of education or training and where teamwork and a high degree of coordination are fundamental to getting work done. (Consider the example from a popular nonfiction book of the early 1980s in box 9.10.) But we can also see concertive control in many large religious organizations, social movements, labor unions, and social advocacy groups—that is, in cases where adherence to core values is a requirement for doing work and the good member is one who is dedicated to and follows closely those values. With all the talk about organizational visions, missions, values, and ethics today, many different kinds of organizations are trying to incorporate this kind of model.

Concertive control can be both exhilarating and burdensome to work under. In a sense, you are being asked to supervise yourself and your colleagues. Self-discipline is necessary. But jobs tend to know no clear limits. In a study of the Grameen (or People's) Bank in Bangladesh, communication researchers Michael Papa, Mohammad Auwal, and Arvind Singhal found that highly dedicated field representatives of this mission-based organization experienced both commitment and exhaustion. They were often ashamed to let colleagues down. Regular meetings and public reports of their progress out in the field reinforced these emotional ties to the organization. The researchers recapped one field-worker's experience of the internal pressures on the job this way:

> Atiqur Rahman is a Grameen Bank field-worker who works on the outskirts of Dhaka. He told us about the pressure he feels from fellow field-workers to retain a high loan recovery rate. When he experienced problems with loan recovery in a particular center (four members had ceased loan repayment), he felt personally

responsible to solve the problem. The four members had taken out a loan for a rickshaw repair business. However, they soon discovered that they could not compete with the more established repair businesses in Dhaka. Rahman met with the nonpaying members and attempted to persuade them to resume loan repayment. When that did not work he offered to help them move their business to an area where they could compete. Rahman eventually wound up working on rickshaw repairs himself to help the loan recipients keep their business functioning.[45]

Box 9.10 An Illustration of Concertive Control
Excerpt from Tracy Kidder's *The Soul of a New Machine* (1981)

Consider this excerpt from Tracy Kidder's book about the computer industry. Here, he vividly describes the recruitment process for a small, high-tech company in the Silicon Valley, California, where an employee's freedom is double-edged. Kidder says: "There was, it appeared, a mysterious rite of initiation through which, in one way or another, almost every member of the team passed. The term that the old hands used for this practice—West [the book's protagonist] invented the term, not the practice—was *signing up*. By signing up for the project you agreed to forsake, if necessary, family, hobbies, and friends—if you had any of these left (and you might not if you had signed up too many times before). From a manager's point of view, the practical virtues of the ritual were manifold. Labor was no longer coerced. Labor volunteered. When you signed up you in effect declared, "I want to do this job and I'll give it my heart and soul." It cut another way. The vice president of engineering, Carl Carman, who knew the term, said much later on: "Sometimes I worry that I pushed too hard. I tried not to push any harder than I would on myself. That's why, by the way, you have to go through the sign up. To be sure you're not conning anybody."[46]

In the passage above, on one hand, there is a great premium placed on individual entrepreneurship and group interdependence. On the other hand, there is tremendous pressure to work long hours and to sacrifice one's family life for the sake of the company and its projects. Work and positions are tied to projects rather than to traditional professional specializations and departments, yet there is a great deal of uncertainty about where a person's job begins and ends. Personality, values, and personal practices of employees become issues in hiring, as the organization tries to select and recruit individuals most likely to succeed and give their all to the company.

Resistance

Talk about *resistance* leads directly to issues of power and language. Resistance implies something being resisted—usually a stronger force, resource, person, or institution. It also implies some identifiable counter-pressure to the locus of power or control. And those who oppose change in organizations are often lumped together as "resistors"—regardless of the personal or professional reasons they may have for questioning some new initiative. Reasons of laziness and ignorance get thrown together with principled, value-based, technically sound reasons. Let's consider the various ways in which the comparatively less powerful members or groups of organizations can confront the more powerful.

Overt Forms

Traditionally, we think of resistance as blatant oppositional tactics, such as strikes by labor unions, sabotage on the assembly line, or simple refusal to obey. All of these strategies involve risks, of course, and can be understood in terms of U.S. economist Albert O. Hirshman's classic typology of exit, voice, loyalty, and neglect.[47] That is, there are certain paths open to unhappy individuals or groups that oppose practices of an organization. Exit is the most dramatic and the most final: quitting. Voice represents an attempt to speak out: as in the case of a whistle-blower who decides to go

Box 9.11 Voices from the Field

The Expression of Dissent in Organizations
Jeffrey Kassing, Arizona State University West

Dissent, or the expression of disagreement or contradictory opinions about workplace policies and practices, can lead to conflict. Researchers in organizational communication have considered both the reasons why and the ways in which employees express dissent.[48] My research considers whether employees express their dissent to management and supervisors (upward dissent), across the organization to fellow coworkers (lateral dissent), or in some instances to family and friends outside of the organization (displaced dissent). Individual, relational, and organizational influences inform employees' decisions about when, how, and to whom to express dissent. Employees consider these influences when determining whether or not they will be perceived as adversarial or constructive and when assessing the risk of retaliation associated with dissenting in one's organization.

Subsequent studies in this line of research have focused particularly on upward and lateral dissent.[49] Findings indicate that employees are more likely to express *upward* dissent when they (a) hold managerial positions, (b) enjoy arguing points of issue, (c) possess relatively high levels of employee commitment and satisfaction, (d) believe they exercise relatively high levels of personal influence in their organizations, (e) believe they control what happens to them, (f) possess higher-quality relationships with their supervisors, and (g) perceive that relatively high levels of workplace freedom of speech exist in their organizations.

In contrast, employees are more likely to express *lateral* dissent when they (a) hold non-management positions, (b) have a tendency to be verbally aggressive, (c) possess relatively low levels of employee commitment and satisfaction, (d) believe they exercise limited personal influence in their organizations, (e) believe that others control what happens to them, (f) possess lower-quality relationships with their supervisors, (g) perceive that relatively low levels of workplace freedom of speech exist in their organizations, and (h) comparatively have worked for their organizations longer.

The factors that distinguish why employees choose to express either upward or lateral dissent are also reflected in attributions we make about dissenters. For example, research findings indicate that organizational members see employees who express upward dissent (in comparison to employees who express lateral dissent) as more satisfied, more argumentative; more effective at exercising personal influence within organizations; more likely to possess higher-quality relationships with their supervisors; and as more likely to see management as open to employee input.

Which factors do you think exert more or less influence with regard to employees' willingness to express upward and lateral dissent? What additional factors might influence employees' willingness to express upward and lateral dissent? When employees express displaced dissent, their opinions are not heard within the organization. What purpose or function do you think this serves for employees?

public about safety violations that might affect the integrity of a consumer product. Loyalty involves largely "swallowing" the concerns while perhaps working quietly to change things. Finally, neglect doesn't have to mean being neglectful; it can represent simply forgetting about or actively ignoring a problem or limitation.

Subtle Forms

Most of the actions discussed above are direct, observable, and fit into Lukes's first level of power (box 9.6). But there can be more subtle forms of resistance at work, such as *symbolic resistance*—that is, trying to take hold of key symbols and to "move" ideas and people in a direction different from the predominant viewpoint. From this standpoint, symbols become the "turf" on which a rhetorical battle is waged. Consider, for example, how a number of gay and lesbian organizations have appropriated the word "queer" to signify collective esteem in place of its usual derogatory connotation, or the ways in which the popular play *The Vagina Monologues* makes use of objectifying words and symbols for the female body in remarkably subversive ways. Also, consider how conservative parties (and advertising campaigns) in many Western countries have succeeded over the past two decades in taking command of the idea of "revolution"—a notion that was historically associated with parties of the left. This is a kind of "symbolic reversal," as Michel Foucault would call it: the symbol gets turned upside down in terms of meaning, yet it retains much of its persuasive force and mythic appeal.[50]

In the United States and in many other parts of the world, after years of declining status as well as membership, organized labor is turning to sophisticated public relations and marketing strategies to take control of certain key symbols, such as "quality," "participation," and "entrepreneurship"—terms that have been more closely associated with management.[51] On the level of work and the shop floor, Gail Fairhurst and her colleagues have been investigating ways that organizational mission statements are exploited by certain segments of employees who are not satisfied with the direction that a company is taking, yet who wish to operate within the frame of loyalty and under the umbrella of protection of the organization's sacred symbols.[52] Of course, behind-the-scenes resistance has been a traditional, potent means of expressing dissatisfaction. This resistance is spoken covertly but explicitly through the "hidden transcripts" of employees and disempowered groups who "play the game" when the king or the boss is around and then "sing their own tune" in the freedom of their own "space." James Scott's fascinating book on resistance shows that this "dual activity" occurs in domains from slavery to secretarial work.[53]

A good example of symbolic resistance came to us from one of our former students who is also a consultant. She was observing a "customer service" training session in a New Zealand public sector organization a few years ago; in the training session, employees were being encouraged to consider other employees as internal customers. The consultant was astonished when one lower level manager jumped up and shouted to the trainer and before the entire group: "Well, if we are all customers, I have to tell you that I'm not going to buy this shit!"

Needless to say, the flow of the meeting was disrupted, as the trainer struggled to regain his composure and then had to go back to basic assumptions behind the whole program. In this case, the type of consensus that had underwritten the seminar—that "customer service" was a wholly good thing and should be understood in certain ways—was called into question by a surprising interruption. The bold supervisor was

Box 9.12 Resistance, Gender, and Customer Service

One of the most important dimensions of resistance is the degree to which any particular act is overt or concealed. Strikes, boycotts, work stoppages and slowdowns, and walkouts from meetings are some of the most vocal and open strategies. Other public acts include posters, mass e-mailings, and refusals to participate in company rituals (like morning physical exercises). "Whistle blowing" is the most public and enlists the media to broadcast charges of impropriety, injustice, or dangerous practices of the organization. At the other end of the continuum are concealed or even private strategies. Concealed strategies include various forms of sabotage and the furtive disruption of workflow (as with computer tampering). Privately, many employees (like many family members) will use passive-aggressive strategies of resistance, perhaps completely unseen by others. So, for example, behind the closed doors of an office or in a quiet corner of the shop floor, an employee may "act out" in a way that is presumably cathartic and defiant yet doesn't directly harm or challenge the organization. Theft from one's employing organization is frequently seen as an act of resistance; rationalized by ill treatment or alienation of the employee (e.g., "I'm just a number here"), it is obviously a concealed strategy.

In the middle of the spectrum are strategies employing irony and reframing—such strategies are both overt and concealed. In Czech popular culture, there's the example of the "good soldier" Svejk, who appears to bumble through his duties, while also quietly undermining the bureaucracy by doing such things as "flannelling" or exaggerating displays of deference and enthusiasm to the point where superiors know that the flanneler is being subversive but have to feign ignorance because if they acknowledge the flanneler, they will be compromising their own positions.[54]

In a study by Alexandra Murphy,[55] a former flight attendant and now professor of communication, we witness just such kinds of "mixed" strategies. In this case, it is a group of mostly female flight attendants who, feeling like they're treated as children by the company, devise a range of strategies to resist organizational control. What is most interesting in this case is the disjuncture between the "public practice" and the less apparent form of resistance itself. Murphy offers a catalog of the resistance strategies she observed and learned about in her interviews and, following the work of James Scott,[56] calls those strategies "hidden transcripts." Besides showing the interaction of gender, organizational power, and demands for customer service in the airline industry, Murphy wants to show how even when employees appear to "go along" they may well be pursuing avenues of resistance.

Table 1: Gender Themes of Hidden Transcripts[57]

Gender Theme	*Public Dominating Practice*	*Hidden Transcript*
Gender regulations of hierarchy and status.	Flight attendants are required to serve the pilots beverage before takeoff to avoid "dehydration."	A flight attendant pokes fun at the pilots when she asks if they need "hydrating" before takeoff.
Gender regulations constraining movement and space.	Female flight attendants are required to report nightly to the training center to document their whereabouts.	Flight attendant trainees break the rules and sign each other in and out of the training center.
Gender regulations of appearance.	Female flight attendants are required to wear shoes with at least a 2-inch heel when off the airplane.	Flight attendants share knowledge of "high risk" areas where one has to wear high heels.

taking a risk, of course, and we don't know the ultimate outcome of either his efforts or the larger organizational change program in that governmental agency. Still, we offer this as a closing example of the ways in which symbols and power are intimately interwoven. What possibilities do you see in your organization for positive change based on the "capturing" of certain symbols?

Snapshot Synthesis

Max Weber got to the heart of our concerns about power in trying explain *uncoerced obedience.* Essentially, Weber tried to answer the question of why do we do things that individuals or institutions tell us to do, or why we do things that are in the interests of some group or organization, but perhaps not so clearly in our own interests. Many theorists have since attempted to explain the workings of power.

While sovereign views of power focus on *who* has power, what is perhaps more interesting and important for our purposes is the *strategic use* of power—that is, power-in-use. While material conditions—such as having control over land or capital—clearly are important, much of the time power is negotiated through communication. Through communication, we use, manage, and augment various bases of power—for example, by attempting to convey an identity of expertise or authority (thus accruing expert power) or attempting to build someone's sense of identification with us (thus gaining referent power). Discursive closure is often exercised through communication so that certain viewpoints never get aired, thus protecting the status quo.

Power comes into play in many of the other topics we discuss in this book. For example, leaders may draw upon diverse forms of power. Additionally, one of the reasons that participation is so important in organizations is so that people share power. And, as we'll see in the next chapter, having substantially different levels of power can both create conflict and make it more difficult to manage.

Key Concepts

- **Authority:** the legitimate use of power in a society
- **Ideal Types of Authority:** according to Weber, these include charismatic, traditional, and legal-rational
- **Alienation:** a concept Marx borrowed from Hegel to describe the historical outcome of the increased division of labor in capitalist societies and processes by which people are separated from their work and each other
- **Organized Expertise:** knowledge about how to organize large-scale projects and institutions; according to Galbraith, the principal source of power in contemporary society
- **Bases of Social Power:** according to French and Raven, these include reward, legitimate, expert, referent, and coercive power; their framework embraces the idea that power resides in the relationship between two people with the key to power being one person perceiving that the other has one or more of these bases
- **Artistic Proofs:** according to Aristotle, the uses of persuasion as available and legitimate means of influence

- **Inartistic Proofs:** according to Aristotle, the use of means other than persuasion as a means of influence, including force, contracts, and specified systems of rewards and punishments, all of which limit human choice
- **Sovereign Uses of Power:** according to Clegg, a view of power that emphasizes the power associated with an individual, a group, or an institution—that is, power that proceeds from a distinct and visible source; from this view, *who* has power is what's important even if that "who" is an institution
- **Strategic Uses of Power:** according to Clegg, a view of power that emphasizes the strategic aspects of power, or power-in-use, as a basic dimension of human relations; from this standpoint, *how* power is exercised is what's most important
- **Lukes's Three-Dimensional Model of Power:** a model that recognizes that power-in-use has more and less obvious aspects that may operate simultaneously; level one includes overt uses of power, such as directives; level two includes less observable aspects, such as people not expressing alternative viewpoints when they hold them; level three includes the least observable aspects of power, such as someone not considering an alternative viewpoint, even though the dominant view may not be in her best interest
- **Discursive Closure:** a process in which certain discussions or discourses feature one viewpoint and close out others, resulting in systematic biases in discussions of particular issues
- **Hegemony**: a process whereby a particular way of seeing and doing things becomes dominant, especially through the participation of diverse groups in society and including those for whom the trend is not in their best interests; in this way, arrangements of power become "commonsensical" and naturalized, even while they are harmful or limiting to certain segments of society or even to society as a whole
- **Systems of Organizational Control:** the basic ways that work and workers are organized and controlled in the interests of the larger organization; major systems of control include *simple, technical, bureaucratic, and concertive* forms
- **Hirshman's Typology of Organizational Responses:** the primary means by which unhappy individuals or groups oppose practices of an organization; these include exit, voice, loyalty, and neglect
- **Symbolic Resistance:** a means of resistance that involves trying to use key symbols to move ideas and people in a direction different from the predominant viewpoint; using this strategy, symbols become the "turf" on which a rhetorical battle is waged

Endnotes

[1] Max Weber, *Economy and Society,* ed. and trans. Guenther Roth and Claus Wittich (Berkeley: University of California Press, 1978).

[2] See Connie Bullis and Betsy W. Bach, "Socialization Turning Points: An Examination of Change in Organizational Identification," *Western Journal of Special Communication* 53 (1989): 273–293; Mark L. Knapp, Cynthia Stohl, and K. Reardon, "Memorable Messages," *Journal of Communication* 31.4 (1981): 27–41.

[3] See Shelby Foote, as quoted in Ken Burns, *The Civil War*, PBS TV series, 1990.

[4] Arvind Rajagopal, *Politics after Television: Hindu Nationalism and the Reshaping of the Public in India* (Cambridge, UK: Cambridge University Press, 2001).

[5] See Steven Lukes, *Power: A Radical View* (London: Macmillan, 1974).
[6] See John Gaventa, *Power and Powerlessness* (Urbana: University of Illinois Press, 1980).
[7] See Albert Memmi, *The Colonizer and the Colonized*, expanded edition, trans. Howard Greenfeld (Boston: Beacon Press, 1991).
[8] Karl Marx, *Capital: A Critique of Political Economy*, ed. Friedrich Engels (Chicago: C. H. Kerr and Co., 1906).
[9] Karl Marx, *The Economic and Political Manuscripts of 1844* (Moscow: Foreign Languages Publishing House, 1961).
[10] Karl Marx and Friedrich Engels, *The Communist Manifesto*, trans. Samuel Moore (New York: Pocket Books, 1964).
[11] See Deidre McCloskey, *The Rhetoric of Economics* (Madison: University of Wisconsin Press, 1984); and Deidre McCloskey, *Knowledge and Persuasion in Economics* (Cambridge, UK: Cambridge University Press, 1994).
[12] See John Kenneth Galbraith, *The New Industrial State*, 3rd ed. (Boston: Houghton-Mifflin, 1979).
[13] See also, Theodore Roszak, *The Cult of Information: The Folklore of Computers and the True Art of Thinking.* (New York: Pantheon Books, 1986).
[14] Theodore E. Zorn and James R. Taylor, "Knowledge Management and/as Organizational Communication," *Issues in Organizational Communication,* ed. Dennis Tourish and Owen Hargie (London: Routledge, in press).
[15] See Kenneth Burke, *Language as Symbolic Action* (Berkeley: University of California Press, 1966).
[16] John R. P. French, Jr. and Bertram Raven, "The Bases of Social Power," *Group Dynamics: Research and Theory*, ed. Dorwin Cartwright and Alvin Zander (New York: Harper & Row, 1968) pp. 259–269.
[17] R. Michael Bokeno and Vernon W. Gantt, "Dialogic Mentoring," *Management Communication Quarterly* 14 (2000): 237–270.
[18] Arnold S. Tannenbaum, *Control in Organizations* (New York: McGraw-Hill, 1968).
[19] Karen Ashcraft, "Identities in Flight," unpublished manuscript, University of Utah, 2003.
[20] Charles Conrad and Mary Ryan, "Power, Praxis, and Self in Communication Theory," *Organizational Communication: Traditional Themes and New Directions*, ed. Robert D. McPhee and Phillip K. Tompkins (Thousand Oaks, CA: Sage, 1985).
[21] Michael J. Cody and Erwin Paul Bettinghaus, *Persuasive Communication*, 5th ed. (International Thomson Publishing, 1997).
[22] Chester I. Barnard, *The Functions of the Executive*, 30th anniv. ed. (Cambridge, MA: Harvard University Press, 1968).
[23] Lukes.
[24] Rosabeth Moss Kanter, *Men and Women of the Corporation* (New York: Basic, 1977).
[25] David Mechanic, "Sources of Power of Lower Participants in Organizations," *Administrative Science Quarterly* 7 (1962): 349–364.
[26] Stewart Clegg, *Frameworks of Power* (London: Sage, 1989).
[27] Bruno Latour, *We Have Never Been Modern*, trans. Catherine Porter (Cambridge, MA: Harvard University Press, 1990).
[28] Stanley Deetz, *Democracy in an Age of Corporate Colonization* (New York: Hampden Press, 1992).
[29] Antonio Gramsci, *Prison Notebooks* (New York: Columbia University Press, 1992).
[30] Dennis K. Mumby, "The Problem of Hegemony: Rereading Gramsci for Organizational Studies," *Western Journal of Communication* 61 (1997): 343–375.
[31] Noreena Hertz, *The Silent Takeover: Global Capitalism and the Death of Democracy* (London: William Heinemann, 2001).
[32] See Michel Foucault, *The Foucault Reader*, trans. Peter Rabinow (New York: Pantheon, 1984).
[33] Marsha Witten, "Narrative and the Culture of Obedience at the Workplace," *Narrative and Social Control: Critical Perspectives*, ed. Dennis Mumby (Newbury Park, CA: Sage, 1997).
[34] Warren Breed, "Social Control in the Newsroom," *Mass Communications*, ed. Wilbur Schramm (Urbana: University of Illinois Press, 1960) pp. 178–194.
[35] Robin Patric Clair, "On the Political Nature of the Colloquialism, 'A Real Job': Implications for Organizational Socialization," *Communication Monographs* 63 (1993): 249–267.
[36] Robin Patric Clair, "The Use of Framing Devices to Sequester Organizational Narratives: Hegemony and Harassment," *Communication Monographs* 60 (1993): 113–136.
[37] Eric Eisenberg, "Ambiguity as Strategy in Organizational Communication," *Communication Monographs* 51 (1984): 227–243; Annette Markham, "Designing Discourse: A Critical Analysis of Strategic Ambiguity and Workplace Control," *Management Communication Quarterly* 9 (1996): 389–421.

[38] Dana Cloud, *Control and Consolation in American Culture and Politics: The Rhetoric of Therapy* (Thousand Oaks, CA: Sage, 1998).

[39] Shiv Ganesh, "Techno-Optimism and 'I.T. Talk': Analyzing Information Technology Discourse in the Context of NGO work in India," paper presented to the Organizational Communication Division, International Communication Association Annual Convention (San Diego, May 2003).

[40] See also Connie Bullis, "Organizational Values and Control," *The Ethical Nexus*, ed. Charles Conrad (Norwood, NJ: Ablex, 1993); Michael J. Papa, Mohammad A. Auwal, and Arvind Singhal, "Organizing for Social Change within Concertive Control Systems: Member Identification, Empowerment, and the Masking of Discipline," *Communication Monographs* 64 (1997): 219–249; and George Cheney, *Values at Work* (Ithaca and London: Cornell University Press, 1999).

[41] Richard Edwards, *Contested Terrain: The Transformation of the Workplace in the Twentieth Century* (New York: Basic Books, 1979).

[42] Phillip K. Tompkins and George Cheney, "Communication and Unobtrusive Control in Contemporary Organizations," *Organizational Communication: Traditional Themes and New Directions*, ed. Robert D. McPhee and Phillip K. Tompkins (Thousand Oaks, CA: Sage, 1985) pp. 179–210; James R. Barker, "Tightening the Iron Cage: Concertive Control in the Self-managing Organization," *Administrative Science Quarterly* 38 (1993): 408–437.

[43] James Barker, *The Discipline of Teamwork: Participation and Unobtrusive Control* (Thousand Oaks, CA: Sage, 1999).

[44] G. Stoney Alder and Phillip K. Tompkins, "Electronic Performance Monitoring: An Organizational Justice and Concertive Control Perspective," *Management Communication Quarterly* 10 (1996): 259–288.

[45] Michael J. Papa, Mohammad Auwal, and Arvind Singhal, "Dialectic of Control and Emancipation in Organizing for Social Change: A Multitheoretic Study of the Grameen Bank in Bangladesh," *Communication Theory* 5 (1995): 189–223.

[46] Tracy Kidder, *The Soul of a New Machine* (New York: Avon, 1981) p. 63.

[47] Albert O. Hirshman, *Exit, Voice, and Loyalty* (Cambridge, MA: Harvard University Press, 1970).

[48] For example, Timothy G. Hegstrom, "Reasons for Rocking the Boat: Principles and Personal Problems," *Business Communication in Europe*, ed. Helmut K. Geissner, Albert F. Herbig, and Eva Wessela (Tostedt, Germany: Attikon Verlag, 1999) pp. 179–194; Jeffrey W. Kassing, "Articulating, Antagonizing, and Displacing: A Model of Employee Dissent," *Communication Studies* 48 (1997): 311–332; Jo A. Sprague and Gary L. Ruud, "Boat-Rocking in the High Technology Culture, *American Behavioral Scientist* 32 (1988): 169–193.

[49] For example, Jeffrey W. Kassing, "From the Look of Things: Assessing Perceptions of Organizational Dissenters," *Management Communication Quarterly* 14 (2001): 443–471; Jeffrey W. Kassing and Todd A. Armstrong, "Examining the Association of Job Tenure, Employment History, and Organizational Status with Employee Dissent," *Communication Research Reports* 18 (2001): 264–273; Jeffrey W. Kassing and Theodore A. Avtgis, "Examining the Relationship between Organizational Dissent and Aggressive Communication, *Management Communication Quarterly* 13 (1999): 76–91; Jeffrey W. Kassing and Theodore A. Avtgis, "Dissension in the Organization as a Function of Control Expectancies," *Communication Research Reports* 18 (2001): 118–127.

[50] Michel Foucault, *The History of Sexuality, Vol. 1: An Introduction*, trans. R. Hurley (New York: Vintage, 1978).

[51] Andrew Gilla, *The Function of Values and Values-related Discourses in Disputes between Socially Responsible Companies and Labor Unions*, diss., U Montana (2001).

[52] Gail Fairhurst, Jerry Monroe Jordan, and Kurt Neuwirth, "Why Are We Here? Managing the Meaning of the Organizational Mission Statement," *Journal of Applied Communication Research* 25 (1997): 243–263.

[53] James C. Scott, *Domination and the Arts of Resistance: Hidden Transcripts* (New Haven, CT: Yale University Press, 1990).

[54] Alexandra G. Murphy, "Hidden Transcripts of Flight Attendant Resistance," *Management Communication Quarterly* 11 (1998): 499–535.

[55] Peter Fleming and Graham Sewell, "Looking for the Good Soldier Švejk: Alternative Modalities of Resistance in the Contemporary Workplace," unpublished paper, U Melbourne, 2001.

[56] Scott.

[57] Murphy.

10

Encountering, Interpreting, and Managing Conflict

Reconsidering Harmony and Discord in Organizational Life

What comes to mind when you think of engaging in conflict? Experts remind us that conflict can be beneficial: it is energizing; it offers the opportunity to release built-up tension; it may stimulate creative thinking; it can strengthen relationships. If all this is true, why do so many people dread conflict? Perhaps the primary reason is that most of us do not have the tools and skills to analyze and work through conflict effectively. As a result, conflict is often painful, and any benefits surface only after uncomfortable interactions.

The Nature of Conflict

Conflict has been defined as "the interaction of interdependent people who perceive incompatible goals and interference from one another in achieving those goals."[1] Notice several things about this definition. First, conflict involves *interaction*, or communication. Conflict is inherently communicative in that people perceive conflict because of the meanings they associate with the other's messages, and they engage in conflict through communication. Even if we try to actively avoid confrontation, we may work to hide our thoughts and feelings. Despite such efforts, those feelings sometimes are still communicated in subtle ways. Second, notice that conflict occurs between people who are *interdependent*. For example, you can believe in centralized organizational structures and I can believe in decentralized structures and we can co-exist nicely with our different points of view *until* we work within the same organization and depend on each other's cooperation. Finally, and perhaps most importantly, conflict is based on *perceptions*. The meanings that we have for each other's actions and intentions are the basis for conflict.

Conflict can vary on many dimensions. First, conflict may vary in *intensity*. Perceiving incompatible goals and interference from another in achieving them can include something as mild as a difference of opinion with a coworker over where to go for lunch. However, it can also include something as serious as an employee filing a grievance for sexual harassment or racial discrimination.

Second, conflict can vary by *level*, that is, by unit of analysis. Conflict between two employees is interpersonal conflict. Conflict between a supervisor and workers is group conflict. Conflict also exists at the organizational level. In professional sports, organizations sometimes engage in bidding wars over the services of a high profile athlete. In fact, large organizations spend a lot of time, energy, and money in attempts to *avoid* conflict—by managing issues and developing strategies to deal with crisis situations.

Third, conflict can vary by how *overt or covert* it is. For example, prior to bidding wars, one organization may not be aware of the other's intentions; the conflict remains covert, at least temporarily. Or, two coworkers may harbor an unspoken dislike for each other and covertly maneuver to avoid or undermine each other.

Fourth, conflict can vary by the degree to which we look at it from a *macroscopic or microscopic* perspective. Notice that the distinction we are drawing here is different from the previous distinctions, in that we are saying that every conflict episode can be seen from both perspectives. More often than not, we take a micro perspective. We consider only the immediate situation—such as the individuals involved, their styles, actions, and intentions. We can also look at the bigger picture—how conflicting parties are embedded within larger systems of work and what conditions constrain their choices and interpretations. The macro perspective can be invaluable in analyzing and managing conflict more effectively.

Fifth, conflict can vary by the degree to which it produces positive or negative *outcomes*. While many of us cringe at the thought of having to deal with conflict, it can be valuable. In addition to the benefits we've mentioned already, conflict can force us to think critically and to examine our positions. Plus it can stimulate positive changes. Conversely, without the skills to manage conflict productively negative outcomes such as resentment, loss of self-esteem, and stress are likely.

Explaining Conflict

In defining conflict, we said that conflict is based in part on perceptions—the meanings that we hold for a situation. Conflict and communication are fundamentally linked. Conflict is created in and develops through communication, as we generate, share, and modify meanings. Communication is also the means by which we resolve or manage conflict. (As an aside, most experts on conflict today prefer the term conflict *management* to conflict *resolution*, since in many cases we may not be able to remove or resolve the fundamental disagreement, but we can find ways to live with or manage the conflict.)

Three particularly useful concepts in understanding how conflict emerges, evolves, and is modified through meanings are attributions, accounts, and discourse. These three concepts, while often treated separately in the conflict literature, are closely linked. At the risk of oversimplifying, we can think of attributions as our internal (or cognitive) explanations for conflict, accounts as our communicative explanations for conflict, and discourses as external influences on our interpretations of (including our explanations for) conflict.[2]

Attributions and Conflict

Attributions are our explanations of the causes of events. We make attributions in order to make sense of, as well as predict, our own and others' behavior. There has been extensive research within psychology and communication studies on attribution processes. The key question on which attribution theorists focus is: Given a particular *observed* behavior, how do we reason backward to the *unobserved causes* of behavior? Thus, attribution theory focuses on how and why individuals interpret the causes of actions. This is very important in understanding conflict, since we view the other party's action, or intended action, as getting in the way of achieving our goals. Furthermore, the attributions we make influence our choices of how to respond to events. If I attribute your getting the lion's share of the bonus in our organization as resulting from your taking personal credit for team efforts, I may respond by refusing to cooperate on future projects.

Explanations for attribution processes generally fall in two categories. First, there are *normative models*, which explain how we would make attributions if we were totally rational and had complete information. In this sense, normative models show how we would like to behave, or think we ought to behave. Second, there are *descriptive models*, which focus more on describing the processes people actually use. These models try to depict what's going on most of the time in the real world. While we sometimes carefully assess the available information and employ the logic of the normative model in attributing the causes of actions, usually our approach is less disengaged. Think about our discussion in chapter 3 of intended rationality and *satisficing*. We may aspire to be perfectly rational, but situational and organizational constraints as well as our own inherent limitations often prevent us from achieving that idealized goal.

Normative models involve logical processes of inference. Much of the research in this tradition attempts to explain our attributions for events as "internal" or "external." Internal (or dispositional) causes include people's traits, motivations, or compe-

Box 10.1 An Attribution Experiment

Think of a recent incident in which someone did something that inconvenienced, hurt, or embarrassed you. Why did they do it? Write down your explanation. Now, think of an incident in which something you did inconvenienced, embarrassed, or hurt someone else. Why did you do it? Compare the two reasons. Our explanation for unacceptable behavior by someone else usually centers on the person: they're lazy, crazy, neurotic, or mean-spirited, for example. Our explanation for our own shortcoming typically centers on the situation: lack of time, lack of options, pressure, or some other element that excuses the action.

tence. External or situational causes include the context, others in the situation, and the task. One of the best-known normative models is Harold Kelley's Covariation Model.[3] According to this model, we consider the person doing the action (that is, the *actor*), the person or thing acted upon (which Kelley called the *entity*), and the *context* of the action in making attributions for an action or event. Then, we consider three kinds of information: *distinctiveness*, *consistency*, and *consensus* information.

For example, imagine that in a staff meeting, you observe that Joan rudely interrupts Jack's presentation. *Distinctiveness* information involves figuring out whether it is the unique combination of this actor with this entity that has led to the action. In this case we might ask: Does Joan act rudely towards everyone? *Consistency* information is information about how consistently the behavior witnessed is displayed by this actor with this entity. In this case, we would ask: Does Joan always act rudely towards Jack? Finally, *consensus* information includes information about how others act toward the entity. In this case: Does everyone act rudely towards Jack?

According to the covariation model, we should consider all three types of information in drawing conclusions. However, we often have neither full information nor the motivation to consider all the information available. Research shows that consistency information is used most frequently by people making attributions, yet it is perhaps the least informative. Consensus information is the least used of the three types.[4] Failure to use all the information available does not mean that the principles of the covariation model are useless. Research shows that we actively use the principles when we try to co-construct attributions for events.[5] Consider the conversation in box 10.2.

Box 10.2 Attribution Principles in Conflict Communication

The project team at a large consulting firm consists of four men and two women who have been working together for about six months. The women feel excluded from certain activities and processes, both at work and outside of work. For example, the men have been going out regularly on Friday evenings to have a drink; they often get together to watch sports on television. The women joined them a couple of times when the project team was initially formed, then quit going. At a staff meeting, three of the men proposed restructuring the team. The women disapproved, and Marie voices their concerns, saying it was another example of men dominating women.

Here are some excerpts from a conversation that took place between John and Marie, after the staff meeting incident.

John: Hey, we're going to have to try to work through our differences with each other before the next staff meeting.

Marie: Fine. But if we're going to work through our differences, these little power plays of yours are going to have to stop.

John: What power plays? I'd say your flying off the handle at every little thing is what has to stop!

Marie: Look, none of the other guys did anything to exclude us [women], at least at work, until you came along.

John: Well, Marie, I could say the same thing: Julie never goes ballistic when I make a suggestion, but you seem to do so quite regularly. And besides, I know from talking to the others that you had these little outbursts long before I came along.

Notice how John and Marie use covariation principles in their conversation to frame the other person as the cause of the problem. Can you identify the distinctiveness, consistency, and consensus information they use?

Descriptive models of attribution processes highlight the biases and errors we exhibit in making attributions. These are particularly useful in understanding conflict; they help us see the tendency to blame the other party as the cause of the conflict. Box 10.3 lists some of the major attribution biases. It is easy to see how these biases can create or intensify conflict and how they can get in the way of managing conflict successfully.

Box 10.3 Attribution Biases

Bias	*Definition and Example*	*Problems Caused*
Fundamental attribution error (FAE)	Tendency to attribute others' behavior to dispositional qualities. *"Tori criticized me because she's a mean person."*	Labeling, categorizing unfavorably; discounting others' explanations; creating defensiveness
Actor-observer bias	Attributing others' behavior to dispositional qualities and our own to external/unstable factors. *"You did poorly on the exam because you're stupid, but I did poorly because the exam was difficult!"*	Same as for FAE; appearing unfair by framing my mistakes as reasonable, others' as unreasonable
Hedonic relevance bias	Tendency to exacerbate the actor-observer bias when others' actions cause us pain, or our own actions provide clear benefits to us. *"You're being so accusatory. Can't you see I only lied because we had a deadline to meet?"*	Same as for actor-observer bias
False consensus effect (or silent majority effect)	We assume others act/think as we do, so actions inconsistent with ours are attributed to internal deficiency. *"Nobody in their right mind would send out a memo criticizing their boss."*	Depict someone with an alternative view as unreasonable/abnormal; unwillingness to entertain other's opinion; imposing your will on others
False uniqueness effect	Assuming we're uniquely gifted, or more skilled/competent than most others; attribute others' superior results to external causes. *"She got lucky. There was no real competition. When I debate, I win in spite of tough opposition."*	Air of superiority; boasting, discounting others' abilities
Self-serving bias (group level = group-serving bias)	Take credit for success (internal attribution); deny responsibility for failure (external attribution). *"I think we've put together a great presentation. If we get a bad grade, it will be because the instructor's having a bad day."*	Conflict after success if others are involved; appear unwilling to take responsibility after failure
Male Gender Bias	Attribute men's success to internal factors such as ability and effort, and women's success to external factors such as ease of task and luck. Conversely, attribute men's failures to external factors and women's failures to internal factors. *"The men's tennis circuit is so much more professional than the women's. You don't have to be that good to be in the top ten of the WTA, but there's very little difference among the top 50 in the ATP."*	Appearance of unfairness toward women; women feel unappreciated, discounted.

Accounts and Conflict

Attributions are cognitive explanations for actions or events; accounts are communicative explanations. Attributions resemble a formula, a logical (or an attempt at logical) deduction. Accounts, on the other hand, are narrative constructions. When we say that someone gave an *account* of his role in an event, we usually mean that person told the story of his or her role. The picture gets a little complicated when we realize that attributions are made visible in accounts. However, accounts demonstrate that the explanations we develop don't emerge independently in our heads; they are constructed through our communication with others.

When we are engaged in conflicts, our accounts are our "truths." We use them to explain past events and to predict future ones (think of our discussion of enactment, selection and retention in chapter 3). However, notice the emphasis on *our* truths, not *The Truth*. Conflict is based in large part on perceptions. While there are sometimes concrete, material causes of conflict, there are almost always multiple accounts that can be given for a conflict episode. Understanding accounts and finding ways for people to see them as their truths—as opposed to The Truth—can be essential to managing conflict effectively.

Theories of accounts often start with the assumption that we create, follow, and use *rules* in interaction. By rules, we mean socially agreed upon standards for what is appropriate, moral, or ethical. Often these rules are unspoken and unarticulated, and only vaguely understood. Examples of rules that most of us would agree to are: (a) it's immoral and unethical to steal, (b) taking something is not stealing if you intend to return it, and (c) an agreement between you and your roommates that you're not to enter each other's rooms without permission must be respected. When we construct accounts, we point to rules that are relevant and use them to explain, justify, or excuse actions.

Importantly, there are multiple rules that may be relevant to any given situation and account. People can differ over which rules are more important. Also, while we defined rules as socially shared, we meant that the general form of the rule is shared—people often disagree about specific applications of a rule. For example, in box 10.2, Marie seems to be using a rule that "coworkers should consult with each other before making proposals that affect them." John, on the other hand, seems to be using a rule that "if a change improves organizational efficiency, people should accept it." While they both might agree with these rules when phrased in general terms, they would likely disagree over which is more relevant in practice and whether it was violated. Their accounts of the conflict that occurred in the staff meeting are likely to be quite different; each sees the other as "wrong" or "unreasonable" since the other is violating standards of good behavior. Their differing accounts lead them to assign blame to the other, resulting in conflict.

People in conflict shape meanings by the language used in their accounts. We lend credibility to one account and dismiss another by the language we use to describe specific behaviors. For example, John could refer to Marie's objection to the proposal as acting with a "chip on (her) shoulder," not being "cooperative," and "flying off the handle." In turn, she could frame his behavior as an attempt to "dominate," as immature, and as a "power play." Language strengthens the speaker's account and frames the other's behavior as unreasonable, which makes the substance of their positions easier to dismiss.

The context for the conflict can also affect our accounts. For example, researchers Nancy Burrell, Patrice Buzzanell, and Jill McMillan studied the images and accounts of conflict expressed by 68 women who worked in state government jobs in the United States.[6] They found that while women tended to frame conflict in common competitive terms such as war or danger, their most common way of dealing with conflict was noncompetitive, evident in expressions of powerlessness, impotence, self-doubt, and vulnerability. The authors found that such feelings were due, among other things, to a bureaucratic context that dismissed them as unfeminine and unprofessional. In an extension of the study a few years later, Patrice Buzzanell and Nancy Burrell found that the context for the conflict—whether the conflict was with coworkers, supervisors, family members, or department members—determined the accounts they were likely to produce.[7] For example, people were more likely to describe conflicts with supervisors in terms of impotence, whereas they described their conflicts with coworkers in terms of war.

While accounts seem to focus on the past, they also project into the future. We consider potential accounts, and they influence our plans. Before we make a difficult choice to act, we consider whether an action will be perceived as acceptable. For example, consider a manager's decision of how to deal with an employee who has committed some offense, such as lying on his expense reports. Should the manager terminate, reprimand, or use some other form of discipline? The manager's decision will be based not only on what she considers the right thing to do but also on possible accounts to explain the decision. For example, if she fires the employee, could she offer a convincing account justifying her actions—one that follows socially accepted rules of appropriate action? Prospective accounts guide behavior. They help us consider whether our actions will be perceived as having merit.

Managing conflict effectively requires those in conflict to acknowledge that *their* accounts are *their* truths, not The Truth. That is, they must acknowledge that their accounts are potentially fallible, potentially influenced by their perceptual biases and attribution errors. A key skill for people in conflict is empathic listening—trying to understand the other party's accounts and their reasons for seeing the situation differently. Based on empathic listening and self-reflection, people in conflict are often able to co-construct an alternative account, a mutually acceptable way to explain what happened (and what should happen next).[8]

Discourses and Conflict

Attributions and accounts are helpful in seeing how two reasonable people or groups arrive at very different meanings for the same set of circumstances. In that process, however, we may overlook the larger social or cultural influences that lead us to construct particular meanings. As we have implied throughout this text there are multiple levels of discourse, ranging from a text (for example, an utterance, conversation, or written statement) to systems of meanings (or underlying logic) shared by a large group of people. In this section, we draw your attention to discourse in the latter sense—systems of logic that are common to particular societies at particular points in time.

One of the discourses we have referred to throughout the book is *marketization*. A primary assumption of those promoting market-based economic systems is that competitive behavior among companies will lead to efficient, effective, and satisfactory production of goods and services for consumers. Market discourse suggests that competition is almost always preferable to cooperation. Marketization also applies market principles to social domains. One domain in which it is frequently applied is the "internal" organizational environment, leading to descriptions of coworkers or other departments within an organization as "internal customers." Extending the market logic leads to viewing each worker as an individual "company" competing with others in this internal marketplace.

Tom Peters's thesis in *The Brand You 50* is that each person must build a "brand image" to create "competitive advantage" because today's workplace is characterized by short-term employment commitments in which employers will recruit and select employees for short-term contracts based on who is most suitable for the position.[9] Given the frenetic pace of the workplace today and the frequency of selection decisions, employers will have little time to thoroughly research these decisions; they will rely on the brand image created by each worker. Accepting or assuming the logic of this discourse creates a very competitive environment ripe for conflict. While a certain amount of competition has always existed between workers in organizations, marketization seems to heighten the competition dramatically and build a climate that encourages conflict. For example, someone's good work (such as a meticulously prepared presentation) may be interpreted by a coworker as competitive behavior or "one-upmanship" that requires a competitive response, which in turn creates or exacerbates a conflict. Managers may perceive destructive conflict between coworkers as the "natural competition" of the market and allow it to play itself out without intervention, if they accept the logic of such marketization.

Prominent discourses influence the meanings we create for events. Accepting a particular discourse may lead us to identify and explain conflict in a situation very differently from what we might explain if we were immersed in a different discourse. For example, imagine what the events highlighted in the previous paragraph would

"It appears we've moved from proactive to preemptive."

look like in an organization that did not emphasize competition. The destructive conflict created by a retaliatory response to a coworker's meticulous presentation takes on a very different meaning in organizational contexts that emphasize cooperation, support, and collaboration.

Sources of Conflict and Communication

As we said above in defining conflict, conflict is based on the meanings we assign to other people, their actions, their words, and their intentions. Moreover, as we have stressed throughout this book, the meanings we have for things are influenced by a variety of factors, both within and external to a situation. When we attempt to identify the source of a conflict, we should look to the particular issues over which people differ. However, we should also take a broader view of the situation and ask what other influences affect the conflict. We can consider the micro-level influences—elements in the conflict such as the personalities of those in conflict, the attributions they construct, the accounts they exchange, and the history of their relationship—in the context of macro-level influences, such as pressures exerted by the organizational culture and the social-cultural discourses in which the participants are immersed.

Individual or Group Sources

While there are endless sources of conflict, some sources tend to recur in organizations. *Different understandings* underlie many other sources of conflicts. For example, if a staff member misunderstands a manager's instructions and therefore does something other than what the manager intended, conflict can result.

Actions of an individual that are threatening or disruptive are a second source of conflict. Communication researchers Cynthia Stohl and Susan Schell describe an extreme form of this dynamic that occurs when a group becomes consumed with the actions of a problem member, a phenomenon that they label the "farrago" (literally, "fodder for cattle"). The farrago is used to describe groups exhibiting a specific set of dysfunctional characteristics that lead members to become collectively confused and ineffective. As Stohl and Schell explain, the farrago dynamic occurs when:

> (a) decision-making procedures are . . . compromised as a result of actions designed to avoid or accommodate one member; (b) issues are redefined against the backdrop of the member; (c) a great deal of energy is expended talking about the particular member . . . ; (d) members become so worn out in dealing with issues related to this one member that they often fail to deal with task issues and priorities become confused; and (e) members often leave such meetings angry, depressed, or frustrated with both the individual and the group.[10]

Both individual habits and properties of the group system contribute to the emergence of the farrago dynamic. Habits of the individual include (a) interpretive omnipotence, claiming the "one correct way" of seeing things; (b) a paternal, "I know what's best for the group" posture, along with dismissing alternative views as misguided or self-serving; and (c) undifferentiated passion, or "approaching social life with an intensity and devotion that far exceeds the emotional investment of others."[11] Top management teams (or TMTs) in organizations may be particularly prone to the farrago phenomenon since they are typically comprised of members with strong power and achievement needs and an individualistic orientation.[12] Simultaneously, they are often under high pressure to perform—both individually and collectively. Importantly, Stohl and Schell argue that the problem individual cannot create the farrago phenomenon without the group system unwittingly supporting it; a group creates the conditions that either perpetuate the farrago dynamic or shut it down.

Role conflict is another common source of conflict. Role conflict occurs when the expectations of, or boundaries between, roles that people perform in organizations are not clear. At a micro level, role conflict is exacerbated because of the tendency toward role expansion. Since roles are never fully defined in job descriptions, people often expand their roles, taking on new tasks and trying new approaches as they attempt to fulfill their job responsibilities. For example, in the business school where Ted works, at one point there was a director of research, a director of e-commerce, and a director of the bachelor of e-commerce degree. While job descriptions were drawn up for each, there was still great potential for role conflict among the three people holding these roles over issues such as research specifically related to e-commerce. Role expansion may be the result of conscious, strategic effort, or simply because situations seem to demand a greater role. As the role expands, it conflicts with other roles. People who are ambitious or have high needs for achievement may be particularly prone to role expansion.

On a broader level, we often find roles to be in structural conflict with one another, meaning that conflict is likely regardless of the persons or personalities involved. An example of this can be found in manufacturing firms where production-oriented departments are frequently in conflict with sales-oriented ones. Production personnel see themselves at "the center" of the organization and view those on the "boundary" with suspicion. On the other hand, sales personnel believe that *they* know

Box 10.4 Role Ambiguity, Role Conflict, and Job Performance

We usually think of role ambiguity and role conflict as being synonymous, and they are related in many ways. At first glance, we would expect both to be negatively related with organizational issues such as job performance. Research, however, presents a more complicated picture. Three decades of research have shown contradictory results, with some studies claiming a correlation between role ambiguity, role conflict and job performance, and others finding no relationship.

Systems theorists Daniel Katz and Robert Kahn help us make conceptual distinctions between role ambiguity and role conflict.[13] For them, role ambiguity is associated with an overall lack of clarity in an organization as to how exactly a particular role is to be played. Role conflict, on the other hand, is associated with actual incompatibility between two or more roles played by a single person. So, at a micro-level, the two phenomena are related, but distinct. Moreover, they have different impacts on job performance.

Travis Tubre and Judith Collins found that the type of job affects the relationship between role ambiguity and job performance. Specifically, the greater the ambiguity associated with professional, technical, and managerial jobs, the more negative the impact on job performance. Interestingly, Tubre and Collins also found that, despite small variations across job types, role conflict does not appear to be meaningfully related to job performance.[14]

What do you think accounts for the relationship between role ambiguity and job performance in professional, technical and managerial jobs? Could it be the inherent complexity of these jobs? What do you think about the finding that role conflict is not related to job performance? Does our expectation to the contrary indicate something about our cultural assumptions about conflict as a negative process?

best because they are closer to the customers. Thus, a structure exists in which conflict can be expected and must be managed creatively.

Limited resources (including financial, material, time, and space) are sources of conflict. For example, there is often a limited pool of money from which budgets or salary increases are drawn, leading individuals and groups to battle to get their "slice of the pie." Similarly, in many organizations, space is at a premium. For example, in all four of the authors' work settings, individuals and departments come into conflict in attempting to garner office space, meeting spaces, and classroom space. Finally, time is a resource over which people come into conflict. For example, competitors vie for meeting time with potential clients. There are any number of personal and situational micro influences; at a macro level, social and cultural values such as competition and speed exacerbate the conflicts.

Conflict also occurs when people perceive that *valued relationships or identities are threatened*. In conversations this can result from a perceived lack of emotional support or "disconfirming messages." Disconfirming messages imply that someone is not important to or respected by the speaker. They can include acts such as (a) ignoring the person; (b) interrupting; (c) responding with tangential or irrelevant comments, (d) using an impersonal tone; and (e) disagreeing repeatedly.[15] Mergers and acquisitions in organizations, for example, can threaten relationships and identities. Box 10.5 describes how conflict created by an acquisition lasted 15 years.

Box 10.5 A Case Study of Conflict[16]

TWA Airlines acquired Ozark Airlines in 1986. The acquisition was contentious from the beginning, producing a great deal of anxiety among the employees of each airline. Prior to the acquisition of Ozark, TWA pilots had backed investor Carl Icahn in his bid to acquire TWA, preferring him to another interested investor, Frank Lorenzo. Soon after Icahn gained control of TWA, he announced his intention to acquire Ozark. The TWA pilots then offered their support for the merger in exchange for control over key means by which the companies would be integrated, such as the creation of seniority lists that determined which pilots got preferred assignments and preferred training. The Ozark pilots, being a much smaller group with control over fewer resources, were faced with a choice of complying with the acquisition and its very unfavorable terms, or losing their jobs. As one former Ozark pilot explained: "They said, if this [contract] isn't signed . . . they [TWA] threatened to take 10 more of our airplanes. They had already taken four of 'em. So they said, 'We're gonna take 10 more of your airplanes and we're gonna furlough 100 more of your pilots.'"

The divisions set up in the acquisition were still apparent 13 years later when communication researchers Tamyra Pierce and Debbie Dougherty analyzed the conflict. The researchers repeatedly witnessed a division between TWA pilots and former Ozark pilots. For example, TWA pilots tended to congregate with other TWA pilots and former Ozark pilots with other former Ozark pilots. The two groups rarely interacted, and when they did the conversations were usually superficial. The former Ozark pilots still wore Ozark service pins while TWA pilots wore TWA and ALPA (the pilots' union) pins, as well as the symbolic colors of the companies' logos. One former Ozark pilot's comments illustrate the depth of feeling: "I always wear my Ozark pin because I'm proud of it. It's sort of like 'Remember the Alamo!' I've always been a bit of a rebel. I don't want them to forget what they did and who we are. I have a tattoo that a few of us now have. It's the three swallows [Ozark logo] in green, on my butt. We all got it about six or seven years ago, way after the merger."

Macro or Cultural Sources of Conflict

As we have emphasized, it is important to consider micro-level conflict in the context of broader cultural patterns. Role expansion may be exacerbated by a competitive or aggressive organizational culture—one in which employees are pushed to work hard and "to beat the competition." Managerial discourses promoting "continuous improvement" and "competitive advantage" encourage the type of role expansion that leads to role conflict. In this sense, the larger culture becomes a "source" for conflict.

Consider particular values promoted by the media. Communication scholar James Chesebro studied prime-time television programs in the United States over a seventeen-year period to determine the values they promoted. He found that leader-centered themes increasingly dominated prime-time programming since 1980–81. Leader-centered dramas or comedies, which included such shows as *Murphy Brown* and *E.A.R.T.H. Force,* emphasized and projected such values as authority, influence, and power.[17] More recently, U.S. "reality" television shows such as *Survivor* or *Blind Date* have emphasized competition as the preferred and acceptable way of resolving conflicts. Whether media programs shape or simply "reflect" dominant values, it is important to understand that our individual approaches to authority and power take place in a culture that places a premium on these values.

The Context of Conflict

The context in which conflict is experienced greatly influences how we understand it and how we attempt to deal with it. Many of our assumptions about communication are based in culture. This is certainly true of conflict. In the 1950s Edward Hall made a now-famous distinction between high-context and low-context cultures. High-context cultures have shared (but largely implicit) assumptions about what is appropriate in a particular context. Rather than expecting each other to have different understandings that need to be expressed, people in high-context cultures expect each other to "read" the context—meaning not only the physical context but also the nature of the interaction taking place and the relationships among the interactants—and to know what actions are appropriate and inappropriate based on this reading. Conflict in high-context cultures is often not verbally acknowledged or managed; rather, it is handled by subtle and indirect, often nonverbal, means. Many East Asian and Oceanic cultures tend to be relatively high context.

In low-context cultures, such as most English-speaking and European countries, people are much less likely to assume that others understand what is appropriate or not, and they are much more inclined to deal with problems explicitly, through direct, verbal means. Two people who are socialized into very different sets of assumptions about conflict may have an even greater difficulty than usual in managing conflicts that occur. Much of the literature on which we draw in this chapter has been developed in low-context cultures that explicitly value verbal interaction as the means to manage conflict. Please keep this cultural bias in mind as you read on.

Beyond national or ethnic culture, *organizational* cultures and climates also influence how we experience and manage conflict. Some organizations may encourage open expression of problems whereas others may discourage such expression. Such differences can have important implications for the quality of employees' work lives and for the organization's ability to detect and deal with problems crucial to its well-being.

Numerous examples of organizational disasters and scandals show the effect of support—or lack of support—of dissent in the organizational culture. Before the U.S. *Columbia* disaster in 2003, there were e-mails about a breach in the heat armor of the left wing, which was struck by a chunk of foam insulation that broke off from the external fuel source 82 seconds after the launch of the space shuttle. The dissent expressed was dismissed. U.S. corporations such as Enron, Xerox, and WorldCom created a "meltdown" in the stock market and in the public's confidence in big business when a series of accounting scandals unfolded in 2001. The cultures of these organizations apparently discouraged at least some employees from speaking up about potential problems.

Power relationships are another important part of the context in which conflict is experienced. National and organizational culture are implicit in such relationships, meaning that culture both influences and is influenced by power. In organizational conflict, asymmetrical power relationships can often mask or suppress the expression of conflict. The ability to control what issues are raised, how conflict is defined, and what criteria or needs are considered legitimate in addressing important issues signals power imbalance. Through *issue control*, power can be exercised covertly and conflict can be avoided or suppressed, thus enabling the interests of more powerful parties to prevail without allowing less powerful parties' voices to be heard. Box 10.6 identifies a number of issue control tactics observed in organizations. Issue control tactics leave the appearance that there is no conflict; they create a *false consensus*, but conflict is just below the surface.

Box 10.6 Issue Control Tactics

- *Directing attention away from an issue:* e.g., "We need to move on to more pressing matters"
- *Limiting access to information:* e.g., "The Privacy Act won't allow me to show you those records"
- *Defining what type of information is considered legitimate:* e.g., "Those people are your sources? Oh, they're totally uninformed" or "Do you have any statistics to back that up or just anecdotal evidence?"
- *Creating fear of raising an issue:* e.g., "Have any of the women here experienced problems with discrimination?" [Asked of the four women present in a room of 20 males, many of whom were senior members of the organization]
- *Creating criteria for decisions or priorities that frame the decision:* e.g., "A good solution will be one that doesn't disrupt work flow"
- *Defining the problem, decision, or conflict in definitive terms:* e.g., "The problem here is that Kathy is not being cooperative or doing quality work"

Conflict as a Process

Conflict is not a single, isolated event. It is a process, and our experiences change as conflict emerges and develops. We begin this section by discussing the inherent ambiguity and confusion that develops around the emergence of conflict and then discuss phases of conflict.

Ambiguity and Misunderstandings in the Conflict Process

Interpersonal communication scholar Alan Sillars argues that our ability to understand, appreciate, and manage conflict is affected by the fact that we mistakenly see misunderstandings between people as something temporary that occurs in unfamiliar situations, so we assume misunderstandings dissolve as we get closer to the person.[18] However, misunderstanding is pervasive in close personal relationships and is often quite normal. The familiarity we develop in close relationships is inherently subjective. The very nature of such familiarity makes it difficult to understand the behavior of peers, family members, or significant others outside the particular labels and identities we have constructed for them. This tendency is exacerbated during explicit conflicts. Interpersonal conflict illustrates clearly that communication as a process is marked by ambiguity (both inherent and strategic).

Sillars argues that ambiguity, disorder, and confusion play central roles in conflict processes.[19] The ambiguity can arise over the *source* of the conflict. For example, take two people in a long-standing work relationship who begin to argue about how often they should meet in order to complete a project. For person A, the conflict could be over an explicit task goal, such as getting the job done on time. Consequently, he or she might view person B as causing the conflict by procrastinating or being obstructive. Person B, however, could see the overall work relationship itself as the source of the conflict by viewing person A in terms of a tendency to dominate or dictate meeting times and places. Ambiguity is also central to conflict processes because *patterns of communication* during conflict are themselves complex. In regular conversation, it is fairly easy to predict the overall nature of the communication and to anticipate the response of the person with whom we are communicating. If you are talking with your roommate about a problem with a professor, for example, you can be fairly sure that the roommate will express support. But this sort of predictability vanishes during a conflict.

The relationship of a message to the one that immediately precedes it (i.e., the nature of its contingency) becomes much more complex in a conflict. For example, we can see *reactive contingency* in conflicts, where one person consistently reacts to the comments of another, as in "You're lazy!" / "No, I'm not!" Or we could see *pseudo-contingency*, where two people are ostensibly talking with each other but in fact are acting out individual scenarios based on imagined frustrations and accusations that have never been articulated. Sometimes we see *delayed contingency*, where one person responds to an earlier comment several interactions later. Also remember that in a typical conflict, contingency shifts, and different people may be using different patterns at the same time! Finally, conflict can be disorganized and confused because of the *context* in which it takes place. Think of the number of times you've thought "Why is this person bringing up this issue *now*? This is hardly an appropriate time!" Since we only have partial knowledge and understanding of other peoples' lives and concerns, it is difficult to predict when and in which context a particular conflict might erupt, and for what reasons.

Because of the ambiguity surrounding conflict episodes, our interpretations of what is happening and why it is happening is very subjective. *Punctuation* is a useful concept in understanding the process of conflict. Just as we use periods and commas to punctuate sentences—that is, to indicate important starting points and transitions—we also tend to punctuate communication processes. Thus, whenever a conflict episode occurs, we find ourselves trying to identify the source or cause of the conflict: When did it start? Who started it? What did they do to start it? However, as we have seen in our discussion of ambiguity, agreeing on how to *punctuate* a conflict episode is a challenge in itself. We often find ourselves saying (or at least thinking) "You started it by doing A!" only to have the other person say, "Well I only did that because you did B!" In other words, each person punctuates the episode differently. Consider again the conversation in box 10.2. In their conversation, John and Marie make several attempts to punctuate their conflict. Marie first implies that the conflict started with John's "power play." But John promptly rejects this explanation, saying that it started with Marie "flying off the handle." They then go on to re-punctuate, suggesting that the conflict started even earlier and again disagree on what actions started the conflict.

Phases of Conflict

While we may not be able to eliminate the ambiguity and confusion that accompanies conflict, we can begin to understand the typical patterns of communication that occur during times of conflict. Management scholar Louis Pondy[20] identified five phases that characterize conflict episodes. His model is helpful in enabling us to see how conflict emerges and develops.

The first phase is *latent conflict*. Conditions for conflict exist, even though no perception of conflict exists and no confrontation has occurred. For example, when two parties value the same limited resources—such as two town officials who both have their eye on an unspent portion of the town budget—latent conflict exists. According to the French philosopher René Girard, this sort of latent conflict is based on what he calls "mimetic desire." Girard argues that mimetic desire, or the desire to have what other people have or to be what other people are, is constitutive of all human societies.[21] Of course, just because latent conflict exists does not mean that the conflict will develop any further. The two officials could find a compatible plan for sharing the money. It's important to recognize that latent conflict nearly *always* exists. The question is, how do we interpret and respond to conditions that *could* produce conflict?

If one or more of the parties becomes aware of the conditions for conflict—that is, one sees another as potentially having incompatible goals and potentially blocking his or her own goal achievement—latent conflict becomes *perceived conflict*. The conflict at this stage is still not overt, but potential problems are sensed by the participants. If one of our two town officials, Katherine, becomes aware of the other's (Scott's) plans for the unspent funds, and Scott's plans differ from Katherine's, perceived conflict exists. Notice in this example that perceived conflict can exist even though Scott is not yet aware of Katherine's plans or concerns.

The perceived conflict phase moves on to *felt conflict* if we begin to personalize the conflict and consider how to address it. As we anticipate making the conflict overt, our emotions become involved. So, as Katherine reflects on and begins to consider how to address Scott's designs on the pool of funds, she is likely to experience more intense emotions—perhaps anger, frustration, or indignation—that sharpen the sense of conflict.

Manifest conflict is when the conflict becomes overt—when one or (likely) both parties express the conflict and attempt to resolve it. This is the stage that we typically think of as conflict, because it is the point at which we see confrontations, bargaining, or problem solving. As Pondy's model makes clear, much that is important in the conflict process occurs prior to the conflict becoming manifest.

Conflict aftermath is the phase that follows manifest conflict. In this phase, participants experience the consequences of the conflict, not only in terms of the agreements or resolutions, but also in terms of consequences for relationships, identities, and perhaps the organizational or group culture. Conflicts often have short-term as well as long-term consequences, as the case of TWA's acquisition of Ozark Airlines in box 10.5 made clear.

Managing Conflict

Thus far we've focused on describing the conflict process—what normally happens when conflict occurs. We now turn our attention to what you can do to manage conflict. We'll focus on what research and theory—plus our own experience—suggest about how you can be more effective in handling conflict situations.

Styles of Conflict

A good starting point for managing conflict is to consider the general approaches available to us. We will differentiate these general approaches, or styles, from more specific tactics of conflict management. A number of researchers have studied styles of conflict. Style is best considered as a behavioral orientation toward conflict, or an expectation about the way conflict should be approached.[22] While we may each use more than one style depending on the situation and we certainly exhibit a variety of specific behaviors during conflict, most of us show a general preference for one or two styles. The diagram below suggests that styles differ in terms of their assertiveness and cooperativeness.[23]

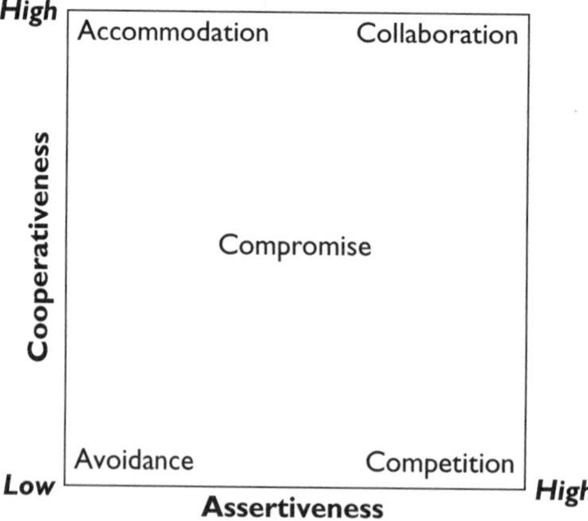

Highly assertive styles emphasize behaviors that reflect a concern for oneself or for "winning" the conflict. Highly cooperative styles are concerned about relationships and include a focus on meeting the needs of the other party in the conflict. As the model shows, however, assertiveness, and cooperativeness are not mutually exclusive. Our style may reflect a high level of both (collaborating style), a low level of both (avoiding style), or even mixed levels, as in the other three styles. Box 10.7 provides some details about each of these conflict styles. Researchers have made subtle distinctions in the styles (as noted in the first column), but for ease of discussion we will retain the focus on the five styles in the diagram.

As is clear from box 10.7, *there is no one best style,* no one-size-fits-all solution. Rather, each of the styles is appropriate in certain situations and inappropriate in others. Interestingly, research shows that regardless of initial style used, most supervisors resort to a dominant style if faced with a non-compliant subordinate.[24]

Box 10.7 Five Basic Styles for Conflict Management

Styles	*What happens when used*	*Appropriate to use when*	*Inappropriate to use when*
Avoidance, denial, or withdrawal	denying existence of a problem or avoiding confrontation	issue is relatively unimportant; timing is wrong; cooling off period is needed; short-term use	issue is important; differing opinions will not disappear and the conflict will build
Accommodation or smoothing over	differences are played down; surface harmony exists; resentment, defensiveness, and possible sabotage may surface if issue remains suppressed	same as above; also when preservation of relationship is the more important concern	reluctance to deal with conflict leads to evasion of an important issue; others are ready and willing to deal with issue
Competition, forcing, or dominance	authority, position, majority rule, or a persuasive minority settles the conflict; results in win/lose perceptions if the dominated party sees no hope for self	power comes with position of authority; when this method has been agreed upon	losers have no way to express needs; could result in future disruptions
Compromise, or meeting half-way	each party gives up something to meet midway; win/lose outcome can still occur if "middle of the road" position ignores the real diversity of the issues	both parties have enough leeway to give; resources are limited; when win/lose stance is undesirable	original inflated position is unrealistic; solution is watered down to be effective; commitment is doubted by parties involved
Collaboration, integration, or problem solving	abilities, values, and expertise of all are recognized; each person's position is clear, but emphasis is on group solution; results in win/win for all	time is available to complete the process; parties are committed and trained in use of process	the conditions of time, abilities, and commitment are not present

Research also suggests that people from individualistic, low-context cultures ("Westerners") tend to prefer direct, assertive styles (competing and collaborating), whereas those from collectivist, high-context cultures tend to prefer less direct styles that allow the other to save face, such as accommodation and avoidance.[25]

With our admittedly Western bias, we would argue that special consideration should be given to the collaborative style. Collaboration is an attempt to work together to find a solution that meets the needs and goals of both parties—that is, a "win-win" solution. Although it may not always be possible to find a collaborative solution, collaboration should be considered when both the issue and the ongoing relationship of the two parties are important. Collaboration probably requires the most complex set of skills of the five conflict management styles. In order to be successful, it also requires the time and commitment of both parties. In box 10.8, we present one useful framework for a collaborative approach to conflict management. Notice how the options presented in the third phase of the model suggest that if an attempt to find a collaborative solution fails, the two parties can always revert to another approach.

There are many books and articles with practical advice about how to manage conflict in a constructive, collaborative manner. While there are some important differences, many of them show a common pattern of identifying a *differentiation* phase, in which the two parties in conflict raise the relevant issues and clarify the differences in their positions and reasons for the differences, then an *integration* phase, in which the parties begin to identify common ground and explore options toward resolution.[26] As one group of experts argued, "Adequate differentiation is a critical prerequisite to constructive conflict management."[27] Participants must clarify their positions, the reasons for them and, most importantly, their underlying goals and interests, so they are clear about what would constitute a satisfactory solution for

Box 10.8 A Collaborative Conflict Management Strategy[28]

***Phase 1*: Explore the other person's viewpoint**
Establish that your immediate goal is mutual understanding, not resolution. Elicit the other person's thoughts and feelings about the issue. Ask for the other person's help in understanding him/her. Try not to defend or disagree. Paraphrase the other person's position to show you understand. Ask the other person to correct your paraphrase if necessary. Repeat these steps until the other person unreservedly agrees that you understand his or her position.

***Phase 2*: Explaining your viewpoint**
Ask for a fair hearing in return. Explain how the other person's thoughts and feelings affect you. Avoid blaming and self-defense. Carefully explain your thoughts and feelings as *your* truth, not *the* truth. Ask for restatements of your position and corrections of factual inaccuracies, as necessary. Review your respective positions.

***Phase 3*: Creating Resolutions**
Affirm your mutual understanding and confirm that you are both ready to consider options for resolution. Brainstorm multiple options. If a mutually agreeable solution is not yet obvious, try one or more of the following options: (1) take time out to reconsider, exchange proposals, and reconvene; (2) agree to neutral arbitration or mediation; (3) compromise between alternate solutions; (4) take turns between alternate solutions; (5) yield (accommodate) once your position is thoroughly and respectfully considered; (6) assert your positional power after thoroughly and respectfully considering the other's position; and (7) agree to disagree and still respect each other.

each party. Notice how the model in box 10.8 very clearly follows this differentiation-integration pattern. In the first two phases, the two parties differentiate before attempting to integrate in the third phase.

Exploring conflict styles is a useful way to begin thinking about and strategizing how to manage conflict. But it is not without its problems. Substantial research suggests that the styles people expect to use in conflict differ substantially from the way they actually behave.[29] Behavior patterns often demonstrate shifts from one style to another during a conflict episode. Thinking of conflict in terms of an individual's style ignores the fact that conflict involves at least two people—and typically more than their rational selves. Rarely do we simply enact a script; to some degree, we improvise in response to the other person's actions.

Negotiation Strategies

Negotiation—sometimes referred to as bargaining—is "a communicative process between interdependent parties with differing goals who are attempting to produce a joint decision."[30] It is a process in which the two parties voluntarily agree to interact in a give-and-take fashion to attempt to reach agreement.[31] Thus, negotiation is a form of conflict management. Sometimes negotiation is considered a more formal process than other attempts to manage conflict. For example, labor-management or other contract negotiators usually establish a set of rules to follow (or implicitly adhere to) and then schedule formal meetings to exchange proposals. However, given our definition above, it is reasonable to consider other, much less formal interactions as negotiations. For example, you might negotiate with a coworker who has a different view on how to handle customer complaints. Or you might negotiate with a business partner on how to distribute profits from your joint efforts. In each case, negotiation involves people choosing to interact and to reach an agreement—versus, for example, taking the problem to a higher authority (the boss or a court of law) as a means of settling the issue.

While there is extensive research and advice on negotiation strategies and tactics, Linda Putnam and Marshall Scott Poole suggest that these can be grouped into two broad approaches. Distributive or *competitive* approaches are "characterized by the appearance of fixed-sum (zero-sum) alternatives; one party must win and the other party must lose."[32] A competitive approach focuses largely on maximizing one's own outcomes, assumes one's own interests are in opposition to the other party's, usually engages in positional tactics (that is, tactics to gain advantage over the other), and tends to focus on short-term goals and tangible issues (such as price and quantity). By contrast, an integrative or *collaborative* approach focuses on maximizing the outcomes of both parties, seeking to find solutions in which both parties are fully satisfied. Rather than assuming oppositional interests, the negotiators assume at least some common interests and engage in a collaborative process of information sharing and trust building rather than positional tactics. Collaborative negotiators focus on long-term and intangible issues, such as preserving the relationship, building trust, and building good will.

Notice the close parallel between the two dominant approaches to negotiation and the styles of conflict management we reviewed earlier. Negotiation, as a form of conflict management, can be seen through the lens of conflict management styles. This suggests that negotiators have at least three other choices beyond competing or collaborating. They can (1) avoid negotiation, choosing other alternatives to deal with the conflict situation; (2) accommodate the other party, give in and allow the other party to have their way; or (3) compromise, which often happens in negotiations. Recognizing the close link between negotiation and conflict management styles also suggests that the model of collaborative conflict management presented in box 10.8 can be useful in negotiations.

Principles and Tactics of Competitive Negotiation[33]

Skilled negotiators who choose to use a competitive approach tend to adopt several key principles to increase their likelihood of a obtaining a successful outcome. Even if you do not choose to use a competitive approach—and there are often practical and ethical reasons *not* to do so—you should be aware of the strategies you may encounter from competitive negotiators.

Since a competitive approach involves the two parties jockeying for position in an attempt to "win" at the other's expense, a key principle is to *maximize your power base*. You should garner the resources necessary to increase the likelihood that you will be in a powerful negotiating position. While there are many resources that can increase one's power base, two of the more important ones are information and alternative options to reaching a settlement. Having good information relevant to the negotiation is critical. One should know as much as possible about the issues to be negotiated, the relevant environment, and the other party's situation. For example, in a recent labor-management contract negotiation at one of our universities, both sides did extensive research on such things as (a) salary structures at comparable universities, (b) the financial health of the university, and (c) the level of satisfaction/dissatisfaction among staff. Since the union knew that the salary structure at this university was low compared to others, that the university was financially healthy, and staff were quite dissatisfied with getting paid less than staff at comparable universities, the union had a strong base of power from which to bargain. The existence of options other than reaching a settlement with a particular party increases one's power base substantially. If you can walk away from the negotiating table and meet your needs elsewhere, you're in a much stronger position to make demands.

A closely related principle is to *make your power base visible*. As we discussed in chapter 9, power is to some degree a matter of perception. We speak of the "visibility" or "legibility" of power and authority in terms of how accessible the resources and strategies are in any particular situation. Thus, making the other party aware of the information and/or other alternatives you have—or creating the appearance of having these—can enhance your negotiating position. For example, in initial negotiations for buying a new car, you might carry an issue of *Consumer Reports* magazine, with business cards from several other dealers clipped to the front. By doing so, you're not so subtly saying, "I've done my homework, and I have other options, so the deal you offer better be good!" Of course, there are ethical implications of *pretending* to have alternatives that do not exist.

Competitive negotiators often adopt another principle: *take extreme positions and minimize movement.* They are especially likely to do so when they sense they are up against an inexperienced negotiator. A colleague who consults with large organizations on negotiations suggests an even more radical proposition: If you're going to compete (and he often cautions them against competitive negotiation), take the most extreme position you can articulate with a straight face.[34] Extreme initial demands tend to set a baseline for expectations. Inexperienced negotiators, or negotiators who do not have good information on which to base their estimates of a likely settlement, may radically adjust their expectations when presented with an extreme opening bid. Research shows—perhaps not surprisingly—that, when a settlement is reached, extreme initial bids combined with relatively small concessions result in more favorable outcomes.[35] However, it also shows that following this principle will decrease the likelihood of reaching a settlement. Thus, following this principle means you're more likely to win big, but you're also more likely to experience total failures—that is, the other party walking away from the negotiating table.

A fourth principle of competitive negotiating is to *work for one-to-one trades of items of relatively equal value*. Think about the previous principle, taking extreme positions and minimizing movement. If you take an extreme position, then quickly back off of it, your position loses credibility. You create the appearance of bluffing or of not taking your own initial bid seriously. In fact, any "free" moves away from the initial position may undermine your stance. However, if your moves away from that position are only made in return for a comparable concession from the other party, the impression that you take your initial position seriously is enhanced. Thus, in buying a used car recently, a friend asked for $1000 off the price. The dealer, after initially refusing, agreed to take off $800, but only if the buyer was prepared to forego the deluxe mag wheels. Making such a concession appears to be an effort to cooperate, thus keeping the buyer's interest, but at the same time is no concession at all; that is, the dealer does not concede anything off the price of the car but simply offers the buyer an option to spend less money, thus retaining the impression the dealer's existing offer is relatively firm.

Finally, competitive negotiators *manage deadlines strategically*. Every few years, one of the professional sports organizations in the United States (the NBA, the NFL, or Major League Baseball) goes through a highly publicized contract dispute. Both sides make strong demands and, often through the media, claim that the other side is being unreasonable. Very little progress is made in the early stages. At some point, a deadline becomes imminent, after which the league's season will have to be delayed or cancelled. Usually, there is a flurry of activity prior to the deadline and agreements are often reached "at the eleventh hour."

The same holds true in other competitive business and even political negotiations. Not only do deadlines have the effect of prompting a settlement, knowledge of a deadline is used strategically, especially if a deadline is more important to one side than to the other. Recently in New Zealand, the high school teachers' union and the Labour government went through a protracted contract dispute that involved strikes and substantial press coverage. As the national election day loomed closer with the dispute still not settled after more than a year, and with opposing parties criticizing the Labour party for its inability to reach agreement, the teachers' union stalled, since they knew that the election day created a prominent deadline for the government but not for them. Finally, days before the election, the government offered to send the dispute to binding arbitration (a neutral party hears both sides and decides the terms of settlement). The union's awareness of the government's deadlines enabled them to hold out and to force the government to change its position.

There are certainly other principles and strategies used by competitive negotiators, but these capture many of the more prominent ones. Box 10.9 provides more specific tactics used in competitive negotiation.

Box 10.9 Competitive Negotiation Tactics

- *Bluff:* fabricating a scenario, such as the phantom buyer; "You'd better take this one quickly, because I have another guy who's really interested."
- *Final offer:* suggesting that the current offer is the last one; "Take it or leave it."
- *Low ball:* sometimes this term is used to describe an extreme offer; we mean it to refer to the tactic of changing the terms of the offer just before closing; "I made a mistake; we can't give it to you for that price after all. It's going to cost you a bit more."
- *Delay:* used to get the other party to invest time in the deal and to increase commitment to settling; "Just wait here while I go check some figures."
- *Limited authority:* often used as the excuse for delay; "I can't lower the price, but wait here while I check with my boss."
- *Good cop/bad cop:* used in cooperation with a partner; the "good cop" appears to be the other party's friend while the "bad cop" makes exorbitant demands; "If you can just increase your offer slightly, I'm sure my partner will calm down and come around."
- *Temper tantrum:* used to upset the other party or to radically change the negotiation atmosphere in hopes that the discomfort caused will get the other party to settle quickly or lower their demands; may be used by the "bad cop"; "I'm *sick* of this crap! If you people aren't serious, then take your business elsewhere!"
- *Pressure to close the deal:* used to get the other party to settle quickly; "Look, this is a one time offer. Either take it now or the deal's off."
- *Emotional plea:* an attempt to play on the other party's sympathy; "Come on, I've got a family to support. Can't you try to be a bit more generous?"

Collaborative Strategies

Box 10.8 presented a collaborative strategy. However, we want to mention several other principles that underlie collaborative negotiation strategies. These principles are largely derived from the work of the Harvard Negotiating Project and the book that emerged from that project, *Getting to Yes,* by Harvard professors Roger Fisher and William Ury.[36]

One key principle is to *separate people from the problem.* This means to treat the issue being negotiated as the focus of the discussion and not treat the other party as if *they* are the problem. Rather than seeing the other party as an adversary, such as we often do in competitive negotiation, the other party becomes a collaborator with whom you work to solve a problem. Closely related is a second principle, *focus on commonalities.* That is, to establish a sense of collaboration, it is important to recognize and draw attention to mutual interests. Even in apparently adversarial negotiation situations, there are usually mutual interests. In Eastern martial arts such as Karate or Taekwondo, participants compete against each other; more significantly, they need and depend upon one another in order to reinforce core values, such as respect, courage, and humility. Focusing on common ground helps reframe the negotiation situation from adversarial to cooperative and can put the negotiators on a path toward building trust.

A critically important principle in collaborative negotiation is to *focus on needs and interests, not positions.* If you think about collaboration as working toward a mutually satisfying solution, you will quickly realize that win-win solutions are not possible if both parties articulate incompatible positions. For example, imagine that our two town officials notice there's an extra $10,000 in the town budget near the end of the year. One official proposes using the money to plant a garden to beautify a particular area of town. The other proposes to use the money to commission a statue that would commemorate war veterans. There is no possibility of a collaborative solution if the two officials stick to their positions. They could compromise, with each getting half the money, but neither could get all of what is wanted. However, if they focus on the underlying needs and interests, not the positions, a collaborative solution is possible. Perhaps what's really important to the first official is improving the particular area of town and what's important to the second one is commemorating the war veterans. With a focus on these underlying interests, a number of collaborative solutions are possible.

This brings us to the fourth principle: *invent options for mutual gain.* To achieve a mutually satisfying outcome, the negotiators should creatively consider ways to meet both parties' needs. Continuing with our city council example, the officials might invent new proposals that address the underlying needs of both partners, such as a veterans' memorial garden or an artistic statue in the designated area of town. Or, they might put their heads together and consider how to expand the amount of money available, such as seeking corporate sponsorship. Or, they might consider jointly sponsoring one initiative this year and the other initiative next year. The point is, once they commit to working to satisfy both of their interests, they can brainstorm a host of options.

Yet another principle that can help collaboration is to *identify objective criteria before solutions.* This is especially useful for very tangible issues that must be negotiated, such as price, quantity of goods, and timing. If the two parties are committed to a collaborative solution, rather than haggling over something such as price, they could agree in advance on some criteria to use to settle the issue. For example, *Consumer Reports* suggested some years ago that a reasonable way to agree on the price for a new automobile is to identify the documented amount of money the dealer has invested in the car and then add three percent. They argued that this ensures the dealer gets a fair profit and the buyer pays a fair price. Notice that such a solution could be agreed upon even before mentioning a specific price. The idea is for the negotiators to agree on areas of cooperation in determining what would constitute a fair settlement rather than engaging in competitive bargaining over all matters.

Finally, collaborative negotiation should include *exchanging information and ideas.* Not only is doing so important to building trust and good will, but it is necessary to being able to develop solutions that meet both parties' needs. While there are obvious advantages to collaborating, negotiators should be cautious—without of course being paranoid or cynical. It is possible for an idealistic negotiator with good intentions to be "taken to the cleaners," or manipulated, by an unscrupulous negotiator who appears to be collaborating only to use the information exchanged to manipulate and take advantage of the other.

All negotiation should be preceded by extensive information gathering and the *creation of a negotiation plan*. The plan should include clear objectives regarding one's underlying interests and goals without committing one to positions that might lead to deadlock. It should include research on the relevant environment and on the other party to ascertain their needs, interests, and constraints, then an inventory of the available resources for bargaining. Notice that research on the other party's situation may suggest possible needs that can be met through resources that would not have been considered relevant before the research was done. For example, the two organizations may plan to negotiate over the purchase of one set of products, but a bit of research may suggest that there are multiple ways the two organizations may be able to benefit each other—and these benefits may come in handy as representatives of the two organizations meet to negotiate.

Intergroup Conflict

Thus far, much of our attention has been devoted to conflict between individuals, or between individuals and an organization. However, the subject of conflict between and among groups in organizations has received a fair amount of academic attention. Putnam and Poole state that there is some danger in assuming that groups can always speak with one voice.[37] That is, what goes on within a group in terms of commonalities and differences between individuals affects how the group itself perceives conflict. As Putnam and Poole also state, intergroup conflict tends to increase when the organization itself is complex, units are interdependent, and perspectives across the units are divergent.[38] This observation makes further sense with reference to other research, which shows that low-conflict organizations are characterized by higher number of inter-group strong ties.[39]

Therefore, when we think about inter-group conflict, we need to be careful about assuming that groups in organizations automatically speak to each other with one voice. Rather, we should focus on the processes by which groups come to share vocabularies and perspectives about their friends and enemies. Putnam and her co-authors conducted an interesting study involving inter-group conflict.[40] Using tenets from the study of organizational culture, namely, "fantasy themes," rites, and rituals, they studied the collective bargaining practices between administrators and teachers in two school districts in the Midwestern United States. Putnam and her colleagues found that the telling and retelling of fantasy themes (stories that develop similar attitudes and emotional responses among members) was the process by which organizational members developed symbolic convergence (similar understandings) on both internal and external enemies and heroes.

For example, in one of the school districts, members tended to see outsiders as villains. They narrated stories about third party intervention, where professional negotiators had taken part in the bargaining process and had to be "shown their place." Putnam and her colleagues found several commonalities in the fantasy themes of both districts, including common desires to make bargaining open, honest, and respectful. Interestingly, there were differences in the way administrators and teachers interpreted bargaining. In one district bargaining over an eleven-day period was considered part and parcel of the everyday work. In the second school district, where bargaining was conducted in one single-day marathon session, bargaining was considered a "necessary evil." The researchers concluded that the different meanings of bargaining in both districts may have had something to do with the fact that bargaining was not merely a means of conflict reduction—it served several other functions such as enhancing group solidarity, balancing power, improving communication, and appeasing various factions.

Stress, Burnout, and Support

We have discussed these strategies and approaches toward conflict resolution in order to stimulate you to think and to deal constructively with conflict as it occurs in your everyday life. One message that all of us often internalize in this regard is "be supportive!" Yet, when we actually look at what the word "support" means, we realize that our everyday use of the concept is somewhat fuzzy and that we actually equate it with simply "being nice!" However, as we will see, there are many forms of support that fulfill different functions. Although the presence of support doesn't eliminate conflict (and probably shouldn't), conflict resolution is easier in a more supportive environment than in a less supportive environment. Usually, we think of social support as being a necessary part of maintaining a healthy organizational climate, and research supports this view. In their classic book *The Social Psychology of Organizations*, Daniel Katz and Robert Kahn state that social support helps ease stress at work.[41] Cynthia Cordes and Thomas Dougherty, in a review of research on stress and burnout at work, say that researchers have found that organizational social support is an important resource for burned-out employees.[42]

Defining Burnout and Stress

Before discussing the issue of organizational social support any further, it is probably a good idea to be a little clearer about what we mean by the terms "stress" and "burnout." It is useful to conceive of burnout as a *form* of stress that has deleterious effects for both the organization and the individual. Most researchers use Christina Maslach's definition of burnout as a starting point for their own work.[43] According to Maslach, there are three things that are involved in burnout. First, burnout is associated with depersonalization, or an inability to be personally involved in one's work. Second, it is associated with diminished personal accomplishment, or a tendency to make negative self-evaluations regarding one's performance at work. And third, it is associated with emotional exhaustion rather than negative emotions per se. It refers to an inability to feel anything at work, including joy or sorrow, elation or despair, love or hate. Stress, on the other hand, has been defined quite simply as a psychological response in which a situation is seen as important, involves uncertainty, and is interpreted as being an opportunity, constraint, or demand.[44] This is an interesting definition because it points toward the fact that stress can be "positive." Can you think of any such situations?

It's important to note that while organizational support helps individuals deal with stress and burnout, the provision of such support does not necessarily end it altogether. Burnout has been associated with such things as overloads, role conflicts, and larger organizational contexts and ideologies. Debra Meyerson, for example, talks about how a professional social work ideology in a hospital led social workers to interpret ambiguity and burnout as a normal, even desirable part of work.[45] So, it should be apparent that while social support processes are helpful to individuals in organizations, we should avoid seeing them as a panacea for larger societal issues such as overwork.

As Katherine Miller and her associates have also found, the experience of stress and burnout varies from occupation to occupation within an organization.[46] In a recent study, Patricia Amason and her colleagues found that not only can stress vary from occupation to occupation within an organization; it can also take on new dimensions when the workplace is multicultural. Hispanic workers faced more stress

"Really, I'm fine. It was just a fleeting sense of purpose—I'm sure it will pass."

at work than Anglo-American employees because of the pressure to *acculturate*, or take on characteristics of Anglo-American culture.[47]

Miller and her associates, who initiated the study of stress, burnout, and social support in our field, have demonstrated that communication plays a large part in moderating burnout.[48] That is, communication processes have a significant role to play in the creation, interpretation, and resolution of burnout. Currently, scholars in the field provide a variety of models for us to conceptualize support. In general, social support is seen as the provision of messages or resources that are intended to be helpful to others. In what follows, we present two models to serve as ways for you to think about the idea of support in more detail and to identify it as it occurs in various forms in a variety of organizations.

Two Models of Social Support

The first typology makes distinctions between various functions of social support.[49] *Emotional support* involves the provision of messages of care and regard for the other person ("you're the best, and I know you'll rock the house at the interview"). *Informational support* involves offering facts, opinions, and advice on matters of concern ("the nearest cafe is four miles away, so make sure you bring some coffee"). *Instrumental* or *material support* involves the provision of tangible resources such as money or lodging ("would you like to take leave for a week while you sort through your problem?"). Finally, *appraisal support* involves evaluative messages that encourage an individual to continue performing well ("you wrote that report really well—it makes our work look excellent").

Communication scholar Myria Watkins Allen developed the second typology of social support. She lists the communication concepts that are related not only to social support in particular but to various forms of organizational support in general.[50] She lists four aspects of organizational communication that affect the extent to which an organizational climate can be considered supportive: conversations with others, job-related feedback, global support-related messages, and decision-making input. Conversations with others significantly influences employee perceptions about the extent of support available at the organization. Positive job-related feedback from supervisors, coworkers, and the organization in general is also related to the amount of support employees feel is available to them. Third, global support-related messages including top management employee policies or the manipulation of symbols in newsletters and other media that are designed to evoke loyalty, also affect the overall supportiveness of the organizational climate. Finally, the amount and manner of decision-making input affects how supportive the organizational climate is—organizations that are more decentralized are usually thought of as being more supportive.

Feminist scholars have made important contributions to our understanding of social support processes. Organizational communication scholar Angela Trethewey demonstrates the importance of different types of social support at work in an interesting feminist study of midlife professional women in the United States.[51] Many of the women who participated in Trethewey's study described their experiences of aging in terms of loss and isolation at work. Trethewey relates this to dominant cultural messages that encourage women to view aging as a process of decline that has to be slowed and controlled. For some women, aging was accompanied by positive experiences: less concern with appearances because they felt greater competence, less concern about comments that men might make, and a realization of greater freedom to do as one pleases. Trethewey advocates that organizations examine the issue of midlife social support more carefully, possibly developing informal support groups, in order to enable women to develop alternative visions of age and work and to deal with disempowerment issues that stem from isolating experiences of aging. How do you think different cultures might interpret the aging process differently, and what effect might this have on organizational policies and programs?

Employee Assistance Programs and Organizational Support

Corporate employee support programs grew tremendously during the 1980s and 1990s. As organizational communication scholar Steve May[52] argues, the rise of a wide range of therapeutic employee assistance programs in the 1990s, from counseling programs to day care and health centers, blurred distinctions that employees would otherwise be able to make between work and home, public and private, and labor and leisure (see box 14.1).[53] Heather Zoller notes that employee assistance programs (EAPs) in the United States that aim to help workers deal with health issues (see box 10.10) can fill other functions.

Arlie Russell Hochschild has found that for many people, especially women, "work is home and home is work."[54] The nature of jobs and salary structures have changed; large numbers of people have to hold down more than one full-time job in order to keep themselves financially solvent. Consequently, they spend more time at work than at home, and maintaining a space for home life, leisure, and community has become increasingly difficult. Given that women are still more often responsible for managing "domesticity," this balancing act is particularly difficult for them. The average family with two income earners in the United States now works about 83 weeks a year, up by 15 weeks since 1969.[55] And in the 1990s, U.S. workers put in more hours on the job than workers in any other industrialized nation.

Box 10.10 Voices from the Field

Analysis of Conflicting Interests, Values, and Goals in Corporate Health Promotion Campaigns

Heather Zoller, The University of Cincinnati

An increasing number of U.S. workplaces offer health promotion initiatives for their employees, and we find similar programs in other parts of the industrialized world (including Japan). Companies like Johnson & Johnson, DuPont, and Coors are building fitness and recreation centers, offering health education, and requiring tests for cholesterol and high blood pressure. Typically, such programs focus on cardiovascular health, nutrition, weight loss, smoking cessation, hypertension control, stress management, or fitness levels. Management and health promoters believe that these programs contribute to the *bottom line.* Improvements in health are expected to increase employee morale and loyalty, lower health insurance costs, and enhance productivity through lower absenteeism and improved job performance. Although there is contradictory evidence about actual outcomes, human resource managers and other proponents often argue, "they're the undisputed feel-good part of employee benefits and human resources programs."[56]

From a managerial perspective, health promotion initiatives are described in *win-win* terms. However, the managerial literature overlooks some potential conflicts that may arise from such programs—especially when viewed from an employee's perspective. Communication scholars William Kirkwood and Dan Brown argue that in health promotion campaigns, *attributing responsibility for illness is a rhetorical, rather than a purely scientific, choice.*[57] For example, even if we accept that cholesterol causes heart attacks, we still must choose among genetics, eating habits, or fast-food advertising as potential culprits for higher cholesterol levels.

Robert Crawford argues that "lifestyle" approaches to health promotion—those that define health in terms of individual choices such as exercise and eating right—obscure the social origins of much illness and disease, including low incomes, discrimination, environmental pollution, and the workplace itself.[58] Such an approach also may encourage *victim-blaming,* because when we are responsible for our health, we are also responsible when we are sick—thus justifying lower health-care expenditures. Although such programs may not improve employee health, Crawford argues, they do promote the values of hard work, self-control, and discipline valued by management. Self-discipline is framed as a moral obligation for the good of the community (in this case, the company) in terms of cost savings. This provides our workplaces with an opportunity to shape employee behaviors and self-concepts.

What values, goals, and interests are potentially or actually in conflict here? Should management have the power to restrict employees' off-work behavior such as diet, exercise, tobacco, or alcohol use? To what degree is a focus on individual wellness, fitness, and "right living" a distraction from larger social, political, and economic problems? How are the same services provided and discussed in other countries? Is the system more responsible for social ills and health problems than individuals?

Practices at work that aim to help workers manage the rest of their lives in consonance with their jobs serve latent conflict reduction functions. Management practices designed to reduce the tension from working long hours—and the increased potential for work-related conflicts as a result of that pressure—sometimes has surreal results. For example, at the Health Care and Retirement Corp in Toledo, Ohio, employees recently went through an eleven-hour seminar on the art of hugging.[59]

To understand issues of employee support we need to examine how they are framed. Issues of employee assistance or human resources management may be individualized or identified with specific segments of employees—as when we focus on how a particular coworker is coping with the demands of the job. Alternatively, we can look at these issues at the level of an organization or even an industry—as when we say that "stresses in the telemarketing field are high." Finally, we could view such issues at a societal level as fundamental conflicts are between the interests of business and labor. As Dana Cloud argues in box 10.11, behind the hype of the "new economy" we should recognize some basic tensions.

Box 10.11 Voices from the Field

Labor and Communication in the Not-so-New Economy

Dana L. Cloud, University of Texas, Austin

Organizational communication scholars have become more interested in commenting on broader work and societal trends, much in the way sociologists and other cultural analysts have done for some time.[60] In this way, organizational communication can broaden its own perspective while making important contributions to the understanding of the times in which we live. After all, this is the way the study of organizations began in the late 19th century: by situating them in the broader landscape of modernity. Since the late 1980s, there has been a great deal of talk of "the New Economy"—suggesting that somehow the high-tech age means that all the old issues of harmful working conditions, industrial waste, and labor-management strife have gone away. To read popular magazines like *Wired*, one would almost think that our economy is now populated exclusively by well-educated, well-paid, independent-minded, technologically savvy entrepreneurs, This emphasis has diverted attention from the issues of labor, especially during the years where unions' power and membership were on the decline in the United States, the United Kingdom, and in number of other industrialized countries.[61] The "new politics" of work rest on the assumption that we are living in a wholly "new" economy that has broken with capitalist relations of the past.[62] Yet the "new" economy is not completely different from what came before: labor-management tensions often persist, different socio-economic classes are often removed from one another, and in the United States the gap between rich and poor is now statistically the greatest for any industrialized nation.[63] Although in all the popular talk about the "new" economy there seem to be no *industrial* workers at all, commodities are still produced around the world on assembly lines by workers who often experience poor working conditions, live in shantytowns, and are denied the right to organize.[64]

Events such as the 1997 UPS (United Parcel Service) strike, late 1990s protests against Nike's treatment of Southeast Asian workers, and the 1999 WTO protests in Seattle show that labor and economic conflict can and will continue to surface, regardless of the myth of a unitary or linear process of globalization. In fact, the international flows of knowledge, labor, and capital are becoming more salient in labor disputes and strikes—in the United States, Canada, Mexico, Venezuela, Argentina, and other countries. In just the last few years scholars as well as political and financial leaders have begun to speak not so much of globalization but of "globalizations" and their discontents. (And, in the same way, we should appropriately speak of "capitalisms").[65] We can look at the discontent on both the broad international level and in specific firms and industries, where strikes and unrest are often explicitly about the effects of economic globalization on workers.

Ultimately, we must see class issues as having fundamental material dimensions as well as apparent symbolic aspects. And, understanding the interrelationships of the material and the symbolic with respect to class and labor is very important. For example, how is it that the material resources themselves, including working hours, make it difficult for some employees to organize? How does the easy movement of capital across international boundaries affect the position and movement of labor? Conversely, how is it that the symbol of "class warfare" is used successfully by U.S. politicians to divert attention from poverty and the increasing concentration of wealth in the hands of a few? And, why do most people like to see themselves as "middle class," almost regardless of income? It is significant that just since 1998, there have been new attempts to organize both "blue collar" and "white collar" workers in the United States and in some other countries, including budding coalitions between previously unlikely allies: U.S. and Mexican labor organizers.

Why do you think that there may be renewed energy for labor organizing? Do work-life balance issues contribute to the need for workers to organize? Where do employee assistance programs fall in the equation? How does the North American situation compare and contrast with what's happening in other parts of the world: in France, with its national 35-hour work week; in Germany, where the national system of co-determination (between government, labor, and industry) has been somewhat weakened, etc.? What does "class" mean to you—in terms of your aspirations, your lifestyle, your associates, and those from whom you may be distanced (both physically and socially or symbolically)? How does contemporary advertising treat class issues and class identities—particularly in its portrayals of technology and luxury

Inter-organizational Conflict

The efforts that large organizations make to reduce the potential for intergroup conflict at work is matched, if not outdone, by the care that they take to reduce the potential for inter-organizational conflict. As we discussed in chapter 5, the rise of "integrated marketing communication" blurs traditional distinctions between such activities as marketing and public relations. One form of public relations that has become an increasingly important way of reducing the possibility of inter-organizational conflict is "issue management."

Issue management differs from traditional conceptions of marketing in that, instead of aiming to reflect the needs and interests of a consumer group, it involves actively working to shape salient public issues and opinion (see box 5.6 on various types of external organizational communication). Large organizations attempt to shape issues in a number of ways—by funding research in particular areas, lobbying politicians, funding political campaigns, and setting up or supporting nonprofit organizations. The Tobacco Institute, for example, which has put out a lot of research on the lack of a connection between smoking and cancer and is at the forefront of the smokers' rights movement, is funded largely by the tobacco industry. In both theory and practice, the management of issues by organizations has focused on the idea of crisis communication, or the nature of an organization's external communication during specific crises.

A corporate *crisis* has been defined as "a situation that runs the risk of escalating intensity, falling under close media or government scrutiny, interfering with the normal operations of business, jeopardizing the positive public image presently enjoyed by the company or its officers, and damaging a company's bottom line in any way."[66] Box 10.12 presents a range of responses to organizational crises. While not all of them are equally effective, Richard Ice argues it is hard to identify one particular response or strategy as being inherently or absolutely better. What appears to matter is the way in which the corporation approaches the crisis and manages its strategies.[67] In this light, David Williams and Glenda Treadaway argue for an overall *proactive* stance as a criterion of effective crisis communication.[68] A proactive approach, for them, involves anticipating the need to communicate during a crisis, initiating communication with various publics, and issuing strong, immediate responses. A second criterion for effective crisis communication for Williams and Treadaway is that the organization must be able to maintain public confidence by attempting to restore trust and build credibility. A key aspect of doing this is to maintain sincere, honest, and open relationships with the press.

In Brinson and Benoit's analysis of an image crisis at Texaco over discrimination against African-American employees by white managers, corrective action and mortification emerged as successful strategies.[69] Strong statements by Peter Bijur, chair of Texaco, helped restore the company's public image. In a news release to the press and in a letter to employees, he announced an immediate investigation into the incident. He also followed up on the initial announcement by announcing punishments for offenders and six specific corrective actions to eliminate discrimination, including diversity training and a confidential hotline. In other statements, he expressed regret and sorrow at the incident. Bijur laid the groundwork for shifting the blame for the incident onto individual managers rather than the structure of management at Texaco itself, as Brinson and Benoit note.

The amount of time and effort that corporations now spend on planning and preparing for potential crisis events is much greater than it was sixty or seventy years ago. Tim Ziaukas has analyzed the overwhelmingly reactive stance that the White Star Line, which owned the RMS *Titanic*, took toward managing the crisis.[70] Ziaukas points out that the company was never in control of information. The story was transmitted by David Sarnoff, a junior employee of the Marconi Company, which controlled the trans-Atlantic wireless system. Philip Franklin, the head of White Star's U.S. operations, heard about the crisis first from reporters. The official message was apparently sent via a telegraph from the *Olympic* (another White Star ship) to Montreal, and from Montreal to the New York Western Union station via a land line, and from there to the White Star offices via a message boy on a bicycle. The pre-launch publicity had trumpeted that the *Titanic* was unsinkable, and the inept reactions after the disaster caused White Star to fail. Corporations today spend much more time, money, and energy trying to control information about potential crises from the outset.

There are a number of ethical issues at stake in crisis communication. Take for example, the inherent assumption that a crisis occurs only when the public and the

Box 10.12 The Example of Image Restoration Discourse

Communication scholars Susan Brinson and William Benoit discuss several self-defense strategies that corporations deploy when they encounter crisis situations.[71] They developed a typology of image restoration discourse, using examples from corporate crises that were covered by the U.S. media in the 1980s and 1990s: the poisonous capsules sold by Tylenol, unnecessary auto repairs at Sears, the Coke-Pepsi rivalry, as well as more generic examples.

Strategy	Key Characteristics	Example
Denial		
Simple denial	Did not perform act	Tylenol did not poison the capsules
Shift the blame	Another performed act	A "madman" poisoned the capsules
Evasion of Responsibility		
Provocation	Responded to the act of another	Firm moved because of new taxes
Defeasibility	Lack of information or ability	Executive not told meeting changed
Accident	Mishap	Tree fell on tracks causing train wreck
Good intentions	Meant well	Sears wants to provide good auto repair service
Reducing Offensiveness of Event		
Bolstering	Stress good traits	Exxon's "swift and competent" cleanup of oil spill
Minimization	Act is not serious	Few animals killed in Exxon oil spill
Differentiation	Act is less offensive than similar acts	Repairs at Sears were preventative maintenance, not fraud
Transcendence	More important values	Helping humans justifies testing animals
Attack Accuser	Reduce credibility of accuser	Coke: Pepsi owns restaurants, competes directly for customers
Compensation	Reimburse victim	Disabled movie-goers given free passes after denied admission to movie
Corrective Action	Plan to solve/prevent recurrence of the problem	AT&T long-distance upgrades: promised to spend billions more to improve service
Mortification	Apologize	AT&T apologized for service interruption

Pick an ongoing example of crisis communication from the media (sadly, there are many!). For example, consider the official responses to corporate scandals in the United States and Western Europe, or the Roman Catholic Church's response to reports of sexual abuse of children by priests, or NASA's public communication in the wake of the Columbia tragedy. What strategies can you see? Are multiple strategies being used simultaneously? Are strategies shifting over time? What do you think about the effectiveness of each strategy? How do large institutions often try to "localize" problems and minimize crises by associating them with "a few bad people" rather than with a larger systemic problem?

media hear about it. This is ethically problematic because it implies that "if no one knows, it's OK." Robert Ulmer and Timothy Sellnow argue that *significant choice* is missing from crisis communication.[72] They define ethical communication between a company and its stakeholders as free-flowing, unrestrained information. The free flow of information allows listeners to discover the "truth" and to make an informed decision (or choice) about the nature of the company. Complicating the picture is the fact that communication as a process is inherently ambiguous and interpretive, making in virtually impossible to arrive at a single definition of a crisis issue. Accordingly, they make a distinction between ethical and unethical uses of strategic ambiguity in communication processes. Ethical strategic ambiguity involves presenting all available data about an issue in order to allow audiences significant choice. Unethical strategic ambiguity involves deliberately posing alternative views that might be minor or erroneous, in order to put a positive spin on an issue and to control public perception. Ulmer and Sellnow point toward the tobacco industry's crisis communication as unethical precisely because it has emphasized research that claims that there is no relationship between smoking and cancer over research that demonstrates that there is a significant correlation between the two.

In his research on crisis communication at Malden Mills in Massachusetts (see chapter 7), Robert Ulmer emphasized the importance of ongoing communication between a company and its stakeholders as a basis for the effective resolution of a public crisis.[73] He focused particularly on the commitment that Aaron Feuerstein, chairman of Malden Mills, demonstrated to various stakeholders over the years, including employees, the local community, customers, and the media. When a fire broke out in December 1995 and workers were at risk of losing their jobs and the community its largest employer, his "discourse of renewal" during his attempts to rebuild the factory turned him from a local hero into a near-mythological figure. Ulmer's research in the Malden Mills case illustrates that it is not the *appearance* of corrective action and mortification that serves as effective crisis communication: it is an *ongoing commitment* that a company has established with its stakeholders that determines how bad news is perceived.

While crisis communication appears to be a dominant form of inter-organizational conflict management today, crises are certainly not the only site of such conflict. Inter-organizational conflict is increasingly an issue in the corporate sector, especially given the growing number of mergers and acquisitions across a range or sectors. Acquisitions are generally seen as having more potential for conflict because, unlike mergers, they explicitly involve larger corporations "taking over" smaller ones (as in the study in box 10.5).

We also see evidence of inter-organizational conflicts in public protests. Students Against Sweatshops, for example, is a student-based movement on many campuses across the United States that uses campus demonstrations, marches, and hunger strikes to influence university policy and public opinion about the work practices of garment manufacturers and distributors. Earth First! is another example of an activist group that attempts high-visibility protests against organizations whose policies they consider environmentally unfriendly. Known for rather uncompromising tactics, the organization uses the defense that the Earth cannot speak for itself. In Missoula, Montana, in June 2002, two protesters stopped a logging truck on a bridge, attached ropes to it, rappelled off the bridge, dangled mid-stream over the Clark Fork River, and unfurled a banner reading "Globalization kills our forests." The group, protesting increased logging in the Bitterroot National Forest, sparked debates in the community over the nature of activism and appropriate civil disobedience. Activist protests often tend to be theatrical precisely because it is an effective (and sometimes the only) way to attract attention to an issue. Paradoxically, the issues themselves are often eclipsed by the controversy over the methods used.

Snapshot Synthesis

Conflict is an inescapable part of our everyday organizational lives and is an inherently communicative issue. It is crucial for individuals who study and practice organizational communication to develop skills to manage conflict effectively. Important among such skills is the ability to analyze and to think about the explanations we develop for conflict, the multiple sources of conflict, and the ambiguity and confusion that surround conflict situations and processes. We should pay attention to both the "macro" and the "micro" elements of conflict situations. That is, we need to analyze how different cultural contexts might affect how conflicts are expressed and resolved, to reorganize the role that popular discourses about markets or gender play in affecting our understanding of conflict issues, and to understand how factors such as class or ethnicity or gender spark or resolve conflicts between individuals. Since conflict processes are tied to perceptions, it is valuable to examine a conflict situation from multiple perspectives, attempting to frame and reframe it in a number of different ways.

Conflict does not take place only between individuals; it also occurs at group and organizational levels. Organizations increasingly go out of their way to prevent conflict situations, using a range of methods including informal support groups, a wide variety of employee assistance programs, and sophisticated plans to resolve potential crises. It is important to recognize that such solutions might not be permanent. Just as organizations might find new ways to contain conflict, individuals might find new ways of communicating dissent.

Key Concepts

- **Conflict:** an inherently communicative phenomenon that occurs between interdependent people and involves differences in perception; it can vary in intensity, level, overtness, scope, and outcome
- **Sources of Conflict:** the underlying causes of conflict are multiple; can include different understandings, threatening actions, role conflict, limited resources, and macro and cultural factors
- **Phases of Conflict:** the typical patterns of communication that occur during times of conflict; according to Pondy, the major phases include latent conflict, perceived conflict, felt conflict, manifest conflict, and conflict aftermath
- **Conflict Style**: a behavioral orientation toward conflict, or an expectation about the way conflict should be approached; typically five styles are discussed: competition, avoidance, accommodation, compromise, and collaboration.
- **Negotiation:** "a communicative process between interdependent parties with differing goals who are attempting to produce a joint decision"[74]

- **Distributive (or competitive) Negotiation:** an approach to negotiation that assumes one party must win and the other party will lose; focuses largely on maximizing one's own outcomes, assuming one's interests are in opposition to the other party's
- **Integrative (or collaborative) Negotiation:** an approach to negotiation that focuses on maximizing the outcomes of both parties, seeking to find solutions in which both parties are fully satisfied; negotiators assume at least some common interests and engage in a collaborative process of information sharing and trust building rather than positional tactics
- **Intergroup Conflict:** conflict between groups or collectives; tends to increase with greater organizational complexity, interdependence, and divergence of perspective
- **Stress:** a psychological response in which a situation is seen as important, involves uncertainty, and is interpreted as being an opportunity, constraint, or demand
- **Burnout:** a form of stress that involves depersonalization, a sense of diminished personal accomplishment, and emotional exhaustion
- **Social Support:** the provision of messages or resources that are intended to be helpful to others; may be informational, emotional, material, or appraisal-oriented and may occur through conversation, job-related feedback, global organizational messages, or decision making
- **Employee Assistance Programs (EAPs):** organizational programs that provide sources of support in organizations but also blur distinctions between work, home, and leisure
- **Crisis Communication:** an organization's external communication during a crisis, or "a situation that runs the risk of escalating intensity, falling under close media or government scrutiny, interfering with the normal operations of business, jeopardizing the positive public image presently enjoyed by the company or its officers, and damaging a company's bottom line in any way"[75]

Endnotes

1 Linda Putnam and Marshall Scott Poole, "Conflict and Negotiation," *Handbook of Organizational Communication: An Interdisciplinary Perspective*, ed. Fredric M. Jablin, Linda L. Putnam, Karlene H. Roberts, and Lyman W. Porter (Newbury Park, CA: Sage, 1987) p. 552; see also Anne M. Nicotera, ed., *Conflict and Organizations: Communicative Processes* (Albany: SUNY Press, 1995).

2 The oversimplification is this: Accounts are in fact forms of discourse, and discourses are not completely external because we participate in and contribute to them.

3 Harold H. Kelley, "The Process of Causal Attribution," *American Psychologist* 28 (1973): 107–128.

4 Susan T. Fiske and Shelley E. Taylor, *Social Cognition*, 2nd ed. (New York: McGraw-Hill, 1991).

5 Brant R. Burleson, "Attribution Schemes and Causal Inference in Natural Conversations," *Contemporary Issues in Language and Discourse Processes*, ed. D. G. Ellis and W. A. Donohue (Hillsdale, NJ: Erlbaum, 1986) pp. 63–85.

6 Nancy Burrell, Patrice Buzzanell, and Jill McMillan, "Feminine Tensions in Conflict Situations As Revealed by Metaphoric Analyses," *Management Communication Quarterly* 6 (1992): 115–149.

7 Patrice Buzzanell and Nancy Burrell, "Family and Workplace Conflict: Examining Metaphorical Conflict Schemas and Expressions Across Context and Sex," *Human Communication Research* 24 (1997): 109–146.

8 John Winslade and Gerald Monk, *Narrative Mediation: A New Approach to Conflict Resolution* (San Francisco: Jossey-Bass, 2000).

9 Tom Peters, *The Brand You 50: Or, Fifty Ways to Transform Yourself from an 'Employee' into a Brand that Shouts Distinction, Commitment, and Passion!* (New York: Knopf, 1999).

[10] Cynthia Stohl and Susan E. Schell, "A Communication-Based Model of a Small-Group Dysfunction," *Management Communication Quarterly* 5 (1991): 91–92.

[11] Stohl and Schell, p. 100.

[12] Theodore E. Zorn and George H. Tompson, "Communication in Top Management Teams," *New Directions in Group Communication Research*, ed. Lawrence Frey (Newbury Park, CA: Sage, 2002). See also David Nadler, "Leading Executive Teams," *Executive Teams*, ed. David A. Nadler and Janet L. Spencer (San Francisco: Jossey-Bass, 1998) pp. 3–20.

[13] Daniel Katz and Robert L. Kahn, *The Social Psychology of Organizations* (New York: John Wiley and Sons, 1978).

[14] Travis Tubre and Judith Collins, "Jackson and Schuler (1985) Revisited: A Meta-Analysis of the Relationships between Role Ambiguity, Role Conflict, and Job Performance," *Journal of Management* 26.1 (2000): 155–169.

[15] Evelyn Sieburg, *Dysfunctional Communication and Interpersonal Responsiveness in Small Groups*, diss., U. Denver, 1969.

[16] Tamyra Pierce and Deborah Dougherty, "The Construction, Enactment, and Maintenance of Power-As-Domination through an Acquisition," *Management Communication Quarterly* 16 (2002): 129–164.

[17] James W. Chesebro, "Communication, Values, and Popular Television Series—A Seventeen-Year Assessment," *Communication Quarterly* 39:3 (1991): 197–225.

[18] Alan Sillars, "Misunderstanding," *The Dark Side of Relationships*, ed. Brian H. Spitzberg and William R. Cupach (Mahwah, NJ: Lawrence Erlbaum Associates, 1998) pp. 73–102.

[19] Alan Sillars and Judith Weisberg, "Conflict as a Social Skill," *Interpersonal Processes*, ed. Michael Roloff and Gerald Miller (Thousand Oaks, CA: Sage, 1987) pp. 140–171.

[20] Louis R. Pondy, "Organizational Conflict: Concepts and Models," *Administrative Science Quarterly* 12 (1967): 296–320.

[21] René Girard, *Violence and the Sacred*, 2nd ed. (Baltimore: John Hopkins University Press, 1979).

[22] Joseph P. Folger, Marshall Scott Poole, and Randall K. Stutman, *Working through Conflict: Strategies for Relationships, Groups, and Organizations*, 3rd ed. (New York: HarperCollins, 1997) p. 185.

[23] Adapted from Folger, Poole, and Stutman.

[24] Charles Conrad, "Communication in Conflict: Style-Strategy Relationships," *Communication Monographs* 58:2 (1991): 135–155.

[25] Stella Ting-Toomey, "A Face Negotiation Theory," *Theories in Intercultural Communication*, ed. Young Kim and William Gudykunst (Newbury Park, CA: Sage, 1988) pp. 213–235.

[26] Folger, Poole, and Stutman. See also Richard E. Walton, *Interpersonal Peacemaking: Confrontations and Third Party Consultation* (Reading, PA: Addison-Wesley, 1969).

[27] Folger, Poole, and Stutman, p. 82.

[28] Adapted from Tom Rusk, *The Power of Ethical Persuasion: Winning through Understanding at Work and at Home* (New York: Penguin Books, 1993).

[29] Conrad, pp. 135–155.

[30] Erwin P. Bettinghaus and Michael J. Cody, *Persuasive Communication*, 5th ed. (Ft. Worth, TX: Harcourt Brace, 1994) p. 309.

[31] Roy J. Lewicki, Joseph A. Litterer, John W. Minton, and David M. Saunders, *Negotiation*, 2nd ed. (Chicago: Irwin, 1994).

[32] Putnam and Poole.

[33] We are indebted to Professor Bob Rineheimer, Duke University, for many of the ideas presented in this section.

[34] Robert Rineheimer, personal communication to Theodore Zorn, November 2, 1994.

[35] Bettinghaus and Cody, p. 327.

[36] Roger Fisher and William Ury, *Getting to Yes* (New York: Houghton-Mifflin, 1981).

[37] Putnam and Poole.

[38] Putnam and Poole.

[39] Reed E. Nelson, "The Strength of Strong Ties: Social Networks and Intergroup Conflict in Organizations," *Academy of Management Journal* 32.2 (1989): 377–402; Giuseppe Labianca, Daniel Brass, and Barbara Grey, "Social Networks and Perceptions of Intergroup Conflict: The Role of Negative Relationships and Third Parties," *Academy of Management Journal* 41.1 (1998): 55–68.

[40] Linda Putnam, Shirley Van Hoeven, and Connie A. Bullis, "The Role of Rituals and Fantasy Themes in Teachers' Bargaining," *Western Journal of Speech Communication* 55 (1991): 85–103.

[41] Daniel Katz and Robert Kahn, *The Social Psychology of Organizations* (New York: John Wiley, 1978).

42 Cynthia Cordes and Thomas Dougherty, "A Review and an Integration of Research on Job Burnout," *Academy of Management Review* 18.4 (1993): 621–656.

43 Christina Maslach, *Burnout: The Cost of Caring* (Englewood Cliffs, NJ: Prentice-Hall, 1982).

44 Randall Schuler, "Definition and Conceptualization of Stress in Organizations, *Organization Behavior and Human Performance* 15 (1980): 184–215.

45 Debra Meyerson, "Interpretations of Stress in Institutions: The Cultural Production of Stress and Burnout," *Administrative Science Quarterly* 39 (1994): 628–653.

46 Katherine Miller, Eric G. Zook, and Beth Hartman Ellis, "Occupational Differences in the Influence of Communication on Stress and Burnout in the Workplace," *Management Communication Quarterly* 3 (1989): 166–190.

47 Patricia Amason, Myria Watkins Allen, and Susan Holmes, "Social Support and Acculturative Stress in the Multicultural Workplace," *Journal of Applied Communication Research* 27 (1999): 310–334.

48 Katherine Miller, Beth Hartman Ellis, Eric G. Zook, and Judith S. Lyles, "An Integrated Model of Communication, Stress and Burnout in the Workplace," *Communication Research* 17 (1990): 300–326.

49 James S. House, *Work Stress and Social Support* (Reading, MA: Addison-Wesley, 1981).

50 Myria Watkins Allen, "Communication Concepts Related to Perceived Organizational Support," *Western Journal of Communication* 59 (1995): 326–346.

51 Angela Trethewey, "Reproducing and Resisting the Master Narrative of Decline: Midlife Professional Women's Experiences of Aging," *Management Communication Quarterly* 15 (2001): 183–226.

52 Steve May, "Therapy at Work: Employee Assistance—Who Benefits? Who Cares?" *At Work* (May/June 1999): 12–13, 23.

53 The provision of such services facilitates employee identification with the organization, see chapter 5.

54 Arlie Russell Hochschild, *The Time Bind: When Home Becomes Work and Work Becomes Home* (New York: Metropolitan Books, 1998); cited in Ibrahim Warde, "End of the New Workplace: Smiling Serfs of the New Economy," *Le Monde Diplomatique* (March 2002): 2.

55 This is in terms of a 40-hour workweek according to Rick Mercier, "Higher Wages and More Time Off," *The Free Lance Star* (3 Sept. 2001), <http://att.nac.net/freelancestar090101.htm>.

56 Deborah Lewis, "Why Wellness Programs Fail," *Financial Executive* 11 (1996): 26.

57 William G. Kirkwood and Dan Brown, "Public Communication about the Causes of Disease: The Rhetoric of Responsibility," *Journal of Communication* 45.1 (1995): 55–76.

58 Robert Crawford, "A Cultural Account of Health: Control, Release and the Social Body," *Issues in the Political Economy of Health Care*, ed. J. B. McKinlay (New York: Tavistock, 1984): 60–103.

59 Warde.

60 David Carlone and Bryan Taylor, "Organizational Communication and Cultural Studies: A Review Essay," *Communication Theory* 8 (1998): 337–367.

61 See Dana L. Cloud, "Laboring under the Sign of the New," *Management Communication Quarterly* 15 (2001): 268–278. Compare: Stanley Aronowitz, *Politics of Identity: Class, Culture, Social Movements* (New York: Routledge, 1992); and Sally Munt, ed., *Cultural Studies and the Working Class* (London: Cassell, 2000). See also: Charles Conrad and Marshall S. Poole, eds., "Communication in the Age of the Disposable Worker," *Communication Research* 24 (Special Issue, 1997); Stanley A. Deetz and Dennis K. Mumby, "Power, Discourse, and the Workplace: Reclaiming the Critical Tradition in Communication Studies in Organizations, *Communication Yearbook* 13 (1990): 18–47.

62 Stuart Hall and Martin Jacques, eds., *New Times: The Changing Face of Politics in the 1990s* (London: Verso, 1989); Robin D. G. Kelley, *Race Rebels: Culture, Politics, and the Black Working Class* (New York: Free Press, 1994); Kevin Kelly, *New Rules for a New Economy* (New York: Penguin, 1999).

63 Contrary to perspectives that regard class as a discursively-produced identity (see Stanley Aronowitz, "Working Class Culture in the Electronic Age," *Cultural Politics in Contemporary America*, ed. Ian Angus and Sut Jhally (New York: Routledge, 1989) pp. 135–150; and Aronowitz). I regard class as an objective relationship to the system in which goods are produced and distributed.

64 See Gordon Marshall, *Repositioning Class: Social Inequalities in Industrial Society* (London: Sage, 1997); Lawrence Mishel, Jared Bernstein, and John Schmitt, *The State of Working America 2000/2001* (Ithaca, NY: Cornell University Press, 2001); Dana L. Cloud, *Consolation and Control in American Culture and Politics: Rhetorics of Therapy* (Thousand Oaks, CA: Sage, 1998); Mike Parker and Jane Slaughter, *Working Smart: A Union Guide to Participation Programs and Reengineering* (Detroit: Labor Notes, 1994).

65 John Gray, *False Dawn* (New York: New Press, 1998).

66 Robert Ulmer and Timothy Sellnow, "Strategic Ambiguity and the Ethic of Significant Choice in the Tobacco Industry's Crisis Communication," *Communication Studies* 48 (1997): 215. Ulmer and Sell-

now's definition is based on Steven Fink, *Crisis Management: Planning for the Inevitable* (New York: AMOCOM, 1986) pp. 15–16.

[67] Richard Ice, "Corporate Publics and Rhetorical Strategies: The Case of Union Carbide's Bhopal Crisis," *Management Communication Quarterly* 4.3 (1991): 341–362.

[68] David Williams and Glenda Treadaway, "Exxon and the Valdez Accident: A Failure in Crisis Communication," *Communication Studies* 43 (1992): 56–64.

[69] Susan L. Brinson and William L. Benoit, "The Tarnished Star: Restoring Texaco's Damaged Public Image," *Management Communication Quarterly* 12.4 (1999): 483–500.

[70] Tim Ziaukas, "Titanic and Public Relations: A Case Study," *Journal of Public Relations Research* 11.2 (1999): 105–123.

[71] Brinson and Benoit. The list of self-defense strategies that they present here is derived largely from William Benoit, *Accounts, Excuses and Apologies: A Theory of Image Restoration Strategies* (Albany: State University of New York Press, 1995); and William Benoit, "Image Repair Discourse and Crisis Communication," *Public Relations Review* 23 (1997): 177–186.

[72] Ulmer and Sellnow, p. 215.

[73] Robert Ulmer, "Effective Crisis Management through Established Stakeholder Relationships: Malden Mills as a Case Study," *Management Communication Quarterly* 14.4 (2001): 590–615; Matthew Seeger and Robert Ulmer, "A Post-Crisis Discourse of Renewal: The Cases of Malden Mills and Cole Hardwoods," *Journal of Applied Communication Research* 30.2 (2002): 126–142.

[74] Bettinghaus and Cody, p. 309.

[75] Ulmer and Sellnow, p. 215.

11

Organizational Change and Change-Related Communication

Pick up any business magazine today or look at any corporate Web site and you're very likely to see one or more articles focusing on organizational *change*. The common wisdom in much of the management literature—what we might call the dominant discourse—is that organizations must change and they must do so *constantly*. Alvin Toffler predicted this emphasis in 1970: *"The acceleration of change in our time is . . . an elemental force."*[1] James March reiterated the effect on discourse in 1995: "The most conventional story of contemporary futurology is a story that observes and predicts dramatic changes in the environments of organizations."2

Many organizations tout their commitment to change in their vision statements and core values. Large consulting firms lead the charge, of course, since their raison d'être is to sell ideas for change to their clients. So, McKinsey and Company's mission is "To help our clients make distinctive, lasting, and substantial improvements in their performance . . ." Similarly, the goal of Accenture (formerly Andersen Consulting) is to "deliver innovations that help clients across all industries quickly realize their visions."[3] These mission statements emphasize the value they place on change. Note that they're counting on their clients valuing change as well. And it's a pretty safe bet. A recent survey by the international consulting firm Bain and Company found that 79% of the more than 400 executives they surveyed responded that getting employees to accept new ways of doing business is one of their major challenges.[4]

The environment in which organizations operate is increasingly *turbulent*—changing rapidly and unpredictably with the globalization of markets and increased competition. Developments in technology contribute to the turbulence because they enable new products and new ways of delivering services. Businesses that might previously have limited their scope to a particular geographic region must expand to retain market share. For example, the New Zealand bookstore chain Whitcoull's now competes with large international bookstores such as U.S.-based Border's plus the Web-based competition such as Amazon. The changing marketplace prompted them to venture into online book sales. Customers are becoming increasingly more demanding and no longer display brand loyalty. Moreover, for government and not-for-profit organizations, taxpayers and sources of funding are increasingly demanding that organizations do more with less.

The recommended response to these pressures is to organize for continuous change—to become a flexible organization that can adapt quickly to changes in the environment. This argument for change has been repeated by popular management "gurus," such as Peter Drucker and Tom Peters, as well as scholars.[5] For example, management scholar Edward Lawler suggests that: "The level of competition today requires high levels and continuous improvement of organizational performance in four critical areas: the quality of goods and services, the cost of producing goods and services, the speed with which products and services are brought to market, [and] innovation in the development of new products and services."[6] Similar arguments have been made for public sector organizations. For example, "The kind of governments that developed during the industrial era, with their sluggish, centralized bureaucracy, their preoccupation with rules and regulations, and their hierarchical chains of command, no longer work very well . . . [they] simply do not function well in the rapidly changing, information-technology-intensive society and economy of the 1990s."[7] The imperative for flexibility amidst change is one of the primary reasons so many organizations in all sectors today are relying on temporary ("temp") workers. But what the organization gains in flexibility with hiring many temps is often counter-weighted by the costs of retraining, diminished individual loyalty, and lessened cohesion.[8]

How do people in organizations engage with the discourse of change and flexibility? What conditions are creating the "imperative" to change and to become more flexible? And how should managers communicate to foster change and flexibility?

Box 11.1 Identifying Your Beliefs About Change

Everyone has a basic set of beliefs—a lay or implicit theory—about change. The following phrases will help you identify some of yours; complete each statement with the first thought that comes to your mind. There are no right or wrong answers, but work quickly. The world is changing fast ;-) !

1. When it comes to making changes, most employees . . .
2. When it comes to making changes, most managers . . .
3. People disagree about whether people are able to change. I believe . . .
4. People resist change because . . .
5. The best way to overcome resistance to change is . . .
6. Sharing information about change before plans are fully developed . . .
7. If I implement a change and discover it is not working out as I expected, I . . .
8. When I am planning a change in my work unit (department, team, or division), I coordinate it with . . .
9. When my boss asks me to implement a change that I think has some problems, I should . . .
10. If I'm part of a group that wants to implement a change before the details have been worked out, I . . .

Look back at your answers; do you see any patterns? What are your beliefs, values, and assumptions about change? What do your answers say about how you see organizations, as well as the world more generally?

What Is Change?

A curious organizational phenomenon is that we often adopt a management trend or value without being clear just what we're embracing. This certainly happens in the case of change, although it's not *unique* to change. We're vague with many things we value, and that's not altogether unreasonable. It allows us to agree in general that something is important, while allowing quite a bit of flexibility in how it's interpreted or implemented.

The Ambiguity of Multiple Meanings

Change is a *polysemous* term—it has multiple meanings. Communication researcher Everett Rogers suggests that change is "the process by which alteration occurs in the structure and function of a social system."[9] Change has also been usefully defined as "the difference(s) between two (or more) successive conditions, states, or moments of time."[10] When we notice that the procedures of a meeting seem very different from past practices, we are thinking about change in those terms.

In addition to these technical definitions, we also use change to refer to a solution. The implication of planned change in organizations, along with related ideas such as "organizational development" and "continuous improvement," is that we can control change. Teams of consultants at large firms often have "wrap-up meetings" at the conclusion of a large project in which they discuss how they can change their practices to be more effective. For example, consultants at Accenture often use a "plus-delta" technique to identify practices that were successful or worked well (the pluses) and those they want to change in the future (the deltas—delta being the Greek symbol for change). Their actions indicate they think they can initiate control and evaluate changes.

At other times, however, people talk about change as if it were something over which we have *no* control, as if it were something that happens *to* us. For example, in discussions about the changing nature of the university system in our three countries (especially the trend toward universities becoming more market oriented), we have each been told that these changes are the "wave of the future" and that you either "ride the wave" or get swamped. Similarly, a Danish manager told Lars that, "It's like biking. You have to keep moving or you'll fall off," suggesting that organizations have no choice but to change.

As we have stressed throughout this text, most important value-based concepts that inspire us or bring us together are ambiguous. Think of how terms like "freedom" or "democracy" or "equality" function in political discourse—both to unite people under certain banners and to gloss over certain differences. Today's popular corporate and business slogans function much the same way. Who can be against "quality"? Yet we may have lots of different ideas about the specific meanings of that term as applied to work processes, products, and services. Ambiguity is a fact of language (and of life in general), although we should be aware of what's going on under broad symbolic umbrellas like change.[11]

The Dialectic of Change and Stability

One way to understand the nature of change is to consider its opposite: constancy, permanence, or stability. We can view change vs. constancy as a *dialectic* where the two ideas are in a natural and inescapable tension; the two extremes are both interdependent and negating (see chapter 6). Such a view implies that both change and constancy are somewhat desirable—but also that they *negate* each other. The more we pursue change, the less constancy we have, and vice versa. The two ideas are interdependent in that we cannot have one pole without the other, and the two concepts are complementary. For organizations, this means that stabilizing measures must follow change. For example, new ways of handling customer complaints are often detailed in procedure manuals so that they become part of the organization's standard operating procedures. Change makes sense only against the backdrop of stability. With this in mind, we can offer another definition of change, one particularly well suited to thinking about *organizational* change: change is "a succession of differences in time *within a persisting identity.*"[12]

Organizations want a measure of permanence. The very structure of an organization, for example, is built upon reliable methods of decision making and dependable sources of expertise and knowledge. This is true even if the organization is not highly bureaucratic. As sociologists Robert Nisbet and Robert G. Perrin write:

> The first major point to make about change is the sheer power of persistence, inertia, or fixity in human behavior. Despite the abundance of phrases in both popular

"So, Jim, where do you see yourself in ten minutes?"

> and learned thought attesting to the omnipresence, the constancy, the timelessness of change, all empirical evidence suggests that in the history of any specific mode of social behavior, persistence and fixity occupy a formidable place.[13]

The concepts of core values or mission statements, so popular today, attest to the not-so-often acknowledged merits of stability and permanence. But organizations want change, too—often for good reasons. As some organizations have experienced, the more they emphasize permanence and stability, the harder it is for them to depart from established practices. Tradition as a source of pride can also constrain choices. For example, IBM in the 1980s was proud of its reputation for secure employment but was forced to change with the rapidly transforming computer market—violating some of its fundamental principles while trying to reinvent itself.

On the other hand, the more an organization strives for continuous change, the more difficult it can be for members to feel a sense of stability, especially when the changes do not follow logically or organically from established missions and strategic plans. Too much change makes a period of relative stability more attractive—even though managers rarely allow themselves to admit this. For example, after a rapid succession of proposals for new programs in the Waikato Management School (where Ted teaches), many staff members called for a moratorium on new proposals. Many business organizations have learned that fundamental changes need to be followed by periods of stability where the changes are implemented and consolidated in organizational practices.

The Social-Historical Context of Change

As the timeline of major trends in chapter 3 illustrated, organizational practices and organizational wisdom have moved through a number of discernible eras. Implicit within each of the various eras are assumptions and attitudes toward organizational change. Ironically, scientific management focused on *changes* that would create efficient *routines*. That is, the emphasis was on cultivating and documenting routine ways of getting work done. Frederick Taylor's time and motion studies provided a technology for systematically documenting "inefficiencies." The idea was that once the efficient means of doing the work was documented, the work would be performed in a repetitive fashion, creating a stable routine. So, while change was an important part of scientific management, the goal was stability or routine. The value of change became more pronounced with open systems theory, which views organizations as existing in a dynamic relationship with their environment—constantly getting feedback and using it to make the necessary adaptations. This theory, however, did not imply that change *per se* is good. With its principle of *homeostasis,* (see box 2.3) open systems theory assumes that organizations strive towards stability or routine. Despite its emphasis on change, open systems theory still assumes that stability and routine are the preferred results.

Nowhere is the celebration of organizational change expressed more explicitly than in the marketing concept established in the 1950s, which urged organizations (public as well as private) to monitor their environments constantly in order to satisfy the "wants" and "needs" of consumers and other relevant publics. The marketing concept advocates a high degree of flexibility and adaptability for all departments of the organization. Only an ultra-flexible organization, according to this view, is able to respond rapidly to changing consumer demands and thus adapt efficiently to the contingencies of a turbulent environment.[14] But even organizations subscribing to the marketing concept may not be as willing to change as we should expect.[15]

The movements that began in the 1970s (organizational culture, quality circles, and Toyotism) all reflect a shift in the change-constancy dialectic toward a greater valuing of change. Quality circles, in which groups of employees met regularly to discuss job-related issues, analyze problems, and recommend improvements or solutions, preceded the emphasis on constantly looking for ways to change that would become central to the total quality management (TQM) trend in the next decade. Toyotism put an emphasis on flexible production, thus explicitly valuing the ability to change quickly based on customers' changing tastes. The organizational culture movement was not explicitly a movement toward greater valuing of change. Since it was greatly influenced by popular books that prescribed a "strong culture" for all organizations, it recommended that organizations change to create such cultures. Ultimately, strong cultures are marked by stability—established patterns of values and practices.

The 1980s and 1990s witnessed TQM, business process reengineering (BPR), and learning organizations. In these movements, the value of change is elevated far above stability and constancy. The central principle of TQM is continuous improvement. Similarly, the learning organization framework assumes that an effective organization is one that is constantly experimenting with new ways of doing things. Finally, BPR is based on the idea that all organizational processes should be studied and reengineered to achieve more efficiency. The key ingredient for success in all these movements is constant change. What remain stable, paradoxically, are structures specifically intended to facilitate change. In the early 2000s, perhaps the most popular trend is e-business. In many ways a realization of the marketing concept and a continuation of the BPR movement, e-business involves using information and communication technologies to achieve goals such as attaining efficiencies, expanding markets, or enhancing customer service. Thus, e-business also places a great deal of emphasis on change.

In our discussion of the dialectic of change-constancy, we have argued that both poles are valued. However, that doesn't mean they're *equally* valued. We have seen historical shifts toward greater emphasis of one pole or the other. Thus, while change has always been praised in modernity, we believe it is valued more today than at any other time in history. This is one of the reasons it is so important to understand change *discourse*. Embedded in our discourse are assumptions and values about what is right and what is important.

A Model of the Change-Related Communication Process

Communication and change are connected in a variety of ways. The model in box 11.2 illustrates the interrelationships between change and communication. Our model builds on previously developed models. For example, Kurt Lewin developed a simple but useful model of the change process using the metaphor of water freezing.[16] Think about snow on the ground that partially melts in the sun, then refreezes into a different texture, such as ice, and takes on other shapes as temperatures change again. Lewin suggested that change is much like this, occurring in four phases: (1) recognition of a felt need for change (unfreezing), (2) development of a change plan (vision),

(3) implementation of the new way (moving), and (4) routinization of the new way (refreezing). Lewin's phases are to some degree reflected in our model. However, we emphasize several important *communicative* features of the change process.

Box 11.2 A Model of Change-Related Communication

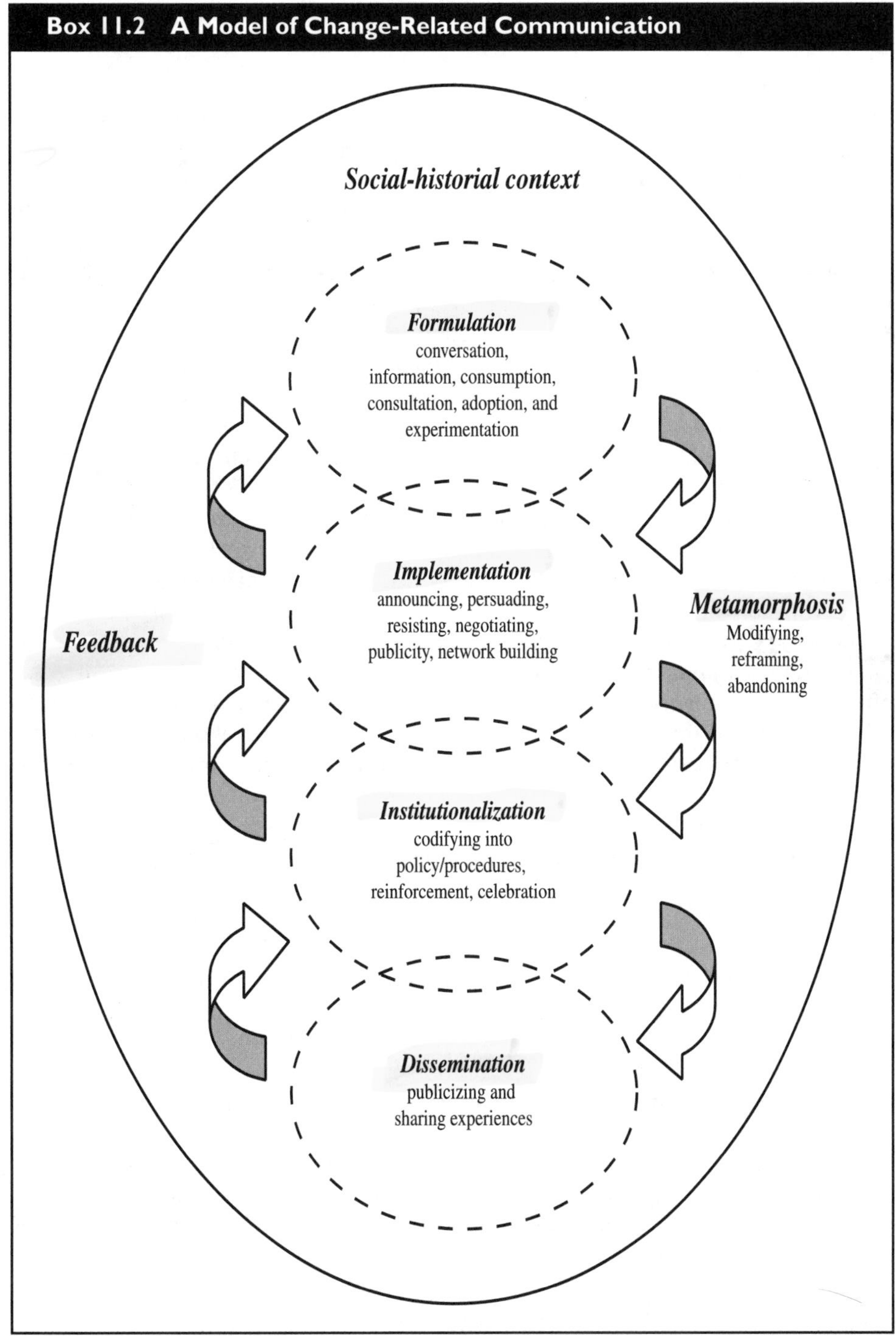

First, communication is more than a tool for change; *communication constitutes change*. We agree with management theorists Jeff and Laurie Ford.

> Change is a . . . process of social construction in which new realities are created, . . . sustained, and modified in the process of communication. Producing intentional change, then, is a matter of deliberately bringing into existence, through communication, a new reality or set of social structures.[17]

Change occurs as a result of people communicating. Because of the important role of conversation and consultation in prompting change, the 3M Company has long provided multiple meeting rooms that encourage informal interactions among employees to discuss possible innovations. Similarly, the popular practice of *benchmarking* is based on the idea that organizations can discover ways to improve by talking with members of other organizations who are known for having "best practices." Benchmarking is a process in which organizations attempt to compare their own systems or practices in a particular area to those of other organizations, thereby discovering ways to improve. For example, a department of a city government organization we studied recently engaged in benchmarking their customer service processes by making visits to several organizations to learn how those organizations earned a reputation for providing outstanding customer service.[18]

Second, organizational *change occurs within a social-historical context*. As we have emphasized throughout this book, the meanings we have for phenomena—in this case, change in general and particular kinds of changes—are influenced by the discursive context in which organizations are embedded. Box 11.3 provides insight into the role of social-historical context and discourse in organizational change.

Third, *discourses related to change are bi-directional;* they flow in and out of the organization. The top ring, *formulation*, includes communication processes such as information consumption. For example, discourse about new management ideas often prompts managers to embrace popular practices of the day, such as outsourcing, knowledge management, or e-business. Managers learn about such practices through management books and magazines, consultants, seminars, and discussions with other managers and are encouraged to initiate such changes in their organizations.[19] The bottom ring of our model, *dissemination*, points to the fact that changes initiated within organizations are communicated to external audiences. For example, major changes are mentioned in annual reports, the business press, and research publications. They are discussed by organizational members with friends and colleagues outside the organization. They may win the Malcolm Baldridge Awards in the United States or the European Quality Award in Europe, programs established to encourage the spread of ideas about improvements in organizational performance. All of these mechanisms contribute to the proliferation of discourse regarding organizational change.

Fourth, *communication is central to the implementation of planned change*. Once a change is decided upon, it must be communicated to others who are affected or who are involved in implementing it. This involves announcing the change, publicizing it, and persuading and negotiating with others to accept it. How change is communicated is often central to whether or not it is successful. We'll focus more on this set of issues later in this chapter.

An important part of implementation is the process of responding *to* changes. People affected by—and those who anticipate being affected by—changes often com-

Box 11.3 Voices from the Field

SeniorNet: An Organization Created for Change
Margaret Richardson, University of Waikato

All organizations must cope with changes. Some organizations are *created* to cope with change. Such is the case with SeniorNet, a learning co-operative for those aged 55 years and older who are interested in learning about computers and computing from their age-peers. SeniorNet was founded in the United States in the 1980s and now has chapters in many countries worldwide. SeniorNet clubs offer face-to-face, age-friendly, formal classroom training that emphasizes learning as an emotionally supportive and mentally stimulating exercise.

The growth of SeniorNet clubs in New Zealand has been phenomenal. Membership has grown from 0 to 94 clubs in 10 years, with a total current membership of more than 22,000. Despite this success, clubs have faced a number of challenges both in their day-to-day operations and in their prospects for long-term survival. Challenges over the years have included a constant battle for funds to upgrade hardware and software as technology changes and resources to meet the increasing demand for services. Resource problems include writing and revising manuals and finding enough similar-age tutors to teach the courses.

SeniorNet clubs, which were created to fill an information void for a generation that grew up without computers, now face a new challenge. Computer learning is now structured into everyday life; succeeding generations have learned computer skills in school and in the workplace. SeniorNet will need to change its focus, perhaps to an emphasis on a sense of community built around some new information and skills void.

What are the various kinds of change apparent in this case? What does this case suggest about how changes in society affect organizational and even personal change? How does SeniorNet participate in change discourse?

municate extensively with one another and with implementers. The following comment from an employee of a large company in the process of downsizing emphasizes this point: "Everyone was trying to figure [the impending layoff] out. When you went on break it was not unusual to find over 30 people in the smoking area talking and talking about it. We wasted more than 140 years of salary in all the time that was spent talking and arguing about what was going to happen. No one could do any work."[20] We'll return to how employees respond to change later in this chapter. Box 11.4 describes an interesting study of change in which we see the importance of communication in change implementation.

A fifth important feature of our model is *metamorphosis*, which highlights the fact that many planned changes don't end as they were originally planned. Changes that are introduced are often reinterpreted, reframed, or even abandoned; the initial proposal often goes through substantial metamorphosis. Communication scholars James Taylor and Elizabeth Van Every, for example, discovered that a major new computer system adopted by the New Zealand Police Force seemed to have been abandoned according to press reports. On closer inspection, however, parts of the system remained—although not always used in the ways that the original implementers intended.[21]

Finally, the ***feedback*** component of the model is intended to suggest that change isn't a simple, linear process. While there is a certain logic as we move from the top to the bottom ring, the overlapping rings and the bi-directional feedback arrows suggest that this process is by no means a neat, step-by-step sequence. Rather, communication during any phase can lead us to reconsider our interpretation of earlier phases. For example, discussions during implementation can raise concerns that force a reconsideration of the original formulation of the problem or idea. The reformulation of an earlier stage in turn affects the movement toward later stages.

Emphasizing the importance of communication to the change process does not dismiss the role that other phenomena play. Certainly equipment, funding, and other material resources matter. However, our understanding of change is constituted in communication, and communication is the central means by which changes occur.

Box 11.4 Voices from the Field

Knowledge and Organizational Change
Timothy Kuhn, University of Colorado at Boulder

Knowledge is important in enabling organizational change to occur, but (as suggested in box 3.5) the "location" of organizational knowledge is not always clear. We usually see it as existing inside the heads of individuals, but it is also possible to see knowledge as a characteristic of a collective.[22] *Collective knowledge* is a characteristic of groups and organizations that affects how individuals think, behave, and evaluate the actions of others. According to structuration theory (see description in chapter 3) there's a dynamic relationship between individual and collective knowledge in organizations; each reflects and influences the other.

In studying planned change in an organization called DPC, my colleagues and I interviewed each employee to assess his or her knowledge about the change. Using the most important concepts from all the employees' combined knowledge, we were able to say what DPC (as a whole) "knew" about the planned change, as well as to describe the similarity between each employee's knowledge and the collective knowledge. We found that when the planned change first got underway, the individual knowledge of employees who were most central in the communication network (e.g., managers) most closely matched the collective knowledge. These employees didn't necessarily have *more* knowledge about the change, but what they knew was very closely aligned with the organization as a whole. But after some important unplanned events—including a major conflict between workgroups, an increase in one workgroup's power, and a sense that the plan was failing to deliver the changes management had promised—the collective knowledge shifted. Topics related to these unplanned events suddenly became more prominent in DPC's collective knowledge, while employees in central network positions no longer found themselves closely aligned with the collective knowledge.

In addition to this finding, we noticed an interesting pattern among the change-related knowledge in individuals. Many practitioners assume that the knowledge of members becomes more similar over time (as seen in phrases like "we need everyone's buy-in"). However, our results showed that while the knowledge of some employees grew more similar, there was simultaneously a divergence compared to other members over time. "Clusters" of people (based on similarities in knowledge about the change) emerged, but these became more distant from one another as DPC's planned change ran into unplanned events.

Why does the knowledge of some people become less (or more) similar to the collective? How does the communication of workgroups affected by conflict change collective knowledge? Does communication about unplanned changes create more or less divergence in collective knowledge?

Dimensions of Change

When we say that change is constituted in communication, we are implying that our *understanding* of what change means is critically important. Think about examples of change in organizations that you have experienced; you can probably list some radically different kinds of changes. Using the university as an example, there can be changes in staffing (a new teacher or secretary is hired), new procedures (a new Web-based enrollment option), and new structures (two departments merging, or a department being eliminated), as well as many others. To be effective in managing and coping with change, we need to understand what differentiates these kinds of changes. Our goal for this section is to explore some of the underlying dimensions of change—what makes one kind change similar to and different from another. We can identify at least six dimensions of change: degree, type (or substance), intentionality, timing, impetus, and control.

Degree

A good starting point for considering dimensions of change is to look at different *degrees* of change. Change can be major or minor—from restructuring an entire company to a change in a customer feedback form. Change can also be abrupt or gradual—from announcing a massive layoff to accumulating the results from a 12-month benchmarking program. For analytical and practical purposes, it is useful to distinguish between what philosopher Gregory Bateson called *first-* and *second-order changes*. You can think of these as the extremes. First-order changes—sometimes referred to as "changes in order not to change"[23]—are minor, incremental changes that any living system has to practice in order to avoid the more fundamental second-order changes (see page 28). Consider, for example, driving a car on a winding country road. In order to avoid ending up in the ditch, destroying the car, and possibly being injured (second order changes), the driver has to make continuous adjustments with the wheel. Such adjustments are first-order changes. Another example is the skin of a chameleon, which changes in color to adapt to its surroundings. These changes are necessary for the chameleon to avoid a second-order change—such as being eaten by a predator. As you can see in these examples, first-order changes are *adjustments* that involve only certain parts of the system; these parts are "loosely coupled" (loosely linked) with the rest of the system. Had they been tightly coupled, the rest of the car would have to bend as much as the wheels, and the chameleon would have to change as radically internally as the changes in its skin color suggest.

Second-order change is rarer and more difficult to monitor by the system itself. A second-order change occurs when the entity becomes something fundamentally different from what it was. Although second-order change is contingent upon events and crises outside the system in question, it is not directly deducible from such external forces. Second-order change, then, is neither necessary in the sense of being inevitable nor continuous in the sense of an ordered series of small steps. Sometimes, second-order changes cannot be anticipated at all.

In work organizations first-order changes happen daily. Someone is hired, fired, or promoted. Forms or work processes are tweaked. A policy is revised. Second-order changes—at least in the extreme—happen less often. A government agency is eliminated. Or, a company files for bankruptcy and goes out of business. Or, a new company or type of organization is formed on the ashes of an old one. In second-order change, different parts of the system—in contrast to the chameleon example—are *tightly* coupled to each other and thus forced to change in concert.

First- and second- order changes can be considered the opposite poles of a continuum. Thus, there are many gradations of change in between, and those seem to be the ones of most interest to managers, at least when they talk about *managing* organization-wide change. The in-betweens could include reengineering organizational operations, developing new products and services, or devising a campaign to change a corporate identity.

Type (or Substance)

Organizational theorist Richard Daft suggested there are primarily four categories of organizational change: (1) *technology*, or the use of new equipment or information processing software to accomplish work (2) *administration*, including organizational structure, policies, work processes, and control systems (3) *products and services*, or the development and modification of those things the organization offers to its clients, customers, or constituents and (4) *human resources*, or the members of the organization and how they're organized.[24] To Daft's categories, we could add *image*. Managers sometimes attempt to shape or change the organization's image. Sometimes this is rather direct, such as by creating new logos or advertisements to convey a desired image of the organization. At other times the attempt is more indirect. For example, an organization might attempt any of Daft's four categories, not primarily because of the desire for their functional benefits, but because of the desire to enhance the organization's or the change agent's image.

We can distinguish what we might call *discursive* change from *substantive* (or material) change. For example, one organization that we're familiar with designed and implemented a new training program on gender relations, with the expressed intent of changing the culture of the organization to make it a more "woman friendly" place to work. However, many of the employees believed that managers had little desire to make substantive changes; rather, they wanted to convey the *impression* that they were becoming a woman-friendly organization, without making the changes most frequently identified as needed to make this happen. To use a contemporary phrase, they wanted to "talk the talk, but not walk the talk."

The substance of the change may also be described in terms of a particular theory, framework, or philosophy guiding the change. For example, adopting new management trends—some of which may be described as management "fashions"—is a prominent way organizations attempt large-scale change today.[25] Thus, some organizations change to be consistent with the principles of total quality management, knowledge management, business process reengineering (BPR), or self-directed work teams. In box 11.5, management scholar Brad Jackson analyzes management fashions and the "gurus" who promote them.

Management fashions often fit Daft's categories of administrative and human resource types of changes; in some cases, these trends could be characterized as technological change. For example, BPR efforts typically change administrative practices by reorganizing the procedures organizations use to accomplish their goals; they often rely on developments in technology to enable these new ways of doing work. Since BPR often involves downsizing or restructuring so that some jobs are eliminated and others are created, there are often human resource changes.

Box 11.5 Voices from the Field

What Role Do Management Gurus Play in Promoting Organizational Change?

Brad Jackson, Victoria University of Wellington

In a recent book and a series of articles, Brad Jackson examined the rise of popular "management gurus" and their role in creating and promoting the performance improvement programs or "management fashions" that have greatly influenced the conduct of organizational life throughout the world. "My experience in management and executive development in North America made me very curious about the formidable power and influence that management gurus exerted on the conduct and practice of management both there and around the world." Following some other recent management scholars, Jackson viewed the gurus as part of a whole management fashion industry, which included other "fashion setters" such as business schools, consulting firms, and the business press.[26]

Jackson used fantasy theme analysis, a dramatistic method of rhetorical criticism, to analyze three management fashions that surfaced during the 1990s: *business process re-engineering* (BPR) promoted by Michael Hammer and James Champy,[27] *effectiveness*, led by Stephen Covey,[28] and the *learning organization*, spearheaded by Peter Senge.[29] While the objectives and content of each of each of the gurus' rhetorical visions was different, they each possessed strong dramatic qualities. A major reason why managers and other followers found these visions compelling was because they could readily relate to the gurus' organizational *dramas*, or the stories they tell. The dramas all contained a familiar cast of characters, a clear and well-developed plot, and a meaningful setting.

For example, Covey's theme makes rich use of the idealized U.S. agrarian past to encourage identification with his vision of effectiveness. Hammer and Champy cast a recalcitrant middle manager at the center of their BPR drama. Action themes tend to take the form of a step-by-step process for achieving managerial and organizational success; Covey's "seven habits"—that is, his principles of developing personal effectiveness—are good examples.

Fantasy theme analyses revealed three fundamentally powerful reasons (or "master analogues") at the heart of every guru's rhetorical vision: *pragmatic, righteous,* and *social.* Each of the management fashions illustrates one of these master analogues. Hammer and Champy's BPR movement, thus, is built on an essentially pragmatic analogue: "You have to do this because it is your *only* choice." To ignore it would mean certain extinction. Covey's vision of effectiveness, by contrast, is rooted in a righteous master analogue that stresses followers should pursue the vision because "it is the *right* thing to do." The vision is founded on principles that are universal and indisputable. Peter Senge's vision of the learning organization is rooted in a social master analogue that urges followers to pursue the vision collectively because "it is a *good* thing to do." In working together to create the common goal of a learning organization, individuals can transcend their differences and find inner peace.

What are the sources of our fascination with gurus both in management and in other fields of endeavor? On balance, do you think gurus have a positive or a negative influence on management thinking and practice? Why are "dramatic" forms of communication so compelling? What are the limitations of this form of communication in managing organizational change?

Intentionality

Some changes, like a change in corporate strategy, are conscious, deliberate, and planned. An example of this would be Xerox's decision in the 1980s to reposition itself from a maker of photocopy equipment to "The Document Company"—an attempt to broaden the scope of the business and to enter new markets. In other cases, to loosely paraphrase a popular expression, "change happens." That is, changes occur all the time in organizations that are not the result of a conscious decision, much less a carefully considered management strategy. The death of a key member of an organization and that person's subsequent replacement is one example. Other examples of unplanned changes are accidents, changes in the workforce because of demographic shifts, and changes in company finances as a result of the rise and fall of the economy.

Timing

Changes may vary from short-term, sudden, abrupt, or immediate to gradual, ongoing, or evolutionary change. An example of the former is what happened when the Hamilton, New Zealand, city management gathered all employees in an auditorium in 1996 to inform them of a major restructuring and downsizing to begin immediately.[30] An example of the latter is Weaver Street Market's decision to implement TQM (see box 11.6), which involved a lengthy process of consultation, followed by pilot testing and gradual change from one system of management to another.

Impetus

The impetus for change may come from a variety of sources. Change can be initiated *externally*; an example would be a regulatory change by the government to which the organization must respond. Or, it may be initiated *internally*, such as when strategists make a decision for a company to enter a new geographical market. Similarly, change can be initiated *centrally* by the strategic planning of a top management team or *non-centrally* from the successful experiments and innovations in the "grassroots" of the organization.

Control

Approaches to implementation of changes vary. The implementation can be controlled (or designed to be controlled) by top management, or it can be evolutionary—allowed to emerge and adapt. That is, implementation may vary from *programmed* to *adaptive*.[31] Programmed implementation involves top management developing a plan for implementation and marshalling the plan throughout its many phases. This is sometimes called a "rule-bound" approach, since the change effort is tightly controlled by rules set by the change agents.[32] Adaptive change implementation involves changes that may be initiated at varying levels of the organization and that are monitored and modified throughout the implementation process as new information about the implementation emerges. With adaptive approaches, organizational members in non-management positions exert influence over the change process by providing feedback on how the changes and implementation of them are perceived.

While these dimensions of change are helpful, we should be careful not to oversimplify. Sometimes a change may appear easy to categorize, but a closer look reveals submerged difficulties. For example, changes that seem at first glance to be abrupt ("We must have a product in that market by next quarter!") turn out to be quite long-term in implementation. Similarly, sometimes people in organizations may try to *frame* changes as being of a particular type for the purpose of creating a positive impression. For example, Southwest Airlines has a slogan of providing "positively outrageous service." A department manager for a city government liked this slogan so much he had it imprinted on employees' name badges, and he often talked of making "positively outrageous"—i.e., radical—changes. However, the researcher who studied the organization saw little evidence of anything she considered outrageous. In one instance, the manager even described a rearrangement of the office furniture as an example of "positively outrageous" changes![33] A recent study showed that managers often tout their efforts to implement TQM (and, we'd suggest, other kinds of changes as well), even when actual change is quite limited.[34] There is, in other words, symbolic value in claiming to use practices that are socially esteemed. Since change is often valued for itself, a manager can present herself as competent or "cutting edge" by claiming to be making radical changes.

Another disclaimer is in order. While we'd often like to know what the change is *really* about, there may not be a conclusive answer. People often develop quite different perspectives on the same change. Sometimes even the same person may see the change differently at different times. In a recent study, George, Ted, and their co-researcher each saw an organization implementing changes focused on teamwork and customer service in radically different ways, depending on what issues and features were prominent at a given time.[35] Sometimes we see the changes as functional and efficient, neces-

Box 11.6 A Brief Case Study

At Weaver Street Market in Carrboro, North Carolina, the Board of Directors created a subcommittee, called the Organization Development Committee (ODC) with the intent of attempting "to improve teamwork, morale, and communication" in the small (55 employees) cooperatively-owned, natural foods grocery store. This initiative was in response to several sources of evidence that suggested employees were generally disgruntled about the quality of work life in the organization.

After surveying employees and other stakeholders, the ODC considered several alternatives, including re-organizing into self-managed teams. Finally, they recommended that the organization adopt total quality management (TQM) as an organizing framework for attaining its goals. Before TQM was officially adopted by the Board, the ODC brought in a business professor to teach them about TQM, invited employees to meetings to learn more about TQM, and finally scheduled an all-day retreat for the managers, with the intention of teaching them TQM management techniques and getting their support. After obtaining the management group's and Board's approval, the implementation process continued.

Among other actions, a consultant was hired to teach group facilitation skills to TQM team leaders, the name of the employee newsletter was changed to reflect the quality theme, and several pilot projects were initiated to test TQM ideas. One of the pilot projects was a project that was already underway; in that case, TQM methods were (to some degree) applied to an existing problem-solving process.

TQM experts have argued that changing to TQM is a five-year process, which requires sustained focus and support. However, after more than a year of TQM with few clear benefits and many other changes taking center stage (such as a major expansion and multiple changes to key personnel), support for TQM within Weaver Street Market waned. After several years, the term TQM was not used any more.[36]

sary to accomplish legitimate organizational goals. At other times we view the changes critically, skeptical about the value of the change and the ethics of the change process. That shift in perspective is a frequent experience. People in organizations are often ambiguous regarding how they see organizational changes, sometimes finding them exciting and energizing, and sometimes viewing them cynically or skeptically.

What Makes Organizational Change Efforts Successful?

There is much practical advice about successful organizational change, as well as extensive research on the subject. However, the answer to the question of what makes change successful isn't at all clear. There are several reasonable criteria one could use in analyzing the results of change. First, we could decide that for a change to be considered successful, it is *accepted* by key stakeholders rather than rejected. However, accept-reject is often too simple a criterion to be useful, as organizational communication scholars Laurie Lewis and David Seibold argue.[37] We can further differentiate acceptance of changes in terms of the *fidelity* and *uniformity* of adoption. Fidelity, here, means there is a match between the intended use of the designer and the actual use of the user. Uniformity means change is accepted similarly across all users. Common sense might suggest that a successful change is one that has high fidelity and uniformity. However, if change agents accept the notion of *adaptive* changes, as discussed above, they would likely consider change efforts successful with low fidelity, but high uniformity.[38]

To judge the success of the change effort, we also would have to consider the initially expressed *goals* of the change agents. For example, many changes are "sold" to stakeholders on the promise of greater profits, greater efficiencies (and thus, savings in time and costs), or higher morale. In box 11.6, a committee promoted TQM as an answer to the organization's yearning for better internal communication and morale. The goals of the change effort later became a point of contention as managers and staff learned more about TQM and became divided on whether the primary goal was to improve customer service (which is more typically a goal of TQM programs) or to improve the quality of work life for staff (which was what prompted the initial change effort). In the end, TQM fulfilled neither set of goals, and the program gradually faded away.

Finally, to judge the success of change efforts, we should also consider the *unintended consequences* of the changes. A systems view of organizations suggests that a change in one part of the system will prompt changes in other parts. Some of these will be anticipated, and some will not be. For example, e-mail technologies were implemented in many organizations with the intended consequence of promoting faster, easier communication among staff and between staff and other key stakeholders (such as customers and suppliers). However, there have typically been unintended consequences of e-mail implementation, such as staff members socializing with friends and family throughout the world and the organization being "spammed" or sent mass e-mailings. While these examples might be considered primarily negative from management's point of view, changes can have positive unintended consequences as well. Thus, determining whether a change is successful is not as simple as it might first appear. It is valuable to spend some time up front assessing the intended goals of the change effort and the potential unintended consequences of the change.

Communicating and Managing Change Effectively

In part because of the complexity of determining when change is successful or effective and in part because of the variability of change, it is difficult to identify a single set of principles for change management. Perhaps the best strategy for developing your skill in managing and communicating change is to become familiar with a variety of strategies that have been successful and to understand which strategy would be most effective in a particular situation.

Our goal in this section is to introduce you to three very different approaches for managing and communicating large-scale organizational change. The first, developed by management scholar Michael Beer and his colleagues, provides a broad strategy for managing innovations and other changes and relies primarily on an *adaptive* approach. The second, developed by communication consultants T. J. and Sandar Larkin, is a set of principles for communicating relatively abrupt changes to staff through a largely *programmed* approach. The third is a set of options for communicating changes to stakeholders (including, but not limited to, staff) developed by communication scholar Laurie Lewis and her colleagues.

Managing Change: An Adaptive Approach

Beer and his colleagues studied large-scale change efforts at six U.S. companies. They found that *programmed* change was the norm but argued that it was often unsuccessful. More successful was what they called a "task alignment" approach (similar to what we referred to above as an *adaptive* approach), which typically was initiated in the grassroots of the organization and led by the general managers of those parts rather than by the CEO. Other research has generally supported this claim.[39] Based on their findings, they recommended five steps to effective change management.

Mobilize commitment to change through joint diagnosis of organizational problems. People in the organization develop a shared diagnosis of the problems that need to be addressed, building their willingness and commitment plus a deep understanding of the roots of the problems faced by the organization.

Develop a shared vision of how to organize and manage for success. The general manager may facilitate but development of the vision or plan should be broadly inclusive and should produce agreement about new roles, responsibilities, and processes that are clearly aligned to the task or solution. Some people will not have participated in the creation of the vision; some will be less enthusiastic and less capable of performing new roles. Change agents therefore must provide the needed support, training, and coaching to address these issues. They must foster consensus for the new vision, competence to enact it, and cohesion to move it along.

Spread revitalization to all departments without pushing it from the top. Executives may be tempted to impose the insights developed in one unit on all other parts of the organization. However, people will be less committed, and the result will not be adapted to the specific situations each work unit faces. Changes should be encouraged in units with which the initiating unit primarily interacts. Those units should be allowed to go through the same process of joint diagnosis and visioning.

Institutionalize revitalization through formal policies, systems, and structures. This is recommended after the new approach is firmly in place rather than at the beginning.

Emphasis is placed on negotiating shared understandings of preferred and workable practices, *then* formalizing them.

Monitor and adjust strategies in response to problems in the revitalization process. The idea is for the team or organization to continually learn and adapt. Like diagnosis and visioning, this should be a shared responsibility, not something for the manager alone. It involves feedback and discussion of those enacting the changes.

Notice the emphasis on communication throughout the steps advocated by Beer and his colleagues. Change was effectively instituted in the organizations studied through constant participation, collaboration, and negotiation. While this research found that change initiated and led from the grassroots is most likely to be successful, the researchers did identify important roles for top management to play. First, top management should create the climate for change by setting high, but reasonable standards and insist on innovative ways to meet them. Second, they should hold up successful units as models to be emulated and provide resources to the successful units. Finally, they should develop career paths that encourage leadership development.

These recommendations are helpful and provocative, but we should ask some questions about them. First, the model assumes that getting consensus on the problem diagnosis and the vision is possible. But is it *always*? In a related way, consensus can often take a great deal of time and energy. These researchers consider that expenditure of time and energy worthwhile, even necessary. But are there times when less democratic processes might be appropriate? And, remember what we discussed in the participation chapter: participative strategies are sometimes used primarily to placate or manipulate. How do organizational members detect insincere attempts to achieve consensus? Finally, could a charismatic CEO be effective and successful in a more top-down process than these authors recommend?

Communicating Changes to Employees

The research by Beer and his colleagues found what other research has supported: that bottom-up or adaptive change implementation is generally more effective than top-down or programmed implementation. Still, while we are tempted to argue for ethical and even practical reasons that changes should rarely be purely top-down, there is little doubt that many change initiatives are mostly just that. Furthermore, many well-known CEOs, such as General Electric's former head Jack Welch, have made their companies quite profitable using top-down approaches. Executives and managers may identify changes to implement, such as downsizing or outsourcing, which are unlikely to be popular or win support. In such changes, bottom-up participation is unlikely to be appropriate. Once a change is decided upon, how should it be communicated so that it gets the results—such as acceptance, commitment, and productivity—that the planners desire?

Larkin and Larkin caused quite a stir when they proclaimed in a *Harvard Business Review* article that most advice about communicating change is wrong.[40] They then provided an alternative recipe for success that many communication professionals since have embraced. Their advice focuses on large-scale, relatively abrupt changes, such as downsizing or a major shift in organizational strategy. The approach, they claim, is also appropriate when the goal is to reach frontline employees, as opposed to middle management. There are three major components to their strategy: "Communicate only facts; stop communicating values. Communicate face-to-face; do not rely on videos, publications, or large-scale meetings. And target frontline supervisors; do not let executives introduce the change to frontline employees."[41]

Just the facts. Larkin and Larkin argue that there is a problem with the contemporary management trend to create vision, mission, and values statements. They argue that employees are often cynical about these concepts—and about management's credibility more generally. Consequently, they suggest management should communicate only the facts during a major change, not try to dress the change up in lofty sounding values, pithy slogans, or vision statements. For example, if the change is downsizing, the critical numbers should be communicated: how many employees will be laid off, how they will be selected, and when the layoffs will occur.

Communicate face-to-face. Larkin and Larkin's second principle is that communication about major changes should happen face-to-face. They cite research and multiple reasons why communication efforts relying on videos and newsletters for such purposes are flawed and suggest that employees prefer face-to-face. In a study of downsizing in an electronics firm, most examples of communication during downsizing took place in one-on-one or small group meetings, and a much higher percentage of the examples that employees considered effective took place in such contexts compared with those they considered ineffective.[42]

Target frontline supervisors. "[T]he first words frontline employees hear about a change should come from the person to whom they are the closest: their supervisor."[43] According to Larkin and Larkin, employees don't usually trust senior managers as much as they do their immediate supervisors. Their finding is consistent with Helena Economo and Ted Zorn's research, which found that 85% of effective examples of downsizing communication involved participants' immediate managers, whereas only 26% of the ineffective examples did.[44]

While we agree that Larkin and Larkin's advice is appropriate in many cases, we doubt whether it is universally appropriate. The advice to avoid communicating values is especially interesting—and perhaps the most controversial of their principles. On the one hand, communicating the values underlying a decision to change should provide employees with useful information: a rationale for the change, a set of reasons for management's decisions. If a parent had decided to move to another city, her children would most certainly want more information than simply when the move will occur and what they are allowed to bring—the equivalent of Larkin and Larkin's "just the facts" advice. Wouldn't most adults be even *more* likely to expect such a rationale? We think so.

However, Larkin and Larkin's advice is useful and sensible up to a point. First, they're emphasizing that employees hearing about a substantial change will be *most* concerned about how they will be affected. Thus, getting to the facts rather immediately—as opposed to presenting a long-winded narrative on the vision and values—seems like good advice. Second, their advice is more understandable when you consider the social-historical context. The idea of communicating vision and values became fashionable in the 1980s based on a sensible idea: groups and organizations would be more effective if they agreed on and were guided by a clear vision and a set of core values. Organizations proudly began to display their vision, mission, and values on plaques at the company reception area, on company letterhead, and on their Web sites. The problem is, many employees see little connection between the values espoused and what actually occurs in the organization, creating cynicism in many cases.

As we see it, there is nothing inherently wrong with explaining changes in terms of vision and values. The problem is doing so when the vision and values (or management themselves) have little credibility—when management has a history of acting inconsistently with values. Another way of saying this is that the problem isn't that managers put too much emphasis on vision and values; the problem is that they don't take them seriously enough. Communicating the vision and values that are the rationale for change makes good sense *when* management has a history of acting consistently with espoused values, or "walking the talk."

Larkin and Larkin's other two principles also have merit, but we need to analyze each situation to determine whether they're appropriate under specific circumstances. For example, what if there's no time for briefing frontline supervisors and then having them meet face-to-face with employees? And what if in-house studies show employees strongly identify with a charismatic CEO?

Communicating Change to Stakeholders

Larkin and Larkin's model focuses on communicating change to employees. However, managers also need to consider communicating to other stakeholders. Communication scholars Laurie Lewis, Stephanie Hamel, and Brian Richardson studied the change communication strategies of nonprofit organizations to identify the variety of strategies used, as well as their advantages and disadvantages.[45] They identified six separate approaches.

Equal dissemination involves disseminating information early and often and equally to various stakeholders, using a variety of media, such as meetings, newsletters, individual phone calls, and listserv postings. This strategy has the advantage of giving everyone fair notice of the change and not catching anyone by surprise, precluding complaints by stakeholders that they were not informed early enough. Disadvantages are that it can be quite costly and time-consuming, plus it may generate unwanted advice or criticism.

Equal participation differs from the equal dissemination strategy in that it involves two-way communication: informing stakeholders and soliciting input from them. This strategy has the advantage of building consensus for the change, but similar disadvantages to the equal-dissemination strategy. Those who reported using this strategy often explained that, while their goal was equal participation, they often gave special attention to some stakeholders.

In the *quid-pro-quo* strategy, implementers communicate primarily with strategic stakeholders who have resources they need or desire, such as money, expertise, or approval power. One executive who used this strategy said, "There's a pecking order with our communication. Whoever pays the most dues, gets listened to the most."[46] This strategy's advantage is efficiency, in that less time is required and fewer points of view need to be accommodated. Of course, the strategy risks alienating those left out of the process.

The *need-to-know* strategy is also selective. Implementers communicate only with those who absolutely have to know or who explicitly express a desire for the information. The advantages and disadvantages are the same as with the quid-pro-quo strategy, plus it avoids overburdening stakeholders with large amounts of information for which they have little use. The key to its success is correctly identifying who needs and wants to know about the change.

Like the previous two strategies, the *marketing* strategy is selective in targeting audiences. However, the key feature of the marketing strategy is designing change communication adapted to each audience. Like a good public speaker, implementers analyze their audiences and design presentations to provide the sort of information and the sort of persuasion most likely to be successful with each audience. The key to success is knowing or identifying what each audience values. This approach is most likely used with substantial or controversial changes. Its advantage is being prepared to deal with the objections each audience raises. The disadvantage is that it may be the most time-consuming of them all. This strategy also does not lend itself well to mass media; it typically requires more targeted communication means, such as meetings. Organizations that primarily rely on media such as newsletters sent to all stakeholders would find this strategy ineffective.

The least planned of all approaches is the *reactionary* approach. In fact, we are reluctant to call this a "strategy," since it involves the implementers responding to concerns as they arise rather than proactively targeting and communicating with various stakeholders. While few respondents in the study by Lewis and her colleagues reported using this approach, the researchers speculated that it might be widely used but that managers are reluctant to admit it. The reactionary approach is most likely to be used when the change is in response to unexpected events, such as funding cuts.

In a similar vein, Lewis, Hamel, and Richardson suggested that many factors might explain the choice of change communication strategies. For example, the scope, novelty, and complexity of the planned change, as well as the nature of the organizational culture and the management style of the implementers, are all likely to be influential. However, many of these influences are indirect. The two factors they claim are most directly predictive of the strategy chosen are the *perceived need for efficiency in communication*[47] and the *perceived need for consensus building*. Implementers are more likely to see a need for communicative efficiency when the organization has limited channels for communicating, there is perceived to be little time for interaction about the change, and when resources are scarce. Implementers are more likely to perceive a high need for consensus building when they perceive changes to be highly controversial or novel and when there is a history of resistance to similar changes. They are also likely to perceive consensus building is needed when stakeholders control critical resources and when stakeholders' on-going cooperation is needed for implementation. Box 11.7 shows the two influential factors and matches them with the five change communication strategies. Since the reactionary approach isn't really a strategy, it is not included. The model in box 11.7 is not intended to be prescriptive. The researchers used the model to describe the choices change implementers *typically* make rather than what they *should* do. However, since it reflects the common sense approaches of a variety of managers, it may be helpful for choosing an appropriate strategy.

Box 11.7 Factors Affecting the Choice of Communication Change Strategies

High Need for Communication Efficiency	need to know	quid pro quo and marketing
Low Need for Communication Efficiency	equal dissemination	equal participation and marketing
	Low Need for Consensus Building	***High Need for Consensus Building***

There are substantial differences in the three approaches reviewed. Some differences appear to be in direct contradiction to each other. For example, Larkin and Larkin's approach dismisses the value of participation and consensus building, whereas Beer's approach considers these processes essential. However, we think all three approaches are valuable, depending on the circumstances of the changes being considered. The approach of Lewis and her colleagues is the most comprehensive, since it encourages an analysis of key situational factors before deciding on a specific strategy. In fact, it is possible to place the other two strategies within Lewis's framework. Larkin and Larkin's approach is very much like the need-to-know strategy, which assumes low need for consensus building and a high need for communication efficiency. Beer's approach, on the other hand, assumes a high need for consensus building and a low need for communication efficiency.

Strategies for Encouraging Innovation

If we accept Beer's findings that the most successful changes are those initiated in the organization's grassroots and that top management's primary role is to create the climate for change, we might ask what can be done to encourage innovation in organizations. While we cannot summarize all of the research here, we will provide some key suggestions that have emerged. In particular, we will focus on three main ideas: (1) networking and the notion of "weak ties"; (2) group process procedures that aid creativity; and (3) organizational culture characteristics that encourage innovation.

Networking and "Weak Ties"

A concept that is quite helpful in encouraging innovation is called the strength of weak ties. This concept refers to the openness of a system or a group to new information from the outside that may well come through relatively weak or undeveloped relationships, as opposed to strong or intimate ones.[48] Think back to our discussion of organizational network density in chapter 6. There we discussed the advantages and disadvantages of being a member of a very dense network in which all the other members are closely tied to one another. Dense networks afford the individual a great deal of support, a sense of a shared past and future, and mutual knowledge.

However, the same system can be closed to the kinds of new information that would come into the system from relatively weak ties or connections with other persons. For example, if you find yourself searching for a job, are you going to gain the most information about possible new job prospects from the people that you talk to every day and with whom you share the same information already? Although they might offer you a lot of emotional support and some concrete assistance, you probably will not gain as much new information from them as you would from say, your next door neighbor's best friend's colleague. That's one example of the strength of weak ties. Within the context of organizational innovation, weak ties become very important because they act as bridges for the flow of new information from other units of the organization or even from other organizations in the environment.

Group Process Procedures that Promote Creativity

Organizations spend a great deal of time and money trying to train staff to interact more effectively in groups. Sunwolf and David Seibold suggest that the training is intended to improve one of four basic group process functions: (1) structuring discussion, (2) analyzing alternatives, (3) encouraging creativity, and (4) managing conflict and agreement.[49] Our primary concern here is with procedures that encourage creativity and innovation.

Procedures such as brainstorming[50] are generally familiar to most people. Students of communication are also likely to be familiar with related procedures such as brainwriting[51] (conducted largely in written rather than oral mode) and nominal group technique (NGT)[52] (silent idea generation rather than oral interaction in the initial stage). These are only a few of many techniques proposed to aid creativity in groups. While the research is not conclusive, it generally shows that techniques incorporating some individual work (such as brainwriting and NGT) produce more ideas and more original ideas than pure brainstorming. However, studies suggest that brainstorming can be more effective when a facilitator leads the group.[53] Based on this research and our experience in facilitating groups, we offer some practical suggestions for creative idea generation in box 11.8.

Box 11.8 Keys to Creative Idea Generation

Getting a group to generate creative, innovative ideas requires that: members feel relaxed and comfortable—unconcerned about their ideas being negatively evaluated; members understand and accept the purpose of generating ideas; there is an atmosphere of energy, comfort, and even humor in the meeting; and the process of idea generation and recording is efficient and energetic.

The following suggestions are roughly in order of importance:

- Review the four rules of brainstorming *prior to* idea generation and enforce them during brainstorming: (1) strive for quantity not quality; (2) freewheel, (say whatever comes to mind); (3) combine and improve ideas; (4) ***no*** evaluation.
- Allow silent idea generation—i.e., preparation or quiet time prior to idea sharing
- Structure the process for efficient, fast-paced, energetic idea generation and recording (for example, use multiple recorders to keep the pace moving; have small groups record their ideas on flip charts to keep everyone in a large group involved)
- Model and communicate high energy and a positive, "can-do" attitude (for example, smile, project your voice, and express your enthusiasm verbally and nonverbally)
- Communicate high expectations (for example, suggest a challenging minimum number of ideas—***do not*** suggest an upper limit; ***assume*** there are more ideas to come—"Let's try to come up with 10 more;" ***not*** "Are there any more?")
- Model and encourage humor and a sense of fun (for example, conduct a frivolous, energizing activity immediately prior to idea generation)

Organizational Culture Characteristics that Encourage Innovation

While there is much that individuals and groups can do to innovate, certainly the context in which they are enmeshed is an important influence on their creativity. Susan Jarboe summarized research on organizational characteristics that encourage innovation. Her conclusions mirror the rules and suggestions concerning idea generation presented above.[54]

- *Absence of fear:* people feel free to express alternative views and, in general, safe to participate in trying out new ideas; there is an absence of surveillance
- *Training for innovation:* people receive training on creativity and innovation skills
- *Rewards and other structures that encourage innovation:* individuals or groups are rewarded through bonuses or other incentives for innovations and work structures that allow alternative paths to achieving goals
- *Support for innovation:* people have the time and resources needed to try out innovative ideas
- *Vision or objectives that highlight innovation:* people perceive that innovation is important in achieving organizational goals
- *Task orientation:* people understand that working hard and focusing on organizational objectives is valued
- *Creative leadership:* leaders encourage and support creativity and avoid behaviors that block or discourage people from innovating

An organizational culture that exhibits these features is likely to encourage the creativity-enhancing procedures and to capitalize on "weak ties" networking practices described above. The combination of individuals networking to bring a steady flow of new ideas into the organization, groups that practice creativity-enhancing techniques, and a supportive organizational culture is likely to enhance innovation.

Responding to Change (or the Politics of Change)

How do employees and other stakeholders react when organizations implement major changes? Sometimes they're energized and excited by the prospects of new, innovative ways of doing things. At other times they're skeptical or cynical; they may be stressed at the prospect of still more change. It's often said that it's human nature to resist change. But in fact, it's human nature to embrace change, too. Positive human aspirations such as learning, growth, and development all involve change. Seeing change and stability as a dialectic, as we suggested earlier in this chapter, means seeing *both* change and stability as valued. However, there is no doubt that stakeholders often resist organizational changes, and this happens often enough and vehemently enough that it may *seem* like resisting change is a fundamental aspect of human nature.

People resist change for a variety of reasons. One reason is because it threatens some valued self-interest, such as established interpersonal relationships, status in the organization, compensation or other rewards, or even employment security. In one nonprofit organization Ted studied, some administrative personnel were threatened by the introduction of a new, centralized database system that would replace familiar, local systems. The administrators were the "experts" with their old systems, and some of them feared losing their expert status while they learned the new system. A second reason people resist change is because it implies criticism and therefore threatens self-esteem. The fact that change is viewed as an improvement may imply that someone's previous performance, abilities, or efforts were inadequate, and therefore not valued or not appreciated.

A third reason for resisting change is because the outcome of proposed changes are often uncertain. Employees may fear that the proposed change will lead to work or

"Can anyone remember what our core business is?"

services that are less satisfying or rewarding. Or, they may fear that the new changes will cause more problems than they solve, or that the anticipated benefits are uncertain. Of course, there may be benefits to the changes that are unknown as well. Importantly, older employees are often targeted for management and peer criticism if they question organizational changes, as Mark Bergstrom and Michael Holmes explain. Rather than exploring whether the questions highlight possible inefficiencies in the proposed change, the assumption is made that the older employee is incapable of learning the new techniques. In fact, the age bias is so strong in some U.S. industries that anyone over 40 is presumed to be insufficiently open to learning.[55] Unfortunately, this bias often ignores the wisdom gained from experience and the fact that many middle-aged and retirement-age persons are deeply engaged with new technologies (see box 11.3).

Fourth, employees may resist because of the frequency of change programs—what might be called the "flavor-of-the-month" response. Every time another change program is marched out as *the* solution or "the way of the future" employees turn their cynicism up one more notch. When management abandons TQM, for example, and embraces Business Process Reengineering (BPR), then abandons BPR in favor of e-business, many employees just shake their heads. As one group of researchers found: "[T]he rhetoric is critical. Failure to stick with one management or organizational change plan and a record of jumping from strategy to strategy in search of the quick fix compounds problems and increases the likelihood of failure as each new approach is met with greater and greater resistance."[56]

Fifth, people may resist changes if the change makers are not trusted. In their study of the acquisition of Ozark Airlines by TWA (see box 10.5) Dougherty and

Pierce found that many of the Ozark pilots resisted using new TWA procedures, in part because they distrusted the management group that had essentially made them second-class citizens of the company.[57] Finally (and closely related to the previous reason), employees balk at organizational changes because there's a common theme to many of the most popular change programs in recent years: people lose their jobs. Box 11.9 gives an example of someone who lost her job through a company's BPR program. When management glosses over the negative impacts of change or frames the changes in upbeat language, the hypocrisy worsens the effect. Pricewaterhouse-Coopers, for example, touts their business process outsourcing (or BPO) process as "a win-win proposition for both the organization and its employees—and . . . it really empowers the employee." They define outsourcing as "the long-term contracting of a company's non-core business processes to an outside service provider."[58] So, while someone may be getting empowered, someone else is losing a job!

Beyond resisting, another possible employee response is to accept the change. One victim of downsizing stated, "Sure, I felt angry, but that doesn't do any good. There was nothing unfair about the corporation's making its operation tighter. Whatever happened, I had to deal with the consequences."[59] Note how he accepts the change as justified. Although he was losing his job, he had "bought" the rhetoric of efficiency and competition.

It is important to realize that resistance to change isn't necessarily a bad thing. Usually in the change management literature, resistance is conceptualized as something to be overcome. However, resistance may be a very helpful indication that the

Box 11.9 A Reengineering Casualty

Alice was hired as an engineer at a major oil company in Texas. After working hard for 5 years, she learned the company had decided to reengineer. She went to one general meeting and met the chief consultant. After that, the junior consultants interviewed employees and managers in small groups, asking "How do you do this job?" "Who do you think is the best employee you know?" The company spent hundreds of thousands of dollars on the consultants, who produced a number of flow charts. Within a year, all employees received a letter: "Report to the HRM director's office on Friday for your 10-minute interview."[60]

Director: Alice, thank you for coming. Your manager will hand you an envelope with your name on it. It will either say you have a new job with us or your job has been terminated. If you are offered a new job, you will be asked if you want to take this job. If you do not, then you will leave today. If the envelope says you no longer have a job, then you will be escorted by security with a cardboard box to collect your things. You are not to touch your computer or any company records. Do you understand these ground rules?

Alice: (nods that she does).

Manager: Alice, here is your envelope. Please open it now.

Alice: (opens the envelope and starts to cry) I liked working here.

Security: I am sorry, but I must escort you from the building. You are not to talk to anyone on your way out.

Alice did not get to say goodbye to the people with whom she had worked. The experience was awful. Even worse, Alice went through an almost identical experience at her next engineering job.

What impact do you expect such practices are likely to have on the "survivors" of the reengineering? What dilemmas would the company face in such a situation? How might they have handled the process more humanely and still achieved their goals?

proposed change is a bad idea! Or, it may be a signal that there are other issues that need to be addressed (for example, management's credibility, or problems stemming from a previous change effort) before the change can be implemented. So, rather than seeing resistance as something to be overcome, an advisable first response should be to listen to the resisters and learn what's behind the resistance. This is especially important if there is a high need for consensus to make the change successful.

Often the concerns and fears that lead people to resist changes are valid. Change imposes costs, and when the perceived costs outweigh the perceived benefits, people may resist. However, people will typically embrace change if they perceive: the intended change as worthwhile, achieving something they value; the change as likely to be effective, accomplishing what's intended; that they can be successful in doing their part; that the amount of effort required of them personally is reasonable; that they will be supported and not meet unmanageable resistance in doing their part; that if they try and fail, the consequences are manageable; and that if they try and succeed, they'll be recognized and rewarded in a way that's valued.

While employees are often suspicious of large-scale change programs initiated unilaterally by management, they are also suspicious when change is absent. Living in a time where the value of organizational change has become so pronounced that few organizations would describe themselves as being resistant to change, members of organizations increasingly expect their workplace to implement changes when needed. And some organizations clearly do this very professionally. As we've seen, however, many organizations embrace a rhetoric of change without doing the necessary follow-up. As a consequence, many employees (at various levels) grow tired of the fact that no matter what they do or what management says it is doing, everything seems to stay the same.[61]

Snapshot Synthesis

Change is associated with both fascination and rejection, hope and anxiety. Although modern society—and contemporary organizations in particular—sometimes seem preoccupied with change, we still view change with great ambivalence. In this chapter we've discussed and illustrated how the preoccupation with change is expressed in a management discourse and practice that often reflects a deep-seated desire for stability and persistence while communicating flexibility and openness toward new possibilities. The dialectic of change-constancy suggests that we value both, even if change tends to be most celebrated in today's organizations. Skillful managers are sensitive to this dialectic, seeking a balance between change and stabilizing initiatives.

Change is constructed in our discourse. We negotiate understandings of what is desirable and undesirable about the status quo, imagine possible future scenarios, and make sense of events in the present and past. So, through our talk, we actually construct what we understand as change (or non-change). Additionally, communication is the means by which change is implemented, as implementers negotiate plans, announce changes, field questions, direct change activities, and so on.

Experts have suggested a variety of strategies for communicating and managing change. While no one strategy is appropriate for every instance of change, there are several management frameworks for particular types of changes. Skillful change managers should assess the context for change thoroughly, including an analysis of its many dimensions, and choose, modify, or create a strategy accordingly.

Key Concepts

- **Change:** the process by which alteration occurs in the structure and function of a social system; the difference(s) between two (or more) successive conditions, states, or moments of time; or, a succession of differences in time within a persisting identity
- **Turbulence:** a term used to describe the rapidly and unpredictably changing environment within which contemporary organizations operate; often used to justify continuous change
- **Change-related Communication:** communication about change as well as communication involved in organizational change processes
- **Change-Constancy Dialectic:** the notion that change and constancy are in a natural and inescapable tension; implies that both are desirable but also that they lean on each other for meaning
- **Homeostasis:** a principle from open systems theory that assumes that organizations strive for stability or routine
- **Benchmarking:** a process through which organizations attempt to compare their own systems or practices in a particular area (e.g., customer service) to those of other organizations, thereby discovering ways to improve
- **First-order Changes**: minor, incremental changes that any living system has to practice in order to avoid the more fundamental second-order changes
- **Second-order Change:** radical change, which occurs when the entity becomes something fundamentally different from what it was
- **Programmed Implementation**: a process of change management in which top management develops a plan for implementing the change and marshals the plan throughout its many phases
- **Adaptive Implementation:** a process of change management that may be initiated at varying levels of the organization and that is monitored and modified throughout the implementation process as new information about the implementation emerges
- **Fidelity (of adoption)**: a standard of evaluating change efforts in which the criterion is the match between the designer's intended use for the change and the user's actual use
- **Uniformity (of adoption)**: a standard of evaluating change efforts in which the criterion is that change is accepted similarly by all users
- **Unintended Consequences**: a concept from systems theory that suggests that a change in one part of the system will prompt changes in other parts of the system, some of which will not be anticipated
- **Strength of Weak Ties:** refers to the openness of a system or a group to new information from the outside that may well come through relatively weak or undeveloped relationships, as opposed to strong or intimate ones

Endnotes

1 Alvin Toffler, *Future Shock* (New York: Bantam, 1970).

2 James G. March, "The Future, Disposable Organizations and the Rigidities of Imagination," *Organization* 2 (1995): 428.

3 <www.accenture.com> accessed 31 March 2002.

4 Darrell Rigby, *Management Tools 2001* <www.bain.com> accessed 31 March 2002.

5 Brad Jackson, *Management Fashions and Management Gurus* (London: Routledge, 2001).

6 Edward E. Lawler, *From the Ground Up: Six Principles for Building the New Logic Corporation* (San Francisco: Jossey-Bass, 1996) p. 8.

7 David Osborne and Ted Gaebler, *Reinventing Government: How the Entrepreneurial Spirit Is Transforming the Public Sector* (New York: Plume, 1992).

8 Loril Gossett, "Kept at Arms Length: Questioning the Organizational Desirability of Member Identification," *Communication Monographs* 69 (2002): 385–404; John W. Jordan, "Sabotage or Performed Compliance: Rhetorics of Resistance in Temp Worker Discourse," *Quarterly Journal of Speech* 89 (2003): 19–40.

9 Everett M. Rogers, *Diffusion of Innovations* (New York: Free Press, 1972) p. 7.

10 Jeffrey D. Ford and Laurie W. Ford, "The Role of Conversations in Producing Intentional Change in Organizations," *The Academy of Management Review* 20 (1995): 541–570.

11 George Cheney, *Values at Work: Employee Participation Meets Market Pressure at Mondragón* (Ithaca, NY: Cornell University Press, 1999).

12 Robert Nisbet and Robert G. Perrin, *The Social Bond* (New York: Alfred A. Knopf, 1977) p. 266.

13 Nisbet and Perrin, p. 269.

14 Ravi S. Achrol, "Evolution of the Marketing Organization: New Forms for Turbulent Environments," *Journal of Marketing* 55 (October 1991): 77–93.

15 Lars Thøger Christensen, "Marketing as Auto-Communication," *Consumption, Markets and Culture* 1.3 (May 1997): 197–227.

16 A more explicitly communication-oriented model of change is that proposed by communication researcher Everett Rogers (see endnote 9 above). He developed the following model specifically to explain organizational innovations. While he presents the stages in his model as a linear process, we could also imagine breaks or even cycles within this process.

1. *Agenda setting*: Members of the organization scan the organization and its relevant environment to define problems facing the organization and potentially useful innovations.
2. *Matching*: Potential innovations are considered together with the organization's problems and a decision made to adopt the innovation or reject it.
3. *Redefining/restructuring*: The adopted innovation as well as organizational structures are modified to create a good fit.
4. *Clarifying:* The modified innovation is put into use and organizational members clarify their understandings of what the innovation means for them.
5. *Routinizing*: The innovation loses its strangeness or novelty and becomes accepted practice.

17 Ford and Ford.

18 Theodore E. Zorn, Deborah Page, and George Cheney, "Nuts about Change: Change-Oriented Communication in a Public Sector Organisation," *Management Communication Quarterly* 14 (May 2000): 515–566.

19 Brad Jackson, *Management Fashions and Management Gurus* (London: Routledge, 2001).

20 Helena Economo and Theodore E. Zorn, "Survivor Perceptions of Communication during Downsizing," *Asia Pacific Public Relations Journal* 1.2 (1999): 19–41.

21 James Taylor and Elizabeth Van Every, "A Historical Analysis of the INCIS Project," unpublished paper, U of Waikato, Hamilton, New Zealand, 2002.

22 Sonja A. Sackmann, "Culture and Subcultures: An Analysis of Organizational Knowledge," *Administrative Science Quarterly* 37 (1992): 140–161; J-C. Spender, "The Dynamics of Individual and Organizational Knowledge," *Managerial and Organizational Cognition: Theory, Methods, and Research*, ed. Colin Eden and J. C. Spender (Thousand Oaks, CA: Sage, 1998) p. 13–39.

23 Gregory Bateson, *Steps to an Ecology of Mind* (New York: Ballantine Books, 1972).

24 Richard L. Daft, *Organization Theory and Design* (St. Paul, MN: West Publishing, 1989).

25 Jackson.

26 In particular, see Erik Abrahamson, "Management Fashion," *Academy of Management Review* 21 (1996): 254–285; Erik Abrahamson and Gregory Fairchild, "Management Fashion: Lifecycles, Triggers, and Collective Learning Processes," *Administrative Science Quarterly* 44 (1999): 708–740.

[27] Michael Hammer and James A. Champy, *Reengineering the Corporation: A Manifesto for Business Revolution* (New York: HarperBusiness, 1993).

[28] Stephen Covey, *Seven Habits of Highly Effective People* (New York: Simon & Schuster, 1990).

[29] Peter Senge, *The Fifth Discipline: The Art and Practice of the Learning Organization* (New York: Currency Doubleday, 1990).

[30] Zorn, Page, and Cheney.

[31] C. Erik Timmerman, "Media Selection during the Implementation of Planned Organizational Change," *Management Communication Quarterly* 16 (2003): 301–340. See also Paul Berman, "Thinking about Programmed and Adaptive Implementation: Matching Strategies to Situations," *Why Policies Succeed or Fail*, ed. Helen M. Ingram and Dean E. Mann (Beverly Hills, CA: Sage, 1980) 205–228; Laurie K. Lewis and David R. Seibold, "Reconceptualizing Organizational Change Implementation as a Communication Problem: A Review of Literature and Research Agenda," *Communication Yearbook*, ed. Michael E. Roloff, vol. 21 (Thousand Oaks, CA: Sage, 1998) p. 93–151.

[32] Lewis and Seibold actually treat programmed-adaptive and rule bound-autonomous as two separate dimensions. For our purposes here, we treat them as one dimension.

[33] Deborah Page, "Constructions of Change-Related Communication: Three Case Studies," diss., University of Waikato, in progress.

[34] Mark J. Zbaracki, "The Rhetoric and Reality of Total Quality Management," *Administrative Sciences Quarterly* 43 (1998): 602–636.

[35] Zorn, Page, and Cheney.

[36] Theodore E. Zorn, "The Uncooperative Cooperative: Attempting to Improve Employee Relations at Weaver Street Market," *Cases in Organizational Communication*, ed. Beverly D. Sypher, vol. 2 (New York: Guilford Press, 1997).

[37] Laurie K. Lewis and David R. Seibold, "Innovation Modification during Intraorganizational Adoption," *Academy of Management Review* 18 (1993): 322–354.

[38] See Timmerman; also, see Bonnie M. Johnson and Ronald E. Rice, *Managing Organizational Innovation: The Evolution of Word Processing to Office Information Systems* (New York: Columbia University Press, 1987); and James Taylor, Carole Groleau, Lorna Heaton, and Elizabeth Van Every, *The Computerization of Work: A Communication Perspective* (Thousand Oaks, CA: Sage, 2000).

[39] Lewis and Seibold, "Reconceptualizing."

[40] T. J. Larkin and Sandar Larkin, *Communicating Change: Winning Employees Support for New Business Goals* (New York, McGraw-Hill, 1994).

[41] Larkin and Larkin, p. 96.

[42] Economo and Zorn.

[43] Larkin and Larkin, p. 101.

[44] Economo and Zorn.

[45] Laurie K. Lewis, Stephanie A. Hamel, and Brian K. Richardson, "Communicating Change to Nonprofit Stakeholders: Models and Predictors of Implementers' Approaches," *Management Communication Quarterly* 15 (2001): 5–41.

[46] Lewis, Hamel, and Richardson, p. 21.

[47] Lewis, Hamel, and Richardson defined communicative efficiency as "the accomplishment of a communicative task with a minimum expenditure of time, effort, and resources" (p. 28).

[48] Mark Granovetter, "The Strength of Weak Ties," *The American Journal of Sociology* 78 (1973): 1360–1380.

[49] Sunwolf and David R. Seibold, "The Impact of Formal Procedures on Group Processes, Members, and Task Outcomes," *The Handbook of Group Communication Theory and Research*, ed. Lawrence R. Frey (Thousand Oaks, CA: Sage, 1999).

[50] Alex F. Osborn, *Applied Imagination: Principles and Procedures of Creative Problem Solving* (New York: Scribner, 1957).

[51] Arthur B. VanGundy, "Brainwriting," <http://www.creativityatwork.com/articlesContent/brainwri.htm> accessed 10 March 2003.

[52] Andrew L. Delbecq, *Group Techniques for Program Planning: A Guide to Nominal Group and Delphi Processes* (Glenview, IL: Scott Foresman, 1975).

[53] For a review of recent research, see Sunwolf and Seibold.

[54] Susan Jarboe, "Group Communication and Creativity Processes," *The Handbook of Group Communication Theory and Research*, ed. Lawrence R. Frey (Thousand Oaks, CA: Sage, 1999) pp. 335–368.

[55] Mark Bergstrom and Michael Holmes, "Organizational Communication and Aging: Age-Related Processes in Organizations," *Handbook of Communication and Aging Research*, ed. Jon F. Nussbaum and Justine Coupland, 2nd ed. (Mahwah, NJ: Erlbaum, in press).

[56] David M. Boje, Grace A. Rosile, Robert Dennehy, and Deborah J. Summers, "Restorying Reengineering: Some Deconstructions and Postmodern Alternatives," *Communication Research* 24.6 (1997): 634.

[57] Tamyra Pierce and Deborah Dougherty, "The Construction, Enactment, and Maintenance of Power-as-Domination through an Acquisition: The Case of TWA and Ozark Airlines," *Management Communication Quarterly* 16 (2002): 129–164.

[58] "What Does 'Employee Empowerment' Really Mean? Corporate America Puts $40 Billion on the Line To Find Out," PricewaterhouseCoopers press release, 2 August 1999. <http://www.pwcglobal.com/extweb/ncpressrelease.nst/DocID/005CD1A76BCB73E6852567C30055AF23>.

[59] Richard Sennett, *The Corrosion of Character: The Personal Consequences of Work in the New Capitalism* (New York: Norton, 1998) p. 29.

[60] Quoted from Boje, Rosile, Dennehy, and Summers, p. 633.

[61] Recall that this is *one* definition of loose coupling as we discussed in chapter 2. See also Karl E. Weick, "Educational Organizations as Loosely Coupled System," *Administrative Science Quarterly* 21 (1976): 1–19. J. Douglas Orton and Karl E. Weick, "Loosely Coupled Systems: A Reconceptualization," *Academy of Management Review* 15 (1990): 203–223.

12

The Meanings and Uses of Organizational Communication Technologies

Contemporary organizations rarely conceive of change independently of technology. Indeed, technology is often seen as synonymous with change. Innovation in higher education, for example, is often *equated* with the implementation of long-distance learning strategies, Web-based course development, and the use of multiple and interactive media. And this is true for most organizations: change-oriented programs typically involve the implementation and uses of new computer-based technologies. Indeed, one of the most prominent ways organizations have changed in recent years is the introduction of "e-business" or "e-commerce." Technology *is* change, it seems. Or is it?

Think for a moment about technologies that have become commonplace in organizations (and beyond) in recent years: electronic (e-) mail, voice mail, Internet and intranet, audio and video conferencing systems, mobile phones, personal digital assistants (or PDAs, like Palm Pilots), electronic calendars, etc. The list seems endless. More importantly, few of these technologies were part of the typical office landscape even as recently as 1990. While most of you have been exposed to such technologies all your adult life, they haven't been around for long. As a child in the late 1960s, Lars sometimes joined his dad at work on Saturdays. His father, who worked in an export firm in Copenhagen, had to check the telex machine to see if there were any messages from overseas partners. Do you know what a telex machine is? Probably not. Generally speaking, a telex is a communications system consisting of teletypewriters connected to a telephone network to send and receive signals. But the most distinguishing feature of the telex, at least as seen from the perspective of a child, was the way messages arrived. They were punched as a pattern of small holes on a long inch-wide roll of paper. One message, thus, could be several yards long. Once received, the pattern of holes was decoded by another part of the machine that would print the message. It sounds complicated, but the machine was fairly easy to handle. Later when he went to college in 1979, Lars was taught to use punch cards to feed into a computer when doing quantitative studies. And even in those days organizations considered themselves sophisticated! The punch cards were soon replaced by computer-based software—much of which, of course, is antiquated today. In the 1980s when Lars wrote his master's thesis, many people used an electric typewriter. Personal computers were around, but not very common among students. That changed very soon, and the story continues: new developments, faster computers, new programs, etc. It's almost a cliché to note how fast things change, how quickly technological equipment becomes obsolete, and to predict how much more sophisticated systems will become in the future. Talk about technology and the future is a constant, prominent part of organizational discourse.

Just as important as the specific features of new communication technologies are the expectations we have regarding their use and their effects. In the organizational context, we typically expect communication technologies to heighten productivity and efficiency, to improve flows of communication, to promote flexibility and responsiveness, and to create administrative and geographic decentralization. Sometimes, perhaps, we even envision that such technologies will increase commitment and solidarity and facilitate participation and egalitarian decision making.

Clearly, communication technologies have brought about many important changes in the workplace. Computer technologies have made it simpler to produce, multiply, distribute, and store written documents; to exchange messages over long distances; and to work together and execute meetings relatively independent of time and space. Computer technology has given us a whole new sense of what it means to deal with "files," thus making possible even greater complexity in organizations. Organizations of all types now rely on electronic databases, electronic collaboration, and virtual meetings. The digital age has changed the content and meaning of those tasks in a number of significant ways. Technologies, however, may have less desirable consequences as well. Some writers warn that communication technologies imply increased management surveillance and control, more standardized work, centralized power, loss of branch autonomy, standardized communication, disrupted group processes and decision making, and increased worker alienation. In this chapter, we will outline and discuss such changes and focus on how new technologies are affecting—and can be expected to affect—the communication of contemporary organizations.

Organizational Communication Technology

What is technology? What is communication technology? And how is communication technology related to interaction patterns and organizing processes of contemporary organizations? As one writer observes, "When one talks of technology most people visualize *machines*."[1] Technology, however, is far more than just machines and material artifacts. Technology is the *application of a specific logic of technique to the domain of human activity and behavior.* Because communication technology changes so rapidly, we need to be careful not to assume that we know a priori

"We have lots of information technology. We just don't have any information."

what technology is and what it can do. Rather, we should take a broader and more abstract perspective. In order to understand the significance of communication technology in the lives of contemporary organizations, it is useful to take a look at the social history of the notion of technology and the more basic notion of "technique."

Technique

According to French sociologist Cornelius Castoriadis, the term *technique* is of Greek origin (*techne*) and goes back to the ancient verb *teucho.* In the writings of Homer, teucho meant to fabricate, to produce, or to construct. Gradually, the meaning of teucho became detached from material production and referred only to the act of causing, bringing about, or bringing into existence. Related to the Greek term for fabrication, we find the notion of creation (*poiesis*), which Aristotle identified with techne. Although technique became associated with creation, it didn't mean the construction of something *entirely* new. Rather, Western philosophy has seen technique as "imitation" or, in the words of Castoriadis, the power to rearrange or bring together existing elements in ways not accomplished by nature itself. [2] Technique, in other words, *has come to mean a non-natural actualization of possibilities inherent in the physical world.*

This notion of technique is evident in the language and culture of the Western world, which typically conceives of technique and technology in narrow instrumental terms. There is an overwhelming bias in our notion of technique toward the accomplishment of tasks, as opposed to, say, the more aesthetic or imaginary dimensions of human existence. Thus, for example, we typically talk about computers as machines that help us do work while ignoring that their presence in an office landscape also signifies power, progress, etc. The emphasis on tasks has stimulated the development of bureaucratic efficiency and scientific approaches to studying human problems in the West, but it has simultaneously blinded us to understanding the full array of human experiences and possibilities.

We need to think of technique not only as an instrument or method of accomplishing tasks but also as an overall orientation. Technique in this sense is a central institution of society that guides the production of meaning in many different contexts. Think of how we often imagine—at least in the Western world—that there are technical solutions to the problems we encounter: genetically modified food, for example, as a solution to hunger and overpopulation or missile shields as a solution to war. Technique, thus, is a mindset, a certain way of looking at and approaching the world. For example, we might say that the "technique" of a farmer is to cultivate and exploit the land, whereas the technique of a landscape architect is to adapt and enhance the land. Each profession has a different orientation, a different posture, toward the earth and its uses. Likewise, the technique of a computer expert is to facilitate the elaboration and exchange of information. The computer industry is especially interesting in terms of orientation. Many professionals speak as though they are dealing only with electrons, bits of information, and knowledge systems—not something material. This attitude supports the general ethos of the "information age" as a period that is wholly post-industrial—as if it were floating above and not dependent on the material world. Pick up a copy of *Wired* magazine, for example, to get a sense of how technology professionals talk about their world.

The most important of all techniques, according to Castoriadis, is social organization itself, "and the mightiest engine ever created by man is the regulated network of social relations."[3] That is, the very way we structure groups, organizations, and societies may be seen as technique—in fact, our highest "technical" accomplishment

Box 12.1 Information as Commodity

In 1986, Theodore Roszak expressed concern that in the so-called "information age" there seems to be an insatiable public need for information and a tendency to worship computers as "emblems of salvation." Whereas information and the handling of information used to have little or no status—data processing responsibilities in most organizations were classified as mundane rather than celebrated—now information has been elevated to new heights in almost all sectors of society.

"Until well into the twentieth century, one looks in vain in magazines for advertisements that feature any sort of data processing equipment, let alone for books and articles celebrating their inventors and manufactures. Compare this with the situation today, when the slickest, most futuristic ads in print and on television are those touting computers for the office, and you have a striking measure of how information has risen in status. The technology of the humble data keepers has finally outmatched the rolling mills, the dynamos, the railroads."[4] As Roszak points out, information is now being proclaimed as the most valuable commodity in business, *any* business.

Why do you think that information has achieved such a high status? Should we concern ourselves with analyzing the types of information we encounter?

according to Castoriadis. This idea corresponds to U.S. economist John Kenneth Galbraith's stress on information and organization as the dominant sources of power in today's world, as we discuss in chapter 9.

Thus, we can think of formal organization itself as a technique—a technique focused on rationalization and control. By linking to the notion of technique we enhance our understanding of technology while capturing a broader understanding of the organization as a tool. Thus, an organizational structure—such as a bureaucracy, on a broad level, or a job interview on a more specific one—may be reframed *as* technology. In this sense, an organization is a tool for shaping the world and creating something new, as we can see when any new corporation or government agency or social movement is born. *Think of an organization you have been involved in—as a student, as an employee, as a member—and consider how technology can be seen both as part of the organization and as the organization itself.* This is a complex issue that we will return to later in this chapter.

Contemporary Communication Technologies

If we look at the office landscape in an average organization in the twenty-first century, we find a host of communication technologies (see box 12.2)—many of which we take for granted or don't even notice any longer. Communication vehicles

Box 12.2 Types of Organizational Communication Technologies

In the organizational setting, communication technology usually refers to four broad categories of technology:

1. *Computer-assisted communication technologies*, including technologies that facilitate the transmission of *text* (electronic mail), *images* (facsimile, computer and video conferencing), and *sound* (voice mail, audio conferencing).
2. *Computer-assisted decision making technologies*, including management information systems, group decision support systems, expert systems, and various kinds of external information retrieval systems.
3. *Networks of computers*, for example, local and wide area networks (LANs and WANs), through which personal computers are linked together for specific work groups or all members of the organization. Intranets are closed user-group networks limited within the physical boundaries of a single organization or organized across several organizational units. Some intranets are "firewalled" from external networks like the Internet.
4. *Networks of networks*, for example, the Internet, which is a complex system of telecommunications linkages that allow major computer facilities to intercommunicate worldwide. The World Wide Web, presently the most sophisticated Internet application, combines text, images, and sound and allows for numerous kinds of information exchange including chat rooms and electronic commerce.

Computer technology, however, is not restricted to the office setting. In advanced manufacturing, for example, computer technology is used to integrate information from external sources (e.g., customers, collaborators, and suppliers) with various aspects of the organization's internal work environment, including decision making, design, and production. We thus need to add a fifth category to our list:

5. *Computer-assisted manufacturing technologies*, including computer-aided design (CAD) and computer-aided engineering (CAE) systems, such as technologies that transform product specifications into machine settings or adjust production flows to changes in demand.

such as the telephone, the fax machine, or the personal pager changed the modern organization considerably when they were introduced. Today, however, these vehicles are rarely thought of as communication technologies. So what do we normally refer to when we talk about communication technology in the organizational setting? We usually reserve the term for media like electronic (e-) mail, voice mail, intra- and Internet, and audio and video conferencing systems. If we are more knowledgeable, we might include information management systems, group decision support systems, and various kinds of so-called "expert systems" that provide technical information related to specific tasks and processes.

Of course, given our suggestion that we should think of technique and technology more broadly than we typically do, we would argue that communication *knowledge* and *skills* also count as communication technology.[5] You may recall our discussion of Fairclough's idea of "technologizing" communication that we reviewed in chapter 6—the idea that communication researchers and trainers identify the components of effective interaction, then teach the techniques to others to enable them to communicate strategically.

Features of Communication Technologies

Communication technologies share a number of important features. Most prominently, these technologies are designed to enhance the *speed* of communication, to facilitate immediate *access to information*, and to enable complex *information exchanges across different geographical locations*.

E-mail and voice mail are delivered in seconds from anywhere on the globe. The same is true for text files and more complex images like pictures and even movies. Communication technologies, it seems, have completely eliminated the influence of *space*. With the possibility of accessing information anywhere, as long as there's an Internet connection, geographical distance is less influential on the communication process than, say, the "chemistry" between people and their willingness to work together. One interesting consequence for organizational communication is that people, in principle, can carry out their work far away from their workplace—a phenomenon also known as "telecommuting."

Our notion of *time* is changed as well. Although communication technologies have not dissolved time constraints and time differentials, they *appear* to have done so in a number of important respects. Whereas communication media like the telephone or face-to-face conversation require the simultaneous presence of the sender and the receiver, technologies like e-mail and voice mail liberate us from such constraints. Thus, we have an important distinction between *synchronous* and *asynchronous* communication. Although we may often prefer synchronous communication because it allows us to get immediate feedback, it confines communication to periods where both parties of the communication process are present or available. One obvious limitation is known as "telephone tag"—the time we spend waiting for the other party to call back. Research has found that telephone tag consumes significant proportions of a normal workday.[6] By contrast, *a*synchronous media, such as e-mail and voice mail, allow the sender the convenience of leaving a message without the requirement of finding the receiver at his or her desk. Asynchronous technologies, thus, make it possible for communication to proceed interactively, outside of "real time," without disruption of the routines of either the sender or the receiver. Many people take advantage of these features by moving through a whole list of contacts before the regular workday begins! Asynchronous technologies facilitate the satisfaction of "checking off" many items on a to-do list—without, of course, being assured that the messages have been received or that something approaching meaningful communication has taken place.

In a similar manner, computer-aided-design (CAD) systems allow, for example, a salesperson and a customer to co-design a custom-made product on a laptop computer and to transmit the design electronically to the factory within minutes. The possibility of obtaining information directly rather than having to go through a gatekeeper—who is located, perhaps, in a different time zone—is another unmistakable benefit of asynchronous technologies.[7] For example, information can be downloaded from a Web site that is available to, say, sales people or the members of a discipline, without the user needing to talk with the producer of the information. At the same time, naturally, opportunities for interaction and the more in-depth understanding that might result are eliminated or postponed.

The features of these technologies and their potential for communication and information exchange, thus, hold considerable promise for a "smoother" functioning work life. Indeed, the writing of this textbook across three continents would have been a far more complicated affair without the compression of space and the redefinition of time offered by these technologies. Think about the advantage of asynchronicity in terms of productivity. Then consider how asynchronicity affects communication patterns and habits, including our respect for other people's time.

There have also been advances in synchronous technologies, creating more opportunities for real-time interactions. Cellular telephones are rapidly spreading to parts of the world that have had little access to the technology previously. In addition, there is growing use of chat rooms, group decision support systems, interactive e-mail, interactive television, and other forms of communication technologies that allow for real-time interaction. Synchronicity and asynchronicity have both produced new conditions for communication in today's world.

Of course, there are other important features of communication technologies. For example, they enable surreptitious *monitoring* and *fast processing* of massive amounts of data. As mentioned in chapter 6, one of the "hottest" applications in business today is customer relationship management (CRM) systems that, among other things, monitor customer purchases, process the data, and then use this data for targeted marketing.

Using Communication Technologies

Technologies, however, are rarely used exactly as envisioned by futurologists, designers, or decision makers—or as feared by techno-phobic social critics. The pages of magazines are filled with examples of both "techno-optimism" (an unbounded faith in the capacity of new technologies to solve our problems) and dire warnings about technology being a kind of Frankenstein out of our control. Put another way, the prognosticators are divided between envisioning *utopian* and *dystopian* futures resulting from technological developments.[8] While both positions have some merit, especially by encouraging us to think of the reasons why we want new technologies, the arguments tend to be too polarized. Most new technologies are really a "mixed bag" in terms of advantages and disadvantages. Rarely do the implementation and use of technologies in organizations live up to the gloomy prophecies of critics who predict, for example, an end to interpersonal interactions in the workplace or an end to employment itself.[9]

There is no simple causality between the technical options and features available to contemporary organizations and the actual use of these technologies in practice. Interestingly, however, we often come across the same *technological determinism* among those who praise the advent of new technologies and those who dread it. Technological determinism is the idea that technology itself is a driving force (perhaps *the* driving force) in human history.[10] According to technological determinists, technological innovations lead predictably and necessarily to certain transformations of society (or organizations). *Both* groups seem to assume that communication technologies have a built-in logic that forces itself more or less automatically on organizations and societies and pushes human interaction in clear-cut and unambiguous directions. Such descriptive determinism does capture some of our experiences with communication technologies: they often seem to develop rather independently of user needs, wants, and influence. For example, think of the constant updates of computer software that sometimes seem more a nuisance than a help, requiring us to learn new features and to re-learn how to do some tasks that had become routine. At the same time, however, technological determinism blinds us to the fact that communication technologies (along with other technologies) achieve their meanings in the context of everyday use.

Perspectives on Communication Media Usage

When researchers have attempted to understand how people use communication technology, they've considered issues including access to various media, availability of communication partners, users' experience with the medium, users' personal style in using media, time and cost advantages, and communication task requirements. Most of the research on the use of communication technology in organizations has focused exclusively on the rational motives of managers when choosing a specific medium, assuming that managers coolly consider the objective dimensions of the medium and task and make a rational decision.

Critical mass theory stresses the significance of a "critical mass" of users for the general diffusion and success of the medium being adopted, accentuating the fact that the usefulness of an interactive medium like the telephone, the fax, or electronic mail increases with universal access. Being the first person in the universe to own a telephone, for example, may have been appealing to some—but certainly not for

Box 12.3 E-mail and Its Users

In 1997, 40 million people in the United States (15% of the population) were using e-mail. In 2002, the number had grown to approximately 135 million (about 50% of the U.S. population). An organization called the Electronic Messaging Association estimated the number of e-mail messages sent in 1997 as 2.7 trillion; the number was predicted to be 6.9 trillion by 2000.[11]

Try to update these figures for your own country. What's the annual increase in e-mail use? Is it possible that the numbers will continue to increase so dramatically?

functional reasons! Critical mass theorists explain the adoption of a medium primarily as a function of the size of the community of users, trying to determine a "tipping point" at which a proportion of users in a community or an organization is sufficiently large to sustain the technology.[12] This is parallel to research by socio-linguists and linguistic anthropologists on the point at which there is a large enough speech community to maintain a rare or isolated language.

Media richness theory, by contrast, takes adoption for granted and analyzes the choice of a medium in terms of a particular task. The central idea of this theory is rooted in the 1930s and 1940s, when consultants and organizational communication scholars tried to match medium (bulletin board, memo, face-to-face interview, telephone, loudspeaker) with the message and the task at hand. Management scholars Richard Daft and Robert Lengel use their media richness model to explain the choice of communication media as a function of the ambiguity of the specific task to be performed.[13] Ambiguity here refers to the possibility for multiple interpretations of the messages. For instance, announcing a meeting time is a relatively straightforward task, but firing an employee or resolving a conflict is a far more complex and sensitive undertaking. Daft and Lengel hypothesize that managers generally will choose a communication medium suitable for handling the level of ambiguity in the task. According to this perspective, firing an employee calls for a rich medium—like a face-to-face meeting—able to provide multiple cues and instant feedback. In contrast, a "leaner" medium like electronic mail is sufficient for scheduling a meeting. Box 12.4 provides a more complete explanation of the media richness model.

Box 12.4 Media Richness Model

The media richness model was proposed by Richard Daft and Robert Lengel as a general framework for understanding the media choices of organizational actors.[14] Media richness denotes the "potential information-carrying capacity of a medium." The information-carrying capacity is defined by four criteria: (1) the possibility for instant feedback, (2) the ability to convey multiple communication cues, (3) the capacity for nonverbal communication (e.g., facial expressions), and (4) the potential to tailor messages to personal circumstances. Communication media that have all or most of these features are referred to as *rich* media. Conversely, media that have none or few of these features are referred to as *lean.* Based on these criteria, we can arrange organizational communication channels along a continuum ranging from very lean to very rich.

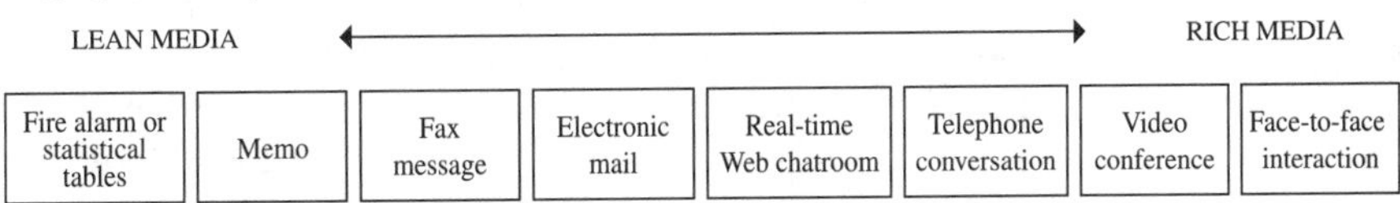

Face-to-face interaction is considered a rich communication medium because it allows immediate, two-way, feedback, combined with the availability of visual (e.g., facial expressions or body language) and linguistic (e.g., tone of voice) communication cues. Because of these features, understandings can be checked and interpretations adjusted. By contrast, statistics or alarm signals are lean media because no additional cues or feedback are possible. Of course, new media are being developed all the time and the features of existing media are being extended.

Where would you place a relatively new medium like text messaging or interactive Webcast (i.e., videoconference via the Web)? Why? Can you think of other features that would affect the richness/leanness of media?

Although the model is generally but only weakly supported by research,[15] its logic and simplicity have an immediate appeal that conforms to our ideals about rational management practice. What is rationality, however, in this context? An organizational actor facing the task of conveying ambiguous, but unpleasant, information to a superior or subordinate may "rationally" choose a leaner medium—like, for example, a letter or an electronic message—that doesn't require face-to-face contact. Conversely, organizational actors may sometimes—for social or other non-task-related reasons—choose a rich medium to convey a comparatively straightforward message. For example, sometimes the primary tasks to be addressed at a staff meeting may be quite straightforward and easily handled via e-mail. However, a manager may choose to have the staff meeting because of the perceived value of staff regularly interacting face to face. And of course, there are abundant examples of insensitive administrators or managers who consistently make poor media choices. In George's consulting with a small city organization, for example, he learned that the chief administrative officer (CAO) often chose e-mail for reprimanding employees and would copy everyone on the organization's distribution list!

As these examples illustrate, the use of communication media may not be rational in the narrow and task-related sense of the term but are very rational if we consider human needs to combine task requirements with social concerns. In spite of these complexities, the model still has its merits. If you were to advise a friend or a colleague on how to deal with a conflict, for example, you'd probably advise against a lean medium and suggest instead a rich one, like a face-to-face conversation.

Other Influences on Media Use

While critical mass theory and the media richness model highlight some important dimensions related to the adoption and choice of specific technologies, we need to ask ourselves whether diffusion patterns and choices surrounding their use accurately describe media usage in organizations. Firstly, the adoption and choice of specific media is not a question settled by organizations or individuals acting in isolation. As Noshir Contractor and Eric Eisenberg state, "Everything about the adoption and usage of media is social."[16] Organizations may prefer certain media—like videoconferences—simply because other organizations have adopted them. Secondly, and related to this observation, we should be sensitive to the possibility that choice behavior with respect to the use of communication technology is not always motivated by efficiency. While we typically justify our media decisions in efficiency terms, our actual use of a medium may be unrelated to that goal. Finally, we need to understand that media adoption and usage are often driven by the people who design, develop, or market the media. Software choices, for example, are typically stimulated by supply rather than demand. Hoping to stay ahead in the competition, designers and providers of communication technology rarely ask end users what they want and need. If they did, those technologies would probably develop much more slowly than they do. As a consequence, most of us know how to use only a small fraction of the features available on our computers (or video players, or cameras, etc.).

To the extent that communication technology options are "given" in advance by designers and producers of such technology, our notion of media "choice" needs to be reconsidered. Moreover, to the extent that the usage of specific media reflect a desire on the part of decision makers to be among cutting-edge and wired organizations, media adoption and usage may reflect expectations, conventions, and motives other than rational task-related choice. Under such circumstances—where choice and necessity become difficult to distinguish—it is obvious that theories that look at adoption and usage in isolation only skim the surface of the phenomenon they are trying to explain.

The social influence model tries to overcome this problem by phrasing the question of choice somewhat differently.[17] In a critique of the implied rationality of traditional media choice models, social influence theorists emphasize that media choices are determined not only by objective task and media characteristics but also by the past experience and the influence of others. Specifically, they suggest that existing communication patterns in the organization along with interactions with peers and coworkers influence people's evaluation and use of new media. Thus, for example, prejudices among close coworkers against a specific medium may prevent or delay the use of that medium even though the medium is most appropriate following rational choice perspectives like the media richness model. Conversely, in work cultures fascinated with technology and new media, such media may be chosen even in situations where other media provide a better match with the task at hand.

It seems only logical that the *perceived* characteristics of a medium and the prevailing norms concerning technology are important predictors for its use in addition to task requirements and more objective media features. Perceptions and norms about media use are exchanged and shared on a daily basis among coworkers, but these perceptions and norms are shaped also by social-historical trends and the general attitude toward technology and media in society. If organizational members are able to choose which communication media to adopt at the workplace, these choices will be shaped both by their work environment and by educational background, family, and the expectations voiced by opinion leaders, business journalists, and experts. The social influences on media choice, in other words, extend far beyond the formal boundaries of the organization. An excellent example comes to us from the research of communication scholar Andrew Flanagin, who finds that the most important factor in predicting Web site adoption and Web design by organizations is what they see other organizations doing![18] *Why do you think this is the case?*

Interestingly, the influence on media choice may well be less concerned with the ability of a specific medium to match the complexity of a message than with its symbolic status. *The dual capacity model* captures this issue by pointing out that every communication medium has the capacity to convey not only data—the primary focus of the rational choice models—but also symbols. In its symbol-carrying capacity, the technology itself becomes the message. This idea parallels Marshall McLuhan's famous dictum that "the medium is the message."[19] Thus, some organizations may choose a medium that is inadequate from a media richness perspective because it symbolizes, for example, a specific organizational culture or management style. For instance, Microsoft PowerPoint and other presentational software have become the standard in many professional circles. Thus, many employees are told that they can't afford not to use the presentational software; they risk being seen as "behind the curve" and will lose credibility if they don't follow the trend. However, all trends fade. In fact, presentation-enhancement technologies have become so common that some presenters "rebel" by returning to traditional outlines, handouts, and overheads. As suggested by the *Wall Street Journal* article in box 12.5, the technology can be as much a curse as a blessing.

Box 12.5 Technology Overkill

From "Pentagon cracks down on . . . PowerPoint"
Greg Jaffe, April 25, 2000, 5:00 PM PT [20]

WASHINGTON—Earlier this year, Gen. Hugh Shelton, chairman of the Joint Chiefs of Staff, issued an unusual order to U.S. military bases around the globe. His message: "Enough with the bells and whistles—just get to the point." It seems that e-mailed military briefings larded with electronic "slides" of booming tanks and spinning pie charts were gobbling up so much of the Defense Department's classified bandwidth that they were slowing more-critical communications between headquarters and units in the field. "The chairman basically told everyone that we don't need Venetian-blind effects or fancy backdrops. All we need is the information," says one senior Defense Department official.

Shelton's order is only the Pentagon's most recent assault on a growing electronic menace: the PowerPoint briefing. Sure, business executives complain about the seemingly endless PowerPoint presentations put on by overeager middle managers in darkened boardrooms across America. But in the military, the Microsoft . . . program, which helps users create computer-based graphics and sound effects, has become one of the most dreaded facts of life. And it's even shouldering the blame for at least some of the armed forces' ills. Congressional support for new weapons programs isn't as strong as expected. Army Secretary Louis Caldera suggests that PowerPoint presentations are alienating lawmakers. "People are not listening to us because they are spending so much time trying to understand these incredibly complex slides," he says. Too many bright, young junior officers are leaving the military for the private sector. A recent survey of captains at Fort Benning, Georgia, cites the "ubiquity of the PowerPoint Army" as a prime reason for their disaffection.

"The idea behind most of these briefings is for us to sit through 100 slides with our eyes glazed over, and then to do what all military organizations hope for . . . to surrender to an overwhelming mass," says Navy Secretary Richard Danzig.

If the spirit moves them they can build in gunfire sound effects and images that explode like land mines. "There is an arms-race dimension to it," says Peter Feaver, a military expert at Duke University and frequent PowerPoint briefer at various war colleges. "If there are three briefings in a row, and you are the one with the lowest production values, you look really lame."

Our observation about the status of media and technological choices clearly extends beyond the organization's boundaries to include options that are influenced and shaped by current trends and norms in the larger business community. While, for example, a perspective like critical mass theory may explain some overall trends related to the adoption of electronic mail, we need other explanations to account for the fact that a growing number of organizations these days feel a strong need to establish and assert their presence on the Internet. In such cases, conceiving of communication technology as a conduit through which messages are transmitted is inadequate. Communication technology is also a code. Although many organizations don't have anything particularly new to tell their audiences that require this new medium, they still insist on "being there" with elaborate Web sites hoping, perhaps, to demonstrate their adherence to a cutting edge, wired community. Even old-time pawnshops in rural Montana have now painted their Web addresses (or URLs) on their storefront windows!

Being present on the Internet and using that medium to demonstrate certain organizational qualities, thus, can be seen as a manifestation of what organizational sociologists John Meyer and Brian Rowan termed "ceremonial conformity."[21] Ceremonial conformity refers to the propensity of organizations to adapt their structures to norms and expectations in their surroundings. As a consequence, many organizations resemble each other. What is ironic, of course, is that in many sectors, and especially in private for-profit companies, the talk is simultaneously about entrepreneurship, creativity, and distinctiveness—as discussed in chapter 5 on organizational identity.

Interpreting the Effects of Organizational Communication Technologies

Early research on the Internet (e-mail began in 1985, and the World Wide Web was launched in 1993) tended to resemble the tradition in media research called "uses and gratifications." That is, the initial studies of the Internet focused on issues such as adoption and the types of uses being made of, say, e-mail by home and office users. This research was based on key questions about the "Why?" and "How?" of Internet use and continues in various forms today.

In line with rationalist explanations of media use, most perspectives on the impact of communication technologies in the organizational setting focus on the *technical* features. Thus, we would expect to be able to predict the social consequences of the automobile or the television or the personal computer (arguably the three most powerful new technologies of the last century) as an extension of the characteristics of the technologies themselves. This is true to some degree; for example, the automobile has "contained" people and "freed" them by its very nature. However, there are other important questions about possible effects of the introduction of a new technology.

Some writers focus on the inhibiting dimensions of mediated communication while others highlight and praise its potential to change and enrich the organization. For example, skeptics argue that electronic media filter out nonverbal cues and therefore inhibit the communication of social and emotional content like, for example, interest, anger, joy, or doubt. Thus, the so-called *"cues-filtered-out" model* has promoted an image of electronic media as impersonal, impoverishing interpersonal relations and reducing the quality of organizational life. *Think of examples that support this view. Consider whether you have personally experienced such a claim.* Proponents of electronic media, on the other hand, emphasize how such media allow organizations to establish new interactive links across organizational boundaries, facilitating open and responsive interactions with internal and external audiences. This is the view expressed in the popular book by Howard Rheingold entitled *Virtual Community*, as he explores the human side of cyberspace.[22] Rheingold is almost wholly optimistic about the capacity for the Internet to foster new forms of connection. Thus he says little about the decline of certain face-to-face communities (such as neighborhoods and civic groups) lamented by political scientist Robert Putnam in his now-famous book *Bowling Alone*,[23] which provides substantial evidence for its claim that civil society has gradually broken down as people have become more disconnected from other individuals, social groups, and society more generally.

So far, however, no research has consistently documented that the use of communication technologies cause the effects envisioned or feared by proponents or critics. A recent study by researchers at Carnegie Mellon University in Pittsburgh reveals mixed effects of Internet use. The project, which tracked a large group of Internet users over time, found that these users felt more, not less, connected with family, friends, and colleagues than for non-users.[24] This finding contrasts with the results of previous research on the social effects of Internet that revealed greater feelings of alienation and loneliness for regular Net users.[25] However, the Carnegie Mellon study also found that regular Internet users reported more stress and hassles in their lives than non-users. This finding is supported by a number of recent commentaries in the popular media, characterizing the wired among us as "relentlessly connected"—and reachable for work even when we're not at work.[26] Other researchers, for instance at UCLA, have already challenged these new findings, especially with regard to stress.[27] Of course, we should inquire whether those who are heavily engaged in e-mail use and surfing the Web are predisposed to be stressed out! The point is that the uses and effects of new technologies are complex and not always easily understood.

One reason for the lack of consistent results is the fact that new communication technologies rarely *replace* existing media. For example, when people are under pres-

"Hi. My name is Barry, and I check my E-mail two to three hundred times a day."

sure and need to meet a deadline, they may choose to e-mail the text transfer followed by a telephone conversation to make sure that the message has been received and understood. This happens frequently in organizations, even when the sender and receiver are located close to each other. Just as electronic mail has not replaced other types of mail, video conferencing has not replaced face-to-face meetings. Most media are complementary; new media may augment existing media without making them obsolete. A good example of this from the second half of the twentieth century is television. It was predicted in 1950, when TV programming and TV sets first became widely available in North America and Western Europe, that this would lead to the demise of radio. Today radio flourishes alongside TV, and both can be accessed through the Web!

Another reason for the lack of consistent research results is that new communication technologies—as we shall see later in this chapter—are not as different from traditional media as they are often assumed to be. Thus, while critics of communication technology tend to glorify face-to-face conversation as the standard by which all new media are evaluated, the proponents—especially within marketing and management—typically describe the interactive features of such media in ways that leave the impression that traditional media are pacifying and non-activating. The fact, for example, that television, radio, and other media do not allow the user to

Box 12.6 What Factors Make Technology Implementation Efforts Successful?

The following is a summary of factors that research has shown to increase the likelihood of successful implementation of new communication technologies. By successful implementation, we mean that the planned technology is installed and those for whom it was intended actually use the technology (primarily) as it was designed. Research from the media richness and social influence models figure prominently in these research findings.[28] Some of these ideas are similar to those discussed in chapter 11 about change in organizations.

- Politically skillful advocates secure top management support for the technology and control strategic resources
- External pressures encourage adoption change
- A strategic vision for implementation exists
- Users perceive the technology as part of a familiar genre of technology (that is, similar in some ways to previously used technologies)
- Users believe that the technology is information rich
- A critical mass of users develops or exists, especially in the immediate context
- People in users' networks have positive attitudes toward the technology
- Users are embedded in a social network that enables access to relevant resources and rules that enable the use of the technology
- Potential users having physical access to the technology and to the network of existing users
- Ongoing facilitation efforts encourage new ways to structure and use the technology
- Change agents experiment, get feedback, and modify the system accordingly
- Change agents encourage "hardiness" among users by enthusiasm, humor in early stages
- Change agents attend to resistance with patience, listening and, when needed, corrective action

Are there other ideas from chapter 11 that you could use to make the implementation of new communication technologies more successful?

talk back directly or to compose individualized information sequences *on* the medium is often taken as an indication that users of such media are passive participants in the communication process. This assumption is wrong. The reception of information is *always* an interactive process in which the receiver co-produces the meaning of the message.[29]

A good example of how new technologies can be a blend of features from more than one medium can be seen with e-mail, which has properties of both oral and written communication. On the one hand, e-mail has been praised for reviving "the lost art" of letter writing; on the other hand, e-mail has certain spontaneous and immediate features that make it akin to "orality." At least people often use e-mail that way. Instead of formulating e-mail messages as formal letters, beginning with a "Dear . . ." or a "Hi . . ." many people simply write the message as if a conversation were already going on. In a sense, e-mail is a new creation; from another point of view it reflects qualities of two known media. Because the technology is less than a quarter-century old, it's still too early to tell exactly which features will dominate. Interestingly, the courts are still arguing over whether standards of "libel" (for written matter) or "slander" (for the spoken word) should be consistently applied to e-mail.

First-level and Second-level Effects

To understand fully the different impacts of communication technology on contemporary organizations, it is useful to distinguish between first-level and second-level effects. First-level or first-order effects are the anticipated technical and practical effects used to justify the adoption of a particular technology. Second-level or second-order effects are those that come about because new communication technology leads people to pay attention to new and different things, organize and interpret relationships differently, and expect different outcomes from their actions.[30] While most of the first-level and some of the second-level effects can be imagined in advance, there are often unintended and unforeseen consequences, both good and bad.

First-level and second-level effects do not overrule each other but may well co-exist as a result of the same management efforts to make the organization more efficient,

Box 12.7 Some Effects of Organizational Communication Technologies

First-level effects:

- Acceleration and regularization of information flows
- Facilitation of information access
- Improvement of organizational flexibility and responsiveness
- Ease of monitoring activities
- New kinds of collaboration across space and time
- Greater capacity for storage of information
- Gains in productivity and efficiency
- Greater participation

Second-level effects:

- Proliferation of information/information overload
- Increased pressure on rapid turnaround on requests
- Increased work pressure
- More boundary-crossing communication
- Reduction in conformity
- Decrease in the power of traditional gatekeepers
- Surveillance and increased control

flexible, and responsive. Thus, for example, an organization may well be able to improve its responsiveness to customers by making it possible for them to e-mail questions to individual employees in the organization. The same possibility, however, may increase work pressure on employees to the effect of reducing their overall efficiency. This is exactly what happened to the Swedish SE Banken in the mid-1990s. Soon after having opened its e-mail channel to customers, it "drowned" in 40,000 unanswered messages!

One of the only things we can be sure about, regarding the introduction and use of a new communication technology, is that there will be surprises! For example, the introduction of the fax (or facsimile) machine in offices in the late 1980s was heralded as a way to transmit documents easily, saving time and postage. Although both benefits were attained, what was not anticipated was the enormous increase in the number of documents transmitted. Simultaneously, the pace of work accelerated. Since results could be transmitted almost instantaneously, people crammed more and more work into the period right up to a deadline. In the provocative book *Why Things Bite Back*, Edward Tenner shows how each new technology has created a number of unintended consequences, reminding us to "be careful what we ask for"![31] Another fine example is the prophecy in 1980 of a "paperless office" by 2000, inspired by confidence in the widespread adoption of PCs (personal computers). Instead, as Tenner observes, offices now consume two or three times as much paper! Indeed, implementing new technologies by no means results in predictable outcomes, as box 12.8 shows.

Box 12.8 Why Do So Many Communication Technologies Fail?[32]

If technology is the solution to so many of our problems, why is the attempt to implement communication technologies in organizations so often unsuccessful?

In early 2001, Ted started a research project focusing on the adoption and implementation of communication technologies. He looked for organizations that were in the early stages of planning or implementation so he could track the process. More than a year into the project, only one of the three projects had implemented the planned system. The other two were terminated before they ever had a chance to produce results—but *not* before they had a chance to soak up thousands of hours and tens of thousands of dollars. And the one that was implemented—the one "success story"—created massive resistance among its users.

Ted didn't start out to study failures or even organizations that looked likely to fail. In fact, he hoped to have a mix of successes and failures, so he could learn more about what facilitates and what obstructs managers' efforts to successfully implement communication technologies. Was he just unlucky? Perhaps, but failures in implementing communication technologies are common. Why is this scenario played out so often?

There isn't one simple answer, but a few insights from his research are worth mentioning. First, these systems are often justified by promised efficiencies; ironically, they typically *increase* the workload substantially, at least in the short term. In the one "successful" organization, many of the user groups had to hire extra staff just to keep up with the extra workload created. In *every* case, the planning, training, trials, and/or modifying took an enormous amount of time. In one of the terminated projects, management just seemed to grow tired of the delay between the time they first approved the project and the time they would receive a payoff.

Second, systems are often designed to do too much. Managers seem to think, "Well, if we're going to put in all this effort, we might as well put in every feature we might possibly use one day." *Big mistake.* Unfortunately, vendors often encourage this sort of thinking, since a bigger, more complex system means a bigger commission for them. The added complexity makes implementing, learning, and using the system that much more difficult. More can go wrong and, in all likelihood, it will. It's often better to design for short-term uses and upgrade and modify later.

Third, there's typically too little attention given to the human aspects of implementation—training and learning are certainly critical but persuading, consulting, coaching, and supporting users and other stakeholders are also necessary and frequently overlooked. One researcher concluded that ICT implementation ought to spend eight dollars on the "soft systems"—that is, the human dynamics—for every one dollar spent on technology. Too often, we forget that the machines are designed for people, not the other way around. Our own frailties—impatience, insecurity, and short attention spans (to name just a few) are often the biggest obstacles to successful implementation. Managers need to put more energy into working with the key stakeholders—particularly the users and key decision makers—and not just the technology.

Like other technologies and technologically-enabled activities, telecommuting can be seen or framed in terms of both first- and second-level effects. Initially romanticized in the late 1980s as universally liberating for employees (first-level effects), telecommuting is now understood to have mixed consequences for home life as well as diverse effects on relations among coworkers and colleagues (second-level effects). But, of course, much depends on how this work practice is understood and applied by each organization. In a fascinating study of the uses of telecommuting in a public-private hybrid organization organizational communication researchers Annika Hylmö and Patrice Buzzanell applied the cultural lenses of integration, differentiation, and fragmentation to reveal the diversity of ways in which telecommuting members understood the organization and what it means to work there.[33]

Personalness, Impersonality, and Hyperpersonality

In a now-classic article, interpersonal communication scholar Joseph Walther[34] offers a number of interesting and counter-intuitive insights into computer-mediated communication and its impact on interaction patterns in organizations. In contrast to the pessimistic notions of electronic media as impersonal, Walther points out that research on the impact of communication technology on interpersonal encounters and exchanges shows no consistent effects.[35] Although the technical features of technologies tend to depersonalize communication by filtering out nonverbal cues, users eventually learn to adapt their behaviors to the medium and thus become more personal when needed. The use of "emoticons" (as mentioned in chapter 6), symbols to indicate emotional intent, such as :-) and :-(in e-mail messages, is one example.

Walther even notes that—sometimes, at least—it is desirable to *foster* impersonal communication. Impersonality stimulates discipline, facilitates brainstorming, and helps focus attention on the immediate task at hand. He cites experiments that demonstrate the superiority of computer-mediated communication (group decision support systems, for example) over face-to-face communication in a number of significant ways, including idea generation and the quality of solutions. In an impersonal, electronic communication environment, people often feel freer to submit ideas and to comment on the quality of others' ideas. As a consequence, the number and the quality of ideas produced in such settings are usually higher. Thus, managers may choose to impose impersonality on specific work groups for strategic reasons.

In addition to its ability to stimulate a strong task-orientation in work groups, computer-mediated communication seems to facilitate more equal participation among organizational members.[36] Without the status cues that infuse and sometimes dominate face-to-face meetings, members of computer-mediated work groups become less conformist and tend to contribute more equally to the generation of ideas and solutions. Younger or lower-ranked members of the organization, for example, who typically hold back on comments and ideas in conventional meetings, feel less restrained in an impersonal communication environment in which their identity is less conspicuous. In this way, computer-mediated communication can "democratize" organizational communication processes. While this equality tends to produce a greater diversity of ideas than we typically find in face-to-face groups, one

Box 12.9 E-mail Use in Organizations

As the most prevalent type of computer-mediated communication, e-mail and its use in the organizational setting can tell us a lot about the social impacts of new technologies. While early research demonstrated a remarkable diversity in the use of electronic mail[37]—some people were extremely adept in using e-mail while others were overwhelmed or out of control—later research has confirmed this finding and added a new level of complexity to our understanding of this medium.[38]

In addition to differences in patterns of individual use, research has found that e-mail may have a "booster effect" at the group level. Work groups that use e-mail typically have a higher level of communication than those who don't, which indicates that e-mail is not a simple substitute for other media. Something new happens in terms of the overall quantity of communication.

At a qualitative level, it has been found that e-mail, because it filters out nonverbal cues, can supply a coordinated focus and thus accommodate bigger work groups than face-to-face interactions. Moreover, the lack of such cues facilitates more open and equal discussion, typically leading to knowledge-based rather than status-based decisions. On the other hand, e-mail may also reduce the value of expertise and may function as an "undiscriminating muffler of all differences."[39] To offset such effects, users sometimes add nonverbal information, for example about status, through their "signatures" (the information that e-mail systems let users design to automatically include at the end of each message, such as job titles or quotations).

E-mail fosters nonconforming behavior and disagreement and generally hinders the emergence of leaders. We see this both in the language used in e-mail (where conflicts and explicit language, "flaming,"[40] are common occurrences) and in the difficulties e-mail groups typically exhibit in reaching consensus. On the other hand, e-mail links people and workgroups over space, time, and other boundaries; this effect helps maintain weaker ties, integrates peripheral members of the organization, stimulates the feeling of belongingness, and eventually relieves workplace stress.

Finally, it's been suggested that e-mail may be (mis)used to organize social events or collective action against management or to disseminate misinformation, rumors, complaints, or jokes. This fear may explain the policy in many organizations against privacy in e-mail communications. While many organizations warn their employees against misuse of e-mail, others routinely monitor e-mail content[41]—even though it has been argued that social use of e-mail facilitates more rapid learning of the system.[42]

What is your opinion of such policies? Think of the consequences in terms of privacy, organizational efficiency and productivity, and quality of work life. Why do you think it is more difficult to reach consensus in e-mail groups?

important drawback of computer-mediated groups is that they generally have more difficulty reaching consensus about decisions than do face-to-face groups.[43]

Walther attributes the differences identified between computer-mediated communication and face-to-face communication to the fact that most experiments involving communication technology so far have taken place in one-time-only work groups with no expectations of future interaction. Where this condition is no longer present—like in most organizational work situations—participants can be expected to gradually adapt their communication behaviors to become more personal. As we know from other kinds of human interaction, our attitudes toward other people are often influenced by the chances that we will meet or work with them again. In other words, expectations about possible future interaction, not the medium itself, determine how personal the interaction will be. Maintaining that face-to-face encounters are the only ideal communication situations thus becomes problematic.

Perhaps it is more realistic, as Walther points out, to compare computer-mediated communication with the construction of a text. Because certain cues are absent in electronic encounters, participants enjoy the freedom to construct and manage their "self" as a text, for example through selective self-presentation. The asynchronicity of some electronic media (for example, electronic mail) underscores this tendency. Computer-mediated communication allows for what Walther calls "hyperpersonal" communication—communication that highlights and stages certain personal characteristics and downplays others. Some people even take on other identities—a different name or another gender, for example—when they surf or chat on the Internet. As we gain experience with new kinds of organizational arrangements, like virtual organizations and "telework," we will no doubt need to be more aware of this interesting second-level effect of communication technology. Finally, the technology-adoption curve, discussed in box 12.10, presents another reason not to be too quick to jump to conclusions about the effects of new technologies.

Box 12.10 Intranets and the Technology-Adoption Curve

An intranet is an application of the "principles and protocols of the Internet . . . to a private network [that] enables people to communicate within organizations."[44] Most large organizations today—including the college or university where you're studying—have an intranet. The network is protected from the outside by "firewalls" or technology that prohibits non-members from accessing its contents. Intranets are often touted as a means to improve employee communication within organizations. However, many organizations use them in a very limited way. One researcher has suggested that there are four phases of intranet development:[45] (1) posting documents, or "brochure ware"; for example, putting the employee handbook online; (2) providing access to personal data, such as number of sick days taken or the amount earned in one's retirement account; (3) enabling one-way transactions, such as allowing employees to enroll in a company-sponsored training program; and (4) employee-to-employee (or "E2E") information sharing, such as "chat rooms" or "bulletin boards" on technical, business, or personal issues.

The fourth phase is where employee communication begins to merge with "knowledge management" (see box 3.5) applications. Some organizations encourage discussions on business or technical issues and attempt to capture the knowledge conveyed and make it available to key decision makers. However, many organizations have not gotten beyond the first phase. One explanation for this is the "technology-adoption curve."[46] This refers to the idea that we tend to use new technologies initially in ways similar to familiar technologies—for example, early PC users treated the PC as a "fancy typewriter." With experience, we begin to experiment and use the new technologies differently, finding innovative applications. As corporate communication specialists gain experience with intranets, they may begin to use them in innovative ways. Certainly some organizations are already doing so. Thus, we need to be careful not to judge new technologies as "failures" too quickly.

Apply the idea of the technology-adoption curve to your own experiences with new technologies (hardware or software). How did your use of the technology change with experience? Can you see how we might explain the technology-adoption curve using structuration theory (see chapter 3)? Can we learn to structure our communication in ways that make better use of the technology's possibilities?

Interacting with the Market

The idea of establishing new interactive and responsive links between organizations and their markets is one of the most prominent expectations associated with contemporary communication technologies. This trend applies not only to private, for-profit firms but also to government agencies, hospitals, labor unions, universities, and charity organizations. We use "market" in a broad sense to include the various stakeholders that form and surround an organization. Based on the ability of media to facilitate fast, two-way communication relatively independent of time and space, many managers and decision makers envision radically new types of exchanges between organizations and their markets—and such exchanges already exist in various forms. Many organizations, for example, conduct business—"e-business"—via the Internet. Products as varied as books, CDs, real estate, and pornography are offered on Web sites. But information technology (including the use of bar codes) can also be used to track sales and thus secure a swifter response to changes in consumer demand.

The inauguration of e-commerce in the 1990s was accompanied by tremendous hype, but now most observers are settling into a more careful, nuanced assessment of its role and appropriateness. In the early 2000s some companies abandoned parts of their e-commerce strategies because such strategies were not profitable or because their customers expressed preferences for telephone-mediated or even face-to-face interactions. In the financial services industry, for instance, many people will not trust their money with a person they do not know, with whom they cannot shake hands. Other companies (like Levi Strauss or Bang & Olufsen) have decided not to do business via the Internet because the Internet as a medium reduces the status or "aura" associated with their products.

Many organizations, however, expect communication technologies to be useful for more than exhibiting and selling products and services. While some organizations exchange information regularly with customers through electronic mail, others maintain chat rooms for stakeholders and other interested parties. For example, Shell Oil has received substantial attention for the "Tell Shell" feature of their Web site, where they post uncensored messages, including those from critics.[47] (Take a look yourself at www.shell.com). Based on the input from such exchanges, organizations are expected to become increasingly responsive to wishes and demands from their surroundings.

Box 12.11 E-Commerce and E-Business

Electronic commerce, or e-commerce, can be seen as a subset of e-business. Whereas the term *e-business* is typically used to describe conducting any aspect of an organization's work online, those aspects of e-business that involve buying and selling information, products, and services are considered e-commerce. E-business has been one of the hottest management trends in the past five years. This is perhaps not surprising, since organizations see the opportunity for expanding existing businesses and developing new ones. The often-touted potential benefits of e-business include:

- Access to a 24-hour worldwide market, all weekdays, all year round (known as "24/7/365")
- Greater number of suppliers, employees, partners, customers
- Faster stock turnover, with streamlined ordering and delivery (efficient "supply chains")
- More complete and immediate market information to guide decisions
- More responsiveness to customers and partners
- More flexibility for and productivity from employees (since they can work at home and use communication technologies to enhance their effectiveness)

Management researcher David Rigby analyzed the rhetoric of large consulting firms in their promotion of e-business in New Zealand.[48] He found the consulting firms tended to portray the "e" economy as chaotic and dangerous yet one that must be embraced for businesses to survive and prosper. Not surprisingly, the consulting firms positioned themselves as uniquely prepared to guide organizations through this chaos. In fact, each offered a set of steps that would lead to success. As Rigby says, the steps outlined for e-business adoption are persuasive because they offer a reassuringly simple, definite path in the face of complexity. Below is an example of steps presented by the consulting firm Cap Gemini Ernst & Young, adapted from Rigby's summary:

Stage One: "eInformation." The company's Web site provides one-way information to customers (product information), suppliers (inventory needs), employees (job postings, online manuals), and shareholders (annual report). "Disseminating information is fast, cheap, reliable; what was once too unwieldy to distribute can now be readily posted."

Stage Two: "eInteraction." Online links with parties inside and outside the company become two-way conduits for information. For example, "greater connectivity fosters customer and vendor feedback, yielding a steady flow of intelligence about products and service levels and enriching relationships."

Stage Three: "eCommerce." Integration of front- and back-office systems so that "companies can fully transact with their constituents." "Data needn't be re-entered at every point and knowledge can be disseminated and leveraged throughout the company." Online transactions, online stock availability, order tracking become possible.

Stage Four: "The eCompany." "The company's borders extend beyond its own doors." Companies bundle services and collaborate with partners. Employees can work from anywhere. "The supply chain reaches new efficiencies which can make holding full inventory unnecessary." "With enhanced connectivity senior management can rapidly assess the profitability of its business relationships, as well as manage the process more dynamically."

Stage Five: "eConomy." The company is positioned as "the central star in a constellation of products and services encompassing related service providers, including perhaps even competitors." A "community" solution is provided, a one-stop-shop offering everything from products and services to knowledge bases, distance learning, question and answer areas, and collaborative capability. Results in "greater pricing efficiencies for both buyer (savings) and seller (competitive advantage)."

In particular, it is often assumed that electronic media will stimulate activity on the part of consumers so that organizations receive more accurate and relevant feedback and thus adapt faster and more efficiently to external changes. This is certainly an important potential of such media. The capacity of contemporary communication technologies for bi-directionality, rapid exchange, larger volume of transaction per time unit (bandwidth), and increases in user activity explain why these media often are referred to as "interactive media." Traditional mass communication media (for example, television, radio, and billboards) confine the receiver within a delineated set of information options; more recent communication technologies (such as decision support systems and the Internet) make it possible for individual users to specify their own information requirements, to compare information across various suppliers, to address suppliers directly, and to receive more rapid responses to their requests. As we've noted, these technologies allow the user to provide feedback in the form of comments or orders to the supplier. Communication technologies, thus, imply more communication links and a higher degree of user control.

This potential, however, is not necessarily realized. The systems of "interactivity" set up by most organizations are often limited to machine interactivity—interactivity with the system without the direct involvement of another person. Other systems include persons but allow simply for increased conversation (chat rooms, for example) without direct implications for organizational practice. Although communication technologies offer unprecedented options for the user to control the *flow* and the *combination* of information, the applications of such technologies in practice rarely move beyond that. As Ian Miles puts it, they primarily allow the user to "select among items of material supplied by information providers, according to the user's requests for information."[49] Moreover, modifications of information for individual needs are typically restricted to the presentation of the information in alternative combinations or alternative forms.

One example is the option offered by some groups of travel agencies to compare prices across firms. On certain Web sites for charter holidays, for example, customers can enter the dates they would like to travel, the maximum amount of money they are willing to pay, and perhaps, their expectations about hotels and services. The Web page then offers a range of options from different travel agencies. Although such options and features are very practical in saving time and providing the user with a general overview of the market, the interactivity they offer typically takes place within a universe largely constructed by producers and *their* ideas about what could be of interest to their audience. As a consequence, the dialogues and responsive measures that organizations set up through the use of Internet-based communication technologies may not necessarily help organizations adapt to external changes.

Perhaps this is because interactivity is not all that new. Without denying differences in interactivity between different media, Miles points out that the potentialities of new communication technologies, like the Internet, are not as unique as often assumed:

> An exchange of conventional letter post might be considered interactive, even if individual media vehicles (letters) present information in a linear sequence. The interactivity between the two parties concerned is here slow and drawn-out over time, but exchanges of letters can be quite conversational. Turning to published products, many people confronted with new interactive media will say that a book is an ideally interactive communication product, since they can rapidly flick through it, examine pages in different sequences, take time to make notes, and so on. . . . In the case of teletext or a printed book, the user's sense of interactivity is

> gained by controlling the information flow through choosing to view particular pages, in a particular order, but not by influencing the content of these pages.[50]

Miles does not reject the idea of interactivity but indicates degrees and possible limits of interactivity among the more well-known communication technologies like the Internet.

Communication scholar Sheizaf Rafaeli[51] argues that interactivity is *not* a characteristic of media. While media and communication channels set some upper bounds for interactivity, it is *the actual use* of a medium that determines the level of interactivity in each particular situation. As a consequence, systems that set up possibilities for feedback do not ensure interactivity *per se.* Interactivity, according to Rafaeli, refers to the extent that communication reflects back on itself—that is, feeds on and responds to past messages. Interactivity is a subset of feedback: "feedback that relates both to previous messages and to the way previous messages related to those preceding them." For full interactivity to take place, communication roles, according to Rafaeli, need to be interchangeable, and turn-taking needs to be non-automatic. *Why do you think Rafaeli highlights these features of interactivity?*

Box 12.12 Voices from the Field

Dance Against the Machine: Cyborg Performances, Masculinity, and Arcade-Based Dance Games in Public Spaces
Cassandra Van Buren, University of Utah

Student unions in many colleges and universities have a new addition to their array of activities: dance machines, which are partly electronic, partly mechanical, and which invite the active but structured participation of users. These machines are sometimes placed next to video games or pinball machines. Other times, they are featured in hallways, corridors, and rooms. In some locations they are in almost constant use, and they attract the attention of many onlookers. In the University of Utah's student union, for example, a large area is dedicated to two of these machines and to the people who crowd around them.

Through the use of time- and pressure-sensitive input devices, arcade-based dance games such as Konami's Dance Dance Revolution (DDR) enable one or two players to compete against the machine or against each other by trying to match precisely the timing and placement of dance steps as represented on the game's display screen. Games such as DDR have also captured the attention of communication scholars working on the ways in which new entertainment technologies engage the concepts of embodiment, simulation, interactivity, and identity within social contexts. Based on preliminary observation of players at video game arcades, the overwhelming majority of players were young males who appeared to use the game as a locus of masculine social interaction. The users have universally serious, almost severe, facial expressions, and the audience usually watches them intently. Matching the findings from scholarship about video games, semiotics, gender studies, and cybernetic systems, it seems that DDR players do not dance so much as they display their ability to simulate robotic athleticism, fully consistent with the traditionally "masculinized" space of the video game arcade.

What do you observe about the popularity of DDR and other dance machines? How do they differ from other arcade games? What sorts of interactions do they allow or encourage? Why do you think the machines are used in the ways Van Buren describes? Is there something about the technology and/or the video arcade tradition that constrains interaction in these ways? What are the implications for public spaces in organizations and communities?

In most cases, what organizations label "interactivity" merely refers to increases in simple reciprocity. To mistake the features of bi-directionality, rapid exchange, and larger volumes of transaction per time unit with interactivity is, according to Rafaeli, to reduce the notion of interaction to *re*action—combined, sometimes, with some options for chitchat. As a consequence, consumers may not be nearly as "powerful" as organizations seem to imagine. Moreover, the kind of feedback that organizations obtain through so-called interactive media may not provide them with the new input necessary to adapt to changing circumstances.

Still, communication technology is often envisioned as an enemy of traditional bureaucracy and as a facilitator of organizational change. However, management researchers Daniel Robey and Ana Azevedo have found that communication technology may stimulate change while at the same time creating persistence in organizational cultures. While technologies have the potential to trigger important organizational transformations, they also "can help to sustain cultural values by

Box 12.13 Communication Technology and Democracy

Many researchers hope that contemporary communication technologies will democratize organizations and societies. Although their notions of democracy vary, they seem to share the expectation that computer-mediated communication will play an important role in the evolution of democracy.[52] While computerization simultaneously allows for increased centralization, surveillance, and control, communication technologies are often seen as enemies of totalitarianism. By facilitating a general access to information in addition to greater possibilities for interaction, and thus more direct forms of participation, communication technologies have important democratic potentials. Research on Web-based community networks, for example, demonstrates that such networks are able to reinvigorate local community life while simultaneously linking their users to issues of global reach and relevance.[53]

Interestingly, however, Web-based networks are often governed in non-democratic ways, allowing members access to information but no *formal* voice in decision making.[54] And even when governance *is* democratic, we need to ask ourselves whether the conversations that they facilitate are inherently democratic. While communication technologies allow for instant responses, they tend to discourage second thoughts and to minimize concern for others. The debates taking place in Web-based discussion forums, thus, are more often characterized by reflex than by reflection, with frequent cases of "flaming" and other forms of verbal harassment. And if we look at the content of debates in many discussion forums, there's a tendency for the growing individualism that we observe in society at large to become even more pronounced. When citizens, for example, address their local politicians via the net they tend to focus more on their private interests than on the community in which the live.[55]

In any case, we need to specify what we mean by "democracy" before we assess the democratizing effects of new communication technologies. Only then can we decide how technologies can be designed to facilitate our democratic goals. If we conceptualize democracy only in terms of information *access*, our model of communication will be significantly different than if we believe democracy is based on direct participation.

What models of communication are implied in these two perspectives? Can you think of alternatives? Does access to information about the happenings in distant communities strengthen or weaken local ties? Do you think Web-based discussion forums contribute to self-interest or to greater concern about joint participation in addressing problems?

embedding them in organizational routines."[56] For example, the CEO of a New Zealand not-for-profit organization worked to design a new knowledge management system that would change the organization toward being more "professional and long-term" in its approach, while social workers in the same organization lobbied to design the system in ways that enabled them to maintain certain cherished values, like branch office autonomy and privacy for clients.[57] Can you think of other examples in which communication technologies can foster or enable resistance to change? Communication technology is marked by paradoxes and ambiguities; its role in organizations and society is by no means clear-cut and settled.

New Organizations?

To conclude this chapter, we will briefly highlight some of the "reorganizing potentials" of new communication technologies. Using the lens of communication technologies provides an opportunity to summarize major findings in the chapter while imagining a number of potential changes in and around contemporary organizations. In fact, several of these changes are already taking place.[58]

Based on Giddens's structuration theory, some writers have argued that communication technology is interrelated with organizational structure.[59] Wanda Orlikowsky, for example, points out that while technology (and technology use) is a product of human action, it also assumes structural properties.[60] Technology, thus, can become a substitute for communication, as when, for example, certain issues and options are not discussed because solutions and decisions are already given by the technology. For example, imagine a drop-down menu on a computer program or an automated answering service, each of which specifies a limited range of options while excluding others you might like to consider. As a consequence of its structuring qualities, communication technology must be seen as both enabling and constraining the organization.

In fact, the very same structuring properties that enable technologies to facilitate organizational responsiveness and change can also be used to prevent change. While technologies, for example, can help organizations establish new communication links with their customers through online services, the same technologies can be used as buffers to avoid the need to respond by directing customers to the FAQ (frequently asked questions) section on the Web. In such examples, we can see how openness and closure are closely linked.

Consequently, we need to reconsider our notion of "rational" technology use. For example, communication technology is often presented as a means to make organizations more effective, either because it allows them to handle more information or because it makes it possible for them to align their activities better with external demands. Indeed, many organizations take advantage of these features. But with the increasing pressure to process more information more quickly, however, information overload is a real danger. Under such circumstances, the tendency to focus on "need-to-know" information that simply confirms established ideas becomes more likely.[61] The inability to cope with the growing mountains of information may imply a new kind of organizational blindness. Although structural change seems to be embedded in the features of new communication technologies, the willingness of organizations to change may not be as pronounced as the techno-optimists tend to assume.

Organizational changes, however, may come about more indirectly from the use of new technologies. That is, new technologies may effect changes in interaction patterns, communication ideals, informality, and other dimensions of organizational culture. For example, in a networked or virtual organization, in which members are linked primarily through computers, the informal or grapevine communication that is so important to the socialization process takes on a new dimension. Additionally, by making it possible to establish new "virtual" types of (sub)organizations and new communities of interest, communication technologies make it easier to maintain weaker ties inside and outside the organization and allow users to blend work and personal relationships. For example, the four of us regularly e-mail colleagues around the world for a source of information or an insight into a problem we're facing in our work.

All these developments, in turn, have significant implications for organizational identity. Identity is, as we've seen, one of the most salient issues for contemporary organizations. Communication technologies, however, tend to blur organizational boundaries and challenge traditional notions of what the organization "is." With the adoption of such technologies, organizations not only face new imperatives to assert their identities, but they also feel a growing pressure to integrate their communications across formal organizational boundaries—to express themselves the same way to different audiences. As organizations, due to their presence on the Internet, feel increasingly transparent to the gaze of various (and often critical) audiences, the managerial emphasis on integration is likely to become more pronounced. One possible outcome of integration is a centralization of communication at the corporate level.

At the same time, however, communication technologies facilitate flatter, and—in some respects—more decentralized structures, which in turn necessitate new types of leadership. On the one hand, communication technologies provide better opportunities for managers and executives to interact with staff and to enact leadership more easily across time and space. Thus, managers may now lead a team with members in several different parts of the planet. On the other hand, the equalizing effects of communication technologies both enable more people to provide leadership and may make it more difficult for someone to lead solely on the basis of their position. Communication technologies, in other words, foster higher expectations for participation across formal boundaries.

Clearly, communication technologies introduce new types of conflict or potential conflicts in organizations. In addition to problems of "flaming" and other kinds of verbal harassment, organizations will have to deal with problems related to the equalizing effects of computer-mediated communication, which allow for more participation but simultaneously make it more difficult to build consensus in decision-making situations. Moreover, due to their increased accessibility to consumers and other external audiences, organizations simultaneously face conflicts outside their formal boundaries. To many managers, these developments call for new forms of control and surveillance inside and outside the organizational setting. Communication technologies make it possible to count keystrokes or to monitor e-mail content inside the organization, just as they facilitate tracking the behavior of external constituencies (for example, customers or competitors). Communication technologies may also control work processes in less obtrusive ways, for example, through the prestructuring, categorization, and labeling of tasks, scenarios, or stakeholders.

Due to communication technologies like the Internet, all organizational communication is potentially global in reach. Indeed, communication technology can be seen as a primary driver of globalization. At the same time, technologies make it possible to emphasize and serve local interests, for example, through Web-based communities. One important challenge to contemporary organizations when communicating in electronic media, thus, is the balancing of local interests and global concerns—for example, maintaining a unified, global image while adapting to local conditions and needs.

There are important ethical challenges as well. In a number of respects, communication technologies put pressure on organizations to strive for more openness, participation, and accountability vis-à-vis internal and external audiences. At the same time, such technologies tend to formalize ethical behavior by standardizing openness, participation, and accountability within a specific format. For example, by using transparency as an explicit strategy (recurrently posting certain types of information, such as environmental reports, on their Web page) some organizations potentially reduce ethics to a marketing issue. Thus, scholars and practitioners of organizational communication need to consider how organizations can face the ethical challenges brought forth by new communication technologies without reducing ethics to window dressing.

Finally, if we look at communication technology as a specific "text" within the organizational setting, we need to develop our ability to "read" such technology—both as a message in itself and as meta-text that talks about certain conditions, values, and expectations in the contemporary "Information Society."

Snapshot Synthesis

Whether we conceive of technology narrowly as tools or machines to accomplish specific ends or more broadly as a mindset or an orientation toward the world, there is no doubt that communication technologies have a tremendous impact on contemporary organizations and societies. While information has become a highly valued commodity, our ability to process information quickly and precisely has improved—and is still improving—significantly. Computer-assisted communication technologies, thus, have made it possible to transmit texts, images, and sound within seconds to any location on the globe. At the same time, computer-assisted decision-making technologies facilitate sophisticated decision-making procedures that require the processing and comparison of large quantities of data. Networks of computers and networks of networks link decision makers and other organizational members effectively with other users within and outside of the organization. Finally, computer-assisted manufacturing technologies allow organizations to transform product specifications into machine settings or to adjust production flows to continuous changes in demand. The reorganizing potentials of current communication technologies are not trivial.

The potentials of communication technologies, however, are rarely realized exactly as their designers envisioned. This is true not only because technologies are implemented differently by different organizations, but also because technology use is only partially rational, because the uses of communication technologies communicate several things at once (e.g., as tools *and* as symbols of status and power), and because there are a host of unexpected outcomes of technology use. As a consequence, the organizational effects of using communication technologies are not clear cut and settled once and for all. While some researchers, for example, have argued that communication technologies limit human communication because they filter out nonverbal and personal cues, others have argued that impersonality in communication is an advantage in decision making because it facilitates a strong task orientation that's more concerned with expertise than with status and tenure. The fears, hopes, and expectations that people hold with respect to technology are interesting in and of themselves, particularly to the extent that our perceptions enact our organizational futures.

Among the most prominent expectations of organizational technology use is the belief that technology will help organizations to develop more responsive communication links with their surroundings, primarily with their customers. While some organizations *have* been able to become more responsive to external audiences by developing sophisticated systems of interactivity, others seem to use the technology to establish new buffers between themselves and their environments. Contemporary communication technologies are truly equivocal media and their role in changing organizations and organizational communication is still in flux.

Key Concepts

- **Technology:** the application of a specific logic of technique to the domain of human activity and behavior
- **Technique:** a non-natural actualization of possibilities inherent in the physical world; derived from the Greek word *teucho*, the act of causing, bringing about, or bringing into existence
- **Organizational Communication Technologies**: computer-assisted (includes electronic mail, fax, computer and video conferencing, voice mail, and audio conferencing); computer-assisted decision-making technologies (include management information systems, group decision support systems, expert systems, and external information retrieval systems); local and wide area networks of computers (for example, intranets); networks of networks (for example, the Internet); and computer-assisted manufacturing technologies (such as computer-aided design and computer-aided engineering) enhance the flow of communication in organizations
- **Features of Communication Technologies**: enhance the *speed* of communication; facilitate immediate *access to information;* enable complex *information exchanges across different geographical locations;* enable *monitoring* of employees; *fast processing* of large amounts of data
- **Asynchronous Communication**: communication that proceeds interactively, outside of "real time"; for example, e-mail and voice mail allow the sender to leave a message without the requirement of the receiver being present
- **Technological Determinism**: technological innovations lead predictably and necessarily to certain transformations of society (or organizations)
- **Critical Mass Theory**: the adoption of a medium as a function of the size of the community of users; a "tipping point" reached when the proportion of users is sufficiently large to sustain the technology

- **Media Richness Theory**: framework for understanding the media choices of organizational actors; hypothesizes that managers choose a communication medium suitable for handling the level of ambiguity of the task
- **The Social Influence Model:** media choices influenced by existing communication patterns in the organization and the influences of peers and coworkers in an ongoing evaluation and use of new media
- **The Dual Capacity Model**: every communication medium has the capacity to convey data and symbols; in its symbol-carrying capacity, the technology itself becomes the message
- **The "Cues-filtered-out" Hypothesis:** the electronic media filter out nonverbal cues, inhibiting the communication of social and emotional content such as interest, anger, joy, or doubt
- **First-level Effects**: technical and anticipated practical effects used to justify the adoption of a particular technology
- **Second-level Effects**: effects that emerge because new communication technology leads people to pay attention to new and different things, to organize and interpret relationships differently, and to expect different outcomes from their actions
- **Flaming**: blunt electronic discussions that can escalate to name-calling and epithets
- **Hyperpersonal Communication**: highlights certain personal characteristics and downplays others
- **The Technology-Adoption Curve**: new technologies initially used in ways similar to familiar technologies, over time innovative applications emerge through experimentation
- **E-commerce and E-business**: e-business is the conducting of any aspect of an organization's work online; aspects of e-business that involve buying and selling information, products, and services are considered e-commerce
- **Interactivity**: the extent to which communication reflects back on itself by reacting and responding to past messages (not a characteristic of the medium itself)

Endnotes

[1] Lucas D. Introna, "Being, Technology and Progress: A Critique of Information Technology," *Transforming Organizations with Information Technology*, ed. Richard Baskerville et al. (Amsterdam: North-Holland, 1994) pp. 277–299.

[2] Cornelius Castoriadis, *Crossroads in the Labyrinth* (Cambridge: MIT Press, 1984).

[3] Castoriadis, p. 242.

[4] Theodore Roszak, *The Cult of Information: The Folklore of Computers and the True Art of Thinking* (New York: Pantheon Books, 1986) p. 8.

[5] See also Karleen H. Roberts and Martha Grabowsky, "Organizations, Technology and Structuring," *Handbook of Organization Studies*, ed. Stewart R. Clegg, Cynthia Hardy, and Walther R. Nord (London: Sage, 1990) pp. 409–423.

[6] Lee Sproull and Sara Kiesler, *Connections: New Ways of Working in the Networked Organization*. (Cambridge: MIT Press, 1992).

[7] Sproull and Kiesler.

[8] Angela Tretheway and Steven Corman, "Anticipating K-Commerce: E-Commerce, Knowledge Management, and Organizational Communication," *Management Communication Quarterly* 14.4 (2001): 619–628.

[9] See, for example, Jacques Ellul, *The Technological Society* (New York: Vintage Books, 1964); Introna.

[10] E.g., Neil Postman, *Technopoly: The Surrender of Culture to Technology.* (New York: Vintage Books, 1992).

11 Ronald E. Rice and Jane Webster, "Adoption, Diffusion and Use of New Media in Organization Settings," *Communication Technology and Society*, ed. David Akin and Caroly Lin (Cresskill, NJ: Hampton Press, 2000) pp. 191–227.

12 Malcom Gladwell, *The Tipping Point, How Little Things Can Make a Big Difference* (Boston: Little, Brown and Company, 2000).

13 Richard L. Daft and Robert H. Lengel, "Information Richness: A New Approach to Managerial Information Processing and Organizational Design," *Research in Organizational Behavior 6*, ed. Barry M. Staw and Lawrence L. Cummings (Greenwich, CT: JAI-Press, 1984) pp. 191–233.

14 Daft and Lengel.

15 Ronald E. Rice and Urs E. Gattiker, "New Media and Organizational Structuring," *The New Handbook of Organizational Communication*, ed. Linda L. Putnam and Fredric M. Jablin (Thousand Oaks, CA: Sage, 2001) pp. 544–584.

16 Noshir S. Contractor and Eric M. Eisenberg, "Communication Networks and New Media in Organizations," *Organizations and Communication Technology*, ed. Janet Fulk and Charles W. Steinfield (Newbury Park: Sage, 1990) p. 143.

17 Janet Fulk, Joseph Schmitz and Charles W. Steinfield, "A Social Influence Model of Technology Use," *Organizations and Communication Technology*, ed. Janet Fulk and Charles W. Steinfield (Newbury Park: Sage, 1990) pp. 117–140.

18 Andrew Flanagin, "Social Pressures on Organizational Website Adoption," *Human Communication Research* 26 (2000): 618–646.

19 Marshall McLuhan and Quentin Fiore, *The Medium is the Message* (London: Allen Lane, 1967).

20 *The Wall Street Journal Online* (abridged). <http://zdnet.com.com/2100-11-502314.html?legacy=zdnn> accessed 9 August 2002.

21 John W. Meyer and Brian Rowan, "Institutional Organizations: Formal Structure as Myth and Ceremony," *American Journal of Sociology* 83 (1977): 340–363.

22 Howard Rheingold, *The Virtual Community: Homesteading on the Electronic Frontier* (New York: Harper Collins, 1994).

23 Robert Putnam, *Bowling Alone: The Collapse and Revival of American Community* (New York: Simon & Schuster, 2001).

24 Robert Kraut, Sara Kiesler, Bonka Boneva, Jonathan Cummings, Vicki Helgeson, and Anne Crawford, "Internet Paradox Revisited," *The Journal of Social Issues* 58:1 (2002): 49–74.

25 Robert Kraut, Vicki Lundmark, Michael Patterson, Sara Kiesler, Tridas Mukopadhyay, and William Scherlis, "Internet Paradox: A Social Technology that Reduces Social Involvement and Psychological Well-Being?" *American Psychologist* 53 (1998):1017–1031.

26 James Gleick, "Inescapably, Obsessively, Totally Connected," *The New York Times Magazine* 22: (April 2001): 62ff.

27 Karen Kaplan, "More Time Online Means Higher Stress," *The Los Angeles Times* (29 July 2001) (as reported in *The Missoulian*, Missoula, Montana, 29 July 2001, p. D1).

28 This summary is abstracted from the following sources: Rice and Gattiker; Tarek Tantoush and Stewart Clegg, "Cadcam Integration and the Practical Politics of Technological Change," *Journal of Organizational Change Management* 14:1 (2001): 9–27; Theodore E. Zorn, "The Emotionality of Information and Communication Technology Implementation," *Journal of Communication Management* 7 (2002): 160–171.

29 Umberto Eco, *The Role of the Reader* (Bloomington: Indiana University Press, 1979); Wolfgang Iser, *The Implied Reader*. (Baltimore, MD: Johns Hopkins, 1974).

30 Sproull and Kiesler.

31 Edward Tenner, *Why Things Bite Back: Technology and the Revenge of Unintended Consequences* (New York: Knopf, 1996).

32 This box is adapted from Theodore Zorn, "Why Do So Many ICT Projects Fail?" *The Dominion* (29 July 2002).

33 Annika Hylmö and Patrice M. Buzzanell, "Telecommuting as Viewed through Cultural Lenses: An Empirical Investigation of the Discourses of Utopia, Identity, and Mystery," *Communication Monographs* 69 (2002): 329–356.

34 Joseph B. Walther, "Computer-Mediated Communication: Impersonal, Interpersonal, and Hyperpersonal Interaction," *Communication Research* 23:1 (1996): 3–34.

35 See also Richard S. Baskerville et al., *Transforming Organizations with Information Technology* (Amsterdam: North-Holland, 1994); Laura Garton and Barry Wellman, "Social Impacts of Electronic Mail in Organizations: A Review of the Research Literature," *Communication Yearbook* 18 (1995): 434–453.

[36] Walther; see also Sproull and Kiesler.
[37] Wendy E. Mackay, "Diversity in the Use of Electronic Mail: A Preliminary Inquiry," *ACM Transactions on Office Information System* 6:4 (1988): 380–397. See also Rob Kling, ed., *Computerization and Controversy*, 2nd ed. (San Diego: Academic Press, 1996).
[38] Garton and Wellman.
[39] Garton and Wellman, p. 441.
[40] "Flaming" refers the escalation of blunt electronic discussions into name-calling and epithets. Sproull and Kiesler (p. 49) explain that electronic mail has made talk, actions, and decisions more extreme and impulsive because communicators lack tangible reminders of the audience and as a consequence tend to forget the norms for appropriate behavior.
[41] Rice and Webster.
[42] Charles W. Steinfield, "Computer-Mediated Communications in the Organization: Using Electronic Mail at Xerox," *Case Studies in Organizational Communication*, ed. Beverly Davenport Sypher (New York: The Guilford Press, 1990) pp. 282–294.
[43] Garton and Wellman; Walther.
[44] Marie E. Murgolo-Poore and Leyland F. Pitt, "Intranets and Employee Communication: PR Behind the Firewall," *Journal of Communication Management* 5:3 (2001): 235.
[45] Harvard Management Update, "The New Uses of Intranets," (May 2000). Reprint no. U0005B; see also Murgolo-Poore and Pitt, 231–241.
[46] Shel Holtz, *Public Relations on the Net: Winning Strategies to Inform and Influence the Media, the Investment Community, the Government, the Public, and More!* 2nd ed. (New York: AMA Publications, 1999); See also Murgolo-Poore and Pitt, 231–241.
[47] Sharon M. Livesey, "The Discourse of the Middle Ground: Citizen Shell Commits to Sustainable Development," *Management Communication Quarterly* 15 (2001): 313–349.
[48] David J. Rigby, "Disseminating E-Business Globally and Locally: A Rhetorical Inquiry into the Role of the "Big Five" Management Consulting Firms," diss., Victoria U of Wellington, New Zealand (2001).
[49] Ian Miles, "When Mediation is the Message: How Suppliers Envisage New Markets," *Contexts of Computer-Mediated Communication*, ed. Martin Lea (New York: Harvester Wheatsheaf, 1992) p. 153.
[50] Miles, p. 151.
[51] Sheizaf Rafaeli, "Interactivity: From New Media to Communication," *Advancing Communication Science: Merging Mass and Interpersonal Processes*, ed. Robert P. Hawkins, John M. Wieman, and Suzanne Pingree (Newbury Park, CA: Sage, 1988) p. 120.
[52] Teresa M. Harrison and Lisa Falvey, "Democracy and New Communication Technologies," *Communication Yearbook 25* (2001): 1–43.
[53] Harrison and Falvey.
[54] Teresa M. Harrison and Timothy Stephen, "Researching and Creating Community Networks," *Doing Internet Research*, ed. Steve Jones (Newbury Park, CA: Sage, 1998) pp. 221–241.
[55] Michael Andersen and Jeppe Nielsen, "Title of Unpublished Master Thesis," diss., Aalborg U, 2002.
[56] Daniel Robey and Ana Azevedo, "Cultural Analysis of the Organizational Consequences of Information Technology," *Accounting, Management & Information Technology* 4:1 (1994): 28.
[57] Zorn, "Emotionality."
[58] See, for example, Kling; see also Gerardine DeSanctis and Janet Fulk, eds., *Shaping Organization Form: Communication, Connection and Community* (Thousand Oaks, CA: Sage, 1999).
[59] E.g., Wanda Orlikowsky, "The Duality of Technology: Rethinking the Concept of Technology in Organizations," *Organization Science* 3 (1992): 398–426.
[60] See also Roberts and Grabowsky.
[61] Lars Thøger Christensen, "Marketing as Communication Technology: Paradoxes and Dialogics," *Consumption, Markets and Culture* 4:1 (2000): 1–21.

13

Communicating in Global and Multicultural Contexts

When we talk about globalization or a global world we often refer to a distinctly *modern* phenomenon related to the rise and spread of capitalism. And indeed, the word *global* has acquired a powerful meaning in today's society based on highly interconnected market economies. Especially since the economic unification of the then-fifteen European Union nations in 1992, it has been fashionable to speak of globalization as a broad-ranging and unstoppable force related to a market-based capitalism. Thus, our talk about this trend, or set of trends, typically focuses on issues like *international trade, multinational corporations, and the spread of consumerism*. But globalization has important social, cultural, political, and religious dimensions as well.[1] Coca-Cola and the Roman Catholic Church are prominent multinational organizations, but so are Amnesty International, The World Court, Physicians for Social Responsibility, and the Al Qaeda terrorist network.

Since 11 September 2001, the meaning of globalization has again come under greater scrutiny. Dramatic differences in outlook about the future of the planet, as well as stark differences in living conditions, have become more apparent. It's difficult to understand globalization in a linear or monolithic fashion, when it's now becoming clear just how many types of fragmentation and conflict exist in the world. Thus, the attitude of many observers toward globalization is now much more sober and more refined than it was 1989 to 1992 when hype overcame analysis in the rush to create new trading blocs as panaceas for the world's ills. In a world with *global awareness*, it is important that we ask searching questions about changing meanings—not only about issues such as employment, productivity, and efficiency but also about equality, democracy, and justice.

Confronting and Defining Globalization

Although the term *globalization* wasn't widely used before the 1960s, a number of significant developments that *pre*date modernity and capitalism had important globalizing effects. The hegemony of the Roman Catholic Church in late medieval Europe, the progress of humanity during the European Renaissance, the development of maps and universal calendars, the spread of colonialism, the formation of nation-states, the creation of time zones, the definition of citizenship, and the two world wars were all processes and events with sweeping consequences for the entire globe. Today, the rapid spread of diseases—from new strains of tuberculosis to SARS to the global scourge of AIDS—offer testimony to the dark side of an interconnected world.

Once modern *Homo sapiens* migrated out of Africa, traces of globalization began. Ancient empires from the Persian Gulf to North Africa flourished from several thousand years B.C.E. Clashes of entire civilizations, as shown dramatically with European conquests of the Americas in the sixteenth to nineteenth centuries and of Australasia in the eighteenth to nineteenth centuries spread—and destroyed—cultures. As early as the seventeenth century, there were a few multinational corporations in the form of state-sponsored imperialistic enterprises like the Dutch East Indies and West Indies Companies. The invention of the mechanical clock, the introduction and spread of money and, much later, the development of electronic media facilitated interaction among diverse peoples and nations. Eventually, formal diplomacy between states, international agreements, legal conventions, international organizations, and cultural links solidified political, economic, and cultural aspects of global interactions.[2] The world, thus, is global in a staggering variety of connections.

With these many different origins, it is no surprise that globalization is an ambiguous and *contested* term—on the street as well as in policy and academic journals. Since the late 1980s, vocal debates have prompted the publication of ideas about globalization and "our" place in history.

At the end of the 1980s, a mid-level U.S. government official, Francis Fukuyama, created a firestorm with his assertion that "we"—meaning the United States and its allies and imitators—had achieved "The End of History."[3] Specifically, he meant that the particular form of market democracy manifested in the United States and in several other parts of the world, had become *the* stable future for the planet. In the 1990s Samuel Huntington, a U.S. political scientist, advanced a very different thesis, now called "The Clash of Civilizations." He argued that we continue to encounter clashes between "incommensurable systems" of cultural, religious, and social beliefs running cross-grain with the processes of globalization.[4] His thesis has also spawned great controversy, especially in the wake of the 2001 terrorist attacks on New York and Washington, largely because Huntington has posited an inevitable collision course between the systems he calls "Western" and "Islamic." Another U.S. political scientist, Benjamin Barber, coined the phrase "Jihad versus McWorld," arguing that market and consumer globalization would necessarily be countered by a number of local and regional trends including reassertion of geographic, ethnic, and religious identities.[5] Later in this chapter, we will consider some refutations to these propositions.

The point here is to not to pick a winner but to make you aware of the contours of these debates, especially in terms of how any one group sees "The Other" and the tempting tendency to lump all others together in convenient categories—for example,

Asia, the Islamic World, the West, etc.—rather than to see the reality of divisions in the outgroup as well as in our own ingroup.[6] This matter will resurface as critically important when we discuss dimensions of intercultural communication later in this chapter.

Box 13.1 Concepts Describing Relationships among Nation-States

The term *colonialism* takes us to a particular period in history—nineteenth- and early twentieth-century European political, economic, and military domination over large areas of the world. It refers specifically to the use of the resources of the colonies to enrich the colonizers. Many scholars argue that the industrial revolution in Europe really took off when the availability of raw materials and labor from the colonies reached a critical mass, and European industries were able to export their finished goods to the developing markets in the colonies. Most colonial encounters were, at least initially, economic and marked by the transfer of political power from local systems to Europe.

The term *development* characterized relationships among nation-states after World War II. While still in use, it is not as central as it once was. The term carries an inherent judgment—an understanding of international politics and economy focused on differences in stages of development. Democracy was usually assumed to be the most developed form of political organization, and, depending on the part of the world you were looking at, either socialism or capitalism were seen as the ultimate stage of economic development. Accordingly, countries in the third world were characterized as developing or underdeveloped, industrializing or underindustrialized. Although there has been substantial criticism of the bias in the designations, development has been a cornerstone of the philosophy of such international organizations as the UN, the International Monetary Fund (IMF), and the World Bank. The terms *first, second,* and *third* worlds are also associated with development. Respectively, they refer to the Industrialized West, the Soviet Bloc and its allies, and former colonies. The use of the terms second and third worlds to refer to rich and ancient cultures and civilizations can be viewed as arrogant; indeed some scholars—notably feminists—use the term "third world" in a subversive manner.

Cultural imperialism is a term that became increasingly controversial in the late 1970s and 1980s. International debates at the UN about the New World Information and Communication Order became heated to the extent that the U.S. pulled out of UNESCO in 1984. Critics who view post-WWII relationships between the "first" and "third" worlds in terms of cultural imperialism point to the ubiquity of Western (especially U.S.) cultural goods and products across the world—the international success of pop stars such as Michael Jackson, Madonna, or Mariah Carey, the popularity of television shows such as *Dallas, Ally McBeal,* or *Friends*, the global spread of Hollywood movies, trends in fashion, the spread of English, and the influence of Western architecture.

The term *globalization* has been increasingly used since the early 1980s and is associated with the increasing spread of free-market capitalism. Although our dominant understanding of globalization is in economic terms, it is tremendously significant in terms of politics and culture.

These four terms represent only a few of the ways in which international systems can be described. Other possibilities include "transnationalism, "postcolonialism," or "neocolonialism." The word *international* itself implies a particular understanding of the world. While the four terms refer to particular historical periods, we can use each of them to think about the contemporary world system.

What would you focus on if you understood the world in which we now live using the description of "colonialism" or "development" or "cultural imperialism?" What term would you choose?

Box 13.2 On the Intentionality of Globalization

As sociology professor Malcolm Waters points out, the notion of globalization is often used and defined in rather vague or tautological ways:

> The definitions of globalization given in general dictionaries are often couched in such unhelpful terms as "to render global" or "the act of globalizing." Even if we delete the tautology as in "to render world-wide" or "the act of diffusion throughout the world" this is misleading from a sociological point of view because it implies intentionality. Many aspects of globalization are indeed intentional . . . including both the increasing level of business planning for global marketing and action by the environmental movement to save the planet. However, many globalizing forces are impersonal and beyond the control and intentions of any individual or group of individuals. The development of Islamic fundamentalism as a response to the effects of Western modernization or the decline of the U.S. car industry are examples of just such effects.[7]

We sometimes ascribe "agency" to a descriptive term as though it is a person or a group with goals, plans, and intentions. What are some practical reasons for this way of thinking? How do we limit the horizons of our imaginations when we say, "Globalization does . . ." or "The Market wants . . ." As Waters asks, what parts of globalization are best seen as intentional? Which are mindless? And which are entirely out of the domain of individual or collective volition?

In everyday usage, globalization evokes a host of different *images* that convey the paradoxical observation that our world is at once expanding and shrinking. These images include Marshall McLuhan's *global village* (see box 13.7), defined and facilitated by television and other media;[8] the *information age*, a term used to express the digitalization of almost all aspects of social life; *post-industrial society*, which suggests we live in a world beyond the material; and *network culture*, which highlights our "interconnectivity." These ideas are usually presented as utopian—diverting our attention from the fact that the world still has sweatshops and smokestacks, automobile exhaust fumes, and chemical wastes. One of the effects of the information age is that many consumers do not view their home computers as material *things*; rather they view them as granting access to the goal of interconnectivity. Only recently, has the full pollution potential of electronic technology begun to be appreciated, as our landfills become receptacles for only slightly outdated equipment. Constant availability of electronic communication is assumed to meet a critical need; lost in the reverence are the realities that interactivity also means constant links to work "24/7/365." We need to examine the rhetoric of globalization carefully.

The spread of mass-mediated images, air transportation, and new communication technologies (like teleconferencing) all foster the impression that the world is becoming smaller geographically. At the same time, the growing *awareness* of interrelated and interdependent actors and processes suggests expansion mentally. One definition of globalization as "a social process in which the constraints of geography on social and cultural arrangements recede and in which people become increasingly aware that they are receding"[9] addresses these important concepts. The definition highlights globalization as a process of perception, understanding, and, by extension, persuasion.

George recently asked one of his classes to describe how they thought about globalization. The students were startled by the question. They had never stopped to assess their beliefs about globalization; they had simply accepted it as one of the aspects of the world in which they live. These 19- to 22-year-olds never experienced a time when globalization wasn't talked about constantly. Technological developments such as personal computers (1980), e-mail (1985), and the World Wide Web (1993), had been regular features of these students' lives. As one of them asked George, "What was the world like before PCs and the Internet?" Just as we discussed in chapter 12, the advance of technology is inextricably bound to our contemporary understandings of an interconnected world.

Of course, the discussion above is about comparatively well-off members of the global society. It's easy to forget that most of the world's population concerns itself with issues far different than how to manage an increasing volume of e-mail. Later in this chapter we will address the uneven and often contradictory effects of globalization. Metaphors such as "a rising tide that will lift all boats" were used in 1994 to promote NAFTA (North American Free Trade Agreement), yet most regions of the world are still striving to feed and house their populations. This issue was one focus of protests against international trade meetings in Seattle in 1999, Genoa in 2000, Quebec City in 2001, and British Columbia in 2002: the "leveling" implied by typical images of globalization hides the material reality of grotesque inequities.[10]

In the context of *organizational communication*, we can think of globalization as the process through which the global economy becomes increasingly *interconnected*,

through which global and domestic organizations merge, and through which communication technologies blur traditional spatial and temporal boundaries.[11] For example, with the adoption of the Euro as a single currency in 2001, most of the European Union nations agreed that their economies would reach a new level of interdependence. For various kinds of commercial firms, this means that the market value of their goods and services is even more standardized than before. The idea of a global network organization is based on connectivity. Janet Fulk uses the term *communality*—the ability of networks to share information—to describe a potential basis for community.[12] Peter Monge points out that global network organizations result in disembeddedness of sorts, because they involve lifting human communication and knowledge out of an everyday, local context, and recontextualizing them at a global level.[13] In this way, certain kinds of interconnection imply disconnection. We can see this vividly in the number of professional elites around the world who are more connected with one another than with most people in their own countries.

In 2000 when George visited Monterrey Tec (the Technological Institute of Monterrey, Mexico) he confronted a dramatic example of the dialectic of interconnection and disconnection. The institution is one of the most elite private universities in all of Latin America; its student population draws from the children of CEOs and diplomats. When George was talking to some of the students informally, he asked them if they personally knew any poor people. A number of them said they didn't, despite the fact that over 80% of the population of Mexico can, by some measures, be termed poor. At the same time, these students readily identified with a well-resourced and well-traveled class of executives and other professionals for whom airports were quite familiar places of entry and exit. The story also illustrates the two sides to what sociologist Manuel Castells has called the network society.[14] Castells argues that the informational global economy is characterized not only by increasing interdependence but also by "exclusionary segmentation"—increasing divisions *within* a society or culture between those who can access the benefits of globalization and those who cannot.

These trends have direct implications for organizational life, as do the diffusion of cultural trends mentioned earlier—such as media images, music, art, and increased travel. In 1973 Wim Wenders released the provocative film *Alice in the Cities*. The acclaimed German film director portrayed vividly how certain parts of culture were being homogenized; the same pop tunes and the same television shows played in many parts of the world. Many refer to U.S. cultural imperialism because so much of what now passes for global culture emanates from New York, Hollywood, and Las Vegas. The French often complain that U.S.-exported culture receives more instant recognition than do ideas and images from Paris. As we will discuss, however, none of these processes are one-sided or straightforward. For example, while the much-parodied U.S. television program *Baywatch* is currently one of the most widely viewed programs in the world, the *meanings* attributed to that show by people from Norway to Turkey to the Philippines to New Zealand differ markedly. We need to understand how people view such shows in the context of their own lives. Indeed, recent statistics on global television viewing show a marked decrease in the popularity of U.S. programming. What might this say about the political climate of 2003?

With all the trends that can be put under the umbrella of globalization, there are some surprising outcomes—some counter-trends toward localism and even tribalism, some reactions against perceived cultural imperialism, and of course tremendous unpredictability. As we will argue, globalization or globalism only makes sense against the reference point of localization and local interests.

The Global and the Local

Along with a growing economic, political, and organizational interdependency and a rapid spread of cultural products and ideas across the globe, we find a tendency for *regional* identities or practices to assert themselves more forcefully. Ironically, the expression of such identities and practices often depends on global media and on a global economy. While the European Union, for example, has been pushing for a more unified Europe in terms of open markets, political principles, common currency, and even a shared identity as a superstate, regional groups have rediscovered or reemphasized their local customs, identities, and allegiances. For example, the Basques and the Catalonians in Spain are using the growing power of the EU to link themselves to the superstate and to gain stronger profiles as regions within states and a superstate. As these minority groups identify with Brussels, they create more separation from Madrid. In today's world, it seems, the notions of the global and the local are so closely interwoven that we cannot conceive of one without the other.

This is true at the market level as well. While globalization continues to be the credo in most private businesses, a growing number of corporations are seeking to *adapt* their products and strategies to local markets. In media terms, this is a kind of "narrowcasting." The Coca-Cola Corporation, for example, keeps selling its classic product across the globe, but it has also developed a range of products adapted to local tastes and preferences. Its yellow Inca Kola, for example, is the most popular soft drink in Peru. McDonald's has developed several locally adapted products—for example, McLaks (salmon) in Norway, spicy Aztec burgers in Mexico, and a range of vegetarian burgers in India. Doing so enables McDonald's to simultaneously co-opt and cater to local tastes and preferences—all the while appearing adaptable and location-friendly.

Although these examples may seem somewhat trivial, they show how some businesses acknowledge that globalization does not (or should not) necessarily homogenize tastes. Roland Robertson uses the (admittedly peculiar) term "glocalization" to refer to this process.[15] The term "*glocal*" comes from blending the terms "global" and "local" and is modeled on the Japanese notion of "dochakuka." *Dochakuka* is originally an agricultural term that referred to the principle of adapting farming techniques to suit a particular area, but it was adopted by Japanese businesses in the 1980s to refer to global localization, or adopting global outlooks to suit local conditions. It thus has a strong marketing connotation and refers to tailoring and advertising global goods and services to suit vastly differentiated local markets.

Globalization is not simply a set of one-way influences; it runs in many directions simultaneously (see box 13.3)—to and from centers and peripheries, sometimes even creating new centers and peripheries. Thus we find examples of market acculturation and adaptation among local companies, for example the marketing of kebab restaurants by German Turks[16] or the adaptation of marketing practices among local business to accommodate diverse ethnic groups.[17] And sometimes small firms can even compete successfully against multinational corporations by using knowledge about local conditions.[18]

Clearly, our understanding of globalization depends on our level of explanation, on which phenomena we foreground or background when we think of globalization. By moving back and forth between the global and the local in the following sections,

Box 13.3 The Dialogics of Globalization

The French sociologist and philosopher Edgar Morin is interested in complexity and especially in the fact that in complex systems like societies, several principles or logics are simultaneously at play. To explain a development in such systems, Morin claims, we need to look not only at trends that support each other in a certain direction but also at divergent forces that contradict each other or point in different directions. The unity of European culture, for example, is not a simple synthesis of its Jewish, Christian, Greek, Roman (etc.) elements but rather the result of complementary, competitive, and antagonistic play among these elements, each of which operates according to its own logic. Even the *idea* of Europe, as first conceived in ancient Athens, had to be put forth against an image of political, cultural, and religious diversity—and that remains the case today. Morin thus prefers to speak of the *dialogics* within the development of any large social system. The dialogic principle signifies, according to Morin, "the symbiotic unity of two logics, which simultaneously nourish each other, compete against each other, live off each other, oppose and combat each other to death."[19]

In what sense can we think of globalization as a process of dialogics? Think of forces that complement each other to make social life more global. Think of opposing forces. If globalization is characterized by one or more dialogics, how can we predict its outcome? Should we even try?

we will see that globalization is a highly ambiguous phenomenon for contemporary societies and organizations and that its interpretation is often nested in our discourses of development and progress.

Forces of Convergence

Globalization is a highly complex term partly because it is surrounded by ideological suspicion. To many, globalization seems to justify the spread and supremacy of Western culture by suggesting that forces beyond human control are transforming the world and making cultures increasingly similar. For some ethnocentric observers, globalization represents the ultimate fulfillment of the eighteenth-century European Enlightenment: Western rationalism and individualism have triumphed and taken over the world. Clearly, although there are counter-tendencies, it would hardly be possible to understand the current phase of globalization without reference to the expansion of Western culture through settlement, colonization, and cultural mimesis (imitation). These processes are shaped by market-based capitalism, and we find Western influence everywhere on the globe, either as a positive preference or point of aspiration or as a negative counter-image.

External Forces

Globalization is typically explained with reference to a number of external forces or trends that push societies and organizations toward similar structures and goals. Known as *the convergence hypothesis*, this perspective holds that a set of imperatives embedded in the global economy—most notably the deregulation of financial markets, the development and availability of new technologies, and the resultant increases in competition—*compel* organizations to adapt similar structuring and production arrangements across markets and nations.[20] For example, the call for contemporary organizations to adopt flexible structures in order to improve responsiveness to external demands—including faster delivery and service, increased information processing, and continuous improvement—is regarded as a necessary and dispassionate reminder of the conditions for organizational effectiveness and survival in today's global world. Increased trade between organizations across national and cultural boundaries gives birth to common markets and to shared languages, common currencies, and similar behaviors. The convergence hypothesis builds on the assumption that although there are differences between nations and between organizations, such differences are relatively insignificant compared to the forces that press societies and organizations to align themselves toward the same economic and technological structures.

We can see this trend in Europe, where the EU has gradually moved from the formation of a common market in the 1950s to the establishment of a shared currency for member countries. As the EU expands to include still more nations in Central and Eastern Europe, this convergence process is going to encompass a growing number of the world's leading industries. Norway, however, whose economy is largely domestic (it is rich because of North Sea oil deposits found in the 1960s) has decided to stay largely outside the EU. Still, it finds that its internal choices (on economic, political, and social matters) are often directly influenced by the EU's decisions, and it therefore needs to maintain an "associate" status with respect to the EU. In other parts of the world as well, trade agreements are developing that are both based on and reinforcing of presumed common regional interests. We see examples in current talks in East Asia as well as in the Americas.

Organizations may vary considerably in structure to begin with, but the convergence hypothesis predicts that as they grow and mature, they will pass through similar developmental stages and eventually develop similar forms. In chapters 2 and 3, we discussed the disconnection between celebrating innovation and entrepreneurship while practicing conformity. As mentioned earlier, an important question is whether these similar organizational forms emerge because of developments in the environment that force organizations to look alike or because central actors tend to have the same expectations about the future. In his seven-year project in the Basque Country, George found that worker cooperatives were becoming more like standard multinational corporations not only because of real market pressures from the "outside" but also because of changes in the managerial ideology on the "inside" (see chapter 8 for a more detailed discussion). Thus, we should be attuned to the real sources of change in any organization, community, or nation, and the fact that they are usually a mixture of external pressures and internal drives.

Although Karl Marx granted some agency to the bourgeoisie (merchant class) and the proletariat (working class), he saw globalization as an inevitable force with its own inherent logic pressing societies and cultures to become increasingly similar. Other sociologists—including Saint-Simon, Durkheim, and Weber—also viewed globalization as intrinsic to capitalism and its constant need to expand beyond national markets. However, while Durkheim and Weber were disturbed by this tendency—Durkheim because of the weakening of local community, Weber because of the spread of modern rationality—both Saint-Simon and Marx saw huge potentials in such convergence. Saint-Simon envisioned a utopian internationalism that included a pan-European government and a universalizing humanistic philosophy. Marx saw globalization as a precursor to a unified and emancipated working class.[21]

Throughout the twentieth century, a number of writers, including U.S. sociologists Talcott Parsons and Daniel Bell, have argued that industrial societies are in fact becoming increasingly similar to one another. While Parsons describes globalization as an "evolutionary process" through which living systems seek to adapt to a changing environment, Bell argues that emerging intellectual technologies will push societies toward a singular post-industrial future without nation-states.

The kind of determinism inherent in the convergence perspective mirrors the impression that most of us have of economic development. *Development* is often seen as the crest of a wave that promises to either lift us or swamp us—depending upon how we react. In either case, we cannot *resist* it. Notice the parallel between deterministic talk about globalization and the idea of technological determinism we discussed in chapter 12. The similarities are not coincidental. Our ideas of globalization are inextricably tied up with a sense of technological advancement. Still, we are left with the profound practical as well as philosophical question: "Who's at the wheel?" In a competitive environment where everybody, urged by other corporations, governments, and interest groups, seeks to move before the wave is actually there—and in this way creates more turbulence—it becomes impossible to determine exactly what triggered the move in the first place.

Institutional Isomorphism

We can attribute the tendency of organizations to become increasingly similar—a process sometimes referred to as "organizational isomorphism"[22]—to several different processes. So-called "institutionalists" distinguish between two different kinds of organizational isomorphism: *competitive* and *institutional*. The first refers to the convergence propelled by competitive market forces; the second looks at influences other than strictly economic. Organizational structures become more similar for a number of reasons. Organizations sometimes converge in order to conform to political standards and to gain legitimacy; thus, *coercive* isomorphism occurs if legal strictures require similarity among organizations. In other cases, organizations converge in order to look like other respected and successful organizations; this *mimetic* isomorphism is visible in imitative mission statements. Finally, convergence may occur as organizations attempt to live up to professional standards in their specific industry; this *normative* isomorphism occurs when professional associations set standards that affect their representatives regardless of where they work. Together these forms of institutional isomorphism often propel organizations to take action without a clear-cut economic or otherwise "objective" imperative in their surroundings. Which external forces can you think of—based on what you've read earlier in this book and elsewhere—that push organizations to become similar? Try to think of examples that distinguish between competitive and institutional isomorphism. What are the most compelling trends in business environments of today?

Pressures toward Divergence

While the convergence in lifestyles, markets and organizational forms appears to be a strong globalizing force in today's world, we can also detect a tendency towards *divergence* if we focus on the significance and meanings given to these and related phenomena. As we shall see later in this chapter, several researchers have demonstrated that managers and employees often display significant differences across cultures and nations in terms of how they experience and behave in various organizational settings. In sum, similarities at the macro level may well coexist with substantial differences at the micro level. For example, some scholars argue that the stronger and more unified a local culture is, the more similarities we will see across organizations and sectors within that local culture. Part of this consistency will come directly from a shared sense of identity, built on the foundation of common cultural practices.[23]

Despite fostering greater connectedness and de-territorialization, globalization potentially increases cultural pluralism by recognizing and drawing attention to ethnic groupings, cultural niches, and local abilities.[24] According to marketing professor Fuat Firat, globalization is not a uniform and universalizing process but a fragmented one.[25] In contrast to conventional views that depict globalization as the spread of one set of lifestyles, products, and consumption patterns—typically North American—across the globe, Firat posits that today there is a weakening of uniformity and universality in people's approaches to living and being. While the tendency to recognize and respect the coexistence of different ethnic, religious, social, and ideological cultures is on the rise in many Western countries, this coexistence of different cultures is itself being globalized. Firat calls this the "globalization of fragmentation."

> Globalization is not a process whereby one form or style dominates over or eliminates all others. Rather, it is the diffusion of seemingly competing forms and styles around the world. The consumer is ready to have Italian for lunch, and Chinese for dinner, to wear Levi's 501 blue jeans for the outdoor party in the afternoon and try the Gucci suit at night to attend a Japanese exhibition, not only changing diets and clothes, but also the personas and selves that are to be (re)presented at each "function."[26]

Although the examples in the quotation are from the upper economic strata of affluent societies, Firat emphasizes that fragmentation is even more pronounced in third-world countries where the coexistence of different lifestyles and products cuts across pockets of both extreme poverty and extreme affluence. While Firat's perspective is interesting and reasonable, can you think of any cultures that are not fragmented in this sense of the term?

While the idea of global convergence sits in tension with the idea of global divergence, we should avoid thinking of them as direct opposites of each other. For example, we could push Firat's perspective further and make the argument that the globalization of fragmentation is itself a uniform and universalizing process. Perhaps it is more productive then, to think of forces of convergence and forces of divergence as coexisting trends in tension. As organizational communication scholar Cynthia Stohl[27] points out, pressures toward divergence are often coterminous (existing together) with a drive toward convergence.

In our efforts to understand the phenomenon of globalization we should look for mixed forms of organization and communication, such as local ways of appropriating global symbols or global ways of dealing with the local. For instance, when the "Japanese economic miracle" of the 1970s and 1980s seized the attention of the industrialized world, everyone asked, "How did they do it?" To answer that question requires a deep exploration of indigenous cultural features (such as the application of the family metaphor in multiple contexts), recent history (Westernization), and two-way influences associated with consulting (such as the adoption of Deming's quality management practices). To label Japanese culture simplistically as "collectivist"—in stark contrast with, say, the individualism of the United States, misses the complexities of both systems as well as the multiple means by which information is diffused and trends established in today's interconnected world.[28]

Popular Discourses on Globalization

As we have seen, most discourses on globalization today are based on market-centered conceptions of its processes and effects. Thus, among both proponents and critics, we typically find globalization explained with references to financial internationalization, trade liberalization, technology, and the development of one global market. Although conclusions differ markedly, most writers seem to share an image of the world as being determined and shaped by powerful economic forces. Below, we shall discuss a number of current perspectives on globalization and see how these discourses may prompt organizations to embark on specific globalization projects.

In an often-cited article in a 1983 issue of *Harvard Business Review*,[29] marketing professor Theodore Levitt argued that in order to survive in a competitive environment, business firms need to operate as if the world were one large market, ignoring what he called "superficial regional and national differences." The crux of Levitt's argument is that although certain regional differences may persist, the world is generally moving towards a converging commonality in terms of tastes, preferences, and lifestyles. According to Levitt, technology is the driving force in this process. He claims technology "has proletarianized communication, transport and travel. It has made isolated places and impoverished peoples eager for modernity's allurements. Almost everyone everywhere wants all the things they have heard about, seen, or experienced via the new technologies."[30] Levitt cites examples of worldwide brands like McDonald's, Coca-Cola, Revlon, Sony, and Levi's jeans available in a wide variety of places on the globe (including Bahrain, Siberia, and Biafra) as an indication of the desire for Western products and lifestyles.

Based on these observations, Levitt urges multinational corporations to become fully global enterprises, abandoning the usual practice of individualizing products for specific regions in favor of one standardized approach. Assuming that the world is moving toward convergence, the global competitor should act as if the entire world were a single entity rather than assuming that the customer who knows his or her own wishes is primary. Following Levitt's view, other writers have added that the Internet is now speeding up the globalization process by making products and services instantaneously available to customers around the globe, augmenting the tendency toward convergence and homogenization. Echoing Levitt's prescriptions, business firms are told "we need global brands to leverage our products across geographic markets."[31]

As you might guess, Levitt's article provoked considerable controversy, especially within the marketing field. While some have focused their critique on the fact that globalization in Levitt's version stresses the production side rather than specific consumer needs and wants, others have refuted Levitt's perspective by showing that consumer preferences *are always locally based*, that the advantages of standardization vary from product to product, and that differences in legislation may prevent marketers from pursuing a fully standardized global approach.[32] Two decades after Levitt wrote his article, few brands and few companies are as global as he envisioned. While we are often told about truly global brands such as Coca-Cola, McDonald's, and

Marlboro, these examples are few in number and rarely represent the marketing concerns of most corporations. In contrast to Levitt's idea, segmentation of customers continues to be a central marketing activity.

The primary weakness of Levitt's argument lies in its circular nature. That is, it is impossible to tell whether global convergence and the homogenization of needs is the cause *or* the effect of global business strategies. While Levitt claims that the globalization of markets is observed as something "out there" to which businesses need to adapt, globalization as a strategy is simultaneously promoted so strongly that organizations following Levitt's creed may end up *enacting* the very phenomena they claim dictates adaptation. So, accepting Levitt's advice that the global corporation actively seeks and works toward global convergence, the discourse on globalization may turn out to be a self-fulfilling prophecy. As an example, George's research on the Mondragón worker cooperatives in the Basque Country found that the industrial co-ops used globalization as its own justification. In essence, some managers told him "We must internationalize because we are international."

Although few proponents of globalization express their viewpoint in the same fundamental all-or-nothing terms as Levitt, most writers on the topic talk about glo-

Box 13.4 "Born Globals"

The internationalization of business firms has traditionally been described as a gradual process that follows a number of stages. Firms aiming for an international market would typically begin this process by expanding their activities to familiar or neighboring markets. Following this model, a Danish firm, for example, would first establish Scandinavian markets (Sweden or Norway) before expanding to other European countries. According to this perspective, internationalization is slow and incremental in nature primarily because firms lack knowledge about foreign markets. The perceived uncertainty causes firms to proceed slowly to avoid risk.

In contrast to this perspective, a group of researchers have suggested that an increasing number of organizations, so-called "born globals," take an international perspective at their inception and begin exporting immediately to geographically or culturally distant markets.[33] Many examples of "born globals" are found in high-tech and research-based industries such as in the biotech industry. U.S. research on "born globals" tends to focus on companies within the IT-industry. Logitech, a producer of computer equipment (keyboards and mice), is often mentioned as an example of a "born global." Research outside the United States, however, has demonstrated that technological sophistication is not the only factor explaining the launch of "born globals." In smaller markets, organizations often need to think globally from day one. The market for specialized fish products, for example, is far too small in Scandinavia to sustain the industry. Most producers therefore target foreign markets immediately. In addition to the general market conditions and technological developments in the areas of production, transportation, and communication, the rise of born globals can be attributed to the international outlook of their founders or entrepreneurs. The more culturally sensitive and interculturally adept the founder is, the more likely he or she is to establish a born global corporation.[34]

Think of examples of organizations that you would describe as born globals. Do they share similar characteristics? With the spread of new communication technologies, most notably the Internet, most businesses are potentially global at birth. Web pages instantly extend the communication reach of organizations. Check out the home pages of a number of firms and discuss whether they project a global outlook.

balization as an *imperative*, implying at once a description of the competitive environment in which contemporary organizations operate and a prescription for their proactive marketing strategies. While we may object that such descriptions/prescriptions are too narrowly focused on economic dimensions (markets, monetary systems, economic integration, legal environments, etc.)[35] this kind of business communication may well set the stage for globalizing processes in the future.

Critics of Globalization

A growing number of voices express concern about the negative consequences of globalization. The primary concerns are political and social; a centerpiece of their arguments is that political and social concerns have been unjustly eclipsed by market-oriented concerns (see also our discussion of market ethics in the next chapter).

Threat to Communities and the Environment

In a book of essays criticizing globalization,[36] the common theme is that organizations and other institutionalized forces of globalization are undemocratic and detrimental to both local communities and the natural environment. In their essay, Ralph Nader and Lori Wallach argue that the General Agreement on Tariffs and Trade (GATT), and the World Trade Organization (WTO) are systems of power "not designed to promote the health and well-being of human beings but to enhance the power of the world's largest corporations and financial institutions."[37] The image of globalization put forth by these writers is an image of unelected bureaucrats and technocrats "sitting behind closed doors in Geneva" working to reduce the power of local or national governments so that unfettered capitalism can sweep the globe and treat it as one common market. Nader and Wallach use the term *corporate globalization* to describe efforts to undermine national sovereignty in terms of its capacity to regulate commerce; they believe it threatens the diversity of local community as well as the local community's power to control decisions, and that this has critical implications for its citizens. To what extent would you say that this description of globalization corresponds to your own experiences as a citizen? Do you feel that critical decisions in your lifetime have been removed from local communities to more impersonal, bureaucratic institutions? In what ways?

Edward Goldsmith argues that the process of globalization is making people vulnerable to distant interests by removing their abilities to freely cooperate and sustain themselves in their local communities. This is evident in such widely different activities as the valuing of currency, the spread of vaccines for new viruses, and the proliferation of terrorism. Against the undemocratic nature of corporate globalization, Goldsmith posits that the institution of democracy, in order to live up to its definition as "government by the people for the people," has to be participatory and locally founded.[38] Based on an image of traditional society as a community where people see their own interests as inseparable from the public good, Goldsmith calls for action to counter globalization through a return to self-sufficient and self-governing communities.

On a micro level, one example of an attempt to promote economic democracy can be seen in several communities in the United Kingdom and the United States that have launched their own local currencies. Commonly called LETS systems,[39] these involve trust-based agreements between locally owned establishments (like

Box 13.5 Some International Development Organizations

The United Nations. The UN was formed in Dumbarton Oaks, near Washington, D.C., in 1943. It is a coalition of nation-states, organized toward realizing "development," or the social, economic, and political welfare of citizens of the member states. The two main bodies are the General Assembly and the Security Council. The major focus of the UN in post-war years was to decrease the dependency that import-heavy colonial economies had bred. The premise was that importing goods and services decreased self-reliance, whereas exporting increased economic production. The overall model was based on "trickle-down" theory—the idea that economic growth would be the engine for political, cultural, and democratic development.

Bretton Woods. A conference, held in Bretton Woods, New Hampshire, in 1944 aimed to ensure the growth of economic infrastructure over the world. The major vehicles of growth were the transfer of technology capital to the third world. The meetings at Bretton Woods led to the formation of the World Bank and the International Monetary Fund (IMF). The World Bank functions through subscription by member nations and investment. The IMF, on the other hand, is a credit-issuing body. From the start, Britain, France, and the United States exercised financial control over both the World Bank and the IMF. Consequently, "first world" evaluation tailored the priorities for "third world" growth. For example, the cultivation of cash crops and cattle were encouraged over basic food production. In other cases, the IMF provided a necessary counterbalance to the unrealistic or unscrupulous promises of political leaders.

GATT. The first General Agreement on Tariffs and Trade (GATT) talks were held in Havana, Cuba, in 1944; implementation began in 1947. The objective was to monitor and reduce the obstacles to free trade, facilitate currency conversion, reduce taxes on imports, etc. There have been seven rounds of tariff agreements. Most have emphasized the reduction of tariffs in industries, but the United States in the 1980s pushed a focus on agriculture as well. The WTO emerged from GATT in 1993–1994.

COMECON. Now defunct, this was the Soviet bloc equivalent of GATT, which included military and industrial aid to developing nations. Competition between COMECON and GATT was one of the reasons behind the Non-Aligned Movement, founded in 1961 to form a third-world force through a policy of nonalignment with either the United States or the then Soviet Union (for more information visit http://www.nam.gov.za/).

UNESCO. A UN organization that focuses on education issues and the free flow of information. Policy development was originally influenced by U.S. academicians until the United States pulled out of UNESCO in 1984. The overall focus of UNESCO is building and funding development communication programs; in 1980 the organization passed a resolution titled the New World Information and Communication Order at the 21st session of the UNESCO General Conference in Belgrade.

grocery or book stores) and consumers. Usually, these systems involve the trade of services (like dry cleaning or plumbing) as well as goods. In Ithaca, New York, for example, the units of currency are called *hours*, in explicit recognition of the time, energy, and labor that go into the production of anything—whether it is a plant sold by a nursery or home nursing care.

Privileging Property over People

Another prominent critic of market globalization, William Greider, has recently argued that movements toward "free trade," such as NAFTA, have actually undermined progress in other arenas, such as environmental protection and labor rights, by privileging property over people and making it difficult, on a practical/legal level, to lodge grievances against the system.[40] Some labor scholars have traced part of the decline of organized labor in the 1980s and '90s to market globalization by showing that unions have been largely unsuccessful in taking their causes to the international level, even as multinational corporations have increasingly ignored national boundaries.[41] There are exceptions, however. In an effort to show solidarity and to adopt an explicitly international strategy, the United Auto Workers (based in Detroit, Michigan) has tried to ally itself with a variety of established and budding unions along the U.S.-Mexican border.

While the market-centered notion of globalization is dominant in today's world, it seems problematic to maintain that the global system is only designed to reduce the power of local governments in order to generate profits for big organizations. Although concerns for profit obviously initiate and control many globalizing efforts, such *conspiracy theories* ignore the many—and sometimes conflicting—political, cultural, and symbolic forces that shape the world. Criticisms of bureaucratic and global institutions that emphasize their undemocratic, impersonal, and distant nature sometimes display a naïve nostalgia for the past—the good old days when democracy was realized through direct participation of citizens in town square meetings. When assessing undemocratic tendencies in organizations, we should consider the question: Is local government always good or better than supranational government? We ask this question because the simple ideal of "local communities" sidesteps the issue of how those local communities interact with and are affected by larger global systems. A more useful definition of democratic participation includes consideration of what happens beyond the boundaries of the local community. Given our pressing global

Box 13.6 The Ruckus Society

Mike Roselle founded the Ruckus Society, a grass-roots organization, in 1995. Its mission is an ongoing fight against institutionalized globalization represented by the World Bank, the International Monetary Foundation, WTO, and multinational corporations. John Sellers, the current leader of the society, claims these institutions dictate our lives, destroy the environment, and exploit poor countries. By training their members to become professional demonstrators, the Ruckus Society hopes to organize and control unrest and commotion in major cities in the interest of affecting global politics and reducing the power of multinational corporations. "It is not our job to enter into any dialogue with these organizations," Sellers claims. "Neither is it our job to find alternative solutions to WTO, the World Bank or IMF. Our role is to rebel against them. WTO is an evil organization."[42] Ruckus also protests violations of human rights in the United States and abroad, and its directors live somewhat unpredictable lives. For example, Nisha Anand, the development and communications director of Ruckus, was arrested by Burma's military junta for demonstrating against human rights violations there; she evaded imprisonment through deportation.

Ruckus has trained more than 3,000 anti-globalization protesters from all over the world, via training camps that it conducts in the United States. Ruckus has an annual budget of $750,000, a lot of which comes from private individuals including Hollywood celebrities Susan Sarandon and Tim Robbins. Media mogul Ted Turner pulled funding after the Seattle protests.

Do organizations such as the Ruckus Society play a significant role in today's globalized world? Do they have any positive impact? What does the emergence of Ruckus say about the "professionalization" of protest movements?

environmental concerns, we have to pay attention to ways in which economic and political practices of local communities are integrated with larger issues of sustainability (using resources in an ecologically sound, economically viable, and socially just manner so that they can be renewed rather than depleted), without compromising the issue of local participation.

Other Voices on Globalization

Is globalization really all that new? Do we live in an era of unprecedented technological change? Doug Henwood, editor of *Left Business Observer*, says no. According to Henwood, rapid technological change has been a constant feature of capitalism for 200 years and the most intensive period of change took place between 1897 and 1947—a period that included the invention of railroads, cars, and communication media like telephones, radios, and television. The world of local self-reliance, typically described by critics of globalization, never really existed. Henwood explains: "Slaves picked cotton for export to Britain, and U.S. industrialization was financed in large part by funds borrowed on London financial markets. The United States was founded by Europeans, who crossed an ocean and stole land from people who'd walked there from Asia some 20,000 or 40,000 years earlier. Like it or not, human beings have rarely stayed put."[43] Moreover, Henwood continues, internationalization in terms of export measures hasn't increased significantly throughout the twentieth century.

Acknowledging this, however, should not lead us to the position that *nothing* new is going on. With the lowering of trade barriers and the rapid movement of people, ideas, and money around the globe, contemporary organizations face new challenges and opportunities that significantly impact their ability to communicate in today's world. Some of these challenges and opportunities are related to economical and material exchanges; others are political or symbolic. While material exchanges increase economic interdependency and political exchanges tie these interdependencies to extended territories, symbolic exchanges more radically liberate relationships from spatial constraints. Such symbolic exchange is evident in the concepts of global reflexivity, interdependence, and the "social imagination."

A Global Reflexivity

Due to new communication technologies, symbols can be produced, reproduced, and transported anywhere on the globe within an instant. Since symbols frequently appeal to basic human needs, they often claim universal significance.[44] Advertisements for products like Microsoft Windows, Coke, Levi's jeans, and McDonald's hamburgers employ universal symbols to reach audiences throughout the world. Even more significantly, the world is increasingly perceived as one single system. Earlier phases of globalization advanced the material interdependencies between cultures and nation-states; recently we have experienced the rise of a reflexive global consciousness—an awareness of the world as an interdependent space *and* an awareness of this awareness. Moreover, as people gradually begin to think of the world as a whole, they increase the probability that the world is reproduced as such.[45]

Box 13.7 Are We a "Global Village"?

More than three decades ago, communication theorist Marshall McLuhan claimed that we live in a "global village" defined by the features of electronic communication. Since electronic communication is almost instantaneous, it is able to link events and locations and create interdependence. McLuhan envisioned electronic media restoring the collective culture of tribalism on a global scale. He wrote:

> Electric circuitry has overthrown the regime of "time" and "space" and pours upon us instantly and continuously the concerns of all other men. It has reconstituted dialogue on a global scale. Its message is Total Change, ending physical, social, economic, and political parochialism. The old civic, state, and national groupings have become unworkable. Nothing can be further from the spirit of the new technology than "a place for everything and everything in its place." You can't go home again.[46]

Although McLuhan's praise of technology may appear somewhat dated, it is interesting to note how his ideas about electronic media foreshadowed the global communication network that we now take for granted, both in our organizations and in our private lives. According to McLuhan, any culture is determined by the medium by which it is transmitted rather than by its content. Thus, he claimed, "the medium is the message."[47] The political implications of his ideas cannot be ignored. While global space is not similar to tribal neighborhoods, the awareness of total interdependence with other members seems to be a necessity whether one lives in a tribal or a global village.

To what extent would you say that such awareness is present in today's world? How would you explain McLuhan's claim that the medium is the message? Think of different examples in your culture that illustrate this observation.

Interdependence and Risk

If the entire globe is linked by communication networks that resemble, in terms of density, the networks of local communities, then our notions of time and space are transformed fundamentally. We begin to think of *where* we are located explicitly in relation to other places, and we even begin think of time in such comparative, reduced terms. Even if this is not entirely the case yet, the spread of new communication technologies implies a gradual "liberation" of time and space that not only connects us instantaneously with distant places but also renders us vulnerable to developments and events across the globe. As sociologist Malcolm Waters points out:

> Security of employment for an Australian sheep shearer, for example, might be affected by trends in Japanese fashions, the Uruguay round of GATT negotiations, the cost of synthetic fibers which is in turn determined by the price of oil which might in turn be determined by American military intervention in the Persian Gulf, and the extent to which the Australian government accepts prevailing global ideologies of marketization and privatization.[48]

Along with the recognition of global interdependence comes a growing awareness of *risk* as an integral dimension of contemporary society. Present-day risks include threats from toxins and pollutants, genetically modified foods, radioactivity, etc. And, of course, terrorism has now emerged as a visible threat in places from New York to Bali; it is no longer seen as a threat localized to areas where armed conflict or all-out warfare is the order of the day. In contrast to the hazards and dangers of previous historical periods, some of the risks that we face today are often the direct consequence of industrialization and overproduction. Also, while usually not perceptible to the senses, present-day risks are not confined to their local origins but threaten to endanger the entire planet. Risk, thus, has a powerful globalizing force that invites us constantly to envision our solutions beyond traditional boundaries. What major risks in your part of the world are direct consequences of globalization? What's the role of communication media in shaping your assessment of those risks?

Interestingly, the interdependence and implied risk of present-day globalization does not run unilaterally from the global to the local. British sociologist Anthony Giddens distinguishes between "globalization from above" and "globalization from below." While the former involves the global spread of financial markets, trade, and technological innovation, the latter refers to the political and social growth of non-governmental organizations (NGOs), interest and pressure groups that increasingly mediate between governments and business corporations and sometimes counterbalance the globalizing force of the market. According to Giddens, such organizations and groups—including consumers—are able to act as a check of both government and business operations.[49]

Based on consumer boycotts of the 1990s—for example, of Shell because of its plan to dump its oil platform Brent Spar in the North Sea and of French wine because of French nuclear testing—it is tempting to argue that consumers have considerable power to affect the decisions of governments and big corporations. It may be objected, however, that this power is confined and easily manipulable. As Will Hutton points out:

> The difficulty is that while consumers clearly have the power to buy or not to buy, it is pretty crude—and only arises when there is a well-publicized flashpoint. Consumers do not have a systematic voice through the democratic process or in the ways companies take decisions . . . perhaps most importantly of all, I am not sure that sufficient consumers are internationalist in their thinking and represent the basis for [a] global civil society.[50]

Does the increased possibility for consumers and various non-governmental groups to respond to forces of globalization imply that such persons and groups are responsible for the decisions made? Consider the possibilities for what are being called "pro-cotts": concerted efforts to support certain businesses on the local level. For example, in cities such as Minneapolis, Boulder, and Salt Lake City in the United States, coalitions of locally owned businesses support one another while trying to solidify a joint clientele in response to inroads being made by multinationals and chains. Think of how these networks of businesses operate differently from those of the past.

Social Imaginations

Scholars of global culture have argued that along with increasing reflexivity and interdependence, global forces are having a profound effect on our cultural imaginations—our collective senses of who we are and what we might become. Cultural anthropologist Arjun Appadurai, for example, appeals to the image of a landscape in characterizing global forces, identifying many diverse "scapes" that characterize our world.[51] For example, "ethnoscapes," focus on ethnic and cultural identities; "financescapes," emphasize the economic dimension; "mediascapes," highlight the roles of mass communication and popular culture, and so forth. A metaphor like this one is useful because it assists us in seeing how various dimensions of globalization have distinctive features and come together to outline possibilities for communities and cultures.

For Appadurai, these "scapes" provide us with the potential to collectively imagine forms of communal existence on an unprecedented scale. For example, Internet Web sites have afforded groups of people new opportunities to communicate and construct their collective identities. In an analysis of online discourse, Shiv found that Hindus who lived in various parts of the world and who came together to discuss politics on a Web site owned and mediated by a corporate news agency constantly debated what it meant to be Indian in a global world. These discussions, enabled by the "financescape" of the news corporation, the "mediascape" of the Internet, and the "ethnoscape" of Hindu cultures, helped members to envision their collective Indianness, resulting in surprisingly conservative expressions of connections between Indianness, Hinduness, and masculinity.[52]

In sum, the issues of reflexivity, interdependence, and imagination demonstrate that globalization inherently involves complex interactions between technology, economy, politics, and culture. How can we judge whether a culture or an organization is globalized or not? What should we look for? Should we judge by the number of McDonald's restaurants across the globe? Or the availability of Coca-Cola in a startling variety of places? Should we focus on the ability of cultures or organizations to retain local customs, values, and ideas in a global world? Or should we look at the extent to which a given culture actively communicates with other cultures? In more general terms, what does globalization imply for the ability of increasingly diverse groups and communities to communicate with each other? Should our focus be sameness or difference—and how do we define these terms? These are some of the questions we take up in the next section.

Intercultural Communication and Diversity in Organizations

Although there are numerous challenges and concerns associated with social life in a global context, it is highly unlikely that organizations will be able to escape the fact that both their operations and their messages are often intercultural at birth. We revisit the topic of intercultural communication in this chapter by proposing a rather counter-intuitive idea: there is nothing tremendously special or distinct about intercultural communication processes. All communication is in a sense intercultural; all forms of communication are about negotiating differences between human beings. As several authors have argued, what appears to be the issue in intercultural research is the degree, or amount, of cultural difference between the people concerned.[53] The sub-field of intercultural communication has grown substantially in the last two decades, due in no small part to the overall emphasis in our field on issues of culture, diversity, and internationalization. Terms such as "intercultural communication," "cross-cultural communication," and "multiculturalism" have become buzzwords, so it is useful to make some tentative distinctions between them.

The term "cross-cultural communication" is usually used in comparative contexts, where scholars attempt to compare broad patterns of communication in one culture with another one. Unlike the term "*inter*-cultural communication" it does not imply the study of actual communication among people with different cultural backgrounds.[54] The notion of "multicultural" communication refers to the idea (which we have already discussed in chapter 4) that it is difficult to refer to a "single" culture in unitary terms. In any given culture, we are likely to find significant subcultures and countercultures. Studies of multiculturalism focus on issues of diversity, minority cultures, and cultural identity.[55] Consequently, studies of multiculturalism imply a commitment to the rights of minorities and, in the context of organizational communication, typically involve considering organizational communication processes in terms of gender, ethnicity, race, and sexuality. It is important to remember intercultural communication, cross-cultural communication, and multiculturalism are closely related to each other. For example, it is almost impossible to study intercultural communication without discussing cross-cultural communication. Moreover, appreciating—and celebrating—intercultural differences implies a commitment (at one level or another) to the idea of multiculturalism. So, both in theory and in practice, we emphasize the intersections rather than the distinctions between each of these terms.

Parochialism

Intercultural communication scholars have emphasized both interpersonal and organizational aspects of intercultural communication. Studies of intercultural communication in organizational contexts—in fact, studies of organizational communication in general—have been called "parochial." Cynthia Stohl finds evidence of parochialism in the fact that a large number of studies have examined intercultural differences in one context (usually between the United States and country X, Y, or Z) and assumed their applicability to all other contexts.[56] This is problematic, she argues, because a theory grounded in one particular cultural context may not "transfer" or "speak" to other situations. Moreover, we often do not acknowledge cultural or political biases that underlie the development of entire research programs. For example, Karen Ashcraft and Brenda Allen argue in box 13.8 that organizational communication scholarship itself has racial foundations.

Box 13.8 The Racial Foundations of Organizational Communication[57]

Organizational communication scholars Karen Ashcraft and Brenda Allen argue that while we have begun to focus on the gendered nature of organizational communication practices, we have yet to focus adequately on its racial contexts and biases. In an analysis of several organizational communication textbooks—selected because textbooks are representations of the current status of the field—they identified five messages that frame how we typically communicate about organizational communication and race.

Race is a separate, singular concept that is relevant only under singular circumstances. Terms such as "race" or "ethnicity" tend to be used only to explain situations that explicitly involve people of color. That is, we tend to explain behavior with reference to ethnicity only when we specifically encounter people who are non-white. Think about the number of times we are likely to encounter issues of race and ethnicity in discussions about diversity, versus the number of times we are likely to hear about it when we discuss other organizational processes. Moreover, when we talk about race, we refer to it in a "singular" way—that is, we see those people who are racially different from us predominantly in terms of this one difference.

Race is valuable insofar as it involves cultural differences that can be identified,

valued, and managed to improve organizational performance. The value of racial and ethnic diversity is usually interpreted with reference to organizational productivity. That is, racial and ethnic differences are not seen as valued organizational goals in and of themselves. Rather, we tend to put issues of race and ethnicity in a positive light only when we emphasize what diversity management can do to boost organizational performance.

All cultural differences are synonymous with international variations. We tend to interpret differences between individuals in terms of our assumptions about differences between national cultures. That is, the notion of "cultural difference" itself usually gets us to think about national-level differences. Consequently, we end up treating ethnicity as synonymous with nationality. Ashcraft and Allen argue that this prevents us from seeing important ethnic differences within national cultures, as well as the critical role that issues of race have played in our overall sensitivity (or lack thereof) toward cultural differences.

Racial discrimination is a function of personal bias, interpersonal misunderstanding, organizational failure to manage cultural differences, and disproportionate demographics. We usually treat racial discrimination as individual-level behavior. Instances of racism are typically explained in terms of individual prejudice, some sort of interpersonal misunderstanding, or the lack of familiarity of individuals with other ethnicities. When we examine the role of organizations in discrimination, we usually focus on how the organization failed to manage individual behaviors, values, and attitudes. This detracts from our understanding of racial inequality as a phenomenon that is trans-individual and embedded in organizational structures and policies themselves.

White (collar) workers and practices constitute universal settings, identities, and practices. As a field, organizational communication tends to direct its prescriptions about effective organizational practice toward white-collar professional work, and in doing so, contains a bias toward white, middle-class life. The very fact that it sounds unusual—and perhaps even ridiculous—to ask about what sort of communication is most effective during unemployment (which is a condition that minorities encounter disproportionately) points to the bias in our field toward treating white (collar), professional work as "good" or "normal."

Competence

Researchers of intercultural communication often focus on the concept of "competence" as a central communication issue.[58] Intercultural miscommunication is seen to occur most often when the people communicating with each other have different perspectives on what counts as competence (effective or appropriate communication). For example, intercultural communication scholar Judith Martin and her colleagues found that Latino university students in the United States regarded approachability and poise as being much more important in intercultural social interaction than did Euro-American students in the same university.[59] The notion of competence is therefore not something fixed and unchanging. It is contextual and extremely difficult, if not impossible, to define as a set of objective characteristics. The context in which intercultural communication competence is defined can be either primarily cultural or situational.[60] That is, cultural prescriptions about the desirability (or lack thereof) of directness and clarity in communication influence what counts as competence. The immediate situation also affects what counts as competent intercultural communication. For example, formality could be considered appropriate in task- or work-related situations such as business deals, and informality might be appropriate in social situations such as a cocktail party. As plenty of people who travel abroad find out to their dismay, however, there are more exceptions than rules!

In addition to framing competence, intercultural contexts also serve to shape the identities of participants. The negotiation of identities through communication in intercultural contexts is a complex issue that varies from situation to situation. However, this does not mean that the lessons we derive from understanding how intercultural differences are negotiated are not translatable. If we are careful about the nature of our assumptions, take into account the possibility that our explanations could be wrong, and avoid using cultural stereotypes as shortcuts toward judging and assessing individual situations, we can cautiously apply lessons learned in one situation to try to understand a new interaction.

For example, Radha Hegde's work with Asian Indian women who have immigrated to the United States helps us understand some of the problems involved in constructing a "minority" identity.[61] Cultural adaptation in intercultural communication is often analyzed at the interpersonal level. For example, Young Yun Kim's model of cross-cultural adaptation argues that, through communication, people undergo a gradual transformation from a monolithic to an intercultural identity in a sequence of stress, then adaptation, then growth.[62] Kim's model assumes that the individual is responsible for his or her participation in the new society and that the individual's sense of efficacy relies on the extent to which he or she has been able to participate and adapt. By contrast, Hegde demonstrates that individual identity is formed as a result of a *range* of factors rather than a single model of individual responsibility. For example, personal identity is connected to how a group or collective identity is articulated. Moreover, identity construction is an ongoing process; it can't be reduced to bipolar terms of adaptation/non-adaptation. Hegde found that three prominent themes structured how Asian Indian women immigrants constructed their identity. The first had to do with how they dealt with stereotypical representations both at the workplace and outside of it; the second had to do with specifically racist encounters; and the third had to do with feelings of isolation. The women Hegde interviewed struggled with images of submissiveness and timidity. One woman, who attended a corporate leadership training program, talked about this process of learning and unlearning: "My mother used to tell me all the time 'don't talk about yourself.' Now when I work with white men I know I have to forget . . . what she told me. I have to learn to be a new person to survive, everything I was raised to be doesn't fit in."[63] "Fitting in" became more complicated when the women encountered racist situations involving their accents, their clothes, their make-up, and their skin color. Adaptation meant, in many ways, coping with a sense of loneliness and isolation that came from trying to tread a fine line between Western individuality and traditional expectations.

The relationship between intercultural communication and identity construction foregrounds the issue of cultural diversity. Studies of communication and diversity have begun to focus on "whiteness" as something that is central to our understanding of diversity in organizations.[64] Jolanta Drzewiecka and Kathleen Wong (Lau) argue, for example, that whiteness is both an enacted and *un*enacted phenomenon in our cultures.[65] The enactment of whiteness refers to the construction of values and practices that are distinct to white cultures, and the "un-enactment" of whiteness refers to the fact that remarkably few white people tend to think of themselves or their identities in terms of whiteness. As Ashcraft and Allen state in box 13.8, whiteness is taken for granted; therefore, it is often unnoticed. Even when it is basic to and dictates the activities of an organization, it remains invisible. In fact, whiteness as a cultural value permeates our understanding of nature itself. Kevin DeLuca identifies conceptions of nature that are associated with white, Western values—the notion of nature as pristine, untouched wilderness. He discusses how this conception has guided the philosophy and activity of environmental organizations such as the Sierra Club.[66]

There are some analogies to be drawn between the notion of invisible whiteness and invisible heterosexuality. Just as white values tend to be both enacted and unenacted, so do we construct a wide variety of policies, procedures, and practices that privilege heterosexuality over homosexuality. While the field of organizational communication has not systematically addressed issues of sexual orientation in the way it has

Box 13.9 Ethnicity and a New Type of Identity

In a provoking and penetrating analysis, sociologist and marketing professor Dominique Bouchet discusses the specific nature of ethnicity today. Typically, ethnicity refers to shared cultural traits—retained customs, languages, or social views—of minority groups with a common ancestral origin. Most often, ethnic characteristics are regarded as fragile—susceptible to the forces of modern society.

Today, the significance of such common identifications has become blurred and unclear. In contemporary, postmodern society, Bouchet argues, ethnicity "has more to do with cultural loss than with cultural ties, more with the loss of a future than with the loss of a past." The question of ethnicity, in other words, highlights the uncertainty of identity in today's world. Bouchet cites the example of young French citizens whose families emigrated from the North African region of Maghreb. These young people have in many ways adopted the culture of the French, even though they reject identifying themselves with French society. While they continue to claim an association with Magrebíes, they reject the traditional values of that society. This situation, which is not uncommon among young second or third generation emigrants in Europe, illustrates that ethnicity does not necessarily indicate commitment to a particular group. Rather, as Bouchet points out, it expresses the *withdrawal* from a group whose common and unique identifications—for instance, music, hairstyles, food, and names—are still used selectively and strategically to express a certain individual style. Bouchet contends that such "*à la carte* ethnicity" has little to do with social unity. The claimed "we" in such contexts is an "I" in disguise. Although Bouchet acknowledges that *bricolage*—the construction of meaning and identity using whatever materials happen to be available—is the only way to navigate in a confused society, he is alarmed that community for many young people in the Western world is defined negatively through rejection:

> When elaborating their personalities and grouping themselves, individuals are influenced mainly by the boredom of their living conditions, the annoyance of their image as perceived by the dominant Other (which includes the mass media), the breakdown of their family structure, the loss of parents' authority, the maladjustment of the education system, the loosening of the social bond, the fascination of consumption, the legitimacy of superfluity and mediocrity, the slackening of political commitment, and the resurgence of violence and force. The virtual impossibility of connecting to an existing social bond at the macro level makes it necessary to unite at the local level.[67]

Can you recognize the tendency to use ethnicity in the á la carte manner described above? What are the implications for organizational culture and participation?

"In the interest of cultural diversity, we've hired Jason, here, who owns a number of hip-hop CDs."

addressed issues of gender, the growing focus on race indicates that issues of diversity will receive more attention. In the last few years, for example, public and private organizations across the United States have begun to provide insurance and other benefits to same-sex partners as well as married couples and heterosexual partners. In fact, the Washington D.C.-based Human Rights Campaign (HRC) has developed an increasingly influential "Corporate Equality Index" that rates large businesses and U.S. branches of multinational corporations on how they treat gay, lesbian, bisexual, and transgender employees. Interestingly, HRC draws much of its funding from corporate sources, including Ford, Nike, American Airlines, IBM, Coors, and Cingular.

Thinking about cultural identities and communication from the point of view of diversity brings some issues into focus that we have already discussed, especially in chapter 8 on participation. Workplace democracy implies that the burden of adaptation should not fall on individuals; rather, democratic participation should be built into organizational structures and policies. As our workplaces become increasingly diverse and differences that were earlier hidden become more public, our notions of effective organization and effective democracy will probably have to change accordingly. In box 13.10, Debashish Munshi and Susan Hafen discuss the implications of "managing" diversity in organizations, rather than seeing it as a fundamental part of organizational lives.

Box 13.10 Voices from the Field

Controlled and Silenced Voices in the Chorus of Diversity
Debashish Munshi, The University of Waikato and
Susan Hafen, Weber State University

As the globalized workforce becomes increasingly multicultural, *diversity management* is becoming a major organizational priority. The trend is reflected not only in the proliferation of books on the subject but also in the inclusion of cultural diversity training programs within workplace routines. The dominant metaphor of diversity management is getting a variety of voices to sing together in a chorus.

The sing-along is, of course, meant to foster workplace harmony. But such "harmony" is often superficial and drowns out issues of *differential power*. As communication scholar Debashish Munshi points out, "while the plurality is formally validated by the presence of a range of musicians, the baton remains in the hands of a Western conductor."[68] Linguistics and pragmatics researchers Jan Blommaert and Jef Verschueren (1998) explain that "management is always in the hands of the powerful, and the management of diversity is not an exception."[69] Munshi's research supports this view by showing how dominant, and in a sense, neo-colonial organizational factions look at diversity as something that needs to be "managed" rather than admitted to the organization on its own terms. Munshi argues this *management* of diversity becomes a process of *controlling* the "other."[70]

Continuing with the music metaphor, communication scholar Susan Hafen asserts that celebrating diversity does not mean just getting a variety of voices from different culture, gender, or lifestyle backgrounds to sing together but also including a whole range of worldviews—even those that question the notion of celebrating diversity. Her research makes a case for "letting all voices, on and (arguably) off key, into the choir, without flinching at discordant notes, without wishing that they would just be silent."[71] Hafen's research tracks both the voices and silences in diversity training discourses. In highlighting the *discursive silences*, Hafen exposes the contradictions between what the advocates and opponents of diversity training programs *say* and *don't say* in their respective arguments. For instance, in talking about the need to learn about other cultures, advocates of diversity programs *essentialize* culture in simple, formulaic terms and ignore the multiplicity of identities. Opponents, on the other hand, often fail to acknowledge the potential of such programs to create a greater awareness of minority identities.

What is your conception of organizational diversity? What role do you think communication can play in creating new organizational values and symbols that involve all? Can bottom-line goals of an organization be in sync with its diversity goals or are they incompatible? What does all this mean for organizational socialization programs?

Celebration of Diversity

Cultural critic Edward Said explicitly argues for a point of view that *celebrates* diversity rather than manages it. In an article titled "A Clash of Ignorance," [72] he argues against the use of oppositional labels such as "Islam" and "The West" in Samuel Huntington's book *The Clash of Civilizations*. In the wake of September 11, Said believes we are even more likely to buy into Huntington's perspective that assumes a "West versus the rest" stance. He argues it is very difficult to arrive at a unitary idea of the West or of Islam:

> The truly weakest part of the Clash of Culture and Civilizations thesis is the rigid separation maintained between them despite the overwhelming evidence that today's world is in fact a world of mixture, of migration, of crossings over, and boundaries traversed. The real question then is whether in the end we want to work for civilizations that are separate, or whether we should be taking the more integrative, but perhaps more difficult path, which is to see them as making one vast whole, whose exact contours are impossible for any person to grasp, but whose certain existence we can intuit and feel and study.[73]

Said ended a lecture at Amherst in 1998 with the quotation on the following page. It helps us understand some of the intersections between the theme of globalization and ideas of intercultural communication and diversity. In advocating a more useful point of view than the "us" versus "them" mentality, Said concluded:

> Much more productive is a new global mentality or consciousness that sees the dangers we face from the standpoint of the whole human race. These dangers include the pauperization of most of the globe's population, the emergence of virulent local, national and religious sentiment as in Bosnia, Rwanda, Lebanon, Chechnya and elsewhere, the decline of literacy and onset of a new illiteracy based on electronic modes of communication, television and the new information global superhighway . . . Our most precious asset in the face of such a dire transformation of history is the emergence not of a sense of clash, but a sense of community, understanding, sympathy and hope . . . the kind of benign globalism already to be found for instance in the environmental movement, in scientific cooperation, in the women's movement, in the universal concern for human rights, in concepts of global thought that stress community and sharing over racial, gender or class dominance.[74]

Snapshot Synthesis

We have noted that globalization is driven by the engine of market economy, but it is far more than that. Although dominant conceptions of globalization are economic, there are other dimensions of globalization that demand our attention. For example, consider the ethnic, religious, political, and social dimensions of peace and war in the Middle East.

In this chapter, we have only begun to scratch the surface of the complexities involved in globalization and communication processes. The term "globalization" is a tremendous abstraction, because it condenses the wide variety of social, political, cultural, economic, and technological processes and events that take place in a bewildering variety of situations. This is not to say that the word "global" is useless (clearly we don't think that is the case since this chapter has emphasized the importance of globalization!). On the contrary, asking yourself what the possible global dimensions are to communication phenomena that you encounter daily in your organizational lives is probably one of the more useful ways in which you can understand and analyze contemporary organizational communication issues.

Key Concepts

- **Globalization:** refers to new and increasing interconnectedness in economic, political, and cultural realms; while economic conceptualizations often dominate, globalization is also inherently political and cultural
- **Convergence Hypothesis**: holds that global forces such as market deregulation have homogenizing effects on organizational practices and forms all over the world
- **Organizational Isomorphism**: the tendency of organizations to become increasingly similar, to imitate one another, and to respond in parallel ways to outside forces

- **Global Imperative:** the idea that globalization is a phenomenon that must happen and cannot be avoided or evaded (illustrated by the metaphor of an ocean wave)
- **Global Reflexivity:** refers to the idea that we are not only aware of the world as an interdependent space, but we are also aware of this awareness
- **Interdependence:** because of globalization, we are intimately connected to events in other parts of the world; thus we are affected by decisions and events in far removed locations
- **Social Imagination:** refers to our collective abilities to conceive of who we are and what we might become; we are affected by a range of financial, technological, mediated, and ethnic forces or "scapes"
- **Intercultural Communication**: communication among people with different cultural backgrounds
- **Intercultural Competence:** effective and appropriate communication in intercultural situations, inherently contextual in nature.
- **Adaptation**: a process by which minority identities adjust to a dominant culture

Endnotes

1 James K. Galbraith, "The Crisis of Globalization," *Dissent* (Summer 1999): 12–16.
2 Roland Robertson, *Globalization* (London: Sage, 1992).
3 Francis Fukuyama, "The End of History?" *The National Interest* (Summer 1989): 3–35.
4 Samuel P. Huntington, "The Errors of Endism," *The National Interest* (Fall 1989): 3–16.
5 Benjamin R. Barber, "Jihad versus McWorld," *The Atlantic Monthly* (March 1992): 53–63.
6 Edward Said, *Orientalism* (New York: Pantheon Books, 1978).
7 Malcolm Waters, *Globalization* (London: Routledge, 1995) p. 2.
8 Marshall McLuhan, *Understanding Media* (New York: McGraw-Hill, 1964).
9 Waters.
10 William Finnegan, "After Seattle," *The New Yorker* (17 Apr 2000): 40–51.
11 Cynthia Stohl, "Globalizing Organizational Communication: Convergences and Divergences," *The New Handbook of Organizational Communication*, ed. Fredric M. Jablin and Linda L. Putnam (Thousand Oaks, CA: Sage, 2001).
12 Janet Fulk, "Global Network Organizations: Emergence and Future Prospects," *Human Relations* 54.1 (2001): 91–99.
13 Peter Monge, "Communication Structures and Processes in Globalization," *Journal of Communication* 48:4 (1998): 142–153.
14 Manuel Castells, *Rise of the Network Society* (Malden, MA: Blackwell, 1996).
15 Roland Robertson, "Glocalization: Time-Space and Homogeneity-Heterogeneity," *Global Modernities*, ed. Mike Featherstone, Scott Lash, and Roland Robertson (Thousand Oaks, CA: Sage, 1997) pp. 25–44.
16 Ayse Caglar, "McDöner: Döner Kebap and the Social Positioning Struggle of German Turks," *Marketing in a Multicultural World: Ethnicity, Nationalism, and Cultural Identity*, ed. Janeen A. Costa and Gary J. Bamossy (Thousands Oaks, CA: Sage, 1995) pp. 209–230.
17 Lisa Peñalosa and Mary C. Gilly, "Marketer Acculturation: The Changer and the Changed," *Journal of Marketing* 63 (July 1999): 84–104.
18 Güliz Ger, "Localizing in the Global Village: Local Firms Competing in the Global Markets", *California Management Review* 41.4 (1999): 64–83.
19 Edgar Morin, *Method: Towards a Study of Humankind: The Nature of Nature*, trans. J. L. Roland Belanger, vol. 1 (New York: Peter Lang, 1992) p. 77.
20 Stohl.
21 Waters.
22 Paul DiMaggio and Walter Powell, "The Iron Cage Revisited: Institutional Isomorphism and Collective Rationality in Organizational Fields," *American Sociological Review* 48 (1983): 147–60.
23 Steven B. Andrews, Carleen R. Basler, and Xavier Coller, "Organizational Structures, Cultures, and Identities: Overlaps and Divergences," *Research in the Sociology of Organizations* 16 (1999): 213–235.

24 See, e.g., Kevin R. Cox, ed., *Spaces of Globalization: Reasserting the Power of the Local* (New York: Guilford, 1997); Ann Cvetkovich and Douglas Kellner, eds., *Articulating the Global and the Local: Globalization and Cultural Studies* (Boulder, CO: Westview Press, 1997); Michael Storper, *The Regional World* (New York: Guilford, 1997).
25 A. Fuat Firat, "Educator Insights: Globalization of Fragmentation: A Framework for Understanding Contemporary Markets," *Journal of International Marketing* 5:2 (1997): 77–86.
26 Firat, p. 79.
27 Stohl.
28 Gideon Kunda, *Engineering Culture: Control and Commitment in a High Tech Corporation* (Philadelphia: Temple University Press, 1993).
29 Theodore Levitt, "The Globalization of Markets" *Harvard Business Review* (May–June 1983): 92–102.
30 Levitt, p. 92
31 H. David Hennessey, "View from Here," *The Ashridge Journal* (July 1999): 23–24.
32 E.g., Susan P. Douglas and Yoram Wind, "The Myth of Globalization," *Columbia Journal of World Business* 22 (Winter 1987): 19–29; Sak Onkvisit and John J. Shaw, "Standardized International Advertising: A Review and Critical Evaluation of the Theoretical and Empirical Evidence," *Columbia Journal of World Business* 22 (Fall 1987): 43–55.
33 Michael W. Rennie, "Born Global," *The McKinsey Quarterly* 4 (1993): 45–52; Tage Koed Madsen and Per Servais, "The Internationalization of Born Globals: an Evolutionary Process?" *International Business Review* 6.6 (1997): 561–583.
34 Tage Koed Madsen, Erik S. Rasmussen, and Per Servais, "Differences and Similarities between Born Globals and Other Types of Exporters," *Advances in International Marketing* 10 (2000): 247–265. Erik S. Rasmussen, Tage Koed Madsen, and Felicitas Evangelista, "The Founding of the Born Global Company in Denmark and Australia: Sensemaking and Networking," *Asia Pacific Journal of Marketing and Logistics* 13.3 (2001): 75–107.
35 E.g., Michael R. Czinkota, Ilkka A. Ronkainen, Michael H. Moffett, and Eugene O. Moynihan, *Global Business*, 2nd ed. (Fort Worth, TX: The Dryden Press, 2001).
36 Jerry Mander and Edward Goldsmith, eds., *The Case against the Global Economy: And for a Turn toward the Local* (San Francisco: Sierra Book Club, 1996).
37 Ralph Nader and Loro Wallach, "GATT, NAFTA, and the Subversion of the Democratic Process," *The Case against the Global Economy: And for a Turn toward the Local*, ed. Jerry Mander and Edward Goldsmith (San Francisco: Sierra Book Club, 1996) pp. 92–107.
38 Edward Goldsmith, "The Last Word: Family, Community, Democracy," *The Case against the Global Economy: And for a Turn toward the Local,* ed. Jerry Mander and Edward Goldsmith (San Francisco: Sierra Book Club, 1996) pp. 501–514.
39 LETS is taken from the invitation, "Let's" and intended to suggest the idea of consent. While the idea of an acronym was an afterthought, LETS is sometimes considered an abbreviation for Local Exchange Trading System. See the LETSystem homepage at http://www.gmlets.u-net.com/home.html.
40 William Greider, "The Right and U.S. Trade Law: Invalidating the Twentieth Century," *The Nation* (15 October 2001): 21–30.
41 Bruce Western, *Between Class and Market: Postwar Unionization in Capitalist Democracies* (Princeton, NJ: Princeton University Press, 1997).
42 John Sellers cited in Jeanette Ringkøbing and Michael Rothenborg, "Økokrigerne," *Politiken* 16 (Aug. 2000): 3.
43 Doug Henwood, "Does Globalization Really Matter?" *In These Times* (31 Mar 1997): 102–105.
44 Waters.
45 Waters, p. 41ff.
46 Marshall McLuhan and Quentin Fiore, *The Medium Is the Message* (London: Allen Lane, 1967) p. 16.
47 McLuhan.
48 Waters, p. 50.
49 Will Hutton and Anthony Giddens, "Is Globalization Americanization?" *Dissent* 47 (Summer 2000): 58–63.
50 "Is Globalization Americanization," p. 62.
51 Arjun Appadurai, "Disjuncture and Difference in the Global Cultural Economy," *Global Culture: Nationalism, Globalization, and Modernity*, ed. Mike Featherstone (London: Sage, 1990).
52 Shiv Ganesh, Mediating the Imagination: Corporate Involvement in the Production of Centralized Subjectivity," *Journal of Communication Inquiry* 24.1 (2000): 67–86.
53 For example, George Barnett, "Cultural Convergence: A Mathematical Theory," *Intercultural Communication Theory: Current Perspectives*, ed. William B. Gudykunst (Thousand Oaks, CA: Sage, 1983) pp. 171–194.

[54] Young Yun Kim, "Searching for Creative Integration," *Methods for Intercultural Communication Research*, ed. William B. Gudykunst and Young Yun Kim (Thousand Oaks, CA: Sage, 1984) pp. 13–30.

[55] See, for example, Will Kymlicka, ed., *The Rights of Minority Cultures* (Oxford: Oxford University Press, 1995).

[56] Stohl.

[57] Karen Lee Ashcraft and Brenda J. Allen, "The Racial Foundation of Organizational Communication," *Communication Theory* 13 (2003): 5–38.

[58] See, for e.g., Myron W. Lustig and Jolene Koester, eds, *Intercultural Communication Competence* (Newbury Park, CA: Sage, 1993).

[59] Judith Martin, Mitchell Hammer, and Lisa Bradford, "The Influence of Cultural and Situational Context on Hispanic and Non-Hispanic Communication Competence Behaviors," *Communication Quarterly* 42 (1994): 160–179.

[60] Lisa Bradford, Renee Meyers, and Kristine Kane, "Latino Expectations of Communicative Competence: A Focus Group Interview Study," *Communication Quarterly* 47 (1999): 98–117.

[61] Radha Hegde, "Swinging the Trapeze: The Negotiation of Identity among Asian Immigrant Women in the United States," *Communication and Identity Across Cultures*, ed. Dolores Tanno and Alberto Gonzalez (Thousand Oaks, CA: Sage, 1998) pp. 34–55.

[62] Young Yun Kim, "Cross-Cultural Adaptation: An Integrative Theory," *Intercultural Communication Theory*, ed. Richard Wiseman (Thousand Oaks, CA: Sage) pp. 170–193.

[63] Hegde, pp. 43–44.

[64] For an overview, see Diane Grimes, "Putting Our Own House in Order: Whiteness, Change and Organization Studies," *Journal of Organizational Change Management* 14 (2001): 132–149.

[65] Jolanta Drzewiecka and Kathleen Wong (Lau), "The Dynamic Construction of White Ethnicity in the Context of Transnational Cultural Formations," *Whiteness: The Communication of Social Identity*, ed. Thomas Nakayama and Judith Martin (Thousand Oaks, CA: Sage, 1999) pp. 198–216.

[66] Kevin DeLuca, "In the Shadow of Whiteness: The Consequences of Constructions of Nature in Environmental Politics," *Whiteness: The Communication of Social Identity*, ed. Thomas Nakayama and Judith Martin (Thousand Oaks, CA: Sage, 1999) pp. 217–246.

[67] Dominique Bouchet, "Marketing and the Redefinition of Ethnicity," *Marketing in a Multicultural World: Ethnicity, Nationalism, and Cultural Identity*, ed. Janeen A. Costa and Gary J. Bamossy (Thousands Oaks, CA: Sage, 1995) p. 88.

[68] Debashish Munshi, "Through the Subject's Eye: Situating the Other in Discourses of Diversity," *Organization↔Communication: Emerging Perspectives*, ed. George Cheney and George Barnett, vol. 7 (Cresskill, NJ: Hampton Press, 2003).

[69] Jan Blommaert and Jef Verschueren, *Debating Diversity: Analysing the Discourse of Tolerance* (London: Routledge, 1998) p. 15.

[70] Debashish Munshi, "The Business of the Other: Representing the Non-west in Management and Media," diss., U Waikato, 2000. In postcolonial theory, the word "other" with a small "o" refers to the "colonized others who are marginalized by imperial discourse." Bill Ashcroft, Gareth Griffiths, and Helen Tiffin, *Key Concepts in Post-colonial Studies* (London: Routledge, 1998) p. 170. The imperial discourse of the colonial times has been replaced by the neo-colonial discourse of business advantage.

[71] Susan Hafen, "Cultural Diversity Training: A Critical (Ironic) Cartography of Advocacy and Oppositional Silences," *Organization ↔ Communication: Emerging Perspectives*, ed. George Cheney and George Barnett, vol. 7 (Cresskill, NJ: Hampton Press, 2003).

[72] Edward Said, "The Clash of Ignorance," *The Nation* 273.12 (2001): 11–13.

[73] Edward Said, "The Myth of the Clash of Civilizations," videotape of a lecture (Amherst, MA: University of Massachusetts Media Education Foundation, 1998).

[74] Said, "Myth."

14

Speaking of Ethics and Values in Organizations

Most textbooks in the social sciences and humanities discuss ethics, but ethics are often treated as an afterthought—just as in many classrooms. "We'll get to ethics at the end of the semester . . . oops—we just ran out of time! I guess the discussion will be brief. But of course, you still know that ethics are important. Be sure to read that last chapter in the text, OK? It's *really* important!" Similarly, most organizations treat ethics either as something to give lip service to or as some "extra" that they can deal with only in good times ("Well, this time we can *afford* to be nice"). In our consulting and research work, we've often heard this argument expressed—although not always so overtly. Some companies, government agencies, and third-sector organizations, however, make ethics an integral part of the way they do business. We will mention a few of the real, inspiring models for action.

We have tried to discuss ethics, ethical issues, and ethical dimensions of organizational lives throughout this book. Sometimes we've explicitly called attention to an important ethical question, such as the importance of having a moral vision of leadership (chapter 7) or the importance of ethics in crisis communication (chapter 10). In other cases, ethics have been present just beneath the surface, as when we talked about decision making in organizations. The study and practice of ethical principles isn't just about moral codes; it concerns choices. In turn, choices suggest values, and values are largely rooted in culture.

In this chapter we present ethics and ethical reflection as part of our everyday experiences and concerns. We'll start with some examples from contemporary organizations, talk about some reasons why ethics are important to all of us today, and then probe deeply into a few issues and cases. Along the way, we'll mention important ethical systems and positions, provide you with some references for further reading and discussion, and give you some tips on how to analyze ethical issues that arise in your own work and lives. Our discussion here is by no means comprehensive, even in our treatment of Western perspectives on ethics. Whenever possible, we urge you to consider points of view other than the Western tradition. Our purpose is not to give you "the right answers" but to offer you some tools for identifying, understanding, and dealing with ethical issues that you face in your (work)life.

Here are some challenging ethical questions involving organizations that have surfaced in recent years.

- Does Nike Corporation have the right to refute charges of abusive child labor practices in Indonesia by arguing that the people there are "better off" with Nike employment than without it?
- To what extent should U.S.-based tobacco companies be held responsible for marketing cigarettes to teenagers in other countries while being required to contribute billions of dollars to government-directed anti-smoking advertising within the United States?
- In what ways should we view aggressive and wide-reaching advertising in China to redefine dandruff as a social problem and therefore set the stage for the sales of anti-dandruff shampoos?
- At what point should firms like Ford Motor Co. and Firestone Tires be required to release information about *potential* defects in products, and how should they do it?
- How should we view attempts by Royal Dutch Shell to refurbish its image, in the wake of problems in Nigeria and the United Kingdom, by presenting itself as a leader in alternative (non-fossil) energy resource development and ecological and cultural sensitivity?
- Do corporations like Exxon/Mobil have rights to free speech—in issuing any sorts of "advertorials" on political and social questions?
- Should there be certain kinds of "litmus tests" for companies that claim to be "socially responsible" or "green" or "employee-centered"?
- Under what conditions, if any, should universities be allowed to alter photos for their brochures that create the impression of greater student diversity at a particular event than was really the case?
- What communicative responsibilities do pharmaceutical companies have in promoting their drugs and in announcing all side effects of them?
- Should advertising always portray the world as it is?
- Should producers of pesticides be held responsible if farmers become ill when using the pesticides against product warnings?
- Under what circumstances, if any, can employees reasonably justify stealing from their employing organizations?
- To what extent should managers be expected to do what they preach, that is, "walk their talk"?
- Should contributions to political campaigns in any countries be *equated* with "free speech" and therefore not have limits?
- How should debates between an ethic of care and the need for efficiency best be conducted in health care institutions?

- Should public hospitals be allowed to prioritize the treatment of their patients so that patients with healthy lifestyles are treated as more important than, say, smokers or drug addicts?
- Should social-movement organizations that preach democracy and sustainability be held to those same values in terms of their *internal* policies and practices?
- How should governments apologize for atrocities committed against other nations, abuses of their own people, or deception of the general public?
- To what degree should Internet music-sharing software be regulated, and what limitations should there be on the free exchange of copyrighted videos and music?

These are just a few contemporary cases and issues that come to mind. Notice, first, how these various cases highlight communication in terms of the construction and use of symbols, messages, and arguments. Most of the cases also have international implications. Many of them involve the clash of two or more ethical (and sometimes legal) principles and may be viewed from more than one perspective. In fact, it is the *clash* of different ethical principles or duties that make many moral decisions difficult. Like King Agamemnon in ancient Greece, who was forced by the gods to choose between love of family and love of country, we often find ourselves in situations requiring difficult moral and practical trade-offs.[1] The work-home tension is one such situation experienced by most people today, as many people around the world struggle to "have a life" while "making a living." In box 14.1 Steve May discusses the ethical questions that surface as boundaries between work and personal issues intersect.

Notice that each question we posed about ethics involves both individual decisions and collective ones. As you consider each question, consider also your personal interests and how they are affected. None of the cases are easy to resolve, although your own belief system may allow you to come to a resolution of some better than others. A good example of such complications is the Napster controversy in 2000–2001, which involved a number of different organizations and institutions and invoked diverse ethical principles.[2] Napster, like other Internet-based companies, created plug-ins that automatically linked distant users so that they could share music and video files. In the United States, lawsuits were filed against Napster by various individuals and music associations, and the net result was the demise of Napster in September 2002. The Napster issue is often framed in democratic terms as "free access" versus the rights of artists and recording labels to recoup "justly deserved royalties." But the issue is even more complex than this. The relevant parties include: recording artists, associations of recording artists, record companies, the courts, private firms (like Napster), users of Napster and other Internet-based companies providing software for sharing MP3 files, and the larger public. The case brings out value questions such as property, privacy, information access, and democracy. What do you think about this case and why? Which values and principles are most important to you in evaluating the case? Why? Which arguments would be the most persuasive or compelling for you, on either side of the issue? If you were adjudicating such a case, how would you rule?

Box 14.1 Voices from the Field

A Question of Boundaries
Steve May

Although many of us tend to maintain distinct divisions between ethical standards and practices in various realms of our life, evidence suggests that we also experience a growing blurring between areas such as public/private, work/family, and labor/leisure. This blurring of boundaries in our lives raises interesting and challenging ethical dilemmas regarding the relationship between employers and employees.

For example, company-sponsored employee assistance programs (EAPs), which have proliferated in the last two decades, raise some difficult ethical questions regarding personal and work boundaries. Originally developed to assist workers with alcohol and drug problems, EAPs now cover almost any physical and psychological problems that may confront an employee. EAPs may assist "troubled workers" with substance abuse and addiction, depression, family problems, grief, gambling, sexual dysfunction, weight gain or loss, and emotions such as anger and resentment, among others. In addition, they may help employees with a variety of health problems through welfare and fitness programs, screenings for cancer, heart disease, and high cholesterol, and so on. In the last decade, EAPs have also introduced counseling sessions for the victims and survivors of downsizing.

Certainly, many employees gain significant benefits from these programs. However, EAPs also pose potential drawbacks, including discrimination (based on physical and mental health), reduced confidentiality of medical information, and constraints on privacy. Recently, for example, both a beer producer and a chocolate manufacturer have fired overweight employees. A trucking company has fired employees for smoking off the job. A national chain restaurant has fired several of its employees for not demonstrating "normal" heterosexual values. An insurance company has barred its employees from engaging in risky leisure activities such as rock climbing, skiing, and in-line skating. An automobile manufacturer has required physical screenings for cholesterol, cancer, and body-fat as a condition of continued employment. When questioned, company executives argue that such practices are in the best interest of both the employer (to improve productivity and reduce health care costs) and the employees (to improve health).

To what extent are EAPs a form of assistance or a form of control? Who should be responsible for the physical and psychological health of employees? Where does the personal autonomy of an employee's body and mind end and the company's interest begin? What realms of life are (and should remain) private, and what realms of life are (and should remain) public? When and where does our labor end and our leisure begin? What are the influences of work upon the family as well as the influences of the family upon work?

Coming to Terms with Ethics

Ethics are a part of life, our jobs, and our organizational activities whether we acknowledge it or not. Even when people insist that something is morally neutral—like "pure information"—they are dealing with ethics. In fact, taking the position that some subject or position on an issue is "value neutral" is a powerful rhetorical strategy that diverts the listener's attention away from the fact that even pure information embodies certain preferences and choices. Numbers, and other kinds of information, never speak for themselves! When we tell an audience that we're offering only pure information about an issue—be it global warming or proposed tax rates or the effects of in-school advertising or the right to own guns—there is necessarily a dimension of persuasion. Or when we say, "differences between men and women are *natural*," we are presenting a particular perspective on gender relationships, even if we claim otherwise. Absolute neutrality is hard to achieve. Thus, the line between "information" and "persuasion" is not so clearly defined, as the ancient Greeks recognized.

Why Do We Need Ethics?

As we discussed in chapter 4, you can't examine what you can't see—what you take for granted. To many people, ethics or morality is an automatic response. They can't isolate their system of beliefs or examine how they came to believe as they do. The focus on "Can I do this?" or "What shouldn't I do?" in the West often reduces democracy to "How far can I push my own rights?" When we are faced with sharply different beliefs or values, however, our own assumptions suddenly stand out. Travel can have this effect, as when a North American confronts a radically different pattern of living in, say, Latin America, Africa, or Central Asia. In all of those regions, the North American is likely to encounter more collectivist, inherently *social* conceptions of values, mores, and notions of "correct" behavior.

In the United States, the U.K., and Australia, problems such as substance abuse or mental illness are defined as *individual* problems rather than a corollary to some aspect of the larger society. In individualistic societies, we blame individuals, sometimes missing the larger patterns and forces at work. From this perspective, most social ills are seen as the result of actions by people who are either "mad" or "bad." In situations of stress or urgency, such as war, we might well label "The Other" as *both* mad and bad. This individualistic perspective frequently narrows ethical discussions to considerations of individual rights rather than collective goals and responsibilities. In a number of Western societies, the talk of "rights" can easily overcome any sense of the commonweal—the ethical well-being of the larger community. As communication theorists James Anderson and Elaine Englehardt explain, organizational rules, norms, and practices do not receive nearly enough attention when we talk about professional ethics; we are far too focused on individual behavior to see the larger context that encourages people to act ethically or unethically.[3] Too often, the egregious acts revealed in corporate, governmental, and other organizational scandals are "contained" through crisis management that confines blame to individuals. The scandal at energy giant Enron in the United States in 2001–02 was largely defused by focusing on individuals.[4]

The need to consider ethics from the perspective of collective goals and responsibilities does not imply that conformity is necessarily a goal or a solution. We can all imagine robot-like adherence to a group norm: most of us have probably witnessed that, or even occasionally done it. But, peer pressure or strong social expectations in themselves are not good reasons for making a particular ethical decision. Ethicists such as Immanuel Kant (1724–1804) do not ask people "to go along with the crowd" but to *arrive* at an individual decision that reflects social concerns through the use of a sound form of ethical reasoning.

Practical Foundations

To ask ourselves about the practical, rather than theoretical, foundations of ethics, we might look across ethical systems and ask: Why does this system exist? For what purpose? These are questions we can ask of ethics in general, and not just of moral prescriptions specific to a particular culture. Listed below are some of the major *practical* reasons for ethics.

- Ethics are for ***coordination.*** They help us organize and prioritize our activities, set certain standards, and have confidence that others, at least most of the time, are going to behave in predictable ways. *Thus, ethics help us get together.*
- Ethics are for ***community*** because moral codes help keep us together and remind one another of what's important. *Ethics help us to get along with one another.*
- Ethics are for ***inspiration,*** when we put forth positive models of behavior and "good work." *Ethics give us hope for betterment*, both on an individual and on a societal level.
- Ethics are for ***social control*** in that they can be used to manage the society, "keep people in line," and regularize activity. *Ethics keep things going.*
- Ethics are for ***emulation,*** as when organizations in one industry set standards that are taken on by others. *Ethics put ideals into practice.*

You may find some of these to be better reasons than others, and you may think of still other reasons that aren't covered by our categories. (While you're reflecting on these points, consider how they apply to your job, or your experience at the university, or your family.) Notice that each of the reasons offered is double-edged. For example, community can be oppressive when it turns into mindless conformity, as we find in some small towns and some religious groups. Moreover, "inspiration" taken from a charismatic leader can lead to exactly the wrong kind of "civic engagement," as in Germany during WWII, in Cambodia in the late 1970s, or the former Yugoslavia during the 1990s. Countless cases of abuses of leadership involved a high degree of organization and efficiency, but the fundamental goals were misguided. One of the most frightening aspects of human experience in the modern world is our capacity, in certain situations, to execute a plan (and, sometimes, people!) in a relentlessly efficient manner, without deep consideration of *what we're doing.* In war trials, we often hear the defendant respond: "I was only doing what I was told to do." Or, "I was only doing my job." Or, "There was a higher authority in which I trusted; they dictated, and I followed." The point is to recognize that multiple things may be going on when people talk about ethics, urge others to be ethical, and try to impose certain standards.

Union Carbide Disaster

Bhopal, India, continues to face ethical and practical issues in the aftermath of the worst industrial accident in world history. In October 1984, a gas leak at a Union Carbide plant killed more than 5, 000 people.[5] A number of community activists have devoted themselves to extraditing and prosecuting former Union Carbide CEO Warren Anderson in India, finding that avenue a more accessible alternative than pressing either civil or criminal charges against the corporation. The government of India has downgraded the charges against Warren Anderson in order to make extradition more likely. Anderson was held briefly by the Indian government in late 1984. After he was released on bail, he never returned to India, despite multiple demands that he face trial there. Meanwhile, the corporation built a huge hospital on the outskirts of Bhopal, while at the same time refusing to release information on the precise contents of the lethal gas. Further complicating matters, many citizens of Bhopal attribute their various illnesses to the disaster, even when some of these problems are caused by non-disaster-related factors (for example, contaminated water). This has made it challenging if not impossible for governmental and health authorities to sort out the relevant cases. The government has created something of a "gas victims' colony," presumably in the interest of helping the many injured families, but this has in fact isolated many citizens from the rest of the community and made it even more difficult than normal for former Union Carbide workers to locate new jobs. There have also been charges of corruption against governmental agencies and private contractors involved in building the six hospitals in and around Bhopal since the accident.

There was also public outrage in the United States after the Bhopal disaster; however, the context for the outrage differed from the one in India. As Debashish Munshi and David McKie argue, the outrage had more to do with *the possibility that a similar accident might occur* in the United States than it did with the complications of the Indian situation per se.[6] Union Carbide in the United States responded by attempting to distance itself from its "Indian counterpart" and argued that safety was a local concern.[7] Bhopal is often cited as "a success story" in public relations textbooks because Union Carbide ultimately escaped with its name and its resources surprisingly intact. But what does this say about our definitions of "success" and about the question of professional ethics in the fields of public relations, issues management, and image management?

The Bhopal case raises the question of authenticity. How do we *know* when a company is "really being ethical" as opposed to just wanting to look that way to a particular group of people? In other words, when a company proclaims itself "socially responsible" and joins an organization like Businesses for Social Responsibility, how do we assess or measure the level of commitment? As far back as ancient Athens, people recognized that "talking the language of justice" could make a government look just.[8] Strong ethical commitments can usually only be assessed over time and in multiple situations. Some marketers, for instance, stress that good reputations can only be earned over the long haul; that it's seldom enough for a firm just to *assert* its values.[9] With globalization, ethical controversies are becoming more visible as they spin themselves out differently in different places. While one culture might view a corporation's actions as ethical, another culture might view them as highly unsatisfactory.

Finally, the Bhopal case also illustrates why the concept of corporate social responsibility (CSR) should be thought of in inter-organizational rather than intra-organizational terms. Over the last few decades, as corporations have become increasingly dominant, CSR has been used to describe the desirability of managing business practices in consonance with larger societal issues and to contribute to the overall well-being of the cultures and communities in which they are embedded. The question of CSR takes on added significance in the context of cases such as Bhopal, which have global dimensions. In Bhopal, the question of Union Carbide's responsibility was negotiated by a range of agencies, including activist groups and the U.S. and Indian governments. As organizational communication scholars Nikki Townsley and Cynthia Stohl argue in an analysis of CSR practices in Sweden, despite the increasingly transnational character of corporate forms of organizing, we cannot conceive of the notion of corporate social responsibility without examining how certain corporate practices are born out of legal frameworks set up by governments.[10] Rhetorical scholar Steve Schwarze (in a study of asbestos contamination caused by a vermiculite mine in Libby, Montana, that claimed more than 200 lives) argues that when we frame corporate irresponsibility as a result of "greedy CEOs," we ignore the fact that such irresponsibility is inter-organizational in nature, co-produced by both corporations and government agencies that failed to do their jobs.[11]

Why Ethical Reflections Matter

Reflecting on ethical concerns is a pressing concern for all of us, and it is useful to consider a range of ways in which individuals, communities, and organizations reflect upon and frame ethical issues. Consider the ways in which people in the world of business might frame the role that ethics can/should play in the workplace. A Cornell Business School survey in 1996 asked executives to rank the values they thought would be important for leaders in the future; *compassion* ranked second only to teamwork. In response to the same question about *current* practice, the executives placed compassion at the bottom. Even more alarming was the fact that top business school students responded to the same survey by ranking compassion *last* in a list of traits needed for leadership in the future![12]

A 2002 *Business Week* article shows another disturbing trend. In a survey conducted by the nonprofit Aspen Institute of nearly 2,000 MBA students at top business schools in the United States, MBA students overwhelmingly put shareholder value above other concerns, including environment, community, customers, and quality products. The survey found that "MBA students [in the United States] enter B-school with relatively idealistic ambitions, such as to create quality products and be of service to consumers. By the time they graduate, though, these goals have taken a back seat to such priorities as boosting their company's share price."[13]

Articulating Basic Values

Part of the difficulty in studying people's ethical frameworks is that it is often not easy to articulate basic values. In an interesting study called "The Moral Muteness of Managers," two management researchers found that part of the reason why business ethics studies lean toward organizational criteria such as efficiency is that most managers have a hard time describing how they make ethical decisions *in any other terms*.[14] That is, there seems to be a lack of alternative visions and ways of conceptualizing problems because a "bottom-line" mentality is so prevalent and little time is spent on reflection. So, here is an important case where the things people don't say, or have difficulty expressing, may be just as important as what they do say. It's what we might call the lack of "the vision thing." Promoting positive role models—not perfect ones, but admirable ones—is one way to encourage people to practice ethical behavior and to think about what choices are available.

Box 14.2 Ethical Reflection and Pedagogy
George Cheney

It's a truism as well as a cliché that our lives are full of surprises. After 23 years of college-level teaching, I'm happy to say that this observation applies fully to the classroom. Some of my greatest joys in teaching have come from surprising turns of events in the course of a discussion with a group of students, however jolting those sharp turns may be at the time.

In the last half of 1998, I had the privilege of teaching and conducting research at the University of Waikato, in Hamilton, New

Zealand. Part of my duties there consisted of offering afternoon and weekend topical sessions in an executive M.B.A. program. One day in November, I was preparing to deliver a half-day lecture about theories of leadership to a group of 20 mid-to-high level Chinese managers. Both in terms of the design of the series of courses and in accord with Chinese cultural norms, a predominately lecture-oriented format was expected. This made the turning point in that class all the more surprising. When I was about half-way through my prepared notes and overheads, one manager politely raised his hand and said: "Professor Cheney: my colleagues and I very much appreciate your presentation and want to read about and discuss this material. But, while we are here together, what I'd most like us to do is make time to discuss the ethical and moral dilemmas in our jobs. You see, we never have time to do that at work, and most of us have no one to confide in even if we did have the time." I looked around the room and saw many nods of agreement.

After checking the understanding and desires of the entire group, I put down my notes, turned off the overhead projector, and sat down in a circle with the students. One spoke about his (all but two students in the class were men) issue; then another; then another. Following the description of each dilemma, there would be lively exchanges among the students, and only occasionally did I intervene with a suggestion like, "Have you considered this . . . ?" or "You know, that relates to such-and-such theory." My role transformed into that of a facilitator for the rest of the afternoon, and the group took full ownership of the space for ethical reflection that they themselves created.

A few days later, especially after returning to some of my notes from recent writings on business ethics, I realized the "space" these managers yearned for was probably the same thing desired by many managers and others around the world. The increased pace of life, the reduction of social concerns to economic ones, and obsession with production in the narrow sense all work against ethical reflection and a quiet, thoughtful consideration of "What really matters."

My thoughts come back to the Chinese managers. What they sought most was what I, in my academic life, take for granted: space and time to reflect. Facilitating a learning environment that allows people to get beyond the taken-for-granted is now my first goal for pedagogy. That is to say, if I can help students find a space to consider what they don't ordinarily consider, to make *opaque* the parts of our society that are usually *transparent* for them, then any information that I transmit to them will be in a sense "gravy."

Work, consumption, home, and civic life should all be subject to reflection and reconsideration. I try to encourage this type of critical thinking now in teaching courses called "Power in Society," "Communication and Ethics," and "Communication and Quality of Work Life." If not in the university, if not in seminars, then where should we expect such reflection and discussion to happen? There's not enough room for it on TV, in cars, on cell phones, or even on the Internet. I'm deeply grateful for the classroom surprise that helped remind me of what's most important in the educational process itself.

Varying Standards

Ethical reflection becomes even more important with greater internationalization, because ethical standards from different parts of the world collide. This sometimes leads to questioning one's own (or one's organization's) ethics. In addition to placing different ethical positions in conflict with one another, globalization also creates *new* ethical problems. Consider, for example, how the U.S.-owned firms along the border to Mexico (called *maquiladoras)* have spawned debates over issues such as wage levels, effects of absentee corporate owners on communities, the flight from rural areas to urban zones that span the frontier, international environmental standards under NAFTA (North American Free Trade Agreement), union organizing across the international boundary, and the flow of labor (that is, people) between the two countries.[15] The example of the *maquiladoras* also illustrates relationships between various institutions, as shown dramatically by the parallel cities along the border—starkly different worlds in juxtaposition. Capital may move freely across the guarded frontier, but not necessarily people or services like water and sanitation. The ethical issues range from the individual choices of managers and employees to multinational contracts and international policies.

The discussion of business ethics has moved beyond the previous gulf between abstract theory completely removed from practice and the practice of trying to be "just one centimeter above the law." The latter phrase has been used by some business ethics professors who argue that ethics is completely a matter of *calculating* one's own personal interests—as we'll discuss later. Fortunately, the literature of business ethics now includes more reasonable scenarios and is more sophisticated in discussing challenges faced in everyday life plus the ethical tensions and trade-offs for employees and managers. Thus, we find realistic casebooks with recent issues and controversies, including for example, Thomas Donaldson and Al Gini's popular *Case Studies in Business Ethics.* This book features examples ranging from mining, to auto-

"Ms. Burney, do we have anything on right and wrong?"

mobile manufacturing, to pharmaceuticals, to hygiene products, to consulting, to taxes, to community responsibility.[16] There are now numerous conferences on business ethics and on important social questions of our day, such as the effects of globalization on local communities. Moreover, we now find articles on ethics written from numerous national and cultural perspectives, from African to Pacific Island points of view. Just a quick look at recent issues of *The Journal of Business Ethics* shows the international scope of today's discussions of ethics. Although Western perspectives still dominate, awareness is broadening as the taken-for-grantedness of certain understandings of ethics is challenged.

Many of the cases cited in the literature say nothing about communication—at least not on the surface: they address issues about oil spills, or chemical gas leaks, or automobile malfunctions. Even in those material cases, however, arguments are made, issues are framed, and judgments are put forth. Robert Jackall's book *Moral Mazes* is a fine example of communication *about* ethics, based on the responses of U.S. managers to questions about what they *actually think about and do* in situations calling for moral decisions.[17] Jackall captured in the managers' own words how they understand and apply ethics in their work and decisions. (We think it would be very interesting to conduct a similar ethnographic study in other national and cultural contexts.) Jackall found that many managers *do* think about ethics, are troubled by the choices they often feel they have to make, and try to do "the right thing." However, many of these same managers use what we might call a language of *constraint* to describe how they feel limited in their actions. Expressed in colloquial language, the position sounds like this: "I would have liked to do the right thing, but the situation didn't allow me that luxury." In some cases, the managers perceive circumstances that prevent them from doing what their consciences tell them they should do. These circumstances include the pressures of deadlines, fear of competitors, expectations of superiors (either real or imagined), and concern for "the bottom line" over social values. Some PR officers interviewed for Jackall's book even expressed the "need" to exaggerate their companies' successes in order to get attention and to win approval for the firm from clients and others.

Proactive Stance

Organizations in all sectors are talking about values. And organizations in all sectors are being much more proactive than before with respect to ethics. This is not to say that organizations are necessarily more or less ethical than in previous periods. Such a claim—in either direction—would be very difficult to prove. Rather, we are noting that ethics as a topic and as a point of reference has become more noticeable. Any large organization today is expected to have both a mission statement and a statement of values or code of ethics. Look at box 14.3 for an example of a code of ethics adopted by one particular organization. What values underlie the various parts of this code? In what ways is the code too specific or explicit, and in what ways is the code not specific or explicit enough? How could codes like this be modified to be more inspirational?

Today organizations do not wait until others ask them about their ethical commitments; they are actively stating their ethics both formally and informally. Ethics, thus, have become part of the corporate portfolio and profile. There are conferences on corporate reputation, corporate citizenship, and corporate social responsibility; numerous books are published each year with those titles. Despite the new

Box 14.3 PRIA Code of Ethics[18]

The Public Relations Institute of Australia (PRIA) is a professional body serving the interests of its members. In doing so, the Institute is mindful of the responsibility that public relations professionals owe to the community as well as to their clients and employers. The Institute requires members to adhere to the highest standards of ethical practice and professional competence. All members are duty-bound to act responsibly and to be accountable for their actions. The following Code of Ethics binds all members of the Public Relations Institute of Australia.

1. Members shall deal fairly and honestly with their employers, clients, and prospective clients, with their fellow workers including superiors and subordinates, with public officials, the communications media, the general public, and with fellow members of PRIA.
2. Members shall avoid conduct or practices likely to bring discredit upon themselves, the Institute, their employers, or clients.
3. Members shall not knowingly disseminate false or misleading information and shall take care to avoid doing so inadvertently
4. Members shall safeguard the confidences of both present and former employers and clients, including confidential information about employers' or clients' business affairs, technical methods or processes, except upon the order of a court of competent jurisdiction.
5. No member shall represent conflicting interests nor, without the consent of the parties concerned, represent competing interests.
6. Members shall refrain from proposing or agreeing that their consultancy fees or other remuneration be contingent entirely on the achievement of specified results.
7. Members shall inform their employers or clients if circumstances arise in which their judgment or the disinterested character of their services may be questioned by reason of personal relationships or business or financial interests.
8. Members practicing as consultants shall seek payment only for services specifically commissioned.
9. Members shall be prepared to identify the source of funding of any public communication they initiate or for which they act as a conduit.
10. Members shall, in advertising and marketing their skills and services and in soliciting professional assignments, avoid false, misleading or exaggerated claims and shall refrain from comment or action that may injure the professional reputation, practice, or services of a fellow member.
11. Members shall inform the Board of the Institute and/or the relevant State/Territory Council(s) of the Institute of evidence purporting to show that a member has been guilty of, or could be charged with, conduct constituting a breach of this Code.
12. No member shall intentionally injure the professional reputation or practice of another member.
13. Members shall help to improve the general body of knowledge of the profession by exchanging information and experience with fellow members.
14. Members shall act in accord with the aims of the Institute, its regulations and policies.
15. Members shall not misrepresent their status through misuse of title, grading, or the designation FPRIA, MPRIA, or APRIA.

Adopted by the Board of the Institute on November 5, 2001, this Code of Ethics supersedes all previous versions.

prominence, there remains a tension between ethics for the sake of some other goal and ethics for its own sake.

This tension is evident in published articles; there are a multitude of contrasting perspectives. Here's one example. An article in *The Strategic Management Journal* argued that for most businesses, ethics or ethical considerations get folded into a cost-benefit analysis. The author explained that short-term considerations tend to prevail over long-term perspectives, meaning that the firm is less likely to bring ethics into view.[19] Another article, this one in the professional magazine *Marketing*, spoke of "the wider benefits of backing a good cause: as firms are rediscovering initiatives linked to good causes are also good for business."[20] How do you feel about these ways to frame ethical responsibility and ethical decision making? How are they realistic but at the same time limiting?

Ethics as an Issue for Organizations

Ethics are a matter of concern not only because of the variety of ways in which we engage in ethical reflection and frame ethical issues, but also because of several trends in the last few decades that have made ethics an issue for contemporary organizations.

The nature of corporate legitimacy (or the basis from which corporations justify their authority or usefulness) has changed dramatically in the past three decades. Prior to 1970, a company could stress that it provided jobs, made a useful or desired product, or fueled economic development without offering further justifications. Some observers like U.S. economist Milton Friedman[21] still believe that the sole responsibility of a business is to make a profit while operating within the bounds of established law. However, there has been a steady increase in arguments about the impact of businesses on their employees, on communities, and on the larger environment. While the traditional reasons for doing business still exist, they are no longer as persuasive as they once were. Part of the explanation is a growing public awareness in some parts of the world of the power of large organizations (especially multinational corporations). Another reason is an underlying skepticism about the basic values of our societies (e.g., growth, efficiency, rationality, etc.). As a consequence, the idea of corporate responsibility is now part of common parlance in organizations. This has positive ramifications for activities such as agenda-setting but negative ones when meaning is diluted because, for example, everyone claims to be "green" and "socially responsible".

There have been high-profile scandals in many sectors. These have occurred in business, government, and in the so-called independent or third sector. When the scandals happen in avowedly values-based organizations—like religious denominations, charities, nonprofit agencies, social movements, etc.—the shock and the media attention are often even greater. People expect organizations based on values, such as churches, to be "above" that sort of thing. When scandals occur in government or in the third sector (for example, in a nonprofit charity organization), we are especially disappointed, in that we expect or somehow hope that greed and other vices will not play so big a role outside private, for-profit firms. Scandals that destroy the credibility of corporations include offering faulty products, concealing important consumer information, mistreating employees, exploiting contacts and inside information, misusing public funds—and the list goes on. While it's difficult to assess whether such incidents are more frequent today than earlier, they perhaps receive more public attention than used to be the case.

In early 2003, reports of a huge scandal at the U.S. Air Force Academy in Colorado Springs emerged. Numerous cases of sexual harassment and rape came to light, along with a massive coverup that had prevented general discussion of the problem for decades. Female cadets at the Academy had been subjected almost uniformly to some kind of aggressive sexual advance by male cadets. In many cases, fear of dismissal led to silence on the part of those injured. As columnist Anna Quindlen wrote, "[H]ow terrible it is that women who must face sexual assault from the enemy as the price of war too often expect to face it from their compatriots in peacetime."[22] The aggravated forms of sexual assault, as well as sexual harassment, should be viewed in terms of power and ethics. As box 14.4 illustrates, sexual harassment is a result of larger processes not isolated, individual actions.

Box 14.4 Communication and Sexual Harassment[23]

Sexual harassment has increasingly become an issue in U.S. workplaces, with over 15,000 charges being filed with the U.S. government in 2000.[24] Although men also experience sexual harassment, statistics show that as many as one out of every two women may have encountered sexual harassment at work.[25] Nearly all communication research on the subject has been based in the United States. One explanation is that the term sexual harassment was coined by U.S. feminist activists in the 1970s.[26]

Communication scholars (notably feminist scholars) have paid attention to how sexual harassment is discursively constructed, experienced, and contested. For example, communication researcher Debbie Dougherty discusses how men and women define and experience sexual harassment differently. In her study of sexual harassment practices in a health care organization in the U.S., she found that men tended to frame sexual harassment using the functional terms of work-related stress, care, and camaraderie, whereas women tended to frame sexualized behavior at work in terms of its dysfunctions.

However, as Nikki Townsley and Patricia Geist argue, U.S. policies about sexual harassment do not adequately deal with the variable contexts and meanings associated with sexual harassment practices.[27] Further, as Robin Clair says, it is difficult to identify and deal with sexual harassment precisely because organizations in the United States have tended to hide, trivialize, or characterize sexual harassment as simple misunderstanding—treating harassment as normal or accepting it as inevitable.[28] Because the underlying message that organizations communicate to victims is "deal with it," victims find it difficult to file charges and resolve the issue.

We should view sexual harassment as not merely a result of interpersonal communication between genders but as a multi-level phenomenon embedded in social structures, cultures, and ideologies. Shereen Bingham delineated four levels at which sexual harassment should be tackled.[29] The first of these is a *socio-cultural*. This level involves addressing bureaucratic and societal systems and arguing for legal and cultural changes. The second level is *organizational*, where changes must be made in internal organizational policies, such as changing policy and procedure manuals to prohibit sexually explicit behavior. Third, collective action should be taken against sexual harassment at the *group* level. This could include building support groups, social and professional networks, and collectively protesting perpetrators of sexual harassment. Finally, the *individual* level includes confronting the harasser face-to-face, writing letters, filing organizational grievances, or filing legal complaints.

How do you think that sexual harassment is dealt with differently by different groups of people? Is it reasonable to expect victims of sexual harassment to take the initiative in reporting cases? How might issues of sexual harassment be framed and resolved differently in various other parts of the world?

Accountability is repeatedly called into question. Interestingly, the legal definition of a "corporation" in the Western industrialized world means that liability is limited and dispersed (Inc. for "incorporated," Ltd. for "limited liability," and S.A. for "anonymous society"). In a sense, we can treat incorporation as a metaphor for the problems of all organizations when it comes to moral accountability. Civil law requires identifying harms and connecting them to the actions of the organization; criminal law usually requires some determination of intent. Intent is difficult to prove, however, when we move from individual to collective levels of analysis.

Organizations tend to accrue power and disperse accountability, making it difficult to discern intention, assign blame, and hold people, as decision makers, responsible for the actions done in the name of the organization. The Ford-Firestone case of 2000–2001 involves complex interrelations about which of the two companies are responsible for the sales of seriously defective tires around the world. This case is still unfolding, and the United States may impose criminal—rather than just civil—penalties on auto and rubber executives for withholding safety information from the public. The collapse of Enron, and especially the realization that much of its presumed worth was fraudulent, called attention to the power of corporations in society. Tens of thousands of employees were left with worthless retirement accounts as a result of the fraud. The world's largest accounting firm, Arthur Andersen, admitted to the deliberate shredding of documents related to Enron's collapse. The criminal conviction of Andersen caused the demise of the company and could result in fines and imprisonment for some senior partners. These cases may mark a transition toward more criminal charges being advanced against corporations and other organizations.

The problem of anonymity in bureaucracy is related to the issue of accountability. As discussed in chapter 2, bureaucracy has many meanings and many different dimensions: some positive, some negative. Part of the strength of bureaucratic organization comes from the fact that it does not rely too heavily on particular persons or groups. The *system* transcends individual contributions, regardless of the power associated with any individuals. As political scientist Robert Lane points out, bureaucracy and the market have a kind of structural impersonality in common: humans are viewed as replaceable in organizational roles and financial transactions.[30] Impersonality is not a new problem. In the late Middle Ages in Europe, guilds brought together groups of craftsmen with common interests in regulating their production and securing a market.[31] Because guilds were designed to transcend individuals in time, resources, and power, they soon became "out of reach" of the very individuals who created them. This type of alienation compounded over generations with the growth of private and public institutions. Practically speaking, organizations "take on a life of their own." Ethically speaking, it then becomes difficult to assign responsibility for a decision or to level blame for a moral lapse or even a crime.

There has been a breakdown of traditional social bonds as many societies have experienced a public-private "split." A key part of modernization is less reliance on traditional forms of authority (religion, autocratic governments, patriarchs or matriarchs, or experts who refuse to explain their conclusions). As we have discussed in other chapters, Émile Durkheim feared that separation and segregation (as occurs with job specialization) would lead to the loss of social solidarity, the loss of a general moral discussion, and alienation.[32] He argued that ethics were not just for individuals to decide for themselves but for communities of people to discuss, affirm, enforce, and modify. Ethical commitments, in other words, are grounded in and supported by values that large groups of people hold in common: ethical frameworks are not a simple formulation stated by a group or organization—as when people talk casually about the "community" of their profession.[33]

Our students regularly apply ethical standards selectively: some for family, some for friends, some for work, etc. They may say: "Well, telling the truth is pretty important when I deal with family and close friends, but not when I'm at work or on the street." Many people would add: "You know, it's a dog-eat-dog world out there, so I just *can't* be as ethical as I would be at home." Such a division is natural, to some extent, but it often gets in the way of reflection on what kind of public sphere we really want. A strict division between private and public life prevents us from seeing just how interdependent we are and the fact that approaching work with the dog-eat-dog expectation can actually be a self-fulfilling prophecy in how we affect others.

Violations of and challenges to trust threaten the foundation of organizations. To a great extent, trust is the foundation for any society and any economy. We often think of the economy as material rather than symbolic. But money actually is a social and symbolic system that relies on confidence.[34] Without a basis of trust and belief in certain symbols, the economy ceases to exist because currency, credit, and future investments depend on understood agreements. With such problems as insider trading on Wall Street and the rise in speculative investments, trust erodes and suspicions rise. This is exactly why consumer confidence is monitored so closely and why fluctuations in the market flow from upsetting news events. Some authors argue that trust may be the single most important element of organizational and inter-organizational culture and that it is best promoted through "trust-cultivating structures" that remind people of their interdependence.[35] From a communication standpoint, this means that much of the work of trust building in organizations should be informal and proactive, rather than legalistic and reactive.

The advice here is consistent with Charles Redding's famous formulation of the "Ideal Managerial Climate" (discussed in chapter 4), the key elements of which are trust, openness, supportiveness, participative decision making, and an emphasis on high-performance goals.[36] Trust is tricky: it's easy to lose but hard to build up. This is why it is such a precious resource for work and organizations, just as it is in friendship, romantic relationships, and families. Trust in others—and in oneself—is at the foundation of an ethical culture. Without trust, anyone, any group can fall into easy justifications for actions that would otherwise be seen as unacceptable or just plain wrong. As the saying goes: "Well, everyone's doing it," or "Hey, I'd better get them before they get me." When you multiply such interpersonal situations by thousands or millions—the erosion of trust can spell disaster. When trust is severely damaged, or when everyone in an organization begins to suspect others' intentions and sees every action through a political lens, true cooperation becomes almost impossible. In 2003, American Airlines asked its three unions to vote to lower wages so that the company would not have to file for bankruptcy. The day after the favorable vote, it was revealed that the corporate board had voted to pay retention bonuses to the CEO, Don Carty, and about six other senior executives, effectively doubling or tripling their salaries for a year. The company also had funded a dormant pension fund for senior executives sheltering their retirement income in the event of bankruptcy. After a firestorm of protests Carty rescinded the bonuses but not the retirement plan. The trust that had led employees to voluntarily take less pay in an effort to work together to save their company was shattered.

Discourse about the economy is increasingly abstract, detaching it from more fundamental human concerns. "The economy" is often discussed as if it were disconnected from people. In New Zealand in 1998, for example, there was an exchange of editorials in the national newspapers about this very issue, in which some commentators spoke of the irony of discussing the unemployment rate as if it had no human face. Discussions of the "Post-industrial Society," the "Information Age," and the "E-economy" are especially prone to this kind of separation. Some of our students have pointed out that the often celebrated images of the "New Economy" are disempowering and even insulting to them because most of them will not be and have no desire to be dot-com millionaires. They note how most jobs and careers are *invisible* in popular discussions. (We'll talk more about this issue when we consider ethics and the market.)

Little understood implications of new technologies produce anxiety. Technology is advancing at a rate faster than our ability to grasp the full implications of these changes. In this sense, the idea of a technological imperative has traction: we develop new technologies simply because we can, often giving little thought to the disadvantages that inevitably accompany advantages. What are the ethical implications of new capabilities such as the private or public nature of e-mail, electronic monitoring of employees at work, or genetic screening of prospective employees for vulnerability to certain chemicals? We are, as *The New York Times* put it a few years ago, "relentlessly interconnected,"[37] without reflecting on why or for what reasons. What are the spillover effects of work where employees are increasingly expected to be connected via cell phones, computers, and palm pilots when off the job (and perhaps on the beach!)? While technology doesn't literally have a life of its own, we often grant it that kind of power by endlessly chasing it. Advertising in the computer industry clearly counts on this kind of *race* metaphor running our lives. One ad warns, "Don't let your grandmother catch up with you!" We connect in lots of ways today, through a wide array of media and technologies, but what is the quality of those connections in many cases, and what connections have been lost?

We confront multicultural and international challenges to accustomed, taken-for-granted routines. Insights from local or indigenous cultures potentially modify or question the business practices imported from more dominant world economies. There is practical, ethical wisdom in the enduring experiences of various communities and cultures of the world, and one of the most important insights is the valuing of social bonds as a means of grounding ethical practice, enforcing standards, and re-embracing wayward members (e.g., rituals of "disentangling," as practiced in some Polynesian societies, where the individual is simultaneously chastised and re-embraced by the community for a wrongdoing).[38]

One of the most challenging issues, it seems, is finding a "common language" to discuss ethics. In many cultures, ethical principles or ideals are implicit and tacit. The question "What is your ethical system?" may produce puzzled reactions in some settings—as happened at a conference on ethics in New Zealand in 2000 attended by representatives of numerous Pacific Island cultures (such as Samoans, Fijians, Tongans, and Maori, the indigenous people of New Zealand). Participants took the opportunity to reflect on cultural differences and to debate the extent to which it was important to articulate an *explicit* set of principles, versus allowing ethics to be part of the fabric of culture and life itself.

What foundation? Whose ethics? For which situations? We increasingly confront these questions. If ethics are essentially agreed-upon standards, what does it mean when different groups cannot agree and all view themselves as upholding ethical practice? What one culture views as a natural emphasis on personal connections in work or politics, another could see as nepotism or as anti-rational. Max Weber observed how such conflicts operated in organizations and societies. While favoring the legal-rational, bureaucratic form and its soft-pedaling of personal preferences and relationships, Weber nevertheless recognized the losses that could result from a march toward rationality.[39] This is just one way in which different ethical systems diverge when applied to the workplace. While this chapter is not about the foundations of ethics, we feel it is important to mention some of the most prominent Western traditions in box 14.5.

Box 14.5 Some Prominent Western Philosophical Traditions in Ethics

- Utilitarianism: achieving maximum happiness while doing the least harm
- Ethical Egoism/Realism: practicing enlightened self-interest over the long term
- *A Priori* Rights/Social Contract Perspectives: emphasizing the actual or implied social bond
- Virtue Ethics: highlighting values as embodied in individuals and a community
- Fairness: focusing on decisions about what kind of society to "construct" (either real or imagined)
- The Golden Rule: featuring role-taking, perspective-taking, empathy
- Kant's Categorical Imperative: treating people as ends in themselves rather than as means to an end
- Feminist: for example, stressing the ethic of care over the ethic of achievement
- Dialogic: emphasizing the communication process as foundational
- Pragmatic: focusing on consequences of adopting one view or another

Recognize, of course, that these brief descriptions do not do justice to any of the perspectives listed. We urge you to pursue further reading: William Frankena's accessible classic, Ethics,[40] *explores the Western tradition.*

Teleological and Deontological Ethics

Speaking generally, the two great traditions in Western ethics are utilitarianism (*teleological* ethics) and the ethics of duty (*deontological* ethics). Reduced to their simplest terms, a teleological perspective focuses on the outcome: "the end justifies the means." Deontological ethics focuses on the process of relating to others. "In this situation, I have a responsibility to protect the rights of . . ." Taken together, these two traditions give us a fairly complete way of analyzing an ethical situation, though each approach has a crucial blind spot. While utilitarianism ignores minority rights and, in some ways, gender issues, the ethics of duty can be simply unattainable for many people and in many situations (and therefore lacks a certain realism). Both traditions have tended to be applied in a "calculating way"—by expressing a principle and producing a judgment (after the fact) or a recommendation (in advance) about people and the specific situation.

A vivid context in which to see the contrast between teleological and deontological ethics is in wartime. While war is usually justified from a utilitarian perspective ("We will destroy the village to save the country"), the ethics of duty often enters in when we later consider what constitute "war crimes"—or excesses even within the setting of war. It's not that big a leap to the domain of business here, where the war metaphor is frequently invoked in arguments about competition, trade, and career advancement. Think about what sorts of business dealings can be justified more easily under the rubric of warfare than they can be with other metaphors.

Ethics of Compassion

In recent years, the overwhelmingly rational or cognitive bias of Western ethical traditions has been complemented with a turn to emotion—an ethics of compassion—an important contribution of Eastern ethics. For example, a number of Buddhist traditions embrace widening circles of compassion to include not only those close to us but also those distant and even our enemies. The same ethical practice extends to other sentient (feeling) beings and the earth itself. In his book *A Passion for Justice*, Robert Solomon argues for an infusion of emotionality into the study and practice of ethics, arguing that out of our very passions come motivations to right wrongs and work toward social justice.[41] Solomon and others who take this position wish not only to counter the overwhelmingly cognitive nature of the Western traditions of ethics but also to highlight how gut feelings can often lead us to do the right thing. Think of the kinds of situations that arouse your sense of anger or sadness and especially the desire to "do something" to help someone or to make a situation better? How can this apply at work? Of course, Solomon's perspective implies a deep confidence in people and their level of civilization. When considering such a perspective, we should ask ourselves when our emotions or "gut reactions" will help guide us toward ethical action.

Thinking about and across Different Ethical Perspectives

In general, the deontological and teleological perspectives can be seen in terms of how they emphasize acts, principles, people, means, and situations. We can represent these five points as a pentagon for "positioning" ethical perspectives, theories, or principles. The diagram is a variation on Kenneth Burke's "Pentad"—act, agent, agency, scene, and purpose.[42] The pentagon is useful because it helps us appreciate the interrelations among ethical perspectives. Using such a framework, we can better compare and contrast various perspectives, seeing their similarities and their differences. From a communication standpoint, we can treat each discourse on ethics in terms of its focus or orientation and the types of assessments to which it typically applies. We can examine the characteristic ways in which a person or an organization *talks about ethics.* Are ethics discussed as coming from *within* a person? Are they imposed from the *outside*? Are they only important when someone else is watching? Do they vary across *setting* and by circumstance? For example, a situational ethic emphasizes scene or circumstances and the kinds of acts that arise from them. Virtue ethics, as developed by Aristotle, feature an agent-act "ratio" in that good acts are associated with virtuous agents or persons (though tied to communities).

Think about how you *talk about ethics* and how you typically justify or excuse your own actions (see box 14.6). Do you, for instance, often *excuse* an action with bad consequences by saying that you had "no choice"? Or, do you often *justify* the same kind of harm by insisting that it was all for a greater good? The sociolinguistic distinction between excuses and justifications is helpful here. *Excuses* tend to take the form: "I know it was wrong or harmful, but I couldn't help it." *Justifications,* by contrast, accept the wrong or the harm and assert, "It had to be done." Sometimes, of course, the wrongfulness or harm is not even acknowledged at all, or may be obscured or minimized. In research on "accounts," sociologists and communication scholars analyze the excuses and justifications used by people ranging from juvenile delinquents, to street gangs, to corporate criminals for "untoward" or unseemly actions. In most cases, people are able to either excuse or justify the action, despite its harms, by appealing to *some system of principles*.[43] That system may not be the one generally accepted by the public, but it is nevertheless salient in the minds of the perpetrators. This realization has transformed the ways some social workers and law enforcement officials deal with street gangs. Instead of viewing gangs as chaotic, uncontrolled, and without order, they see them as responding to a different (and admittedly misguided) set of principles—and in reaction against the order of the society from which they feel alienated. The implications for addressing street violence are clear: the grounds for the motivations and plans of gangs must be removed as well as applying traditional means of law enforcement against crimes committed by them.

Box 14.6 Ethical Pentagon

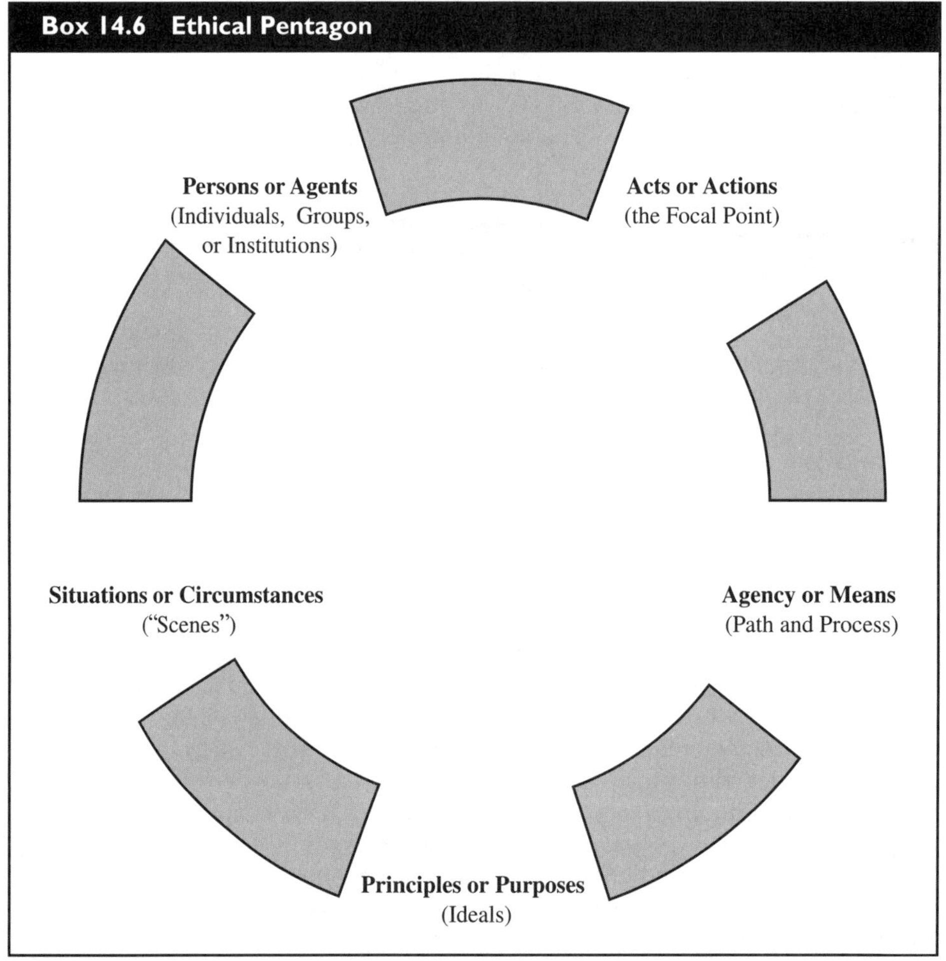

Different ethical systems focus on different behaviors. This is important to remember when we compare and contrast ethical perspectives. For example, in recent years the Western media have given practically no attention to the fact that in the Islamic ethical tradition, broadly speaking, there is great concern for economic imbalances, the concentration of wealth, and poverty.[44] Instead of observing *varieties* of Islam, and highlighting this attention to economic justice, Western commentators have tended to paint all of Islam with a fundamentalist brush, focusing on the extreme subordinate position of women in certain Islamic-run societies. The point here is that we need to see ethics as multi-faceted, not just within our own camps but in those of others. In fact, by comparing and contrasting different ethical systems, we can help to understand better our own blind spots and our convenient ways of compartmentalizing ethics. So, for example, ethical discussions in the United States can expand to pay more attention to economic disparities both within the country and between richer and poorer parts of the world. This has implications for the internal practices of organizations as well. In the United States people have become accustomed to justifying enormous differences between "top" and "bottom," with salary ratios far exceeding what we see in other parts of the industrialized world. Only in the last few years has criticism of this growing gap received attention in the mainstream media.

Think about your own preferred ethical theories or perspectives and try to place them on the diagram above. How do you explain noble acts? What is your assessment of acts that are commonly viewed as unacceptable? Do you see any patterns in your ethical discourse?

What about Communication?

Linking communication to ethics is not new. Plato, for example, recognized that persuasion could be very seductive in terms of encouraging people to "short circuit" rational reflection and to be tempted by an attractive but ultimately harmful idea. Aristotle saw ethics as bound up in every appearance of an orator on a platform and in every message that was issued to the public. More recently, philosophers from various parts of the world have come to a view that if communication (in certain respects) is distinctively human then it entails certain ethical assumptions—e.g., about veracity (or accuracy), honesty (or truthfulness), etc. We can talk about the relationship between ethics and communication from several angles: we can examine *language* itself as inherently ethical; we can look at communication and ethics in terms of *values*, and we can look at *levels* at which ethics and communication are linked.

There is a whole line of thought where ethics are seen as *inherent* in communication processes.[45] One famous example of this comes from twentieth-century philosopher Martin Buber, whose reflections on "I/Thou" help us appreciate our deepest assumptions about ourselves and our relations to others.[46] Another comes from the foremost contemporary proponent of critical theory, Jürgen Habermas, who sees the communicative act as the basis for our ethics and for a theory of social practice.[47] While Buber's approach is more emotional (more metaphysical), Habermas's is logical and rational. Both of these ethical understandings, however, stress dialogue. True dialogue, they say, involves perspective taking (from the cognitive standpoint) and empathy (from a more emotional standpoint). There are at least three aspects of language that bind it inextricably with questions of ethics.

"Honesty is the best policy, Fernbaugh, but it's not company policy."

Language as an Ethical Choice

Language, as we've emphasized throughout this book, always has a *persuasive* dimension, even when it appears to be or is presented as "just information" or "just the facts." Labeling an issue calls attention to it and frames it in a particular way. Think of names for wars, social movements, opposition groups, organizational change, etc. Language is persuasive—it suggests choices and options; the fact of choice implies ethics.

Ambiguity is an inherent part of language, even when we strive for precision.[48] But there are degrees and types of ambiguity. In some cases being deliberately ambiguous can be viewed as ethical, even necessary. For instance, how else do we unite diverse groups of people except under ambiguous banners by talking about values like "justice," "progress," "freedom," etc.? In other cases, though, we consider intentional ambiguity to be unethical. Consider cases where organizations and their leaders avoid taking responsibility for an action or its consequences by speaking in very vague terms—what some politicians and businesspeople call "plausible deniability."[49]

Emotionality is a third dimension of language. As we've discussed we often contrast emotionality with rationality; in fact, that distinction characterizes much of the Western philosophical tradition. But the presence of emotion in language and other symbols cuts both ways. Sometimes, the use of emotionally charged labels can be used to short-circuit reasoning processes. This is certainly the case with lots of political ads on television. Other times, emotionality is essential in helping us focus our attention on something important. Recall Solomon's statement that we can have a passion for justice.[50] Justice is not just something we think about and decide upon; in many cases, it is also something we feel. Think of persons who speak out in meetings and are eloquently and forcefully able to convey the importance of an issue.[51]

The Role of Values in Ethics

Let's turn our focus to values as *undefined master symbols or sacred points of reference*—considering in particular, the ways we talk or communicate about values. Values and value-based slogans command great allegiance for decision making even when their multiple meanings and practical senses go unexplained (box 14.7). Value-related or value-implicative terms are *indices for entire domains of meaning and yet are simultaneously devoid of meaning.* Values are often indexed or referenced at a vague, emotionally rich level that cannot be achieved by more specific symbolic appeals. Values are *emotionally charged*; many organizations elicit warm feelings in their audiences or stakeholders with references to such things as "family friendly," "environmentally friendly," or "child conscious." And, some value expressions operate as a means of *pacification and denial of problems* (e.g., "We are *all* equal"). This is a subtle point, probably best made by Indian economist Amartya Sen,[52] when he observed how value-related terms such as equality can be asserted to mask endemic or persistent differences.

From a communication standpoint, ethics has two levels. First, we can focus on an *ethical issue* in organizational communication practice, for example: electronic

Box 14.7 Organizational Expressions of "Value(s)"[53]

- Arranging a *hierarchy of commitments* ("people first")
- Advocating *specific values* ("customer service"), especially with new campaigns
- Celebrating simply *having values* (in political discourse, "family values")
- Imitating *(mimesis)* values of other organizations ("They have *excellence*; we need it, too!")
- Values/ethics *as style or fashion* (often with secular-mythological or religious symbolism)
- Values as *premises for decision making and as building blocks of future persuasive efforts* (in issue management, establishing common ground often with only vague references or images)
- Values as means of *employee motivation and horizontal control* in organizations ("concertive" organizing around visions, missions, etc.)
- Values as representing or encapsulating the *tradition* of an organization (appeals to founding principles); in contemporary terms, values as central to *corporate branding, identity, and reputation*
- Values as *undefined master symbols or sacred points of reference* ("Quality is our most important product")
- Values as *inappropriate assertions of consensus* ("We at Acme all believe")
- Values as *checks or benchmarks against which performance is evaluated*
- Values as *sites of resistance* (employees' subversive use of the organization's mission by turning it upside down)
- Value-based logic as *the rationality* of the organization (reflexive organizations that revisit their own values; the idea of organizational integrity)
- Values as *embedded in social practices* (journalistic objectivity as enacted by ritual); values as *implicit in or inferred from entire patterns of behavior or whole relationships* (trust)
- *Transformation of values*, both "within" or "under" key terms and across them (evolution of the term *consumer* in twentieth century)

monitoring at work; when companies should notify "downsized" employees of impending layoffs; whether journalists should reveal confidential sources of information; the degree of openness required of superiors in dealing with subordinates. Sissela Bok's book, *Lying*,[54] reveals the role of communication in identifying ethical issues. The book puts a laser beam on a variety of types of communication situations—many involving organizations and work—and asks, "How and under what circumstances can a lie be justified?" Bok examines many different circumstances: "white lies," lies for "the good of the country," lies to one's enemy or competitor, deception in social research, lies to a terminally ill family member, lies as exaggeration, and so forth. In the end, she suggests it's very difficult to justify lies of any kind.

A second way to consider ethics and communication is by *reflecting on the ways ethics and values are discussed* in popular as well as in professional discourses: for example, how does a particular philosophy of business allow for or encourage ethical practice? Should business be socially responsible? Should accounting practices take values other than cost savings into account? All of these examples concern the "framing" of ethics: how ethics are seen, what definitions of ethics will prevail, if there are boundaries around the application of ethics, and so forth. Examples of everyday sayings that reveal a particular perspective on ethics are: "All's fair"; "Blood is thicker than water"; "It's just business." In each of these cases, an overall or *meta*-ethical standard is put forth.

The ways we think and talk about "The Market" (similar to our earlier discussion of abstracting the economy) provide some useful illustrations of what we mean here. As we discuss the market, we imbue it with certain characteristics, even agency; we grant it power as a social actor, we give it authority over our actions, etc. This is a bit ironic in light of the fact that the market is actually made up of people—or more precisely, lots of relationships and transactions between people (and of course, between organizations!). Consider the various ways we talk about the market and the implications for ethics of these various ways of seeing it (box 14.8).

Once again, we must be attuned to *national and cultural differences in ethical practices*. What becomes "common sense" with respect to ethical practice or expecta-

Box 14.8 Meanings Attributed to "The Market"[55]

- Exigency or Pressure ("The market made us do it")
- The One Best Way (to order the economy and society)
- "The End of History" (global hegemony)
- Market as God (or ultimate source/answer to questions)
- Amoral Frame for Action ("It's just business")
- Domain of Relationships (as in the marketplace)
- Arena of Consumer Choice (representing "freedom')
- Global Network (especially of organizations)
- Arena of Symbolic Play (e.g., investment clubs)
- "The Real World" (in contrast with . . .)
- Myth or Meta-narrative we Tell about Ourselves (our tradition)
- Everyday Social Practice ("modern day hunters and gatherers at the mall")

How do you think about and talk about the market? What difference does it make in terms of ethics? In what ways do you see the market as a social agent that has attitudes, intentions, and goals? How does this view both make sense and lead us astray? How is the market moral? Amoral? Immoral?

tions for moral conduct is culturally and even legally shaped. For example, in the United States, many presumed acts of ethical corporate behavior may be in direct response to the requirements of existing laws, or to the fear of litigation, or in anticipation of higher standards to be enacted either formally or informally. The notion of corporate ownership of property, for example, has far stronger legal standing in the United States than it does in countries with (formerly) socialist policies, such as Sweden or India. At the same time, we find companies and government agencies looking over their shoulders to see what other organizations are doing before determining their own standards.

To summarize, a communication-oriented approach to ethics recognizes not only that some ethical issues (like the notification about an impending layoff, or supervisors' openness) have communication dimensions but also that the very ways we discuss ethics have important implications.

Postmodern Challenges to Ethics

Most of what is said and written about ethics is framed within a modern perspective, a perspective that takes for granted that "underneath" different expressions we all aspire to the same goal (or *telos*) and, as a consequence, ethics has universal dimensions. A *post*modern sensibility implies that we are hesitant to accept any one ethical system as being applicable to everyone and for all time—that there's a healthy skepticism toward overarching views. This perspective, attuned to the reality of multiple belief systems, is not the same as relativism, where all frameworks or positions are treated as being just as good as one another. Adopting a postmodern attitude means that we can no longer see society and its moral standards as completely unified or completely consistent in the way that we once did. Consider the following example. After the student rebellions in Paris in 1968, a French philosopher remarked: "There was no bloodshed, thus nothing happened." To this the Italian (and postmodern) philosopher Mario Perniola said something like: "Isn't this typical for the modernist attitude, that all changes need to be soaked in blood—that if there has been no bloodshed, *nothing* has happened?" What Perniola expresses here is a fundamental doubt in the values and goals of modernity and a growing suspicion of what we call "progress" and "development."

This kind of doubt and suspicion is not at all incompatible with religious belief systems and ethical frameworks. For example, what some religious perspectives on ethics and the key insights of postmodernism share is a radical questioning of the Enlightenment, or the *certainty* with which "progress" has been pursued over the past two hundred years or so. The greatest difference is that a postmodernist perspective doubts the possibility for any single overarching and enduring perspective.

With a postmodern perspective we move outside our comfort zone, where our ethical and moral positions are not taken for granted. If the end (or the goal) no longer justifies the means, how should we orient ourselves toward the future? And how do we establish our ethical principles? Many postmodernists decline to provide answers to such questions. Far from being wholly cynical, however, a postmodernist perspective can point us toward a return to a contingent, value-based rationality that considers ethics in specific life-situations. In this sense, ethics can become local or a small narrative—constantly invented and reinvented by a community—as opposed to modernity's grand narratives of progress, individuality, and rationality.[56] In this sense, our ethical practice becomes an ongoing reflection about our values, ends, and means rather than an automatic application of a general framework. Whether humankind is ready for such challenge, however, is another question. All of these issues can be seen as the backdrop for the organizational and professional settings within which ethical decisions are made.

Organizational Culture and Ethics

To conclude this chapter, we would like to offer you a few pragmatic suggestions about examining ethics in the organizational cultures in which you participate. When looking at an organizational culture from the point of view of its ethics, what stands out the most are formal attempts to codify ethical behavior in organizations. So, a good place to start examining the ethical dimensions of organizational culture is to look at a professional code of ethics. Consider the quotation below from 1890 and think how easily it could have been written today:

> The more the dimensions of societies increase and the more markets expand, the greater the urgency of some regulation to put an end to this instability. [This is because] the more . . . the society extends beyond the individual, the less can the individual sense within himself the social needs and the social interests he is bound to take into account. Now, if these professional ethics are to become established in the economic order, then the professional group . . . must be formed or revived.[57]

What did Durkheim mean, and how is what he said relevant today? Formal ethical codes are important for several reasons, and these reasons are related to the reasons listed at the beginning of this chapter: (1) they unite a community of professionals; (2) they offer a basis for making important distinctions; (3) they are used to sanction violators; and (4) they offer standards for ethical excellence. Review box 14.3 on the code of ethics for the Public Relations Society of Australia. Ask yourself what underlying principles of ethics can be inferred? How might informal ethics in the organization differ from its formal ethical code? Can such codes be enforced? If so, how? How might such a code have been different say, fifty years ago? Finally, what theories of ethics can you see operating in the code?

In addition to codes of ethics, here are some other questions about the organizational culture that are useful to consider when focusing on ethics.

- *The vision or concerns* of the organization: What do decision makers in the organization regularly think about and what things do they announce as important?
- *Organizational structure*: How does the structure of the organization allow or disallow for ethical discussion, debate, and dissent?
- *Informal norms and socialization*: To what extent do issues of character and moral leadership come to the fore during management training?
- *The status of (negative as well as positive) role models*: Whose example "matters," and how is mentorship conducted?
- *Habit or routine*: What patterns become established or become the taken-for-granted ways of dealing with problems?
- *Tests*: How do the organization and its decision makers respond to crises?

Box 14.9 Voices from the Field

A Case Study on Corporate Social Responsibility and Communication about It

Sasha Grant, The University of Waikato

The Body Shop International, PLC is a values driven, high quality skin and body care retailer operating in 50 countries with over 1,900 outlets.[58] The Body Shop was founded by entrepreneur Anita Roddick (OBE) who, in 1976, started retailing home-made naturally inspired products with minimal packaging from a small shop in Brighton on the South coast of England. Franchising created rapid growth and internal expansion. The Body Shop's ethics are rooted in Roddick's personal beliefs and agenda—to dedicate business to the pursuit of social and environmental change—and are fundamental to the way the organization operates. In 1999, The Body Shop brand was voted the second most trusted brand in the United Kingdom by the Consumers Association. In 2000, The Body Shop enjoyed worldwide retail sales that totaled £634.6m and a pre-tax profit of £31.5m.[59]

The Body Shop is a pioneer in the Business for Social Responsibility Movement. Roddick has spoken openly about the role of business in society:

> I would love it if every shareholder of every company wrote a letter every time they received a company's annual report and accounts. I would like them to say something like: "Okay that's fine, very good. But where are the details of your environmental audit? Where are the details of your accounting to the community? Where is your social audit?"[60]

Trading relationships with communities in need (The Body Shop Community Trade Programme) and campaigns for the environment, animal protection, and human rights make The Body Shop distinct from its competitors. Social and environmental auditing and reporting presented The Body Shop with a powerful rhetorical vehicle for establishing and building on value premises. The Body Shop Values Reports in 1995 and 1997 were recognized by the United Nations Environmental Programme and Sustainability as "trailblazing," and ranked highest in their reviews of international corporate environmental reports. In 1994, Roddick started the New Academy of Business: "Our vision is to help build the next generation of business education based on responsibility, accountability and respect for diversity."[61]

In order to maintain a consistent and unified identity, The Body Shop has had to demonstrate its commitment to and self-improvement on issues like environmental protection, animal protection, and human rights to both internal and external audiences. Intense media scrutiny tested The Body Shop's identity in 1994 with the publication of a controversial article that questioned the organization's values. Additionally, The Body Shop's policy on transparency and open communication provided the template for imitators and competitors to position their identities on The Body Shop image, threatening the organization's position as a leader in its field.

In 1998, the turn to more conventional business professionals resulted from the growth in size of the company, the need to improve financial performance, and the need for more experience in conventional business operation. This decision led to the organization's first round of redundancies, a shift toward conventional marketing, and a new Chief Executive Officer.

Is there a need for a corporate code of conduct? Who should develop and oversee these codes of conduct? How important is ethical leadership to an organization's success? Is there a direct relationship between ethical leadership and socially responsible business? Are the personal values and ethics of leaders central to the organization's identity, and if so, does it always have to be this way? What happens to the organization, its identity, and its future when the leader leaves (the classic problem of succession)?

While it is difficult to provide a set of general guidelines to promote ethical practices and debates in organizations, here are a few rules of thumb that we can follow to build an organizational culture that is self-conscious about its ethical standards. First, discussion and debate around core organizational values should be promoted. Second, formal standards and codes of ethics should be both inspiring and up to date. Third, avoid casting ethics primarily as a formal issue; instead, treat it as part of the informal culture of the organization. One way of doing this is to offer living examples of ethical standards. Fourth, authorize ethical ombudspersons who can give advice and facilitate discussion of ethical issues. Fifth, focus on the multiple benefits and outcomes of ethical debates. Sixth, develop checks on corporate and top-down power.

Finally, encourage orientation toward the "triple bottom line": where the organization considers its own profits and growth, its responsibility to employees, and its roles in the wider community and environment. The triple bottom line is a fairly commonly used indicator of social responsibility. The index refers, first, to the responsibility to make a profit and satisfy investors; second, to the responsibility toward employees with respect to benefits, work environment, and voice; and third, to the responsibility toward the wider community and environment in terms of various impacts. This index is now widely supported by associations of businesses for social responsibility in numerous countries.

Snapshot Synthesis

In this chapter, we have attempted to provide you with an overview of the reasons why ethics are important in both theory and practice. The practice of organizational communication is inherently ethical in nature; in order to become more effective practitioners, we must also become more ethical ones. As the dimensions of organizational communication shift from context to context and era to era, so do ethical practices and reflections. In our current globalized world, the nature of ethical reflection and the importance of ethical issues in organizations have shifted considerably and become simultaneously more urgent, more complex, and more challenging.

Key Concepts

- **Corporate Social Responsibility (CSR):** asserting that good business practices take into account their impact on communities, society, the economy, and nature
- **Corporate Legitimacy**: framework through which corporations justify their role, authority, and usefulness in society
- **Teleological Ethics (utilitarianism):** a perspective that focuses on the aims and outcomes of ethical decisions
- **Deontological Ethics (ethics of duty):** a perspective that emphasizes transcendent duties and responsibilities and a focus on process
- **The Ethical Pentagon:** a variation on Kenneth Burke's pentad to compare and contrast various perspectives on ethics, especially the degree to which they emphasize persons, acts, situations, agency, and purpose/principle in evaluating ethical situations

- **Ethical Dimensions of Language:** aspects of language that bind it inextricably with questions of ethics, including persuasiveness, ambiguity, and emotionality
- **Levels of Ethics and Communication:** level one focuses on ethical issues in communication practice; level two focuses on how ethics and values are framed and discussed by a perspective or across perspectives
- **Modern Perspective (on ethics):** perspective that assumes a universal ethics—a common goal (or telos)
- **Postmodern Perspective (on ethics):** in contrast to the modern perspective, skepticism toward universal ethical frameworks; assumes ongoing reflections about ethical practices in specific life situations

Endnotes

1 Martha Nussbaum, *The Fragility of Goodness* (New York: Cambridge University Press, 1986).

2 See, e.g., Charles C. Mann, "The Heavenly Jukebox," *The Atlantic Monthly* (Sept. 2000): 39–59.

3 James A. Anderson and Elaine E. Englehardt, *The Organizational Self and Ethical Conduct* (Fort Worth: Harcourt, 2001). See also Charles Conrad and George Cheney, "Notes on Agency in the Ethics of Recent Corporate Scandals," Texas A&M University and University of Utah, September 2002.

4 Charles Conrad, "Notes on the Enron etc. Case," unpublished paper, Texas A&M U, 2002.

5 Amy Waldon, "Bhopal Seethes, Pained and Poor 18 Year Later," *The New York Times* (21 September 2002): A3.

6 Debashish Munshi and David McKie, "Different Bodies of Knowledge: Diversity and Diversification in Public Relations," *Australian Journal of Communication* 28.3 (2001): 11–22.

7 Richard Ice, "Corporate Publics and Rhetorical Strategies," *Management Communication Quarterly* 4 (1991): 341–362.

8 James Boyd White, *When Words Lose Their Meaning* (Chicago: University of Chicago Press, 1984).

9 Stephen Robertson, "Good Reputation Must Be Earned in the Long Term," *Marketing* (7 Jan 1999): 10.

10 Nikki Townsley and Cynthia Stohl, "Contracting Corporate Social Responsibility: Swedish Expansions in Global Temporary Work," *Management Communication Quarterly* 16.4 (2003).

11 Steve Schwarze, "Corporate-State Irresponsibility, Critical Publicity and Asbestos Exposure in Libby, Montana," *Management Communication Quarterly* 16.4 (2003).

12 Thomas R. Dyckman, "Study: Executive Compassion on the Rise," *Bridge News* (22 Nov 1996).

13 Mica Schneider, "Learning to Put Ethics Last," *Business Week* (11 March 2002).

14 Frederick B. Bird and James A. Waters, "The Moral Muteness of Managers," *California Management Review* 32 (Fall 1999): 73–88.

15 These issues were widely discussed in academic and popular writings in the late 1990s, with U.S. labor unions, along with Latin American advocacy groups, paying increased attention to the poor working conditions of many Mexicans employed in U.S.-owned factories along the border.

16 Thomas Donaldson and Al Gini, *Case Studies in Business Ethics*, 4th ed. (Upper Saddle River, NJ: Prentice-Hall, 1996).

17 Robert Jackall, *Moral Mazes* (New York: Oxford University Press, 1988).

18 *PRIA Code of Ethics*, Public Relations Institute of Australia, 3 Feb. 2003 <http://www.pria.com.au/ethics/code/html>.

19 Bernhard Schwab, "A Note on Ethics and Strategy: Do Good Ethics Always Make for Good Business?" *Strategic Management Journal* 17 (1994): 499–500.

20 Sue Adkins, "The Wider Benefits of Backing a Good Cause," *Marketing* (2 Sept 1999): 20–21.

21 Milton Friedman, *Capitalism and Freedom* (Chicago: University of Chicago Press, 1962).

22 Anna Quindlen, "Battlefield Rape Is Less a Concern Than It Is in Service at Home," *The Salt Lake Tribune* (5 April 2003): A15.

23 Thain Hagan, University of Montana, contributed to this text box.

24 Joann Keyton, Pat Ferguson, and Steven C. Rhodes, "Cultural Indicators of Sexual Harassment," *Southern Communication Journal* 67 (2001): 33–50.

25 Sandy Welsh, "Gender and Sexual Harassment," *Annual Review of Sociology* 25 (1999): 165–190.

26 Susan Brownmiller, *In Our Time: Memoir of a Revolution* (New York: Delta Books, 1999).

27 Nikki Townsley and Patricia Geist, "The Discursive Enactment of Hegemony: Sexual Harassment and Academic Organizing," *Western Journal of Communication* 64 (2000): 190–217.

[28] Robin Clair, "The Use of Framing Devices to Sequester Organizational Narratives: Hegemony and Harassment," *Communication Monographs* 60 (1993): 113–136.

[29] Shereen G. Bingham, "Communication Strategies for Managing Sexual Harassment in Organizations: Understanding Message Options and Their Effects," *Journal of Applied Communication Research* 19 (1991): 88–115.

[30] Robert Lane, *The Loss of Happiness in Market Democracies* (New Haven, CT: Yale University Press, 2000).

[31] James S. Coleman, *Power and the Structure of Society* (New York: Norton, 1974).

[32] Émile Durkheim, *The Division of Labor in Society*, trans. George Simpson (New York: Free Press, 1933).

[33] Peter Dahler-Larsen, "What 18 Case Studies of Organizational Culture Tell Us about Counter-Intentional Effects of Attempts to Establish Shared Values in Organizations," *Current Topics in Management*, vol. 3 (Westport, CT: JAI Press, 1998) pp. 151–173.

[34] Andrew Bard Schmookler, *The Illusion of Choice* (Albany: SUNY Press, 1993).

[35] Andrew Brien, "Professional Ethics and the Culture of Trust," *Journal of Business Ethics* 17 (1998): 391–409.

[36] W. Charles Redding, *Communication within the Organization* (New York: Industrial Communication Council, 1972).

[37] James Gleick, "Inescapably, Obsessively, Totally Connected," *The New York Times Magazine* (23 April 2001): 66ff.

[38] Karen A. Watson-Gegeo and Geoffrey M. White, *Disentangling: Conflict Discourse in Pacific Societies* (Stanford, CA: Stanford University Press, 1990).

[39] Max Weber, *Economy and Society* (Berkeley: University of California Press, 1978).

[40] William Frankena, *Ethics* (Englewood Cliffs, NJ: Prentice-Hall, 1963).

[41] Robert Solomon, *A Passion for Justice* (New York: Addison-Wesley, 1990).

[42] Kenneth Burke, *A Grammar of Motives* (Berkeley: University of California Press, 1969).

[43] Marvin B. Scott and Stanford M. Lyman, "Accounts," *American Sociological Review* 33 (1968): 46–62.

[44] Azim Nanji, "Islamic Ethics," *A Companion to Ethics*, ed. Peter Singer (Oxford: Blackwell, 1993).

[45] Richard Johannesen, *Ethics and Human Communication*, 5th ed. (Prospect Heights, IL: Waveland Press, 2001).

[46] Martin Buber, *I and Thou* (New York: Scribner's, 1970).

[47] Jürgen Habermas, *A Theory of Communicative Action* (Boston: Beacon Press, 1984).

[48] Kenneth Burke, *A Rhetoric of Motives* (Berkeley: University of California Press, 1969).

[49] Eric M. Eisenberg, "Ambiguity as Strategy in Organizational Communication," *Communication Monographs* 51 (1984): 227–242.

[50] Solomon.

[51] Howard F. Stein, *Nothing Personal, Just Business: A Guided Journey into Organizational Darkness* (Westport, CT: Quorum Books, 2001).

[52] Amartya Sen, *Inequality Reexamined* (1992; Cambridge, MA: Harvard University Press, 1995).

[53] George Cheney, "Arguing about Values and Ethics in Market-oriented Discourses," *New Approaches to Rhetoric*, ed. Steven Goldzwig and Patricia Sullivan (Thousand Oaks, CA: Sage, in press).

[54] Sissela Bok, *Lying* (New York: Pantheon Books, 1978).

[55] Cheney, "Arguing."

[56] Jean-Francois Lyotard, *The Postmodern Condition: A Report on Knowledge*, trans. Geoff Bennington and Brian Massumi, (Minneapolis: University of Minnesota Press, 1984).

[57] Émile Durkheim, *Professional Ethics and Civic Morals* (Westport, CT: Greenwood Press, 1983).

[58] The Body Shop, *Annual Report and Accounts* (West Sussex, UK: The Body Shop, 2000).

[59] The Body Shop.

[60] Anita Roddick, *Body and Soul* (London: Ebury Press, 1991) p. 252.

[61] Anita Roddick, *Business as Unusual* (London: Thorsons, 2000) p. 257.

15

Analyzing Organizational Communication

With Daniel J. Lair

Having worked your way through the fourteen chapters of this book, you'll be able to "read" organizations very differently than you did before. Theories *do* affect how we look at organizations. As you began reading this textbook, you already had your own theories about organizations and communication; you just may not have known it! Now you can see the very broad range of possible concepts and principles and how they develop and are supported or modified and sometimes dismissed. Theories do many things for us: they aid us in making sense of many different cases and situations; they sensitize us to issues we otherwise take for granted or rarely discuss; they provide us with a more professional lens for our observations; and they equip us with a more refined and nuanced terminology to present our findings.

We chose to highlight five themes throughout this book. We restate them here as the foundation for the applications discussed in this chapter. When analyzing organizational communication, it is important to remember:

- the interdependence of internal and external forms of organizational communication;
- global and multicultural perspectives on organizational communication;
- the disciplinarity and multi-disciplinarity of organizational communication;
- the unity of theory and practice in organizational communication; and
- critical thinking as essential in the analysis of organizational messages and discourses.

The four of us find organizational communication to be a vibrant field. Working in it requires extensive planning, careful decisions, and much work—but it's also a great deal of fun. We hope you will be inspired to contribute to the ongoing flow—to step into the stream of organizational communication and to change its course, informed by a worldview that recognizes diverse perspectives and is mindful of the potential effects of organizational decisions on people.

We stressed at the beginning of this book that theories are very practical. In this chapter we attempt to do something different with the conclusion of an organizational communication textbook. While much of our discussion in the previous chapters has emphasized goals such as understanding, analysis, and criticism, we believe it's important to end the book with some practical advice about how to analyze communication in an organization. Informed analysis provides a sound basis for effective change. We will discuss some important aspects of language and other symbols and then present a few means of data gathering and analysis. Because of space limitations, we can touch only briefly on the philosophy of method underlying different choices for gathering and analyzing data. In your classroom discussions, you will find opportunities to elaborate and fill in the gaps, while also discovering which strategies and techniques are most useful and appealing to you.

What's in "Communication"?

When we ask what communication is and where we can find it, we are asking fairly fundamental questions about exactly what constitutes organizational communication and where we should look for it. Some argue that an organization itself can be interpreted in the form of a text. Think about this idea carefully. If we realize that what we do with a "text" is interpret it, then we can think of organizations themselves as texts that can be "read."

When we try to read an organization we discover just how central communication is but also that communication is fraught with ambiguity, tensions between different meanings, and transformations in meaning over time. The metaphor of text draws our attention to how much of an organization is written, spoken, and, thus, constructed by its members through the linguistic and other symbolic resources available to them. Hence, the way we grant technology power, through language, is perhaps as important as the material presence of technology in our lives and work. This is why James R. Taylor and his colleagues urge us to see the full possibilities for "reading" an organization—including how its members talk about material aspects of work.[1] In a similar way, as we discussed in chapter 4, the entire culture of an organization can be "read"—and inferences can be drawn about what is unspoken or implicit (what we have referred to, in chapter 9, as "deep structures").

At an even more basic level, as François Cooren explains, we can understand not only the communication-related aspects of organizations but also how language itself has certain "organizing properties" that affect such things as how a sense of joint activity emerges (with the slippery nature of "we"), how authority is constructed (with notions of "representation," or who stands for whom and what), and how all sorts of objects (including architecture, technology, animals, and social forces) are "mobilized"—or granted the capacity of social agents/actors, through our speech.[2] Thus, it is interesting and important to see how we *position* the environment of the organization as being something more than simply other organizations.[3]

Here's an example to probe more deeply: how might you read authority as people in organizations talk about it? Recall that messages can be read as authoritative on at least two levels: in terms of their explicit content (say, advice or directions) and in terms of what they suggest about how the source of the message ought to be regarded in the future (as an authority). Consider the links between words like "author" and "authorize" and authority as formally ascribed or sanctioned power. When we look at authority this way, we recognize how it is *interactional* and how it can be "heard" or "read" in several different ways in each situation. From this perspective, we can ask:

- Where does authority emerge in situations that are basically informal? For example, how do emergent leaders begin to convey a sense of authority and the ability to speak for the group in a way that others can accept?
- How is authority constructed in a situation, with both material and symbolic means? For instance, what resources of language, visual imagery, and the physical environment establish authority at the beginning of a celebrity interview?
- How is authority gradually assumed over time for an individual, group, or institution, in terms of patterns of talk? How is this accomplished in the courtroom and in other legal contexts?
- What parts of authority or power are directly "readable" or "legible"—that is, how accessible are the structures of power? Are the apparent rules really disguises for unspoken norms?
- What parts of authority or power have to be understood by "reading between the lines"—such as the *real* reason behind a new organizational initiative?
- What parts of authority or power exist as "sub-texts," or concealed instances of resistance—like potential oppositional votes in a cabinet meeting?
- What parts of authority and power exist as "meta-texts," or broad commentaries on relationships? For instance, how does an argument over how to use the new photocopier represent something deeper about a relationship between peers at work?[4]

When we read an organization, we are *de*mystifying its structures and processes; we make accessible its important meanings; and we explicitly recognize the roles of its many "authors." So we might ask—what is an organization's "reputation"? From one perspective, the reputation is built up from *many* interactions between the company and employees, consumers, and other groups. If those interactions, and various messages, are seen over time as honest, open, consistent, and reliable, then various groups of stakeholders will come to associate a positive reputation with the company. Think about how your individual encounters with a governmental agency or a multinational corporation or a religious institution affect your view of the whole organization?

As we discussed in chapter 9, one useful way of understanding power and authority is to conceive of a *second order* of messages—"what they say" about relationships. Similarly we may want to ask how structures and interactions can be read, how organizational identities present themselves as texts, how rationality has both textual and "meta-textual" qualities, etc. Above all, we may want to know what counts or passes as an organizational message and when we should pay special attention to it.

Let's think back to the range of things we've called "organizational communication" earlier in this text.

- *Symbols*, including logos, artifacts, architecture, uniforms, etc.
- *Structures,* such as rules and standard operating procedures
- *Patterns* of practices, like the typical ways news gets spread
- *Discrete Messages*, such as memos, ads, and announcements
- *Interactions*, as in a performance appraisal interview
- *Relationships,* as between a manager and subordinates
- *Narratives,* as in the tales about the company's founder
- *Meetings*, as both sets of messages and as messages themselves
- *Networks,* like the formal representative structure of a workers' council, or informal "bitch sessions"
- *Rituals,* like the morning physical exercises before work
- *Campaigns*, say, accompanying the launch of a new product line
- *Myths,* or stories plus ideology, "Everyone at Acme can someday be as rich as the CEO"
- *Broad discourses,* such as the multiple ways an industry expresses and sustains its faith in technology

Some forms of communication come in neat "packets" (think of memos) while others have fuzzy or indefinite boundaries (for example, an organization's ongoing communication about change). To understand organizational communication, it's often important ***not*** to focus on a single message but rather to look at a broad pattern. Indeed, this is exactly the way many media analysts and sociologists are now approaching the study of advertising. Instead of asking, "How persuasive is this ad?" they may ask, "What are the effects of seeing lots of these types of ads?" In a similar manner, researchers on violence in the media have looked for patterns—for example, the impact of routinely seeing murders on television programs on one's view of society or one's evaluation of the relative safety of stepping out on to the street. Thus, it's not only a question of what a particular image of violence "does" to a child or an adult; it's more about the overall impact of seeing thousands of violent acts portrayed on television. Through exposure over time, we may assume a more violent world than the one that actually exists.

Communication isn't just the single messages we can set apart from one other but the totality of interactions that form our context for understanding. How many of the key messages that shaped your worldview can you isolate or remember? What are some of the repeated messages you receive a work? How do these make you feel or see the world?

Dimensions of Organizational Messages

Generally speaking, we can consider the following *dimensions* of organizational messages:

- from micro to macro,
- as having a certain channel or direction,

- as flowing through a particular medium,
- as being comparatively formal or informal,
- as having an explicit or implicit purpose, and
- as manifesting one or more levels of meaning.

A memo has relatively clear features—a discrete, micro-level message in a written or electronic medium, perhaps issued downward from the "boss," somewhat formal, having a stated and perhaps an unstated purpose—and subject to analysis for meaning. While most of the characteristics of the memo could be identified in a straightforward way, its purpose(s) and meaning(s) might involve some subtleties. The memo may ostensibly be about the agenda for an upcoming meeting, yet the message could have the "silent" purpose to insure that one specific issue is on the agenda and others are excluded. Thus, the chair of the meeting may use the memo to control the discussion process by setting in advance the list of legitimate items for consideration.

In addition to the features of messages already mentioned, we can ask about the extent to which messages reflect and contribute to general trends. When is a message a "*representative* anecdote" (in Kenneth Burke's terms)[5] with respect to a broad trend? For example, at the level of a business, when should a particular meeting be seen not only as the usual and recurrent gathering but as a "turning point" that signals a new way of doing business, perhaps by moving members away from old goals and toward new ones? During a recent budget cutback at Lars's university, for example, one meeting between department chairs suddenly marked a detour from the usual practice of dividing financial reductions evenly among activities. To many, this meeting indicated a significant turning point.

When is a message a *symptom* of a problem? For example, consider what William Arnold and Jeanne Plas called "the golden gripe" (or the special complaint).[6] The golden gripe is the kind of criticism that surfaces and resurfaces in an organization and that merits sustained attention from managers. For example, in some organizations committees are continuously formed to address problems although their reports are consistently ignored by the very CEOs or administrators who created the committees in the first place. Committee members repeatedly express dissatisfaction—not that specific recommendations are rejected but that the committee is ignored. This meta-message can be very damaging to the overall culture of trust in the organization.

When does a message have almost *material force*? For example, when does a symbol, such as nation's flag, become an extension of the nation itself? With respect to language, when does the invocation of a corporate mission embody the entire organization? To put the matter in the terms of the General Semantics movement of the mid-twentieth century: "When does the map *become* the territory?"

Language and Other Symbols

Linguists recognize some basic dimensions of language; we can apply each of these terms to our analysis of larger patterns in an organization. *Grammar* refers to the structure of a sentence, but it can also be used to refer to "the grammar" (structure) of an organization's core set of values. For example, if a company tries to chart its activities from a professed set of values, those values become a kind of grammar for the organization's practices. This is exactly what many companies are trying to do with rules for consistent application of core values (as we discussed in chapter 14). *Semantics* stresses meaning and can be applied to an individual message or to whole sets of messages—for example, the meaning(s) of a particular advertisement or an entire advertising campaign. *Syntax* refers to the order of the elements of a message, independent of their logical relationships (grammar). Here we can think of the importance of the *sequence* of messages or events. In advertising, we may consider the advantages of "primacy" or "recency" in terms of the placement of a key idea, just as we consider the same thing with respect to a public address. Finally, *pragmatics* captures the real or potential effects of a message—the persuasive possibilities for language in use. With pragmatics, we are asking, "What difference does it make to call something this or that?" Another way to put it is: How is the audience supposed to think, feel, or behave when confronted with this type of message?

Just as we are often unable to *see* technologies because we take them for granted in everyday life, so we tend to see through language. Our everyday expressions such as "Talk is cheap" or "Put your money where your mouth is" reinforce this tendency by asserting that language isn't something of real substance. This is what Kenneth Burke calls "naïve verbal realism": the view that language is merely "added on" to reality as opposed to being a constituent part of reality itself.[7] But, this everyday logic overlooks the fact that something like *history* (as a "story") is built up of symbols, and that those symbols are created and advanced from particular points of view. This is not to throw the idea of *facts* out the window, but it is a reminder that what we call "facts" in any given case should always be weighed against the role or potential role of human subjectivity in focusing on (that is, isolating and expressing) these particular facts. What we choose to call "facts"—or how we choose to label something—can have profound, wide-ranging implications, as discussed in box 15.1. On the one hand, we should overcome our "lay" perspective on language, which devalues it as "not real"; at the same time, we need to remember that symbols can't do everything!

With *images*, all four dimensions of language are transformed somewhat because of the immediacy of an image. For example, when a celebrity advertises a product (even if that person has few qualifications to know anything about the product), immediacy bypasses ethos. We might call this "trans-ethos"—meaning that the traditional means of building credibility for a speaker or source of communication is short-circuited with an appeal to something familiar or powerful. Political ads often do this with national symbols; automobile ads do it with demonstrations of power.

The use of a *metaphor*—say, "deadwood" to represent a segment of a company's workforce about to be "downsized" or laid off—is a form of encapsulation. It condenses rational processes by combining ideas from different contexts. With a strong emphasis on emotionality, reasoning processes may take a "back seat" when metaphors are at play. For example, in the video made for public television called *The Ad and the Ego* in 2000, several sociologists and communication theorists make the powerful observation that the essential message (or meta-message) of all advertising is "You're not okay." That is, nearly all ads speak to a certain feeling of inadequacy—the "problem"—that can be satisfied with the "solution"—the product or service being promoted. This sense is played up through images of the body and environments where anxiety is produced. In most cases, "the answer" is presented in the acquisition of more stuff. Thus, we need to pay close attention to entire ranges of messages and to the interaction of words and visual imagery within them. In recent years, media analysts have helped us begin to understand the role of visual images in our society—in contexts ranging from political campaigns to marketing to advocacy of social causes.

Semiotics provides the most advanced treatment of symbols. As the theory and analysis of "signs" and their life in society, semiotics aids us in examining the interre-

Box 15.1 Voices from the Field

The Interrelations of the Symbolic and the Material: "It's Not Easy Being Green"
Connie Bullis, University of Utah

The environmental impacts of our industrial and post-industrial ways of life are becoming painfully evident. Thus, we are profoundly affected when we cannot drink untreated water from streams, cannot be sure that breathing city air is safe for our health, and cannot assume that the food we eat is grown on uncontaminated soil. Some economists have pointed out that with growth as an unquestioned *good*, we count many questionable practices on the *positive* side of the balance sheet. When we send *more* children to the hospital for asthma treatment, bottle *more* water so people can drink safely, and use *more* toxic chemicals to increase food production, we mark these as positive because they "grow the economy."[8] On the other hand, life-enhancing systems such as forests and wetlands are typically not counted as positive, but rather as used or even wasted resources.

As students of organizations and institutions, we have often conceived of organizations as though they exist separate from "objective" reality. Across organizational studies, for example, "the environment" refers to other *organizations* rather than to the substance and life of the planet. We organizational communication scholars have largely ignored the connections between organizational processes and the environmental consequences, preferring to celebrate symbols and "social construction" to the point of almost ignoring the earth's material limits.[9]

We can justifiably turn to business as one sector from which solutions must spring. One response is simply to deny the problem: "environmentalists" are labeled "radicals," air pollution is called "haze"; the economy is pronounced to be "information-based." Another reaction is to "green the talk" while maintaining existing production, transportation, and waste elimination processes. Products are marketed as "green" whether or not there is any substantial truth to the claim. Many corporations, however, are taking more proactive approaches by exceeding regulatory requirements and implementing processes to upgrade their environmental practices. Total Quality Environmental Management and the Triple Bottom Line are two comprehensive approaches. Ultimately, we may insist not only that companies provide better products while not degrading the environment but also reconsider our blanket commitment to *unending* economic growth—to a market that never stops expanding.

As corporate spokespersons often claim, corporations are merely creating the products that consumers demand. If consumer demand doesn't support industrial practice, the practice will not survive. For example, we all know that sport utility vehicles (SUVs) create more air pollution than many other cars. Yet, demand for these vehicles continues to grow—far surpassing the projections of leading automakers. Thus, our greatest challenge may be to change our personal choices while also looking to innovative organizational approaches. After all, the term and concept *lifestyle* was self-invented (in the 1920s). So, why can't we change it?[10]

How can we understand environmental problems without uniquely blaming either corporations or consumers? How should environmental problems be framed and expressed? How do certain patterns of communication actually contribute to environmental problems? Can they be used to foster change? How do we understand material constraints on symbols, and vice versa?

"We're interested in words, not deeds."

lationships of various images—be they different parts of a televised advertisement for a car or the components of a corporate logo.

In writings dating back to the late nineteenth century, philosopher (and semiotician) Charles Sanders Peirce described the signifying process (*semiosis*) as a dynamic relation between three elements: a sign, an object and an interpretant. Peirce described the relation this way:

> A sign . . . is something, which stands to somebody for something in some respect or capacity. It addresses somebody, that is, creates in the mind of that person an equivalent sign, or perhaps a more developed sign. That sign which it creates I call the *interpretant* of the first sign. The sign stands for something, its *object.* It stands for that object, not in all respects, but in reference to a sort of idea.[11]

The sign can, in principle, be anything—a gesture, a logo, an advertisement, a slogan, a product, a package, a narrative, a written text, a set of behaviors, or even an entire persuasive campaign. The object, which the sign stands for, is sometimes also called the *referent*—an equivalent to the notion of the world as it "is," objectively speaking. Finally, the interpretant can be thought of as a mental image in the mind of the interpreter created or stimulated by the sign—an image that links the sign to the object or referent, just as the word "IBM" creates a mental image that links the three letters I, B, and M with a large corporation that produces computers. The relation between the three elements in the signifying process can be illustrated this way:

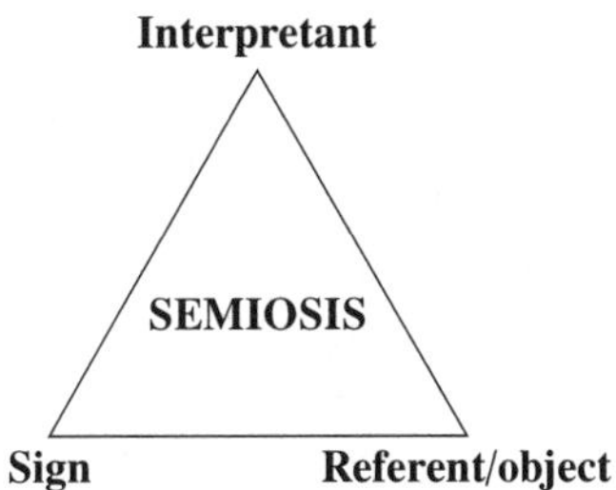

Just as a map can only inform us about certain dimensions of a landscape, the sign only highlights, as Peirce explains, certain aspects of the referent. Some signs, however, are more "naturally" or logically linked to their referents than others. Peirce distinguishes between three classes of signs: *icons, indices,* and *symbols.* An *icon* is a sign that has certain qualities in common with the object it stands for: a picture of a person has iconic qualities because it is a sign that references a particular person through *resemblance*. Onomatopoeia in language is another example: the name mimics the sound of something, like "cuckoo" or "tweet-tweet." An *index* is a sign that refers to its object because it is being affected by that object in some way: footprints on the beach, for example, are affected by the feet of somebody walking there, just as smoke is often caused by fire. The relation between an index and its object is, in other words, based on causality or physical connection. Both icons and indices are to some degree "motivated"[12] by the objects or referents for which they stand. In contrast, a *symbol* is a conventional sign—it stands for an object only because of a rule or a principle. Think, for example, of Coca-Cola's slogan "The Real Thing." The only reason why this well-known sign is taken to represent the object Coca-Cola, and is able to create in our minds images of a particular soft drink, is convention—the same convention Coca-Cola now, ironically, has to work against in order to convince us that their more recent slogan "Always" refers to the same object.

We find icons, indices, and symbols in many sign systems, but *language* is mainly symbolic—related to its object through conventions, which are in large part arbitrary. In a dynamic society associations are constantly changing, and certainly the associations related to corporate symbols and communications change with time, cultures, and the people who create them. We have briefly reviewed the nature of language and other symbols (especially visual images) as a foundation for analyzing organizational communication. Next we'll consider some reasons for analyzing various aspects of communication in organizations and then look at strategies and techniques for gathering data and analysis.

Some Purposes/Reasons for Analyses of Communication

We have made the case that "talk is *not* cheap"; in fact, it can be very expensive. As we mentioned in chapter 4, our communication about 11 September 2001 in the United States—whether we call the events a "terrorist act," "an act of war," "an attack on the United States," or "a crime against humanity"—makes a big difference, not only in terms of how we make sense of those events but also in terms of how we respond to them. Calling something a "crime" suggests a "police action"; labeling the same event "an act of war" points to military mobilization. The government of the

United States as well as governments of other nations are debating the types of trials or other outcomes for the several thousand suspects who have been apprehended and detained in relation to "9/11." Can you think of other examples where a seemingly simple choice of a label can have huge implications down the road?

You might wonder why you should learn to analyze organizational communication. Isn't it more important to be trained to produce the messages that we are required to create in any particular position we hold (say in public relations or marketing)? There are a number of good reasons for being "literate" about organizational communication. Part of this literacy is *appreciating* the variety of ways communication can be approached, examined, and understood. One of the greatest difficulties students of communication typically have is making the transition from describing to systematically analyzing the content of a message or episode. To describe well is a very useful skill, but a deeper analysis takes one beyond the literal content of messages to consider their context, their relationship to other messages, and certain criteria such as effectiveness, ethics, etc. Some practical aspects of "analysis" are listed below.

- An analysis *goes beyond reporting or listing* the components or sections of something—such as an interview or an ad campaign or an organization.
- An analysis involves *selecting or highlighting* the most important or interesting features of the object of analysis. All parts of what's under investigation are not given equal attention or weight. For example, Pierce and Dougherty's study[13] looked at relationships between TWA and Ozark pilots in terms of dominance (chapter 10). If the authors had focused on communication about coordination, a different study might have emerged.
- An analysis is *informed by relevant theoretical material or concepts*. For example, if analyzing leadership in teams, articles or books on the topics provide the theoretical background. For example, Ted's research on leadership today draws on both the traditional models in that area as well as an understanding of contemporary trends.
- An analysis is *flexible and inductive*, allowing interesting observations or insights to emerge from the object of study—such as new ways of looking at work and organizations witnessed in a particular organization.
- An analysis is *divided into sub-topics*. For instance, an organization undergoing restructuring may be examined in terms of sub-topics such as leadership philosophy and practice, communication networks and patterns of interaction, and principles of teamwork.
- An analysis should incorporate *a variety of types of evidence or data*. Depending on availability, these include quotations and paraphrases, statistics and other types of general assessments, examples from experience, etc. Shiv's study of an NGO in India, for example, looked both at documentary data in the form of reports, publications, memos, and research studies, as well as interviews with key informants.[14]
- An analysis should *make comparisons and contrasts* with other such objects of analysis. Linda Putnam and her coauthors studied (see chapter 10) the bargaining rites and fantasy themes of two different school districts, drawing tentative conclusions from the comparison.[15]

- An analysis should *be provocative*, noting surprises, ironies, contradictions, or paradoxes—for example, inconsistencies between an organization's promotion of creativity and its other practices. As we saw in chapter 8, Cynthia Stohl and George Cheney noted a number of paradoxes in attempts at employee participation, teamwork, and workplace democracy.
- Finally, an analysis can make *value judgments*—positive and negative—and include recommendations where appropriate. But, that judgment should be firmly grounded in accessible criteria.

As we consider any message (such as a mission statement), or set of messages (like a PR campaign), or even a broader discourse (like the contemporary hype of technology—or "techno-optimism"), the specific aims of our analysis may include any or all of the following seven purposes. For the sake of illustration, assume the object of analysis is a message, such as a slogan or ad, or a set of messages such as a change initiative.

1. *Description*. For example, what exactly is in the message? What is its literal meaning? What does it not mention?
2. *Prediction*. What can we tell about the future (likely or probable events) from a message? What effects can we imagine? What does the message "do," practically speaking? For instance, will a new corporate identity campaign really change people's minds about the "environmental sensitivity" of an oil company?
3. *Understanding*. How does a message increase our awareness of some issue, problem, situation, person, or group? Can a message be used to advance interpersonal or inter-group understanding (in the deepest sense)?
4. *Insight*. What special knowledge of an issue, problem, person, group, or situation can be learned through a message? For example, consider a message that offers a fresh perspective on a familiar problem, or a message that reverses an accustomed meaning.
5. *Intervention*. How can understanding of the message aid us in penetrating and working on a problem? For example, one organization we've worked with was committed to using democratic principles but had operated very autocratically. A consultant helped them learn the skills of meeting facilitation and, based on their newfound awareness, the management team was attempting to reach consensus on all decisions. They brainstormed 162 issues they needed to address, but two months later were still focusing on issue number two, with 160 still to go! Based on an analysis of their messages (that is, their expressed desires and communication patterns), a researcher reframed their task as identifying the issues on which consensus was important and which could be best handled by a range of other decision-making styles. Thus, the analysis facilitated an intervention that enabled more satisfying communication for the group.
6. *Deconstruction*. While a negative connotation is sometimes attached to this term, it refers to an open-ended analysis of messages that sees meaning as malleable and changeable. From this perspective, words and images are like putty: the possibilities for their transformation are not limitless but they are many. Take, for example, the transformation of "quality" from setting high

standards for production and service (excellence) to getting one's organization in line with what others are doing by adopting programs such as total quality management (*mimesis*).

7. *Transformation*. Is there an element in a message that transcends a situation? For example, Kenneth Burke[16] speaks of the use of humor in many instances to help parties in conflict move to a different plane of understanding and interaction. Conflict in a meeting can be diffused when someone reframes a point of contention as trivial in the broader scheme of things.

Data Gathering

The sheer variety of potential messages that can be studied make it important that you ask yourself what it is, exactly, that you want to analyze. Objects of analysis could include: a newspaper editorial, an order, a commercial, an episode from a television program, a corporate document such as an annual report, a magazine ad, a conversation, an interview, a speech, a debate, a meeting, a PR campaign, a social movement, etc. Broadly speaking, there are four categories of gathering data: artifacts, surveys, interviews, and observation.

Artifacts

As organizations conduct their day-to-day business, they inevitably leave traces of their activities in the form of concrete artifacts: advertisements, Web pages, corporate mission statements, minutes from meetings, or confidential memos that surface years later. And as we discussed in chapter 4, there's also the literal architecture of the organization itself! These artifacts are often a rich source of data and can provide a unique window into the life of an organization.

Artifacts work well as messages to analyze for several reasons. First, they are convenient: advertisements and Web pages, for example, are readily available (confidential memos, such as those that have helped sink the large tobacco companies are clearly more difficult to obtain!). Artifacts fit our earlier description of neat "packets"—tidy objects of analysis, with clear boundaries. Artifacts provide tangible, objective evidence for your analysis. For some organizations, for example, art collections are important representations of what the organization is—or aspires to be.[17]

There are limitations, however, on what artifacts—by themselves—can tell us. For example, from an artifact alone, we can only speculate about the intentions of the artifact's producer(s). We can't, for example, know what the producers of an advertisement were attempting to accomplish from watching the ad alone. Similarly, we can only speculate on an artifact's effects on audiences, both intended and unintended: watching that same advertisement alone will in other words tell us little about how its audience might react. Finally, when considered by themselves, artifacts are somewhat static; they represent a snapshot of an incident of organizational communication at a specific point, rather than a cinematic unfolding of that communication as a *process*.

Surveys

The type of research most frequently encountered by the general public is survey research. Most of us have participated in some type of public opinion poll or market survey. While surveys may take many different forms, what they have in common is that they ask a group of people (carefully selected through sampling) a number of standardized questions, allowing for comparison between—and across—individual answers.

Surveys are very useful in the study of organizations. For example, surveys play a prominent role in the International Communication Association (ICA) Communication Audit, an instrument designed to provide organizations with an assessment of their current communication practices in order to improve future communication. The ICA Audit questionnaire survey includes a base of 116 items asking members to assess the current state of communication within the organization as well as the *ideal* state of communication. Questions deal with topics such as the flow of information in the organization, employee satisfaction with the amount and types of information received, and openness with supervisors. Thus, a typical question asks respondents about their *degree of satisfaction with the information received from their supervisor*. The audit varies in topics and format, and it sometimes includes in-depth interviews and sophisticated network analyses. (A representative version of the audit instrument is available to instructors and students on our Web site: http://www.organizationalcommunication.com. This will give you an idea of the types of questions often used, as well as the topics covered.)

As a method of studying organizational communication, surveys possess several important strengths. First, their nature makes it possible to study a relatively large group, or sample, of people. Surveys also facilitate a comparison of individuals' answers within and across organizations. One of the original purposes of the ICA Communication Audit, for example, was to make possible the comparison of communication in many different organizations.[18] Surveys rank high in the traditional measure of reliability, largely because they reduce researcher bias in observations of the behavior (or in this case, the answers) of a respondent. However, it's often overlooked that participant responses in the first phase of a survey can be used to construct or reconstruct the survey as the research process develops. So, the presumption of "distance" between the questionnaire items and the meanings reported by respondents really is a matter of degree.

Surveys, however, are also limited by several factors. First, they are somewhat limited in terms of depth—while they may record perceptions held by organizational members, they rarely identify reasons *why* those perceptions are held. Similarly, surveys don't describe the social context in which respondents find themselves, yielding a less nuanced, less rich picture of organizational life that can typically be obtained from, say, open-ended interviews.[19] Finally, surveys are inherently artificial, to varying degrees. People generally do not conceive of their opinions on a Likert scale, yet surveys ask them to pick the number (or descriptive phrase) on a 5- or 7-point scale that best represents their opinion. And the mere fact of asking a question in a particular way—and this is true of interviews as well—can produce an artifact of the methodology itself. A respondent who really doesn't think or care about an issue may suddenly be led to have an opinion on a kind of soap, or a new film, or an aspect of the economy, or a problem at work. (If you plan on conducting a survey as a part of your research into an organization, our Web site offers advice for developing your standardized questionnaire.)

Interviews

Another way to enhance understanding of organizational communication is interviewing an organization's members directly. Surveys occasionally take on some characteristics of interviews, such as when a census worker appears on your doorstep to ask you more detailed questions. Here, however, we conceive of interviews in a more specific sense—a moderately open-ended discussion between interviewer and interviewee, a discussion with a purpose.[20]

Interviews come in many varieties. One of the most useful interview formats for conducting qualitative organizational communication research is often "semi-structured" (sometimes called "moderately scheduled"). Neither highly structured (as in an interview that consists of all closed-ended questions) nor unstructured (as in the dreaded interview opener, "Tell me about yourself"), semi-structured interviews offer topics and questions to the interviewee. But they are carefully designed to elicit the interviewee's ideas and opinions on the topic of interest, as opposed to leading the interviewee toward preconceived choices. They rely on the interviewer following up with probes to get in-depth information on topics of interest. (Our Web site offers suggestions for designing and conducting semi-structured interviews.)

One of the main strengths of conducting interviews is that they allow the researcher access to detailed descriptions of participants' thoughts, beliefs, and values. In interviews, organizational members have the opportunity to describe their experiences fully and *in their own words.* Additionally, interviews allow the researcher access to topics that other means would not. For example, in an interview, a researcher could ask a supervisor why she chose to e-mail a subordinate rather than talking to him in person—eliciting more information than a simple observation of the communication incident would reveal. Finally, the open, interactive nature of an interview allows participants to bring up subjects that may be vitally important but that the researcher never anticipated.

The main disadvantage of conducting interviews is *reliability*. Because interviews are open and interactive, each interview will be different. Accordingly, making direct comparisons between participants' answers is somewhat more difficult than in survey research. Because interviews are so personal and so interactive, the researcher—and all of her biases—is more present in the data, from creation to analysis. All of us have seen how leading or even loaded questions are used on television interviews: for example, "Even though you disagree with the administration's policy, you'll of course be patriotic and support it—won't you?" In short, the researcher not only leaves his traces on the ultimate analysis of the data—but also in the generation of the data to be analyzed! Finally, be warned (plan ahead!) that the process of creating interview transcripts—essential to the analysis of any interview—tends to be a very time- and labor-intensive process.

Observation

The process by which a researcher goes to an organization (enters the "field") and watches (or even participates in) organizational life as it unfolds is observation. By observing an organization and its members as they carry out their day-to-day activities, the researcher is able to paint what anthropologist Clifford Geertz calls a "thick description" (see chapter 4), a vivid picture of the organization as it appears to the researcher.

As a means of collecting messages for analysis, observation includes a range of possibilities. Raymond Gold suggests that researchers can adopt several different roles, which differ in the researcher's degree of participation.[21] *Complete participants* are those who engage in the day-to-day activities of an organization without revealing their identity to organizational members. The *participant-as-observer* is known by

Box 15.2 Voices from the Field

"Native" Organizational Research: The Advantages and Disadvantages of "Being There"

Jill J. McMillan, Wake Forest University

One of the most compelling aspects of studying organizational communication is that we are all, to greater or lesser degrees, experts. From work to school to sports clubs to political parties to labor unions, we have been organizational members in a number of contexts. As a result, we know much more about organizational communication than we think we do. Therefore, I urge my organizational communication students to "go native"—to start to practice organizational analysis in their own groups—those organizations they know best. To that end, I have received some extraordinary analyses on a title-winning baseball squad, a fraternity, a dance team, and even the communication department.

The advantages of formally examining one's own organization are numerous: you *know* the organizational culture already, and there is no problem of access; members are usually willing to talk; and data are abundant and easy for a bona fide member to obtain. The greatest advantage, however, is that you *care*—you are inherently interested in this group by virtue of your membership there, leading almost invariably to the "thick description" that Clifford Geertz recommends for rich cultural analysis.

Native research is not without its challenges, however, and after two decades of using my own institution as a lab, I have learned the pitfalls well: people may be too willing to talk, especially the chronically dissatisfied; access to critical data may be restricted; the researcher may experience mild schizophrenia—a conflict of interest between being a researcher and/or being a member; a low-ranking researcher may fear punitive action from an unfavorable report; and institutional politics may prevent a thorough analysis and public airing (for example, report or publication).

A recent study[22] is a case in point. In 1995, my university entered into a plan with technology giant IBM to become one of its "major modeling sites." Because a colleague and I were part of a research team studying the effects of computerization on our campus, we faced certain methodological and philosophical dilemmas: Would the "real" decision makers talk to us? Would the critical objects of this effort—students and faculty—come clean about their successes and failures with technology? Would our research interests compromise our own authentic participation? And because the stakes for success were so high, would we be free to report the "good, the bad, and the ugly" of the computer initiative, which was our original agreement with the administration.

A full account of the politics of our study goes beyond the purview of this brief forum, but suffice it to say that throughout the study we walked a tightrope between interested participation and relatively objective research. We suspect that by most standards we experienced remarkable cooperation from institutional actors who stood to lose big from unfavorable accounts of the technological initiative. Only once was there the veiled suggestion of censorship, and the only response from the university president to the pre-publication article was why hadn't we used his *real* name! We learned firsthand, however, that the landscape of native research is fraught with political minefields.

Recall the last notable event in your group or organization that captured well what it's like to be a member there. How would you go about studying the group or organization? How open would members be to your questions/investigation? How receptive would members be to a public account of this event? What practical things could you accomplish by taking your findings back to the group or organization?

members to be a researcher, but participates in their day-to-day activities to gain a fuller understanding of what those activities mean to members.[23] *Observers-as-participants* are researchers who are known to organizational members as researchers but primarily watch, rather than engage in a social scene. Such researchers are nevertheless "participants," because their presence affects the social context (as illustrated by the Hawthorne experiments, see chapter 3). Finally, *complete observers* are those who watch a social scene unfold, unknown to the participants. The complete observer role can create problems, however. Without a connection to participants, one gains little insight into the participants' understanding of their world; ethically, the researcher is less likely to feel an obligation to those studied.

Observation as a professional means of obtaining messages for analysis possesses several advantages. First, it allows the researcher to provide full, vivid, "thick" descriptions of organizational life. Participant observation in particular affords the researcher the opportunity to experience at least some part of the lives of those studied. According to organizational ethnographer John Van Maanen, "by means of such sharing a rich, concrete, complex, and hence truthful account of the social world being studied is possible."[24] By observing organizational communication as it unfolds, the researcher can access important details that might otherwise be missed.

Like interviews, observation suffers somewhat from the problem of reliability: because the method relies so heavily on the researcher's perceptions in defining and collecting the data—even if the researcher's participation is minimal—a researcher inevitably introduces her biases into the research. Accordingly, she must pay careful attention to what those biases are and how they might affect the collection and ultimately the analysis of messages. In addition, observation is essentially watching organizational life unfold over time; as a result, it requires a large investment of time in gathering the data. Finally, each observation is a unique process of interaction between researcher and participants, making comparison of observations in different contexts a nearly impossible task. (If you are planning on conducting observation of an organizational meeting or other event, our Web site lists several suggestions to make your observations as fruitful as possible. The guidelines assume an "observer-as-participant" role.)

Each of the four primary data-gathering methods represents a wide range of traditional ways to collect messages for analysis. Box 15.3 raises some important issues about the way in which the methods that deal with people directly (surveys, interviews, and observation) conceive of those who are being researched. Each of the different ways of describing those whom we study has different implications.

Box 15.3 Subjects, Informants, Respondents, and Participants

In conversations about methodology, we often pay so much conceptual attention to the process of gathering data (via surveys, interviews, observation, and questionnaires, etc.) that we forget to adequately conceive of the groups of people who produce the data. Different types of research conceive of the groups of study in different ways. Each of these terms, or metaphors, usually involves a particular worldview and methodology.

The metaphor of a "subject" is probably the most common way to describe people being researched. Most people are aware of terms such as "research subjects," and all U.S. universities have a "human subjects" office that deals with legal, ethical, and policy-related issues involved in data collection. The word "subject" is usually connected to quantitative studies of organizational communication. It is especially evident in experimental studies where people's behavior is watched (or "controlled") for responses to specific stimuli.

The "informant" metaphor is another common way to describe people being researched. Studies that follow a "key informant" approach usually focus on people who have a lot of experience with a phenomenon as compared to people around them, or who have access to what the researcher considers expert knowledge.

The "respondent" metaphor is also widely used by researchers. It is usually used in studies that aim to get a range of opinions and information about a particular phenomenon. Here, rather than consider individuals as "key informants" who have specialized or expert knowledge about a phenomenon, individual responses are treated as one of a potentially large set of responses. Several forms of survey research use a "respondent" approach, as do smaller qualitative studies that aim to gather a range of interpretations of a phenomenon.

Finally, the "participant" metaphor is increasingly used in qualitative approaches to organizational communication. Here, rather than assume a deductive framework where the researcher pre-understands the phenomenon being studied, the knowledge that is generated by the study is assumed to be co-constructed by the researcher and the people being researched—hence the term *participant*. Thus, researchers who engage in qualitative observation and consider themselves an integral part of the situation being observed refer to their activity as "participant observation." Similarly, qualitative researchers who conduct ethnographic interviews consider them "conversations."

Other Ways of Gathering Messages

Several other methods of data gathering involve talking directly to organizational members. In some respects, these methods are variations of the more traditional methods described above; in others, they stand on their own as unique tools to access organizational members' understandings of their environments and experiences.

Metaphor elicitation/pictures. In our consulting as well as our research, we have found the simple technique of asking people to "draw your organization with you in it" to be very helpful. While the exercise may seem trivial or silly, it can be quite revealing. For example, George has seen pictures as diverse as fortresses, encampments, and buildings without windows in a single organization. Such drawings can aid us in appreciating how different the many experiences of a single organization are, how individual members conceive of their relationship to the organization, and what ways people conceptualize the organization as a whole. In addition, consistency or difference across messages is quite revealing in itself—a useful tool for the interpretive researcher just as for the pragmatic change agent. Likewise, Ted asks organizational members to draw the organization as it is now and then as they'd like it to be in five or ten years' time. This sort of exercise can work well in seminars on creative visualization, where people project themselves into the future and then "work backwards" in time to consider what needs to happen to make that vision a reality.

Critical incident/memorable message. The "Critical Incident Technique" is based on the assumption that certain positive or negative events will be influential in a person's memory and (work)life. Given all the problems with accuracy in recall,[25] this technique is not designed to yield perfect reflections of past events, even as experienced from one person's standpoint. Rather, the technique works (1) as a prompt to elicit salient memories and stories in one's work life and (2) as a means of identifying key issues at work. Also, the technique has an advantage over more purely open-ended questions (e.g., "How is your job?") because it narrows the range of recall and response to something manageable. When asked, for example, to recall "a meeting during the past year that went particularly well" (or "badly," for that matter), most employees are able to describe an event in a fair amount of detail. While doing so, they also reveal their basic assumptions or philosophies regarding their work and the organization for which they work. Too, the researcher is able to uncover key narratives that have emerged among the workforce, when their telling transcends time and individual, personal experiences.

On a conceptual level, the critical incident technique parallels the concept of "memorable messages"[26] (see chapter 4). George, for example, learned on a committee studying the experiences of transfer students that they were most likely to bond with the university if someone took the time to help them or just be nice to them during the crucial first days at the institution. Other parallel concepts include "turning points"[27] and "critical junctures,"[28] all of which reference "key moments" at which either individual experience or an interpersonal relationship is fundamentally affected and perhaps shifted by a message or a larger event. (Our Web site offers guidelines for conducting research using the "Critical Incident Technique.")

Account/protocol/retrospective. Recall our discussion of the role of accounts in chapter 10. Individuals and organizations describe what they've done, what they're currently doing, or what they're planning for the future through accounts. As Charles Conrad has found,[29] organizations often tend to provide self-serving accounts for how they're doing: for example, crediting themselves entirely for financial success and blaming "fierce competition" for their downturns or losses. For organizations, as with individuals, accounts for decisions and actions are revealing in

"The employees have to assume a share of the blame for allowing the pension fund to become so big and tempting."

terms of the values emphasized, how they "position" the social actors (e.g., heroes and villains), and what logical connections they make. Asking participants to provide their accounts for organizational phenomena—then looking for common themes and important differences in the accounts—can help us understand a great deal about organizational life.

Role playing. Role playing can be a useful exercise and a means of eliciting messages, in several ways. First, as conflict management researchers and professional mediators appreciate, putting each party in the other's shoes can foster insight. Second, role switching (even for a day), as done in some organizations, can help employees understand what's going on in other parts of the organization, and thereby encourage more effective collaboration. Third, role playing and role switching can aid organizations that desire "flatter" structures by reducing the amount of hierarchical distance between levels. Thus, role switching is a highly interventionist technique—whether used for research or consultation or organizational development. Interesting and sometimes valuable data can be generated during these exercises, as various members come to terms with what it means to walk in someone else's shoes or to see work and the organization as others see it.

Unobtrusive measures of communication. In the 1970s researchers in the social sciences became interested in the pursuit of unobtrusive measures for social phenomena.[30] These are measures that are non-intrusive yet indicative of certain aspects of social life. For empirically oriented researchers, these techniques emerged as alternatives to lab experiments, surveys, and structured interviews, but we can see such measures as data to be added to any strategy (including the collection of organizational documents—which is often unobtrusive in itself). A few examples of unobtrusive measures are: the patterns of worn carpet in hallways or corridors, the number of times certain office doors open during the day, and the amount (not the type!) of mail in someone's box. All of these unobtrusive measures can be used to assess in gross ways the amount or flow of messages. These and similar indicators can be used, sometimes in interesting ways, to supplement other means of data gathering. Can you think of other kinds of unobtrusive measures? What about your own observations of persons' eye gazes during meetings? What can that tell you?

Importance of Choices in Data Gathering

Each of the data-gathering techniques presented above has strengths and weaknesses. Use our discussion to help guide you in determining when it is most appropriate to use which method and what other methods might complement the choice. Many studies rely on multiple methods of data collection to paint a full, vivid picture of communication in an organization. The strategy of employing multiple methods is often called "triangulation." Just as we might use several theories to explain a single phenomenon, we may use several research methods to examine it.[31] The researcher must pay careful attention to what method is being chosen—and why—because these choices ultimately impact the outcome of any study.

Think back to the earlier section of this chapter where we discussed some purposes and reasons for conducting analyses of communication. Each of these purposes and reasons ultimately affect a study's outcome. By selecting or highlighting certain features (as all analyses inevitably do), we ignore others. By informing our analyses with certain theories, we inevitably shape our conclusions (a study of a major labor strike, for example, would be quite different if approached using neo-Marxist rather than prevailing management theories). By aiming to predict an organizational outcome rather than describe what is happening, we shape the direction of our study from the beginning. In short, each decision we make along the way while conducting research affects the outcome. Box 15.4 illustrates how the manner in which one particular study was conducted ultimately determined its conclusions. The lesson? Think carefully about the decisions you make as you design your research project—each decision will play a crucial role in the conclusions you ultimately make.

Box 15.4 Voices from the Field

"What is Knowledge?"

Barbara Schneider, University of Calgary

I recently examined the research that two managers in an educational organization carried out in order to produce knowledge that would be used for decision making in the organization.[32] The managers interviewed all the teachers in one of their educational programs, took notes on the interviews, analyzed the data using thematic analysis, and wrote a report that recommended changes in the programs. I taped all interviews and meetings at which the report was discussed, collected copies of all notes and drafts of the report, and analyzed in detail how the managers were implicated in the production of knowledge that would allow them to write a report that promoted their view of the organization as the reality of organizational life.

A brief analysis of the following excerpt from one of the interviews illustrates my approach.

Director: How do you feel about the general quality of instruction within the program?

Teacher: Like each teacher, what they do?

Director: Yeah, not asking for a breakdown of each teacher individually, but are you generally comfortable that there is a good standard of instruction, good teachers doing good work, or do you have concerns about it?

Teacher: I would think they do good work, but I have never heard anybody . . . I don't know exactly how many we have in the program, who is in the program. I heard [other teachers'] students because we had a few recitals together, so what I heard I liked, but I am not sure, is that it or is there more to it, or did everybody play.

Notice how the director *participates in the production* of the teacher's answer. He instructs the teacher in how to answer the question so that the answer will be relevant to the managers' goals in conducting the research. The answer is thus not the teacher's alone but is a collaboration of interviewer and interviewee. The answer is then compressed and transformed in the notes the managers record: "Think they do good work . . . Hears other teachers' students in recitals. Likes what she hears." All of the uncertainty the teacher expressed in her answer has been removed in the notes, leaving the impression that she does think the other teachers are doing good work.

Although the managers are implicated in the production of both the interview answers and the notes of those answers, the notes become the "facts" on which the report is based. The conclusions and recommendations for change proposed in the report are legitimated by the inclusion of quotes from the teachers' own words as represented by the notes. Thus the managers construct knowledge that supports their view of organizational reality and allows them to carry out their jobs as managers.

What are the implications of Schneider's arguments for managers and communication professionals? Is it possible to generate objective knowledge through interviews or through other methods? If not, how do we justify doing research to solve problems?

Data Analysis

Inevitably, as you gather messages, you will begin to analyze them. You'll think about the meaning of an advertisement as you select it, connect the content of a memo you've just gathered to an article you recently read for class on employee participation, speculate on the ultimate effectiveness of a corporate Web page you've just surfed. In each of these examples, you'd be conducting some form of analysis—however preliminary—while you were in the process of gathering data. By dedicating sections of this chapter to "Data Gathering" and "Data Analysis," we certainly don't mean to suggest that there is a clear division between the two activities. Nevertheless, at some point, you'll have a pile of messages in front of you waiting to be analyzed in a more formal sense.

Reading Messages as a "Text"

Near the beginning of this chapter, we discussed the idea of "reading" an organization as a "text." Quite similarly, the messages you've selected can be read as one text (which may include, in a very literal sense, a number of texts): your object of analysis. As you begin your analysis, or your reading of the text of messages you've collected, there are three initial questions you need to address: the nature of the object of analysis, the focus of analysis, and goal(s) of analysis.

Nature of object of analysis. What are the special features of your object of analysis? For example, a corporate annual report typically possesses a self-promotional tone and includes elements such as a letter from the CEO or top administrator.[33] Conversations usually have expectations for turn taking, topic change, talk time, etc. Advertising often exaggerates a problem or a choice. Each of these features will influence what you are ultimately able to do with your analysis. Thus, it's important at the outset of your analysis to describe carefully what you see as the most apparent or distinguishing features of the communication you're analyzing.

Focus of analysis. Are you emphasizing particular aspects of the object of analysis or simply exploring it in a largely inductive manner? For example, is there an issue you want to consider with respect to the object of analysis, such as the portrayal of women in advertising, or references to organizational growth in a company magazine, or the success of job applicants who use certain terms or tell certain stories? Do you have a theoretical framework in mind as you approach the analysis?

Goal(s) of analysis. Identify your objectives, or "research questions," as specifically as you can. Do you want to describe the content of your object of analysis, carefully recording only what was said or expressed? Do you want to analyze its content, moving to a level of inference about its components and meaning and significance? Do you want to criticize its content, making informed value-based judgments about it? Are you attempting to support, elaborate, refute, or create a theory? Are you analyzing the object simply because it is distinctive or important in itself? Do you foresee some practical extensions or applications of your analysis and your findings? Your goal(s) and your basic assumptions will dictate to some extent how you proceed from the data to the development and expression of conclusions.

Answering these questions will help inform the way you ultimately read your "text" of collected organizational messages. Additionally, think about the "level" at which you plan to read your "text." Danish psychological researcher Steinar Kvale suggests that any interview text can be analyzed at three levels: (1) *a self-understand-*

ing level of interpretation (what the *interviewee* is trying to convey; (2) a *common-sense level of interpretation* (how what is said relates to broader trends and common interpretations by other people); and (3) *a theory level of interpretation* (how does data from the interview support your hypothesis).[34] While Kvale's suggestions pertain particularly to interviews, they can be applied equally to other sorts of messages as well.

Content Analysis

There are many different types of content analysis, and the term itself has a long history in the social sciences.[35] Here we talk about content analysis in the broadest sense—referring to the multiple ways to approach a message or set of messages in terms of identifying and classifying content. In this sense, content analysis may be conducted largely without theory—or at least without *explicit* theoretical assumptions or adherence to a particular theoretical framework. We may simply want to probe what a certain domain of communication "is like." (Box 15.5 includes several possible interpetations of the dialogue between a research worker and his manager.)

George and Greg Frenette (one of his students) decided to investigate the actual value-based terms present in corporate documents after finding that most studies simply *made assumptions* about those themes without much empirical investigation. They found an overwhelming emphasis on *growth* through the internal (house organs) and external documents (annual reports)—in fact growth was mentioned in every single document in the representative sample of corporations.[36] Only later did George and Greg link their findings to theory and to some critical observations of the notion of unlimited growth. On the other hand, content analysis may well be accompanied by a theoretical perspective. For example, we could look at television "sitcoms" in terms of how they portray work, beginning with the assumption that today's stresses at work are minimized on television. Or, we could use CEO letters in corporate annual reports for a "reading" of leadership in contemporary business, with the assumption that today's CEOs emphasize entrepreneurship and that this complements the kind of workplace insecurity that has accompanied rapid economic shifts. The point is that our "sampling" of communication should fit with our overall goals for analysis.

Generally speaking, we can see content analysis in two steps: first, carefully documenting what's "in" the messages; second, moving to the level of interpretation. In

Box 15.5 Analysis of an Interaction

This interaction originally appeared in a 1965 *Harvard Business Review* article on subordinancy.[37]

Dr. Richard Dodds, a newly hired physics research worker in a company laboratory, entered the office of his superior, Dr. Blackman, and showed him a letter. This letter was from Professor Wilkin of another research institution, offering Dodds a position. Blackman read the letter.

Dodds: "What do you think of that?"

Blackman: "I knew it was coming. He asked me if it would be all right if he sent it. I told him to go ahead if he wanted to."

Dodds: "I didn't expect it, particularly after what you said to me last time. I'm really quite happy here. I don't want you to get the idea that I am thinking of leaving. But I thought I should go and visit him—I think he expects it—and I wanted to let you know that just because I was thinking of going down, that did not mean I was thinking of leaving here, unless, of course, he offers me something extraordinary."

Blackman: "Why are you telling me all this?"

Dodds: "I didn't want you hearing from somebody else that I was thinking of leaving here, because I was going for a visit to another institution. I really have no intention of leaving here, you know, unless he offers me something really extraordinary that I can't afford to turn down. I think I'll tell him that, that I am willing to look at his laboratory, but unless there is something unusual for me, I have no intention of leaving here."

Blackman: "It's up to you."

Dodds: "What do you think?"

Blackman: "Well, what? About what? You've got to make up your mind."

Dodds: "I don't consider too seriously this job. He is not offering anything really extraordinary. But I *am* interested in what he has to say, and I would like to look around his lab."

Blackman: "Sooner or later you are going to have to make up your mind where you want to work."

Dodds replied sharply: "That depends on the offers, doesn't it?"

Blackman: "No, not really; a good man always gets offers. You get a good offer and you move, and, as soon as you have moved, you get other good offers. It would throw you into confusion to consider all the good offers you will receive. Tell me, isn't there a factor of how stable you want to be?"

Dodds: "But I'm not shopping around. I already told you that. He sent me this letter; I didn't ask him to. All I said was I think I should visit him, and to you that's shopping around."

Blackman: "Well, you may choose to set aside your commitment here if he offers you something better. All I am saying is that you will still be left with the question. You've got to stay some place, and where is that going to be?"

Dodds: (after some discussion of how it would look if he changed jobs at this point): "Look, I came in here, and I want to be honest with you, but you go and make me feel guilty, and I don't like that."

Blackman: "You are being honest as can be."

Dodds: "I didn't come in here to fight. I don't want to disturb you."

Blackman: "I'm not disturbed. If you think it is best for you to go somewhere else, that is O.K. with me."

Dodds: (after another lengthy exchange about what he really wants and how his leaving would look to others): "I don't understand you . . . All I wanted was to show you this letter, and let you know what I was going to do. What should I have told you?"

Blackman: That you had read the letter and felt that under the circumstances it was necessary for you to pay a visit to Wilkin, but that you were happy here and wanted to stay at least until you had got a lot of work done."

Dodds: "I can't get over it. You think there isn't a place in the world I'd rather be than here in this lab . . ."

The audience for the original article was managers who needed assistance in coping with the more subtle forms of discontent of subordinates. The author, Abraham Zaleznik, was trying to explain problematic psychological dynamics in the communication between managers and members of their workforces. These patterns are portrayed strictly as *weaknesses* that should be perceived, managed, and ultimately overcome. Interestingly, Zaleznik sees four such problems as manifest in the text of this interaction: (1) (self-)doubt, (2) attitude reversal, (3) hidden aggression, and (4) denial of responsibility. For example, he describes the admission by the employee of both positive and negative feelings toward a single object as "attitude reversal" and states that it goes hand in hand with doubting. Zaleznik offers no critique of the manager's role—except to say that that the manager should recognize the "compulsiveness" in the employee's behavior and should try to promote a kind of "subordinancy *with* responsibility"[38] within the organization where all employees will rise above the weaknesses shown here.

In his 1980 book *Authority*, Richard Sennett takes the same dialogue segment and reverses the interpretation.[39] From Sennett's critical perspective, the original interpretation of the interaction is lopsidedly in favor of the manager. And the whole exchange illustrates a form of authority that Sennett calls autonomy, authority without love. Sennett's analysis of authority and power in society is distinctive because it considers them in terms of the emotional as well as the rational bonds that relations of authority or power involve. Thus, paternalism is seen by Sennett as an authority of false love in that it appears to be wholly in the other's "best interests," but it often serves the interests of the powerful by creating an unhealthy dependence. Autonomy, on the other hand, is part of many relations in modern, industrialized societies where aloofness, coolness, and "professionalism" are valued. This way of being is clearly promoted in many bureaucracies (as suggested in chapter 3), but it also can be found in a variety of informal as well as formal situations in numerous industrialized countries. In Sennett's analysis of the exchange between Dodds and Blackman, he comments that unlike the case of paternalism, where the employer draws attention to himself, Blackman "consistently focuses the employee back upon his *own* responses, aspirations, and feelings. The employer avoids dealing with his employee person-to-person through a technique . . . of reversed responses" (emphasis added).[40] For instance, Blackman responds to Dodds's mention of the possibility of another offer *indirectly*, with a question: "Why are you telling me all this?" The manager distances himself from the situation and calls into question the feelings of the employee.

But, there are other interpretations of the episode to consider. For example, we could base the analysis on gender or culture. The fact that both of the interactants are male is important with respect to the *likelihood* of acknowledging a social bond ("I don't need others") and to the proscription against displaying professional weakness ("I'm confident, strong") and to the idea of personal marketability ("I'm valuable, mobile"). So, we could recast Zaleznik's idea of "weakness" and Sennett's interpretations about autonomy and distance by imagining a mixed-gender or female-female interaction.

Given the time the article was published, it's likely that the interactants were white U.S. males. The casting of professional behavior in coolly bureaucratic terms, where personal histories and social attachments are pushed from view, may be seen as part of the ethos of an industrialized society that has generally regarded many emotional expressions as excessive and inappropriate in the organizational setting. This cultural tendency would *perhaps* not be as pronounced for, say, two African-American managers or two Latino managers, though we have to be careful not to generalize across *any* groups. That is, while we may find certain cultural tendencies toward valuing emotional expression or privileging relational dimensions of interaction, the specific combination of such tendencies with organizational norms and individual inclinations will vary a great deal. With all of its managerial myopia, Zaleznik's interpretation does remind us that individual personality can play a big role in a situation such as this. So, ultimately, we should look to the interplay of personal, organizational, and societal factors in trying to understand broadly as well as deeply "what's going on" in a text or an interaction.

These analyses offer several possible interpretations of the dialogue. Does your analysis differ?

What sources of power are featured in the exchange? How is power exercised by the manager and by the employee? What strategies—conscious or unconscious—does each person use? What emotional aspects—both explicit and implicit—can you see in this interaction? How might the larger context of this one-on-one interaction, the organization's culture, be relevant to analyzing the case? Could there be some accustomed ways of handling situations like this one? Given the constraints of the situation, could the employee have pursued another strategy with greater success?

his critique of structural semiology, Umberto Eco said that you could not really make such clear distinctions (as one can between, say, the denotative and the connotative levels of meaning), a point which is worth keeping in mind as you devise categories for analyzing the content of any messages. Most manuals for content analysis[41] elaborate the first step (we summarize their recommendations on our Web site). The remainder of this section elaborates the second step, offering suggestions for different ways to interpret the content of the messages you are analyzing.

Thematic analysis, as defined by communication scholar William Foster Owen, is an attempt to identify and interpret "the discourse participants use in conceptualizing their current, ongoing relational episodes."[42] The idea is to "actively enter the worlds of native people and to render those worlds understandable from the standpoint of a theory that is grounded in the behaviors, languages, definitions, attitudes, and feelings of those studied."[43] While Owen focused on themes in relationships, his method may be used to understand people's interpretations of any sort of phenomena. For example, one study using this method examined the motivational communication attempts by sales team managers as recalled by the sales staff.[44] Thematic analysis allowed the researchers to identify the most frequent and prominent motivational communication strategies used by the managers.

Centering resonance analysis (CRA) is a text analysis method that represents a given instance of discourse as a network of words.[45] It relies on the fact that speakers and authors intend to convey meaning when they communicate and accordingly structure their utterances to be meaningful within the context of other utterances they are making at the time. CRA uncovers this structure using computational linguistics and uses it to construct a network of relationships between important words in the text. The *influence* of different words in the text is determined by their position in the overall network. CRA networks, then, represent the main ideas in the text, their relative importance in making the text coherent, and how the author or speaker organizes them.

CRA was originally designed as a research tool for organizational communication. Organizations produce huge quantities of messages; communication researchers—even those using the most broad-scale methods like ethnography—can only study a tiny portion of the communication taking place. If a method like CRA can represent and process this communication via computerized methods, then it becomes possible to think about studying organization-wide communication rather than isolated instances of talk. It may be possible to see important relationships between simultaneous instances of communication in multiple locations, for example. There would be little hope of ever studying such a phenomenon with traditional methods of organizational communication research.

CRA can also help us understand how large-scale discourse systems change over time. Kevin Dooley and Steven Corman used CRA to analyze more than two months of news coverage by Reuter's of the 9/11 terrorist attacks.[46] They found that the coverage followed six main themes: the attack itself, air security, international politics, military response, economic impact, and anthrax. These themes varied over time, suggesting a process in which events are followed by institutional responses, which are followed by sense-making in the public and press.

CRA is not only a research tool; it also has practical applications in organizations, especially those that have large quantities of unstructured text containing valuable information and know-how.[47] For knowledge management applications, it is possible to compute *resonance* between CRA networks and use this information to group texts together based on similar content. In cases where the texts represent the work of particular people, it is possible to search for cases where people have similar expertise but don't know one another. Connecting such people potentially improves the "know who" network of the organization.

In recent years, various software programs have been developed to structure and assist the content analysis of messages. The most sophisticated ones allow for treatment of the "co-occurrence" of words and phrases, allowing the researcher to consider how clusters of terms and concepts operate in a discrete message or in a larger body of discourse. For example, suppose we want to know how employees talk about change versus how management discusses it over the course of a series of strategy sessions in a company. We can use the software program to analyze large volumes of discourse, after recording and inputting it, to discern "constellations" of concepts around the idea of change and thus make comparisons and contrasts across groups. (One example of such a program is "Hilighter," developed by Dor Orgad, and it is referenced on our Web site.)

Features of the Language Itself

Earlier in this chapter, we discussed the importance of language in determining what a "fact" is and how it is presented to constitute reality. We also presented some basic dimensions of language. Here, we focus specifically on some key ways in which language is deployed in organizational messages that may help inform your analysis.

- *Relational versus content dimension of a message.* Language can be used—often unintentionally—to mask or obscure deep-seated problems by describing them at a surface level. An apparent argument over the agenda for a meeting, for example, may indicate a deeper power struggle. Thus, the ostensible agenda for that meeting (the budget) may not be the real issue for the employees but rather one of control in general.
- *Active versus passive voice.* Organizations frequently use passive voice—again, often unintentionally—to enhance their mystery and power. For example, organizations will often announce: "It has been decided that the new policy will take effect immediately." Notice how the passive voice masks the decision makers and suggests a neutral air of authority. While a person can be questioned or challenged, "It has been decided" leaves no one to question.
- *Agency and subject position.* Agency refers to the capacity of a person, group, or thing to initiate action ("to be able to do something"): "We had no choice but to raise electricity rates." Subject position often refers to an implied audience. Car ads try to construct an appealing identity for the prospective buyer and driver ("You're the kind of driver who likes . . .").
- *Metaphor.* Metaphors describe one thing in terms of another and, in so doing, bring with them a host of associations with the "new" term. Consider, for example, the positive and negative aspects of treating an organization like a "happy family," or a "dynamic team," or a "finely tuned machine."
- *Use of pronouns.* Pronouns can be used as more general ways of describing people, or groups of people. Accordingly, it is often important to pay special

attention to who is included in the use of a particular pronoun. One of us, for example, worked at a retail store where every morning the manager would announce whether or not "we" (meaning all of the store's employees) had made the previous day's sales goal; when it came time to reward "us" for achieving those goals, however, "us" included only management.

- *Personification.* It's very common to try to treat non-human things as human ("The market was disappointed yesterday"). In the 1988 movie *Bull Durham*, the minor league baseball manager informs baseball players who are being let go that "The Organization has decided to make a change," as if the organization were itself a living being.
- *Coherence/cohesion.* How do messages hang together? And how much do they take for granted? Are they heavily "intertextual" as many ads are—that is, referencing other messages?[48] For example, what missing parts are the readers/listeners encouraged to supply? A useful concept to think of when considering the coherence or cohesion of a message is Aristotle's *enthymeme* (see chapter 3). An enthymeme typically includes an argumentative premise that is not stated; instead, the audience is left to infer the conclusion. For example, when corporations make arguments about what will and will not affect the bottom line, the premise usually left unstated is that decisions should be made according to their impact on the bottom line, *above other factors*.
- *Narrative or story telling.* Narratives are defined by having characters, a plot, a climax, and a moral or a conclusion.[49] Narratives crop up in all sorts of messages from advertising to stories told over and over again within organizations (see chapter 4). Organizational communication theorist Dennis Mumby analyzed one such narrative, told repeatedly at IBM, where the CEO was stopped from entering a restricted area by a security guard because he did not have the appropriate identification with him at the time.[50] The ultimate effect of this retelling was to impart a sense that at IBM, "nobody is above the law," while at the same time subtly reinforcing the power of the CEO in the first place.
- *Expressiveness.* This refers to the emotionally evocative dimension of language; to the deliberate or unnoticed uses of terms that heighten the emotional power of a message. Thus, some Benetton ads will have very simple verbal by-lines, in order to enhance the power of their images, as the corporation seeks to identify itself with issues like the struggle against AIDS or hunger.

Discursive Strategies

Themes and features of language focus fairly specifically on what words are used, where, and how often. At a broader level, analysis can tackle the more general question of *how* language is deployed in a message by focusing on discursive strategies at work. Discursive strategies are exactly that—strategic. By employing language creatively (even if that creativity is unintentional!), the sender of a message can effectively shape the issue at the heart of their message in an advantageous manner. Here is a list of particular discursive strategies that you should look for as you conduct your analyses.

- Identification: linking one issue with another; *"Sex and violence on television" is often expressed as an indivisible unit—so much that they are seldom separated in public criticisms of television programming.*
- Differentiation: declaring an issue to be unrelated to another or separating the organization from responsibility; *"Guns don't kill people; people kill people."*
- Juxtaposition: simply putting one thing next to another, regardless of connection; *Advertisements place a beautiful woman on top of a sleek new car.*
- Strategic Ambiguity: using language to obfuscate; *"We cannot say for certain that smoking causes cancer."*
- Denial: asserting that the issue is not relevant or is not even an issue; *"The loss of that part of the workforce will have no effect on quality."*
- Containment: minimizing an issue; *"Don't mind his flirting and talking about sex at work. He's harmless."*
- Reification: treating something as solid and unchangeable; *"Women have never been allowed at Augusta [Georgia] National Golf Club."*
- Enhancement: stressing the importance of an issue; *"We are in a crisis—that much is certain!"*
- Substitution or diversion: trying to move the discussion to another issue; *"The problem with energy resources is not over-consumption but under-exploration."*
- Bolstering or self-promotion: building the status or credibility of the organization; *"In the union's generous proposal to management yesterday, we offered to cut wages by one percent."*
- Dismissal: denigrating an opposing viewpoint or opposing source; *"Only feminazis, eco-terrorists, and right-wing lunatics will fail to endorse this policy."*
- Partial reporting: taking a statistic or a result out of context; *"The unemployment rate is at an all-time low."*
- Totalizing: declaring a concern to be overriding, of superordinate importance, or overshadowing all other issues; *"Global warming is unquestionably* the *most important issue of our time."*
- Apology: using excuses or justifications for harmful past actions; *"We admit we made a few mistakes but have already taken action to correct them."*
- Misrepresentation: offering highly questionable assertions or conclusions from data; *"The proposed tax cut will benefit* all *Americans."*
- Concealment of identity: hiding or renaming the source of a message; *Think of ads that barely mention the source, give it a misleading name, or don't even list it: e.g., "The U.S. Committee on Energy Awareness," a group of nuclear power companies.*
- Self-expansion: suggesting that an organization or a consensus is really larger than it is; *"Our employees overwhelmingly support the new performance appraisal system."*
- Reframing and reversal: using an ironic or surprising shift to create a new idea; *"The tax cuts in the proposed budget are another instance of corporate welfare."*
- Non-response: ignoring an issue that has been raised by a person or group; *In U.S. presidential debates, questions about one issue are often answered by a two-minute soliloquy on a completely different topic.*

- Propaganda: suggesting that only one view is reasonable or possible; *"You can buy this new product or be left behind."*

Our summary of approaches to data collection and analysis is by no means comprehensive. We have provided a sample of some methods but want to stress that there is no one best way to study a communication phenomenon.

Overall Research Orientations

As our discussion of methodology (and our text, for that matter!) draws to a close, we'd like to step back and offer some general suggestions. What follows are several orientations that you can take as you conduct your research. Consider them "viewpoints" or "angles" from which you can read the text of messages that you gather. Each of these orientations serves as a guide to help you make decisions as you conduct your analysis, both about what you're looking for and why you're looking for it.

Noting the absence of certain things. Most analyses of communication content emphasize what ***is*** said or what ***is*** present in the "text" (whatever the object of analysis may be). In some cases, however, there might be important elements that are notable for their absence: for example, the exclusion of a particular topic on a meeting's agenda, the disappearance of a certain image in television advertising over time, the departure from past terminology, etc. In each of these cases, what is ***not*** said may well be more important than what actually ***is*** said. This perspective becomes especially important in dealing with issues such as power and conflict in organizations. "Reading between the lines" can help us understand a relationship, event, or situation more fully; however, we must also take care not to let our critical selves get the better of us and start imagining power relations or tensions where they don't really exist.

Singling out particularities/exceptional characteristics. This is the traditional strategy of much of humanistic research. The orientation works in isolating and examining a great work of art, a powerful public address, or a significant piece of literature. But the strategy also applies on a micro level and can be seen in the organizational context when we, for instance, explore special aspects of a particular leader's philosophy and practice, or we try to uncover what is distinctive or even unique about a particular organization's culture. Of course, a study that begins with an emphasis on particularity can end up emphasizing universality (generalizability), or a combination of the two. This is exactly what happened for George during his seven-year study of the Mondragón worker cooperatives in the Basque Country, Spain. Initially, he sought to understand the special aspects of and challenges to employee participation and workplace democracy there; over time, though, he became open to the fact that the market pressures, the managerial approaches, and the rising consumerism in the culture all represented features that "spoke" not only to the case of Mondragón but also to many other organizations and contexts around the world.

Looking for underlying patterns/causes of communication. Causal reasoning is an important component of scientific explanations and approaches to social phenomena. We have no space here to retrace the long debate over the type of causation most appropriate to the social sciences. Suffice it to say that the issue is complex and that causation can mean a variety of different things. We know from basic inferential statistics, of course, that correlation (or co-occurrence) does not necessarily establish a causal relationship between two different things. We also know that many presumed causal relationships end up being reversed or complicated by other variables, for example, the causal relationship between job satisfaction and productivity that was investigated extensively during the Human Relations movement. That relationship is intuitively appealing and certainly has instances of support. However, after finding a consistently weak positive correlation between the two factors (around .17 on the average), researchers began to realize that sometimes the relationship is the reverse—that is, the productive worker is the happy worker—and that other variables like work climate and reward systems greatly affect whether "the happy worker will be the productive worker" consistently over time. The point here for methodology is that we should be aware of multiple routes to the same results and the possibilities for diverse kinds of interrelationships. This makes the technique of causal inference from textual data (like a series of board meeting minutes) questionable but still doable. We should consider the nature of our data, their completeness, their richness, and then (re)visit our own claims.

Examining internal inconsistencies/contradictions/paradoxes. We discussed the element of surprise in the earlier chapters on rationality, participation, and technology. The concept of "unintended consequences" captures vividly the fact that "the best laid plans" of people and organizations often lead to both negative and positive results—results that could not have been imagined beforehand. Will our new reward system actually reinforce the wrong behaviors? Will the introduction of a new technology turn out to have at least as many disadvantages as advantages? Will our new team-based participation program actually turn out to limit employee involvement rather than to stimulate it? These are the kinds of outcomes to which we should be attuned. None of this is to say that we should cultivate a kind of cynicism that sees only opportunities to reverse meanings or undermine projects. But looking for ironies, conflicts, contradictions, and paradoxes is an important feature of research methodology just as it is a crucial dimension of research conceptualization. And the more messages we analyze in any organization, of course, the more likely we are to find, for instance, that the professed public identity of the organization is quite different from the images and identities held by employees.

Making comparisons with other types/analyses of organizational communication. Although the comparative case study method has long been a mainstay of methodology in sociology and political science, it has been used relatively infrequently in organizational communication or in organizational studies generally. One reason is the amount of time and effort required for even one in-depth case study. If that problem can be solved, the comparative method is very revealing. The trick is to decide carefully what characteristics to hold constant across the two or more cases and which to vary. So, for instance, we might look at the uses of decision-support technologies in two or more organizations, but we still have to decide on the types of organizations. Should they be from the same sector? The same industry? Of the same size? And, so forth? These are the kinds of decisions to weigh deliberately in choosing a comparative case study method; the choices will depend on what we hope to learn.

Assessing effectiveness of messages. In the early years of the twentieth century, rhetorical study distinguished itself from the field of English and more specifically from literary criticism on the basis of emphasizing the effect of messages. In other words, the primary concern of rhetorical critics was the actual or potential persuasive impact of a message, as opposed to, say, the message's aesthetic qualities. To a great extent, rhetorical investigation has maintained its emphasis on effect, and in this way rhetorical analyses parallel those in pragmatics (as a sub-field of linguistics) and critical discourse analysis (as an interdisciplinary approach to language that highlights power relations). We know from studies of organizational effectiveness (and individual competence) that effectiveness can be judged in a variety of ways. Consider how publicly traded companies present themselves and interpret the last year's results in their annual reports, or look at the multiple ways universities define themselves as successful. The same is true of "effect" and "effectiveness" with respect to messages. Several distinctions are helpful for the analyst of organizational communication: *(1) the distinction between the impact of a single message and a larger discourse or pattern of messages, (2) between short-term effect and long-term impact, and (3) between intended effect and unintended results*. Look at Box 15.6 for an example of how these three issues are evident in a single study. Here, the researcher identified a particular set of messages on Girl Scout cookie boxes, contextualized them with reference to a "Brand Voice" discourse, outlined two important unintended effects of these messages, and speculated on potential long-term impacts.

Box 15.6 Voices from the Field

The Girl Scout Cookie Sale

Kenlyn Kjesbo, The University of Montana

The Girl Scouts of the United States of America (GSUSA) is the largest organization for girls in the world, boasting over fifty million past and present members worldwide.[51] It is also home to one of the most recognizable fundraisers in the U.S.: the Girl Scout cookie sale. The 2002–03 cookie boxes and sales material reflect state-of-the-art marketing practices, leaning heavily on a set of training programs called "Brand Voice" that are designed to standardize and market Girl Scout values to external audiences.[52] The cookie box images feature professionally photographed, ethnically diverse, happy and active girls who either wear Girl Scout uniforms head-to-toe or feature the approved Girl Scout "Brand Voice" logo and tagline. The intended effect of these messages is, of course, to show the world the opportunities that the organization offers girls who join it. However, the effectiveness of the corporate "Brand Voice" should not be judged solely by an analysis of its impact outside the organization; there are also two important unintended effects on audiences inside the organization that should be considered.

The first effect was evident amongst membership specialists I interviewed, who voiced a tension between their commitment to providing the best possible experience for girls in the organization and their dependence on the sale as a fundraiser for council operations. The branding of the cookie sale often resulted in an emphasis upon sales and promotion over learning and experience, and staff members sometimes questioned whether the girls personally gained anything from participating in the cookie sale. The second effect was evident in focus groups I conducted with Girl Scouts. Their comments about the boxes and the girls featured in them indicated that they did not identify with the branding practices that were so visible on the cookie boxes. Among other things, they emphasized that the boxes overemphasized young girls and that the models on the boxes didn't seem like "real" people.

We therefore have a paradox: a program designed to promote the interests of the organization has potentially alienating effects on the very people it is ostensibly serves. Of course, this is not to say that managers and directors at GSUSA cynically exploit girls for their own narrowly defined organizational interests. On the contrary, GSUSA's willingness to experiment with recent programs like Studio 2B (a program that is designed to reduce the hierarchy between girl scouts and their leaders) [53] makes it clear that it has the interests of its members at heart, and intends to remain a place "where girls grow strong." Good organizational communication research can help ensure that these good intentions result in equally good effects.

Can you think of a situation where an organization designed a series of messages for an external audience that had unanticipated consequences for an internal audience? How would you design a study that examined the effects of such messages?

Epilogue

As we explained in chapter 1, theories and practices should always be engaged in conversation with one another. Everyday practices of leadership, for example, can be informed by theories, and new or modified perspectives on leadership can develop out of actual situations. Real-world experiences often challenge our theories, encouraging us to develop new models, and theories provide the basis for thinking critically about those real-world situations. As each of us goes through life, we find ourselves modifying our theories of love, power, success, goodness, and so forth. Taking stock of our theories helps us to see "the bigger picture" of the world in which we live. For instance, it's easy to forget that formal organizational structures are born out of informal communication, like a small set of personal relationships. Once established, the formal organizational structures of, say, a community business network will both affect and rely upon informal relationships for the continuity of the new organization of organizations. Thus, informal/formal practices exist in a dialectical interdependence where each plays off the other—and, in fact, each makes sense in terms of the other.

Throughout the text we have highlighted a number of dialectics, including: change/constancy, interconnectedness/alienation, openness/closedness, autonomy/control, novelty/predictability, fairness/individuality, instrumentality/morality, and equality/inequality. Communication is the means by which these and other dialectics are manifested and managed. For example, in board meetings about productivity and profit we can learn a great deal about the priorities of an organization and whether those two objectives are tempered or counter-balanced by social concerns (for employees, for the community, for the environment). We urge you to consider and confront various tensions in organizational practices. Reflect critically on what it means to talk about a topic like conflict in ways that make it seem totally unacceptable; the kinds of terms, images, and metaphors that are used to describe employees and their relationships with management (e.g., "a family," "a partnership," "a team"); the ways initiatives or policies for technology are framed by managers or administrators; the unintended consequences of a public corporate identity campaign for consumers; how diverse cultures and sub-cultures try to express themselves within or against a larger organizational plan for socialization; the instances in which we hear people say "It's just business" or "the market dictates that . . ." to exclude ethical considerations from view. These are just a few examples of situations and subjects where you can begin to analyze the organizational communication all around you. We hope this final chapter offers you some valuable tools for looking more closely and carefully at specific organizational messages and broader discourses. And we hope that the textbook inspires you to understand your own roles in today's organizational world and to try to make organizations better.

Endnotes

[1] James R. Taylor, *Rethinking the Theory of Organizational Communication: How to Read an Organization* (Norwood, NJ: Ablex, 1993).

[2] François Cooren, *The Organizing Property of Communication* (Amsterdam and Philadelphia: John Denjamins, 1999).

[3] Connie Bullis and George Cheney, "On the Ecological Boundaries of Organizational Communication," article prepared for journal review.

[4] Richard Sennett, *Authority* (New York: Random House, 1980).

[5] Kenneth Burke, *Permanence and Change: An Anatomy of Purpose*, 3rd revised ed. (1935; Berkeley: University of California Press, 1984).

[6] William Arnold and Jeanne Plas, *The Human Touch* (New York: Wiley, 1993).

[7] Kenneth Burke, *Language as Symbolic Action* (Berkeley: University of California Press, 1966).

[8] See <www.adbusters.com>.

[9] Connie Bullis and George Cheney, "The Ecological Limits of Organizational Communication," International Communication Association annual meeting, Acapulco, Mexico, June 2000.

[10] Stuart Ewen, *Captains of Consciousness* (New York: McGraw-Hill, 1976).

[11] Charles Sanders Peirce, "Logic as Semiotic: The Theory of Signs," *Semiotics: An Introductory Anthology*, ed. Robert E. Innis (Bloomington: Indiana University Press, 1897–1910/1985) p. 5. See also Jørgen Dines Johansen, "Prolegomena to a Semiotic Theory of Text Interpretation," *Semiotica* 57.3/4 (1985): 225–288.

[12] Roland Barthes, *Image, Music, Text*, ed. and trans. Stephen Heath (New York: Hill and Wang, 1977).

[13] Tamyra Pierce and Deborah Dougherty, "The Construction, Enactment, and Maintenance of Power-as-Domination through an Acquisition: The Case of TWA and Ozark Airlines," *Management Communication Quarterly* 16 (2002): 129–164.

[14] Shiv Ganesh, "The Myth of the Non-Government Organization: Governmentality and Transnationalism in an Indian NGO," in *Organization ↔ Communication: Emerging Perspectives, Volume 7*, ed. George Cheney and George Barnett (Cresskill, NJ: Hampton Press, in press).

[15] Linda Putnam, Shirley Van Hoeven, and Connie A. Bullis, "The Role of Rituals and Fantasy Themes in Teachers' Bargaining," *Western Journal of Speech Communication* 55 (1991): 85–103.

[16] Kenneth Burke, *A Rhetoric of Motives* (Berkeley: University of California Press, 1969).

[17] Annamma Joy, "The Modern Medicis: Corporations as Consumers of Art," *Research in Consumer Behavior* 6 (1993): 29–54.

[18] See two versions of this instrument, plus others relevant to the analysis of organizational communication, in Rebecca R. Rubin, Philip Palmgreen, and Howard E. Sypher, eds., *Communication Research Measures: A Sourcebook* (New York: Guilford, 1994).

[19] Earl Babbie, *The Practice of Social Research*, 9th ed. (Belmont, CA: Wadsworth/Thomson Learning, 2001).

[20] Thomas R. Lindlof, *Qualitative Communication Research Methods* (Thousand Oaks, CA: Sage, 1995).

[21] Raymond L. Gold, "Roles in Sociological Field Observations," *Social Forces* 36 (1958): 217–223.

[22] See Jill J. McMillan and Michael Hyde, "Technological Innovation and Change: A Case Study in the Formation of Organizational Conscience," *Quarterly Journal of Speech* 86 (2000): 19–47. Data from this case are also utilized in an upcoming issue of *Southern Communication Journal*, special issue on "Organizational Discourse and Citizenship."

[23] Robert M. Emerson, Rachel I. Fretz, and Linda L. Shaw, *Writing Ethnographic Field Notes* (Chicago: University of Chicago Press, 1995).

[24] John Van Maanen, *Tales of the Field* (Chicago: University of Chicago Press, 1988) p. 3.

[25] K. Anders Ericsson and Herbert Simon, *Protocol Analysis: Verbal Reports as Data*, rev. ed. (Cambridge: MIT Press, 1993).

[26] Cynthia Stohl, "The Role of Memorable Messages in the Process of Organizational Socialization," *Communication Quarterly* 34.3 (1986): 231–249.

[27] Connie Bullis and Betsy Wackernagel Bach, "Socialization Turning Points: An Examination of Change in Organizational Identification," *Western Journal of Speech Communication* 53.2 (1989): 272–293.

[28] Sally Planalp, "Critical Junctures in Interpersonal Relationships," unpublished paper, U of Utah, 2002.
[29] Charles Conrad, ed., *Ethical Nexus* (Norwood, NJ: Ablex Publishing. Co., 1993).
[30] Eugene J. Webb, Donald T. Campbell, Richard D. Schwartz, and Lee Sechrest, *Unobtrusive Measures: Nonreactive Research in the Social Sciences* (Chicago: Rand McNally, 1966).
[31] Norman Denzin, *The Research Act: A Theoretical Introduction to Sociological Methods* (Chicago: Aldine, 1970).
[32] Barbara Schneider, "Managers as Evaluators: Invoking Objectivity to Achieve Objectives," *Journal of Applied Behavioral Science* 36 (2000): 159–173; Barbara Schneider, "Constructing Knowledge in an Organization: The Role of Interview Notes," *Management Communication Quarterly* 15 (2001): 227–255; Barbara Schneider, "Theorizing Structure and Agency in Workplace Writing: An Ethnomethodological Approach," *Journal of Business and Technical Communication* 16 (2002): 170–195.
[33] George Cheney and Jill McMillan, "Organizational Rhetoric and the Practice of Criticism," *Journal of Applied Communication Research* (18)2 (1990): 93–114.
[34] Steinar Kvale, "Om tolkningen af kvalitative forskningsinterviews," *Tidsskrift for Nordisk Forening for Pædagogisk Forskning* (1984): 55–66. See also, Steinar Kvale, *InterViews: An Introduction to Qualitative Research Interviewing* (Thousand Oaks, CA: Sage, 1996).
[35] See Ole R. Holsti, *Content Analysis for the Social Sciences and the Humanities* (Reading, MA: Addison-Wesley, 1969).
[36] George Cheney and Greg Frenette, "Persuasion and Organization: Values, Logics and Accounts in Contemporary Corporate Public Discourse," *The Ethical Nexus*, ed. Charles Conrad (New York: Ablex, 1993).
[37] Abraham Zaleznik, "The Dynamics of Subordinancy," *Harvard Business Review* (May–June 1965): 119–137.
[38] Zaleznik, p. 124.
[39] Sennett, pp. 97–104.
[40] Sennett, pp. 100–101.
[41] E.g., Holsti.
[42] William F. Owen, "Interpretive Themes in Relational Communication," *Quarterly Journal of Speech* 70 (1984): 274.
[43] Owen, citing Denzin.
[44] Theodore E. Zorn and Sarah E. Ruccio, "Motivational Communication in College Sales Teams," *Journal of Business Communication* 35 (1998): 468–499.
[45] Steven R. Corman, Timothy Kuhn, Robert D. McPhee, and Kevin J. Dooley, "Studying Complex Discursive Systems: Centering Resonance Analysis of Communication," *Human Communication Research* 28 (2002): 157–206.
[46] Kevin J. Dooley and Steven R. Corman, "The Dynamics Electronic Media Coverage," *Communication and Terrorism: Public and Media Responses to 9/11*, ed. B. Greenberg (Cresskill, NJ: Hampton Press, 2002) pp. 121–136.
[47] Robert D. McPhee, Steven R. Corman, and Kevin J. Dooley, "Organizational Knowledge Expression and Management: Centering Resonance Analysis of Organizational Discourse," *Management Communication Quarterly* 16.2 (2002): 274–281.
[48] Lars Thøger Christensen, "Intertextuality and Self-Reference in Contemporary Advertising," *Advertising Research in the Nordic Countries*, ed. Flemming Hansen and Lotte Yssing Hansen (København: Samfundslitteratur, 2001) pp. 351–356.
[49] Mary Helen Brown, "Defining Stories in Organizations: Characteristics and Functions," *Communication Yearbook* 13 (1990): 162–190; Mary Helen Brown and Jill J. McMillan, "Culture as Text: The Development of an Organizational Narrative," *Southern Communication Journal* 57:3 (1991): 49–61; David Boje, *Narrative Methods of Organizational Research* (Thousand Oaks, CA: Sage, 2001).
[50] Dennis K. Mumby, *Narrative and Social Control: Critical Perspectives* (Thousand Oaks, CA: Sage Publications, 1993).
[51] National Historic Preservation Center, *Highlights in Girl Scouting 1912–1996* (New York: Girl Scouts of the United States of America, 1997).
[52] Girl Scouts of the United States of America, *Brand Voice: A Training Manual for Executive Directors* (New York: Author, 1999).
[53] Girl Scouts of the United States of America, "Studio 2B: Frequently Asked Questions," unpublished manuscript, New York, 2003.

Name Index

Subject Index